T0325020

Social and Human Elements of Information Security:
Emerging Trends and Countermeasures

Manish Gupta
State University of New York, Buffalo, USA

Raj Sharman
State University of New York, Buffalo, USA

INFORMATION SCIENCE REFERENCE

Hershey · New York

Director of Editorial Content: Kristin Klinger
Managing Development Editor: Kristin M. Roth
Assistant Development Editor: Deborah Yahnke
Editorial Assistant: Rebecca Beistline
Director of Production: Jennifer Neidig
Managing Editor: Jamie Snavely
Assistant Managing Editor: Carole Coulson
Typesetter: Cindy Consonery
Cover Design: Lisa Tosheff
Printed at: Yurchak Printing Inc.

Published in the United States of America by
        Information Science Reference (an imprint of IGI Global)
        701 E. Chocolate Avenue, Suite 200
        Hershey PA 17033
        Tel: 717-533-8845
        Fax: 717-533-8661
        E-mail: cust@igi-global.com
        Web site: http://www.igi-global.com

and in the United Kingdom by
        Information Science Reference (an imprint of IGI Global)
        3 Henrietta Street
        Covent Garden
        London WC2E 8LU
        Tel: 44 20 7240 0856
        Fax: 44 20 7379 0609
        Web site: http://www.eurospanbookstore.com

Library of Congress Cataloging-in-Publication Data

Social and human elements of information security : emerging trends and countermeasures / Manish Gupta and Raj Sharman, editor [sic].

        p. cm.

Includes bibliographical references and index.

Summary: "The book represents a compilation of articles on technology, processes, management, governance, research and practices on human and social aspects of information security"--Provided by publisher.

ISBN 978-1-60566-036-3 (hbk.) -- ISBN 978-1-60566-037-0 (ebook)

1. Computer crimes. 2. Computer security. 3. Security systems. I. Gupta, Manish, 1978- II. Sharman, Raj.

HV6773.S63 2009

658.4'78--dc22

                        2008013115

British Cataloguing in Publication Data
A Cataloguing in Publication record for this book is available from the British Library.

All work contributed to this book set is original material. The views expressed in this book are those of the authors, but not necessarily of the publisher.

List of Reviewers

Deapesh Misra
George Mason University, USA

Kris Gaj
George Mason University, USA

Mahil Carr
IDBRT, Hyderabad, India

Mahi Dontamsetti
m3security Inc.

Anup Narayanan
First Legion Consulting, India

Shambhu Upadhyaya
CSE, SUNY Buffalo, USA

Madhusudhanan Chandrasekaran
CSE, SUNY Buffalo, USA

Chandan Mazumdar
Jadavpur University, West Bengal, India

Mridul S. Barik
Jadavpur University, West Bengal, India

Anirban Sengupta
Jadavpur University, India

Nick Pullman
Citi Group, USA

Arunabha Mukhopadhyay
IIM Kolkata, India

Samir Chatterjee
Claremont Graduate University, USA

JinKyu Lee
Oklahoma State University, USA

Jingguo Wang
University of Texas, USA

David Porter
Detica Corporation, UK

Tejaswini Herath
SOM, SUNY Buffalo, USA

Donald Murphy
M&T Bank Corporation, USA

Robert Franz
M&T Bank Corporation, USA

Jessica Pu Li
SOM, SUNY Buffalo, USA

Lawrence Harold
IIT Madras, India

Siddhartha Gupta
IBM Global Services, Gurgaon, India

David Porter
Detica Corporation, UK

4 Anonymous Reviewers

Table of Contents

Section I
Human and Psychological Aspects

Section II
Social and Cultural Aspects

Section III
Usability Issues

Section IV
Organizational Aspects

Detailed Table of Contents

Section I
Human and Psychological Aspects

Chapter I

Deborah S. Carstens, Florida Institute of Technology, USA

With the increasing daily reliance on electronic transactions, it is essential to have reliable security practices for individuals, businesses, and organizations to protect their information (Vu, Bhargav, & Proctor, 2003; Vu, Tai, Bhargav, Schultz, & Proctor, 2004). A paradigm shift is occurring as researchers are targeting social and human dimensions of information security as this aspect is seen as an area where control can be exercised. Since computer security is largely dependent on the use of passwords to authenticate users of technology, the objectives of this chapter are to (a) provide a background on password authentication and information security, (b) provide a discussion on security techniques, human error in information security, human memory limitations, and password authentication in practice and (c) provide a discussion on future and emerging trends in password authentication to include future research areas.

Chapter II

Marcus Nohlberg, School of Humanities and Informatics, University of Skövde, Sweden

This chapter introduces the concept of social psychology and what forms of deception humans are prone to fall for. It presents a background of the area and a thorough description of the most common and important influence techniques. It also gives more practical examples of potential attacks and what kind of influence techniques they use, as well as a set of recommendations on how to defend against deception and a discussion on future trends. The author hopes that the understanding of why and how the deceptive techniques work will give the reader new insights into information security in general, and deception in particular. This insight can be used to improve training, to discover influence earlier, or even to gain new powers of influence.

Chapter III

Mahi Dontamsetti, President, M3 Security, USA
Anup Narayanan, Founder Director, First Legion Consulting, India

This chapter discusses the impact of the human element in information security. We are in the third generation of information security evolution, having evolved from a focus on technical, to process based to the current focus on the human element. Using case studies, the author's detail how existing technical and process based controls are circumvented by focusing on weaknesses in human behavior. Factors that affect why individuals behave in a certain way, while making security decisions, are discussed. A psychology framework called the conscious competence model is introduced. Using this model, typical individual security behavior is broken down into four quadrants using the individuals' consciousness and competence. The authors explain how the model can be used by individuals to recognize their security competency level and detail steps for learning more effective behavior. Shortfalls of existing training methods are highlighted and new strategies for increasing information security competence are presented.

Chapter IV

Ryan West, Dell, Inc., USA
Christopher Mayhorn, North Carolina State University, USA
Jefferson Hardee, North Carolina State University, USA
Jeremy Mendel, North Carolina State University, USA

The goal of this chapter is to raise awareness of cognitive and human factors issues that influence user behavior when interacting with systems and making decisions with security consequences. This chapter is organized around case studies of computer security incidents and known threats. For each case study, we provide an analysis of the human factors involved based on a system model approach composed of three parts: the user, the technology, and the environment. Each analysis discusses how the user interacted with the technology within the context of the environment to actively contribute to the incident. Using this approach, we introduce key concepts from human factors research and discuss them within the context of computer security. With a fundamental understanding of the causes that lead users to make poor security decisions and take risky actions, we hope designers of security systems are better equipped to mitigate those risks.

Chapter V

Alison Adam, University of Salford, UK
Paul Spedding, University of Salford, UK

This chapter considers the question of how we may trust automatically generated program code. The code walkthroughs and inspections of software engineering mimic the ways that mathematicians go about assuring themselves that a mathematical proof is true. Mathematicians have difficulty accepting a computer generated proof because they cannot go through the social processes of trusting its construction. Similarly, those involved in accepting a proof of a computer system or computer generated code cannot go through their traditional processes of trust. The process of software verification is bound up in software quality assurance procedures, which are themselves subject to commercial pressures. Quality standards, including military standards, have procedures for human trust designed into them. An action research case study of an avionics system within a military aircraft company illustrates these points, where the software quality assurance (SQA) procedures were incommensurable with the use of automatically generated code.

Section II
Social and Cultural Aspects

Rauno Kuusisto, Finland Futures Research Center, Turku School of Economics, Finland
Tuija Kuusisto, Finnish National Defense University, Finland

The purpose of this chapter is to increase understanding of the complex nature of information security culture in a networked working environment. Viewpoint is comprehensive information exchange in a social system. The aim of this chapter is to raise discussion about information security culture development challenges when acting in a multicultural environment. This chapter does not introduce a method to handle complex cultural situation, but gives some notes to gain understanding, what might be behind this complexity. Understanding the nature of this complex cultural environment is essential to form evolving and proactive security practices. Direct answers to formulate practices are not offered in this chapter, but certain general phenomena of the activity of a social system are pointed out. This will help readers to apply these ideas to their own solutions.

Paul Drake, Centre for Systems Studies Business School, University of Hull, UK
Steve Clarke, Centre for Systems Studies Business School, University of Hull, UK

This chapter looks at information security as a primarily technological domain and asks what could be added to our understanding if both technology and human activity were seen to be of equal importance. The aim is therefore to ground the domain both theoretically and practically from a technological and social standpoint. The solution to this dilemma is seen to be located in social theory, various aspects of which deal with both human and technical issues, but do so from the perspective of those involved in the system of concern. The chapter concludes by offering a model for evaluating information security from a social theoretical perspective, and guidelines for implementing the findings.

Chapter VIII

This chapter attempts to understand the human and social factors in information security by bringing together three different universes of discourse—philosophy, human behavior, and cognitive science. When these elements are combined, they unravel a new approach to the design, implementation, and operation of secure information systems. A case study of the design of a technological solution to the problem of extension of banking services to remote rural regions is presented and elaborated to highlight human and social issues in information security. It identifies and examines the concept of the 'other' in information security literature. The final objective is to prevent the 'other' from emerging and damaging secure systems rather than introducing complex lock and key controls.

Social engineering refers to the practice of manipulating people to divulge confidential information that can then be used to compromise an information system. In many cases, people, not technology, form the weakest link in the security of an information system. This chapter discusses the problem of social engineering and then examines new social engineering threats that arise as voice, data, and video networks converge. In particular, converged networks give the social engineer multiple channels of attack to influence a user and compromise a system. On the other hand, these networks also support new tools that can help combat social engineering. However, no tool can substitute for educational efforts that make users aware of the problem of social engineering and policies that must be followed to prevent social engineering from occurring.

As software becomes more and more entrenched in everyday life in today's society, security looms large as an unsolved problem. Despite advances in security mechanisms and technologies, most software systems in the world remain precarious and vulnerable. There is now widespread recognition that security cannot be achieved by technology alone. All software systems are ultimately embedded in some human social environment. The effectiveness of the system depends very much on the forces in that environment. Yet there are few systematic techniques for treating the social context of security together with technical system design in an integral way. In this chapter, we argue that a social ontology at the core of a requirements engineering process can be the basis for integrating security into a requirements driven software engineering process. We describe the i* agent-oriented modeling framework and show how it can be used to model and reason about security concerns and responses. A smart card example is used to illustrate. Future directions for a social paradigm for security and software engineering are discussed.

Section III
Usability Issues

End users often find that security configuration interfaces are difficult to use. In this chapter, we explore how application designers can improve the design and evaluation of security configuration interfaces. We use IEEE 802.11 network configuration as a case study. First, we design and implement a configuration interface that guides users through secure network configuration. The key insight is that users have a difficult time translating their security goals into specific feature configurations. Our interface automates the translation from users' high-level goals to low-level feature configurations. Second, we develop and conduct a user study to compare our interface design with commercially available products. We adapt existing user research methods to sidestep common difficulties in evaluating security applications. Using our configuration interface, non-expert users are able to secure their networks as well as expert users. In general, our research addresses prevalent issues in the design and evaluation of consumer-configured security applications.

This chapter highlights the need for security solutions to be usable by their target audience and examines the problems that can be faced when attempting to understand and use security features in typical applications. Challenges may arise from system-initiated events, as well as in relation to security tasks that users wish to perform for themselves, and can occur for a variety of reasons. This is illustrated by examining problems that arise as a result of reliance upon technical terminology, unclear or confusing functionality, lack of visible status, and informative feedback to users, forcing users to make uninformed decision, and a lack of integration amongst the different elements of security software themselves. The discussion draws upon a number of practical examples from popular applications as well as results from survey and user trial activities that were conducted in order to assess the potential problems at first hand. The findings are used as the basis for recommending a series of top-level guidelines that may be used to improve the situation, and these are used as the basis assessing further examples of existing software to determine the degree of compliance.

The Internet has established firm deep roots in our day to day life. It has brought many revolutionary changes in the way we do things. One important consequence has been the way it has replaced human to human contact. This has also presented us with a new issue which is the requirement for differentiating between real humans and automated programs on the Internet. Such automated programs are usually written with a malicious intent. CAPTCHAs play an important role in solving this problem by presenting users with tests which only humans can solve. This chapter looks into the need, the history, and the different kinds of CAPTCHAs that researchers have come up with to deal with the security implications of automated bots pretending to be humans. Various schemes are compared and contrasted with each other, the impact of CAPTCHAs on Internet users is discussed and to conclude, the various possible attacks are discussed. The author hopes that the chapter will not only introduce this interesting field to the reader in its entirety, but also simulate thought on new schemes.

Chapter XIV

Sylvain Castagnos, LORIA—Université Nancy 2, Campus Scientifique, France
Anne Boyer, LORIA—Université Nancy 2, Campus Scientifique, France

This chapter investigates ways to deal with privacy rules when modeling preferences of users in recommender systems based on collaborative filtering. It argues that it is possible to find a good compromise between quality of predictions and protection of personal data. Thus, it proposes a methodology that fulfills with strictest privacy laws for both centralized and distributed architectures. The authors hope that their attempts to provide a unified vision of privacy rules through the related works and a generic privacy-enhancing procedure will help researchers and practitioners to better take into account the ethical and juridical constraints as regards privacy protection when designing information systems.

Section IV
Organizational Aspects

Chapter XV

C. Warren Axelrod, US Trust, USA

Traditionally, the views of security professionals regarding responses to threats and the management of vulnerabilities have been biased towards technology and operational risks. The purpose of this chapter is to extend the legacy threat-vulnerability model to incorporate human and social factors. This is achieved by presenting the dynamics of threats and vulnerabilities in the human and social context. We examine costs and benefits as they relate to threats, exploits, vulnerabilities, defense measures, incidents, and recovery and restoration. We also compare the technical and human/social aspects of each of these areas. We then look at future work and how trends are pushing against prior formulations and forcing new thinking on the technical, operational risk, and human/social aspects. The reader will gain a broader view of threats, vulnerabilities, and responses to them through incorporating human and social elements into their security models.

Chapter XVI

This chapter addresses the issue of electronic workplace monitoring and its implications for employees' privacy. Organisations increasingly use a variety of electronic surveillance methods to mitigate threats to their information systems. Monitoring technology spans different aspects of organisational life, including communications, desktop and physical monitoring, collecting employees' personal data, and locating employees through active badges. The application of these technologies raises privacy protection concerns. Throughout this chapter, we describe different approaches to privacy protection followed by different jurisdictions. We also highlight privacy issues with regard to new trends and practices, such as teleworking and use of RFID technology for identifying the location of employees. Emphasis is also placed on the reorganisation of work facilitated by information technology, since frontiers between the private and the public sphere are becoming blurred. The aim of this chapter is twofold: we discuss privacy concerns and the implications of implementing employee surveillance technologies and we suggest a framework of fair practices which can be used for bridging the gap between the need to provide adequate protection for information systems, while preserving employees' rights to privacy.

Achieving alignment of risk perception, assessment, and tolerance among and between management teams within an organisation is an important foundation upon which an effective enterprise information security management strategy can be built. We argue the importance of such alignment based on information security and risk assessment literature. Too often, lack of alignment dampens clean execution of strategy, eroding support during development and implementation of information security programs. We argue that alignment can be achieved by developing an understanding of enterprise risk management plans and actions, risk perceptions, and risk culture. This is done by examining context, context and process. We illustrate this through the case of LeCroy Corp., illustrating how LeCroy managers perceive risk in practice, and how LeCroy fosters alignment in risk perception and execution of risk management strategy as part of an overall information security program. We show that in some circumstances diversity of risk tolerance profiles aide a management teams' function. In other circumstances, variances lead to dysfunction. We have uncovered and quantified nonlinearities and special cases in LeCroy executive management's risk tolerance profiles.

Chapter XVIII

Manish Gupta, State University of New York, Buffalo, USA
Raj Sharman, State University of New York, Buffalo, USA
Lawrence Sanders, State University of New York, Buffalo, USA

Information security is becoming increasingly important and more complex as organizations are increasingly adopting electronic channels for managing and conducting business. However, state-of-the-art systems design methods have ignored several aspects of security that arise from human involvement or due to human factors. The chapter aims to highlight issues arising from coalescence of fields of systems requirements elicitation, information security, and human factors. The objective of the chapter is to investigate and suggest an agenda for state of human factors in information assurance requirements elicitation from perspectives of both organizations and researchers. Much research has been done in the area of requirements elicitation, both systems and security, but, invariably, human factors have not been taken into account during information assurance requirements elicitation. The chapter aims to find clues and insights into acquisition behavior of human factors in information assurance requirements elicitation and to illustrate current state of affairs in information assurance and requirements elicitation and why inclusion of human factors is required.

Chapter XIX

Neil F. Doherty, Loughborough University, UK
Heather Fulford, Loughborough University, UK

Information is a critical corporate asset that has become increasingly vulnerable to attacks from viruses, hackers, criminals, and human error. Consequently, organizations have to prioritize the security of their computer systems in order to ensure that their information assets retain their accuracy, confidentiality, and availability. While the importance of the information security policy (InSPy) in ensuring the security of information is acknowledged widely, to date there has been little empirical analysis of its impact or effectiveness in this role. To help fill this gap, an exploratory study was initiated that sought to investigate the relationship between the uptake and application of information security policies and the accompanying levels of security breaches. To this end, a questionnaire was designed, validated, and then targeted at IT managers within large organizations in the UK. The findings presented in this chapter are somewhat surprising, as they show no statistically significant relationships between the adoption of information security policies and the incidence or severity of security breaches. The chapter concludes by exploring the possible interpretations of this unexpected finding and its implications for the practice of information security management.

Foreword

During the past two decades, the Internet has evolved from a technologically sophisticated tool to a commonly used and accepted medium for communication. The promise of interconnectedness has been realized, providing unprecedented access to people and information. Despite its promising and meteoric rise to prominence, Internet technology also presents great challenges. The open nature of the Internet is highly insecure, leading to new questions about the security and quality of information. Moreover, the promise of interconnected access raises the potential for new threats, causing us to rethink the meaning and value of privacy in this environment. Individuals and organizations are potentially endangered in new ways by threats that may emanate from both internal and external environments.

Information security encompasses a broad range of topics and forms. It is, nonetheless, defined by the common aim of preserving the integrity, availability, and confidentiality of information system resources. With the introduction of information technology and the resulting security challenges that organizations face daily, it has become essential to ensure the security of the organization's information and other valuable assets.

Enterprises facing security threats demand powerful and flexible approaches that can match the dynamic environment in which these threats emerge. Challenges related to telecommunications and data security within the computer and transmission network include threats from online fraud, identity theft, illegal content, hacking, and piracy, to name a few. Security breaches such as distributed denial-of-service attacks and virus infections have highlighted the vulnerability of the information systems as end-users become more dependent on these systems. Complicating the issue is the fact that computer attacks can access personal information, raising both privacy and economic costs for individuals and organizations. Such costs can be expected to escalate as data generation and reliance by individuals and organizations increase on a daily basis.

Many organisations beginning to advocate security policies are relying purely upon technical solutions. However, information security is only partly about technology. A lack of understanding persists about the strategic importance of managing information security and the need to address security from a people, processes, and technology standpoint in order to implement a successful security strategy. Information security is not a problem which needs to be solved, but a process to be managed proactively. This process does not only require safeguarding information from the development and design stage of the new systems to their implementation, but it also requires a more holistic emphasis that goes beyond technology to address the social and human dimensions of communications, psychology, marketing, and behavioural change.

This holistic approach encompasses technical and procedural controls involving technology and human factors—the people who purchase, implement, use, and manage that technology. The human element can become the leaky faucet that spills sensitive information, as employees are often the weakest link when it comes to information security. People who manage and implement information security strategies must take this reality into account as they respond to vulnerabilities that ultimately impact the effectiveness of the organisation.

This book attempts to close this gap between technology and human factors by exploring the development and implementation of information security strategies. Information security is not merely a technological issue—it is also a human issue. As such, it invokes all of the complexity, unpredictability, and wonder that human beings bring to their creative enterprises.

Sylvia Kierkegaard
President
International Association of IT Lawyers (IAITL)

Sylvia Mercado Kierkegaard *(BA, MA, MSc International Business and Law Summa cum laude, PG Dipl. Law, LLM, PG Dipl. EU Law, PhD) is the author of over 2000 publications. She is the editor-in-chief of the Journal of International Commercial Law (DOAJ-access), International Journal of Private Law (Inderscience) and associate editor and editorial board member of over 20 international journals, including the Computer Law and Security Report (Oxford-Elsevier), where her articles regularly appear. She is the president of the International Association of IT Lawyers (IAITL) and chairs numerous international conferences dealing with information technology and law. She is also the EU senior legal expert on information security for the EU-China Info Society project. Her international experience includes working in Europe, the Middle East, North America, and Asia advising clients on a broad range of legal issues. She is a frequent invited speaker in conferences and a member of study committees which recommend and draft policies and legislations.*

Preface

More often than not, it is becoming increasingly evident that the weakest links in an information-security chain are the people because human nature and social interactions are much easier to manipulate than targeting the complex technological protections of information systems. Concerns and threats regarding human and social factors in organizational security are increasing at an exponential rate and shifting the information security paradigm. This book brings together publications on very important, timely, and critical issues of managing social and human aspects of information security. The book aims to provide immense scholarly value to, and contribution in, information technology discipline. Despite being an emerging threat to information security, there is dearth of quality literature in the area. The key objective is to fill a gap in existing literature on human and social dimensions of information security by providing the readers one comprehensive source of latest trends, issues and research in the field. The book provides high-quality research papers and industrial and practice articles on social and human aspects of information security. The book covers topics both on theoretical (research) aspects of securing information systems and infrastructure from social engineering attacks and real-world implications and implementations (practice) of the research.

BEYOND TECHNOLOGY AND POLICY, TOWARDS COMPREHENSIVE INFORMATION SECURITY

With the abundance of confidential information that organizations must protect, and with consumer fraud and identity theft at an all time high, security has never been as important as it is today for businesses and individuals alike. An attacker can bypass millions of dollars invested in technical and non-technical protection mechanisms by exploiting the human and social aspects of information security. While information systems deal with human interactions and communications through use of technology, it is extremely infeasible to separate the human elements from the technological ones. Because of this, organizations and individuals alike must be equipped with the knowledge of what information can be used to initiate attacks, how information divulged could precipitate further attacks and compromise their states of systems, and how to discern and mitigate against such attacks. Businesses spend billions of dollars annually on expensive technology for information systems security, while overlooking one of the most glaring vulnerabilities—their employees and customers (Orgill, 2004; Schneier, 2000). Research has indicated that human error makes up as much as 65% of incidents that cause economic loss for a company and that security incidents caused by external threats such as computer hackers happen only 3% or less of the time (Lewis, 2003; McCauley-Bell & Crumpton, 1998). Information security cannot be achieved purely from a technology standpoint alone but from understanding human behavior and the social context in which humans are embedded (Dhillon, 2007).

The 2007 CSI Computer Crime and Security Survey reports that insider abuse of network access or e-mail (such as trafficking in pornography or pirated software) edged out virus incidents as the most prevalent security problem, with 59% and 52% of respondents reporting each, respectively. The survey also finds that there have been too many data breaches driven by simple human error and carelessness. On a new question that was added in this year's survey, asking what percentage of the security budget was allocated for awareness training. Almost half—48%—spend less than 1% of their security dollars on awareness programs. For the first time this year, the survey also asked about measures organizations had adopted to gauge the effectiveness of their security awareness training programs (CSI/FBI Survey, 2007). The survey shows that 18% of respondents do not use awareness training, implying that 4 out of 5 respondent organizations do in fact engage in training their employees about security risks and appropriate handling of sensitive data (CSI/FBI Survey, 2007). Although a strong majority performs this kind of training, many of the respondent organizations (35%) make no effort to measure the effect of this training on the organization. A quarter of them learn anecdotally from reported staff experiences; roughly one third (32%) administer tests to see whether their lessons have taken hold (CSI/FBI Survey, 2007). Only about one in ten (13%) of the respondents say they test the effectiveness of the training by checking whether employees can detect internally generated social engineering attacks (CSI/FBI Survey, 2007). These numbers quite clearly indicate that human and social elements are not given enough consideration in design and implementation of security programs. While only a small portion (20%) are conducting security training and awareness programs, even fewer (10%) are actually measuring effectiveness of the programs. All the same, we see that damages and threats from non-technical and non-procedural elements of information security are higher than ever. No system is immune to human ingenuity. Effective information security must be culturally ingrained and backed by strategies and processes that are continually tested, taught, measured, and refined (Lineberry, 2007). Businesses spend a significant portion of their annual information technology budgets on high-tech computer security. But the firewalls, vaults, bunkers, locks, and biometrics those dollars buy can be pierced by attackers targeting untrained, uninformed, or unmonitored users. Some of the best tools for fighting social engineering attacks are security awareness training and social engineering testing (Lineberry, 2007), but as we just saw, organizations have a long way to implement an effective information security awareness program and also measure its performance. Research by Belsis, Spyros, and Kiountouzis (2005) also suggests that although successful security management depends on the involvement of users and stakeholders, that knowledge on information systems security issues may be lacking, resulting in reduced participation.

Reformed computer criminal and security consultant Kevin Mitnick popularized the term social engineering, pointing out that it is much easier to trick someone into giving you his or her password for a system than to spend the effort to hack in (Mitnick & Kasperavičius, 2004). He claims it to be the single most effective method in his arsenal. In another recent survey of black hat hackers, social engineering ranked as the third most widely used technique (Wilson, 2007). The survey results indicate that 63% of hackers use social engineering, while 67% use sniffers, 64% use SQL injection, and 53% use cross site scripting. Social engineering is an attack to break into a corporate network and applications by manipulating human and social elements. Along with issues surrounding social engineering, there are several other facets to human and social elements such as usability issues, organizational aspects, social and psychological aspects, and privacy issues that the book covers in detail. The book brings to readers an excellent compilation of high quality and relevant articles on technology, processes, management, governance, research, and practices on human and social aspects of information security. The book brings together articles from researchers and practitioners in the financial, legal, technology, and information security fields through original papers on all aspects of roles and effects of human and social dimensions of information security.

ORGANIZATION OF THE BOOK

The nineteen chapters of the book are organized into 4 sections based on the following broad themes:

I.   Human and Psychological Aspects
II. Social and Cultural Aspects
III. Usability Issues
IV. Organizational Aspects

The section on *Human and Psychological Aspects* focuses on some of the most important issues in information security that relate to human, behavioral, and psychological aspects. In this section, we explore some of the interesting phenomena associated with password authentication and how human and social factors interplay with passwords in determining security of a system or environment; particularly human errors and human memory characteristics. We also look into concept of social psychology and what forms of deception humans are prone to fall for, while providing a background of the area and a thorough description of the most common and important influence techniques. This section also presents a case study *detailing how exploiting weaknesses in human behavior can circumvent existing technical and procedural controls. Another case study is presented to* raise awareness of cognitive and human factors issues that influence user behaviour when interacting with systems and making decisions with security consequences. Lastly, an action research case study is presented in this section that illustrates that quality standards, including military standards, have procedures for human trust designed into them in light of trust issues with automatically generated program codes. The second section on *Social and Cultural Aspects* contains chapters that explore and present interesting findings on information security culture as a social system, an international perspective on social aspects of information security, a case study to elaborate and highlight human and social issues in information security, effects of digital convergence on social engineering attack channels, and a social ontology for integrating security and software engineering. The third section on *Usability Issues* comprises of chapters on research on prevalent issues in the design and evaluation of consumer-configured security applications, security usability challenges for end-users, the impact of CAPTCHAs on Internet users, and the various possible attacks and issues with privacy rules when modeling preferences of users in recommender systems based on collaborative filtering. The final section of the book, *Organizational Aspects*, investigates topics on threats, vulnerabilities, and responses to them through incorporating human and social elements into their security models through an adaptive threat-vulnerability model and the economics of protection, issues surrounding employee surveillance and privacy protection, issues related to aligning IT teams' risk management to business requirements, under-acquisition of human factors in information assurance requirements elicitation, and an exploratory review of effectiveness of information security policies.

OVERVIEW OF CHAPTERS IN THE BOOK

With the increasing daily reliance on electronic transactions, it is essential to have reliable security practices for individuals, businesses, and organizations to protect their information (Vu, Bhargav, & Proctor, 2003; Vu, Tai, Bhargav, Schultz, & Proctor, 2004). A paradigm shift is occurring as researchers are targeting social and human dimensions of information security, as this aspect is seen as an area where control can be exercised. Computer security is largely dependent on the use of passwords to authenticate users of technology. In light of the significance of authentication issues, Dr. Deborah Sater Carstens of Florida Institute of Technology, USA, in her chapter (Chapter I), "*Human and Social Aspects of Password Authentication*," provides a background on password authentication and information security, discusses security techniques, human error in information security, human memory limitations, and password authentication in practice, and provides a discussion on future and emerging trends in password authentication to include future research areas.

Chapter II, "*Why Humans are the Weakest Link?*" introduces the concept of social psychology and what forms of deception humans are prone to fall for. It presents a background of the area and a thorough description of the most common and important influence techniques. It also gives more practical examples of potential attacks and what kind of influence techniques they use, as well as a set of recommendations on how to defend against deception and a discussion on future trends. The author, Marcus Nohlberg (University of Skövde, Sweden), hopes that the understanding of why and how the deceptive techniques work will give the reader new insights into information security in general, and deception in particular. This insight can be used to improve training, to discover influence earlier, or even to gain new powers of influence.

Chapter III, "*Impact of the Human Element on Information Security*" discusses the impact of the human element in information security. We are in the third generation of information security evolution, having evolved from a focus on technical, to process based to the current focus on the human element. Using case studies, the authors, Mahi Dontamsetti of M3 Security, USA and Anup Narayanan of First Legion Consulting, USA, detail how existing technical and process based controls are circumvented by focusing on weaknesses in human behavior. Factors that affect why individuals behave in a certain way while making security decisions are discussed. A psychology framework called the conscious competence model is introduced. Using this model, typical individual security behavior is broken down into four quadrants using the individuals' consciousness and competence. The authors explain how the model can be used by individuals to recognize their security competency level and detail steps for learning more effective behavior. Shortfalls of existing training methods are highlighted and new strategies for increasing information security competence are presented.

The goal of Chapter IV, "*The Weakest Link: A Psychological Perspective on Why Users Make Poor Security Decisions* is to raise awareness of cognitive and human factors issues that influence user behaviour when interacting with systems and making decisions with security consequences. This chapter is organized around case studies of computer security incidents and known threats. For each case study, the authors, Ryan West, Dell Inc., USA, Dr. Christopher B. Mayhorn, North Carolina State University, USA, Dr. Jefferson B. Hardee, North Carolina State University, USA, and Dr. Jeremy Mendel, Clemson University, USA, provide an analysis of the human factors involved based on a system model approach composed of three parts: the user, the technology, and the environment. Each analysis discusses how the user interacted with the technology within the context of the environment to actively contribute to the incident. Using this approach, the authors introduce key concepts from human factors research and discuss them within the context of computer security. With a fundamental understanding of the causes that lead users to make poor security decisions and take risky actions, the authors hope designers of security systems are better equipped to mitigate those risks.

Chapter V, "*Trusting Computers through Trusting Humans: Software Verification in a Safety-critical Information System,*" considers the question of how we may trust automatically generated program code. The code walkthroughs and inspections of software engineering mimic the ways that mathematicians go about assuring themselves that a mathematical proof is true. Mathematicians have difficulty accepting a computer generated proof because they cannot go through the social processes of trusting its construction. Similarly, those involved in accepting a proof of a computer system or computer generated code cannot go through their traditional processes of trust. The process of software verification is bound up in software quality assurance procedures, which are themselves subject to commercial pressures. Quality standards, including military standards, have procedures for human trust designed into them. Dr. Alison Adam of University of Salford, UK and Dr. Paul Spedding, of University of Salford, UK present an action research case study of an avionics system within a military aircraft company that illustrates these points, where the software quality assurance (SQA) procedures were incommensurable with the use of automatically generated code.

The purpose of Chapter VI, "*Information Security Culture as a Social System: Some Notes of Information Availability and Sharing*" is to increase understanding of the complex nature of information security culture in a networked working environment. Viewpoint is comprehensive information exchange in a social system. The aim of this chapter is to raise discussion about information security culture development challenges when acting in a multicultural environment. The authors, Dr. Rauno Kuusisto, Turku School of Economics, Finland and Dr. Tuija Kuusisto, Finnish National Defense University, Finland give some notes to gain understanding, what might be behind this complexity. Understanding the nature of this complex cultural environment is essential to form evolving and proactive security practices. Direct answers to formulate practices are not offered in this chapter, but certain general phenomena of the activity of a social system are pointed out. This will help readers to apply these ideas to their own solutions.

In Chapter VII, "*Social Aspects of Information Security: An International Perspective,*" authors, Dr. Paul Drake and Dr. Steve Clarke of University of Hull, UK, look at information security as a primarily technological domain, and ask what could be added to our understanding if both technology and human activity were seen to be of equal importance. The aim of the chapter is to ground the domain both theoretically and practically from a technological and social standpoint. The solution to this dilemma is seen to be located in social theory, various aspects of which deal with both human and technical issues, but do so from the perspective of those involved in the system of concern. The chapter concludes by offering a model for evaluating information security from a social theoretical perspective, and guidelines for implementing the findings.

Chapter VIII, "*Social and Human Elements of Information Security: A Case Study,*" attempts to understand the human and social factors in information security by bringing together three different universes of discourse—philosophy, human behavior, and cognitive science. When these elements are combined, they unravel a new approach to the design, implementation, and operation of secure information systems. A case study of the design of a technological solution to the problem of extension of banking services to remote rural regions is presented and elaborated to highlight human and social issues in information security. The author, Dr. Mahil Carr, Institute for Development and Research in Banking Technology, India, in the chapter, has also identified and examined the concept of the 'other' in information security literature. The final objective is to prevent the 'other' from emerging and damaging secure systems rather than introducing complex lock and key controls.

Social engineering refers to the practice of manipulating people to divulge confidential information that can then be used to compromise an information system. In many cases, people, not technology, form the weakest link in the security of an information system.

In Chapter IX, "*Effects of Digital Convergence on Social Engineering Attack Channels,*" the authors, Dr. Bogdan Hoanca and Dr. Kenrick Mock of University of Alaska Anchorage, USA, discuss the problem of social engineering and then examine new social engineering threats that arise as voice, data, and video networks converge. In particular, converged networks give the social engineer multiple channels of attack to influence a user and compromise a system. On the other hand, these networks also support new tools that can help combat social engineering. However, no tool can substitute for educational efforts that make users aware of the problem of social engineering and policies that must be followed to prevent social engineering from occurring.

As software becomes more and more entrenched in everyday life in today's society, security looms large as an unsolved problem. Despite advances in security mechanisms and technologies, most software systems in the world remain precarious and vulnerable. There is now widespread recognition that security cannot be achieved by technology alone. All software systems are ultimately embedded in some human social environment. The effectiveness of the system depends very much on the forces in that environment. Yet there are few systematic techniques for treating the social context of security together with technical system design in an integral way. In Chapter X, "*A Social Ontology for Integrating Security and Software Engineering,*" the authors, Dr. E. Yu and Dr. J. Mylopoulos of University of Toronto, Canada and Dr. L. Liu of Tsinghua University, China, argue that a social ontology at the core of a requirements engineering process can be the basis for integrating security into a requirements driven software engineering process. Authors describe the i* agent-oriented modeling framework and show how it can be used to model and reason about security concerns and responses. A smart card example is used to illustrate. Future directions for a social paradigm for security and software engineering are discussed.

End users often find that security configuration interfaces are difficult to use. In Chapter XI, "*Security Configuration for Non-experts: A Case Study in Wireless Network Configuration,*" Cynthia Kuo and Dr. Adrian Perrig of Carnegie Mellon University and Jesse Walker of Intel Corporation, USA explore how application designers can improve the design and evaluation of security configuration interfaces. The authors use IEEE 802.11 network configuration as a case study. First, the authors design and implement a configuration interface that guides users through secure network configuration. The key insight is that users have a difficult time translating their security goals into specific feature configurations. Our interface automates the translation from users' high-level goals to low-level feature configurations. Second, the authors develop and conduct a user study to compare our interface design with commercially available products. The authors adapt existing user research methods to sidestep common difficulties in evaluating security applications. Using authors' configuration interface, non-expert users are able to secure their networks as well as expert users. In general, the research addresses prevalent issues in the design and evaluation of consumer-configured security applications.

Chapter XII, "*Security Usability Challenges for End-users,*" highlights the need for security solutions to be usable by their target audience and examines the problems that can be faced when attempting to understand and use security features in typical applications. Challenges may arise from system-initiated events, as well as in relation to security tasks that users wish to perform for themselves, and can occur for a variety of reasons. This is illustrated by examining problems that arise as a result of reliance upon technical terminology, unclear or confusing functionality, lack of visible status and informative feedback to users, forcing users to make uninformed decision, and a lack of integration amongst the different elements of security software themselves. Dr. Steven M. Furnell of University of Plymouth, UK discusses a number of practical examples from popular applications, as well as results from survey and user trial activities that were conducted in order to assess the potential problems at first hand. The findings are used as the basis for recommending a series of top-level guidelines that may be used to improve the situation, and these are used as the basis assessing further examples of existing software to determine the degree of compliance.

The Internet has established firm deep roots in our day-to-day life. It has brought many revolutionary changes in the way we do things. One important consequence has been the way it has replaced human-to-human contact. This has also presented a new issue, which is the requirement for differentiating between real humans and automated programs on the Internet. Such automated programs are usually written with a malicious intent. CAPTCHAs play an important role in solving this problem by presenting users with tests that only humans can solve. Chapter XIII, "*CAPTCHAs—Differentiating between Human and Bots*" looks into the need, the history, and the different kinds of CAPTCHAs that researchers have come up with to deal with the security implications of automated bots pretending to be humans. Various schemes are compared and contrasted with each other, the impact of CAPTCHAs on Internet users is discussed and to conclude, the various possible attacks are discussed. The author, Dr. Deapesh Misra of Verisign, USA, hopes that the chapter will not only introduce this interesting field to the reader in its entirety, but also simulate thought on new schemes.

Chapter XIV, "*Privacy Concerns when Modeling Users in Collaborative Filtering Recommender Systems*" investigates ways to deal with privacy rules when modeling preferences of users in recommender systems based on collaborative filtering. It argues that it is possible to find a good compromise between quality of predictions and protection of personal data. Thus, it proposes a methodology that fulfills with strictest privacy laws for both centralized and distributed architectures. The authors, Dr. Sylvain Castagnos and Dr. Anne Boyer of LORIA—Université Nancy 2, Campus Scientifique, France, hope that their attempts to provide an unified vision of privacy rules through the related works and a generic privacy-enhancing procedure will help researchers and practitioners to better take into account the ethical and juridical constraints as regards privacy protection when designing information systems.

Traditionally, the views of security professionals regarding responses to threats and the management of vulnerabilities have been biased towards technology and operational risks. The purpose of this chapter is to extend the legacy threat-vulnerability model to incorporate human and social factors. This is achieved by presenting the dynamics of threats and vulnerabilities in the human and social context. Dr. Warren Axelrod of US Trust, USA, in his chapter (Chapter XV), "*An Adaptive Threat-Vulnerability Model and the Economics of Protection*" examines costs and benefits as they relate to threats, exploits, vulnerabilities, defense measures, incidents, and recovery and restoration. The author also compares the technical and human/social aspects of each of these areas. The author then looks at future work and how trends are pushing against prior formulations and forcing new thinking on the technical, operational risk, and human/social aspects. The reader will gain a broader view of threats, vulnerabilities, and responses to them through incorporating human and social elements into their security models.

Chapter XVI, "*Bridging the Gap between Employee Surveillance and Privacy Protection*" addresses the issue of electronic workplace monitoring and its implications for employees' privacy. Organizations increasingly use a variety of electronic surveillance methods to mitigate threats to their information systems. Monitoring technology spans different aspects of organizational life, including communications, desktop, and physical monitoring, collecting employees' personal data, and locating employees through active badges. The application of these technologies raises privacy protection concerns. Throughout this chapter, Dr. Lilian Mitrou and Dr. Maria Karyda of University of the Aegean, Greece, describe different approaches to privacy protection followed by different jurisdictions. The authors also highlight privacy issues with regard to new trends and practices, such as tele-working and use of RFID technology for identifying the location of employees. Emphasis is also placed on the reorganization of work facilitated by information technology, since frontiers between the private and the public sphere are becoming blurred. The aim of this chapter is twofold: it discusses privacy concerns and the implications of implementing employee surveillance technologies and suggests a framework of fair practices which can be used for bridging the gap between the need to provide adequate protection for information systems, while preserving employees' rights to privacy.

Achieving alignment of risk perception, assessment, and tolerance among and between management teams within an organisation is an important foundation upon which an effective enterprise information security management strategy can be built. Authors of Chapter XVII, "*Aligning IT Teams' Risk Management to Business Requirements*," Dr. Corey Hirsch of LeCroy Corporation, USA and Dr. Jean-Noel Ezingeard of Kingston University, UK, argue the importance of such alignment based on information security and risk assessment literature. Too often, lack of alignment dampens clean execution of strategy, eroding support during development and implementation of information security programs. Authors argue that alignment can be achieved by developing an understanding of enterprise risk management plans and actions, risk perceptions, and risk culture. This is done by examining context, context and process. Authors illustrate this through the case of LeCroy Corp., on how LeCroy managers perceive risk in practice and how LeCroy fosters alignment in risk perception and execution of risk management strategy as part of an overall information security program. They show that in some circumstances diversity of risk tolerance profiles aide a management teams' function. In other circumstances, variances lead to dysfunction. Authors have uncovered and quantified nonlinearities and special cases in LeCroy executive management's risk tolerance profiles.

Information security is becoming increasingly important and more complex as organizations are increasingly adopting electronic channels for managing and conducting business. However, state-of-the-art systems design methods have ignored several aspects of security that arise from human involvement or due to human factors. Manish Gupta, Dr. Raj Sharman, and Dr. Lawrence Sanders aim to highlight issues arising from coalescence of fields of systems requirements elicitation, information security, and human factors in their Chapter, XVIII, "*Systems Security Requirements Elicitation: An Agenda for Acquisition of Human Factors.*" The objective of the chapter is to investigate and suggest an agenda for state of human factors in information assurance requirements elicitation from perspectives of both organizations and researchers. Much research has been done in the area of requirements elicitation, both systems and security, but, invariably, human factors are not been taken into account during information assurance requirements elicitation. The chapter aims to find clues and insights into acquisition behavior of human factors in information assurance requirements elicitation and to illustrate current state of affairs in information assurance and requirements elicitation and why inclusion of human factors is required.

Information is a critical corporate asset that has become increasingly vulnerable to attacks from viruses, hackers, criminals, and human error. Consequently, organizations have to prioritize the security of their computer systems in order to ensure that their information assets retain their accuracy, confidentiality, and availability. While the importance of the information security policy (InSPy) in ensuring the security of information is acknowledged widely, to date there has been little empirical analysis of its impact or effectiveness in this role. To help fill this gap, Chapter XIX, *"Do Information Security Policies Reduce the Incidence of Security Breaches: An Exploratory Analysis"* presents an exploratory study was initiated that sought to investigate the relationship between the uptake and application of information security policies and the accompanying levels of security breaches. To this end, authors, Dr. N.F. Doherty and Dr. H. Fulford of Loughborough University, UK, designed, validated, and then targeted a questionnaire at IT managers within large organizations in the UK. The findings presented in this chapter are somewhat surprising, as they show no statistically significant relationships between the adoption of information security policies and the incidence or severity of security breaches. The chapter concludes by exploring the possible interpretations of this unexpected finding and its implications for the practice of information security management.

The book is aimed towards primary audience of professionals, scholars, researchers, and academicians working in the field of fast evolving and growing field of information security. Practitioners and managers working in information technology or information security area across all industries would vastly improve their knowledge and understanding of critical human and social aspects of information security.

REFERENCES

Belsis, P., Kokolakis, S., & Kiountouzis, E. (2005). Information systems security from a knowledge management perspective. *Information Management & Computer Security, 13*(3), 189-202.

CSI/FBI Survey. (2007). *Twelfth annual CSI/FBI computer crime and security survey*. Retrieved September 22, 2007, from http://i.cmpnet.com/v2.gocsi.com/pdf/CSISurvey2007.pdf

Dhillon, G. (2007). Principles of information systems security: Text and cases. Danvers: John Wiley & Sons.

Lewis, J. (2003). Cyber terror: Missing in action. *Knowledge, Technology & Policy, 16*(2), 34-41.

Lineberry, S. (2007). The human element: The weakest link in information security. *Journal of Accountancy, 204*(5). Retrieved from http://www.aicpa.org/pubs/jofa/nov2007/human_element.htm

McCauley-Bell, P. R., & Crumpton, L. L. (1998). The human factors issues in information security: What are they and do they matter? In *Proceedings of the Human Factors and Ergonomics Society 42nd Annual Meeting*, USA (pp. 439-442).

Mitnick, K., & Kasperavičius, A. (2004). *CSEPS course workbook*. Mitnick Security Publishing.

Orgill, G. L., Romney, G. W., Bailey, M. G., & Orgill, P. M. (2004, October 28-30). The urgency for effective user privacy-education to counter social engineering attacks on secure computer systems. In *Proceedings of the 5th Conference on Information Technology Education CITC5 '04*, Salt Lake City, UT, USA, (pp. 177-181). New York: ACM Press.

Schneier, B. (2000). *Secrets and lies*. John Wiley and Sons.

Vu, K. P. L., Bhargav, A., & Proctor, R. W. (2003). Imposing password restrictions for multiple accounts: Impact on generation and recall of passwords. In *Proceedings of the 47th Annual Meeting of the Human Factors and Ergonomics Society,* USA (pp. 1331-1335).

Vu, K. P. L., Tai, B. L., Bhargav, A., Schultz, E. E., & Proctor, R. W. (2004). Promoting memorability and security of passwords through sentence generation. In *Proceedings of the Human Factors and Ergonomics Society 48th Annual Meeting*, USA (pp.1478-1482).

Wilson, T. (2007). *Five myths about black hats, February 26, 2007*. Retrieved April 15, 2007, from http://www.darkreading.com/document.asp?doc_id=118169

Section I
Human and Psychological Aspects

Chapter I
Human and Social Aspects of Password Authentication

Deborah S. Carstens
Florida Institute of Technology, USA

ABSTRACT

With the increasing daily reliance on electronic transactions, it is essential to have reliable security practices for individuals, businesses, and organizations to protect their information (Vu, Bhargav, & Proctor, 2003; Vu, Tai, Bhargav, Schultz, & Proctor, 2004). A paradigm shift is occurring as researchers are targeting social and human dimensions of information security, as this aspect is seen as an area where control can be exercised. Since computer security is largely dependent on the use of passwords to authenticate users of technology, the objectives of this chapter are to (a) provide a background on password authentication and information security, (b) provide a discussion on security techniques, human error in information security, human memory limitations, and password authentication in practice, and (c) provide a discussion on future and emerging trends in password authentication to include future research areas.

INTRODUCTION

With the increasing daily reliance on electronic transactions, it is essential to have reliable security practices for individuals, businesses, and organizations to protect their information (Vu et al., 2003; Vu et al., 2004). A paradigm shift is occurring as researchers are targeting social and human dimensions of information security, as this aspect is seen as an area where control can

be exercised. Since computer security is largely dependent on the use of passwords to authenticate users of technology, the mission of this chapter is to addresses the human and social aspects of password authentication (Wiedenbeck, Waters, Birget, Brodskiy, & Memon, 2005). Users are challenged to remember long and random passwords and therefore too often choose passwords that may have low security strength or be difficult to remember (Wiedenbeck et al., 2005; Yan, Blackwell, Anderson, & Grant, 2004). As the number of individuals using computers and networks has increased, so has the level of threat for security breaches against these computers and networks. Carnegie Mellon's computer emergency response team (CERT) (2007) has collected statistics showing that six security incidents were reported in 1988 compared to 137, 529 in 2003. Furthermore, CERT (2007) reported that 171 vulnerabilities were reported in 1995 in comparison to 8,064 in 2006. In addition, the Federal Bureau of Investigation (FBI) conducted a survey in which 40% of organizations claimed that system penetrations from outside their organization had increased from the prior year by 25% (Ives, Walsh, & Schneider, 2004).

The rapid expansion in computing and networking has thus amplified the need to perpetually manage information security within an organization. Events such as 9/11 and the war on terrorism have also underscored an increased need for vigilance regarding information security. Organizations, government, and private industry are currently trying to adjust to the burden of this heightened need for information security, and, as an example of this, the U.S. Department of Homeland Security (2002) has focused particular efforts on ensuring information security. In light of the current context of universal computing and the realistic threats that exist to organizations' information systems, there is a strong need for more research in the field of information security. The main objectives of this chapter are to (a) provide a background on password authentication and information security, (b) provide a discussion on the main thrust of the chapter, human and social aspects of password authentication, which include the topics of security techniques, human error in information security, human memory limitations, and password authentication in practice, and (c) provide a discussion on future and emerging trends in password authentication to include future research areas and concluding

remarks in the area of human and social aspects of password authentication.

Password Authentication Background

In this world of ever increasing technological advances, users of technology are at risk for developing information overload as the number and complexity of passwords and other electronic identifiers increase. Previous investigations of the National Institute of Standards and Technology (NIST, 1992) have suggested that more than 50% of incidents that occur within government and private organizations have been connected to human errors. The role that people play in maintaining information security is an important one that the literature has only begun to address. As researchers improve their understanding of how social and human factors limitations affect information security, they can provide organizations with insight into improving information security policies. Passwords adopted by users are too easily cracked (Proctor, Lien, Vu, Schultz, & Salvendy, 2002). In particular, organizations can benefit from research revealing how best to minimize the demands that passwords place on the human memory system while maintaining the strength of a password (Carstens, McCauley-Bell, Malone, & DeMara, 2004).

The application of human factors and specifically, cognitive theory principles, can be used to positively influence system security when organizations follow password guidelines that do not exceed human memory limitations. Ultimately, user memory overload can be minimized when all aspects of a password authentication system have been designed in a way that capitalizes on the way the human mind works and also recognizes its limitations. As Hensley (1999) wrote, "Password(s) do little good if no one remembers them." Nevertheless, the exponential growth in vulnerabilities and security incidents as suggested by the CERT (2007) underscores that the design of password guidelines should be part of a comprehensive approach that still maintains strength of passwords as necessitated by the information technology (IT) community. Human and social factors in organizational security, such as human error on information security, are important issues that left unresolved can have adverse effects on industry.

Information Security Background

Ensuring effective information security involves making information accessible to those who need the information while maintaining the confidentiality and integrity of that material. There are three categories used to classify information security risks: (a) confidentiality, (b) integrity, and (c) accessibility or availability of information (U.S. Department of Homeland Security, 2002). A security breach in *confidentiality* can be defined as occurring when sources not intended to have knowledge of the information have been provided with this knowledge. Sending sensitive data to the wrong person is an example of this category. A security breach in *integrity* is an incident where there is an unauthorized or incorrect change made to an information source, such as a financial accounting error that causes the information in the database to be inaccurate. A security breach in *accessibility* occurs when either access for those entitled to a system is denied or access is given to those who are not authorized to access the system. An example of this category would be an authorized user of a system who is unable to access a system due to forgetting his or her password. Given the definitions, a *human error security incident* is defined as any human error related event that compromises information's confidentiality, integrity, or accessibility (Carstens et al., 2004).

The development of security is similar to any other design or development process in that the involvement of users and other stakeholders are crucial in the success of an organization's security policies. Research by Belsis, Spyros, and Kiountouzis (2005) suggests that although successful security management depends on the involvement of users and stakeholders, that knowledge on information systems security issues may be lacking resulting in reduced participation. Organizations seek to retain knowledge in their operations, but the extent to the knowledge captured on security related topics is not necessarily handled with the same consistency and rigor. Often, the process is an ad hoc one in gathering security knowledge through either the hiring of external consultants or depending on random internal security experts. Security knowledge can exist in both the form of tacit and explicit knowledge in four modes. The first mode is *socialization* and results strictly in tacit knowledge. This type of knowledge occurs when individuals interact with each other while sharing their knowledge. The second mode is *externalization*, which results in tacit knowledge being transformed into explicit knowledge. This type of knowledge results in the creation of metaphors, models, and analogies that an organization will use. The third mode is *combination*, resulting in knowledge sharing through documents, meetings, and better structuring of existing knowledge. As the term combination implies, both tacit and explicit knowledge exists within this mode. The fourth mode is *internalization*, whereby explicit knowledge becomes tacit knowledge. This occurs when an individual works frequently on a certain project where documented knowledge is utilized as well as the individual's experience expanding as an individual gains more familiarity with their work. The four modes together relate to how knowledge transformation within an organization occurs and contributes to the organizational memory. Lahaie (2005) discusses the threat of corporate memory loss when individuals leave an organization. Therefore, an information system knowledge management system could be deployed within an organization to ensure that knowledge, specifically in the area of security, is documented and assessable to aid in the success of an organization's security policy (Belsis et al., 2005).

An organization's security policy is becoming an increasingly important topic as a source to protect organizations' information assets. Risk analysis can be used to determine threats and identify processes to secure computer assets (Gerber, von Solms, and Overbeek, 2001). However, securing computer assets is no longer adequate in the information society of today and therefore we must also identify alternative approaches to securing information assets. Proactive security measures should be undertaken due to the degree of sensitive information within organizations and their constantly changing technological environment (Sanderson & Forcht, 1996). Information security management personnel are facing unprecedented challenges to ensure the safety of information assets within an organization (Hong, Chi, Chao, & Tang, 2003). By looking at theories on security policy, risk management, control and auditing, management system, and contingency theory, practitioners and researchers can work together to build a comprehensive theory of information security management and specifically password management. A security policy focuses on planning information security requirements, forming consensus in an organization, drafting and implementing a policy and revising the policy as deemed necessary. Risk management is concerned with the evaluation of organizational security risk factors for the purpose of ensuring that the level of risk at any given time for an organization is acceptable. Control and auditing theory investigates and implements security standards for an organization as a mechanism to control systems. The auditing segment of the theory provides for a means to assess control performance to ensure the standards are being maintained across an organization. Management system theory places value on the need for information security documentation in an organization as a tool and guide to ensure control and protection

of information assets. Contingency theory as it relates to information security management is to establish guidelines on how an organization will prevent and respond to system threats and vulnerabilities. The birth of an integrated theory occurs through ensuring that all of the theories are considered by information system practitioners and researchers in meeting organization security objectives. Therefore, organization's culture in the area of security policy could shift to an integrated theory involving multiple personnel to come together in the development and maintenance of the security policy.

The next section of the chapter discusses the main issues, controversies, and problems in the area of information security and specifically, password authentication. By comparing and contrasting what has been accomplished in the past with what is currently being undertaken, solutions and recommendations for organizations in regards to managing their information assets will be uncovered.

HUMAN AND SOCIAL ASPECTS IN PASSWORD AUTHENTICATION

Security Techniques

Research on passwords is necessitated in spite of a movement towards alternative security techniques, such as bioidentifiers, individual certificates, tokens, and smart cards. Smart cards communicate directly with the target system and run the authentication procedure themselves. A survey of 4,254 companies in 29 countries was conducted by Dinnie (1999) to identify a global perspective of information security. The survey indicated that password authentication in the USA is the preferred security method utilized 62% of the time, as opposed to smart card authentication only being used 8% of the time and certificates 9% of the time. In Australia, password authentication is used 67% as opposed to smart card authentication only being used 9% of the time and certificates 5% of the time. The remaining countries surveyed showed password authentication at 58% with smart card authentication at 4%. However, the problem with password authentication, smart cards, and tokens is that these provide the ability to have the information that is requested but not the ability of identifying the person (Harris & Yen, 2002). Therefore, bioidentifiers will likely become increasingly popular as it is the only way to identify who the person is rather than what they have or know. The main problems of bioidentifiers are the cost, inconvenience of users needing to prepare to be scanned and needing to be enrolled at multiple computer systems, potential to fool systems leading to unauthorized access, and fear individuals have with their biometric data being stolen. Therefore, password usage for both professional and personal use is still a common means of authentication necessitating the need to further understand the human and social aspects of information security.

Human Error in Information Security

Research has indicated that human error makes up as much as 65% of incidents that cause economic loss for a company and that security incidents caused by external threats such as computer hackers happen only 3% or less of the time (Lewis, 2003; McCauley-Bell & Crumpton, 1998; NIST, 1992). However, there is only a minimal effort to address the human error risks in information security, which is among the highest cause of information security incidents (McCauley-Bell & Crumpton, 1998; Wood & Banks, 1993). A common challenge faced by individuals today is the need to simultaneously maintain passwords for many different systems in their work, school, and personal lives. Research conducted by Wiedenbeck et al. (2005) suggests that stringent rules for passwords lead to poor password practices that compromise overall security. Human limitations can compromise password security because users

are unable to remember passwords and therefore keep insecure records of their passwords, such as writing a password down on paper (Yan et al., 2004). Organizational security policies need to be adhered to by employees to ensure protection of organization's information assets. Therefore, changes in security policies using integrated theory should be considered resulting in policies being better followed.

A survey in the area of the human impact on information security indicated that 37% of survey participants never change their work and/or school passwords and that 69% of survey participants never change their personal passwords (Carstens et al., 2004). The same research suggests that when prompted to replace a current password, 43% of survey participants changed their work and/or school passwords back to a password they had used in the past; 33% of survey participants indicated changing their personal passwords back to an old password as well. The survey research suggests that with the IT community stressing the importance of using secure passwords, not writing passwords on paper, changing passwords often, and using different passwords for all systems, a person may compromise the strength of their password due to human information processing limitations. Proctor et al. (2002) performed experiments testing passwords between five characters and eight characters in length. The research suggests that increasing password character length to a minimum of six to eight characters reduces crackability and therefore password strength, in terms of security. Another study conducted suggests that crack-resistant passwords were achieved through the use of a sentence generation password method including the user to embed a digit and special character into the password (Vu et al., 2004). However, memorability issues occurred with users from adding the digit and special character to the password.

Human Memory Limitations

Miller's (1956) chunking theory and Cowan's (2001) research is useful to consider, regarding human and social factors in organizational security, specifically when developing a model for password guidelines. This theory classifies data in terms of chunks and indicates that the capacity of working memory is 7±2 chunks of information. More recent research suggests that a mean memory capacity in adults is only three to five chunks with a range of two to six chunks as the real capacity limit (Cowan, 2001). A chunk of data is defined as being a letter, digit, word, or different unit, such as a date (Miller, 1956). A chunk is further described as a set of adjacent stimulus units that are closely tied together by associations in the user's long-term memory. Miller suggests that merely turning information into a meaningful chunk of data can increase a person's short-term memory capacity. This occurs because chunking data places the input into subsets that are remembered as single units. A person's short-term memory capacity is reduced if a person tries to remember isolated digits or letters rather than grouping or recoding the information into chunks of data. Chunking then becomes useful in the development of passwords in creating a meaningful sequence of stimuli within the total string of data; that is, chunks serve as an integral representation of data that are already stored in a person's long-term memory.

Similar to Miller's chunking theory, Newell, Shaw, and Simon (1961) suggest that highly meaningful words are easier for a person to learn and remember than less meaningful words, with *meaningful* being defined by the person's number of associations with the word. Vu et al. (2003) suggest that passwords could be more memorable if users comprised their passwords with familiar characters such as phone numbers. Memorizing a string of words that represent complete concepts is easier to remember than an unrelated list of words suggests Straub (2004). Building on Miller's work,

Golbeck (2002) suggests that schemas can serve as the basis for chunks because they provide a meaningful method for grouping information. A schema is defined as a mental model that makes recall of an item easier for users. Mental models are sets of beliefs that a person has on how a system works and therefore interacts with a system based on these beliefs (Norman, 1988).

Research suggests that turning information into a meaningful chunk of data can increase a person's short-term memory capacity. For example, a study conducted by Loftus, Dark, and Williams (1979), which tested short-term memory retention among ground control and student pilots through an examination of communication errors, found that recall was better when material was chunked. In addition, Preczewski and Fisher (1990) studied the format of call signs made up of any series of letters and digits used by the military in secure radio communications. The findings indicate that the size of the chunks influenced the accuracy of short-term retention. Furthermore, mixing letters and digits within one-chunk was more difficult to recall than just having letters or digits make up the chunk because the mixed chunk of letters and digits lacked meaning. This research therefore suggests that memory is enhanced when the person can make meaning of the data string.

Wickens (1992) suggests that chunking should be used whenever possible because of people's working memory limitations. Further, he describes chunking as a strategy or mnemonic device that may be taught. This mnemonic aspect is what makes chunking a helpful way for organizations and individuals to develop passwords that do not exceed human memory limitations. Therefore, system designers, or in this case, system password guideline designers, should not exceed the low end of Miller's 7±2 chunk scale. Proctor et al. (2002) performed research where Miller's chunking theory (1956) was a consideration in testing different length passwords between five characters to eight characters due to Miller's 7±2 chunk scale. In a study conducted by Vu et al.

(2004), a sentence generation method was utilized to produce a crack resistant password through the user being required to embed a special character and digit into the sentence. User memorability of these generated passwords declined as it took users two times longer to recall the passwords, made users perform twice as many errors in recalling the password, and resulted in users forgetting the password twice as often. The researchers suggest that the errors occurred due to users forgetting the sentence generated and the special character and/or digit embedded in the sentence. Furthermore, participants experienced difficulty with remembering the digit and/or symbols which researchers attributed to the symbols and/or digits not being meaningfully related to the sentence. Vu et al. (2003) conducted a different study to analyze the effects of password generation and recall utilizing multiple accounts suggesting that increasing demands on human memory leads to the level of remembrance of the password to be decreased.

Carstens, Malone, and McCauley-Bell (2006) performed a study at a large federal agency to determine whether a difference exists in people's ability to remember complex passwords with different difficulty levels. Four different types of passwords were tested. The first password did not use chunking theory and participants were required to follow the following guidelines: password must be at least seven characters in length; password must have a combination of symbols and letters; password cannot use the same term more than twice; password must not spell out a dictionary word or proper noun; and password can't be relevant data such as individual's social security number, street address, birth date, and so forth. The second password was a two-chunk password and required participants to use the following guidelines: password must contain the participants' first and last initials using a combination of both uppercase and lowercase letters (first chunk); password must contain participants' federal agency start date using dif-

ferent types of symbols as day, month, and year separators (second chunk). The third password was a three-chunk password requiring participants to use the following guidelines: password must contain participants' first and last initials formatted using a combination of both uppercase and lowercase letters (first chunk); password must contain participants' federal agency start date using different types of symbols as day, month, and year separators (second chunk); password must contain participants' mother's first name initial in uppercase and maiden name initial in lowercase (third chunk). The fourth password tested was a four-chunk password comprised of the following criteria: Participants selected two meaningful dates that were not easily accessible to the public, using a symbol of choice to be used as day/month/year separators (2 chunks); participants selected two sets of initials that contained at least one uppercase and one lowercase letter (2 chunks). For each of the passwords tested, different guidelines were given. All of the guidelines mandated study participants to choose passwords with a combination of numbers, letters, and special characters. The passwords tested that included chunking theory, which were the second, third, and fourth passwords, gave participants written guidelines informing participants how their password should be developed, such as with the use of their mother's maiden name initials. However, only in the four-chunk password was verbal training given to participants in how to create meaningful passwords. The results indicate that a password comprised of meaningful chunks is easier to recall than a password with random data such as the seven character password tested, even if the password contains additional characters. Individuals were better able to recall the passwords in the two-chunk password and three-chunk password as well as in the four-chunk password, which indicates that data in the actual passwords could be meaningfully chunked together for the individual. Furthermore, the results indicate that an individual is able to recall a two-chunk password as easily as a three-chunk or even a four-chunk password. Results further suggest that as long as information in a password is composed of meaningful information unique to an individual, human memory capabilities enable an individual to recall up to four-chunks of data consisting of up to 22 characters.

Password Authentication in Practice

This chapter offers guidance to those that design security policies by providing a practical guide to password management as displayed in Figure 1. The first component of password management is to use integrated theory in the development of security policies. Integrated theory insists on pulling individuals from different areas within an organization along with expertise within many important disciplines such as risk, security, control and auditing, management and contingency theory. This enables a systematic approach to the management of passwords and overall security within an organization.

The second component of password management is to provide guidelines for individuals within organizations to follow that result in secure passwords. Previous research by Carstens et al.

(2006) developed secure password guidelines that are listed:

- Passwords must be a combination of symbols, numbers, and letters.
- Passwords cannot use the same character more than twice.
- Passwords must not spell out words that are found in a dictionary or use a proper noun such as a name of a person, pet, place, or thing.
- Passwords can not contain information easily accessible to the public which include but are not limited to a social security number, street address, family members' birthdays, and wedding anniversary dates.
- Passwords contain two to four chunks of data and are comprised of 10 to 22 characters in length, which will be dependent on the character length capabilities of any given system.

The purpose of the password guideline research was in evaluating the impact of password demands as a means of authentication and to mitigate risks that result when these demands exceed human capabilities. The intent was to develop password guidelines that do not exceed human memory limitations, yet that maintain

Figure 1. Password management guidelines

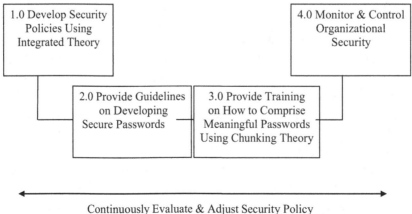

Continuously Evaluate & Adjust Security Policy

strength of passwords. The password guidelines developed in the research had individuals compose their passwords of relevant and meaningful data that are not accessible to the public. Some industries do suggest to system users to compose passwords of meaningful data. However, specific guidelines or password training have not been established to aid users in how to comprise a password that is both secure and meaningful. The research provided value to information security literature through testing the usefulness of chunking theory being applicable to the development of passwords. When followed, these guidelines result in (a) reduced vulnerabilities in information systems within organizations and (b) increased trust in the users of information technology. These guidelines provide users with a password that is both secure and easy to recall in terms of it being stored effectively in an individual's long term memory. The password guidelines were created that do not exceed human memory limitations, yet maintain strength of password as necessitated by the information technology community. The two criteria for ideal password development are (a) passwords contain meaningful and personally relevant data for the user and (b) passwords are strong passwords in terms of the IT community's standards. It is important that these guidelines be utilized in conjunction with training that assists the user in creating a password composed of meaningful data chunks and in managing multiple passwords.

The third component of password management is to provide some degree of training to individuals in creating a meaningful password. Providing training to individuals within organizations will provide assistance in the creation of passwords that are meaningful and therefore more easily remembered. The training guides employees on how to compose passwords that are comprised of meaningful chunks of data unique only to that employee. Research by Yan et al. (2004) suggests that password security can be significantly improved through educating users on how to better

comprise a password. First, the instructor should define what it means to compose a password of meaningful chunks and may discuss how many chunks of data can easily be recalled by users (i.e., two, three, or four). It would also be helpful if the instructor encouraged different employees to comprise their passwords of different lengths so that potential hackers would be unable to discover a consistent password length among employees. For example, an instructor might inform employees in one class to have a system specific password between 7-9 characters in length and in another class might recommend a password between 10-12 characters in length. Instructors should also stress the importance to not have the same password used for more than one system. Employees should also be encouraged to select one chunk of a password to be considered as a core of every password. The core or one-chunk would then be part of all passwords. For example, if a person wanted to create a two-chunk password, a person could select "Mb#=43," which translates to my basketball number equals 43, as one-chunk within their password. The person could then select the second chunk of data such as "iemf," which translates to industrial engineering major in Florida. The two chunks could be combined, "Mb#=43iemf" to form one password that an individual uses to access their university portal. The person could then select "GMCBHS," which translates to go minuteman at Cocoa Beach High School. Once again, the two chunks could be combined, "Mb#=43GMCBHS" and used as an individual's password for their social network account such as myspace.com or facebook.com, since these systems often link former high school friends together. Therefore, one-chunk of every password for an individual could remain constant. It is the second chunk of the password that could vary and be composed of information that is directly linked to the system or device where it is used. An individual could then have multiple passwords in both their professional and personal lives that have one familiar chunk which never varies. However, from a security perspective, any additional chunks used in the password should vary. From a human memory limitations perspective, linking the second chunk to the system being used in a unique and non-obvious matter would enable an individual to obtain a password that is strong yet easy to recall.

The fourth component of password management is to monitor and control organizational security. This component typically resides with the security administrator (Higgins, 1999). Some organizations may have different administrators such as one for a gateway, network, and so forth. However, it is every individual's job to ensure that the security policy is being adhered to throughout the organization. Routine audits should be scheduled by the administrator. The audits would result in the identification of any vulnerability that may be present within organizations' information assets. Additionally, the use of publicly available hacking techniques should be tested to ensure that the information assets can withstand the trials. Users should be prompted by their systems to change passwords periodically. Requiring that passwords request at several gates, from remote access, network, applications, and files enhances security as well, according to Higgins (1999). The use of scanner or cracker programs could also be used to ensure strong passwords are chosen by individuals. Lastly, it is important for all organizational security personnel to ensure that time is spent to continuously evaluate and adjust the security policy as new technologies and individuals become part of an organization. These guidelines are applicable to a variety of uses such as information systems, document passwords, corporate portals, and mobile devices. However, the guidelines are not applicable to legacy systems due to the recommended character length. Although, the other aspects of the guidelines could aid legacy system users to better recall their passwords.

TRENDS IN PASSWORD AUTHENTICATION

Emerging and Future Trends in Password Authentication

There are many trends in the area of passwords that can be classified as either emerging or future. Emerging trends are in the area of securing information assets for organizations as displayed in Figure 2. This is a basic model for human factors practitioners and information technology professionals to use in determining the vulnerabilities that password practices are producing on their information systems. This is an initial model and additional research is ongoing to validate and enhance the model. A great need in the area of information security is to uncover methods to manage information assets which begin through uncovering information threats and system vulnerabilities. Vulnerabilities have the potential to cause harm to information which is the core of any organization, as knowledge is power. Without confidentiality, integrity, and accessibility of information within organizations' systems, an organization's competitive advantage could be violated. Organizations still primarily utilize passwords as a means of user authentication for information technology. The password issues consist of an individual being expected to remember many different passwords, multiple systems that required different or similar passwords for an individual to obtain access, and the complexity of password guidelines that individuals are expected to follow in the development of their passwords. These issues produce system vulnerabilities, such as weak passwords (e.g., dictionary words), common passwords (e.g., using the same password for more than one system), visible passwords (e.g., an individual writing their password on a sticky note hanging on their computer), and security policies not being followed due to the complexity of the password guidelines. Currently, the model identifies workload concerns as well such as overload of information. Together, the workload and password issues produce system vulnerabilities that could result in the potential of insecure information assets. Identification of the causes of the vulnerabilities are important, as once the causes are known, security personnel can then take the appropriate actions to decrease the vulnerabilities through reducing or eliminating workload and password concerns.

The integrated theory approach is another emerging trend that focuses on security policy, risk management, control and auditing, management system, and contingency theory can be used to build a comprehensive security policy that is more likely to be followed by individuals in an organization and ensure that security within an organization is maintained (Hong, Chi, Chao, & Tang, 2003). As technology continues to pulse through the daily lives of individuals, the behavioral aspects of humans at work and play continues to be explored resulting in more technology in terms of products to help organize individuals. Along with new technology, new and changing security policies will be implemented in organizations which are responsible for growth in the field of information technology.

A future trend will be the development of a tool or better method for password management. Password management issues causes organizational help desks personnel to be extremely busy on Mondays and after holidays due to the number of employees that forget their passwords. This will continue to be a problem, if not even an increasing problem, as the number of passwords individuals are required to remember increase due to the degree of technology in society. It is anticipated that alternative security options such as those discussed in the *security techniques* section will continue to be developed to enable more organizations to utilize alternatives to passwords for work related systems. A future trend will likely be to develop a wireless device that could serve a person for all of their password authentication needs. The problem, of course, with such a device would be if the device is ever lost, which is why the device would likely be some type of biometric device that is able to accurately and efficiently distinguish one individual from another without concern by users of their identity being stolen. This will continue to be an important topic for practitioners and researchers until a solution is found. In the interim, there is research that can be performed to make the life of those individuals

Figure 2. Understanding the vulnerabilities present with information assets in an organization

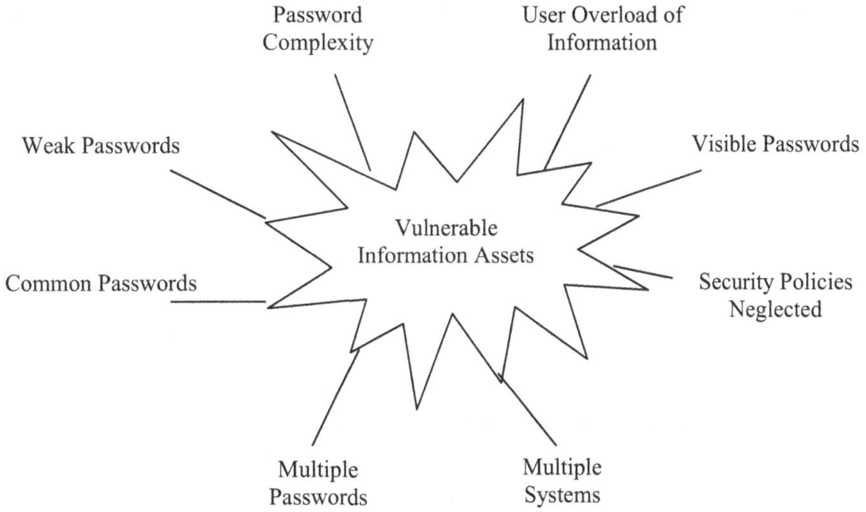

required to maintain multiple passwords easier. Future password authentication research will be discussed next.

FUTURE PASSWORD AUTHENTICATION RESEARCH

The world has been revolutionized by the amount of information that makes its way into the daily lives of individuals and ultimately organizations. It is therefore necessary that research continues to identify specific ways that assist individuals in handling the abundance of information. Future research in password authentication practices should continue to explore the human and social factors in organizational security. Organizational and individual password usage, as new technology emerges, will likely increase the memory demands placed on individuals daily. Research will need to be continuously conducted to keep a pulse on the password demands being placed on individuals to identify techniques that assist humans with the management of their passwords. Determining the links between password issues and other newly identified issues on human memory limitations and strategies to reduce the potential for vulnerabilities produced will be crucial for organizational success. Future research in the social and human side of information security will further support the need for organizations to have password guidelines that do not exceed human memory limitations. Having password guidelines that do not exceed human memory limitations will enable organizational security policies to be better followed and eliminate the need for individuals to write their passwords on a piece of paper or use the same password for multiple systems. Identification of the links between password issues and possibly workload issues on human memory limitations will further educate organizations on the vulnerabilities present. As vulnerabilities are identified, organizations will be able to better guard against the vulnerabilities

present in systems and therefore positively contribute to impacting the security of information within systems.

CONCLUSION

Although there are many alternatives to password authentication, individuals have multiple passwords that are used daily, as password authentication is still considered to be the most common form of authentication. Therefore, an issue for information security personnel is to reduce the information load faced by individuals trying to maintain numerous passwords for recall. A password-creation system that does not impose additional demands on a person's attention capacities and short-term memory, since passwords are composed of information that already exists in an individual's long-term memory, is perhaps a mechanism that individuals can use until a better and more affordable alternative to authentication exists. When individuals have passwords that do no exceed human memory limitations, employees can be trusted to follow organizational security policies. The more instruction and education that can be given to employees will have positive benefits in enabling them to form strong passwords that are easy to recall. The use of password guidelines reduces the likelihood of an organization being subject to a security breach since individuals would be less likely to engage in practices that render an organization vulnerable, such as using the same password for multiple systems or writing their passwords on paper. The recommendations and suggestions for improvement to security policies discussed in this chapter support the use of Miller's (1956) chunking theory and Cowan (2001), when developing password guidelines and training on password development. Through simple password guideline changes and employee password security training, organizations can better guard against human error while maintaining secure practices for user authentication that guard against external threats. Until passwords are no longer in use, it is important that practitioners and researchers continue their efforts as a building block for future research that focuses on the human side of information security and specifically the human and social aspects of password authentication.

REFERENCES

Belsis, P., Kokolakis, S., & Kiountouzis, E. (2005). Information systems security from a knowledge management perspective. *Information Management & Computer Security, 13*(3), 189-202.

Carnegie Mellon Computer Emergency Response Team (CERT). (2007). *Computer emergency response team statistics.* Retrieved April 25, 2007, from http://www.cert.org/stats/cert_stats. html#incidents

Carstens, D. S., Malone, L., & Bell, P. (2006). Applying chunking theory in organizational human factors password guidelines. *Journal of Information, Information Technology, and Organizations, 1*, 97-113.

Carstens, D. S., McCauley-Bell, P., Malone, L., & DeMara, R. (2004). Evaluation of the human impact of password authentication practices on information security. *Informing Science Journal, 7*, 67-85.

Cowan, N. (2001). The magical number 4 in short-term memory: A reconsideration of mental storage capacity. *Behavioral and Brain Sciences, 24*(1), 87-185.

Dinnie, G. (1999). The second annual global information security survey. *Information Management & Computer Security, 7*(3), 112-120.

Gerber, M., Solms, R. V., & Overbeek, P. (2001). Formalizing information security requirements. *Information Management & Computer Security, 9*(1), 32-37.

Golbeck, J. (2002). *Cognitive load and memory theories.* Retrieved April 2, 2007, from http://www.cs.umd.edu/class/fall2002/cmsc838s/tichi/printer/memory.html

Harris, A. J., & Yen, D. C. (2002). Biometric authentication: Assuring access to information. *Information Management & Computer Security, 10*(1), 12-19.

Hensley, G. A. (1999). *Calculated risk: passwords and their limitations.* Retrieved April 2, 2007, from http://www.infowar.com/articles/99article_120699a_j.shtml

Higgins, H. N. (1999). Corporate system security: towards an integrated management approach. *Information Management & Computer Security, 7*(5), 217-222.

Hong, K. S., Chi, Y. P., Chao, L. R., & Tang, J. H. (2003). An integrated system theory of information security management. *Information Management & Computer Security, 11*(5), 243-248.

Ives, B., Walsh, K., & Schneider, H. (2004). The domino effect of password reuse. *Communications of the ACM, 47*(4), 75-78.

Lahaie, D. (2005). The impact of corporate memory loss. *Leadership in Health Services, 18*, 35-48.

Lewis, J. (2003). Cyber terror: Missing in action. *Knowledge, Technology & Policy, 16*(2), 34-41.

Loftus, E. F., Dark, V. J., & Williams, D. (1979). Short-term memory factors in ground controller/pilot communication. *Human Factors, 21*, 169-181.

McCauley-Bell, P. R., & Crumpton, L. L. (1998). The human factors issues in information security: What are they and do they matter? In *Proceedings of the Human Factors and Ergonomics Society 42nd Annual Meeting*, USA (pp. 439-442).

Miller, G. A. (1956). The magical number seven plus or minus two: Some limits on our capacity for processing information. *Psychological Review, 63,* 81-97.

National Institute of Standards and Technology (NIST). (1992). Computer *system security and privacy advisory board* (Annual Report, 18).

Newell, A., Shaw, J. C., & Simon, H. (1961) *Information processing language V manual.* Edgewood Cliffs, NJ: Prentice-Hall.

Norman, D. A. (1988). *The psychology of everyday things.* New York: Harper & Row.

Preczewski, S. C., & Fisher, D. L. (1990). The selection of alphanumeric code sequences. In *Proceedings of the Human Factors Society 34th Annual Meeting* (pp. 224-228).

Proctor, R. W., Lien, M. C., Vu, K. P. L., Schultz, E. E., & Salvendy, G. (2002). Improving computer security for authentication of users: Influence of proactive password restrictions. *Behavior Research Methods, Instruments, & Computers, 34,* 163-169.

Sanderson, E., & Forcht, K. A. (1996). Information security in business environments. *Information Management & Computer Security, 4*(1), 32-37.

Straub, K. (2004). Cracking password usability exploiting human memory to create secure and memorable passwords. *UI Design Newsletter*, Retrieved April 2, 2007, from http://www.humanfactors.com/downloads/jun04.asp

U.S. Department of Homeland Security. (2002). *Federal information security management act.* Retrieved April 2, 2007, from http://www.fedcirc.gov/library/legislation/FISMA.html

Vu, K. P. L., Bhargav, A., & Proctor, R. W. (2003). Imposing password restrictions for multiple accounts: Impact on generation and recall of passwords. In *Proceedings of the 47th Annual Meeting of the Human Factors and Ergonomics Society,* USA (pp. 1331-1335).

Vu, K. P. L., Tai, B. L., Bhargav, A., Schultz, E. E., & Proctor, R. W. (2004). Promoting memorability and security of passwords through sentence generation. In *Proceedings of the Human Factors and Ergonomics Society 48th Annual Meeting,* USA (pp.1478-1482).

Wickens, C. D. (1992). *Engineering psychology and human performance* (2nd ed.). New York: HarperCollins Publishers.

Wiedenbeck, S., Waters, J., Birget, J. C., Brodskiy, A., & Memon, N. (2005). PassPoints: Design and longitudinal evaluation of a graphical password system. *International Journal of Human Computer Studies, 63,* 102-127.

Wood, C. W., & Banks, W. W. (1993). Human error: an overlooked but significant information security problem. *Computers & Security, 12,* 51-60.

Yan, J., Blackwell, A., Anderson, R., & Grant, A. (2004). Password memorability and security: Empirical results. *IEEE Security and Privacy, 2*(5), 25-31.

Chapter II
Why Humans are the Weakest Link

Marcus Nohlberg
School of Humanities and Informatics, University of Skövde, Sweden

ABSTRACT

This chapter introduces the concept of social psychology, and what forms of deception humans are prone to fall for. It presents a background of the area and a thorough description of the most common and important influence techniques. It also gives more practical examples of potential attacks, and what kind of influence techniques they use, as well as a set of recommendations on how to defend against deception, and a discussion on future trends. The author hopes that the understanding of why and how the deceptive techniques work will give the reader new insights into information security in general, and deception in particular. This insight can be used to improve training, to discover influence earlier, or even to gain new powers of influence.

INTRODUCTION

A computer crime starts, and ends, with a human, no matter which method is chosen for the attack. Many successful computer crimes could have been prevented if the people involved had been more vigilant, more security conscious, or aware of their own weaknesses. This chapter deals with human weakness. It can be perceived as a "how-to-manual" for the aspiring attacker, but just as well as a "know-yourself" guide that can be used by both individuals and professionals in order to improve their personal and organizational defenses. It might also give a little more understanding for the victims. When researching successful attacks from the comfortable position of the outside observer, most of us are prone to throw the first stone against what can be seen as gullible humans. The fact is that almost everyone is susceptible to the techniques and weaknesses described in this chapter, simply because the attacks play on human emotion rather than logic.

BACKGROUND

We humans are complicated beings, with some interesting shortcuts in our behavior. In recent years there have been multiple studies on deception in general and influence in particular. These studies have been done in, amongst others, the field of economics and most notably in social psychology. In order to stay as close to the human element as possible, this chapter will focus on the social psychological aspects that can be practically used by the attacker. There are ample theories and work being done in a more theoretical setting, but this chapter will focus on the techniques that the perpetrators might use. Cialdini (2001) has written one of the most influential books in this area, and this chapter will follow his use of the six basic rules of influence, together with some other added aspects of influence. In order to facilitate a better understanding of the concepts, examples will be given, both from the literature and from real life. When applicable, the terms will be tied together with information security as far as possible. Not all the information here will be from research, some will also be added from online sources, guides on what to explore and attack written for the aspiring social engineer. While this information has not been judged against academic standards, it is still relevant, because it is the information attackers will try to use for their attacks and therefore important to know.

Deception is a powerful tool for any attacker, but also for any parent, teacher, salesman, or most of us in our everyday lives. We buy and sell goods, we court romantic interests, and we try to raise our kids in a good way without them loathing us too much when we try to get them to do their chores. In all of these examples, and many more, deception is the key element. Deception can be defined as:

Everything done to manipulate the behavior of the other side, without their knowledge of the friendly intent, for the purpose of achieving and exploiting an advantage is deception. The "what" of deception is the manipulation of behavior. The "why" is to exploit the advantage achieved (Feer, 2004).

There are two different kinds of deception. There is dissimulation, which concerns the hiding of the truth (Bowyer, 2003). The truth can be hidden in three ways. It can be hidden by masking the information, for instance, by hiding nefarious features in a piece of software. It can also be hidden by repackaging the information, for instance, by hiding a Trojan horse in legitimate software. Finally, information can be dissimulated by dazzle, to shock or surprise, for instance, by sending nude pictures in an e-mail. The other kind of deception, simulation, deals with exhibiting false information. Simulation can be done by mimicking, which is spoofing or imitating reality, for instance, as done in a phishing attack. It can also be done by inventing, which is the creation of a new reality, for example, false messages from Microsoft that a certain bug must be patched as soon as possible. The final method of simulation is decoying, where a diversion is done to create a diversion from the real object, such as a false warning of a different attack than the one you are exposed to at the moment.

HUMANS AND DECEPTION

Most of us, and indeed probably you, the reader, consider ourselves exceptionally resistant to manipulation. We are better than the average at detecting lies, and can spot a con a mile away. When asked about our friend's susceptibility to deception, however, we find them to be far more gullible (Levine, 2003). Obviously, we are misjudging our own capacities, as influence in general is highly effective, which is proven by the huge profits it generates for advertisers, corporations, and religious groups, among others, that use these techniques.

The reason people misjudge their own abilities to spot deception is because of "lie detector bias" where individuals almost always overestimate their ability to detect lies (Marett, Biros, & Knode, 2004). This is further complicated by the truth bias, which is the widespread assumption that most people are telling the truth (Martin, 2004). Humans also tend to think that bad things, such as death, accidents, crime, natural disasters, and so forth, generally only happen to others (Levine, 2003). To further highlight our vulnerabilities, another interesting weakness in the human psyche is the "fixed-action patterns." They are most easily studied in animals, where certain specific conditions, "trigger features," trigger a predetermined response. For instance, a certain breed of bird will instantly start to care for any egg-like object, even if it is obviously not an egg but instead perhaps a painted volleyball (Levine, 2003). While "fixed-action patterns" might seem impractical, for animals in particular, they save time, energy, and mental capacity. Even for humans, certain "fixed-action patterns" are beneficial, for instance, giving thanks when receiving a gift, doing what police officers say you should, and so forth. In normal circumstances, the "fixed-action patterns" are usually correct and beneficial to us. They start to become a major problem when someone starts to use them as a weapon against ourselves.

So basically, we humans believe that we are good at spotting lies, that people seldom lie to us and that bad things mostly happen to others. We are also mostly blissfully unaware that we have certain "fixed-action patterns" that will make us react almost without thinking to certain requests. This is the stage for the great game of influence.

THE BASICS OF INFLUENCE

The easiest, and many times the most efficient means of influencing others are simply to be kind.

A bit of kindness goes a long way, since most average users really want to be helpful (Granger, 2002). A slightly more advanced method is to add the illusion of a reason behind the request. The illusion of a reason can be just as effective as a good reason. When asking people to do something, it was found that simply using the word "because" in the question is just as effective as using it in together with an actual motivation (Cialdini, 2003). In order to develop deeper skills of influence, any single one of, or combination of, the following techniques can be used.

Authority

People are likely to respond obediently to authority. We are generally brought up to respect authority and ever since we were kids it has been beneficial to do as the authorities want us to do; both in school, at home, in church, in the army, and in the workplace. Listening to authority is seldom detrimental to anyone. In extreme circumstances this can push people to do dreadful things, as was shown by the famous Stanley-Milgram experiment (Obedience to Authority Study). In the study, subjects thought that they were administering electric shocks to another (fake) subject in order to punish them for errors. The real study was to test their willingness to administer painful, or even potentially lethal, doses of electricity while being told to do so by an authoritative test supervisor. The study showed that a disturbingly high percentage (65 %) were willing to continue the experiment even though they, to the best of their knowledge, were administering extremely painful and potentially lethal doses of electricity to another subject who was screaming in pain and complaining about intense chest pains (Blass, 2002).

But authority is not only someone telling us what to do. Other aspects than verbal orders are also influencing who we think is a person of authority. One example of this is uniforms. Uniforms are a cheap and simple way to be perceived as a person of great authority (Mitnick, 2002). Uniforms can be of the obvious kind (police uniform, doctor's coat, soldiers uniform), but perhaps the most effective kind of uniforms are those that we do not normally perceive as a uniform. Examples of this kind of uniforms are technicians' and maintenance personnel's clothing and the clothing worn by cleaners. Cleaners and maintenance staff are groups of people that often tend to have full access to most areas, often at times when there are few or no other employees around. They are also often employed by someone else than the organization in which they work, a subcontractor. This gives them full access, and they are rarely questioned, making them a risky element. Reasonably normal clothing is also a kind of uniform, especially the style and message of the outfit. For instance, a nice, tailored suit sends a different message than a "nerdy" Linux t-shirt, but they are both efficient as uniforms in a particular context. Another kind of uniform is the title of a person, where an impressive title, such as professor, doctor, lord, sir, and so forth, can influence the amount of authority we perceive that someone has (Cialdini, 2003). Real titles often take years of hard work to achieve, but to acquire a fake title only takes seconds. Even fake diplomas can be bought cheaply, making it even more difficult to judge the value of a mentioned title.

Other examples of things that make us perceive someone as having authority are purely material artifacts, such as wealth, fancy clothing, jewelry, and expensive cars, and certain other human traits such as length and tone of voice. Humans are easily influenced by these things, and having the right clothes can make a big difference, something which is well known by con men (Cialdini, 2003).

The practical consequences of this human weakness for uniforms and fancy attributes, except for the sad fact that the imagery in hip-hop videos actually works well to influence our perceptions of the artists as important, are that an attacker would benefit from using either a specific uniform to make desktop hacking easier, or for instance, specific titles to make a social engineering attack over the telephone be more efficient. This was made chillingly obvious in a study where nurses were called over the telephone by a person introducing himself as a doctor responsible for one of the patients, then proceeding to tell the nurse to administer a dangerously high dosage of medicine to the patient. Without requesting further identification most nurses, 95 %, complied, and were stopped by the researchers on their way to the medicine cabinet (Levine, 2003).

Scarcity

When told that something they want is in short supply, people tend to want it even more. The information that others might be competing for the same thing triggers the sense of competition. This can be observed in ads everyday, where terms as "limited supply" are frequently used. Time is always a stressing factor, it is efficient to make the market see that time is in limited supply, thus leaving less time for reflection (Cialdini, 2003). Our reactions to scarcity also mean that the things that are hard to possess are valued higher and perceived as better than those that are easy to possess. This has interesting consequences for how people value information that is banned or made secret. When information is banned, humans have a greater desire to acquire it, and they also have a more favorable attitude towards it than before it was banned. Humans also have a greater interest in what has become scarce, rather than what has always been scarce (Cialdini, 2003). That people value banned information more is a noteworthy piece of information for organizations that begin to employ more strict secrecy policies, or who have a rigorous security classification. It also explains some of the basics for the so called "hacker culture." Information wants to be free, because if it is secret, it must be interesting. It also means that information might actually be more secure if it is not classified as secret at all. The very classification of secret makes people want it, because then it is limited, and if it is limited, it is good. This principle can also explain why people lust to get into exclusive night clubs, even if queuing might take all night, why people work so hard to get accepted into more or less exclusive social clubs, why the value of art goes up when the artist is dead, and why almost everything nowadays is sold in "limited editions," products ranging from sodas to cars. This is because if supplies really are limited, we do not want to miss the chance to buy the product. Scarcity works because we learn historically that the good things really are in short supply. And if they are in short supply, we lose the freedom of choice, something we as humans resent (Cialdini, 2003).

Scarcity could be used by attackers by providing a "limited service offer" or by pressing on time: "Sure, I could help, but I'm leaving soon, so we'll have to fix it quickly." Another consequence is that making information harder to get could actually make more users interested in it, actually making it less secret.

Liking and Similarity

People favor others that are like themselves. If we share similarities, then we are prone to react favorably to a person similar to ourselves only because of the similarity. Another particularly influencing factor here is the physical attractiveness of a person. A person who is very attractive can be perceived as a purely attractive person, where attractiveness is the dominating characteristic of the person. This is called the "halo effect" and it makes attractiveness a very influential factor (Cialdini, 2003). In fact, an attractive physical appearance can make us believe that the person is smarter, kinder, stronger, and of a higher moral character, but we are also oblivious of our mostly automated preference towards attractive people (Levine, 2003). If you are blessed with an attractive physical appearance, you will find that influencing people is easier.

Similarity can be of several different kinds; for instance, how a person is dressed and a person's background and interests. So when choosing how to dress when trying to deceive is basically up to whether to use authority, or to dress like the victims and use similarity (Cialdini, 2003). The importance of liking is also emphasized in neuro-linguistic programming, NLP, where a great focus is on developing rapport between people. In NLP rapport means being "in sync" with the person you are talking to. The common techniques are matching of body language, breathing (frequency), and maintaining eye contact (O'Connor & McDermott, 1996). Creating rapport increases liking, and is a powerful weapon of influence.

Other ways to increase liking is to have frequent contact with the target, as familiarity increases liking, a tactic which is also used in examples by Mitnick (2002). What is interesting here is that familiarity works without victims noting that it occurs, so we tend to like people frequently featured in the media, or those that we see often at work, for no other reason than that we see them often. An effective method among strangers to quickly achieve liking is to share a common "enemy," something most army recruits have experienced when sharing the dislike for certain officers is a sure way to get conversation started. If the attacker manages to leverage himself and the victim in a situation where they cooperate in order to gain mutual benefits, such as helping each other, liking will also increase. As our senses are tied together with our overall experience of the situation, it is also interestingly enough effective to meet while eating. The positive experience of the food will strengthen liking. Most importantly, it is important to avoid meeting under bad conditions, as the negativity of the condition will affect the liking of the persons involved, as do being the bearer of bad news. We are also easily affected by compliments, even if we realize that the compliments are given with an ulterior motive (Cialdini, 2003).

This knowledge would be used by an attacker to befriend the targets, to build a liking, rapport, with the target, for instance, sharing an enemy (perhaps the boss), or by sharing a remarkable amount of interests and background. How come most car salesmen are so similar to their customers, with children roughly the same age?

Reciprocation

The rule of reciprocation is hard wired in us, and might indeed be the very reason we are humans; our ancestors learned to share, which lead to civilization. The rule is quite simple: If someone provides a favor for us, we feel that we must repay that favor, even it we did not ask for it. It is more or less an automated reaction and it is frequently used, and abused by, for instance, car salesmen. They tell the customer that they are doing them a favor by lowering the price, or by including rust proofing, or even by selling them the car without any commission. This makes the customer feel an urge to repay them, and what better way to do so than to buy a car?

Reciprocation is a very powerful technique that in many cases can be directly responsible for successful influence (Cialdini, 2003). One of the classic examples is the flowers that are given out by Hare-Krishnas. The flower is free, they say, but it is customary to give a small donation in return. Even if the receiver of the flower does not want it, or even likes the Hare-Krishnas, he will feel obliged to return the favor, and to give a donation. In fact, this technique is so powerful that it is one of the major reasons for the success of the Hare-Krishnas (Cialdini, 2003). The same thought is behind the free samples often given out at super-markets. Not only do they let the customers taste the product, they also have the aura of a gift around them, making it hard for people to resist buying the product after receiving a sample as a gift from the nice lady.

What should be noted especially here, is that people's sense of reciprocation will stand even if the gift is very small, and the request for return is far greater than what would be reasonable (Cialdini, 2003). A variation of the reciprocation rule is called the "rejection-then-retreat" technique. It consists of making an initial, extreme, offer that is sure to be rejected, and then retreat to a lower, more sensible request that was the initial goal with the request. An example would be to ask someone to buy a $50 painting to support the arts, and upon rejection, offer them to buy a $5 set of postcards. Not only does the "rejection-then-retreat" technique increase the possibility that the request will be accepted, it also makes the target more probable to carry out the request, and to fall for such requests in the future (Cialdini, 2003).

An attacker could use this by stating that he has helped the victim in a small matter without prior request, or by giving the victim privileged information that he did not ask for.

Commitment and Consistency

No one wants to be known as a failure. If a person has promised to do something, he will try his best to do it, so as to not be regarded by his peers as untrustworthy. Therefore, people try hard to act in ways that are consistent to the way they have acted before and to the choices they have made. In the same way, people find that they are more willing to stand by their decisions when they have been made public in some way, when a stand has been taken. This is why a gambler is far more certain of the odds after placing a bid than before and also why so many charities collect signatures on lists (Cialdini, 2003).

In order for a commitment to be most effective, it should be active, public, and demand a certain degree of effort, and if a person is to accept responsibility for it afterwards, it should also be made without strong outside pressures (Cialdini, 2003). This has the interesting spin-off effect that it actually is harder to convince someone into cooperating for a longer period of time using a large bribe, or a really violent threat, than it is to give a smaller bribe and a more feasible threat. This is something that was well known during the cold war, where most recruited traitors actually did not get paid a great deal of money. It was more efficient for the foreign power to get them to supply classified information for relatively little money, as they then would justify their treason not just because of monetary gains but also by ideological support. This would get them to feel more personally responsible and to have a greater commitment to the relationship, making them easier to exploit as resources for a long time.

Someone wanting to use this knowledge to influence someone could do it by trying to get the target to express public support for the concept, as well as not making the support too easy to express. If offering a bribe, it would be relatively small, and any threat made should be of the reasonable kind, not too spectacular, but threatening enough to "tip the edge." If it is too threatening, the mark will not feel obliged to follow through as soon as the immediate threat is removed.

Social Proof

When people have to make a decision on the proper behavior in a situation when they are uncertain, they do this by seeing how people, especially those that are similar to themselves, in their vicinity act. Usually it is correct to do the same thing as the people around you. This is the phenomenon known as "social proof." Social proof can cause people to do things not in their own self-interest, such as purchasing products because of their popularity, or sharing passwords with coworkers because "everyone else in the department is doing it." What is even worse, it can lead to a phenomenon called pluralistic ignorance (Cialdini, 2003). Pluralistic ignorance is when everyone is trying to see how everyone else is acting, leading to a situation where no one acts at all. This is most horrifying in cases where crimes are committed in an area with a lot of witnesses around and no one acts to help the victim, or when someone

gets sick in the middle of the street and no one stops to check to see if they are OK. On the other hand, when someone stops to actually check if the person in the street is OK, several others might help out almost instantly, as I myself discovered while helping an elderly lady who had fallen off her bike. After the first couple of volunteers had arrived, the crowd started to snowball, and soon people had to be told to leave in order not to create a traffic hazard.

This could have a major impact on the security of any organization, because people will adapt to the general attitude towards security in the organization, rather than to what is written in a policy. Even if management wants to have a high degree of security, the employees can nullify any attempts, unwittingly, by social proof. Examples of this are organizations where the sharing of passwords, while expressly forbidden in the policy, still is a sign of trust among employees. Not sharing would stigmatize a person as untrusting, paranoid, and not a part of the group, as sharing is seen as a matter of trust (Brostoff, Sasse, & Weirich, 2002).

An attacker could use this to enforce the techniques of persuasion by telling the target that everyone else is doing whatever she asks the target to do, such as giving out login information. If there is proof, or if the target believes this to be true, it would be very hard to resist the demand.

Other Weaknesses

When the person asked to perform something has very little interest in it, they generally have low involvement. As they are detached from the task they are being asked to perform, they may be especially easily influenced by logical reasons for the task, urgency, or authority. Examples of people with low involvement can be security guards, cleaners, or receptionists (Harl, 1997). This group of people does not care as much about the quality of the arguments, but more about the quantity; the more the better (Harl, 1997).

In contrast, people with a high involvement, for example, systems administrators, are persuaded more by the quality of the arguments than the quantity (Harl, 1997).

Another powerful factor to elicit the desired compliance is to use strong affect (Gragg, 2002). If the victim is feeling a heightened sense of anger, surprise, or anticipation, he will be less likely to think through the arguments presented to him. This can be done either by aggravating the mark or simply by surprising him with a demand that was completely unanticipated. Similar to surprise is overloading (Gragg, 2002). When someone has to deal with a great deal of information and does not have enough time to think about it, this lowers the ability to think critically about the situation. An example of this would be to present and require a lot of technical information from a person with very little technical knowledge. The basis for all more advanced deception tricks is to use deceptive relationships (Gragg, 2002). It is a very powerful psychological trigger to establish a relationship with someone, solely to exploit that person. This can be done effectively by sharing information and a common enemy, as discussed under liking. The attacker does this by using techniques for creating rapport for a long time, actually building up a (false) relation with the target, befriending her, and then slowly starting to use the relationship for nefarious gain. This technique was especially popular with foreign intelligence services, as it also leads victims to rationalize their actions internally, thus being more committed to the case.

HOW TO ACT WHEN INFLUENCING OTHERS: A PRACTICAL EXAMPLE

The mentioned techniques and examples might sound convincing, but in order to illustrate how they can be used, an example is given. This example is based on the premises that a perpetrator wants to get either information, in the form of login information, from the mark (victim), or to get the mark to perform some action at the perpetrator's request. This is a classical social engineering attack. The techniques should work best when trying to influence someone from a Western culture. Many of the same techniques can be used against persons from other cultures too, but they might, due to cultural differences, be ineffective or even insulting (Levine, 2003).

The perpetrator begins by either creating a person of authority, or by exploiting existing relationships. If the perpetrator knows the mark or someone who knows the mark, he can use this or make it up, but a real reference is far more useful. If that is not possible, the perpetrator may create a person of authority, such as a doctor, researcher, or other successful person, as suggested. In this case, the attacker chooses to be a systems administrator:

The attacker describes himself as a senior systems administrator (authority) from a high profile consultancy firm hired to investigate critical network problems of the organization (scarcity). He phones the mark, introduces himself, notes the accent of the target, and asks where the target is from. Whatever city the mark answers, the attackers' wife is from the same town (similarity). He then asks if the mark could consider spending a couple of minutes helping him fix the network (commitment), then he starts to describe the problem with the network, by using technical jargon and ample statistics (authority). He explains that the mark's computer must be taken off-line for a couple of days, maybe a week, while they fix the problem. This is if the mark cannot help them with some technical services, the way many of his colleagues have today (social proof), notably by typing in an increasing complicated series of commands in the DOS-prompt (overloading). The perpetrator then offers to do the mark a favor by fixing the problem, as he is to leave for a week of vacation in a couple of minutes (scarcity). The mark must do a small favor to the perpetrator (reciprocation) by not telling anyone of this, as the attacker could lose his job over it due to the mark's really strict boss (liking, by finding common enemy). The best way to fix the situation is if the mark could bring his computer to the fictitious office of the attacker, just an hour away by car, and then bring his personal ID papers, a signed letter of recommendation from a co-worker, and a written history of what the mark has done with his computer the last year, as is the policy in the consultancy firms. Or, perhaps, if it can be kept just between them, the mark could just give the attacker his login information (contrast).

This is a simple and classic example of a social engineering attack. As demonstrated, it is deceptively simple, however, as it uses most of the manipulative techniques available, even though it does not delve too deeply in any one of them. Against the right kind of mark, using the right kind of setting, this attack is highly efficient.

How the Attacker Can Be Persuasive

Levine (2003) believes that there are three key elements to being persuasive as a person. They are authority, honesty, and likeability. The other techniques described can be used to strengthen influence, but on an interpersonal level, only these three are crucial. There are some easy ways for the attacker to strengthen the way the mark perceives his offerings in these elements.

If actually meeting the mark face to face, it is always important to maintain eye contact. This will make the attacker seem far more honest and authoritative. While maintaining eye contact, it is also useful for the attacker to act as if he is engrossed in what the mark is talking about. It is, however, not good if the attacker actually is engrossed, as this will limit his perception. When preparing for an attack, the attacker will consider the clothes he will wear closely. They are a kind of uniform, signaling authority, and will be carefully selected to reflect the particular kind of authority the attacker aims toward. Classic examples of this are doctor's coats, police uniforms, but do not forget that normal clothing is also a kind of uniform. For instance, a nice, tailored suit sends a different message than a "nerdy" Linux t-shirt, but they are both efficient as uniforms in a particular context.

Speaking with confidence and using ample technical jargon will make the attacker seem more knowledgeable, and therefore more authoritative, especially if the mark does not know much about the area the perpetrator is talking about. The same is valid with statistics; so the attacker can use them to further his argument, as people tend to believe more in arguments supported by statistics, even if the statistics are false or irrelevant. The attacker should also always show both sides of the argument, as this will makes him seem less pushy and more honest. The attacker will try to find similarities with the mark, such as the same hobbies, kids the same age, have relatives in their hometown, and so forth. He will also mimic the behavior and speech patterns of the mark somewhat. This builds rapport, which leads to liking.

Be wary of new acquaintances displaying several of the mentioned characteristics.

Defending Against Deception

In this section you, the reader, is given a concrete set of tips on how to avoid being influenced. While simply reading about the techniques and vulnerabilities presented in this chapter will make you more resistant to manipulation, simply theorizing around the concepts are of limited use to organizations and those responsible for security. Levine (2003) suggests two basic approaches to enhance resistance. The first is "the sting," where people are put in situations when they are influenced to act against their own preferences, and when they comply, they are informed of the influence tactic and what has just happened. This has the benefit of pushing the subjects out of their comfort zone, making their vulnerability more obvious to them.

What is critical here is that the subjects should be made to acknowledge their own personal susceptibility (Levine, 2003).

The second method is a little less intrusive than "the sting," and more manageable in a business context. The goal here is to expose the subjects to weaker forms of persuasions, which then acts much like an inoculation does to an immune system; it prepares it for the real threat. The most important issue to consider here is to get support from management and in the information security policy for such efficient counter measures as "the sting" and inoculations. When support is acquired, a small roll-out, especially of inoculations is preferred, and in high risk scenarios, stings can also be enacted. While it can sound cruel and unethical, it is also one of the easiest ways to practice some kind of resistance to these attacks. Deception against one's own employees has been used, with some success, at both West Point Military Academy (Dodge & Ferguson, 2006), and the New York state (Bank, 2005). In the West Point case, students were sent an e-mail from a person claiming to be a colonel, ordering them to click on an attached link to verify their grades. This approach got 80 % compliance among the students, who were later informed of the risks of their acts. In the case of the New York state, 15 % of the employees tried to enter their passwords into a special online "password checker" after receiving an e-mail from the "Office of Cyber Security and Critical Infrastructure Coordination," urging them to do so. A follow-up to this a couple of months later, with a similar approach, got a lower compliance rate (8 %).

In order for you to be better prepared against attacks using specific vulnerabilities discussed, a short guide of defenses is given.

To defend against authority, it is best to remove the element of surprise from authority. Be suspicious of authority power, and remember the influence power of authority. There are two questions that might help with this: Is the person really a person of authority? If he is, then how truthful do you think that person is (Cialdini, 2003)?

While the scarcity principle is easy to learn about, it is hard to counter. One method is to try to learn to recognize the feel when the competitive cogs in our brain starts to whirl, but it might not be enough. Learning to think about the scarce object from a more utilitarian standpoint can also help. Do we want the object because it is rare, or do we believe that the object will be better because it is rare? Then we should remember that rare things are rarely better (Cialdini, 2003).

Due to the vast spectra of possibilities to influence liking, it is hard do develop a broad spectrum of defenses. Instead Cialdini (2003) recommends a simple approach: Allow to be swept away by the liking of others, but when it comes to decisions, consider how long the person who is asking you to make a decision has been in contact with you, and whether or not you like him, to a reasonable extent, based on this time. If you adore someone who is trying to get you to give him some information after only knowing him for a couple of minutes, there is probably foul play in the works.

Reciprocity is a very effective influence technique, and very hard to defend against. A too strict rule against accepting any kind of gifts will make you seem socially awkward. A more efficient method is to redefine gifts given, to their real meaning. A sales person giving you a gift is really exposing you to marketing, and thus you do not need to return the favor. A stranger offering you help over the telephone with something you did not request or know that you needed is most likely up to no good.

To protect against consistency, you also have to reach inside yourself. Cialdini (2003) mentions two kinds of methods to spot when someone is exploiting your consistency. The first is to identify when we get the feeling that we are pushed into performing actions we know that we do not want to perform. The second method is to consider whether or not we would make the same commitment, if we could travel back in time.

Social proof is something that is most often useful to you. In fact, in most new situations you would be well advised to follow the behaviors of others. There are, however, certain situations when social proof can lead to your being tricked into performing harmful acts. In order to avoid this, there are two tricks. Be aware of what are obviously faked situations, such as found in ads with groups of people praising a product, or when someone claims that the people around you are doing something you doubt that they are doing. You should also remember that the actions of others are not to be taken as the sole reason for your actions (Cialdini, 2003).

FUTURE TRENDS

This is an area that has been studied extensively in other areas of science than information security. There are ample material in fields ranging from literature, to social sciences, to marketing and economics. There is a broad range of researchers working in the field, but within the field of information security, this area remains rather unexplored. While problems with software, networks, and other technical artifacts no doubt will be of a high importance in the foreseeable future, there is a growing trend when it comes to more human aspects of information security. It is notable that an industry icon such as Bruce Schneier has begun to put interest in the field, and there are emerging academic conferences such as the HAISA (Human Aspects of Information Security & Assurance) conference.

One of the challenges for those of us working in the field of the human element of security is how we can argue that our work is both important and whether or not it actually improves security. This has always been easier for technical products, as they often can argue efficiency based on statistics. When the buyer has to choose from a product promising a 99.99 % protection against "millions" of computer viruses, or an education program that might prevent one case of social engineering, the choice is often simple for the purchaser. It is thus, sadly, our task as researchers, professionals, and students to help point out that the single attack might very well be the most damaging attack imaginable, far more than a random virus attack.

The increased attention gained in this field will probably bring greater awareness, among both professionals and ordinary users. When users become more resilient towards the easy tricks, such as those described in this chapter, the attackers will have to either get more advanced themselves, which is quite hard due to the increased complexity of the skills needed, or find other ways to attack. If attackers have to develop their skills of influence to a level high enough to influence even humans well aware and trained against influence techniques, they might as well leave the field of crime and seek more lucrative employment as influence professionals, such as salesmen or politicians.

CONCLUSION

This chapter has showed how easy it is to use influence to get people to do things that they may not want to do. The goal has been to give concrete examples of well-established techniques and methods, together with practical uses. Hopefully the reader now has a greater insight in both the manipulation techniques used by computer criminals and the techniques used by the everyday deception professionals.

One of the major points of this chapter is just how easy the techniques are to learn and to implement. In fact, just by reading through this chapter, you, the reader, now probably have most of the tools you need to influence people around you to a far greater extent than before. This is of course knowledge that should be used with some caution. While in most cases it is rather easy to influence people, the counter reaction from people who just understood that they have been manipulated is generally rather severe. Good relationships are not built on deception.

Still, there is a lot of merit in using deception, albeit on a small scale, against one's users and subordinates in an organization. As long as the use of deception of one's own employees and co-workers is practiced with afterthought and a clear goal, and ample feedback and information is given, it might serve well as an educational and training tool. Do remember that these are the techniques the bad guys are using. If we do not prepare against the methods used, we will easily fall victims to them.

REFERENCES

Bank, D. (2005). "Spear phishing" tests educate people about online scams. *The Wall Street Journal.* Retrieved March 2, 2006, from http://online.wsj.com/public/article/SB112424042313615131-z_8jLB2WkfcVtgdAWf6LRh733sg_20060817.html?mod=blogs

Blass, T. (2002). The man who shocked the world. *Psycology Today.* Retrieved March 9, 2006, from http://www.psychologytoday.com/articles/pto-20020301-000037.html

Bowyer, B. (2003). Toward a theory of deception. *International Journal of Intelligence and Counterintelligence, 16,* 244-279.

Brostoff, S., Sasse, A., & Weirich, D. (2002). Transforming the "weakest link": A human-computer interaction approach to usable and effective security. *BT Technology Journal, 19*(3), 122-131.

Cialdini, R. (2001). *Influence: Science and practice.* Needham Heights, MA: Allyn & Bacon.

Dodge, R., & Ferguson, A. (2006). Using phishing for user e-mail security awareness. In S. Fischer-Hübner, K. Rannenberg, L. Yngström, & S. Lindskog (Eds.), *Proceedings of the IFIP TC-11 21st International Information Security Conference (SEC 2006)* (pp. 454-458). New York: Springer Science + Business Media Inc.

Feer, F. (2004). *Thinking about deception.* Retrieved March 11, 2006, from http://www.d-n-i.net/fcs/feer_thinking_about_deception.htm

Gragg, D. (2002). A multi-level defense against social engineering. *SANS Institute.* Retrieved September 17, 2003, from http://www.sans.org/rr/papers/index.php?id=920

Granger, S. (2001). Social engineering fundamentals. *Security Focus.* Retrieved September 18, 2003, from: http://www.securityfocus.com/printable/infocus/1527

Harl (1997). *The psychology of social engineering.* Retrieved March 12, 2006, from http://searchlores.org/aaatalk.htm

Levine, R. (2003). *The power of persuasion.* Hoboken, NJ: John Wiley & Sons Inc.

Marett, K., Biros, D., & Knode, M. (2004). Self-efficacy, training effectiveness, and deception detection: A longitudinal study of lie detection training. *Lecture Notes in Computer Science, 3073,* 187-200.

Martin, B. (2004). Telling lies for a better world? *Social Anarchism, 35,* 27-39.

Mitnick, K. (2002). *The art of deception.* Indianapolis, Indiana: Wiley Publishing, Inc.

O'Connor, J., & McDermott, I. (1996). Principles of NLP. London: Thorsons.

Chapter III
Impact of the Human Element on Information Security

Mahi Dontamsetti
President, M3 Security, USA

Anup Narayanan
Founder Director, First Legion Consulting, India

ABSTRACT

This chapter discusses the impact of the human element in information security. We are in the third generation of information security evolution, having evolved from a focus on technical, to process based, to the current focus on the human element. Using case studies, the authors detail how existing technical and process based controls are circumvented, by focusing on weaknesses in human behavior. Factors that affect why individuals behave in a certain way, while making security decisions are discussed. A psychology framework called the conscious competence model is introduced. Using this model, typical individual security behavior is broken down into four quadrants using the individuals' consciousness and competence. The authors explain how the model can be used by individuals to recognize their security competency level and detail steps for learning more effective behavior. Shortfalls of existing training methods are highlighted and new strategies for increasing information security competence are presented.

KNOWLEDGE & INFORMATION SECURITY

We live in an information age. Companies that are successful are those that are able to harness and utilize information to their competitive advantage. Along the same lines, economies and countries that are successful in this age are the ones who are networked; information based and those who empower their population. The electron (information based economy) has replaced the atom (nuclear power) as the true indicator of strength of a country. Given the wide spread and critical nature of information, protecting information, that is, information security, is essential for maintaining competitive advantage and business sustenance.

The threats to information are varied. They are technical, physical, and human in nature. To counter these threats, information security has evolved over the past few decades. We are today, in the third generation (3G) of information security. It has evolved from its initial focus on technology, to its focus on processes (standards, best practices) and to the current focus on the human element that manages or uses the technology and processes.

The shift in focus from technology to processes, and subsequently the human element, has come with the realization that technology and processes are only as good as the human beings that use them.

The evolution of the information security model has occurred due to the evolution of the type of threats that businesses are faced with on a day-to-day basis. The threats have evolved and become more sophisticated. Typical threats that occurred during the technology implementation phase were viruses, worms, distributed denial of service (DDOS), and so forth. Use of firewalls, anti-virus, and IPS systems grew as a means of

countering those threats. Human element related threats during this phase were device misconfigurations, excessive trust in security technology, and security flaws within the technology itself. For example, attitudes like, "I have this anti-virus, so I am secure, now let me look at other non-security issues" were common place. The other major problem was security flaws within the technology itself. For example, security flaws within the software that were installed in firewalls, anti-viruses, and so forth.

Typical threats during the process implementation phases were: too much reliance on documentation and absence of actual practice. This phase does justice to the saying "documented but not practiced." For example, organizations invested time and money in documenting policies, processes for information security, especially during the periods of legal regulations and compliance. The result was that there were numerous documents that helped the organizations to comply to legal regulations but did not substantially reduce information security risk.

The main reason why technology and processes have not managed to effectively bring down the instances of information security incidents is because the people entrusted with managing the technology and processes were not motivated, aware, responsible, and qualified for information

Figure 1. Evolution of information security

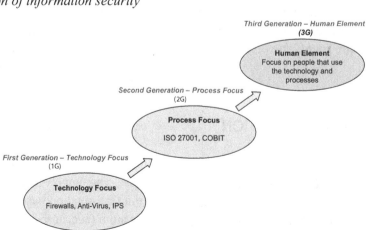

security management. The rest of this chapter explores this in detail.

The Human Element: The Reason and Catalyst

Security threats (attacks, exploits, tactics, etc.) have changed over the years, with the most significant changes occurring over the past 5 years. A look at media coverage shall reveal that instead of massive worm and virus attacks that had prominence 3-5 years back, the focus today is on:

- **Online frauds:** Examples include capturing online banking user ID's and passwords, using key loggers.
- **Phishing:** Crafting e-mails that pretend to be from banks, auction Web sites, and so forth, requesting the recipient to correct some faults with their online logging credentials by enticing the user with a URL and a Web page that resembles a reputable Web site.
- **Spam:** Unsolicited junk e-mails that are an irritant and consumes bandwidth.
- Social engineering: psychological tactics used by attackers to make human beings reveal information. phishing (mentioned) is one such a tactic.
- **Spyware & malware:** Malicious software that gets installed when a user clicks on an illegitimate URL or by installing software. The user is often enticed towards installing the software using social engineering techniques.

Examining the reasons behind the success and propagation of these attacks reveal that most all of these attacks target individuals. The human element is the reason and catalyst for the success of these attack techniques. The reasons can be further distilled to two factors:

- **Human error:** Inadvertent actions performed by people that have an impact on security.

Examples include accidental deletion of data, revealing of passwords because the source of the request appears genuine, and so forth.
- **Human fraud:** Willful actions aimed at destroying information. Examples include sabotage, information theft, and so forth.

While fraud is beyond the scope of this chapter, the reason for human error can be explored and corrected using well-designed and refined techniques.

The Human Factor in Information Security

How do people think and feel about information security? Finding answers to this question determines success or failure of information security management both at a personal as well as organizational level. Organizations are constantly challenged by the irrational behavior of employees when they fail to secure intellectual information, customer information, computers, and other sensitive information or systems.

CASE STUDY ONE

An information security consultant was hired by an organization to determine the information security awareness of employees. The consultant, after a brief initial study of the organization, designed a simple test that focused on two psychological aspects:

- **Obedience to authority:** This is a behavioral factor exhibited by people, especially when they live in a society that accepts a hierarchical structure
- **Self preservation:** This behavioral factor is common to all human beings. The desire to survive and sustain is inherent in all human beings.

The consultant executed the test as follows. With the CFO's permission, the consultant used the intercom (telephone) of the CFO and dialed a few employees in random, and employed the following dialogue—"Hi, I am your new ERP consultant and I am calling from the CFO's room. We have just finished implementing a new salary module for processing your salaries next month onwards. If you don't mind, we need your domain login ID and password to integrate your salary processing for the next month."

The test was done on five subjects and all five subjects revealed the passwords (some of them even spelt the passwords for the consultant's benefit!).

CASE STUDY TWO

A company has a card access system for all employees to gain access to the building. They also have a regularly scheduled fire evacuation drill conducted in conjunction with the local fire department. The fire evacuation drill involves triggering of a fire alarm, general evacuation announcement on the building PA system, evacuation of all employees from the building, routine building checks by the fire department, subsequent cancellation of the fire drill, and re-admittance of all the employees back into the building.

Given the large number of employees the company had in their building (several hundred), the security guards usually deactivated the swipe card access system during employee re-admittance after a fire drill. This was done to reduce the inconvenience factor, since it would take a substantial amount of time for all employees to be re-admitted using the two lane swipe card access system. The security guards tried initially to enforce the policy, but due to a large number of complaints from employees, they chose to de-activate the system.

An intruder, knowing the fire drill schedule, would wait in the parking lot, mingle with the employees when they came out, and then subsequently gain access during re-admittance.

The mentioned scenarios raise the question, "Is information security a technical solution?" If it was purely a technical issue, then which technical controls were circumvented in the mentioned scenarios? Obviously, information security goes beyond purely technical or process issues. For example, there is a very high chance that the organization in the first case study would have had technical security controls such as passwords, document access controls, and so forth. Still the very purpose of these controls was negated by a psychological tactic that exploited human weaknesses. Similarly in the second case study, a security control existed, namely the card access system. But the long delays, frustrations, and complaints by employees led the guards to de-activate the system. While the first case study exploited the obedience to authority and self preservation aspect of the individual, the second case study exploited the "reduce inconvenience" and "need to be liked" aspects of an individual.

The market today is cluttered with vendors, who sell excellent solutions such as firewalls, which can process millions of packets per second, intrusion detection systems (IDS's), which can perform in-depth attack-detection, worm and virus control mechanisms, and biometric and multiple factor authentication systems. We also have multiple security standards and processes such as ISO27001, CoBIT, HIPAA, and so forth. Organizations have their own security policies and procedures defined to meet their security goals.

But from the case study presented, attempt to answer the following questions:

- Do technical solutions effectively mitigate information security incidents?
- After reading the above scenario, do you think that the human perception of a potential threat scenario can be improved?
- What are the potential factors that could have avoided the above scenario?

The case studies show how excellent technical controls (first case study) and good security processes and procedures (second case study) can be defeated due to the human element.

The "Reality" and "Feeling" of Security

Why do human beings commit errors that influence information security?

The question can be answered by analyzing the difference between the "reality" & "feeling" of security.[1] For a security practitioner, security is a reality that could be calculated in mathematical terms, for example—risk. For a non security practitioner, security is a feeling, a few examples of which are shared. This probably explains the following:

1. An individual feels more secure driving a car on his own rather than being driven by another driver, though there is no statistic to prove that driving on your own reduces the risk of an accident.
2. An individual feels more secure inside a car rather than in an airplane though statistics prove that there is a higher chance of getting killed in a road accident than an air crash.

The two behavioral examples mentioned are influenced by perception, which is in turn influenced by external factors such as media, peer group, culture, work practices, and so forth. This is explained diagrammatically:

An individual when faced with a situation whereby he/she has to make a decision that influences personal security or organizational security is influenced by his/her "feeling" of security. This could be either a "conscious" or "unconscious" decision. This decision may either be a decision that may have a positive impact on security (security is not compromised) or it could be a security tradeoff. Security "tradeoff" is examined in more detail in the next section.

Security Tradeoffs: Influenced by the Feeling of Security

Individuals make security tradeoffs every day. In fact, this is by far one of the most critical issues for information security managers and individuals responsible for information security implementation. A few examples of security tradeoffs that often worry an information security officer responsible for security practices are listed:

*   Individuals share passwords to get work done quickly.

Figure 2. The feeling of security and the influences

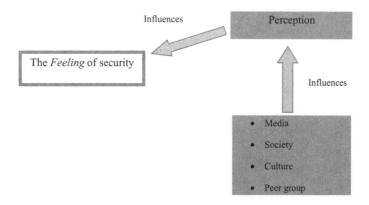

- Individuals write down passwords or stick them in easily accessible places so that they do not forget them.
- Individuals connect to unauthorized wireless access points for free Internet access.
- Individuals click on unknown URL's in phishing e-mails, introducing spyware or providing information that compromises privacy.

The reason for security tradeoffs is often personal convenience/inconvenience and other factors such as self preservation, fear, and so forth. For the purpose of this chapter, let us explain the "convenience/inconvenience" factor. For example—when asked whether they would like their blood samples tested for malaria every week, most persons would say NO. Now when the same question is asked with a different context—"The company wants to send you on a United Nations project to the Amazon River basin." The answer could be different. Hence, when confronted with a "cost," people reduce or avoid "security tradeoffs." This is illustrated in Figure 3.

Given a security decision point where one of the choices causes great personal inconvenience, an individual is more probable to choose the option that causes the smaller inconvenience. In fact, the greater the inconvenience caused, the higher the security risk of the option chosen by the individual. Similarly, when faced with a security decision point, where one of the choices has a higher personal cost (decision has big im-

pact—positive or negative on life, money, career, etc.) associated with it; an individual is more probable to choose the option that has the higher personal cost. The higher the personal cost of a decision, the lower the security risk of the option chosen by the individual.

Security trade-offs are often made unconsciously based on perception that we explored earlier. This "perception" factor can be explained in-depth by using the "conscious competence" model that is explained in the next section.

The Conscious Competence Model

The "**conscious competence model**[2] is a matrix that links states of human awareness with knowledge ("competence" and "incompetence") and links them to decision making abilities.

Table 1 identifies four "levels" that a person can be when presented with a scenario that requires an intelligent decision to be made. For the purpose of our discussion, the aim of studying the "conscious competence model" is to understand how individuals behave (react) in a scenario that contains potential information security threats and associated risks. The decision making (reaction) or the security tradeoff the individual makes would be influenced by the "conscious competence quadrant" the individual is operating in, either consciously or unconsciously, at that particular moment of time. We will analyze each of the four quadrants.

Figure 3. Security tradeoff, personal inconvenience, and cost

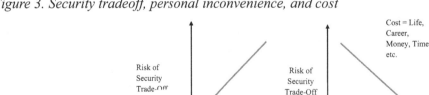

Table 1.Conscious competence model

Knowledge Level	Awareness Levels	
	Unconscious	Conscious
Incompetence	**Quadrant 1** You don't know that you do not know.	**Quadrant 2** You know that you do not know.
Competence	**Quadrant 3** You can do it without thinking about it.	**Quadrant 4** You can do it if you think about it.

Quadrant 1

Unconscious + Incompetence	In this "level," the person is totally ignorant of the potential risks associated with a scenario. The person is unaware of the existence or relevance of a skill. The person is unaware of the particular skill deficiency. The person denies relevance or utility of the skill.
Example from real life	A toddler playing with a sharp instrument Incompetence in this instance is lack of knowledge that the instrument is sharp and that sharp instruments can hurt. Unconscious is playing with the instrument without forethought

Quadrant 2

Conscious + Incompetence	In this "level," the person is aware that he is "ignorant." The person is aware of the existence and relevance of the skill. The person is aware of his/her deficiency in the skill.
Example from real life	Deciding to ask for assistance in a foreign country (foreign language not understood) Incompetence in this instance is lack of knowledge of foreign language; consciousness is recognition of the fact that the individual does not know the foreign language.

Quadrant 3

Unconscious + Competence	In this "level," the person is aware without being conscious about it.
	The skill becomes automatic, is second nature.
	It becomes possible for certain skills to be performed while doing something else, for example, knitting while reading a book.
	Skill is instinctual; the person might have difficulty in training or explaining to another person how it is done.
	The need to ensure this behavior is checked regularly against new processes.
	Difficult to unlearn, since it is instinctual.
Example from real life	Automatically looking at both sides of the road based on sensory cues while crossing the road while the mind may be actively engaged on other thoughts (e.g.. talking on a cell phone while crossing the street, driving, sports activities, typing, etc.)
	Competence in this instance is the knowledge that one needs to look at traffic before crossing a road, unconsciousness is applying knowledge without forethought and effort.

Quadrant 4

Conscious + Competence	In this "level," the individual is aware, but must force himself/herself to be so.
	The person will need to concentrate and think in order to perform the skill.
	The person can perform the skill unassisted.
	Demonstrable skill, but not teachable by a person.
Example from real life	In a foreign land, while crossing the road, consciously forcing yourself to think that driving directions may be different.
	Competence in this instance is the knowledge that driving directions may be different. Conscious is applying this knowledge with forethought.

Now, let us analyze the link between the various quadrants of the "conscious competence model" and "security tradeoffs."

Is it possible to reduce the risk of "security tradeoffs" using the "conscious competence model" as a baseline? Let us explore this in more detail in the next section.

Reducing Risk of "Security Tradeoffs" using the "Conscious Competence" Model as a Guideline

To use the "conscious competence model" as a guideline for reducing risk of "security trad-

eoffs," we must view the model from a different perspective. In the previous section, we linked the model with "security tradeoffs." In this section, we are viewing the "conscious competence model" from a positive perspective by adding three more factors:

- Can behavior that reduces security risk be learned?
- Pitfalls and/or challenges
- Positives

In Table 3, we have identified whether behavior can be modified. The next obvious question is,

Table 2. The link between "conscious competence model" and security tradeoffs

Quadrant	Reason for security tradeoff	Contributing factors	Example in the context of information security
Unconscious + Incompetence	The individual is ignorant and hence influenced by perception.	Perception is influenced by culture, society, peer group, and so forth.	An untrained employee clicking on a URL provided within a "phishing" e-mail.
Conscious + Incompetence	The individual possibly knows the risks but still makes a decision that has a security risk which impacts information security.	Personal convenience/ inconvenience	An employee being unable to identify whether an e-mail is genuine or not. Rather than take the time to verify authenticity of the e-mail, the employee trusts their "gut" and could make a decision with a high security risk.
Unconscious + Competence	The individual is knowledgeable and makes a decision without conscious awareness.	Self perseverance and/or there is a cost involved	Pressing "Ctrl+Alt+Delete" while leaving the desk since it has become a habit (the reason could be a company security policy that imposes a penalty).
Conscious + Competence	The individual knows the risks but makes a conscious decision to accept the risk.	"I don't care" mentality, lack of respect for security policies	Not bothering "swiping" the access card and tail-gating behind a colleague

Table 3. Correcting security tradeoffs using conscious competence model

Quadrant	Reason for security-tradeoff	Contributing factors	Example in the context of information security	Can reduced security risk behavior be learned?	Pitfalls and/or challenges	Positives
Unconscious + Incompetence	The individual is ignorant and hence influenced by perception.	Perception is influenced by culture, society, peer group, and so forth.	An untrained employee clicking on a URL provided within a "phishing" e-mail	Yes	The individual has to be trained and educated afresh and this involves effort and time.	You have a fresh and impressionable mind to work with.
Conscious + Incompetence	The individual possibly knows the risks but still takes a decision that has a security risk which impacts information security.	Personal convenience/ inconvenience	An employee being unable to identify whether an e-mail is genuine or not. Rather than take the time to verify authenticity of the e-mail, the employee trusts their "gut" and could make a decision with a high security risk.	Yes	The individual may or may not be willing to acknowledge lack of competence.	The subject may have a positive attitude and willingness to correct weaknesses
Unconscious + Competence	The individual is knowledgeable and makes a decision without conscious awareness.	Self perseverance and/or there is a cost involved	Pressing "Ctrl+Alt+Delete" while leaving the desk since it has become a habit (the reason could be a company security policy that imposes a penalty).	Yes	Set perceptions have to be changed.	The individual has a competence (an advantage) that can be enhanced further.
Conscious + Competence	The individual knows the risks but makes a conscious decision to accept the risk.	"I don't care" mentality, lack of respect for security policies.	Not bothering "swiping" the access card and tail-gating behind a colleague.	Yes	The individual may have a negative attitude with respect to information security, which requires strong corrective measures.	A good opportunity to define strong information security disciplinary policies.

"What are the techniques to modify behavior" or strategies that could be used? It is best to answer this question by analyzing the effectiveness of current approaches.

Current Approaches and Their Effectiveness

The various initiatives undertaken by organizations to reduce risk of security tradeoff's are:

- **Training** (classroom & electronic)
- **Visual content**—posters, notices, videos, and so forth

Security Policies

Though the mentioned activities have been in use for some time, they are not effective beyond a certain point. The possible reasons for the ineffectiveness of current information security awareness and training approaches are:

Quality of content: Organizational information security training programs focus primarily on security policies and procedures. Though this is important and has to be conveyed to the employees, the content tends to be dry and monotonous

Absence of focus: Organizations need to ask themselves the question: What are we trying to achieve?—Increase security awareness or convey security policies. Without this focus, trainings tend to be drab affairs

Fear: Organizations play on their employees fear by conveying the following message in a subtle manner—"If you don't do this (follow security policies), then you will suffer the following consequences (repercussions or disciplinary procedures)." This creates hypocrisy within the organization, because on one side the organization conveys the message to employees that they are the organization's biggest assets and on the other side, the organization conveys the message that the employees are a "security threat."

Coverage: For large sized organizations it is often difficult to cover all employees in their information security training program. Reasons for this are employees could be at a customer location, absent from work, attending to urgent project deadlines, and so forth. Moreover, it is important to ensure that perimeter personnel (security guards), support personnel (janitors, catering), and external contractors attend the training and this is often missed.

Quality of trainer: Often organizations confuse the role of an IT expert or information security expert with that of a trainer. This often happens when a system administrator or information security engineer is asked to train employees. Though they may be experts in their domain, they may not possess the communication skills that are so essential to convey the importance of information security. Moreover, the trainers themselves may be stressed by handling their existing task as well as handling training.

Measurement of retention: Information security awareness as practiced by organizations today is often limited to conducting a training session. The training sessions are not followed up with a strategy to measure how much the employees have "captured" and "retained."

So, is it possible to have a more effective strategy to reduce security tradeoffs? The answer is yes and the strategy is to focus on "security competence."

Information Security Competence

The approach to reducing security tradeoffs must focus on the development of individual and organizational information security competence. Information security competence can be defined as a blend of intelligence, feeling, skills, and organizational relationship. This is elaborated in the following diagram.

- **Security perception**—understanding the reason and logic for information security.

- **Security acceptance**—adopting information security and allocating mind-share.
- **Applying security**—integrating security practices into day-to-day work.
- **Commitment to the organization**—respecting security policies and practices of the company.

Strategies for Increasing Information Security Competence

Step 1: Set Goals

The goals for improving information security competence can be defined as:

- Make every individual as "responsible & aware" of information security as possible.
- Subsequently reduce security incidents (security tradeoffs) due to human factor.
- Promote a positive feeling about information security and consequently gain more acceptance of information security practices into day-to-day work practices.
- Create a management system for monitoring, measuring, and improving human impact on information security.

Step 2: Increase Security Perception by Conveying Concepts

For effective human impact management for information security, it is important to understand the impact of the three factors on information security namely:

- Culture
- Organizational ecosystem
- Individual work practices

The concepts can be summarized as follows:

- Individuals imbibe the culture of the society they live in, and the environment surrounding them.
- They carry this culture to the organization they work in, where it is integrated with the work culture.
- At a micro level, there are behavioral characteristics unique to each individual.

Step 3: Increase Security Acceptance

Security acceptance can be increased through strategic intervention techniques that are "active"

Figure 4. Core approach to enable information security competence

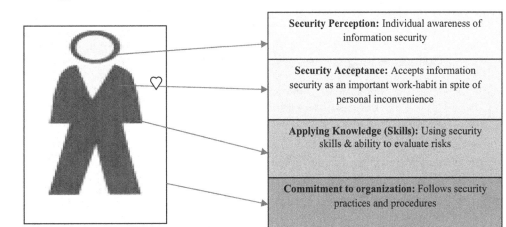

rather than "passive" in nature. For example, a regular information security awareness training program is "passive" in nature as the audience participation is limited. Security acceptance can be increased using "active" techniques that make the end-user "THINK" about information security. Examples of such techniques are:

• Vision building exercises
• Mind-mapping sessions
• Coaching/ mentoring sessions
• Security perception surveys
• Quizzes and games that require active participation
• Tools that simulate realistic attacks and test participants

An example of a mind-mapping session is provided:

A mind map, as per the definition in Wikipedia, is a diagram used to represent words, ideas, tasks, or other items linked to and arranged radially around a central key word or idea. It is used to generate, visualize, structure, and classify ideas, and as an aid in study, organization, problem solving, and decision making. The mind-mapping technique can be used to make a person analyze the impact of his or her own "at-risk" information security behavior. For the purpose of this example,

let us use a mind-map to analyze the impact of "password sharing."

The mind map shown is generated from a real life information security awareness session with a group of employees in an organization. The security trainer gave the group a simple phrase— "sharing of passwords" to think about. Next, the trainer asked the members of the group to talk about the thoughts that came to their minds when they heard the phrase "sharing of passwords." The group members provided answers such as "unauthorized entry," "account misuse," and so forth (highlighted in red). Further, the trainer asked them to think about these phrases in an organizational context. This simulated the audience to think and share their ideas on how—for example—"unauthorized entry" could impact the organization. For example, the group members enumerated "unauthorized entry" could be into systems, e-mail accounts, file servers, corporate intranet, and so forth.

The session concluded with the audience being able to appreciate the impact of a security breach, such as sharing of passwords, that looks trivial when performed, but when taken in an organizational context has impact such as "impact on customer confidence,, "fines & penalties," and so forth (highlighted in green).

Figure 5. Concepts behind information security practices

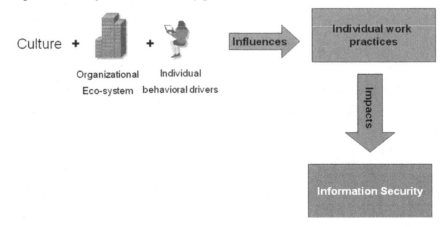

Step 4: Applying Security Skills

The desired consequence of "step 3—increasing security acceptance" is to promote the application of security skills. This can be conveyed through awareness sessions on using security tools or adopting security practices into day-to-day work practices. This can again be achieved through strategic awareness sessions that accomplish a particular goal. For example:

- Choosing strong passwords
- Identifying phishing or SPAM e-mails
- Best practices for keeping systems "malware" free

Step 5: Linking Security with the Organizations Goals

The ultimate purpose of information security is to ensure that security errors and accidents do not compromise the business goals of the organization. This can be accomplished by conveying the following message in an example format to the workforce.

The message is important to convey the link between business goals and security targets so that the end-user is able to understand and appreciate the importance of information security to achieve business goals of the organization.

Step 6: Continuous Measurement

The strategies that are used to increase security competence must be continuously measured and improved. The word measurement brings the term "metrics" to almost every manager's mind. But what types of metrics exist to measure information security competence? The issue is quite challenging since what has to be measured is knowledge, competence, and awareness, which are not concrete and difficult to measure. The best answer is that an organization must determine what best suits them. For example, an organization may choose the metric "number of security incidents before strategic awareness sessions and after awareness sessions." Another organization may choose an external penetration tester and perform a series of social engineering tests before and after awareness sessions and use the

Figure 6. Mind-map: Analysis of own "at-risk" behavior (password sharing)

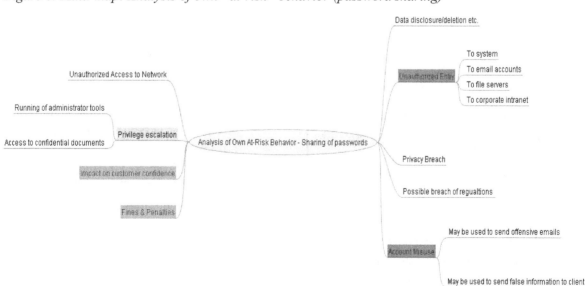

results as a metric. The best bet is to choose an approach and measurement technique that best fits the business requirement. A discussion for measuring improvement in information security awareness is provided.

Discussion

This discussion focuses on the usage of metrics for measuring information security awareness. Organizations have to decide how they want to address the following questions:

- What types of metrics are used—qualitative or quantitative?
- What is the measurement approach—direct measurement or indirect measurement?

Let us evaluate a few real-world examples:

- ABC Inc. conducts a series of information security audits. The audit findings are listed:
- The number of information security incidents being reported is few.
- Awareness of basic information security practices such as not sharing passwords,

Figure 7. The link between business goals and security

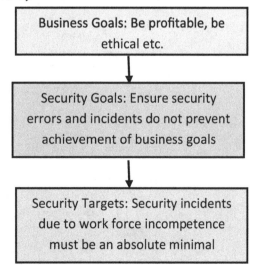

```
Business Goals: Be profitable, be
ethical etc.
```

```
Security Goals: Ensure security
errors and incidents do not prevent
achievement of business goals
```

```
Security Targets: Security incidents
due to work force incompetence
must be an absolute minimal
```

locking systems while leaving the desks, and so forth, is very poor.
- Reluctance to follow security regulations (for example—not bringing personal media players and storage devices) is high.

Subsequently, ABC Inc. conducted a series of innovative information security awareness sessions that included mind-maps, animations, coaching dialogues, and so forth.

Subsequently, another audit was conducted and the audit results are listed:

A glance at the results would make a security manager happy. But metrics are a double edged sword and could often be misleading, providing a false sense of security. Let us look at the same table and ask some probing questions.

The table highlights two important aspects while using metrics to measure increase in information security awareness:

- Do not trust an individual metric. Always corroborate a metric with another metric or data to reach a more accurate conclusion. For example, in the table, the first metric on information security incidents would have pointed a reviewer in the wrong direction, but with a probing question being asked, it the led the reviewer in a much more meaningful direction.
- Perform direct and indirect measurements. For example, the metric—"attitude towards security regulations and rules" can be measured by a simple perception survey by asking the respondents a sample question as follows—"Do you feel information security is important now that you have attended the training? Would you stop using personal electronic storage devices at the work place?" Respondents may say "yes." But without corroborating evidence, trusting this "yes" alone invites a false sense of security. Hence, in the table, this metric is further probed with a question that focuses on an indirect

Description	Results (with metrics)	
	Previous Audit	Current Audit
Number of information security incidents reports by employees	12 in 6 months	39 in 6 months
Awareness of basic information security practices by employees (example—not sharing passwords, locking systems)	Poor	Good
Attitude towards security regulations and rules	Negative	Positive
Description	Results (with metrics)	
	Previous Audit	Current Audit
Number of information security incidents reports by employees	12 in 6 months	39 in 6 months
Comment: While users are reporting more incidents (which means more awareness), the number of information security incidents has also increased (which is bad). Is this a case of new security incidents that are occurring or a case of security incidents that were happening previously, not reported in the audit due to lack of awareness?		
Awareness on basic information security practices by employees (example—not sharing passwords, locking systems)	Poor	Good
Comment: The mentioned audit results must be supported by a review of incident reporting logs. For example—how many reports of password sharing are available in the incident logs? How many reports of unlocked systems are available in the incidents logs? If sufficient information is not available, we must wait for a few more months and perform another audit before clearly identifying an improvement in awareness on information security among the workforce.		
Attitude towards security regulations and rules	Negative	Positive
Comment: The mentioned audit results must be supported by a review. For example—what is the number of personal devices available with the employees within the work area at any given time? Is it lesser than what it was prior to the awareness sessions		

metric—verification of security practices by auditing the number of personal devices being carried by people.

A good model for performing information security management using metrics is ISM3 (information security management maturity model)[3] that is available at www.ism3.com.

CONCLUSION

Information security has evolved to its current focus on the human element. The important factors to be understood are: the reasons why an individual behaves in a particular manner when confronted with a situation that poses a potential information security risk. In this context, the "reality" and "feeling" of security must be understood.

Further, it is important to understand that almost all of us make security tradeoffs on a day-to-day basis based on our perception. This perception is fed by various factors including society, media, workplace behavior, culture, and so forth. The conscious competence model is a good guide that can be used to understand the impact of security tradeoffs and also to define corrective measures. Further, the corrective measures themselves must focus on increasing security competence through strategic techniques that convey the reasons for corrective actions and these strategies must be subject to continuous revision and improvement.

It is safe to surmise that the human element must be addressed to ensure that businesses stay sustainable and successful over the course of time.

REFERENCES

Gordon Training Institute. *Conscious competence learning model.* www.gordontraining.com

ISM3. *Information security management maturity model.* www.ism3.com

Schneier, B. (2007). *The psychology of security.* www.schneier.com/essay-155.html

Chapter IV
The Weakest Link:
A Psychological Perspective on Why Users Make Poor Security Decisions

Ryan West
Dell, Inc., USA

Christopher Mayhorn
North Carolina State University, USA

Jefferson Hardee
North Carolina State University, USA

Jeremy Mendel
North Carolina State University, USA

ABSTRACT

The goal of this chapter is to raise awareness of cognitive and human factors issues that influence user behavior when interacting with systems and making decisions with security consequences. This chapter is organized around case studies of computer security incidents and known threats. For each case study, we provide an analysis of the human factors involved based on a system model approach composed of three parts: the user, the technology, and the environment. Each analysis discusses how the user interacted with the technology within the context of the environment to actively contribute to the incident. Using this approach, we introduce key concepts from human factors research and discuss them within the context of computer security. With a fundamental understanding of the causes that lead users to make poor security decisions and take risky actions, we hope designers of security systems are better equipped to mitigate those risks.

INTRODUCTION

Humans are fallible. That means exploitable. Recorded in every religious text and mythology is the evidence of human imperfection. We lose our wallets, forget our passwords, and drive over the speed limit when we are in a hurry. Yet somehow, we managed to develop manifestations of pure logic in the form of computing systems. At the helm of all this technical sophistication and complexity, unfortunately, is a user.

True Story:

"Company X" is a large nationwide hotel chain across the United States. Each hotel has two wireless networks, one accessible to hotel guests and one accessible to hotel employees. The hotel employees use this for reservations, reporting, and so forth. Once a month, a number of reports are rolled together by the IT manager, who puts them into a presentation for his upper management. The executives present this report as part of a monthly presentation to the parent company who owns the hotel chain. The parent company and the hotel chain have different policies and firewall settings, and the IT manager for the hotel chain has not, in 3 years, been able to figure out how to make them mesh without causing breakages down the line. As a result, once a month, when the executives give their presentation, the IT manager drops the firewall for the hotel chain for the duration of the presentation.

User error and poor human factors design contribute to many of the top computer security risks faced today. According to a recent CSI/FBI computer crime and security study, losses due to computer security incidents were estimated to total more than $52 million across the 313 companies surveyed (Gordon, Loeb, Lucyshyn, & Richardson, 2006). Of the most common security incidents reported in the study, losses related to viruses or malware totaled an estimated $15.7 million, losses associated with the unauthorized

access of information totaled $10.6 million, and losses caused by laptop or other hardware theft totaled $6.6 million.

When it comes to data loss within organizations, it appears that users are more of a problem than hackers or malware. According to a 2007 report from the IT Policy Compliance Group, mistakes made by internal employees accounted for approximately 75% of all data losses (Gaudin, 2007). In contrast, malicious activity such as Internet-based threats, attacks, and hacks, accounted for about 20% of data losses.

On the home front, a 2004 survey from AOL and the National Cyber Security Alliance reported that 72% of home users surveyed did not have a properly configured firewall (America Online and the National Cyber Security Alliance, 2004). In addition, approximately 40% of users with home wireless networks had no encryption configured.

In all of these cases, there are human factors issues associated with the acceptance and usability of security mechanisms, user perceptions of risk and how it motivates their behavior, and decision making strategies which pit convenience against security.

The focus of this chapter is not on the technologies of computer security but on the psychology of those who use them. Human decision-making has been a topic of study in social sciences for well over a century (Goldstein & Hogarth, 1997). The research shows that individuals are often less than optimal decision-makers when it comes to reasoning about risks (Simon, 1956). Not only do internal factors such as prior experience and knowledge specific to the decision maker influence the quality of decisions but many naturalistic or environmental factors such as time pressure (Hammond, 2000) and situational context (Klein, 1998) also effect decisions. Thus, there are a variety of data sources available to describe the nature of predictable and exploitable characteristics in the human decision making process. Understanding these principles and how users come to make security decisions may suggest how we can develop interventions to improve the outcome of the decisions. Recent evidence suggests that decision-making within the domain of computer security does not qualitatively differ from decision-making processes used in other contexts (Hardee, West, & Mayhorn, 2006). Thus, much of the knowledge gleaned from the classical decision-making literature can be used to understand the pre-existing biases that might place users at risk in user-security scenarios.

We hope the reader develops insight into the user-security problem through a better understanding of the cognitive mechanisms that underlie the human side of the equation.

The goal of this chapter is to raise awareness of cognitive and human factors issues that influence an end user's behavior when he or she is interacting with a system and making decisions or taking actions that have security consequences. With a fundamental understanding of the causes that lead users to make poor security decisions and take risky actions, designers of security systems may be better equipped to mitigate those risks.

To this end, this chapter is organized around case studies of documented computer security incidents and known threats. For each incident, we will provide a post-mortem analysis of causal factors involved. In this fashion, we will introduce key concepts from human factors research and discuss them within the real world context of information security. In addition, we will discuss human factors issues related to potential solutions that might be considered to mitigate the incidents described in the case studies.

SYSTEM MODEL APPROACH TO UNDERSTANDING SECURITY INTERACTIONS

Human factors as a scientific discipline often uses a systems approach to conceptualize all aspects of a problem (Helander, 1997). Within the sys-

tems approach, the user-machine-environment attributes are all considered to interact during the production of task-specific behavior. The "user" refers to operator characteristics such as expertise, competence, age, or motivation. Here, a thorough understanding of the abilities and the limitations of the user is important in determining how information is perceived and processed. Equally important is the "machine" component which consists of the characteristics of any extraneous tool that is being used to aid the human operator in performing the designated task. Human-machine interactions range from simplistic tasks where someone is using a hammer, to much more complex relationships involving automated systems (Sanders & McCormick, 1993). Lastly, all user-machine interactions occur within the "environment," which describes the task as well as the context in which it is performed. Thus, the social/organizational climate of a company as well as the ambient (e.g., stress, heat, etc.) characteristics of the environment might also influence task performance.

The systems approach has proven to be an effective tool in improving safety within a variety of contexts. Human error in diverse situations ranging from the 1984 Bhopal chemical spill in India to the 1986 Chernobyl nuclear reactor disaster have been analyzed using this approach (Reason, 2000). More recently, attempts to reduce errors within the healthcare industry have greatly benefited from the realization that medical errors are the product of multiple factors. Bogner (2004) successfully illustrated that the traditional rule within the healthcare industry of "blaming the provider" for adverse events such as infusion pump mishaps, medication administration errors, and surgical blunders is not an effective means for preventing such incidents in the future. Rather, an understanding of the interactions between the provider, the equipment, and the organizational/physical environments is necessary for formulating effective error reduction through informed intervention. For instance, common transfusion errors have been reduced through more effective labelling of samples at the blood bank (Linden, 2004). Moreover, efforts to reduce medication adherence errors in older adults have been informed by knowledge of how cognition and perception change with age (Park & Skurnik, 2004) and how technology such as personal digital assistants might be designed to facilitate adherence (Mayhorn, Lanzolla, Wogalter, & Watson, 2005).

Given this consistent level of previous success, it seems appropriate to bring this technique to bear in understanding how computer security errors occur. We envision the user-security scenario as a system which can be modelled with three parts: the user, the technology they are interacting with, and the environment/context in which the interaction takes place. These three things together, determine how a user will respond in a given situation. It also provides a framework for us to categorize and discuss a myriad of factors in user-security scenarios.

For each security incident case study described in this chapter, we will discuss causal factors involved based on this systems approach. Each explanation will discuss how the characteristics of the user interacted with the technology within the context of the environment to actively contribute to the occurrence of the security incident.

PHISHING FOR RECRUITS: WEST POINT MILITARY ACADEMY E-MAIL STUDIES

In 2004, researchers at the United States Military Academy at West Point, New York, conducted a study in which a sample of cadets received e-mails from a fictitious senior officer asking them to click on an embedded link for information about their grades (Ferguson, 2005). The goal behind the study was to actively test the effectiveness of the school's security awareness training program which all cadets were required to take. Over 400

of the 512 cadets sampled for the study (more than 80%) clicked on the embedded link.

In a follow up study 1 year later, students were sent one of three types of phishing e-mails which encouraged them to either click on an embedded link in the e-mail, open an attached file supposedly pertaining to their grades, or worst of all, to submit their social security numbers through a Web site (Jackson, Ferguson, & Cobb, 2005). Of the 1,010 phishing e-mails sent encouraging cadets to click on an embedded link, roughly 30% of cadets did so. This was a large decrease from the previous year but a significant number of cadets proved to be vulnerable to phishing. Of the 1,014 phishing e-mails sent encouraging cadets to open an attached file, approximately 48% of cadets did so. Finally, of the 456 phishing e-mails sent trolling for social security numbers, roughly 47% of cadets provided them.

What factors account for these high numbers despite having participated in mandatory security awareness training and having been fooled once before?

User Factors

A common concern of IT organizations is that users fall prey to viruses and other malware distributed through e-mail. Why is this attack vector so successful? In the case of the West Point e-mail, what factors led to cadets believing the message was real and taking the action requested of them? A little background first.

Satisficing and Problem Solving

Humans have limited information processing capacity and routinely multi-task. As a result, few tasks or decisions receive our full attention at any given time. Humans allocate mental processing resources judicially and try to accomplish the most while using the least.

To conserve mental resources, we tend to favour quick decisions based on learned rules and heuristics. These are aided by pattern recognition, which is cheap and easy in terms of mental effort. In fact, pattern recognition is what the human brain does best. In contrast, careful and deliberate concentration requires focused attention, a great deal of scarce short-term memory resources, and is very expensive in terms of mental effort.

When considering a problem, humans usually develop a solution that meets the needs of the problem to a satisfactory degree. This is called *satisficing* (Simon, 1957). We settle on choices we can arrive at quickly and that seem good enough, not decisions that are the best. While decision-making is not optimal, it is highly efficient. It is efficient in the sense that it is quick, it minimizes effort, and the outcome is good enough most of the time. Of course, this willingness to settle for a less than optimal solution may leave us open to error.

Returning to the West Point e-mails, we can expect that cadets do not scrutinize the authenticity of every e-mail they receive, or consider the consequences of opening attachments, embedded links, and so forth. It would be extremely counterproductive in terms of time and effort, especially when considering the low frequency of genuine security incidents.

Representativeness as a Decision Making Heuristic

Representativeness refers to a decision-making heuristics people employ where decisions are made by classifying the problem as a known type based on experience (Tversky & Kahneman, 1974). The decision is made based on memory of past decisions with a category of problems rather than evaluating of the options each time.

In the case of the West Point e-mails, if the e-mail looks similar enough in appearance and content to previous e-mails, users accepted their legitimacy with little doubt. While the bogus e-mails created for the West Point study had suspicious cues intentionally added in the content, such as a fictitious colonel and office address (Figure 1), they were too subtle to be noticed by a cadet skimming through all of their e-mails.

Feedback and Learning from Security-Related Decisions

For a user to effectively learn to produce secure computer-related decisions, the feedback from the interface used to make a security or risk de-

Figure 1. Example of a fictitious phishing e-mail used in the 2004 West Point phishing study. The only clues to the fraudulent nature of the e-mail are the fictitious colonel and building

From: sr1770@usma.edu [mailto:sr1770@usma.edu]
Sent: Tuesday, June 22, 2004 4:57 PM
To: cadet@usma.edu
Subject: Grade Report Problem

There was a problem with your last grade report. You need to:

Select this link Grade Report and follow the instructions to make sure that your information is correct; and report any problem to me.

Robert Melville
COL, USCC
sr1770@usma.edu
Washington Hall, 7th Floor, Room 7206

cision must be conducive to the human learning processes. In a typical learning situation, behavior is shaped by positive reinforcement when we do something "right." When we do something successfully, we are usually rewarded immediately so that the connection between our action and the consequence is clear (Grice, 1948). This temporal contiguity is missing in the case of security, when the user does something correctly (e.g., makes a secure choice); the reinforcement is that bad things are less likely to happen. There is no immediate reward or instant gratification, which can be a powerful reinforcement in shaping behavior.

In another common learning situation, behavior is shaped by negative reinforcement when we do something "wrong." We do something bad, we immediately suffer the consequences. In the case of security, when the user does something bad, the negative reinforcement may not be immediately evident. It may be delayed by days, weeks, or months if it comes at all. From previous research, it is known that the introduction of a delay between the behavior and the bad consequences will result in less suppression of the behavior (Baron, 1965). Thus, cause and effect is learned best when the effect is immediate and anti-security choices often have no immediate consequences. This makes learning consequences difficult except in the case of spectacular disasters and near disasters.

Technology Factors

Credibility

Exactly what was it about the e-mails that made them seem so credible? Both the sender of the e-mail and the e-mail address were bogus yet the cadets made an error in judgment by responding inappropriately with their personal information. This scenario is an illustration of one area where the attributes of the system or technology might influence the thought processes of the user. When a user encounters a Web site and has to judge its authenticity from limited information (e.g., its

appearance, etc.), studies show that users report the "design look" as the most important indicator of credibility (Stanford, Tauber, Fogg, & Marable, 2002). Given the simple heuristic approaches that user employ to establish the veracity of online information, it should be no surprise that users are generally bad at judging the credibility of information sources like Web pages and so forth, based on domain names or official seals/logos as well (Wogalter & Mayhorn, 2006).

Personal Relevance

It is likely the content of the e-mail dealing with cadet grades made the e-mail personally relevant to the recipients. Therefore, they were motivated to perform any action requested. It stands to reason that this kind of specific and targeted content would be much more relevant and motivating than generic spam content dealing with money from royal families in Nigeria or pictures of celebrities.

Environmental Factors

In addition to the user factors and technology factors, the context around the incident played an equally important role. In the first study, the fake e-mail was sent to students just before the end of a semester when grades were on all cadets' minds. In addition, by chance, cadets had received an e-mail regarding grades a few days before the fake e-mail was sent. Thus, there was a very credible context surrounding the receipt of the fake e-mail, which added to its perception of legitimacy.

Time Pressure

Because cadets were undergoing both academic and military training, they might be considered as a special population in terms of their level of community engagement and activity. Arguably, these cadets were engaged in a very busy life style that required them to multi-task on a regular basis. It seems likely that time pressure may have played a role in complying with the bogus e-mails and made cadets more likely to rely on rote decision making heuristics when evaluating the e-mails.

Also, because the cadets were actively engaged in military training that conditioned them to obey the commands of a superior officer; they were predisposed to comply with the seemingly credible request. Within the military environment, subordinates may be very used to receiving frequent orders from superiors with little advance notice. Such environmental factors might combine with the technology and user variables to elicit security behavior which, in retrospect, might be considered inappropriate.

Evaluating Potential Solutions

Evaluating potential solutions to these problems from a user-technology-environment perspective allows a more holistic approach to assessment and calls attention to user and environmental factors that might otherwise go overlooked.

In systems engineering, designers often try to design error out of the system by eliminating dependencies on components with high failure rates and working well within component tolerances. The approach that reduces the greatest source of error in the system may be to eliminate the user from the interaction where possible. For example, automatically scanning attached files before opening or before downloading to the user's machine would be a more robust way to mitigate malware than relying on users to pay attention to what they are doing.

Attempts to build systems that detect and warn users about phishing Web sites have fallen short of useful, partially due to problems with users noticing the alerts from such systems (Dhamija & Tygar, 2005). Notification of risk is a critical area in user-security interaction and we will address that in more detail later. In the meantime,

it is surprising what people can overlook when engaged in an activity.

Inattention Blindness

Inattention blindness is a well studied psychological phenomenon where observers may not perceive details in a scene that are not part of the task at hand. Seemingly un-ignorable features of a scene are often ignored, features much more obvious than the subtleties between "http" and "https" or icons. For example, Simons and Chabris (1999) provide a striking demonstration of this in a study where they showed that study participants asked to watch a video of a basketball game and count the number of passes, did not notice a gorilla who walked through the middle of the players, stopped in the center of the scene, turned toward the camera, and beat on its chest.

Turning back to phishing tricks, not only are users prone to fall for lures that are highly similar to sites or e-mail they are familiar with and trust, but attempts to warn users will go unheeded unless they capture and hold users' attention.

Unfortunately, there may be easier ways for users to infect their computers or organization's networks than opening attachments or downloading files. They might install them physically. Several cases document the dangers of removable storage devices to networks and the inherent curiosity of end users.

CURIOSITY KILLED THE NETWORK: DELIVERING MALWARE THROUGH STORAGE DEVICES

As part of a security audit for a bank in 2006, security consultants seeded the parking lot, smoking areas, and break rooms with USB key drives containing a safe Trojan that called home when the USB drive was inserted into an employee's machine. Of the 20 USB Trojans planted, 15 (75%) were found and used in the bank's personal computers over a three day period (Stasiukonis, 2007).

In a similar story, a UK based computer training company handed out 100 CDs in London's financial district and told recipients that if they ran the CDs on their computers, they would be entered into a contest for a free vacation (Kirk, 2006). Contained on the CD was a program which launched a Web browser and reported home. Although all CDs had printed warnings on the front cover instructing users to check with their corporate security policies before running the CD, 75 of the 100 CDs (75%) handed out called home. Included in the transmitted information were IP addresses of several high profile London companies.

Perhaps the most stunning example of the risk posed by removable storage devices occurred in 2005 with the near theft of over £200 million ($423m) from the world's second largest bank, the Sumitomo Mitsui Bank (Ilet, 2005; Sturgeon, 2005; Betteridge, 2005). According to the British National Hi-Tech Crime Unit who foiled the plan, hackers accessed the computer systems at the London offices of Sumitomo Mitsui using information gathered from keystroke logging programs which permitted them to acquire passwords and other sensitive account information.

While neither bank officials nor representatives for the National Hi-Tech Crime Unit fully explained how the keystroke logging software was installed on Sumitomo Mitsui computers, there was much speculation over the use of small USB storage devices. One theory explored by the investigating agency was that the hackers gained physical access to the computers via a company insider or housekeeping staff and was able to insert USB drives into the back of computers which injected the key logging software.

Given the apparent reliability with which end users will insert found objects into their corporate computers, coercing bank employees or facilities people into the plot would seem an unnecessary step. The thieves could have handed them out to unsuspecting employees who were ignorant of any felonious intentions.

Do end users not care about the security of the systems they use? After all, the CDs handed out on the streets of London did have warnings on the cover instructing people to make sure they were in compliance with their corporate security policies before running them. Why is this attack vector so successful? We might as well ask why the Trojan army hauled the Greek's wooden horse into the city of Troy.

User Factors

Users do not Think They are at Risk

A possible explanation is that these users were unaware of the dangers at hand. More importantly, however, even if the dangers were known, they were probably perceived as very unlikely events. People often believe that they are less vulnerable to risks than others. Most people believe that they are better than average drivers and that they will live beyond the average life expectancy (Slovic, Fischhoff, & Lichtenstein, 1986). This belief that one is more capable than their peers is known as *optimism bias* (Dalziel & Job, 1997; Dejoy, 1987). Another mistaken belief is known as the *third person effect* (Perloff, 1993) where some people believe that they are less susceptible to hazards than other people (Adams, Bochner, & Bilik, 1998). Given these biases, it stands to reason, then, that any computer user has the pre-set belief that they are at less risk of computer vulnerability than others. While people generally do know that there are viruses, hackers, and other computer risks out there, they inherently believe it is less likely to happen to them than others.

Safety is an Abstract Concept

When evaluating information to make a decision, results that are abstract are less persuasive than results that are concrete (Borgida & Nisbett, 1977).

This is essential to conceptualizing how users perceive security and make decisions. Often the pro-security choice has no visible outcome and there is no visible threat. The reward for being more secure is that nothing bad happens. Safety in this situation is an abstract concept. This, by its nature, is difficult for people to evaluate as a gain when mentally comparing cost, benefits, and risks.

Compare the abstract reward (safety) garnered from being more secure against a concrete reward like satisfying curiosity, entering a contest, and so forth, and the outcome does not favor security. This is especially true when a user does not know what his or her level of risk is or believes he or she is initially at less risk than others. Returning to the principle of satisficing, the user is also more likely to make a quick decision without considering all of the risks, consequences, and options.

Technology Factors

In these cases, there are obvious technology factors which could be addressed. First, end users were allowed to attach portable storage devices to their desktop computers or use portable storage media. It would have been possible to mitigate this risk by preventing users from doing so either by hardware configuration or by user account access controls.

While possible, it may not always be practical to have desktop computers without USB ports or CD drives or to deny users access rights to them. Another possibility would have been to automatically scan all removable storage devices or storage media for potential malware and alert the user or automatically block its use.

Environmental Factors

Outside of the human-computer loop, there are environmental factors involved as well. One has to wonder what the general security ethos of these organizations was. While employees in these organizations were doubtlessly exposed to security awareness information and even training perhaps, did they feel they had a personal responsibility? This is something with which all IT organizations struggle.

Diffusion of Responsibility

Diffusion of responsibility is a well known social behavior that occurs in groups where individuals tend to neglect responsibility or fail to take action believing that someone else in the group will (Darley & Latané, 1968). In restaurants, for example, large groups of diners tend to leave less money in tips, as a proportion of the bill, than smaller groups (Freeman, Walker, & Latané, 1975). The reasoning is that in larger groups, more people shortchange the tip believing the difference will be made up by someone else who will over tip. In smaller groups, the members know their contribution is significant. Related to computer security, it is easy for end users in an organizational setting to believe that security is not their responsibility and defer it to someone else who must know more about it than they do, must be watching for security problems, and must know what to do when one occurs.

Evaluating Potential Solutions

One solution to the problems described in the stories may be to impose a corporate security policy that users cannot use portable USB storage devices. From a human factors perspective, this is unlikely to be successful for several reasons:

- Users may not respect the policy because they do not understand the risk involved.
- They may not be aware of the policy or forget the policy.
- Environmental situations may arise where the users have to use a removable storage device.

- If they try it once and there are no negative consequences, they will likely continue to do it in the future.

A more reliable way to prevent the risk is to take the user out of the equation. It would be possible to prevent users from using removable storage devices or scan any such device or media for malware when discovered. This would reduce the risk that users accidentally inject malware into network.

Those steps might reduce these specific risks but what about the overarching issues around risk perception and diffusion of responsibility from which many other risks descend? In these cases, raising user awareness of security issues and making them actively engaged in the process are needed.

Many security administrators and IT professionals responsible for security know the best time to ask for funding for a security project is right after a major virus outbreak or security breach. Incidents heighten everyone's security awareness and create an environment with less user induced risk for some time, until the panic settles down and the original base level returns. The challenge is to raise users' base level of awareness in an effective and meaningful way without creating an environment of paranoia. This should be a goal of simple and recurring training campaigns.

Systems Approach to Training

Designers of security systems might consider adopting the systems approach to training which is often considered a standard practice in the field of human factors and ergonomics (Helander, 1997; Mayhorn, Stronge, McLaughlin, & Rogers, 2004).

In the systems approach to training, the characteristics of the person, the environment, and the technology itself are considered through a series of sequential stages: needs assessment, task/person analysis, selection and design of

training programs, and evaluation. The initial step of needs assessment determines the content of training materials by exploring whether training is necessary, what skills need to be taught, and the characteristics of those who will benefit most from training. Task and person analyses follow needs assessment and are conducted to determine the functional characteristics of the technology and users.

Specifically, a task analysis defines the step-by-step procedure for operating a device such as a computerized security application and yields a list of requirements and abilities that are essential to effectively operate that device. Of equal importance is the person analysis that defines the capabilities and limitations of the target of the training, in this case the individuals who will learn to use the security application. From the results of the task and person analyses, the most appropriate design and selection of training options can be used to facilitate learning. Training techniques such as the provision of well-organized written instructions may assist in reconciling the differences between task requirements and personal limitations.

Once a training program is in place, evaluation of that program is necessary to ensure that training is effective. To evaluate a program, measures of successful learning such as retention of information and usability should be examined. If a training program is deemed ineffective, a new needs assessment should be conducted and new training techniques should be considered during an iterative process (design, test, redesign, test, etc.).

COMMUNICATION OF SECURITY RISK

While the previous sections have mainly focused on the attributes of the user and the environment, this section will describe some preliminary efforts to manipulate the properties of the system to effectively communicate the nature of the security risk through warnings. In general, one of the goals of the human factors discipline is to increase safety (Sanders & McCormick, 1993). One approach to pursuing this goal includes the use of warnings systems (see Wogalter, 2006 for a comprehensive review) such as pop-up dialog boxes to deliver risk communication messages during computing. Recently, researchers in the area have concluded that advances in new and emerging technologies promise to revolutionize these efforts possibly leading to safer, more secure user behavior (Wogalter & Mayhorn, 2005).

To explore these issues, a pilot study is currently being conducted by the authors of this chapter to explore the decision making process that users undergo when they encounter security messages. To summarize the procedure of the study, participants were asked to perform a cover task while the experimenter left the room to run an errand. On the participant's computer ran a program to display a simulated security warning 10 minutes into the cover task. The security warning contained a message requesting the user's permission to close an unsecured port. Due to the absence of the experimenter, participants were forced to respond to the warning without any guidance. After a period of time, the experimenter returned and questioned the participant about his or her experience performing the cover task then the security dialog. Preliminary results indicate that the majority (approximately 76%) of participants dismiss the warning quickly without reading the security-related message or seeking further information. Even more striking may be that, in several cases, participants did not recall seeing any security message or dialog at all. This may have been due to inattention blindness.

User Factors

Within the literature, a variety of models have been presented to describe how users generally interact with warnings that they encounter (e.g.,

Lehto & Miller, 1986; Edworthy & Adams, 1996; Rogers, Lamson, & Rousseau, 2000; Wogalter, Dejoy, & Laughery. 1999). Most models agree that secure behavior is heavily reliant on the capacity of the human perceptual and cognitive processes to first notice a warning, then comprehend the message content, and finally making the decision of whether or not to comply with the security system instructions.

Base Rate and Response Bias

Security message dialogs are displayed less often than all the other message dialogs issued by the operating system and applications taken together. This means that non-security message dialogs have a higher base rate of occurrence than security message dialogs. Because non-security dialogs have a higher base rate, users develop a *response bias* to the general category of message dialogs. That is, users learn to accept the default decision or always click "OK" when they receive any kind of message dialog without paying much attention to what it says. In this way, users come to automatically ignore security message dialogs when they look similar to other message dialogs. Such dismissive behavior might be due to habituation (Wogalter & Mayhorn, 2005). When an individual is repeatedly exposed to a given stimulus (e.g., a warning), habituation occurs such that less attention is given to that stimulus during subsequent exposures.

Technology Factors

As mentioned before, effective warnings capture and maintain the attention of the user through the process of noticing. Thus, the most basic way a warning such as a security message dialog can fail a user is to be non-distinctive in the sense that it blends into the background noise and does not communicate a sense of importance or urgency. Such design failures often lead users to ignore and dismiss the warning before reading the message

(Figure 2).

The high rate of occurrence for all system message dialogs is, itself, a technology factor contributing to the problem. In our pilot study with security dialogs, one participant told of his experience with an anti-virus program that continually alerts a message dialog with an offer to renew his update service as the reason he quickly dismissed the experimental warning. He has been conditioned to disregard the warning and, in his mind, the warnings all blurred together. The constant alerting of messages which carry no real perceived value creates a noisy environment to which users adjust, sometimes with drastic measures. This behavior has been observed in many human factors domains. Fighter pilots, for example, have been known to actually disable cockpit alarms with high false alarm rates by pulling out the electrical fuses and train engineers have been known to tape over auditory alarms to muffle their sound (Sorkin, 1988).

Environmental Factors

Environmental factors at work within this pilot study include the dual nature of the task itself. Users were initially assigned a primary task to complete within a specific time frame. When presented with the secondary task of responding to the warning, users conserved time by mostly ignoring the warning. As previous research within the naturalistic decision making literature suggests, time pressure frequently decreases the quality of decisions (Hammond, 2000).

Another environmental factor at work during this pilot study was the use of a computer that was not the personal property of the user. Because the experiment was conducted in the university setting, many users may have believed that they did not have the authority to make security decisions regarding a university-owned machine. In this case as with the examples of malware installed via USB devices or free CDs, users may have

Figure 2. Examples of security dialogs

felt a diffusion of responsibility for any negative consequences to the computer.

Evaluating Potential Solutions

As previously described, security functions should be designed such that end users have few alternatives except to make the secure decision. To address potential solutions that might increase behavioural compliance with the security information relayed to them via message dialogs, a number of technological changes might be put into place to attract attention and optimize user comprehension of the security situation via message content.

For instance, the ability to dismiss a warning is a system design flaw that can be easily remedied. Previous research indicates that interactive warnings that cannot be dismissed but require a forced choice, often result in warning compliance (Duffy, Kalsher, & Wogalter, 1995). Thus, a message dialog that can be minimized or dragged to the periphery of the display is much more likely to be ignored than a dialog box that requires user feedback in the form of an explicit response.

Other attempts to attract the user's attention might focus on modifications to the message dialog itself. Previous evidence from the warnings literature suggests that personalized warning signs incorporating the person's name led to higher rates of compliance than non-personalized warning signs (Wogalter, Raciot, Kalsher, & Simpson, 1994).

Lessons from other areas of human factors might be instrumental in finding techniques to capture the attention of users as well. For instance, the use of multimodal alarms has been successful during medical monitoring procedures where anesthesiologists are immediately alerted to changes in critical patient vital signs by the use of auditory alarms that supplement integrated visual displays (Sanderson, 2006). Such a use of other non-visual modalities of communication within the security domain might manifest themselves in the form of vibratory computer mice or auditory "earcons."

To optimize the impact of the message content of a warning, the ability of the user to comprehend the message must be tested. Thus, the designers of security message dialogs should test the readability of their warnings to ensure that risk communications are comprehensible to the end user. For example, the use of technological jargon must be avoided so that users are not predisposed to ignore the messages (Mayhorn, Rogers, & Fisk, 2004). Because the human factors research literature indicates that warnings may not be understood by members of the at-risk population at levels expected by the designers (Mayhorn, Wogalter, &

Bell, 2004; Wolff & Wogalter, 1998), it is important that comprehension testing be conducted to determine the effectiveness of proposed warnings *before* they are implemented for use.

Published standards have provided guidance for warning designers by quantifying what level of comprehension constitutes acceptable message content. The American National Standards Institute (ANSI Z535.3, 2002) requires that at least 85% of the answers from a sample of 50 or more people should correctly identify the message content being communicated. Furthermore, the sample should generate no more than 5% critical confusions which are defined as answers that are opposite to the intended concept or wrong answers that lead to behavior resulting in adverse consequences (ANSI, 2002).

DISASTERS WAITING TO HAPPEN

To this point in the discussion, the actions of the end user's interaction with the technology of the system have been examined exclusively. Whether the user will make secure decisions when faced with security message dialogs or whether they respond to phishing e-mails by providing confidential personal information are important, yet the actions of others within the broader system must also be considered to fully describe the sources of error. According to Reason (2002), the errors of the end user can be classified as active errors because the resulting consequences are directly tied to the behavior of the end user. For instance, the UK incident reported by Kirk (2006) illustrates that the active error occurred when users in the London financial district ignored the printed warning regarding corporate security policies and inserted the CDs.

To fully analyze such a situation, Reason (2002) made a distinction between these active errors and latent errors which result from the activities of other people such as interface designers, managers, and high level corporate decision makers who are removed in time and space from the interface where the user decision is made. The consequences of such latent errors may lie dormant in the system for a long time before they combine with other factors such as end user action to initiate a system security breach. For instance, high level corporate decision makers may have contributed to the vulnerability of the system and the increased likelihood of a security incident by adopting a rather lax security policy that allowed employees to use external storage devices from unknown sources.

Oops, Lost the Hard Drive

True story:

"Company Y" wants to be a good corporate citizen when it de-commissions hardware during its regular hardware refresh cycle. According to federal regulations in its industry, the company must completely wipe all hard drives from de-commissioned systems (laptops, desktops, servers, portable drives, devices, etc.) in a very specific way. These hard drives must be wiped using a very specific type of technology and must be wiped a very specific number of times before they are considered to be safe. There is no automated way to do this process, so company Y's solution is to pull all the hard drives from anything about to go into the community, and store them in a room until someone has the time to complete the wiping process. To date, the process has not been completed and the room is filled with thousands of hard drives waiting to be processed.

This is a security breach waiting to happen. Consider the following:

In the summer of 2006, a stolen hard drive belonging to a Veteran's Administration employee made headlines as the second-largest data breach in U.S. history and the largest breach of social security numbers ever (Mark, 2006). The laptop was the property of a data analyst who took the *external*

hard drive to his home where it was stolen. The external hard drive contained personal information on roughly 26 million veterans including names, social security numbers, birth dates, and addresses. Although the hard drive was recovered and no sensitive data was comprised, the Veteran's Administration faced multiple class action lawsuits as a result of negligence.

In 2007, Empire Blue Cross and Blue Shield of New York blamed human error when they accidentally lost a CD of customer data en route to a third party research company (Washkuch, 2007). The CD contained names, social security numbers, and the medical histories of roughly 75,000 insurance customers.

We can view these latter two cases with respect to our human-technology-environment model and see that the users directly involved probably considered the potential security problems as very unlikely events. At the technology level, there were simple solutions that could have been imposed to prevent the mishaps and there would certainly have been environmental factors at play such as a need to work from home or a rush to deliver the CD of data. However, these cases also suggest deeper level and latent problems in the environmental factors around the organizations' corporate security policies or federal regulations.

Can I have your Social Security Number Please?

At the end of 2005, financial services company, H&R Block inadvertently embedded social security numbers within tracking codes printed on packaging that was used to mail customers free copies of its tax preparation software (Vijayan, 2006). In the beginning of 2006, Blue Cross and Blue Shield of North Carolina made the same mistake and exposed social security numbers belonging to more than 600 of the insurance company's customers by printing them along with the street address on a mailer sent to the customers (Vijayan, 2006). A month after the Blue Cross Blue Shield incident, the Boston Globe accidentally exposed the names, credit card numbers, and bank account information of more than 200,000 subscribers when sensitive documents were reused to print routing labels attached to bundles of newspapers (Vijayan, 2006).

The companies involved in these incidents all claimed human error as the responsible culprit. However, the reality is more complex and harder to fix. Guaranteed, the users involved will not make the same mistakes again, and there may be technology level changes, but there will likely be other incidents in future. Again, these are cases where many people were involved who had opportunities to prevent the errors before they happened. These are not cases of computer network or database compromises, but system failures where latent errors combined in a way that resulted in the breach.

Evaluating Potential Solutions

There are numerous techniques that can be used to address latent errors within a system (see Reason, 2002 for a comprehensive review). One such method that may prove useful to designers of security systems is the technique for human error rate prediction (THERP). In THERP, vulnerabilities within the human-machine systems could be caused by human error alone or in conjunction with equipment functioning or operational procedures and practices (Swain & Guttmann, 1983).

THERP employs fours steps to mitigating the likelihood of human error:

1. Identify system functions that can be influenced by human error.
2. Perform a detailed task analysis to obtain a list of human operations.
3. Estimate error probabilities for each item on the list via expert judgment or available data.

4. Estimate the effects of human failure on the system then alter the characteristics of the system to minimize human error. Iteratively recalculate the probability of human error to determine the utility of each system modification.

Human reliability assessment methods such as THERP have been used in many realms to help design and assess human-machine systems by identifying opportunities for user error and steps where error detection and recovery are critical.

CONCLUSION

Users are generally considered to be the weakest link when it comes to computer security. There are many stories of user actions leading to security incidents beyond the small number discussed here. While the user problem in computer security is well known, less has been offered to explain why.

In this chapter, we have attempted to call attention to cognitive and human factors issues that influence an end user's behavior when interacting with a system or making decisions with security consequences. It is not possible to eliminate users from the control loop in computer security and, as a result, they will always provide a source of errors in the system. The most elegant and intuitively designed interface does not improve security if users ignore warnings, choose poor settings, or unintentionally subvert corporate policies. The challenge in developing robust security systems is take this into account and minimize the potential for error on the user end through intelligent design on the technology end.

Human factors research methodologies have provided many contributions towards the reduction of user error and promotion of system safety in high risk domains ranging from medicine to nuclear power. We feel there is much potential for these approaches to be incorporated into the design and evaluation of user-security systems.

By conceptualizing the system as an inter-related mechanism that relies on the interactions between human, technology, and environmental factors, security professionals might be able to develop interventions that work to strengthen the weak links.

We would like to extend a special thank you to Leslie Johnson for the "true stories" based on her experience as a user experience researcher working in the human-security interaction realm.

REFERENCES

Adams, A., Bochner, S., & Bilik, L. (1998). The effectiveness of warning signs in hazardous work places: Cognitive and social determinants. *Applied Ergonomics, 29*, 247-254.

American National Standards Institute (ANSI). (2002). *Criteria for safety symbols* (Z535.3-Revised). Washington, DC: National Electrical Manufacturers Association.

America Online and the National Cyber Security Alliance (2004). *AOL/NCSA online safety study.* http://www.staysafeonline.info/news/safety_study_v04.pdf

Baron, A. (1965). Delayed punishment of a runway response. *Journal of Comparative and Physiological Psychology, 60,* 131-134.

Betteridge, I. (2005). Police foil $420 million keylogger scam. *eWeek.com.* http://www.eweek.com/article2/0,1895,1777706,00.asp

Bogner, M. S. (2004). *Misadventures in health care: Inside stories.* Mahwah, NJ: Lawrence Erlbaum Associates.

Borgida, E., and Nisbett, R. E. (1977). The differential impact of abstract vs. concrete information on decisions. *Journal of Applied Social Psychology, 7,* 258-271.

Dalziel, J. R., & Job, R. F. S. (1997). Motor vehicle accidents, fatigue and optimism bias in taxi drivers. *Accident Analysis & Prevention, 29,* 489-494.

Darley, J. M. & Latané, B. (1968). Bystander intervention in emergencies: Diffusion of responsibility. *Journal of Personality and Social Psychology, 8,* 377-383.

Dejoy, D.M. (1987). The optimism bias and traffic safety. In *Proceedings of the Human Factors and Ergonomics Society* (Vol. 31, pp. 756-759).

Dhamija, R., & Tygar, J. D. (2005). The battle against phishing: Dynamic security skins. In *Proceedings of SOUPS* (pp. 77-88).

Duffy, R. R., Kalsher, M. J., & Wogalter, M. S. (1995). Increased effectiveness of an interactive warning in a realistic incidental product-use situation. *International Journal of Industrial Ergonomics, 15,* 169-166.

Edworthy, J., & Adams, A. (1996). *Warning design: A research prospective.* London: Taylor and Francis.

Ferguson, A. J. (2005). Fostering e-mail security awareness: The West Point Carronade. *Educause Quarterly, 28,* 54-57.

Freeman, S., Walker, M. R., & Latané, B. (1975). Diffusion of responsibility and restaurant tipping: Cheaper by the bunch. *Personality and Social Psychology Bulletin, 1*(4), 584-587.

Gaudin, S. (2007). Human error more dangerous than hackers. *TechWeb.* http://www.techweb.com/showArticle.jhtml?articleID=197801676

Goldstein, W. M. & Hogarth, R. M. (1997). *Research on judgment and decision-making: Currents, connections, and controversies.* Cambridge, UK: Cambridge University Press.

Gordon, L. A., Loeb, M. P., Lucyshyn, W., & Richardson, R. (2006). *2006 CSI/FBI computer crime and security survey*. Baltimore: Computer Security Institute.

Grice, G. R. (1948). The relation of secondary reinforcement to delayed reward in visual discrimination learning. *Journal of Experimental Psychology, 38,* 1-16.

Hammond, K. R. (2000). *Judgments under stress.* New York: Oxford University Press.

Hardee, J. B., West, R., & Mayhorn, C. B. (2006). To download or not to download: An examination of computer security decision-making. *Association of Computing Machinery: Interactions, 13*(3), 32-37.

Helander, M. (1997). The human factors profession. In G. Salvendy (Ed.), *Handbook of human factors and ergonomics* (2nd ed., pp. 3-16). New York: Wiley.

Ilet, D. (2005). Inside the biggest bank raid that never was. *Zdnet.* http://news.zdnet.co.uk/security/0,1000000189,39191956,00.htm.

Jackson, J. W., Ferguson, A. J., & Cobb, M. J. (2005, October 12-22). Building a university-wide automated information assurance awareness exercise. In *Proceedings of the 35th ASEE/IEEE Frontiers in Education Conference,* Indianapolis, IN, (pp 7-11).

Kirk, J. (2006). Free CDs highlight security weaknesses. *PC World.* http://www.pcworld.idg.com.au/index.php/id;2055135135;fp;2;fpid;1

Klein, G. (1998). *Sources of power: How people make decisions.* Cambridge, MA: The MIT Press.

Lehto, M. R., & Miller, J. M. (1986). *Warnings, volume 1: Fundamentals, design, and evaluation methodologies.* Ann Arbor, MI: Fuller Technical.

Linden, J. V. (2004). The trouble with blood is it all looks the same: Transfusion errors. In M.S.

Bogner (Ed.), *Misadventures in health care: Inside stories* (pp. 13-25). Mahwah, NJ: Lawrence Erlbaum Associates.

Mark, R. (2006). Teens charged in VA laptop theft. *Internetnews.* http://www.internetnews.com/bus-news/article.php/3624986

Mayhorn, C. B., Lanzolla, V. R., Wogalter, M. S., & Watson, A. M. (2005). Personal digital assistants (PDAs) as medication reminding tools: Exploring age differences in usability. *Gerontechnology, 4*(3), 128-140.

Mayhorn, C. B., Rogers, W. A., & Fisk, A. D. (2004). Designing technology based on cognitive aging principles. In S. Kwon & D. C. Burdick (Eds.), *Gerotechnology: research and practice in technology and aging* (pp. 42-53). New York: Springer Publishing.

Mayhorn, C. B., Stronge, A. J., McLaughlin, A. C., & Rogers, W. R. (2004). Older adults, computer training, and the systems approach: A formula for success. *Educational Gerontology, 30*(3), 185-203.

Mayhorn, C. B., Wogalter, M. S., & Bell, J. L. (2004). Are we ready? Misunderstanding homeland security safety symbols. *Ergonomics in Design, 12*(4), 6-14.

Park, D. C., & Skurnik, I. (2004). Aging, cognition, and patient errors in following medical instructions. In M.S. Bogner (Ed.), *Misadventures in health care: Inside stories* (pp. 165-181). Mahwah, NJ: Lawrence Erlbaum Associates.

Perloff, R. (1993). Third person effect research 1983-1992: A review and synthesis. *International Journal of Public Opinion Research, 5,* 167-184.

Reason, J. (2002). *Human reason.* Cambridge, UK: Cambridge University Press.

Rogers, W. A., Lamson, N., & Rousseau, G. K. (2000). Warning research: An integrative perspective. *Human Factors, 42*(1), 102-139.

Sanders, M. S., & McCormick, E. J. (1993). *Human factors in engineering and design* (7th ed.). New York: McGraw-Hill Inc.

Sanderson, P. (2006). The multimodal world of medical monitoring displays. *Applied Ergonomics, 37,* 501-512.

Simon, H. A. (1956). Rational choice and the structure of the environment. *Psychological Review, 63,* 129-138.

Simons, D. J., & Chabris, C. F. (1999).Gorillas in our midst: sustained inattentional blindness for dynamic events. *Perception, 28*(9), 1059-1074.

Slovic, P., Fischhoff, B., & Lichtenstein, S. (1986). Facts versus fears: Understanding perceived risks. In D. Kahneman, P. Slovic, and A. Tversky (Eds.), *Judgment under uncertainty: Heuristics and biases* (pp. 463-489). New York: Cambridge University Press.

Sorkin, R. D. (1988). Why are people turning off our alarms? *Journal of Acoustical Society of America, 84,* 1107-1108.

Stanford, J., Tauber, E. R., Fogg, B. J., & Marable, L. (2002). Experts vs. online consumers: A comparative credibility study of health and finance websites. *Consumer WebWatch.* www.consumerwebwatch.org

Stasiukonis, S. (2007). Social engineering, the USB way. *Dark Reading.* http://www.darkreading.com/document.asp?doc_id=95556&WT.svl=column1_1

Sturgeon, W. (2005). Foiled £220m heist highlights spyware threat. *Zdnet.* http://news.zdnet.co.uk/security/0,1000000189,39191677,00.htm

Swain, A.D, & Guttmann, H.E. (1983). *Handbook of human reliability analysis with emphasis on nuclear power plant applications. NUREG/CR 1278.* Albuquerque, NM: Sandia National Laboratories.

Tversky, A, & Kahneman, D. (1974). Judgment under uncertainty: Heuristics and biases. *Science, 185*(4157), 1124-1131.

Vijayan, J. (2006). "Human error" exposes patients' social security numbers. *Computerworld.* http://www.health-itworld.com/newsletters/2006/02/14/18209?page:int=-1

Washkuch, F. (2007). Newspaper: Medical information of 75,000 Empire Blue Cross members lost. *SC Magazine.* http://scmagazine.com/us/news/article/643807/newspaper-medical-information-75000-empire-blue-cross-members-lost/

Wogalter, M. S. (2006). *Handbook of warnings.* Mahwah, NJ: Lawrence Erlbaum Associates.

Wogalter, M. S., Dejoy, D. M., & Laughery, K. R. (1999). *Warnings and risk communication.* London: Taylor and Francis.

Wogalter, M. S., & Mayhorn, C. B. (2005). Providing cognitive support with technology-based warning systems. *Ergonomics, 48*(5), 522-533.

Wogalter, M. S. & Mayhorn, C. B. (2006). Is that information from a credible source? On discriminating Internet domain names. In *Proceedings of the 16th World Congress of the International Ergonomics Association.* Maastricht, The Netherlands.

Wogalter, M. S., Racicot, B. M., Kalsher, M. J., & Simpson, S. N. (1994). The role of perceived relevance in behavioral compliance in personalized warning signs. *International Journal of Industrial Ergonomics, 14,* 233-242.

Wolff, J. S., & Wogalter, M. S. (1998). Comprehension of pictorial symbols: Effects of context and test method. *Human Factors, 40,* 173-186.

Chapter V
Trusting Computers Through Trusting Humans:
Software Verification in a Safety–Critical Information Society

Alison Adam
University of Salford, UK

Paul Spedding
University of Salford, UK

ABSTRACT

This chapter considers the question of how we may trust automatically generated program code. The code walkthroughs and inspections of software engineering mimic the ways that mathematicians go about assuring themselves that a mathematical proof is true. Mathematicians have difficulty accepting a computer generated proof because they cannot go through the social processes of trusting its construction. Similarly, those involved in accepting a proof of a computer system or computer generated code cannot go through their traditional processes of trust. The process of software verification is bound up in software quality assurance procedures, which are themselves subject to commercial pressures. Quality standards, including military standards, have procedures for human trust designed into them. An action research case study of an avionics system within a military aircraft company illustrates these points, where the software quality assurance (SQA) procedures were incommensurable with the use of automatically generated code.

INTRODUCTION

They have computers, and they may have other weapons of mass destruction. Janet Reno, former US Attorney General

In this chapter our aim is to develop a theoretical framework with which to analyse a case study where one of the authors was involved, acting as an action researcher in the quality assurance procedures of a safety-critical system. This involved the production of software for aeroplane flight systems. An interesting tension arose between the automatically generated code of the software system (i.e., 'auto-code'—produced automatically by a computer, using CASE [Computer Aided Software Engineering] tools from a high level design) and the requirement of the quality assurance process which had built into it the requirement for human understanding and trust of the code produced.

The developers of the system in the case study designed it around auto-code—computer generated software, free from 'human' error, although not proved correct in the mathematical sense, and cheaper and quicker to produce than traditional program code. They looked to means of verifying the correctness of their system through standard software quality assurance (SQA) procedures. However, ultimately, they were unable to bring themselves to reconcile their verification procedures with automatically generated code. Some of the reason for this was that trust in human verification was built into (or inscribed into [Akrich, 1992]) the standards and quality assurance procedures which they were obliged to follow in building the system. Despite their formally couched descriptions, the standards and verification procedures were completely reliant on human verification at every step. However these 'human trust' procedures were incompatible with the automated production of software in ways we show below. The end result was not failure in the traditional sense but a failure to resolve incom-

mensurable procedures; one set relying on human trust, one set on computer trust.

Our research question is therefore: How may we understand what happens when software designers are asked to trust the design of a system, based on automatically generated program code, when the SQA procedures and military standards to which they must adhere demand walkthroughs and code inspections which are impossible to achieve with auto-code?

The theoretical framework we use to form our analysis of the case study is drawn from the links we make between the social nature of mathematical proof, the need to achieve trust in system verification, the ways in which we achieve trust in the online world, the methods of software engineering, and within that, the software quality movement and the related highly influential domain of military standards.

In the following section we briefly outline the social nature of mathematical proof. The next section discusses the debate over system verification which encapsulates many of the ideas of mathematical proof and how such proofs can be trusted by other mathematicians. The chapter proceeds to consider 'computer mediated' trust, briefly detailing how trust has been reified and represented in computer systems to date, mainly in relation to the commercial interests of e-commerce and information security. Trust is particularly pertinent in the world of safety-critical systems, where failure is not just inconvenient and financially damaging, although commercial pressures are still evident here, but where lives can be lost. The model of trust criticised by e-commerce critics is more similar to the type of trust we describe in relation to safety-critical systems, than one might, at first, expect. Understandably, we would like to put faith in a system which has been mathematically proved to be correct. However computer generated proofs, proofs about correctness of computer software, and automatically generated code are not necessarily understandable or amenable to inspection by people, even by experts. The question then arises of whether we can bring ourselves to trust computer generated proofs or code, when even a competent mathematician, logician, or expert programmer cannot readily understand them.

Following this, we describe the evolution of software development standards and the SQA movement. We argue that the development of quality assurance discourse involves processes of designing human ways of trusting mathematical evidence into standardisation and SQA. Military standards are an important part of the SQA story, having consequences far beyond the military arena. Standards are political devices with particular views of work processes inscribed (Akrich, 1992) in their design. We note the way that military standards, historically, moved towards formal verification procedures only to move back to rely more on 'human' forms of verification such as code walkthroughs and inspections in the later 1990s. The story is shot through with a tension between finding ways to trust the production of information systems and finding ways to control them. Formal methods, based on mathematical proof offer the promise of control, but only if we can bring ourselves to trust a proof generated by a machine rather than a proof constructed by another person. We present the background to the case study in terms of a description of the complex 'post cold war' military and commercial environment. This is followed by a description of the action research methodology employed in the project, an outline of the case study and an analysis of the case study findings in terms of our theoretical framework. In the conclusion we briefly note that mathematicians and others are gradually finding ways of trusting computers.

THE SOCIAL NATURE OF MATHEMATICAL PROOF

At first sight, the concept of mathematical proof appears to be relatively simple. The idea of a logical and rigorous series of steps, leading from one or more starting positions (previous theorems or axioms) to the final conclusion of the theorem seems to be the basis of mathematics. The concept of mathematical proof leading inexorably to true and incontrovertible truths about the world is very compelling. It is not surprising that we would like to apply the apparent certainty and exactness of mathematical approaches to computer programming. However if we consider briefly how agreement on mathematical proof and scientific truth is achieved by communities of mathematicians, then the social and cultural dimension of proof, as an agreement amongst trusted expert witnesses, reveals itself.

With the epistemological and professional success of mathematical proof, many of the cultural processes which go into making a proof true sink from consciousness and are only rendered visible in times of dispute; for example as in claims to the proof of Kepler's conjecture or Fermat's last theorem (Davies, 2006; Kuhn, 1962; Singh, 1997). Only on the margins then do we call into question our ability to trust these people when a mathematical proof cannot be agreed to be true by an expert community of mathematicians, as sometimes happens.

The apparently pure and abstract nature of mathematical proof fairly quickly breaks down when we inspect it more closely. In particular, when there is disagreement about a proof, the nature of proof is revealed as a social and cultural phenomenon; the matter of persuading and convincing colleagues. DeMillo, Lipton, and Perlis (1977, p. 208) wrote

Mathematicians talk to each other. They give symposium and colloquium talks which attempt to convince doubting (sometimes hostile) audiences of their arguments, they burst into each others' offices with news of insights for current research, and they scribble on napkins in university cafeterias and expensive restaurants. All for the sake of convincing other mathematicians. The key is that other mathematicians are inclined to listen!

This traditional approach towards mathematical proof, which could be described as one of *persuasive rigorous argument between mathematicians leading to trust,* is not the only way to address the idea of proof. A quite different approach appeared in the 1950s and was based on the work on logic developed by Bertrand Russell and others in the 1930s and used the newly invented electronic computer. This new logic-based approach was not dependent on the computer, but the computer's speed and accuracy had a major impact on its application to the proof of theorems in replacing the persuasive rational argument of competent mathematicians with a *formal* approach which sees any mathematical proof as a number of steps from initial axioms (using predicate logic), to the final proof statement (based purely on logical inference) without the requirement of a human being.

Many proofs can be completed by either method. For instance, many persuasive rigorous argument proofs can be converted to formal proofs (MacKenzie, 2004). It should be emphasised, however, that there is a real difference between the two types of proof. We are not simply talking about a machine taking on the role of a competent mathematician. Some proofs which are readily accepted by mathematicians rely on arguments of symmetry and equivalence, analogies, and leaps of imagination, which humans are very good at understanding but which a formal logic approach cannot replicate. Symmetry and analogy arguments of this type cannot be established by formal methods based on logical progression because symmetry relies on understanding semantics and cannot be gleaned from the syntax of a proof.

Whereas the persuasive rigorous argument, the 'human' approach, has been used for thousands of years, the formal or 'computer generated' approach has been in use for only about half a century. Clearly, the two methods are not treated in the same way by the expert community of mathematicians. With a rigorous argument type of proof, although one may expend much energy convincing one's colleagues of the validity of the proof, the *potential* for coming to agreement or trust of the proof is there. Essentially, in trusting that a mathematical proof is correct, mathematicians are demonstrating their trust in other competent mathematicians. However, expert mathematicians clearly have trouble bringing themselves to trust computer proofs, for good reason, as a computer cannot explain the steps in its reasoning (Chang, 2004).

COMPUTER SYSTEM VERIFICATION: TRUST AND THE SOCIAL

The preceding section contrasted the *use* of computer technology in a claimed proof: the formal method and the human 'rigorous argument' approach to proof. Although this is not the same thing as the proof or verification of a computer system *itself*, in other words the formal, computer generated proof that the computer system matches the specification, the question of whether we can trust the computer is exactly the same.

The idea of *proof* or *verification* of a program is quite different from simply testing the program. Typically, a large suite of programs might have thousands or millions of possible inputs, and so could be in many millions or even billions of states. Exhaustive testing cannot be possible. If a computer system is to be used in the well-funded and high-profile military field to control a space craft, aeroplane, or a nuclear power station, it is highly desirable if the system can be actually *proved* to be correct, secure, and reliable. Since testing, although vital, can never prove the system's correctness, more mathematical methods involving the notion of proof became of great interest in the late 1960s and have remained so ever since.

In fact the history of the verification of computer systems echoes that of mathematical proof, with basically the same two approaches: those who support the rigour of formal methods and those who believe that the purely formal, mechanised proof lacks the crucial element of human understanding (Tierney, 1993). In a paper to an ACM Symposium, DeMillo et al. (1977) argued that the two types of proof were completely different in nature, and that only the persuasive rigorous argument proof with its strong social aspect will ultimately be believable and capable of earning *trust.*

COMPUTER-MEDIATED TRUST

In ethical terms, trust is a complex phenomenon and is essentially a human relationship (Nissenbaum, 1999; Stahl, 2006). We think of trust in terms of a trustor who does the trusting and a trustee who is trusted. The trustee does not of course have to be human, but Nissenbaum (1999) suggests that the trustee should be a being to whom we ascribe human qualities such as intentions and reasons, what might be termed an 'agent.' Trust allows meaningful relationships and a vast range of intuitions to work. Nissenbaum (1999) argues that when we are guaranteed safety trust is not needed: 'What we have is certainty, security, safety – not trust. The evidence, the signs, the cues and clues that ground the formation of trust must always fall short of certainty; trust is an attitude without guarantees, without a complete warrant.' Intrusive regulation and surveillance are attempts at control and bad for building trust.

This generalised definition of trust clearly maps onto our description of mathematicians trusting proofs. They may not have complete certainty over the correctness of a mathematical proof, but they have good reason to trust a competent member of the community of expert mathematicians. Therefore they can trust the proof supplied by such a person.

Understandably, there has been much interest in trust in the online world, both in terms of online security and trust in e-commerce transactions. Nissenbaum (1999) suggests that excessive safety

controls, say in e-commerce, may encourage participation but they limit experience: 'Through security we may create a safer world, inhospitable to trust not because there is distrust, but because trust cannot be nourished in environments where risk and vulnerability are, for practical purposes, eradicated.'

Stahl's (2006) take on trust in e-commerce shows another example of the intangible human nature of trust, which has become reified and commodified, so that it can be measured and exchanged in machine transactions. Like Nissenbaum (1999), Stahl points to the way that a trustor does not have complete control over a trustee; vulnerability and uncertainty must be accepted in a trusting relationship. This of course includes business transactions, and is especially important in e-commerce as many of the traditional ways of developing trust are absent from online transactions. Trust becomes a way of generating profit; small wonder that trust, including technological ways of creating trust and maintaining it, has been of so much interest in e-commerce. In the world of e-commerce research, trusts lose its relational aspects and becomes a form of social control. 'If trust is limited to calculations of utility maximisation in commercial exchange, then most of the moral underpinnings of the mechanisms of trust become redundant. Trust changes its nature and loses the binding moral quality that it has in face-to-face interaction.' (Stahl, 2006, p. 31)

Although, on the face of it, Nissenbaum's and Stahl's arguments on the problems of online trust in e-commerce are not the same as the issue of trust described in the body of this chapter, there are important congruencies which are very directly applicable to our characterisation of trust. Whether it is a human trusting another human or an expert mathematician trusting another expert mathematician to supply an accurate proof, the same relationship between trustor and trustee obtains.

For Nissenbaum and Stahl, the issue is what happens to trust when it is commodified within an online relationship. In other words, what happens when the human-trusting-human relationship is mediated by technology? In this chapter we also consider what happens when the human-trusting-human relationship—in terms of a human trusting another human's mathematical proof, or computer program—is replaced by a human having to trust a machine. Of course, in this trustor-trustee relationship, the trustee, that is, the machine, cannot be understood in the way that another person can be.

The pressure to create computer-mediated trust is completely bound up with commercial pressures. The maximisation of profit drives the reification of trust in e-commerce. Similarly in the world of military avionics we describe, it is the commercial pressure of building systems more cheaply and faster which provides the impetus to turn over proofs, testing of programs, and automatic generation of code to a machine. A third aspect of similarity between Stahl's and Nissenbaum's view of computer-mediated trust and ours relates to the tension between trust and control. This is clearly present in the debate over trust in e-commerce. But it is also present in software quality discourse as we discuss below.

In the following section we briefly discuss some of the ways in which human trust has traditionally been built into procedures designed to verify program correctness, and how this can be seen to mirror an ideal group of mathematicians agreeing upon a mathematical proof.

BUILDING TRUST INTO A COMPUTER SYSTEM

We argue that, historically, much of the development of the software engineering discipline can be understood in terms of the development of procedures, through which we can convince ourselves to trust, and control, the development of information systems and the production of software. For instance, Myers' (1979) classic

book on software testing explores the topic of human testing in detail, justifying methods such as formal *code inspections* and *code walkthroughs*. The differences between the two methods depend on different usages of the terms 'inspection' and 'walkthrough,' but the important point is that both involve a small group of professionals carefully reading through code together. We argue that this can be viewed as an imitation of the social (persuasive rigorous argument) form of proof described earlier where 'mathematicians talk to each other' in symposia and colloquia and so on (DeMillo et al., 1977). The original programmer should be in the group, analogous to the mathematician demonstrating a proof or principle to expert colleagues. The aim (as originally suggested by Weinberg [1971]—an 'egoless' approach) is to discover as many errors as possible rather than to try to demonstrate that there are none. So the team is to act as an idealised group of 'Popperian' scientists looking for 'refutations' (Popper, 1963). Under such an approach, one can never be entirely sure that the code is correct. But, as the walkthrough proceeds, the original programmer and the code inspection team can gradually come to trust the code as bugs are weeded out and fixed.

Myers claims positive advantages of code inspections and walkthroughs, including the value of the original programmer talking through the design (and thus spotting the errors). He also notes the ability of human testers to see the causes and likely importance of errors (where a machine might simply identify symptoms) and also the likelihood that a batch of errors will be identified simultaneously. Also the team is able to empathise with and understand the thought processes of the original programmer in a way which a machine arguably cannot. Importantly, the team can be *creative* in its approach. In working together they also, inevitably, form something of a sharing and trusting community (even if it is disbanded after a day or two).

The lesson gleaned from human verification techniques, such as walkthroughs and code inspections, is that these have been regarded, for some time, as reliable, if not exhaustive, ways of ensuring reliability of software.

SOFTWARE QUALITY ASSURANCE AND MILITARY STANDARDS FOR SOFTWARE

The software verification techniques of code walkthroughs and inspections are important parts of the armoury SQA. Effectively, we argue that SQA is a branch of software engineering which formalises and standardises the very human methods of trust, and ultimately control outlined above, which we need to build into software engineering procedures. The SQA movement is an important part of the story of the growth of software engineering because of its quest for rigour and control of potentially unruly programs and programmers.

First of all, SQA offers a promise of rational control over software, the software development process, and those who produce software. Software quality criteria include features for directing, controlling, and importantly, measuring the quality of software (Gillies, 1997). 'Qualification' is achieved when a piece of software can be demonstrated to meet the criteria specified in these quality procedures. An important aspect of SQA involves demonstrating that software meets certain defined independent standards.

The development and adherence to software standards is a very important part of the story of SQA. Generic industry standards are available, but also of much interest—particularly for the case study set out later in the chapter—are military standards. Indeed, the defence industry is so influential that Tierney (1993) argues that military standards influence software engineering far beyond applications in defence. Hence military standards are a very important part of SQA, and ultimately are important in formalising ways in which designers of computer systems can

come to trust the systems and the production of correct software.

A number of military standards have been developed to regulate and control the use of software in defence applications. For instance, US standards DOD-STD-2167A (1988), MIL-STD-498 (1994), and ISO/IEC 12207 (1995) respectively established the requirements for software development and documentation in all equipment to be used by the US military (and effectively that of all Western armed forces), introduced object oriented development (OOD) and rapid application development (RAD), then broadened the scope of international standards to include acquisition and maintenance. (DSDM Consortium, 2006).

The relevant UK standard 00-55, (MoD, 1997) *Requirements for Safety Related Software in Defence Equipment,* was published in 1997 and echoes much of MIL-STD-498, but moves the discussion on provably correct software in a particular direction. At first sight, this seems highly significant to the current argument, because it clearly expressed a preference for *formal* methods, in other words mathematical procedures whereby the software is proved to be correct by a machine (MacKenzie, 2001).

Tierney (1993) argues that the release of UK Defence Standard 00-55 in draft in 1989 had the effect of intensifying the debate over formal methods in the UK software engineering community. It devoted as much space to regulating and managing software development labour processes as the techniques and practices to be used for formal designs. This reinforces our argument that SQA is concerned with control of work processes and those who perform them, the software developers. On the one hand, many argued that mathematical techniques for software development and verification could only ever be used sparingly, as there simply was not enough suitable mathematical expertise in most organisations and it increased software quality at the expense of programmer productivity. On the other side, those from a more mathematical camp argued that there was commercial advantage in proving software correctness as errors could be trapped earlier in the software development cycle (Tierney, 1993, p. 116).

Designed into the MoD (UK Ministry of Defence) standard was a view of safety-critical software as an important area of regulation and control. Some of the reason for this was a change in its own organisation from the 1980s. The UK government sought to open up work traditionally done in-house by the MoD in its own research establishments to private contractors (Tierney, 1993, p. 118). Given that it had to offer its software development to the private sector, it built in ways of controlling it within its defence standards (Tierney, 1993, p. 118). Further political impetus was offered by the introduction of consumer protection legislation in the UK in the late 1980s which required software developers to demonstrate that their software had not contributed, in the event of an accident enquiry, and that they had demonstrably attended to safety. Thus we can see that in Def Stan 00-55, politics, in the shape of the MoD's need to open up software development to the private sector and also to avoid being held responsible for inadequate software in the event of an accident, played an important role.

However, more significantly, this document has itself been superseded in 2004 by (draft) standard 00-56 (MoD, 2004). Def Stan 00-55 has now become obsolete. The changes involved in Def Stan 00-56 are of great interest, in that the preference for formal method is lessened. In the new standard, it is accepted that provably correct software is not possible in most cases and that we are inevitably involved in a human operation when we attempt to show that code is reliable in a safety-critical environment. Without a more detailed consideration of the history of formal methods in the UK over the last decade, which is beyond the scope of the present chapter, a strong claim that the move back to more human methods of verification might be difficult to sustain.

Nevertheless it is interesting to note the way that Def Stan 00-5, with its emphasis on formal approaches and attendant onerous work practices, has been consigned to the history books with a clear move back to human verification.

CASE STUDY CONTEXT

The case study relates to a large European military aircraft company (MAC) with which one of the authors was engaged as a researcher in a joint research project, lasting around three years, during the mid to late 1990s. A high proportion of the senior management were men and its culture was masculine in style, particularly emphasising an interest in engineering and technical mastery (Faulkner, 2000). Indeed there was much interest, pleasure, and admiration for elegant products of engineering (Hacker, 1991). When one of their fighter planes flew over (an event difficult to ignore on account of the engine noise), offices would clear as employees went outside to admire the display of a beautiful machine. A certain amount of military terminology was used, sometimes ironically, in day-to-day work. A number of employees had links with the armed forces. MAC was exclusively involved in the defence industry, with the UK's MoD being its largest customer and other approved governments buying its products.

As a manufacturing company in an economy where manufacturing was in steep decline and with its ties to the defence industry, if a major defence contract went elsewhere, jobs would be on the line. Despite the 'hi-tech' nature of its work, MAC had a traditional feel to it. The company had existed, under one name or another, right from the beginning of the avionics industry. The defence industry, and within that the defence aerospace industry, faced uncertain times as the UK government was redefining its expectations of the defence industry in post-Cold War times. It quickly came to expect much clearer demonstrations of value for money (Trim, 2001).

Therefore, the 'peace dividend' brought about by the end of the Cold War meant uncertain times for the defence aerospace industry as military spending was reduced significantly (Sillers & Kleiner, 1997). Yet, as an industry contributing huge amounts to the UK economy (around £5 billion per annum in export earnings Trim (2001, p. 227)), the defence industry is hugely important in terms of revenue and employment. Defence industries have civil wings (which was the case with MAC) and it was seen as important that the defence side of the business did not interfere with civil businesses. For instance, BAE Systems is a partner in a European consortium and was pledged £530 million as a government loan to develop the A3XXX aircraft to rival the USA's Boeing 747 (Trim, 2001, p. 228).

Although not strictly a public sector organisation itself, its location in the defence industry put MAC's business in the public sector. However, in the UK, views of public sector management were undergoing rapid change in the mid 1990s and it was seen as no longer acceptable that the taxpayer should underwrite investment (Trim, 2001). Such firms were required to be more competitive and to be held more accountable financially. Hence, quality management and value for money were becoming key concepts in the management repertoire of the UK defence industry from the mid 1990s onwards. As we discuss in the preceding section, this was at the height of the UK MoD's interest in formal approaches to the production of software. In a climate where post-Cold War defence projects were likely to demand a shorter lead time, there was considerable interest in speeding up the software development process.

Computer technology and related activity clearly played a central role in MAC. One division of MAC, the Technical Directorate (TD), developed most of the airborne software (much of it real-time). This software clearly has a central role in ensuring aircraft performance and safety. Around 100 people were involved in developing systems computing software. It was in this divi-

sion that Software Development System (SDS), a safety-critical airborne software system for flying military aircraft, was developed.

Research Methodology

The methodological approach of the research was based on action research (Myers & Avison, 2002). As several successful participant observation studies in technology based organisations have been reported in the literature (Forsythe, 2001; Low & Woolgar, 1993; Latour & Woolgar, 1979), an ethnographic approach holds much appeal. However, a strict ethnographic approach was neither feasible nor desirable in this study. As someone with technical expertise, the researcher could not claim to be the sociologist or anthropologist, more typical of reported ethnographic studies of technological systems (Low & Woolgar, 1993; Forsythe, 2001). This also meant that he was not 'fobbed off' by being directed into areas that the participants thought he wanted to look at or where they thought he should be interested in as happened in the Low and Woolgar (1993) case study. Based in the Quality Assurance Division (QAD) in the SQA team, early in his research, the researcher proved his technical credentials by helping run a workshop on software metrics and this helped to gain him full inclusion in the technical work. Although as a technical researcher, rather than a social researcher, it was arguably difficult for him to maintain the 'anthropological strangeness' which ethnographers look for in explaining the common sense and every day logistics of working life. In any case, he had been invited, through this research, to make a contribution to the improvement of SQA procedures. Therefore the research can be characterised as a form of action research (Baskerville & Wood-Harper, 1996), where potential improvements to SQA were to be seen as the learning part of the action research cycle.

Although action research receives a mixed press from the IS research community (Baskerville & Wood-Harper, 1996; Lau, 1999), it is nevertheless seen as a way of coming to grips with complex social settings where interactions with information technologies must be understood within the context of the whole organisation. Baskerville (1999) notes the growing interest in action research methods in information systems research. Two key assumptions are that complex social settings cannot be reduced for meaningful study and that action brings understanding (Baskerville, 1999). The culture of MAC was extremely complex, as we characterise above and discuss again in what follows. Arguably, key elements would be lost were the researcher to have adopted a more distant role, relying on interviews and questionnaires rather than becoming fully immersed and contributing to the detail of the project. The researcher adopted an interpretivist approach, looking to the interpretations of the other participants of the research. But by allowing for social intervention he became part of the study, producing shared subjective meanings between researcher and subjects as coparticipants in the research (Baskerville, 1999).

For a period of over one year out of the three that the whole project lasted, the researcher spent, on average, one day per week working with MAC staff with access to a variety of staff across the organisation, and was therefore able to participate in a range of meetings and workshops and to gain a familiarity with the individuals concerned. This could not easily have been gained from interviews or surveys. These events included meetings where software quality staff considered quality policy, such as the implication of international standards, to broader meetings where technical staff were considering development methods in detail. Free access was allowed to relevant policy and development documents. This permitted an overview of the detailed practices and culture of this large and complex organisation.

Analysis of Case Study Findings

The initial remit of the researcher was to work with staff to optimise the use of software quality assurance within the organisation. The use of cost benefit analysis was originally suggested by senior management. Given our characterisation of the UK defence industry's particular focus on management of quality and value for money, as described above, it is entirely in keeping with the industry's changing needs that the researcher was initially directed into these areas. The researcher viewed it as problematic to assign monetary cost to SQA activities, and even harder to assign monetary benefits. However, these concerns were never addressed directly in the project as it soon emerged that there was greater interest in a new approach to software development being pioneered by MAC.

Ince (1994, p. 2-3) tells the story of a junior programmer's first day in a new job. A senior programmer shows him around, advising him where to buy the best sandwiches at lunchtime, where to find the best beer after work, and other similarly important matters. Then the senior colleague points to a door. 'Whatever you do don't go through that door, the people there have been given the job of stifling our creativity.' The door, of course, led to the quality assurance department.

The staff of MAC's Quality Assurance Division expressed some similar feelings, albeit less dramatically. They wanted to act as consultants, offering a measure of creativity to the technical development process, although safely wrapped in appropriate quality assurance processes, but all too often they felt like the police. The strong awareness of the safety-critical nature of software development, and the related fairly advanced organisation of quality assurance in MAC, thanks in no small measure to the necessity to adhere to MoD standards, meant that SQA was never going to get quite the negative press that it attracted in Ince's (1994) anecdote. Nevertheless, there was still some feeling that the Quality Assurance Division could be brought on board in a project some time after the Technical Division had time to do the creative part.

Hence, TD had been prototyping the new SDS system for about a year when they decided to bring in Quality Assurance Division. As we explain below, the newness of the style of development in SDS made it unclear how it was to be quality assured. Unsure of how to proceed, the SQA manager turned to the researcher for suggestions. The researcher now became involved in investigating the use of the new software development approach, which would involve the inclusion of computer generated program code ('auto-code') in safety-critical airborne software systems, leading to the approval of the new approach and its incorporation into MAC's software quality assurance systems.

Although there has been a long tradition of using computers to aid the process of software engineering itself, such CASE tools (Pressman, 2005) have not generally been used to generate safety-critical code (this was always written by human programmers). The new MAC SDS was an ambitious system whose targets were principally to reduce avionics systems development time by 40% and the cost by 30%, whilst maintaining the very high quality standards necessary for computer-based system which fly—and therefore can crash—military aircraft.

A key aspect of SDS was process integration using an integrated modeling environment. There was consequentially a heavy reliance on automated methods. A specification was developed in a formal modeling language and this generated programming code automatically. In particular, automatic code generation was eventually to lead to aircraft flying 'auto-code' in safety-critical systems. Two aspects of SDS stand out in the climate of defence spending of the mid 1990s. First, there was pressure to reduce costs and show value for money. Second, the use of formal methods in computer programming received a

huge boost in the mid-1990s through the Defence standard DEF Stan 00-55 which mandated the use of formal methods base approaches in safety-critical software. It is not surprising that there was considerable interest in a system which offered the promise of considerably reduced software production times.

MAC invested a great deal of money and time in SDS in the hope that the improved time-scales which SDS promised, together with reduced costs, could keep major current aircraft developments on course. This was particularly important in an environment of political intervention and considerable public interest and concern over escalating costs and delivery times in the public sector, including the defence industry. These benefits could only accrue to MAC if the quality, that is, correctness of the software, could be assured.

SDS was heavily dependent on software (CASE) tools. MAC had used these for many years, and had procedures in place for their qualification (i.e., acceptance) in certain circumstances. However, these applied to mission-critical rather than safety-critical systems. Furthermore, the movement towards auto-generated code led to a different environment than one where tools improved and speeded up the design process, but where failure would show up and be merely time-wasting. There was seen to be a need for a major improvement/update of these procedures, a quantum change, before they would be acceptable for safety-critical applications.

Some tools being used had major world-wide user communities, associated academic conferences, and came from supposedly secure and reliable suppliers. Others might not be so well supported, both intellectually and commercially. (For instance, it might be no use having an ideal tool if the supplier was small and unlikely to survive for many years.) Methods already existed for supplier qualification. These methods were undertaken by software quality staff. However, the qualification of these suppliers could be a crucial issue in the qualification of the tool and ultimately the integrity of the avionics system. The issue was not merely one of qualification, it was also one of *demonstration* of qualification to customers. Ultimately, the need in some sense to *prove* the new methods became paramount. Hence we can see that quality procedures did not just involve procedures, such as code walkthroughs through which software teams could persuade themselves to trust program code, they also applied to the question of choosing and trusting suppliers.

A number of meetings took place with members of the SDS team. This discussion was very useful for an understanding of SDS and gave the researcher a richer understanding of the SQA needs. It soon became apparent that the necessary fundamental problems with SQA in SDS were going to be difficult to answer.

The difficulties were centred around two conflicting ideas. The first of these was that for the *persuasive rational argument* approach to be successful there would be a need for a group of professionals to participate in code walkthroughs, with consequent discussion and persuasion. On the face of it, this was simply not possible, since the computer which wrote the auto-code could not take part in such a discussion. Alternative approaches were considered. Clearly there would be a stage before the auto-code (at the requirements specification level) where human agents were involved, but this was found to be too high level to meet the relevant military standards (the US MIL-STD-498 [1994] and the UK standard 00-55 [MoD, 1997]). Both standards are very specific about the exact conduct of the necessary walkthrough. It had to be a *code* walkthrough.

On the other hand, for the *formal proof* approach method to work, there would first need to be such a formal proof. This did not seem within the capability of the QAD itself, despite the division being quite well resourced. MAC referred back to the auto-code tools suppliers, but once again there was no such proof and no realistic possibility of achieving such a proof. Although

MAC was an important customer for the auto-code tool suppliers, they were not prepared to expend the necessary resources. Furthermore, a 'weakest link' argument demonstrates a fundamental flaw with the formal approach in computer systems. If the auto-code tool itself could be formally verified, it would then become necessary also to consider the operating system on which the tool would run and the hardware systems involved. Potentially this could involve a seemingly infinite regression of hardware and software systems having to be proved correct, where the system is only as good as its weakest link. Frustration grew as no solution was forthcoming and ultimately SDS was shelved indefinitely.

We have argued that mathematical proof is essentially a human achievement between members of the expert mathematical community who are persuaded of the correctness of mathematical proofs because they trust each other. These processes of trust are replicated in the procedures that have been developed in software engineering, and within that, software quality assurance. As part of the defence industry, developing safety-critical systems, MAC had highly developed SQA procedures which were obliged to follow international military standards. Their code walkthroughs, which are analogous to the ways mathematicians achieve trust in a proof, were an important part of such quality procedures. Formal methods offer the promise of an attractive certainty and control over software production and hence control over the work processes of human programmers. They also offer the promise of automatic verification of software systems which, potentially, could be much cheaper than traditional human based approaches to the verification of software through traditional SQA procedures.

SDS achieved very little despite the huge efforts put into it by the many people working for MAC. Although it was not, at the time, formulated in such stark terms, success was elusive because an attempt was being made to achieve the impossible: namely using auto-code whilst being held to quality assurance procedures which demanded code walkthroughs which could not possibly be achieved in an auto-code system. Attempts were made to consider formally proving the correctness of the auto-code. In addition to supplier reluctance, this raised the spectre of the infinite regress. If one looks to proving the auto-code correct, then the operating system must be proved correct, the hardware platform and so on.

This was at the height of interest in formal methods for safety-critical systems for defence, a view embodied in Def Stan 00-55. The rise of formal methods is crucially linked to the defence industry. The interest in formal methods and automated approaches arrived as pressure mounted on Western governments to prove cost effectiveness due to the changing nature of defence developments after the end of the Cold War and the need to avoid litigation for software that might be implicated in an accident. Yet the difficulties of applying formal methods in systems of any level of complexity and the need to trust the program code acted as a spur to maintain complex human centred software quality assurance procedures.

CONCLUSION: TRUSTING COMPUTERS

There is much evidence that we already *do* trust computers in many walks of life without formal proof or other formal demonstration, even to the extent of trusting safety-critical systems such as the 'fly by wire' software in the Boeing 777 airliner, two million lines of code which have not been fully proved (Lytz, 1995). Expert mathematicians have begun to accept computer generated proofs, albeit in qualified ways (Chang, 2004). As MacKenzie (2001, p. 301) argues, 'moral entrepreneurs' of computerised risk ensure that warnings about computerised risk are heeded so that safety-critical software is avoided and,

where it is unavoidable, much care is taken over its development. Military standards, so detailed about the use of formal methods in software design and attendant work processes in the 1990s, have moved a decade later to be much less prescriptive about the work methods of ensuring software quality, thereby allowing for the crucial element of human inspection in order that the software may be trusted. As Collins (1990) notes, we are remarkably accommodating to computers, making sense of them and involving them in our social networks, and will continue to find imaginative ways of doing so. This echoes Nissenbaum's (1999) view that we may trust computers if we can treat them as 'agents.' We may meaningfully ascribe intentions and reasons to them.

In this chapter we have sought to tell a story of trust, in particular how software may be trusted when it is not produced by a human programmer. This involves consideration of a complex set of discourses including the question of mathematical proof and how proof is achieved within mathematical communities. We see a similar need to replicate such human processes of trust in trusting computer systems. We have argued that the making of standards to be applied within software quality assurance procedures shows ways in which mechanisms of trust are inscribed in software standards. Our case study, an action research project in a military aircraft company, demonstrates the difficulties which occur when quality assurance procedures involving code walkthroughs—procedures with built-in human trust mechanisms—are incommensurable with a system which relies on auto-code. The climate of defence research and spending was a major influence, both on our case study and the wider development of standards. There is a continued tension between needing to trust and trying to control: trusting the software and controlling its production. The story which we tell here is one of continuing human ingenuity in finding ways of trusting computer software.

REFERENCES

Akrich, M. (1992). The de-scription of technical objects. In W. E. Bijker & J. Law (Eds.), *Shaping technology/building society: Studies in sociotechnical change* (pp. 205-224). Cambridge, MA/London: MIT Press.

Baskerville, R. Investigating information systems with action research. *Communications of the Association for Information Systems, 19*(2). Retrieved October 5, 2006, from http://www.cis.gsu.edu/~rbaskerv/CAIS_2_19/CAIS_2_19.htm

Baskerville, R., & Wood-Harper, A.T. (1999). A critical perspective on action research as a method for information systems research. *Journal of Information Technology, 11*, 235-246.

Chang, K. (2004, April 6). In math, computers don't lie. Or do they? *New York Times.* Retrieved October 5, 2006, from http://www.math.binghamton.edu/zaslav/Nytimes/+Science/+Math/spherepacking.20040406.html

Collins, H.M. (1990). *Artificial experts: Social knowledge and intelligent machines.* Cambridge, MA: MIT Press.

Davies, B. (2006, October 3). Full proof? Let's trust it to the black box. *Times higher education supplement.*

De Millo, R.A., Lipton, R.J., & Perlis, A.J. (1977). Social processes and proofs of theorems and programs. In *Proceedings of the 4ᵗʰ ACM Symposium on Principles of Programming Language* (pp. 206-214).

DSDM Consortium. (2006). White papers. Retrieved October 5, 2006, from *http://www.dsdm.org/products/white_papers.asp*

Faulkner, W. (2000). The power and the pleasure? A research agenda for 'making gender stick.' *Science, Technology & Human Values, 25*(1), 87-119.

Forsythe, D.E. (2001). *Studying those who study as: An anthropologist in the world of artificial intelligence.* Stanford University Press.

Gillies, A.C. (1997). *Software quality: Theory and management* (2ⁿᵈ ed.). London/Boston: International Thomson Computer Press.

Hacker, S. (1989). *Pleasure, power and technology: Some tales of gender, engineering, and the co-operative workplace.* Boston: Unwin Hyman.

Ince, D. (1994). *An introduction to software quality assurance and its implementation.* London: McGraw-Hill.

Kuhn, T.S. (1962). *The structure of scientific revolutions.* University of Chicago Press.

Latour, B., & Woolgar, S. (1979*). Laboratory life: The social construction of scientific facts.* Princeton University Press.

Lau, F. (1999). Toward a framework for action research in information systems studies. *Information Technology & People, 12*(2), 148-175.

Low, J., & Woolgar, S. (1993). Managing the socio-technical divide: Some aspects of the discursive structure of information systems development. In P. Quintas (Ed.), *Social dimensions of systems engineering: People, processes and software development* (pp. 34-59). New York/London: Ellis Horwood.

Lytz, R. (1995). Software metrics for the Boeing 777: A case study. *Software Quality Journal, 4*(1), 1-13.

MacKenzie, D.A. (2001). *Mechanizing proof: Computing, risk, and trust.* Cambridge, MA/London: MIT Press.

MacKenzie, D.A. (2004). *Computers and the cultures of proving.* Paper presented at the Royal Society Discussion Meeting, London.

Ministry of Defence (MoD). (1997). Requirements for safety related software in defence equipment

Retrieved October 5, 2006, from http://www. dstan.mod.uk/data/00/055/01000200.pdf

Ministry of Defence (MoD). (2004). Interim defence standard 00-56. Retrieved October 5, 2006, from http://www.dstan.mod.uk/data/00/056/01000300.pdf

Myers, G.J. (1979). *The art of software testing*. New York: Wiley.

Myers, M.D., & Avison, D.E. (Eds). (2002). *Qualitative research in information systems: A reader*. London: Sage Publications.

Nissenbaum, H. (1999). Can trust be secured online? A theoretical perspective. *Etica e Politica, 2*. Retrieved October 5, 2006, from http://www.units.it/~etica/1999_2/nissenbaum.html

Popper, K.R. (1963). *Conjectures and refutations*. New York: Harper.

Pressman, R. (2005*). Software engineering: A practitioner's approach* (6th ed.). London/New York: McGraw Hill.

Sillers, T.S., & Kleiner, B.H. (1997). Defence conversion: Surviving (and prospering) in the 1990s. *Work Study, 46*(2), 45-48.

Singh, S. (1997). *Fermat's last theorem*. London: Fourth Estate.

Stahl, B.C. (2006). *Trust as fetish: A Critical theory perspective on research on trust in e-commerce*. Paper presented at the Information Communications and Society Symposium, University of York, UK.

Tierney, M. (1993). The evolution of Def Stan 00-55: A socio-history of a design standard for safety-critical software. In P. Quintas (Ed.), *Social dimensions of systems engineering: People, processes and software development* (pp. 111-143). New York/London: Ellis Horwood.

Trim, P. (2001). Public-private partnerships and the defence industry. *European Business Review, 13*(4), 227-234.

Weinberg, G. (1971). *The psychology of computer programming*. New York: Van Nostrand Reinhold.

This work was previously published in International Journal of Technology and Human Interaction, Vol. 3, Issue 4, edited by Bernd Carsten Stahl, pp. 1-14, copyright 2007 by IGI Publishing, formerly known as Idea Group Publishing (an imprint of IGI Global).

Section II
Social and Cultural Aspects

Chapter VI
Information Security Culture as a Social System:
Some Notes of Information Availability and Sharing

Rauno Kuusisto
Finland Futures Research Center, Turku School of Economics, Finland

Tuija Kuusisto
Finnish National Defense University, Finland

ABSTRACT

The purpose of this chapter is to increase understanding of the complex nature of information security culture in a networked working environment. Viewpoint is comprehensive information exchange in a social system. The aim of this chapter is to raise discussion about information security culture development challenges when acting in a multicultural environment. This chapter does not introduce a method to handle complex cultural situation, but gives some notes to gain understanding, what might be behind this complexity. Understanding the nature of this complex cultural environment is essential to form evolving and proactive security practices. Direct answers to formulate practices are not offered in this chapter, but certain general phenomena of the activity of a social system are pointed out. This will help readers to apply these ideas to their own solutions.

INTRODUCTION

Information security issues can be considered as balancing between information availability and confidentiality. Organizations should be able to understand what kind of information shall be and will be available to ongoing and future activities and which parts of that shall be secured. This information depends on situation and those phenomena that emerge from the complex networked working environment. Information security culture affects behind security management and technology. Understanding the nature of this complex cultural environment is essential to form evolving and proactive security practices. Direct answers to formulate practices are not offered in this chapter, but certain general phenomena of the activity of a social system are pointed out. This will help readers to apply these ideas to their own solutions.

System can be considered as a comprehensive wholeness that is constructed of nodes and connections between them (Castells, 1996). Nodes can be human beings, organizations, communities, technological systems, natural systems, or sub-systems of various entities (e.g., Checkland & Holwell, 1998; Checkland & Scholes, 2000). Information is something that is required to launch activity while moving between nodes. Security can be considered as a comprehensive concept that enables activities to be conducted in an environment that is stable and predictable enough to gain desired objectives. Culture is a social structure that tends to maintain certain patterns. This pattern maintenance is driven by information called values and valuations. Each actor has their own kind of cultural structures and values and their interpretation of other values (Schein 1992). It is obvious that a system contains several cultural phenomena that are exchanging value and other information. Culture itself is thus a *complex system* that evolves during time while various interacting actors are exchanging information.

The theoretical background is based on the theory of communicative action by Jurgen Habermas (1984, 1989). In this theory, Habermas is constructing a communicative system consisting of structures, activities, and information interacting in a social context on the basis of the sociological ideas of Talcott Parson. We are using this systemic construction as a basis, against which we are applying the concept of information security

culture. Some examples of information sharing practices of various actors are presented to learn certain phenomena concerning the development of information security culture.

Interest in the security of information and knowledge has increased together with the development of coalitions between states and networks between public and private organizations. It is obvious that security activities are needed for protecting information vital to the functions of the states and organizations. (e.g., Finnish Government 2003 & OECD, 2002) The emphasis of security activities has been on the means to protect the confidentiality and integrity of information flows on those networks. However, keeping information confidential is not as challenging as the identification of critical information and core knowledge from all of the information available. That is the reason why we focus here on information availability. Modern societies and organizations depend on information and knowledge. They need to identify critical information and core knowledge and put them available either for internal use or for external use visible to customers, partners, and competitors to survive or to gain competitive advantage. So, states and organizations have to find a balance between the confidentiality and availability of information. They need this balance to identify and communicate information that suits their goals.

Information security culture can be seen as a concept that provides means to reach the balance between confidentiality and availability of information. Edward Waltz (1998) defines three major information security attributes as follows:

1. Availability provides assurance that information, services, and resources will be accessible and usable when needed by the user.
2. Integrity assures that information and processes are secure from unauthorised tampering (e.g., insertion, deletion, destruction, or replay of data) via methods such as encryption, digital signatures, and intrusion detection.

3. Confidentiality protects the existence of a connection, traffic flow, and information content from disclosure to an unauthorised user (Waltz, 1998).

Whitman and Mattord (2003) define availability as follows: "Availability enables users who need to access information to do so without interference or obstruction, and to receive it in the required format." Users in their definition are not only humans but computer systems, as well. According to their thinking, availability does not mean that information is automatically accessible to any user, but it needs verification of the user to become reachable to that nominated user. "The information is said to be available to an authorised user when and where needed and in the correct format" (Whitman & Mattord, 2003).

According to the concept of information security culture, the confidentiality, integrity, and availability of information shall not be based only on norms such as information security policies, but on a shared organizational culture. The aim of this chapter is to increase understanding about the development of information security culture for multicultural states and organizations acting in global environments. The theoretical background of the chapter is based on Habermas' (1984, 1989) theory of communicative action. Some notes will be made by referring Luhmans (1990) ideas of the difference of the various functions of the society of interpreting the reality seasoned with Schein's (1992) nearly classical ideas about organizational culture. Cultural aspects will be approached both literature review, and empirical results on information sharing in different decision-making situations.

Security is considered as a whole, but the focus is set on the socio-cultural viewpoint. The meaning of security culture forming, and approaches to create a holistic security cultural atmosphere are discussed. The basic assumption is that a multicultural organization is able to achieve a unified information security culture,

but this culture reveals itself in different way to the various actors of the network. Cultural aspects will show themselves in dynamic way, as well. Culture seems to change during time and from one situation to another.

The research approach is hermeneutics pursuing to gain understanding about the process of forming a culture. Information systems security is studied mainly in social context and research approach is empirical theory creating. Research is completed by first analysing the concept of information security culture and explaining the main content of selected theories of social systems. Aspects of information security culture are combined to these theories. Secondly, discussion based on case studies is presented. Finally, we will ponder what information shall be communicated to gain unity in a security culture and what kind of challenges will arise during the process of forming the culture.

INFORMATION SECURITY CULTURE

Networked working environment set new kinds of challenges to information system security area. Interaction between various actors is dynamic and emergent. Flexibility and certain kinds of meta-policy processes have risen into vicinity (Baskerville & Siponen, 2002). That is obvious, because to understand what is required at organization level or at its sub-levels, the completeness of the overall system behavior shall be understood at least to some degree.

Dhillon (1997) has a broad view to the term "security culture." He defines that security culture is the behavior in an organization that contributes to the protection of data, information, and knowledge (Dhillon, 1997). Data are typically defined to be known facts that can be recorded. Data are suitable for communication, interpretation, or processing by humans or artificial entities. Information is usually defined as structured data useful for analysis (Thierauf, 2001). When structured, data are turned into information, for example, Niiniluoto (1997). Awad and Ghaziri (2003) state that information has a meaning, purpose, and relevance. They emphasized that information is about understanding relations.

Knowledge is defined as "the ability to turn information and data into effective action" (Applehans, Globe, & Laugero, 1999). Previously, the security of data and information has been emphasized when security practices in organizations have been developed. However, the protection of core knowledge is as critical as the protection of key data and information for an organization. Knowledge is distinctly different from data and information. Knowledge is the ability to turn information and data into effective action (Applehans et al., 1999). It is a capacity to act (Sveiby, 2001). According to Maier (2002), "Knowledge comprises all cognitive expectancies that an individual or organisational actor uses to interpret situations and to generate activities, behaviour and solutions no matter whether these expectancies are rational or used intentionally." In cognitive expectancies "observations have been meaningfully organised, accumulated and embedded in a context through experience, communication, or inference" (Maier, 2002). Knowledge grows through the whole life of an actor, and all new perceptions are interpreted against the organised, understood, and accepted field of information. This very same idea about knowledge is found in the production of Merleau-Ponty (1968) and Bergson (1911). Incoming information is interpreted through a mental filter that consists of the internalised perception history of the entity.

Von Solms (2000) included *information security culture* development in the third wave of information security, that is, in the institutionalization wave. The aim of the institutionalization wave is to build information security culture in such a way that information security becomes a natural aspect of the daily activities of all employees of the organization. It covers standardization, certification, measurement, and concern of the

human aspect to information security (Von Solms, 2000) (Figure 1).

Most of the recent papers approach information security culture from theories and models of organizational culture (Nosworthy, 2000; Chia, Ruighaver, & Maynard, 2002; Martins & Eloff, 2002, Schlienger & Teufel, 2002; Zakaria & Gani, 2003). Chia et al. (2002) based their work on a general framework of an organizational culture developed by Detert, Schroeder, and Mauriel (2000). Martins and Eloff (2002) define that information security culture is the assumption about acceptable information security behavior and it can be regarded as a set of information security characteristics such as integrity and availability of information. They outlined information security culture model consisting of organizational, group, and individual levels. The aim of their work is to support an organizational information security culture evaluation. Martins and Eloff (2002), Schlienger and Teufel (2002), as well as Zakaria and Gani (2003) adopted Schein's (1992) organizational cultural model. Schlienger and Teufel (2002) and Zakaria and Gani (2003) give examples of information security issues related to each of the elements of the model. Zakaria, Jarupunphol, and Gani (2003) have the management perspective to the studying and applying of the organizational culture into information security management.

Figure 1. Relation of effectiveness and required time to develop information security

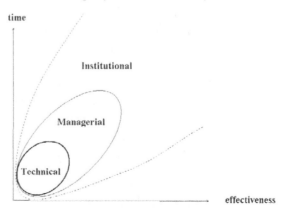

They regard an information security culture as a subculture in an organization. As a summary, the authors stress an organizational information security culture model development and security culture evaluation.

Nosworthy (2000) emphasizes that the organizational culture plays a major role in information security, as it may resist change or direct what types of changes will take place. Schlienger and Teufel (2002) argue that a corporate culture including an information security culture is a collective phenomenon that is changing over *time* and it can be designed by the management of an organization. So, there is a need to understand fundamentals of culture when aiming to develop information security culture in an organization.

Culture is most commonly defined as a set of shared values, shared understanding, or even shared methods of problem solving (Bell, 1998; Habermas, 1984, 1989; Hofstede, 1984), but some still use a definition of culture that is all-encompassing and abstract in manner and which provides very little help in the identification of cultural properties. Values are the commonsense beliefs about right and wrong that guide us in our daily lives (Fisher & Lowell, 2003). Straub, Loch, Evaristo, Karahanna, and Strite (2002) argue that information systems (IS) research nearly always assumes that an individual belongs to a single culture. They proposed social identity theory to be used as a grounding for cultural research in IS. Social identity theory suggests that each individual is influenced by plethora of cultures (Straub et Al., 2002). When applied to information security culture research, this means the interpretation of information security culture is influenced by several cultures (Figure 2).

An individual belongs to several ethical, national, organizational, and information security cultures. They have an effect on the way the individual interpret the meaning and importance of information security culture. These individual cultural aspects are rather solid and they describe the world of values of each individual actor.

Figure 2. The interpretation of information security culture is influenced by plethora of cultures

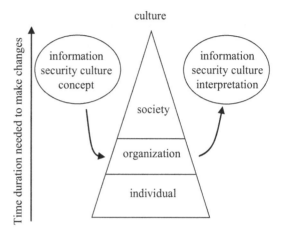

Anyhow, it could be stated that interaction with several other actors emerges somewhat unpredictable cultural phenomena at *network* level. Network, while interchanging all kind of information, produces an ever changing combination of activity patterns that gets its force from each actors' cultural phenomena and interaction. It is obvious that this kind of situation is more or less difficult to control. That is the reason why different kinds of methods of managing this ever changing combination of different valuations are now under development.

DYNAMIC ORGANISATION MODEL

Habermas (1984, 1989) bases his thinking on information classification in the theories of social sciences. He combines critically theories about society, a human being as a part of the society, and system theories. This approach will fit rather well into organisational and inter-organisational features such as *information security culture*. Habermas (1989, referring to Talcott Parsons production) states that there are four basic classes of information, which are directing an actor's activity. These are values, norms, goals, and external facts. These same basic items can be found from the background of any purposeful act at any level—from individuals via working-groups to organisations, from individuals via families to societies. Those items contain information, which—when used—will orient an actor to adapt its behaviour to better fit into the surrounding. So, actors in a system will interact with each other via exchanging these four types of information. That information will fulfill demands of pattern maintenance, integration, goal attainment, and adaptation functions. Figure 3 depicts these dependencies.

The arrow, which is named "information flow," describes the direction of information, which is coming in to the information refining process of an actor. It shows that values have effects on norms, which both have effects on goals and the attainment of those, and further on, all those have effects on exploiting external information. Vice versa, the arrow called "energy flow" describes those activities, which are taking place from using external information to change values. An actor has a certain variety of resources, means and facts to put in practice to achieve goals (Habermas, 1989).

Information concerning values will determine a general system of culture. The function of culture is to maintain certain patterns of activity. These patterns consist of cognitive interpretation schemes, symbolic expressions, and value standards, like standards of solving moral-practical and cognitive-instrumental problems, as well as appreciations. Cultural orientations are both normative and motivational, the first containing cognitive, appreciative and moral and the latter cognitive, mental-emotional and evaluative (Habermas, 1989). Information about values forms the long-lasting basis of information creation. Information about values is changing rather slowly and it is more or less dependant on the culture of concern (Bell, 1998; Hofstede, 1984; Schneider & Barsoux, 1997).

Norms will determine mutually expected rules, among which the subjects of community will perform their interactions. Norms will entitle the members of community to expect certain actions from each other in certain situations. That will obligate members of this community to meet the legitimate expectations of others. Norms will build up a system of controls and orient actors' activities to fulfill normative validity claims. The acceptance of norms will lead to full adaptation and further development of patterns (Habermas, 1989). The understanding of norms without acceptance will lead to various ways of action from seemingly total adaptation in the context of norm-setting community to total ignorance of norms and drifting outside of that community. The latter will happen if norms are not understood, as well. There, the dilemma of subjective and objective

Figure 3. Information and energy flows and functions using the information in an actor approached as a social system (Habermas, 1989)

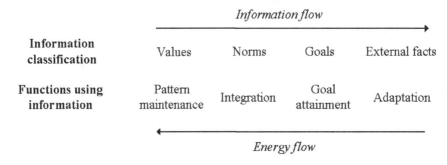

		Information flow		
Information classification	Values	Norms	Goals	External facts
Functions using information	Pattern maintenance	Integration	Goal attainment	Adaptation
		Energy flow		

world will be seen. The adaptation to the community will depend on the value-based judgement of the acceptance of those norms, which are set by the community.

Goals will determine the desired end-state of actions. Goals are directing resources and means to gain success as effectively as possible. Goals will provide information of polity, about those choices, which are made by top management of an actor. This actor can be, for example, a state, an organisation, a team, or even an individual. Finally, means and resources are used to put such activity in practice, which will lead the actor to fulfill its goals as optimally as possible. The user of those resources is here called an "institution" (Figure 4). Originally in Habermas' theory, this structure is economy. Anyhow, it could be thought that depending on the viewpoint, this resource-using structure may just as well be something else. For example, from the viewpoint of an enterprise, the institution will be, for example, marketing, production, and/or research and development department.

The structural phenomena of this systemic approach contain culture, community, polity, and institutions. Information flows and actions described above will take place in these structures, which are subsystems of the whole system. Cultural systems are more solid than communities, which are again more solid than a polity structures. This ontology may be applied

to organisational environment, as well. Organisational culture will remain at least partly in spite of organisational changes, both ontological and normative. Policy, which determines goals, will change among the demands of the surrounding environment and information offered by norms. Finally, exploiting external information, and using resources and means will be mostly dependant on goal setting.

To form a systemic model of information exchange of a general actor, some other assumption shall be done. Systems will produce activity, when the right kind of information is fed into their structures. This activity again acts as input information for the system to produce new activity (Figure 5). This feature has been discovered very early (Aristotle) and it can be found both in literature (e.g., Maier, 2002) and in practical life.

In addition, Habermas (1989) describes that a *social system* contains *time* and space dimension. System has initial state and goal state. Its *communication* orientation is oriented both internally and externally, as well. A model that contains information, activity, and structure, as well as temporal and spatial orientation of information exchange can be formulated. This very rough model is depicted in Figure 6 (earlier published, e.g., Kuusisto, 2004; Kuusisto, Nyberg, & Virtanen, 2004; Kuusisto, 2006).

This model consists of a four-field situated in time and space axis. Time axis contains initial

Figure 4. Information and energy flows and structure of an actor approached as a social system (Habermas, 1989)

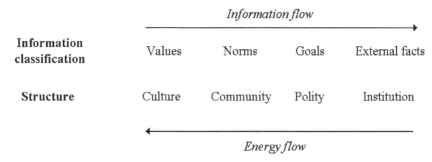

Information classification	Information flow			
	Values	Norms	Goals	External facts
Structure	Culture	Community	Polity	Institution
	Energy flow			

Figure 5. Information-driven activity cycle in structure

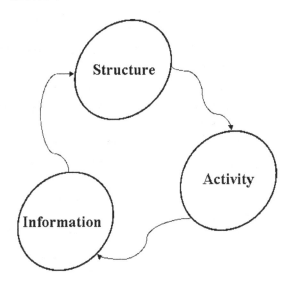

Figure 6. Systemic model of an organization in time and space

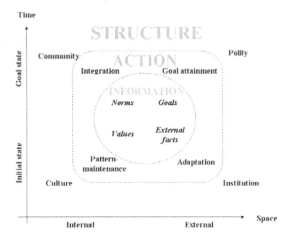

state and futures' state and space axis contain internal interaction and external interaction. Each field contains a certain kind of information, structure, and activity. Interactivity relationships of those four fields exist between their neighboring fields. Now these ideas can be formed into a holistic systemic model of organizational *dynamics*. This model is presented in Figure 7. With help of this systemic model, we can reach

towards understanding of those phenomena that may be important when examining the *complexity* of security issues in an organization.

As can be seen on the model, information of different functional parts of the system is a combination of the influence of neighbor parts of the system and external input of each subsystem of the comprehensive system. It can be easily recognized that this kind of system is *complex*, thus being emergent. Depending on what is the viewpoint of an actor, it deals with somewhat different information. For example, institution adapts to the overall system by interpreting information about cultural activities (pattern-maintenance), organizations' goal attainment, and those external facts that it collects from the other systems (e.g., stakeholders). Polity structures (e.g., strategic management of an organization) form their worldview by using information of organizations features and competence, their stakeholders' activities and those goals that has set to the organization. Those two viewpoints are rather different. It is obvious that the forming understanding about security culture is not so straightforward. This model gives a good starting point of evaluate those challenges that are faced, when attempting to formulate such actions that will guarantee as functioning security activities as possible.

Habermas (1989) claims that the judgment basis of the information exploitation and activity practices varies from one subsystem to another. On the institution viewpoint, universalism is important judgment basis. People in the organization want be "saved," they are willing to see themselves continuing their existence in a safe environment. They are willing to obey their cultural heritage, act in an environment, where such decisions are made that ensure this continuous existence in mental space, as well. They make their perceptions of outer world against this mental basis. On the other hand, polity structures make their judgments on the basis of performance. A community and its members should be governed so that the overall performance of the completeness

Figure 7. Model of organization dynamics

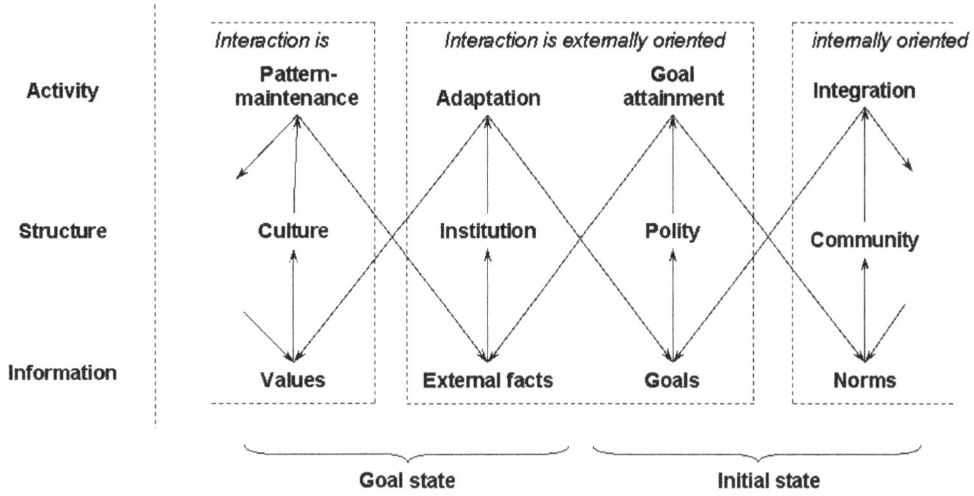

is as optimum as possible. So, the orientation of these two subsystems to the complete system is different. Niklas Luhmann (1990) has same kind of idea. He claims that different functions of a society have different basis for judging the plausibility of activity. He claims that, for example, for economy, this basis is to own—not to own, for law it is right—wrong, for science true—untrue, for politics it is right political program—other programs, for religion it is good—bad (behavior), or joy—fear, and for education this basis is right attitude and competence versus wrong attitude and competence. On the basis of these ideas, it can be claimed that different actors have different ways to interpret the world that they face every day. It could be assumed that in an organization management, marketing, production, and research and development personnel have different judgment basis to issues that they face in their every day activities. This happens on the area of security and security culture, as well.

Over a *time*, an actor such as a state or an organization approached as a *social system* will attempt to reach a goal state, which contains a normatively unified community, which is setting mutually accepted goals in a policy process. This state will be constructed on cultural structures

manifested by communicating values, and on the use of available resources. The system shall be able to maintain itself both internally and externally. Information concerning values and norms will determine the interaction against the system itself. The system, weather it is, for example, an organisation or society, contains information about values and norms. This information will guide goal forming and the use of resources. Information about goals and resources will guide the social system to perform suitable interaction with the outer world.

Culture can be seen as a structural phenomenon, which aim is to maintain suitable patterns of a *social system* to form a solid enough basis for orienting towards the future. Culture is communicated by values. A continuous process of the evolution of values and reconstruction of norms will be present in the system itself. Having an effect on the objective world will be done by policy-making and institutional structures. In an organisation environment, this means the will of the top management, and the optimal use of organisational resources, like information, *time*, material, personnel, and money. Interaction takes place in a situation via a communicative process, where information about various items is shared between subjective actors using mutually understood codes. The whole interacting process is a series of situations, where mutual adaptation of interacting actors will take place.

Information security culture in an organisation is most obviously a part of an organisational culture. The development of an information security culture can be seen equal to any culture forming process. When referring to Habermas' theory, forming a structure called culture will require a lot of energy. If it is thought that energy will be transferred via information, a subsequently great amount of information shall be delivered. Therefore, it will demand a certain period of time to perform changes in cultural structures. Seemingly, it is very important to understand what kind of information is available to form this cultural basis.

Organization culture determines how the nature of reality is seen in the organisation. According to Habermas' theory, culture is the structural phenomenon, which will act as a platform, from which the information about the basic nature of the organisation will rise. On the other hand, culture will be the ultimate structural frame of the memory of the organisation, where all that information, which is considered the most valuable and preferable, is stored during the entire life of the organisation. So, culture is a structure, where the most long-effecting information, that is, values of the organisation will be stored. The energy to form the cultural structure will come via norms. Norms determine those rules, which will be followed inside the organisation to be able to work together as smoothly as possible. Norms and values are the inside information of an organisation, but they will be shown outside by performing activity via those goals that organisation has. This means that the values of the organisation will be communicated to the surrounding through its activities.

On practical level, it is a question about how to perform social process between organization polity structures, organization members, and stakeholder community. Finally, it is question about how to reach understanding of security policy and practices and personal interpretations of threat? How possible is it to reach understanding of divergently oriented subject of a comprehensive system? For a member of an organization, his/her feeling of security is real, and for management its action to make community more safer place to perform organizations´ functions is real. Community contains a good selection of those realities.

MODELING THE INFORMATION SHARING OF AN ORGANIZATION

Next, a general information content model of shared situation understanding is presented. The ultimate origin of the model is classic Greek philosophy (Aristotle) as depicted in Figure 8.

The information model that is used to analyze the dynamism of organizations behavior in different situations is described in Table 1. Rows describe the temporality and abstraction degree of information. Information at the upper row is relatively most abstract, future oriented and its effects are long-lasting. The lowest level contains information that updates fast, is concrete, and is observable as immediate events. The column at left contains cultural information described by Schein (1980, 1991). The next left column contains actors' internal information. The next right contains information of expressed conclusions made by the actor. The right column describes information that comes from outside of an actor or is remarkably affected by the world outside the actor itself. Rough contents of the information categories are described in the table, as well. The idea of forming this framework is described, for example, in Kuusisto (2004) and Kuusisto (2006). The main idea to use this kind of model is to show how very divergent is the information space, when organizations or other actors move from one kind of situation to another.

Figure 8. Classic approach to making choises (idea adopted from Aaltonen & Wilenius, 2002, referring to Malaska & Holstius, 1999) compared to information categories suggested by Habermas

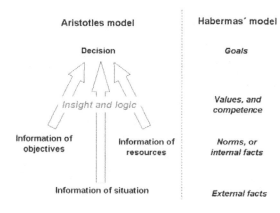

Every layer of the model has a specialized task in the overall process of forming the understanding of working environment and using information in decision-making process. The layer that deals with event information produces all the time an updated picture of events compared to the physical features of the organization. On the next layer upwards, the constraints are sorted out. This means the restrictions and possibilities that the environment will produce and the behavior and properties of actor have, when it is interacting with its environment. Conclusions at this level are abstracted analysis about restrictions and possibilities for activity. The next two layers contain information of resources and means of an actor

Table 1. Information categorization model

Values	Internal facts	Conclusions	External facts
Basic assumptions Hidden assumptions that will guide the behavior of an actor.	**Mission, vision** An end-state of the actor.	**Decision** A solution based on thinking and assessment.	**Task** Given activities or work to be performed. For example, activities originated by upper-level management or by the development of a situation.
Socially true values Those assumptions that are mutually accepted in a certain group to be a basis of thinking and executing activities.	**Means** Activities or methods to reach an aim or fulfill a purpose.	**Alternatives to act** Description of possibilities or proposals to act.	**Foreseen end states** Future situations most certainly reached when activities are finished.
Physically true values Those assumptions that can be accepted to be valid in certain physical environment.	**Resources** Available material and human resources such as people, financial resources, material, and office space and time.	**Possibilities to act** Describes a thing, event, or development that can be taught or is expected. Possibilities to act are derived from strategies and resources.	**Anticipated futures** Describes possible paths to the goal that the actor can choose and that provide something new to the actor. For example, strategy alternatives.
Social artifacts Structure of a social system, principles of interaction, and description of nodes and their mutual positions, and observable behavior.	**Action patterns** Describes how an actor can behave. Are stored on databases or is tacit knowledge, for example, process descriptions, manuals, instructions, and action plans.	**Restrictions** Things that have to be concerned before planning the use of resources and means. For example, restrictions placed on activities and conditions of information acquisition.	**Environment** Describes an area or a space that affects an actor. For example, activities of media, market trends, national trends, global trends, and higher-level decisions.
Physical artifacts Results of activity, like technical results of a group, written and spoken language, symbols, and art.	**Features** Describes properties of objects such as the properties of an organization or equipment. Are stored in databases or is tacit knowledge, for example, infrastructure descriptions, properties of equipments, and competencies of people.	**Event model** A description that enables the outlining of the pattern of a situation. For example, reports, documents, analyzed conclusions such as quality reports, statistics, pictures, and maps.	**Events** Describes time-limited events caused by actors. For example, meetings, accidents, and hostile activity.

combined with futures expectations of the overall system, including stakeholders. These input facts as well as information about events and environment, and knowledge about the composition and the development of the situation and possible end-states are used as basis. The possibilities to act and information about alternate ways to operate are refined. The chain of deduction can be continued until the ultimate decision-making layer is reached. There, all output information from the lower layers shall be available. Conclusions of a neighbor layer are relatively more meaningful than information on the other layers. The whole spectrum of cultural information shall be available for the decision-maker. The decision-maker must be able to know the action patterns, anticipate the change of the situation, foresee the end-state of the action, and deeply understand the meaning of the mission as a part of the bigger continuum of action.

INFORMATION AVAILABILITY REQUIREMENTS AND SHARING PRINCIPLES IN PRACTICE

We present four different information sharing cases to demonstrate the divergence of the requirements of acting in emergent networked environment. Those cases lead reader to the world of not only the *complexity* of *networked structures*, but also to the complexity of using and producing information and to those challenges that are faced in *dynamic* acting environment. Understanding this manifold complexity is important for two reasons. First, it gives some ideas to understand how to perform security activities to ensure information availability, integrity and confidentiality. Second, it gives hints to understand those challenges that can be faced, when security culture is attempted to create in emergent environment. Those four cases are: starting a new activity, building up a network, moving from normal "steady-state" situation to a situation where fast decision-making is required,

and guidance by values. Research targets have been government and agency level organizations including military, as well as state provincial search and rescue organizations. Results have revealed challenges concerning information exchange practices and organizational aspects. This shows the complexity of the challenges that are faced when implementing information security culture in multinational, multi-actor dynamic networked working environment.

Cases are presented rather briefly, because for the purpose of this study it is not relevant to describe those in details. The most interesting conclusions are described here to show how different the information sharing and exploiting world is when dealing with different kinds of situations. Those conclusions are then analyzed using models of organization dynamics and information categorization presented earlier.

Thirty crisis management specialists were asked what issues they have found challenging when planning and beginning practical cooperation on the field (SHIFT WS#1, 2006). Specialists were from different countries and they represented both governmental and non-governmental organizations. The people that answered the questions represented the practical experience of planning and executing operations in a multi-actor environment. The idea of this very brief survey was to find out most important structure, activity, and information related challenges that those actor had faced during their operations.

Answers were categorized in three major classes that were "structural items," "activity items," and "information items." Information items were further on, categorized on the basis of the model described earlier. Structural challenges were focused on the nature of the working environment, (self) organizing of the actors on the field, information access and sharing structures, as well as user-friendly technological support. Activity challenges were focused on finding the way to discuss—to share the needed information to build up the overall structure to act in a proper way. Challenges of activity seem to concentrate on information management in a *complex* and emerging structure in a rather divergently acting network of various actors.

Challenges concerning information sharing concentrated mainly in five classes:

- Socially true values
- Social artifacts
- Action patterns
- Features
- Environment

To some degree challenges were faced on the area of:

- Physically true values
- Mission and vision
- Means
- Resources
- Possibilities to act
- Event model
- Foreseen end-states
- Events

It can be seen that most of the information content expressions are situated in five categories that present socially oriented values, feature phenomena of all actors and environmental facts. This tells us that actors are interested in the information that is not necessarily dependant of them, but is essential to know to be able to work successfully on the field. They have been experienced that the phenomena of the working environment and phenomena of other actors are essential to know. This means that cultural information is necessary. Further on, to "elicit cultural competence" requires a lot of discussions at personal level with all those actors that are involved to common activity. At the departing phase of an operation, the information about the working environment and working partners or other actor on the field is rather essential to find the optimal way to deploy own activity.

To find out how organizations will start their information exchange when they are reorganizing their cooperative relationships in suddenly changing situations, we studied the information exchange practices in a search and rescue exercise (SAR, 2007). Several various organizations and about 100 personnel from rescue, medical, law, and other authorities as well as volunteers were involved to the exercise. We surveyed 30 people of that network of actors. People were asked what information they want to have from their cooperative counterparts, what information they are willing to share, and what information they want to have more. We analyzed the content of answers by using the information categorization model described earlier. Main conclusions were as follows:

1. Information sharing situations are complex by nature.
2. Information about past (what has taken place and how those events have affected to activity), present day (events), and the future (intentions) is relevant. This relevance differs from depending on the information users' viewpoint.
3. Information content relevance depends on the activity that an actor is performing. Content interests are very divergent.
4. Depending on the role of an actor, the interest to information varies quite a lot. Role is here understood like, for example, situation awareness, analyzing the meaning of information content, planning of the operation, and decision-making. Referring to the information exchange categorization model, the following features exist:
a. Situation awareness role concentrates to events, event models, environments, restrictions and partly tasks, and decisions.
b. Those who analyze the basic information for planning purposes focus on their information gathering interests to events, environment,

resources, as well as features of actors, action patterns, and anticipated futures.

c. Planners concentrate on resources, anticipated futures, foreseen end-states and possibilities, and alternatives to act.

d. Decision-makers focus their interest on means, tasks, foreseen end-states, mission, vision, possibilities to act, and decisions.

Those actors, who are on the management level, are much more interested in futures information (anticipated futures and foreseen end-states) and action possibilities that those who perform the field activities at the operative level. Planners and decision-makers want to see to the future.

Those actors that are performing tasks on the operative level are much more interested on decisions that concern them than those ones who these decisions have done. Operative actors want to know what they are expected to do.

Information interest varies depending on if the information shall be accurate and certain or shall it be updated quickly enough according to the development speed of the situation. Accuracy of information is emphasized on conclusions category and at the events-features end of the model. Especially, events information and decisions are required to be as accurate as possible. Updating speed is kept important at the level of combining the information of resources and means to the futures information about the development of the situation to create alternatives to act. Most important is to achieve updated information about tasks and continuous ability to evaluate the requirements of the mission (see Kuusisto, Kuusisto, & Nissen, 2007).

Challenges in *information sharing* are focused on three items:

a. Willingness to share information in networks. It seems that about 20% of information exchange is directed to networking partners. The rest of the information exchange takes place inside own organization structure.

b. There are differences between the information that actors are willing to share and the one they are willing to receive. In general, more information is wanted of features, action patterns, events, environment, and anticipated futures. Also, information of resources, possibilities to act, and foreseen end-states are kept relevant to get. Willingness to share information focuses on event model and decisions. This leads to the dilemma of wishes and wills. Different information is wanted that shared. Information sharing challenges focus on the categories of events, resources, means, event models, features, action patterns, and anticipated futures.

c. Organizing of actors does not basically support networked information sharing. Actors tend to keep in organizations structures, where they are used to act on long-term. Willingness to organize ad-hoc, or to form task-based organizations, or self-organize is limited and takes time. Information sharing structures are trust-based and they are developed on long-term.

It seems that building up a *network* is rather challenging. In spite of the fact that all actors involved in this exercise knew each other somewhat well, certain viscosity to form new kinds of networks was observable. This means that in such situations where actors are joining and departing the network, a certain amount of *time* will elapse before networked actors will understand each other in new kind of network structure. Further on, if certain structure produces certain activity, the evolving network produces different kinds of actions depending on what kind of actors have joined into the network. If it is question about security culture, it reveals itself in a new form when actors of the network change. Security culture evolves during time.

An empirical study about situation awareness in crisis management was conducted in governmental organizations in Finland in 2005.

A research report of that study is published in Kuusisto et al. (2007). This brief conclusive text is based on that report. The aim of the study was to collect information for improving interagency collaboration services and processes of crisis management. The study focused on the changes in situation awareness when moving from normal situations to disruptive situations and exceptional conditions. The method of the study was semi-structured interview. Eleven people representing governmental authorities were interviewed. The interviewees were active actors in the area of domestic and international security, or tightly related to these actors.

The interviewees assessed the changes in the priority of information contents when moving from normal situations to disruptive situations and exceptional conditions. The interviewees were asked to select those information contents that priority increases and those information contents that priority decreases, in crisis situations.

Analysis of the material was completed and the following recommendations were sorted out. Both the forming of basis for decision-making and decision-making itself require a wide understanding of large systems having a structure, activities, and information potential. When forming the basis for decision-making, this need is visible, especially in task analysis. The forming of the basis for decision-making activities will be supported by future study methods suitable for situations where immediate activities are needed. Information about resources is a prerequisite for future orientation. In addition, information and experience on features, action patterns, anticipated futures, foreseen end states and mission, and vision supports the producing of information about futures. Capability needed for forming the basis for decision-making is the creation of new information and knowledge. This is different from capabilities needed for decision-making. These capabilities are combination of existing information and willingness to make decisions.

As a conclusion, the forming of basis for decisions as well as decision-making have to be supported by the following information based activities:

- Analyses of the development of real-time situation
- Presenting of the continually updated resource information
- Practices for informing tasks immediately
- Processing of future scenarios—finding of plausible development paths and foreseen end states
- Realistic analysis of tasks and forming of missions
- Forming, presenting, and analysis of alternatives to act
- Sharing of decisions

In conclusion, it can be stated that free information sharing, understanding the ongoing situation and pro-activity are important when decision-makers are acting in rapidly changing situations.

OECD (2002) stresses a somewhat solid ethical and value based basis for security measures implementation and development in organizations and states. The paper gives a good selection of values that are suggested to give guidance for organizations to promote long-lasting security development. Next, values and value-based statements were found from the paper:

- Taking account of all network members' interests
- Confidence among all networked actors
- Ethical values (develop and adopt best practices and to promote conduct that recognizes security needs and respects the legitimate interests of others)
- Co-operation and information sharing (especially sharing information about threats and vulnerabilities)

- Personal privacy
- Freedom to exchange thoughts and ideas
- Free flow of information
- Confidentiality of information and communication
- Protection of personal information
- Openness and transparency
- Security is a fundamental element of all products, services, systems, and networks
- Security is an integral part of system design and architecture
- Forward-looking responses to emerging threats
- Seeing evolution of risks

Those values are meant to give guidance to organizations to promote good practices in developing and implementing security policies, practices, measures, and procedures. The values that are described can be abstracted in four main categories:

- Understanding that it is question about a comprehensive system where security is an integral part of that system
- Free *information sharing* concerning security issues
- Understanding that personal and organizational privacy and confidentiality requirements exist
- Pro-activity

It is interesting to see that these issues are rather alike of those that have been discovered in those three studies of using information in decision-making in different situations.

CONCLUDING REMARKS

Culture is a structure, which exist to maintain patterns by the information called values. Values have effects on norms. Norms are information, which determines the mutually understood

policy to perform collaboration successfully. To change values, the norms must be accepted and internalised first.

Time shall be taken into account. Unified structures in complex environments will not arise suddenly. They need a certain amount of time to manifest themselves. The development of a culture always causes more or less changes to personally understood values. The aim of forming a culture is to gain such structure, on which a solid base for all activities can be constructed. To be unified, the information gluing this structure together, that is, values of individuals and organisations shall be as close to each other as possible. The more divergent they are, the longer the duration will be to unify them.

Habermas (1984, 1989) argued that those who take part in interaction, for example, *communication*, should have at least one shared item of knowledge. This guarantees that they have a potential to construct their shared situation coherently. Shared knowledge is information by which models for creating mutual understanding can be formed. Without these models, creating of understanding is not possible. A prerequisite is that people commit to believe in the models. This requires that information concerning the models is communicated.

Successful communication requires that values, experiences, knowledge, and emotions of people involved are shared. It is rather challenging to share knowledge about commonly agreed values and appreciations in multi-cultural *networks*. It seems obvious that during a short period of *time*, it is impossible to create commonly understood values. Organizations must be able to create and communicate believable, attractive, and acceptable pictures about them over the long haul. By this—in advance communicated—image, organization can attract people to fulfill, or at least understand those objectives like the confidentiality, integrity and availability of information and knowledge, which it appreciates. This kind of communication needs lots of information about the future expectations. So, an organization must be able to communicate its valuations in advance. This forms the basis for *information security culture* development.

The more communication is future-oriented, the longer the communication process takes. The longer communication will last, the more information it needs and the more information is abstracted. Time-divergent *communication* contains communicating of the organization's future, current, and past activities (Figure 9).

Communicating about the future is needed to create shared mental models about the information security. It includes communicating about the organization's image, valuations, values, and expectations in the long-term. The aim of long-term communication is to have an effect to way the other organizations in the business *network* approach information security. Communicating about the current activities includes communicating about technical and managerial level information security activities such as reflections to the implementation of information security

policy. Communicating about past achievements includes putting information security policy, information security process descriptions, or information security audit results available to partner organizations.

Research and experience has proven that availability of information about situation, competence, actors' features, futures development, and decisions is relevant. Anyhow, unbalance between released and required information is considerable. People are willing to release different kinds of information than they wish to receive from others.

Traditional organizing of actors does not basically support networked information sharing. In practical situations, actors tend to keep in organizations structures, where they are used to act on long-term. Willingness to organize ad-hoc, or to form task-based organizations, or self-organize is limited and takes time. *Information sharing* structures are trust-based and they are developed on long-term. Lessons learned emphasize that information exchange between organizations is

Figure 9. Time-divergent communication for information security culture development (the idea in He-lokunnas & Kuusisto, 2003a, see also an applications in Ahvenainen, Helokunnas, & Kuusisto, 2003 and Helokunnas & Kuusisto, 2003b). Measurable results of activities concern information security policy, process descriptions, and audit results. Managing activities and objectives concern the implementation of information security policy and vision of course is pointed towards the information security culture.

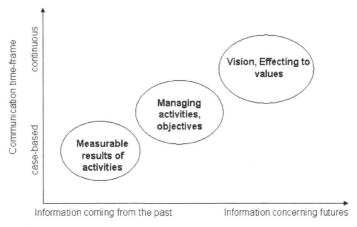

limited and creating trusted information sharing processes is time consuming. Functioning information sharing procedures cannot be developed during operative activity. They shall exist beforehand, at least to some degree.

Culture evolves. It shows itself in different ways to different actors in a network. Actors come into and depart from the common network. Each structural change of the network will change the information content of the network, as well. Cultural changes cannot be made during a short period. Forming understandably unite security culture is possible, but it will prerequisite at least either long period of time to communicate desired values, or possibility to exploit existing unity of values.

Networking is an obvious future trend. Networking is here understood as forming various ad hoc organizations to deal with some special case. These cases can be, for example, businesses, international politics, and hobbies. Networks include several perspectives and viewpoints, because every network member has its own way to act and interact. Different information is required in different phases of inter-working in networks. A new member offers and requires different information that one who has acted a longer period in network.

It seems that unified security culture or even the same kind of orientation to security culture is somewhat impossible to achieve in evolving networks. Security practices can be improved in two ways. First, those basic principles how an organization deals with information security issues shall be communicated long-term. This tells to other network members the orientation of an organization to security issues and makes its behavior more understandable. Second, some basic values shall guide the behavior of all organizations or actors that are working together on the same network. Rather good candidates of those values might be the four that were found from OECD recommendations. These are supported by practical observations of various decision-making situations:

- Understanding that, it is a question about a comprehensive system where security is an integral part of that system
- Free information sharing concerning security issues
- Understanding that personal and organizational privacy and confidentiality requirements exist
- Pro-activity

Culture is an evolving informational system. To be able to work successfully in emerging networks, the structure and nature of those networks shall be understood. So, to develop good security practices, systemic nature of the world shall be studied.

REFERENCES

Aaltonen, M., & Wilenius, M. (2002). *Osaamisen ennakointi*. Helsinki, Finland: Edita Prima Oy.

Ahvenainen, S., Helokunnas, T., & Kuusisto, R. (2003). Acquiring information superiority by time-divergent communication. In B. Hutchinson (Ed.), *Proceedings of the 2nd European Conference on Information Warfare and Security* (pp. 1-9). Reading, UK: MCIL, Reading.

Applehans, W., Globe, A., & Laugero, G. (1999). *Managing knowledge*. Boston: Addison-Wesley.

Awad, E., & Ghaziri, H. (2004). *Knowledge management*. Upper Saddle River, NJ: Prentice Hall.

Baskerville, R., & Siponen, M. (2002). An information security meta-policy for emergent organizations. *Journal of Logistics Information Management, 15*(5/6), 337-346.

Bell, W. (1998). *Foundations of futures studies, vol II, values, objectivity, and the good society*. New Brunswick, London: Transaction Publishers.

Bergson, H. (1911). *Creative evolution*. Lanham, MD: Henry Holt and Company, University Press of America, TM Inc.

Castells, M. (1996). *The information age: Economy, society and culture: Volume I, The rise of the network society*. Padstow, Cornwall: T.J. International Limited.

Checkland, P., & Holwell, S. (1998). *Information, systems and information systems—making sense of the field*. Chichester, New York, Weinheim, Brisbane, Singapore, Toronto: John Wiley & Sons Ltd.

Checkland, P., & Scholes, J. (2000). *Soft systems methodology in action*. Chichester, New York, Weinheim, Brisbane, Singapore, Toronto: John Wiley & Sons, Ltd.

Chia, P.A., Ruighaver, A.B., & Maynard, S.B. (2002). Understanding organizational security culture. In *Proceedings of PACIS2002*, Japan. Retrieved February 20, 2007, from http://www.dis.unimelb.edu.au/staff/sean/research/ChiaCultureChapter.pdf

Detert, J. R., Schroeder, R. G., & Mauriel, J. (2000). Framework for linking culture and improvement initiatives in organisations. *The Academy of Management Review, 25*(4), 850-863.

Dhillon, G. (1997). *Managing information system security*. Chippenham, Wiltshire, GB: Anthony Rowe Ltd.

Finnish Government Resolution. (2004). *Strategy for securing the functions vital to society*. Helsinki, Finland: Edita Prima Oy.

Fisher, C., & Lovell, A. (2003). *Business ethics and values*. Harlow, London, New York, Boston, San Francisco, Toronto, Sydney, Singapore, Hong Kong, Tokyo, Seoul, Taipei, New Delhi, Cape Town, Madrid, Mexico City, Amsterdam. Munich, Paris, Milan: Prentice Hall.

Helokunnas, T., & Kuusisto, R. (2003a). Strengthening leading situations via time-divergent communication conducted in Ba. *The E-Business Review, 3*(1), 78-81.

Helokunnas, T., & Kuusisto, R. (2003b). Information security culture in a value net. In *Proceedings of the 2003 IEEE International Engineering Management Conference* (pp. 190-194). Albany, NY, USA.

Habermas, J. (1984). *The theory of communicative action, volume 1: Reason and the rationalization of society*. Boston: Beacon Press.

Habermas, J. (1989). *The theory of communicative action, volume 2: Lifeworld and system: A critique of functionalist reason*. Boston: Beacon Press.

Hofstede, G. (1984). *Culture's consequences: International differences in work-related values*. Beverly Hills, London, New Delhi: Sage Publications.

Kuusisto, R. (2004). *Aspects on availability*. Helsinki, Finland: Edita Prima Oy.

Kuusisto, R. (2006). Flowing of information in decision systems. In *Proceedings of the 39th Hawaii International conference of System Sciences* (abstract on p. 148, paper published in electronic form). Kauai, HI: University of Hawai'i at Manoa.

Kuusisto, T., Kuusisto, R., & Nissen, M. (2007). Implications of information flow priorities for interorganizational crisis management. In L. Armistead (Ed.), *Proceedings of the 2nd International Conference on I-Warfare and Security* (pp. 133-140). Monterey, CA: Naval Postgraduate School.

Kuusisto, R., Nyberg, K., & Virtanen, T. (2004). Unite security culture—may a unified security culture be plausible. In A. Jones (Ed.), *Proceedings of the 3rd European Conference on Information Warfare and Security* (pp. 221-230). London: Academic Conferences Limited.

Luhmann, N. (1999). *Ökologishe Kommunikation, 3. Auflage*. Opladen/Wiesbaden: Westdeutcher Verlag.

Maier, R. (2002). *Knowledge management systems. Information and communication technologies for knowledge management*. Berlin, Heidelberg, New York: Springler-Verlag.

Malaska, P., & Holstius, K. (1999). Visionary management. *Foresight, 1*(4), 353-361.

Martins, A., & Eloff, J. (2002). Information security culture. In *Proceedings of IFIP TC11 17th International Conference on Information Security* (pp. 203-214). Cairo, Egypt: IFIP Conference Proceedings 214.

Merleau-Ponty, M. (1968).*The visible and invisible*. Evanston, IL: Northwest University Press.

Niiniluoto, I. (1997). *Informaatio, tieto ja yhteiskunta, Filosofinen käsiteanalyysi*. Helsinki, Finland: Edita.

Nosworthy, J. (2000). Implementing information security in the 21st century—do you have the balancing factors? *Computers and Security, 19*(4), 337-347.

OECD. (2002). *OECD guidelines for the security of information systems and networks: Towards a culture of security*. Adopted as a recommendation of the OECD Council at its 1037th session on July 25, 2002. Retrieved April 11, 2007, from http://www.oecd.org/dataoecd/16/22/15582260.pdf

SAR. (2007). A *survey* of sharing information in a search and rescue excercise. A co-operative exercise, where rescue, law and medical organizations and non-governmental organizations rehearsed together in a case of airliner accident at Helsinki airport on January 25, 2007 (Research report not published).

Schein, E. H. (1980). *Organizational psychology* (3rd ed.). Englewood Cliffs, NJ.: Prentice-Hall.

Schein, E. H. (1992). *Organizational culture and leadership* (2nd ed). San Francisco: Jossey-Bass.

Schlienger, T., & Teufel, S. (2002). Information security culture: The socio-cultural dimension in information security management. In *Proceedings of IFIP TC11 17th International Conference on Information Security* (pp 191-202). Cairo, Egypt: IFIP Conference Proceedings 214.

Schneider, S., & Barsoux, J-L. (1997). *Managing across cultures*. London, New York, Toronto, Sydney, Tokyo, Singapore, Madrid, Mexico City, Munich, Paris: Prentice Hall.

SHIFT WS#1. (2006). *Group survey*. Conducted in workshop of a project that deals with information sharing in networked crisis management environment (SHIFT = Shared Information Framework and Technology) on November 13-16, 2006 (Research report not published).

Straub, D., Loch, K., Evaristo, R., Karahanna, E., & Strite, M. (2002). Toward a theory-based measurement of culture. *Journal of Global Information Management, 10*(1), 13-23.

Sveiby, K-E. (2001). *A knowledge-based theory of the firm to guide strategy formulation*. Retrieved February 15, 2003, from http://www.sveiby.com/articles/Knowledgetheoryoffirm.htm

Thierauf, R. (2001). *Effective business intelligence systems*. London: Quorum Books.

Von Solms, B. (2000). Information security—the third wave? *Computers and Security, 19*(7), 615-620.

Waltz, E. (1998). *Information warfare: Principles and operations*. Boston & London: Artech House.

Whitman, M. E., & Mattord, H. J. (2003). *Principles of information security*. Boston: Thomson™ Course Technology, printed in Canada.

Zakaria, O., & Gani, A. (2003). A conceptual checklist of information security culture. In B. Hutchinson (Ed.), *Proceedings of the 2nd European Conference on Information Warfare and Security* (pp. 365-372). Reading, UK: MCIL, Reading.

Zakaria, O., Jarupunphol, P., & Gani, A. (2003). Paradigm mapping for information security culture approach. In J. Slay (Ed.), *Proceedings of the 4th Australian Conference on Information Warfare and IT Security* (pp. 417-426). Adelaide, Australia: University of South Australia.

Chapter VII
Social Aspects of Information Security:
An International Perspective

Paul Drake
Centre for Systems Studies Business School, University of Hull, UK

Steve Clarke
Centre for Systems Studies Business School, University of Hull, UK

ABSTRACT

This chapter looks at information security as a primarily technological domain, and asks what could be added to our understanding if both technology and human activity were seen to be of equal importance. The aim is therefore, to ground the domain both theoretically and practically from a technological and social standpoint. The solution to this dilemma is seen to be located in social theory, various aspects of which deal with both human and technical issues, but do so from the perspective of those involved in the system of concern. The chapter concludes by offering a model for evaluating information security from a social theoretical perspective, and guidelines for implementing the findings.

INTRODUCTION

Within this chapter, we first look at the dominant approach to information security (ISec), establishing it as a domain in which technological factors predominate, and insufficient consideration is given to human issues. Building on this foundation, a picture is presented of the complexity of ISec, from which it is argued that the practice *ought* to pay more attention to the ways in which differing perceptions might give rise to a different ISec practice.

The tensions in ISec are presented as occurring between theory and practice on the one hand, and social and technological on the other. From this position, the question posed becomes: "How can we build an ISec practice which is grounded theoretically, and which addresses both technological and social issues?"

The source of a solution to this dilemma may be found in social theory. Various aspects of social theory deal with both human and technical issues, but do so from the perspective of those involved in the system of concern. Our approach, therefore, has been to build models to evaluate and implement ISec, both based explicitly on theories of social action.

BACKGROUND TO INFORMATION SECURITY

From a Technological to a Human-Centred Perspective

Currently, the practice of information security (ISec) aims primarily to protect information and to ensure it is available to those authorised to access it. This approach is emphasized by the well established definition of information security to be found in the U.S. Department of Defense "Orange Book" (DOD, 1985):

In general, secure systems will control, through use of specific security features, access to information such that only properly authorised individuals, or processes operating on their behalf, will have access to read, write, create, or delete information.

Within the United Kingdom, a similar perspective on ISec can be seen in UK government publications, for example the Communications-Electronics Security Group[1] (CESG 1994), The British Standard for Information Security Management (ISO 2000; BSI 2003), and in the documentation and practice within a large number of organisations who have adopted information security practices. In all of these cases, the primary concern is to protect the *confidentiality*

and *integrity* of *information,* and to restrict its *availability*: the so called "CIA" of ISec.

So, this is ISec practice—but where has this practice come from? A brief look at the development history of the British Standard, outlined, gives an indication of this in the UK.

The sources of the Standard (BS7799) are traceable to the 1990s, when a group of security professionals formed a committee under the auspices of the British Standards Institute, and with the support of the UK government's Department of Trade and Industry, to document current "best information security practice" based on the current experience, knowledge, and practice of those contributing. The product of this effort was the Code of Practice for Information Security Management (BSI, 1993). The committee continued to work towards maintaining and improving the code of practice, and today it has developed into the British Standards for Information Security (ISO, 2000; BSI, 2002). The same committee continues to maintain and revise this Standard. During the various iterations, Part 1 of the Standard has been accepted by the International Organization for Standardization, commonly known as ISO, as an international standard, ISO-17799.

Part 1 of the Standard (ISO, 2000) is a code of practice which contains around 130 controls to be considered and implemented. Part 2 (BSI, 2003) contains the same number of controls but *specifies* their use and is therefore auditable. Both parts of the Standard provide guidance for the development and implementation of a risk-based management system that allows the continued assessment and management of risks. This is delivered through an information security management system (ISMS) that incorporates a cycle which, in essence, compiles a list of the 130 controls and determines whether the absence or inadequate implementation of these controls is likely to harm the organisation and if so, by how much. Proper management of risks and correct implementation of applicable controls can attract certification to the Standard and the right to use the

Table 1. Analysis of information security literature in the current domain

Reference	Title	Approach	Category/Bias
Baskerville (Baskerville, 1988)	Designing information system security	Checklist-standard based approach to securing systems	Operational/Technical
Cooper (Cooper, 1989)	Computer and communications security: Strategies for the 1990s	Analytical and strategic tools to understand security issues and implementing an effective security programme	Operational/Technical
Peltier (Peltier, 2001)	Information security risk analysis	Basics of risk management including breakdown of threats and mitigation techniques	Risk management
Russell and Gangemi (Russell & Gangemi, 1991)	Computer security basics	Fundamental principles and concepts of information security	Operational/Technical
Langford (Langford, 1995)	Practical computer ethics	Maps out ethical problems of computer use and strategies for dealing with them	Pseudo-humanistic
Gollman (Gollman, 1999)	Computer security	Comprehensive review of security technologies together with some interesting explorations of the meaning of a secure systems—for example, whether controls should focus on data, operations or users	Operational/technical
Warman (Warman, 1993)	Computer security within organisations	Discussion of computer security from organisational and management perspective including recognition that managing the security of people is just as important as managing security of technology	Business/organisational
Forrester and Morrison (Forrester & Morrison, 1994)	Computer ethics	Exploration of ethical issues surrounding hacking, writing viruses, artificial intelligence, and data protection	Pseudo-humanistic
Neumann (Neumann, 1995)	Computer related risks	Comprehensive review of computer failures, why they occur, and what can be done to avoid recurrences	Risk management
Wylder (Wylder, 2003)	Strategic information security	Guidance on integrating information security requirements with the business goals of the organisation to ensure the success of the security practice	Business/Organisational

continued on following page

Table 1. continued

Reference	Title	Approach	Category/Bias
Killmeyer-Tudor (Killmeyer-Tudor, 2000)	Information security architecture: An integrated approach to security in the organisation	Guidance on setting up an information security practice including technical controls and strategic business alignment	Business/Organisational
Birch (Birch, 1997)	The certificate business: Public key infrastructure will be big business	Suggests forward-looking technological solutions for current information security problems, for example, ID cards to secure transactions	Operational/Technical
Baum (Baum, 1997)	The ABA digital signature guidelines	American Bar Association guidelines on securing transactions	Operational/Technical
McCauley (McCauley, 1997)	Legal ethics and the Internet: A U.S. perspective	Exploration of ethical issues surrounding publication of information on the Internet, especially concerning publication of personal information and the lack of controls around publication	Pseudo-humanistic
Leng (Leng, 1997)	Internet regulation in Singapore	Controlling access to "objectionable" content and the ethical questions of, for example, censorship, that arise	Pseudo-humanistic
Longbough (Longbough, 1996)	Internet security and insecurity	Technical "how to" guide for computer hackers	Operational/Technical
Northcutt (Northcutt et al., 2002)	Inside network perimeter security: The definitive guide to firewalls, VPNs, routers, and intrusion detection systems	Technical controls required to secure an organisation's internal computer network against external threats	Operational/Technical
Kuong (Kuong 1996)	Client server controls, security and audit (enterprise protections, control, audit, security, risk management and business continuity)	Technical controls required to secure an organisation's internal computer network, and attached systems, against external or internal attack	Operational/Technical
Wright (Wright 1993)	Computer security in large corporations: Attitudes and practices of CEOs	Highlights the dangers of insufficient focus on information security within organisations	Business/Organisational

British Standard kite mark to signify appropriate management of information security.

So, BS7799 has grown out of ISec practice to become, arguably, the measure by which all UK information security is judged. But are there any other reasons for believing that we can categorise a particular approach to ISec? During the course of this study, we researched the relevant literature extensively, and the result of this is summarised in Table 1, which classifies nineteen key ISec texts, and Figure 1, which is an analysis of a wide representative sample of such texts.

Figure 1 represents further analysis of the literature within the information security domain. This is the result of a search of a sample of currently available information security literature which is considered representative on the basis of a quantitative literature review, which is broadly in line with the expectations of both the author and other key information security practitioners with whom this has been discussed.

The pattern which has emerged is of a domain that includes some broad risk-based theory, but is technically biased, with only cursory reference to business and human-centred domains. How successful these human-centred excursions have been is unclear as they typically focus (see Table 1) on what may be regarded as superficial ethical issues such as data privacy, and how to get people to accept the required information security practice. Business-aligned literature tends towards the attainment of resources to maintain the security practice rather than a true attempt to align security with the business objectives, or, in a wider sense, the needs of the people within the organisation. In terms of quantity of literature, there is a massive bias towards technical and operational controls within the domain. In fairness, as technology continues to evolve, there is an almost continual need to update the technical security literature base to keep pace. However, this does not adequately explain the paucity of social literature within what is essentially a domain that radically affects people and how they are expected to behave.

Looking back again from this perspective to the British Standard, its very presence seems to be one of the problems with the information security domain as it stands today. British Standards generally can be shown to be useful tools in differentiating between one *product* and another. Many assume that the presence of the BSI kite mark on a child's safety harness for example, will mean that the target product is more reliable than one that does not have a kite mark. It is assumed that certain criteria are observed in the manufacture of certified products and that their quality and reliability is tested using established industry practices. Few consumers probably know the detailed tests, tolerances, and manufacturing practices that are used to gain and maintain certification. Most probably *trust* that the product will be "better" and perhaps even as good as it is possible to get as a result of certification. However, it is unclear how these certification principles that seem to work so well with products can be satisfactorily applied to services, processes, and controls such as those embodied in BS7799 to achieve a better result than one which does not meet the certification requirements. Other British standards appear to exhibit the same problem. For example, the standard for quality management (ISO, 2000), the

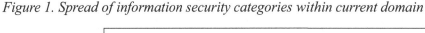

Figure 1. Spread of information security categories within current domain

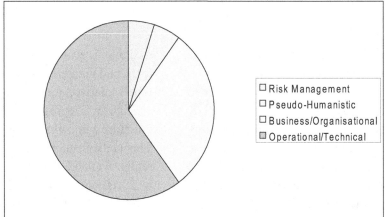

standard for environmental management (ISO, 2000), and the standard for service management (BSI, 2002; BSI, 2003) all suffer, it is argued, by trying to bring standardisation to a domain where standardisation does not readily fit. The key problem here is that, where there is human free will present in a domain, the opportunities to truly remove variability through standardisation are constrained by the unpredictable nature of human behaviour.

In the case of the information security standard, as well as the examples cited, the response from the standard and from ISec practice is to further constrain human behaviour within a rule-based framework of technical controls. This seems perilous in a domain where social issues would appear to be significant, if not dominant. To ignore social issues within the information security domain is to imply that the security of an information system is not changed if all of the people involved in it, or affected by it are changed. This implication seems insupportable given that two of the three guiding principles of current information security practice are that information should be accessed only by *people* who are authorised to access it, and that steps should be taken to ensure information is available when authorised *people* need it. This theme of social issues within the information security domain is THE central issue of this study.

ISSUES AND PROBLEMS

Towards a Determination of the Success of Current Practice

Before moving on to addressing the lack of consideration of human issues in ISec, there was one further task we wanted to complete in the study. If ISec's technical focus is insufficient to address the problems of the IS domain, this ought to be reflected in the success or failure of that practice.

There is good quality quantitative data available to demonstrate trends in information security and the use of BS7799. Every 2 years the DTI sponsors an Information Security Breaches Survey (DTI, 2000; DTI, 2002; DTI, 2004). Table 2 summarises the results pertinent to information security generally and BS7799 in particular. The table provides an indication of the seriousness with which information security in general, and BS7799 in particular appears to be taken. An information security policy is considered a fundamental and first step towards current information security practice. This can be contrasted with the importance that senior managers say they place on information security and the effects of not paying sufficient attention in this domain. The industry sectors shown are the largest represented in the sample. Further detailed analysis of the results appears below the table.

It can be seen that, in spite of significant increases in the number of UK businesses that have suffered security breaches (24% in 2000, 44% in 2002, almost doubling to 78% in 2004), the number of organisations with a security policy remains low, at a third in 2004. Remarkably, amongst those responsible for information security, only 12% were aware of the contents of BS7799 in the 2004 survey. This shows a slight drop from the 2002 survey! The number of businesses who have implemented BS7799 also remains a disappointing 5%. However, the number of organisations who have installed anti-virus software has significantly increased to 93%. Other areas showing significant improvements include the perceived importance of information security and the number of organisations that have carried out a risk assessment. Clearly, the disappointing awareness and use of the standard is not matched by the perceived importance of information security, the need for risk assessment, and the value in investing in key protective measures such as anti-virus software. So what is causing this lack of interest in the standard? The 2002 and 2004 surveys both cited the top reason given by respondents—the cost of

Table 2. Information security breaches surveys

	2000 Survey	*2002 Survey*	*2004 Survey*
Number of UK businesses with a documented (Avison) security policy	14%	27%	33%
Number of those responsible for IT security that are aware of contents of BS7799	No data	15%	12%
Number of UK businesses that have BS7799 implemented	No data	5%	5%
Amount of IT budget spent on (information) security	No data	2%	3%
Number of UK businesses believe information security is high priority for senior management	53%	73%	75%
Number of UK businesses have suffered at least one malicious security breach in past year	24%	44%	78%
Number of UK businesses that have implemented anti-virus software	No data	83%	93%
Number of UK businesses that have carried out a detailed risk assessment of their IT systems and the threats to them	37%	66%	No data
Number of staff employed by respondents. a) 1-49, b) 50-249, c) 250+	No data	a) 51% b) 29% c) 20%	a) 51.9%, b) 31% c) 17.1%
Sample size	1000	1000	1000
% of respondents in manufacturing sector	No data	24%	24%
% in retail & distribution	No data	15%	15%
% in technology	No data	14%	14%

purchasing the standard. When you consider that the cost of ISO17799 is currently £94 and the cost of BS7799 is currently £56, that is a little surprising. You can also buy them both for a discounted £110. The second most common reason cited is that the standard is seen to be only relevant to large organisations. If that is the case then the uptake in large organisations might be expected to be significant. The proportion of people responsible for information security in large organisations was 42% in the 2002 survey and dropped back to just over a third in the 2004 survey.

A further problem is that, for information security, there is no measurement within current practice in terms of whether an implementation of information security practice has been successful.

Whilst the practice will often include *quantitative* measurement (for example the number of controls implemented, how long it took to implement them, and how much it cost), there is very little *qualitative* measurement such as how successful the implementation was in reducing risk. There are also means whereby the presence or absence of controls can be audited and certified. It can be determined whether security failures have become greater or reduced following implementation of controls.

However, this does not seem a very acceptable means of measuring success, as any reduction could be due to some unknown factor outside of the scope of the practice. Consequently, there seems to be no effective means of determining whether a system is fully secure or even more secure as a result of deploying information security controls. Nor does there seem to be any way of establishing how much security is enough to afford the protection that an organisation may desire to have. Information security and the supporting British Standard represent best available practice in ensuring the confidentiality of sensitive information, and the integrity and availability of important business information. With such high claims one would expect BS7799 to have received great attention and to be an essential tool in the armoury of any successful organisation.

Information Assurance: A Survey

The purpose of this section is to further validate the outcomes of the analysis of the information security breaches surveys presented in the previous section.

The Information Assurance Advisory Council (IAAC) surveys corporate leaders, public policy makers, law enforcement, and the research community to address the challenges of information infrastructure protection. They are engaged in the development of policy recommendations to government and corporate leaders. IAAC recommendations tend to be influential because their sponsors and members comprise leading commercial end-users, government policy makers, and the research community. IAAC's stated aim is to work for the creation of a safe and secure information society.

In October 2002 the IAAC published a survey (Modhvadia, Daman et al., 2002) which explored the concept of information assurance, contrasted it with information security, and surveyed organisations' awareness of the British Standard for information security (ISO, 2000; BSI, 2002). The survey was undertaken only amongst IAAC members. A total of 58 surveys were distributed; all were followed up by telephone. Full responses

in writing and in telephone interviews were received from 16 members (31% response rate). Approximately half the organisations surveyed were large, a quarter medium-sized, and a quarter small. The survey contains no further information on the meaning of large, medium and small organisations. The organisations were simply asked to categorise themselves. The following sectors were represented: Finance, 8%; Government, 15%; Retail, 4%; Risk Management, 15%; IT, 23%; Telecoms, 12%; Utilities, 12%; Manufacturing, 7%; and Legal, 4%.

The study provides a comparison between the terms "information security" and "information assurance." The study suggests that the term information security often leads to an over-emphasis on confidentiality whilst missing other aspects of the problem, for instance: integrity, accessibility, and reliability. Moreover, use of the term security and an emphasis on IT often mean that this type of risk is too easily seen as a low-level and niche activity, which falls outside the interests of senior management and the board of directors.

It is clear that those surveyed do not see BS7799 as being sufficient to cover all business requirements; the lack of other standards is leading many organisations to develop in-house, bespoke standards and processes. Nearly two-thirds of respondents found that BS7799 does not go far enough in protecting information systems and there is a clear demand for further standards and clearer guidance.

From detailed responses to the survey, it was found that the companies who thought there was no better alternative did so not because of the merits of BS7799 but because of the lack of alternatives. (Modhvadia, Daman et al. 2002) propose a recasting of information security as "information assurance" with less emphasis on confidentiality and more on other aspects such as integrity, availability, and reliability. However, they still strongly propose a controls biased approach driven by the assessment of risk.

This exploration of current practice has surfaced a surprising willingness in the literature and in the practice of organisations to accept information security as a concept even though the tools available to implement it are often considered lacking.

Through a detailed examination of the British Standard and an extensive review of available information security literature, a model has emerged which clearly shows a domain which is dominated by a set of practical controls which are seen as rigid, unclear, and largely irrelevant to the business needs of most organisations. This view is largely supported by the findings of the two surveys (outlined previously).

What has become clear, even within some recent developments that have sought to provide a more accessible model for managing information such as information assurance, is that all current practice is centric around the needs of the technology and of information rather than the needs of people in general and users in particular. Where human issues are explored in this domain, it is to confer responsibilities and education on people to conform to the needs of the system and to regulate their behaviour.

What emerges then is a domain which is to all intents and purposes technological, as proven by the absence of sufficient consideration for human issues, and a domain dominated by pragmatism as demonstrated by the way in which the principle models in the domain were constructed and are maintained. That is, constructed through the collation of the practical experiences of practitioners, and maintained through practical experiences of practitioners and by reference to surveys and in response to user groups and new regulatory frameworks.

Moving from the Standard to current information security literature, a similar pattern emerges of a domain that includes some broad risk-based theory and becomes progressively more specific and technically biased over time, although with some excursions into business and human-centred domains. How successful these human-centred excursions have been is unclear as they typically focus on superficial ethical issues such as data privacy, and how to get people to accept the required information security practice. Business-aligned literature tends towards the attainment of resources to maintain the security practice rather than a true attempt to align security with business objectives. In terms of quantity of literature, there is a massive bias towards technical and operational controls within the domain. In fairness, as technology continues to evolve there is an almost continual need to update the technical security literature base to keep pace. However, this does not adequately explain the relative absence of social literature within what is essentially a domain that radically affects people and how they are expected to behave.

So, through a detailed examination of the British Standard (together with a review of ISO and the DOD Orange Book) and an extensive review of available information security literature, a model has emerged which clearly shows a domain which is dominated by a set of practical controls which are seen as rigid, unclear, and largely irrelevant to the business needs of most organisations. What has become clear, even within some recent developments that have sought to provide a more accessible model for managing information such as information assurance, is that all current practice is centric around the needs of the technology and of information rather than the needs of people in general and users in particular. Where human issues are explored in this domain, it is to confer responsibilities and education on people to conform to the needs of the system and to regulate their behaviour.

Figure 2 summarises the position reached so far, and gives some idea of the complexity of the issues.

Figure 2. The complexity of information security

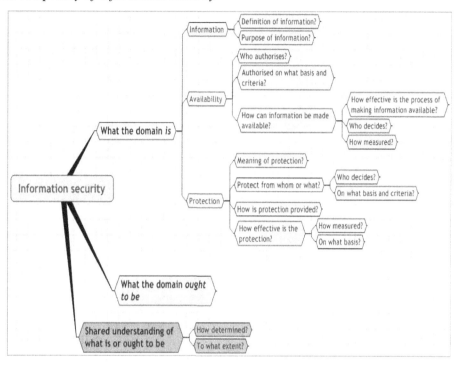

SOLUTIONS AND RECOMMENDATIONS

Towards an Improved Information Security Practice

Figure 3 summarises how a different mix of social/technical and theoretical/practical approaches to ISec might be characterised.

In terms of Figure 3, information security can best be represented currently as a technical practice, with scant regard to social needs. What we have been pursuing in our research programme is a way of moving this view of ISec to an action-oriented approach to the domain. This has involved two key stages, both of which are explicitly based on declared social theory:

1. Development, testing, and refinement of a model for evaluating current information security practice

2. Development of an implementation model to action the findings of the evaluation

In the next section, this is carried forward by presenting an evaluative model for Information Security which is true to these tenets.

An Evaluative Model for Information Security

The model for evaluating information security, presented in Figure 4, is the result of an ongoing research and development programme which is currently of some 8 years duration. The grounding for the model is drawn from a foundation in critical theory, and whilst it is not necessary to detail this within this short chapter, there are certain issues which are important to the analysis. In particular, we will be referring later in the chapter to issues of "decolonisation": these relate specifically to the work of Weber and Marx (Historical Materi-

Figure 3. Theoretical vs. practical and social vs. technical comparison grid

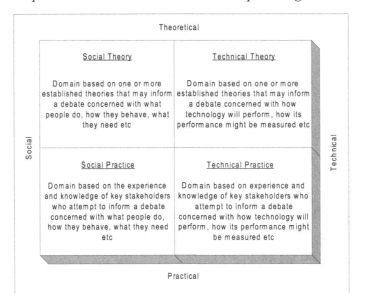

alism, Marx & Engels, 1968), and are grounded in a critical theory which is traceable to Kant. In terms of the model it is important, for example, to recognise where the public sphere is allowed to be colonised—an example of the impact of which is given. For the purposes of this text, a brief description of the model is given; for those who wish to look more deeply into the background to its production and wider use, please see Drake (2005).

The model is derived by combining three concepts from social theory:

1. Habermas' systems/lifeworld and public/private spheres of influence. In outline, this theory helps us to understand how human action becomes systematised within organisations. The outcome is that the system functions (e.g., the technical aspects of information security) come to dominate, whilst lifeworld functions (e.g., aspects of wider social interaction) are overridden.
2. Parsons' AGIL model.
    *   Adaptation (A) is concerned with securing and distributing the means from

the environment for social systems' survival. In terms of information security, this is related to issues such as gaining organisational support though funding and developing channels of improvement.

*   Goal-attainment (G), concerned with defining and prioritising social system goals: in information security related to such issues as determining short term and long term needs; differentiating between local/on-site security requirements from the needs for remote working.
*   Integration (I): the co-ordinating of relationships within the social system: in information security—demonstrating to stakeholders that risks are managed and resources are being used appropriately; appreciating the concerns of the practitioners implementing the system
*   Latency (L): motivating the desired behaviours and managing tensions within social systems. Frequently

reviewing the information security system (policies, procedures, etc.) to ensure the administrative processes support and align with organisational objectives; establishing a culture of security within the organisation, and so on.

1. Merton's concept of latent and manifest action and outcomes.

How the Model Works

The power of the model rests in no small way on its dynamic nature, enabling it to adapt to changing circumstances. The evaluative model provides a more culturally enriched means of shifting practice towards lifeworld by navigating *around* the AGIL media. It can be argued that the lines horizontally and vertically through the AGIL part of the model form actual barriers to navigation. It is not possible to move from a system-dominated

domain into a lifeworld-dominated one just by deciding that it is desirable to do so. That is the purpose of the cycle that runs around the outside of the AGIL functions in Figure 4. If it is desired to move away from the system-dominated domain then the individuals within the system have to be influenced. The private spheres which represent those individuals and their families, work groups, and so forth, have to be modified. Once all the actors have been "privately" influenced the organisation can "go public" through engagement in the public sphere which is when the organisation starts to win back some of the richness of the lifeworld. This is analogous to "winning hearts and minds" in organisational/leadership terms.

Once lifeworld-bias has been achieved care must be taken to guard against accidentally (or deliberately) restricting the physical manifestations of where this lifeworld exists. For example, if an environment where the lifeworld exists is changed, a communal area for example, then the

Figure 4. Evaluative model for information security practice (A representation of Habermas' and Merton's contribution to Parsons' model, showing public and private spheres, system and lifeworld boundaries, and manifest & latent functions)

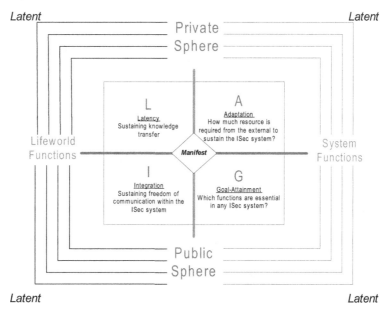

public sphere is being destroyed because people will stop congregating there. The public sphere is a big part of lifeworld. If it is allowed to be colonised then the dependent lifeworld(s) will be too. The manifest vs. latent function idea basically operates when a lifeworld is deliberately colonised (manifest) vs. when it happens by accident because someone has not thought through the consequences or is not paying enough attention (latent).

The point is that decolonisation is not just a simple decision which can be taken by managers. To achieve this in action requires that research is informed from other domains, including organisational culture, management and organisational

theory, change management, boundary theory and so on.

To demonstrate how this model works, it is applied below to BS7799. This task was undertaken as part of the research project in order to provide a benchmark for the domain. Each of the 130 controls in the Standard has been assessed individually against the model, making possible a detailed analysis of the elements of the model explicitly addressed by the Standard. One of the most startling outcomes of this was that only 64 of the 130 controls emerged as relevant to information security, and of this 64, over half (33) are related to goal attainment.

Case Analysis of the Evaluative Model

Clearly, the application of the model to BS7799 raises some interesting questions about information security practice. To consolidate this, further analysis was carried out within a UK local government organisation.

One of the more significant findings of this research has been the clear opportunity to shift the practice towards a more socially-aware lifeworld biased approach. The metaphorical approach taken here was specifically selected as a contrast to the "controls counting" approach used in the review of the British Standard and in the other case studies employed in this research. The enhancement required to the evaluative model surfaced through this empirical research is the addition of representation of what ought to be rather than just what currently is. The addition of this enhancement is also in line with a critically informed study which underpins this research.

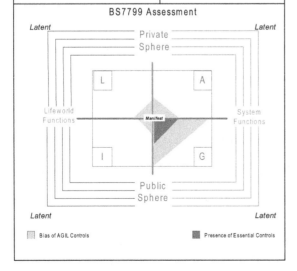

Evaluating BS7799

The evaluation of BS7799 against the model showing how strongly the Standard focuses on goal directed issues. The relevance of this will become clearer as we look at some case examples later in the chapter.

INTERNATIONAL PERSPECTIVE

BS7799 Assessment

Latent — Private Sphere — Latent
L — A
Lifeworld Functions — *Manifest* — System Functions
I — G
Latent — Public Sphere — Latent
Bias of AGIL Controls   Presence of Essential Controls

THE FUTURE: IMPLEMENTING INFORMATION SECURITY BASED ON SOCIAL CONSIDERATIONS

So much for the task of assessing the position of information security in an organisation, but how is

CASE
EXAMPLE

INFORMATION SECURITY IN U.K. LOCAL GOVERNMENT

With some 14,000 staff this organisation is the largest employer in the county in which it is located, providing services such as schools, roads and transport schemes, libraries and care for the most vulnerable in society. Around half of its £500 million annual budget is spent on education and a further quarter on social care.

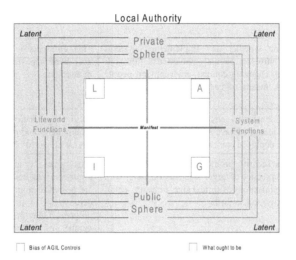

One of the directorates within the organisation provides services to the authority itself such as information technology (IT), human resources and finance. The IT department incorporates the local authority's information security practice which forms the subject of this research.

Unlike the BS7799 analysis, the above result was derived by engaging with participants in the system, using primarily a process of metaphorical exploration. The dotted shading shows participant views of where the organisation was at the time of the analysis, whilst the lined shading is their view of where they ought to be. The 'ought' analysis indicated a significant opportunity for a shift towards lifeworld functions. The Integration function is about co-ordinating relationships within the social system and Latency is about motivating the right behaviours and managing tensions within the social system. How the metaphors worked can be seen in outline from the metaphors which participants felt were best for describing the current situation. Ideas such as the unseen driver, the engine that pushes from the back which is forgotten about by the driver, and the inability to stop the train once it is moving are all highly indicative of system biased functions in general and the Goal-attainment function in particular. The train taking passengers well out of their way is also suggestive of the Adaptation function indicating insufficient resources. This is particularly helpful in terms of moving towards the lifeworld biased functions where an ability to make changes in the route to avoid trouble spots is again suggestive of co-ordinating relationships (amongst passengers), motivating the right behaviours towards a common good and managing tensions within the social system.

The strong bias towards adaptation and goal-attainment controls indicates that the organisation did not consider social issues when developing its security practice and did not create or maintain a broad culture of information security. The organisation is significantly biased towards the adaptation and goal-attainment functions which is in line with the organisation's observed security practice and intent to pursue BS7799 certification.

Table 3. Adapted approach to information security

Number	Step	Comments
1	Assess presence of essential controls. If there are gaps they should be implemented unless good reason not to.	Absence of essential controls puts the organisation at risk of loss of information and access in a way that cannot be addressed through application of sociologically-biased controls.
2	Assess security practice of organisation against evaluative model and create security profile map. Compare this profile with other organisation of similar size, industry sector, complexity, and so forth.	As more organisations are assessed the baseline of organisations' security profiles will grow and provide this additional dimension of analysis.
3	Determine whether any implemented system-biased controls can be easily converted to lifeworld-biased by changing context, environment, people involved, means of capturing feedback, and so forth.	This represents the easiest step to moving the very common goal-attainment focused security practice to a lifeworld focused one.
4	Determine whether any of the lifeworld-biased controls identified have not been implemented but could be deployed reasonably easily.	If an organisation has built its practice around audit requirements and/or functional concerns, it is quite likely that not all lifeworld-biased controls have been implemented.
5	Reassess security profile and compare with the previous practice of target organisation along with other organisations of similar size, industry sector, complexity, and so forth.	This gives a new baseline from which to measure improvements towards a lifeworld-biased approach. There are few measurements available as the practice changes but deployment of lifeworld controls is a useful indicator of progress. Other specific measures such as user satisfaction, number of security incidents, and so forth, should be formulated on a case by case basis. Have regard for the outcomes that are sought by the organisation.
6	Identify neutral (N), counter-productive (C), and other-responsibility (O) controls and eliminate or reassign.	It is critically important that N and C controls are not just dropped and ignored. Careful thought should be given to determine whether they are correctly classified and consideration of whether they are important to some other organisational function (in which case, presumably, they would be reassigned as O). If O controls remain a dependency after they have been reassigned, the dependency must be surfaced and appropriate service levels agreed and documented.
7	Use the action loop through public and private spheres to drive the security practice towards a lifeworld focus	This action step is key to maintaining a focus on both technical and human centred issues throughout the life of an information security system.
8	Reassess security profile and compare with last baseline. Redo action loop at action step 6.	This becomes a long-term (perhaps continual) process to achieve desired outcomes and sustain the required focus.

this to be made use of? Implementation requires a more longitudinal study into the impact of the approach, but initial indications suggest that the procedure outlined in Table 3 is a helpful approach to implementing a security practice based on the findings and use of the evaluative model.

Figure 5 provides some structure to these steps, indicating that the process through these steps should be continuous. It also shows that in terms of priority, getting the essential controls in place is highest priority because failure to do this would most likely undermine the whole security practice irrespective of its social/technical biases. The next priority is to make sure the practice is continually reviewed to ensure it is meeting the means of its users and the businesses. Thirdly, use the evaluative model to identify opportunities to move the practice towards a more socially

Figure 5. Revised framework for applying security practice

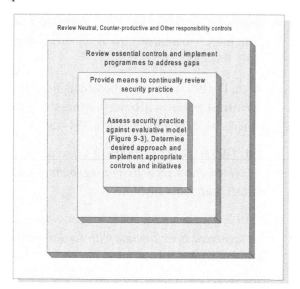

aware, life-world biased approach. Underpinning all of this is the need to identify and deal with neutral, counter-productive, and other-responsibility biased controls. The general ways that these would be dealt with are to remove neutral and counter-productive controls altogether and to reassign other-responsibility to the appropriate department within the organisation but clearly maintain such controls as dependencies for the information security practice.

CONCLUSION

Information security is a domain which has hitherto been dominated by technologically-biased, operationally-focused, pragmatic controls. Deeper research of the domain is revealing a set of largely ignored human considerations, in respect of which methods informed by social theory are proving of value.

The approach adopted in this chapter gains its credibility from an explicit basis in social theory, from which an evaluative model and method of implementation have been crafted.

Shortcomings, derived from the application of the evaluative model, in one of the key standard approaches to information security, and in the application of information security within a large organisation, have further improved our understanding of how strategies can best be derived and managed in this domain.

- Information security is a domain dominated by pragmatic, technology-based methods.
- By acceding to these methods, both the British Standard and industrial practice has favoured a short-term, operationalist approach.
- Human factors are seen as largely external to the information security "system."
- This chapter reports a research study from which has been derived an evaluative model and implementation approach which takes account of human factors by drawing specifically on social theory.
- The outcome is a more human-focused information security, with methods which enable the current status to be determined and improved upon.

This study has focused on what might be termed an evolutionary shift from system-biased controls to lifeworld-biased controls. This shift can best be characterised as a removal of system-biased controls, deployment of lifeworld-biased controls, and a recasting of existing system-biased controls as lifeworld-biased ones.

The evaluative model provides a more culturally enriched means of shifting practice towards lifeworld by navigating *around* the AGIL media. It can be argued that the lines form actual barriers to navigation. It is not possible to move from a system-dominated domain into a lifeworld-dominated one just by deciding that it is desirable to do so. That is the purpose of the cycle that runs around the outside of the AGIL functions. If it is desired to move away from the system-dominated domain then the individuals within the system have to be influenced. The private spheres which represent those individuals and their families, work groups, and so forth, have to be modified. Once all the actors have been "privately" influenced, the organisation can "go public" through engagement in the public sphere which is when the organisation starts to win back some of the richness of the lifeworld. This is analogous to "winning hearts and minds" in organisational/leadership terms.

Once lifeworld-bias has been achieved, care must be taken to guard against accidentally (or deliberately) restricting the physical manifestations of where this lifeworld exists. For example, if an environment where this lifeworld exists is changed, a communal area for example, then the public sphere is being destroyed because people will stop congregating there. The public sphere is a big part of lifeworld. If it is allowed to be colonised then the dependent lifeworld(s) will be too. The manifest vs. latent function idea basically operates when a lifeworld is deliberately colonised (manifest) vs. when it happens by accident because someone has not thought through the consequences or is not paying enough attention (latent).

The point is that decolonisation is not just a simple decision which can be taken by managers. To achieve this in action requires that research is informed from other domains, including organisational culture, management and organisational theory, change management, boundary theory, and so on. Further research informed from these perspectives, within a critical approach would seem to be of value.

REFERENCES

Avison, D. E. (1989). An overview of information systems development methodologies. In R. L. Flood, M. C. Jackson, & P. Keys (Eds.), *Systems prospects: The next ten years of systems research.*(pp. 189-193). New York: Plenum.

Baskerville, R. (1988). *Designing information system security.* Wiley.

Baum, M. (1997). The ABA digital signature guidelines. *Computer Law & Security Report, 13*(6), 457-458.

Birch, D. (1997). The certificate business: Public key infrastructure will be big business. *Computer Law & Security Report, 13*(6), 454-456.

BSI. (1993). *DISC PD0003: A code of practice for information security management.* London: British Standards Institute.

BSI. (2002). BS7799-2:2002. *Information security management. Specification with guidance for use.* British Standards Institute.

BSI. (2003). BS15000-2:2003 *IT service management. Code of practice for service management.* British Standards Institute.

CESG. (1994). *CESG electronic information systems security: System security policies* (Memorandum No.5).

Cooper, J. (1989). *Computer and communications security.* New York: McGraw-Hill.

DOD. (1985). *DoD trusted computer system evaluation criteria (The Orange Book).* (DOD 5200.28-STD). United States Department of Defense.

Drake, P. (2005). *Communicative action in information security systems: An application of social theory in a technical domain.* Hull: University of Hull.

DTI. (2000). *Information security breaches survey 2000: Technical report.* London: Department of Trade & Industry.

DTI. (2002). *Information security breaches survey 2002: Technical report.* London: Department of Trade & Industry.

DTI. (2004). *Information security breaches survey 2004: Technical report.* London: Department of Trade & Industry.

Forrester, T., & Morrison, P. (1994). *Computer ethics*. MIT.

Gollman, D. (1999). *Computer security*. Wiley.

ISO. (2000). *BS ISO/IEC 17799:2000, BS7799-1:2000. Information technology. Code of practice for information security management*. International Standards Organisation.

Killmeyer-Tudor, J. (2000). *Information security architecture: In integrated approach to security in the organisation*. CRC Press.

Kuong, J. (1996). *Client server controls, security and audit (enterprise protection, control, audit, security, risk management and business continuity)*. Masp Consulting Group.

Langford, D. (1995). *Practical computer ethics*. McGraw-Hill.

Leng, T. (1997). Internet regulation in Singapore. *Computer Law & Security Report, 13*(2), 115-119.

Longbough (1996). *Internet security and insecurity*. Management Advisory Publications.

Marx, K., & Engels, F. (1968). *Selected works in one volume*. London: Lawrence & Wishart.

McCauley, J. (1997). Legal ethics and the Internet: A US perspective. *Computer Law & Security Report, 13*(2), 110-114.

Modhvadia, S., Daman, S. et al. (2002). *Engaging the board: Benchmarking information assurance*. Cambridge: Information Assurance Advisory Council.

Neumann, P. (1995). *Computer related risks.*, Addison-Wesley.

Northcutt, S. et al. (2002). *Inside network perimeter security: The definitive guide to firewalls, virtual private networks (VPNs), routers, and intrusion detection systems*. Que.

Peltier, T. (2001). *Information security risk Analysis*. Auerbach.

Russell, D., & Gangemi, G., Sr. (1991). *Computer security basics*. O'Reilley.

Warman, A. (1993). *Computer security within organisations*. MacMillan.

Wright, P. (1993). Computer security in large corporations: Attitudes and practices of CEOs. *Management Decision, 31*(7), 56-60.

Wylder, J. (2003). *Strategic information security*. Auerbach.

ENDNOTE

[1]   CESG is a UK government sponsored body that provides advice to both government and industry on best practice approaches to the delivery of information security.

Chapter VIII
Social and Human Elements of Information Security:
A Case Study

Mahil Carr
Institute for Development and Research in Banking Technology, India

AI can have two purposes. One is to use the power of computers to augment human thinking, just as we use motors to augment human or horse power. Robotics and expert systems are major branches of that. The other is to use a computer's artificial intelligence to understand how humans think. In a humanoid way. If you test your programs not merely by what they can accomplish, but how they accomplish it, they you're really doing cognitive science; you're using AI to understand the human mind.

Herbert Simon

ABSTRACT

This chapter attempts to understand the human and social factors in information security by bringing together three different universes of discourse – philosophy, human behavior and cognitive science. When these elements are combined they unravel a new approach to the design, implementation and operation of secure information systems. A case study of the design of a technological solution to the problem of extension of banking services to remote rural regions is presented and elaborated to highlight human and social issues in information security. It identifies and examines the concept of the 'Other' in information security literature. The final objective is to prevent the 'Other' from emerging and damaging secure systems rather than introducing complex lock and key controls.

INTRODUCTION

Information security falls within the broad category of security. All the while when designing systems, designers employ an underlying model of the "human being" who is either an "attacker," "adversary," "eavesdropper," "enemy," or "opponent," apart from the normal user of a system who is a "beneficiary," "customer," or "user." For the sake of simplicity, let us call the human being who interacts with the information system in the normal, authenticated, and authorized user mode as a legitimate "user." Let us call a human being who interacts with the system performing some illicit operations not within the legitimate framework as the "other." It is important to understand that the same person may switch between different modes from user to the other depending on the context. Most security systems employ a model of the "other" in relation to which the security features of systems are designed.

This chapter focuses on fundamental underlying premises that are implicitly or explicitly employed while constructing secure information systems. This chapter attempts to open the door for a new approach to the study of information security. It examines the human and social factors in information security from the perspective of a model of human behavior and cognitive science. A real world case study is the basis from which insights are drawn from the process of its design (but not actual implementation). We attempt to outline three distinct universes of discourse and frames of reference and try to relate them together. First, we look at the underlying broad philosophical assumptions of security frameworks in general. Second, we choose a model of human behavior from a systems perspective and situate a cognitive science approach within it. Third, we analyze the technical fabrication of information security protocols in the context of human and social factors, drawing insights from a case study. We discuss and highlight issues in providing secure messaging.

The philosophy of security section discusses the reason why at all we need secure systems. Secure systems are products of a particular time, space, and the level of technology currently available in a society. From the nature of humanity we draw the conclusion that all human beings have the potential to create security hazards. However, whether a person is a legitimate user of the system or the "other" (at the individual level) is determined by his or her cognitive (rational) capacities, emotions (affective states), intent (will), spirituality (belief systems adhered to), and the overt behavior of the individual that is expected of him or her. This provides an explanatory framework to understand why individuals who are intelligent opt to undertake malicious activities (e.g., "hackers" and "terrorists"). The social setting in which the individual is embedded to a great extent determines his or her predisposition to choose act the role of "the user" or the "other." The expression of the "collective conscience" of the community to which he or she belong gives sustenance to the emotional basis, the formation of will, the spiritual basis, and specifies public action that is encouraged. Though these particular human and social factors are not treated in depth in this chapter, it points out that these factors have to be studied seriously and an approach should be taken to prevent the emergence and continued presence of the "other" in the social space. This probably is a more secure way of ensuring implementation of security features.

We look at a case study where information security is of key concern in a modern financial system. The case study outlines a design process for remote banking that offers several technical and managerial challenges. The challenge is to be able to extend banking to communities that hitherto have had no experience in banking and to those who are illiterate. This chapter outlines the technical issues that need to be addressed to make remote banking a reality. From this case study, we draw conclusions of how the "other" is present in the design of the project. We have only emphasized and dealt with the cognitive model of the "other" among the several human and social factors involved in providing a secure financial system. We conclude the chapter paving the way for a deeper social science research that needs to the address the problem of the causes of formation of malicious or subversive intent, process of its sustenance, its expression, presence, and persistence. This will enable creation of secure systems.

PHILOSOPHY OF SECURITY

To understand human factors in information security we must have a framework to comprehend both the "human" and "security." Let us first address the question "Why security?" A simple description of the human being and human nature gives us the answer. Human beings are products of nature and interact with nature. Humans have the ability to create or fashion things out of natural material. They have the power to destroy forms and recreate newer forms, for example, they can melt iron, make steel, build edifices, and construct cars and aircrafts. Humans have the power to break and make things. This human potentiality makes them destroyers while at same time being creators (e.g., cutting trees to make furniture). The potential threat while safeguarding an artifact or a possession comes from other humans (and possibly from his or her own self too). A layer of security is therefore necessary to protect an entity from being destroyed accidentally or deliberately. Borders are an essential security feature that preserves the form of an entity and provides an inner secure space ("privacy"). Borders delineate and define distinct spaces. What is within and what is outside. Humans have the capability to break open "security" features (the husk, shell, case, or skin that covers and protects a seed or fruit).

In their quest to attain mastery over the universe, humans have developed tools that are efficient in interacting with nature intimately.

Whenever humans develop a new tool that is technologically advanced than the current level of technology, then the new technology can also be deployed as a weapon. The invention of knives gave rise to swords, dynamite for mining gave rise to grenades, the capability to generate nuclear power gave rise to nuclear weapons, and so on. When a certain technology becomes out of date the weapons also become outdated, for example, we no longer use bows and arrows, swords and even firearms—we no longer witness duels or fencing. Security frameworks of yesteryears are no longer meaningful today—castles and fortresses are no longer strongholds, they have been replaced by different types of defense establishments (e.g., the Windsor castle and many fortresses dotted all over India). Previously, photographing a dam was thought to be a security risk. But with today's satellite capabilities and inter continental ballistic missiles, the information of the location of a dam cannot be kept secret (e.g., Google Earth). The security frameworks of a particular time are contingent upon the level of technology that the society has achieved.

Since humans have the innate potentiality to destroy and consume, if something is to be preserved from destruction then it is necessary to safeguard it with a layer of security. Particularly with respect to information security, one needs to be clear whom you need to protect information from. What are the threats to information security—where does it arise from? The employee, customer, the competitor, or the enemy? Malicious attacks from "hackers" or even from your own self? While constructing systems, it has to be taken into account that:

A human being will exploit a vulnerability in a system, if there is a vulnerability existing in the system, to his or her advantage at cost of the system.

All security frameworks are built with the *other* and the *other's* capability in mind.

HUMAN FACTORS: A BEHAVIORAL MODEL

When we talk about "human" factors that influence information security, we first need to identify and define what we mean by "human" factors. Human factors are taken into account in a wide variety of fields, for example, aeronautics, ergonomics, human-computer interaction, medical science, politics, economics, and so forth. Each of these fields considers human factors from several different aspects. In aviation, human factors mean cognitive fidelity, whole body motion, and physiological stress (Garland, 1999). Ergonomics deals with user interface design, and usability—making products in the workplace more efficient and usable. Anthropometric and physiological characteristics of people and their relationship to workspace and environmental parameters are a few of the human factors taken into consideration in ergonomics. The other factors may include the optimal arrangement of displays and controls, human cognitive and sensory limits, furniture, and lighting design.

We need a model of the "human" in the context of information security. Models provide us with important relationships between variables. Philosophical positions give us a foundation to construct scientific models over empirical data. While scientific models are often reductive in nature (i.e., entities are studied in isolation), systems models study interactions between components. The sum of parts is greater than the whole. The systems model of human behavior gives us a possible basis to identify the sources of threat to information security. Information security cannot be achieved purely from the standpoint of cryptographic algorithms (lock and key mechanisms) alone, but from understanding human behavior and the social context in which humans are embedded (Dhillon, 2007).

The systems model of human behavior identifies three major components of the mind as well as the biological and spiritual underpinnings

(Huitt, 2003). Eysenck (1947), Miller (1991), and Norman (1980) provide empirical support for the three dimensions of mind (or human personality) for example:

1. Cognition (knowing, understanding, thinking—processing, storing, and retrieving information);
2. Affect (attitudes, predispositions, emotions, feelings); and
3. Conation (intentions to act, reasons for doing, and will).

These three components of the mind can be used to address several issues that can arise in the context of information security. An individual's thinking (cognition), feeling (affect), and willingness (volition, conation), as well as overt behavior and spirituality are constituents that interact to give appropriate human responses to stimuli from the environment. A second characteristic of the systems model of human behavior is that human beings do not operate in isolation; they are products of a variety of contexts—environments that surround the individual human being that he or she is in constant interaction play a major role in the individual's responses and interactions with the world (see the next section on social factors for a detailed discussion).

There are therefore five major components of the human being in the systems model of human behavior (Huitt, 2003):

1. **Cognitive component:** Perceives, stores, processes, and retrieves information
2. **Affective component:** Strongly influence perceptions and thoughts before and after they are processed cognitively
3. **Conative component:** The intent of the human actor
4. **Spiritual component:** How humans approach the mysteries of life, how they define and relate to the sacred and the profane

5. **Behavioral system:** Explicit action of the human being and the feedback received from other members of the community.

Of these, the major component that we are concerned with is the cognitive component. We would like to explore this cognitive component from the framework of cognitive science. Briefly, here we will outline how other components are influential in information security. Human emotions, the basis of the affective component is a subject that has been explored in psychology (Huitt, 2003). A variety of emotions impact how humans relate with information systems. Anger, fear, and anxiety are known to influence the adoption and usage of information systems (Athabasca University, 2000), for example, the introduction of computerized systems in the banking industry in India faced organized, stiff resistance during the initial phases as bank employees had apprehensions of threats of job loss and retrenchment (Goodman, 1991). The conative component (human will) determines at what level an individual or a group of people will adopt information technology. The human being can be influenced by cultural factors ("we" and "they"), the religious position he or she has abided by (spirituality), and also the collective memory (social factors) in which he or she has been contextualized.

While this chapter essentially focuses on a cognitive science perspective, it also admits the limitations of cognitive science in general. In this chapter we have taken a limited attempt to study only the cognitive component of the mind as opposed to treating other components such as the affective, the conative, the spiritual, and the overt action of the human being. There are philosophical criticisms raised by Dreyfus (1992) and Searle (1992) to cognitive science. They claim that this approach is fundamentally mistaken in the sense that cognitive perspective does not take into account (Thagard, 2004):

- The *emotion* challenge: Emotions can be the basis for action in human thinking.
- The *consciousness* challenge: The ability to do what is good and what is evil influences the cognitive model of the human being.
- The *world* challenge: The physical environment in which a human being is located influences his or her thought.
- The *body* challenge: Health conditions can determine one's thought patterns.
- The *social* challenge: Human thought is always embedded in symbol, ritual, and myth and is part of a collective conscience.
- The *dynamical systems* challenge: The human mind is a continuous dynamic system, and does not always compute in the traditional sense.
- The *mathematics challenge*: Human thinking is not mathematical—the brain does not compute using numeric quantities will making calculations, for example, the speed at which a human being drives a car is not computed using equations.

The systems model of human behavior does accommodate all the criticisms to a pure cognitive science approach.

SOCIAL FACTORS (SYSTEMS AND ECOSYSTEMS)

Systems cannot be completely understood without understanding the ecosystem within which they are embedded. Human behavior is not merely a function of an individual's cognitive components. There are three levels of ecology that are identified by the systems model of human behavior (Huitt, 2003). Huitt's framework is discussed. The first level of the ecology or the context of human behavior is the micro-system. The family, the local neighborhood, or the community institutions such as the school, religious institutions, and peer groups form part of the micro-system where individual formation occurs. The second level is the meso-system. This influence arises from social institutions or organizations where the human being does work (employment) or obtains pleasure (entertainment). The micro-system institutions filter and mediate the influence of these meso-systems and institutions with which the individual interacts. The third level is the macro-system. The third level of influence relates to the international region or global changes or aspects of culture. Ecological parameters can influence human behavior significantly. The German defeat in the First World War that led to an economic catastrophe leading to the Second World War is a case in point. All human actions of individuals in the German world or the Allied world had to be influenced by the war during the world wars.

The sources of security threats can emerge from the global environment, the meso-system, or the micro-system. An individual's motivation to destroy can emerge from any of these sources. In a context of war between two communities, each may perceive the other as a threat (e.g., world wars). Two organisations may compete against each other for their share of the market (e.g., Microsoft vs. Apple). Families may have animosities with other families (e.g., the Capulets and the Montagues). Therefore, each of these of these ecological levels may strongly impact as to whom the individual treats as the "other."

Cognitive Science and Security

Cognitive science emerged when researchers from several fields studied complex representations and computational procedures of the mind. Cognitive science is the interdisciplinary study of mind and intelligence, embracing philosophy, psychology, artificial intelligence, neuroscience, linguistics, and anthropology (Thagard, 2004). The computational-representational approach to cognitive science has been successful in explaining many aspects of human problem solving, learning, and language use.

Cognitive scientists build computer models based on a study of the nature of intelligence, essentially from a psychological point of view. This helps comprehend what happens in our mind during problem solving, remembering, perceiving, and other psychological processes. AI and cognitive science have been able to formulate the information-processing model of human thinking (Association for the Advancement of Artificial Intelligence, 2007). Rapaport (2000) puts it this way:

The notion that mental states and processes intervene between stimuli and responses sometimes takes the form of a 'computational' metaphor or analogy, which is often used as the identifying mark of contemporary cognitive science: The mind is to the brain as software is to hardware; mental states and processes are (like) computer programs implemented (in the case of humans) in brain states and processes.

Whereas when we talk about human factors in information security, we are primarily interested in the human information processing model. An understanding of human information-processing characteristics is necessary to model the *other's* capability and action. Characteristics of the human as a processor of information include (ACM SIGCHI, 1996):

- Models of cognitive architecture: symbol-system models, connectionist models, engineering models
- Phenomena and theories of memory
- Phenomena and theories of perception
- Phenomena and theories of motor skills
- Phenomena and theories of attention and vigilance
- Phenomena and theories of problem solving
- Phenomena and theories of learning and skill acquisition
- Phenomena and theories of motivation

- Users' conceptual models
- Models of human action

While cognitive science attempts to build a model of the human as an information processor (HIP model), it deals with only one individual unit as its basis. However, the design of security features in information systems design has to take into account two or more processing units as the basis of the model. The technical fabrication of secure systems incorporates a model of the "Other." A careful analysis of the Global Platform (see case study) or EMV standards reveals the process of how the designer attempts to build secure financial information systems where the "attacker" is always present in the scenario. The cognitive model of the "attacker" is the human factor that the system attempts to protect itself against (Fig. 1). The *other's* technical competence is assumed to be equivalent to that of the designer. The destructive capability—the computational-representational model of the "other" is the source of threat for the designer, to protect against whom the designer designs his or her security features.

THE CASE STUDY: FINANCIAL INCLUSION USING INFORMATION TECHNOLOGY

Financial inclusion means extending banking services at an affordable cost to the vast sections of disadvantaged and low-income groups. Financial Inclusion Task Force in the UK has cited three priority areas requiring serious attention: access to banking, access to affordable credit, and access to free face-to-face money advice (Kumar, 2005). The Reserve Bank of India (RBI) has noticed that more than eighty percent of adult rural Indians (245 million, roughly the size of U.S. population) do not hold a bank account (Nair, Sofield, & Mulbagal, 2006). The Reserve Bank of India has mandated that banks extend their outreach taking banking service to the common man (Reserve Bank of India, 2005).

Extending banking to the rural areas where there are no bank branches, consistent power supply, or communication links such as telephones or Internet is a daunting task. This calls for newer approaches in taking banking to remote regions. One solution that RBI has come up with is to enable customers' intermediate banking facilities through business correspondents who act as agents on behalf of banks (Reserve Bank of India, 2006). As law mandates, any transaction on an account involving cash has to be made within the physical premises of the bank. The business correspondents are appointed by the banks and have the authority to accept deposits or make cash payments when customers would like to withdraw or deposit money from or to their accounts at locations other than bank premises.

The experience of microfinance institutions in India while taken into account suggested that cash management is a problem in rural India. The

Figure 1. Cognitive model of the designer of secure information systems

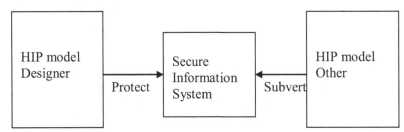

transport of cash is expensive and dangerous. A solution was sought whereby the cash that is available in the villages could be circulated and kept within the region would lead to less security hazards in cash management. Instead of opening full-blown brick and mortar bank branches in remote districts (an expensive proposition), it was proposed that with the help of modern information technology and managerial capabilities of business correspondents, banking functionalities could be extended to remote regions. It is known that information technology solutions to deliver banking services have been able to reduce transaction costs (e.g., ATMs). The business requirements for the proposed solution are outlined. We also discuss in the next section how these requirements could possibly be implemented using information technology as a vehicle.

Business Requirements for the Financial Inclusion Initiative

The basic idea of the financial inclusion initiative is to extend banking services to the un-banked and under-banked rural population. The rural communities that reside in remote regions were the target beneficiaries of the scheme.

Information technology should enable banks to provide services that have the following business requirements:

- Banking services such as deposits, withdrawals, and funds transfer are to be provided.
- Each customer must be identified uniquely by some means especially fingerprints. Biometric authentication using fingerprints proved to be more secure than personal identification number (PIN) based authentication. As most customers are illiterate, they would not be able use PINs to authenticate themselves (in some pilots it was noticed the rural customers who could not keep their PIN secret had written it down on the card itself!).
- Both online and off-line transactions must be possible.
- Balance enquiry and mini-statement showing last ten transactions must be possible at all terminal locations.
- No transaction should be lost in the entire system.

Technical Implementation Issues (Problems and Solutions)

The model solution proposed for the financial inclusion initiative is outlined in Figure 2. Each customer is given a smart card with his primary account number and other personal details such as address, nominee details, and contact information stored within it. The smart cards are to be used at bank terminals owned by banks and operated by business correspondents. The

Figure 2. Model solution for the financial inclusion initiative

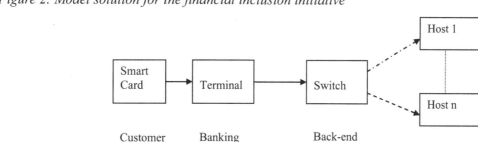

customer is authenticated using the biometric fingerprint of the customer stored in the smart card. These terminals have connectivity through GSM, CDMA, PSTN, or Ethernet depending upon the type of connectivity available at the local place of operation. However connected, the communication finally happens through an IP connectivity to the back-end switch. The network switch connects a particular terminal with an appropriate bank host. All customer details and account information including current balance is held at the bank host. The smart card is used for customer authentication whenever transactions are made at bank terminals. Figure 3 provides an overview of the technological solution to the financial inclusion initiative.

The technical issues addressed in the design of the system:

- The choice of the appropriate smart card (ISO 7816, Global Platform)
- The internal layout and file structure of the smart card (personalization)
- The choice of the terminal (Level 1—EMV certified)
- The communication protocol between the terminal and the smart card (EMV)

Figure 3 Technological solution for financial inclusion—an overview

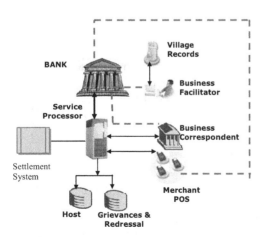

- The communication protocol between the terminal and the switch (ISO 8583)
- The customization of the switch software
- A card management system
- A terminal management system

The Smart Card

Smart cards have been widely used in various sectors such as transport, retail outlets, government, health (insurance), mobile telecom, and in the financial sector. Smart cards come in different flavors with differing operating systems, memory capacities, and processing power (Rankl & Effing, 2003). Smart cards come with different operating systems like MultOS, Payflex, or Java. Certain operating systems are vendor specific. Smart cards differ in terms of the memory capacity that is available within them. There is a tradeoff between the cost and the level of security required. A crypto card that uses public key infrastructure (PKI) offers more security and is relatively more expensive than a smart card that permits only static data authentication.

A wide range of smart card with different memory capacities exist from 8K, 16K, 32K, and 64K. It was a business requirement specification that the customer's fingerprint templates need to be stored in the smart card. Also, since the last 10 transaction details had to be stored within the smart card for balance enquiry and mini-statement, a smart card with as much EEPROM memory as possible was needed. The fingerprint template ranges from half a kilobyte to one kilobyte in size. Considering the storage of templates for four fingers, this would take about four kilobytes of space. A normal, rudimentary software application on the smart card takes about four kilobytes. Therefore, the final choice was a 32K card. Smart cards were specified to adhere to ISO 7816 standards (physical characteristics and cryptographic requirements).

The information contained in the smart card is to be held securely, only to be read and updated using secure symmetric keys. This solution using symmetric keys, though weaker than a PKI solution, was adopted mainly due to cost considerations. A PKI enabled, Europay MasterCard Visa (EMV) compliant cryptographic smart card costs four times as much as a normal card. The affordability of the customer determined the level of security that could be offered. Since the account balances were anticipated to be low—a lock costlier than the value it protects was discarded. A secure access module (SAM) at the terminal provided the necessary computational security to read and access the information in the smart card. Derived keys and diversified keys are used for this purpose (Rankl & Effing, 2003).

Smart cards can contain multiple applications. Global platform is an industry wide standard that provides a layer of management while handling multiple smart card applications. Global platform specifies the security requirements that a card and the application should have while making secure smart card applications. Table 1 samples some of the security requirements that global platform card security specification addresses (GlobalPlatform, 2005).

Corporations such as Visa and MasterCard have built their own EMV standard applications such as Visa Smart Debit/Credit (VSDC) or MChip, respectively. The design issue is whether to adopt one of these applications (with suitable customization) or to build a custom application from scratch. Adopting any of these standard applications has the advantage of worldwide interoperability. But the price is heavy in terms of licensing and royalty fees that the poor rural customer has to bear when every transaction is made.

Table 1. Sample from global platform perception of security threats

1.	High level threats are classified security concerns as: - The manipulation of information on card including modification of data, malfunction of security mechanism, - The disclosure of information on card - The disclosure of information of card as design and construction data.
2.	*The cloning of the functional behavior of the smart card on its ISO command interface is the highest-level security concern in the application context.*
3.	The attacker executes an application without authorization to disclose the Java card system code.
4.	An applet impersonates another application in order to gain illegal access to some resources of the card or with respect to the end user or the terminal.
5.	The attacker modifies the identity of the privileged roles.
6.	An attacker prevents correct operation of the Java card system through consumption of some resources of the card: RAM or NVRAM.
7.	The attacker modifies (part of) the initialization data contained in an application package when the package is transmitted to the card for installation.
8.	An attacker may penetrate on-card security through reuse of a completed (or partially completed) operation by an authorized user.
9.	An attacker may cause a malfunction of TSF by applying environmental stress in order to (1) deactivate or modify security features or functions of the TOE or (2) deactivate or modify security functions of the smart card. This may be achieved by operating the smart card outside the normal operating conditions.
10.	An attacker may exploit information that is leaked from the TOE during usage of the smart card in order to disclose the software behavior and application data handling (TSF data or user data). No direct contact with the smart card internals is required here. Leakage may occur through emanations, variations in power consumption, I/O characteristics, clock frequency, or by changes in processing time requirements. One example is the differential power analysis (DPA).

Issues in Storing Value in the Smart Card

Permitting off-line transactions (as connectivity is poor) require that account balance information be carried within the smart card. The value stored in the cards has to be treated as electronic money or currency. However, apart from technicalities of implementing an electronic purse, there are legal constraints. Electronic currency has not yet been afforded the status of legal tender. Electronic wallets have so far been unsuccessful in the market in Europe (Sahut, 2006).

Certain types of smart cards have an e-purse facility implemented in the card itself. The common electronic purse specifications (CEPS) standard outlines the business requirements, the functional requirements and the technical specifications for implementing e-purses. However, CEPS is considered as a dead standard in the industry. Whenever there is a situation where the value of currency can be written by the terminal onto the card, the security risk dramatically increases. Therefore, the possibility of offering offline transactions as a business requirement had to be compromised.

Issues in Customer Authentication using Biometric Identification

In today's payment systems scenario in India, a normal magnetic stripe card that is used for debit or credit applications. The magnetic stripe card holds the customer's primary account number (PAN), name, and some authentication information (such as enciphered PIN). No account balance information is held in the card. These cards facilitate only online transactions.

The business requirements for this initiative demanded that off-line transactions should be accommodated since connectivity is poor in rural India. This meant that the card needed to carry the account balance to allow offline transaction facilities. Therefore, the option of a smart card was taken. The smart card is to carry biometric (fingerprint) identification details, customer information, and bank account information. However, since the card should also possibly be used with other existing financial networks, a magnetic stripe was also needed in the card (e.g., using the same cards in ATMs apart from the terminals). So a combination of chip and magnetic strip solution was proposed.

The fingerprint template was to be stored in the card so that every time the customer wanted to do a transaction, a fingerprint scanner could extract the image and terminal could compute the template for feature matching. The biometric validation process could either take place at:

- **The card:** The biometric fingerprint template is held within the card. The terminal reads the fingerprint and creates the template. The templates are compared inside the card using the intelligence within the card.
- **The terminal:** The terminal reads the biometric fingerprint and converts it to a template, and it is compared with the template stored read from the smart card into the terminal. Terminals also have memory requirements and limitations.
- **The back-end host:** The back-end stores both the image and the template. The comparison is made with the biometric template stored within the smart card. This solution is costly in terms of telecommunication costs since the fingerprint template needs to be communicated to the back-end host over wired or wireless telecommunication networks for every transaction the customer makes.

The Terminal

The interaction between the card and the terminal is specified in the Europay, MasterCard, and Visa (EMV) standard. The terminal was chosen to be one with Level 1—EMV compliant hardware. The software on the terminal had to be Level 2—EMV compliant software. An EMV Level 2 certification guarantees software on the terminal that is reasonably secure. The software handles the communication between the smart and the terminal communication. The EMV process is discussed in section below.

EMV Standards for Smart Card: Terminal Communication

EMV standard is a specification of a protocol that governs the communication between the terminal and the smart card (EMVCo, 2004). Essentially, terminal verifies whether the card belongs to the acceptable family of cards, the card authenticates whether the terminal is a genuine one, and finally, the cardholder has to be authenticated, that is, whether the cardholder is the one whom he/she claims to be. There are several steps in the EMV process:

1. Initiate application
2. Read application data
3. Data authentication
4. Apply processing restrictions
5. Cardholder verification
6. Terminal action analysis
7. Card action analysis
8. Online/off-line processing decision
9. If online, then issuer authentication and script processing—go to step 11
10. If off-line process the transaction
11. Completion.

Though there are several steps (we will not delve into the details here), we discuss only the process of static data authentication (SDA) as an example of an EMV process. The terminal verifies the legitimacy of the data personalized in the card. This is to detect any unauthorized modification or tampering of the data after personalization of the card (Radu, 2003).

The public key of the certificate authority (CA) is stored in the terminal. The CA signs the public key of the card issuer (e.g., a bank) using the CA's private key and this certificate is stored in the smart card. The issuer uses its private key to digitally sign the static data (those data items that are to be protected from tampering). The signed static data is stored on the card. When the terminal wants to verify the authenticity of the data the following steps are done:

1. The terminal retrieves the certification authority's public key.
2. The public key of the issuer is retrieved from the certificate.
3. Retrieve the signed static data.
4. Separate the static data and its signature (hash result).
5. Apply the indicated hash algorithm (derived from the hash algorithm indicator) to the static data of the previous step to produce the hash result.
6. Compare the calculated hash result from the previous step with the recovered hash result. If they are not the same, SDA has failed. Else SDA is successful.

This procedure verifies whether the card has been tampered with or not. The cardholder verification method (CVM) verifies whether the card belongs to the cardholder or not. Traditionally, the cardholder uses a personal identification number (PIN). In the financial inclusion project it is envisaged to use biometric fingerprint authentication for the CVM.

Terminal: Host Communication

Once the user is authenticated, the terminal communicates with the host to make transactions. The transactions include deposit, withdrawal, and funds transfer or utility payments. ISO 8583 is the protocol that governs this communication between the smart card and the terminal. ISO 8583 defines the message format and communication flows. ISO 8583 defines a common standard for different networks or systems to interact. However, systems or networks rarely directly use ISO 8583 as such. In each implementation context, the standard is adapted for its own use with custom fields and custom usages. In the financial inclusion project, the message arrives in the switch in the EMV format. The message is stripped of EMV formatting and encryption; a customized ISO 8583 message is generated and passed on to the host. The communication between the terminal and the switch happens over the air or over the wire using a telecommunication network. Table 2 provides a small sample of messages.

HUMAN AND SOCIAL FACTORS IN INFORMATION SECURITY

Before outlining the possible abuses of the system by its various participants, it is important to note that in a complex information system as discussed in the case could be compromised by both the insider (personnel who construct and maintain the system) and people who are end users of the system (outsiders). We briefly dwell upon the problem of insider threats before addressing the possible problems created by outsiders to the system.

The Insider

Shaw, Ruby, and Post (1998) identify the sources of threats can emerge from employees (full time and part time), contractors, partners, and consultants in the system. People who are emotionally distressed, disappointed, or disgruntled can be manipulated and recruited to commit damaging acts. Introverts (people who "shy away from the world while extroverts embrace it enthusiastically"—H. J. Eysenck) like intellectual pursuits rather than interpersonal relationships are vulnerable to act destructively. Profiles of possible perpetrators of security threat are people who are socially isolated, computer dependent, and gain emotional stimulation and challenge through breaking security codes consequently beating security professionals. High rates of turnover reduce loyalty of employees to particular organizations. Moreover, computer professionals have weak ethics and they see any unprotected data as fair game for attack. Certain predisposed traits in individuals when exposed to acute, stressful situations produce emotional fallout that leads them to act in ways subverting the system.

A study of illicit cyber activity in the banking and financial sector (United States Secret Service, 2004) reveals that most of the security incidents required very little technical training and skills. In 87% of the cases studied, simple and legitimate user commands were used to create the security incidents and 13% of cases involved slightly more sophistication like writing scripts or creating "logic bombs." About 80% of the users were authorized users. Only few (23%) were employed in technical positions. Most of the system subversion activities were planned in advance by the perpetrators and their intent of the actions were known to other people such as potential beneficiaries, colleagues, friends, and

Table 2. Sample ISO 8583 messages (Source: http://en.wikipedia.org/wiki/ISO_8583)

Message Type Indicator	Type of Request	Usage
0100	Authorization request	Request from a terminal for authorization for a cardholder transaction
0200	Acquirer financial request	Request for funds
0400	Acquirer reversal request	Reverses a transaction
0420	Acquirer reversal advice	Advises that a reversal has taken place

family. Most of the attacks were carried out during normal business hours and at the work place. Revenge, dissatisfaction with company policies, desire for respect, and financial gain were some of the motivating factors identified by the study.

Threats, whether they emerge from inside or outside, whatever be the source of their motivations (the different ecological levels and individual dispositions that influence human behavior), at the point of attack the perpetrator applies logic or a heuristic strategy to make his or her move. Therefore, the designer needs to anticipate the possible scenarios where the system can be compromised. The designer therefore has an anticipated intricate model of the *other's* cognitive thought processes and possible "moves." Against this backdrop, the designer secures the system in the best possible manner (like building a fortress), for example, "bus scrambling"—individual bus lines are not laid out in sequence in a smart card microcontroller, rather they are scrambled so that the potential attacker does not know which bus line is associated with which address bit or function (Rankl & Effing, 2003). In this respect, cognitive science can play a significant role in uncovering, mapping, and addressing the heuristics, the strategies, and the logic employed by potential attackers.

The modern banking system, on the whole, is rather vulnerable as it is heavily dependent and exposed to various consultants and vendors. Vendors take care of security risks within their organizations, for example, smart card manufacturers have to secure the entire process of production of smart card, key management process, transport and distribution process, and card personalization process. The banking electronic system relies heavily on outsourcing certain key functionalities such as database management where "ethical" and regulatory aspects do not govern the interface and interaction. Every time a vendor "opens" a banking database either for maintenance or for troubleshooting, the risks of exposure are quite phenomenal.

We have discussed the technicalities of secure financial transactions that can happen in the financial inclusion project in the earlier section. If there occurs a security breach or incident, either in the authentication process using the smart card or in the interaction between the cardholder and the business correspondent, the entire system will collapse. Any of the human participants in the financial system can attempt to subvert the system—the outsider to the system, the customer, or the business correspondent. We discuss three possible scenarios that could lead to comprising of the financial system.

First, we look at a masquerader who either steals or obtains a smart card that is in use in the project. Second, we look at problems a customer can create when offered facilities for off-line transactions. Third, we consider the case of a dishonest business correspondent who can exploit the illiteracy (vulnerability) of the customer.

The Outsider

The outsider to the system who obtains a card may be able to use the card to his or her advantage. Since the EMV standard does not provide for biometric fingerprint authentication, this has to be incorporated with the cardholder verification method (CVM). In the extreme case, it may be possible for the outsider to alter the biometric of a card and use it to masquerade as the user.

The Other Customer

Secondly, in the case where off-line transactions were to be permitted, the card has to carry financial information such as account balance. The possibility of abuse or misuse by the customer had to be accounted for. The customer could make several offline transactions and claim to loose the card. If the card were to be reissued to customer with balances available at the host (not as yet synchronized with the offline terminal information), then the bank stands to loose financially.

One could not trust the customer not to resort to this avenue.

The Other Banking Correspondent

Thirdly, the problem of dishonest business correspondents (those operating terminals doing transactions on behalf of the bank) came to the fore. Suppose a rural customer who was illiterate would like to withdraw cash from his/her account then the business correspondent can debit a larger value than what was disbursed to the customer. Though a printed receipt would be made available to the customer, since the customer is illiterate this would not be of any practical use. This gives rise to a flaw in the system. This technical loophole could only be overcome with some form of social surveillance as well as taking care to appoint trustworthy business correspondents. A possible administrative solution was to provide a hotline for customer complaints of this kind of system abuse by business correspondents. Once a business correspondent is identified as committing fraud, the bank authorities could take appropriate action.

This financial inclusion project highlights the limitations of approaching information security from the viewpoint of technicalities alone. It requires a solution whereby all the parties involved are bound by ethics as well appropriate social controls (administrative procedures to handle disputes and violations). Human and social factors have to be taken into account to be able to provide a good solution to the problem of remote banking.

CONCLUSION

This chapter attempts to place the human and social elements of information security within a wider context. It discusses some philosophical underpinnings underlying security ventures. The chapter takes the systems model of human behavior as a basis and situates a cognitive science approach within. It discusses the design a real world case of a secure financial system of how it characterizes and accounts for the "other." The design of the technical system is entirely based on the current level of information technology today and how it is employed in a remote banking application scenario.

The source of much of our technical aspects and capabilities (e.g., cryptography) in information security emerged in the historical context of world wars—battling with a real, flesh and blood "enemy." But today systems designers' battles with the "other" in their imagination to construct secure systems. This chapter attempts to outline the need for a broader approach to information security incorporating philosophy, social and cognitive sciences. Security should be approached from first principles. This approach may provide different ways to handle security. The implications for information security may be derived from a general philosophy of security. Since security is essentially a psychological, political, social, and historical phenomenon, there is a need to "model" the human (and the "other") in the frames of references of these sciences. This will better able societies and organizations to understand the source and nature of threats and deal with them at that level, rather than at the level of technical fabrication alone, for example, deep-seated emotional memory wounds of lost battles long ago may stir and motivate a "hacker" or a "terrorist." The philosophical question to address is "How do you prevent the "other" from emerging and operating adversely in the world?" The social and moral fabric of society needs as much attention as the design of security of protocols.

REFERENCES

ACM SIGCHI. (1996). *Curricula for human-computer interaction*. Retrieved March 20, 2007, from http://sigchi.org/cdg/cdg2.html#2_3_3

Association for the Advancement of Artificial Intelligence. (2007). Cognitive science. Retrieved on March 20, 2007, from http://www.aaai.org/AI-Topics/html/cogsci.html

Athabasca University. (2000). *Ergonomics resources.* Retrieved April 17, 2007, from http://scis.athabascau.ca/undergraduate/ergo.htm

Dhillon, G. (2007). *Principles of information systems security: Text and cases.* Danvers: John Wiley & Sons.

EMVCo. (2004). *EMV integrated circuit card specifications for payment systems, Book 2.* Retrieved March 20, 2007, from http://www.emvco.com/

Ericsson, K. A., & Simon, H. A. (1993). *Protocol analysis: Verbal reports as data* (Rev. ed.). Cambridge, MA: The MIT Press.

Eysenck, H. (1947). *Dimensions of personality.* London: Routledge & Kegan Paul.

Garland, D. J., Hopkin, D., & Wise, J. A. (1999). *Handbook of aviation human factors.* Mahwah, NJ: Lawerence Erlbaum Associates.

Global Platform. (2005). *GlobalPlatform smart card security target guidelines.* Retrieved March 20, 2007, from http://www.globalplatform.org/

Goodman, S. (1991). *New technology and banking: Problems and possibilities for developing countries, actor perspective.* University of Lund, Sweden: Research Policy Institute.

Huitt, W. (2003). A systems model of human behavior. *Educational Psychology Interactive.* Valdosta, GA: Valdosta State University. Retrieved March 20, 2007, from http://chiron.valdosta.edu/whuitt/materials/sysmdlo.html

Kumar, K. G. (2005). *Towards financial inclusion.* Retrieved April 16, 2007, from http://www.thehindubusinessline.com/2005/12/13/stories/2005121301240200.htm

Miller, A. (1991). Personality types, learning styles and educational goals. *Educational Psychology, 11*(3-4), 217-238.

Nair, V., Sofield, A., & Mulbagal, V. (2006). *Building a more inclusive financial system in India.* Retrieved on April 16, 2007, from http://www.diamondconsultants.com/PublicSite/ideas/perspectives/downloads/India%20Rural%20Banking_Diamond.pdf

Norman, D. (1980). Twelve issues for cognitive science. *Cognitive Science, 4,* 1-32. [Reprinted in Norman, D. (1981). Twelve issues for cognitive science. In D. Norman (Ed.), *Perspectives on cognitive science* (pp. 265-295). Norwood, NJ: Ablex Publishing Corp.]

Radu, C. (2003). *Implementing electronic card payment systems.* Norwood: Artech House.

Rankl, W., & Effing, W. (2003). *Smart card handbook.* Chichester, England: John Wiley and Sons.

Rapaport. W. J. (2000). Cognitive science. In A. Ralston, E. D. Reilly, & D. Hemmindinger (Eds.), *Encyclopedia of computer science* (4th ed.) (pp. 227-233). New York: Grove's Dictionaries.

Reserve Bank of India. (2005). *RBI announces measures towards promoting financial inclusion.* Retrieved April 16, 2007, from http://www.rbi.org.in/scripts/BS_PressReleaseDisplay.aspx?prid=14069

Reserve Bank of India. (2006). *Financial inclusion by extension of banking services—use of business facilitators and correspondents.* Retrieved April 20, 2007, from http://www.rbi.org.in/scripts/NotificationUser.aspx?Mode=0&Id=2718

Sahut, J. M. (2006). Electronic wallets in danger. *Journal of Internet Banking and Commerce, 11*(2). Retrieved April 16, 2007, from http://www.arraydev.com/commerce/JIBC/2006-08/Jean-Michel_SAHUT.asp

Social and Human Elements of Information Security: A Case Study

Shaw, E. D., Ruby, K. G., & Post, J. M. (1998). The insider threat to information systems. *Security Awareness Bulletin, 2*- 98. Retrieved September 5, 2007, from http://rf-web.tamu.edu/security/sec-guide/Treason/Infosys.htm

United States Secret Service. (2004). *Insider threat study: Illicit cyber activity in the banking and finance sector.* Retrieved September 5, 2007, from http://www.secretservice.gov/ntac_its.shtml

Chapter IX
Effects of Digital Convergence on Social Engineering Attack Channels

Bogdan Hoanca
University of Alaska Anchorage, USA

Kenrick Mock
University of Alaska Anchorage, USA

ABSTRACT

Social engineering refers to the practice of manipulating people to divulge confidential information that can then be used to compromise an information system. In many cases, people, not technology, form the weakest link in the security of an information system. This chapter discusses the problem of social engineering and then examines new social engineering threats that arise as voice, data, and video networks converge. In particular, converged networks give the social engineer multiple channels of attack to influence a user and compromise a system. On the other hand, these networks also support new tools that can help combat social engineering. However, no tool can substitute for educational efforts that make users aware of the problem of social engineering and policies that must be followed to prevent social engineering from occurring.

INTRODUCTION

Businesses spend billions of dollars annually on expensive technology for information systems security, while overlooking one of the most glaring vulnerabilities—their employees and customers (Orgill, 2004; Schneier, 2000). Advances in technology have led to a proliferation of devices and techniques that allow information filtering and encryption to protect valuable information from attackers. At the same time, the proliferation of information systems usage is extending access to more and more of the employees and customers of every organization. The old techniques of social engineering have evolved to embrace the newest technologies, and are increasingly used against this growing pool of users. Because of the widespread use of information systems by users of all technical levels, it is more difficult to ensure that all users are educated about the dangers of social engineering. Moreover, as digital convergence integrates previously separated communications channels, social engineers are taking advantage of these blended channels to reach new victims in new ways.

Social engineering is a term used to describe attacks on information systems using vulnerabilities that involve people. Information systems include hardware, software, data, policies, and people (Kroenke, 2007). Most information security solutions emphasize technology as the key element, in the hope that technological barriers will be able to override weaknesses in the human element. Instead, in most cases, social engineering attacks succeed despite layers of technological protection around information systems.

As technology has evolved, the channels of social engineering remain relatively unchanged. Attackers continue to strike in person, via postal mail, and via telephone, in addition to attacking via e-mail and online. Even though they arrive over the same attack channels, new threats have emerged from the convergence of voice, data, and video. On one hand, attacks can more easily combine several media in a converged environment, as access to the converged network allows access to all media types. On the other hand, attackers can also convert one information channel into another to make it difficult to locate the source of an attack.

As we review these new threats, we will also describe the latest countermeasures and assess their effectiveness. Convergence of voice, data, and video can also help in combating social engineering attacks. One of the most effective countermeasures to social engineering is the continued education of all information systems users, supplemented by policies that enforce good security practices. Another powerful countermeasure is penetration testing, which can be used to evaluate the organization's readiness, but also to motivate users to guard against social engineering attacks (see for example Argonne, 2006).

Throughout this chapter we will mainly use masculine gender pronouns and references to maleness when referring to attackers, because statistically most social engineering attackers tend to be men. As more women have become proficient and interested in using computers, some of the hackers are now female, but the numbers are still small. Nonetheless, there are some striking implications of gender differences in social engineering attacks, and we discuss those differences as appropriate.

SOCIAL ENGINEERING

Social engineering includes any type of attack that exploits the vulnerabilities of human nature. A recent example is the threat of social engineers taking advantage of doors propped open by smokers, in areas where smoking is banned indoors (Jaques, 2007). Social engineers understand human psychology (sometimes only instinctively) sufficiently well to determine what reactions they need to provoke in a potential victim to elicit the information they need. In a recent survey of black hat hackers (hackers inclined to commit computer crimes), social engineering ranked as the third most widely used technique (Wilson, 2007). The survey results indicate that 63% of hackers use social engineering, while 67% use sniffers, 64% use SQL injection, and 53% use cross site scripting.

Social engineering is used so widely because it works well despite the technological barriers deployed by organizations. Social engineers operate in person, over the phone, online, or through a combination of these channels. A report on the

Australian banking industry in *ComputerWorld* claims that social engineering leads to larger losses to the banking industry than armed robbery. Experts estimate these losses to be 2-5% of the revenue, although industry officials decline to comment (Crawford, 2006). Social engineering is also used in corporate and military espionage, and no organization is safe from such attacks. A good overview of social engineering attacks and possible countermeasures can be found on the Microsoft TechNET Web site (TechNET, 2006).

According to Gragg (2003), there are some basic techniques common to most social engineering attacks. Attackers tend to spend time building trust in the target person. They do that by asking or pretending to deliver small favors, sometimes over an extended period of time. Sometimes, the trust building is in fact only familiarity, where no favors are exchanged, but the victim and attacker establish a relationship. Social engineering attacks especially target people or departments whose job descriptions include building trust and relationships (help desks, customer service, etc). In addition to asking for favors, sometimes social engineers pretend to extend favors by first creating a problem, or the appearance of a problem. Next, the social engineers can appear to solve the problem, thus creating in a potential victim both trust and a sense of obligation to reciprocate. They then use this bond to extract confidential information from the victim. Finally, social engineers are experts at data aggregation, often picking disparate bits of data from different sources and integrating the data into a comprehensive, coherent picture that matches their information gathering needs (Stasiukonis, 2006b; Mitnick & Simon, 2002).

Although the description might seem complex, social engineering can be as simple as just asking for information, with a smile. A 2007 survey (Kelly, 2007) showed that 64% of respondents were willing to disclose their password in exchange for chocolate (and a smile). Using "good looking" survey takers at an IT conference led

40% of non-technical attendees and 22% of the technical attendees to reveal their password. Follow up questions, drilling down to whether the password included a pet name or the name of a loved one elicited passwords from another 42% of the technical attendees and 22% of the non-technical ones. While the survey respondents might have felt secure in only giving out passwords, user names were easier to obtain, because the full name and company affiliation of each survey respondent was clearly indicated on their conference badge. An earlier survey cited in the article reported similar statistics in 2004.

Another paper urging organizations to defend against social engineering illustrates the high levels of success of even simple social engineering attacks. Orgill (2004) describes a survey of 33 employees in an organization, where a "researcher" asked questions about user names and passwords. Only one employee of the 33 surveyed escorted the intruder to security. Of the 32 others that took the survey, 81% gave their user name and 60% gave their password. In some departments, all the employees surveyed were willing to give their passwords. In one instance, an employee was reluctant to complete the survey. A manager jokingly told the employee that he would not get a raise the next year unless she completes the survey. At that point, the employee sat down and completed the survey. This is a clear indication that management can have a critical role in the success or failure of social engineering attacks.

Statistically, an attacker needs only one gullible victim to be successful, but the high success rates mentioned above indicate that finding that one victim is very easy. If such "surveys" were to be conducted remotely, without a face to face dialog or even a human voice over the phone, success rates would likely be much lower, but the risks would also be lower for the attacker. Convergence of data, voice, and video allows attackers to take this alternative route, lower risk of detection at the expense of lower success rate. Given the ability to automate some of the attack avenues using converged media, the lower success rate is not much of a drawback. We will show how most social engineering attacks resort to casting a broad net, and making a profit even of extremely low success rates.

The basic tools of the social engineer include strong human emotions. Social engineers aim to create fear, anticipation, surprise, or anger in the victim, as a way to attenuating the victim's ability to think critically. Additionally, information overload is used to mix true and planted information to lead the victim to believe what the social engineer intends. Reciprocation is another strong emotion social engineers use, as we described earlier. Finally, social engineers combine using guilt (that something bad will happen unless the victim cooperates), transfer of responsibility (the social engineer offers to take the blame), and authority (where the social engineer poses as a supervisor or threatens to call in a supervisor). These are basic human emotions used in all social engineering attacks, whether using converged networks or not. This chapter will focus on how attackers use these emotions on a converged network, combining data, voice, and video.

SOCIAL ENGINEERING ON CONVERGED NETWORKS

Social engineering has seen a resurgence in recent years, partly due to the convergence of voice, data, and video, which makes it much easier to attack an organization remotely, using multiple media channels. The proliferation of computer peripherals and of mobile devices, also driven by network convergence, has further opened channels for attacks against organizations. In this section we discuss new attack vectors, combining some of the classical social engineering channels (in person, by phone, by e-mail) and show how they have changed on a converged network.

Social Engineering Attacks Involving Physical Presence

The classical social engineering attack involves a social engineer pretending to be a technical service person or a person in need of help. The attacker physically enters an organization's premises and finds a way to wander through the premises unattended. Once on the premises, the attacker searches for staff ID cards, passwords or confidential files.

Most of the in-person social engineering attacks rely on other information channels to support the in-person attack. Convergence of voice and data networks allows blended attacks once the attacker is within the victim's offices. Before showing up at the company premises, the attacker can forge an e-mail message to legitimize the purpose of the visit; for example, the e-mail might appear to have been sent by a supervisor to announce a pest control visit (applekid, 2007). Alternatively, the attacker might use the phone to call ahead for an appearance of legitimacy. When calling to announce the visit, the attacker can fake the telephone number displayed on the caller ID window (especially when using Voice over IP, Antonopoulos & Knape, 2002).

After entering the premises, an attacker will often try to connect to the organization's local area network to collect user names, passwords, or additional information that could facilitate subsequent stages of the attack. Convergence allows access to all media once the attacker is connected to the network; even copiers now have network connections that a "service technician" could exploit to reach into the organization's network (Stasiukonis, 2006c). Connecting to the company network using the port behind the copier is much less obvious than using a network port in the open. Finally, another powerful attack may involve a social engineer entering the premises just briefly, connecting a wireless access point to the organization's network, and then exploring the network from a safe distance (Stasiukonis, 2007).

This way, the attacker can remain connected to the network, but at the same time minimize the risk of exposure while in the organization's building.

Social Engineering via Email, News, and Instant Messenger

One example of how convergence is changing the information security threats is the increased incidence of attacks using e-mail, HTML, and chat software. This is attractive to attackers, because it bypasses firewalls and allows the attacker to transfer files to and from the victim's computer (Cobb, 2006). The only requirement for such attacks is a good understanding of human weaknesses and the tools of social engineering. The attackers spend their time devising ways to entice the user to open an e-mail, to click on a link or to download a file, instead of spending time breaking through a firewall. One such attack vector propagates via IRC (Internet relay chat) and "chats" with the user, pretending to be a live person, assuring the downloader that it is not a virus, then downloading a shortcut to the client computer that allows the remote attacker to execute it locally (Parizo, 2005).

Because of the wide use of hyperlinked news stories, attacks are beginning to use these links to trigger attacks. In a recent news story (Naraine, 2006b), a brief "teaser" concludes with a link to "read more," which in fact downloads a keylogger by taking advantage of a vulnerability in the browser. This type of attack is in addition to the fully automated attacks that involve only "drive by" URL, where the malicious content is downloaded and executed without any intervention from the user (Naraine, 2006c). Analysis of the code of such automated attacks indicates a common source or a small number of sources, because the code is very similar across multiple different attack sites.

Convergence allows e-mail "bait" to use "hooks" in other applications. For example, an e-mail message with a Microsoft Word attach-ment may take advantage of vulnerability in Word and rely on e-mail as the attack channel (McMillan, 2006). Other vulnerabilities stem from more complex interactions between incompatible operating systems and applications. The recently released Microsoft Vista operating system has vulnerabilities related to the use of non-Microsoft e-mail clients, and requires user "cooperation" (Espiner, 2006). As such, Microsoft views this as a social engineering attack, rather than a bug in the operating system.

Other attacks are purely social engineering, as in the case of e-mail messages with sensationally sounding subject lines, for example, claiming that the USA or Israel have started World War III, or offering views of scantily clad celebrities. While the body of the message is empty, an attachment with a tempting name incites the users to open it. The name might be video.exe, clickhere.exe, readmore.exe, or something similar, and opening the attachment can run any number of dangerous applications on the user's computer (Gaudin, 2007). Other e-mail messages claim that the computer has been infected with a virus and instruct the user to download a "patch" to remove the virus (CERT, 2002). Instead, the "patch" is a Trojan that installs itself on the user's computer. The source of the message can be forged to make it appear that the sender is the IT department or another trusted source.

Finally, another way to exploit news using social engineering techniques is to send targeted messages following real news announcements. An article on silicon.com cites a phishing attack following news of an information leak at Nationwide Building Society, a UK financial institution. Soon after the organization announced the theft of a laptop containing account information for a large number of its customers, an e-mail began circulating, claiming to originate from the organization and directing recipients to verify their information for security reasons (Phishers raise their game, 2006). This is a much more pointed attack than the traditional phishing attacks (described next), where a threatening or cajoling email is sent to a large number of potential victims, in hope that some of them will react. Such targeted attacks are known as "spear phishing."

Phishing

Phishing is a special case of e-mail-based social engineering, which warrants its own section because of its widespread use (APWG, 2007). The first phishing attacks occurred in the mid 1990's and continue to morph as new technologies open new vulnerabilities. The classical phishing attack involves sending users an e-mail instructing them to go to a Web site and provide identifying information "for verification purposes."

Two key weaknesses of the user population make phishing a highly lucrative activity. As a larger percent of the population is using Web browsers to reach confidential information in their daily personal and professional activities, the pool of potential victims is greatly increased. At the same time, the users have an increased sense of confidence in the information systems they use, unmatched by their actual level of awareness and sophistication in recognizing threats.

A survey of computer users found that most users overestimate their ability to detect and combat online threats (Online Safety Study, 2004). A similar situation is probably the case for awareness of and ability to recognize phishing attacks. As phishers' sophistication increases, their ability to duplicate and disguise phishing sites increases, making it increasingly difficult to recognize fakes even by expert users.

More recently, pharming involves DNS attacks to lure users to a fake Web site, even when they enter a URL from a trusted source (from the keyboard or from a favorites list). To mount such an attack, a hacker modifies the local DNS database (a hosts file on the client computer) or one of the DNS servers the user is accessing. The original DNS entry for the IP address corresponding to a site like www.mybank.com is replaced by the IP

address of a phishing site. When the user types www.mybank.com, her computer is directed to the phishing site, even though the browser URL indicates that she is accessing www.mybank.com. Such attacks are much more insidious, because the average user has no way of distinguishing between the fake and the real sites. Such an attack involves a minimal amount of social engineering, although, in many cases, the way the attacker gains access to the DNS database might be based on social engineering methods.

In particular, pharming attacks can rely on converged media, for example, using an "evil twin" access point on a public wireless network. By setting up a rogue access point at a public wireless hotspot and by using the same name as the public access point, an attacker is able to hijack some or all of the wireless traffic though the access point he controls. This way, the attacker can filter all user traffic through his own DNS servers, or more generally, is able to mount any type of man-in-the-middle attack. In general, man-in-the-middle attacks involve the attacker intercepting user credentials as the user is authenticating to a third party Web site and passing on those credentials from the user to the Web site. Having done this, the attacker can now disconnect the user and remain connected to the protected Web site. True to social engineering principles, these types of attacks are targeted at the rich. Evil twin access points are installed in first-class airport lounges, in repair shops specializing in expensive cars, and in other similar areas (Thomson, 2006).

Social Engineering Using Removable Media

In another type of social engineering, storage devices (in particular USB flash drives) might be "planted" with users to trick them into installing malicious software that is able to capture user names and passwords (Stasiukonis, 2006a). This type of attack is based on the fact that users are still gullible enough to use "found" storage devices or to connect to "promotional" storage devices purporting to contain games, news, or other entertainment media. Part of the vulnerability introduced by such removable storage devices is due to the option of modern operating systems to automatically open certain types of files. By simply inserting a storage device with auto run properties, the user can unleash attack vectors that might further compromise their system. In addition to USB flash drives, other memory cards, CDs, and DVDs can support the same type of attack.

Social Engineering via Telephone and Voice Over IP Networks

Using telephone networks has also changed. The basic attack is often still the same, involving a phone call asking for information. Convergence, in particular the widespread use of digitized voice channels, also allow an attacker to change his (usually) voice into a feminine voice (bernz, n.d.), which is more likely to convince a potential victim. Digitally altering one's voice will also allow one attacker to appear as different callers on subsequent telephone calls (Antonopoulos & Knape, 2002). This way, the attacker can gather information on multiple occasions, without raising as much concern as a repeat caller.

The wide availability of voice over IP and the low cost of generating and sending possibly large volumes of voice mail messages also enable new types of attacks. Vishing, or VoIP phishing (Vishing, 2006) is one such type of attack that combines the use of the telephone networks described with automatic data harvesting information systems. This type of attack relies on the fact that credit card companies now require users to enter credit card numbers and other identifying information. Taking advantage of user's acceptance of such practices, vishing attacks set up rogue answering systems that prompt the user for the identifying

information. The call number might be located in a different location than the phone number might indicate.

The use of phone lines is also a way for attackers to bypass some of the remaining inhibitions users have in giving out confidential information on the World Wide Web. While many users are aware of the dangers of providing confidential information on Web sites (even those who appear genuine), telephone networks are more widely trusted than online channels. Taking advantage of this perception in conjunction with the widespread availability of automated voice menus has enabled some attackers to collect credit card information. Naraine (2006a) describes an attack where the victim is instructed via e-mail to verify a credit card number over the phone. The verification request claims to represent a Santa Barbara bank and directs users to call a phone number for verification. The automated answering system uses voice prompts similar to those of legitimate credit card validation, which are familiar to users. Interestingly, the phone system does not identify the bank name, making it possible to reuse the same answering system for simultaneous attacks against multiple financial institutions.

A vishing attack even more sophisticated than the Santa Barbara bank attack targeted users of PayPal (Ryst, 2006). PayPal users were sent an e-mail to verify their account information over the phone. The automated phone system instructed users to enter their credit card number on file with PayPal. The fraudulent system then attempted to verify the number; if an invalid credit card number was entered, the user was directed to enter their information again, bolstering the illusion of a legitimate operation. Although this type of multi-channel attack is not limited to VoIP networks, such networks make the automated phone systems much easier to set up.

As VoIP becomes more prevalent we may begin to see Internet-based attacks previously limited to computers impact our telephone systems (Plewes, 2007). Denial of service attacks can flood the network with spurious traffic, bringing legitimate data and voice traffic to a halt. Spit (spam over Internet telephony) is the VoIP version of e-mail spam which instead clogs up a voice mailbox with unwanted advertisements (perhaps generated by text to speech systems) or vishing attacks. Vulnerabilities in the SIP protocol for VoIP may allow social engineers to intercept, reroute calls, and tamper with calls. Finally, VoIP telephones are Internet devices that may run a variety of services such as HTTP, TFTP, or telnet servers, which may be vulnerable to hacking. Since all of the VoIP phones in an organization are likely identical, a single vulnerability can compromise every phone in the organization.

SOLUTIONS AND COUNTERMEASURES TO SOCIAL ENGINEERING ATTACKS

Following the description of attacks, the chapter now turns to solutions. The first and most important level of defense against social engineering are organizational policies (Gragg, 2003). Setting up and enforcing information security policies gives clear indications to employees on what information can be communicated, under what conditions, and to whom. In a converged network, such policies need to specify appropriate information channels, appropriate means to identify the requester, and appropriate means to document the information transfer. As the attacker is ratcheting up the strong emotions that cajole or threaten the victim into cooperating, strong policies can make an employee more likely to resist threats, feelings of guilt, or a dangerous desire to help.

In addition to deploying strong policies, organizations can use the converged network to search for threats across multiple information channels in real time. In a converged environment, the strong emotions associated with social engineering could be detected over the phone or in an e-mail, and adverse actions could be tracked and stopped

before an attack can succeed. In other words, convergence has the potential to help not just the social engineer, but also the staff in charge of countering such attacks.

Anti-Phishing Techniques

A number of anti-phishing techniques have been proposed to address the growing threat of phishing attacks. Most anti-phishing techniques involve hashing the password either in the user's head (Sobrado & Birget, 2005; Wiedenbeck, Waters, Sobrado, & Birget, 2006), using special browser plugins (Ross, Jackson, Miyake, Boneh, & Mitchell, 2005), using trusted hardware (for example on tokens) or using a combination of special hardware and software (e.g., a cell phone, Parno, 2006).

All the technological solutions mentioned involve a way to hash passwords so that they are not reusable if captured on a phishing site or with a network sniffer. The downfall of all of these schemes is that the user can always be tricked into giving out a password through a different, unhashed channel, allowing the attacker to use the password later on. A good social engineer would be able to just call the victim and ask for the password over the phone. Additionally, even though all these solutions are becoming increasingly user friendly and powerful, they all require additional costs.

Voice Analytics

We discussed earlier the negative implications of VoIP and its associated attacks (vishing). A positive outcome of data and voice convergence in the fight against social engineering is the ability to analyze voice on the fly, in real time as well as on stored digitized voice mail.

Voice analytics (Mohney, 2006) allows caller identification based on voice print, and can also search for keywords, can recognize emotions, and aggregate these information sources statistically with call date and time, duration, and origin. In particular, voice print can provide additional safeguards when caller ID is spoofed. At the same time, given that the social engineer has similar resources in digitally altering her voice, the voice analytics could employ more advanced techniques to thwart such attacks. For example, the caller could be asked to say a sentence in an angry voice or calm voice (to preempt attacks using recorded voice data). Attacks by people who know and avoid "hot" words can be preempted by using a thesaurus to include synonyms.

Blacklisting

Another common technological solution against social engineering is a blacklist of suspicious or unverified sites and persons. This might sound simple, especially given the ease of filtering Web sites, the ease of using voice recognition on digital phone lines, and the ease of using face recognition (for example) in video. However, maintenance of such a list can be problematic. Additionally, social engineers take precautions to disguise Web presence, as well as voice and physical appearance. Even though a converged network may allow an organization to aggregate several information sources to build a profile of an attack or an attacker, the same converged network will also help the social engineer to disperse the clues, to make detection more difficult.

Penetration Testing

Penetration testing is another very effective tool in identifying vulnerabilities, as well as a tool for motivating and educating users. As mentioned earlier, users tend to be overconfident in their ability to handle not just malware, but social engineering attacks as well. By mounting a penetration testing attack, the IT staff can test against an entire range of levels of sophistication in attack.

An exercise performed at Argonne National Labs (Argonne, 2006) involved sending 400

messages inviting employees to click on a link to view photos from an open house event. Such e-mail messages are easily spoofed and could be sent from outside the organization, yet they can be made to seem that they originate within the organization. Of the 400 recipients of the e-mail, 149 clicked on the link and were asked to enter their user name and password to access the photos, and 104 of these employees actually entered their credentials. Because this was an exercise, the employees who submitted credentials were directed to an internal Web site with information about phishing and social engineering.

A more complex and more memorable (for the victims) example of penetration testing was reported on the DarkReading site (Stasiukonis, 2006d). The attacker team used a shopping card to open the secure access door, found and used lab coats to blend in, and connected to the company network at a jack in a conference room. Several employees actually helped the attackers out by answering questions and pointing out directions. As part of the final report, the team made a presentation to the employees, which had a profound educational impact. Six months later, on a follow up penetration testing mission, the team was unable to enter the premises. An employee, who first allowed the attackers to pass through a door she had opened, realized her mistake as soon as she got to her car. She returned, alerted the security staff and confronted the attackers.

Palmer (2001) describes how an organization would locate "ethical hackers" to perform a penetration testing exercise. The penetration testing plan involves common sense questions, about what needs to be protected, against what threats, and using what level of resources (time, money, and effort). A "get out of jail free card" is the contract between the organization initiating the testing and the "ethical hackers" performing the testing. The contract specifies limits to what the testers can do and requirements for confidentiality of information gathered. An important point, often forgotten, is that even if an organization performs a penetration testing exercise and then fixes all the vulnerabilities identified, follow up exercises will be required to assess newly introduced vulnerabilities, improperly fixed vulnerabilities, or additional ones not identified during a previous test. In particular, despite the powerful message penetration testing can convey to potential victims of social engineering, there is always an additional vulnerability a social engineer may exploit, and there is always an employee who has not fully learned the lesson after the previous exercise.

Additionally, social engineering software is available to plan and mount a self-test, similar to the Argonne one reported earlier (Jackson Higgins, 2006a). Intended mainly to test phishing vulnerabilities, the core impact penetration testing tool from Core Security (www.coresecurity.com) allows the IT staff to customize e-mails and to use social engineering considerations with a few mouse clicks (Core Impact, n.d.).

Data Filtering

One application that may address social engineering concerns at the boundary of the corporate network is that proposed by Provilla, Inc. A 2007 Cisco survey identified data leaks as the main concern of IT professionals (Leyden, 2007). Of the 100 professionals polled, 38% were most concerned with theft of information, 33% were most concerned about regulatory compliance, and only 27% were most concerned about virus attacks (down from 55% in 2006). Provilla (www.provilla-inc.com) claims that their DataDNA™ technology allows organizations to prevent information leaks, including identity theft and to maintain compliance. The product scans the network looking for document fingerprints, on "every device...at every port, for all data types," according to the company. The channels listed include USB, IM, Bluetooth, HTTP, FTP, outside email accounts (Hotmail, Gmail, etc). Conceivably, the technology could be extended to include voice over IP

protocols, although these are not mentioned on the company Web site at this time.

Reverse Social Engineering

Another defensive weapon is to turn the tables and use social engineering against attackers (Holz & Raynal, 2006). This technique can be used against less sophisticated attackers, for example, by embedding "call back" code in "toolz" posted on hacker sites. This can alert organizations about the use of such code and about the location of the prospective attacker. Alternatively, the embedded code could erase the hard drive of the person using it—with the understanding that only malevolent hackers would know where to find the code and would attempt to use it.

User Education

Among the tools available against social engineering, we saved arguably the most effective tool for last: educating users. Some of the technologies mentioned in this section have the potential to stop some of the social engineering attacks. Clearly, social engineers also learn about these technologies, and they either find ways to defeat the technologies or ways to circumvent them. Some experts go as far as to say that any "no holds barred" social engineering attack is bound to succeed, given the wide array of tools and the range of vulnerabilities waiting to be exploited. Still, educating users can patch many of these vulnerabilities and is likely to be one of the most cost-effective means to prevent attacks.

We cannot stress enough that user education is only effective when users understand that they can be victims of attacks, no matter how technologically aware they might be. Incidentally, penetration testing may be one of the most powerful learning mechanisms for employees, both during and after the attack. Stasiukonis (2006c) confesses that in 90% of the cases where he and his penetration testing team get caught is when a user decides to make a call to verify the identity of the attackers. The positive feelings of the person "catching the bad guys" and the impact of the news of the attack on the organization are guaranteed to make it a memorable lesson.

Educating the users at all levels is critical. The receptionist of a company is often the first target of social engineering attacks (to get an internal phone directory, to forward a fax or just to chat about who might be on vacation, Mitnick & Simon, 2002). On the other hand, the information security officers are also targeted because of their critical access privileges. An attacker posing as a client of a bank crafted a spoofed e-mail message supposedly to report a phishing attack. When the security officer opened the e-mail he launched an application that took control of the officer's computer (Jackson Higgins, 2006b). A social engineering attack may succeed by taking the path of least resistance, using the least trained user; at the same time, an attack might fail because one of the best trained users happened to notice something suspicious and alerted the IT staff.

Educational efforts often achieve only limited success and education must be an ongoing process. A series of studies by the Treasury Inspector General for Tax Administration (2007) used penetration testing to identify and assess risks, then to evaluate the effectiveness of education. The study found that IRS employees were vulnerable to social engineering even after training in social engineering had been conducted. In 2001, the penetration testers posed as computer support helpdesk representatives in a telephone call to IRS employees and asked the employees to temporarily change their password to one given over the phone. Seventy-one percent of employees complied. Due to this alarming rate, efforts were made to educate employees about the dangers of social engineering. To assess the effectiveness of the training, a similar test was conducted in 2004, and resulted in a response rate of 35%. However, another test in 2007 successfully convinced 60% of employees to change their password. One bright spot is that

of the 40% of employees who were not duped by the social engineers, 50% cited awareness training and e-mail advisories as the reason for protecting their passwords, indicating that user education has the potential for success. In response to the latest study, the IRS is elevating the awareness training and is even emphasizing the need to discipline employees for security violations resulting from negligence or carelessness.

Clearly, user education is not limited to social engineering attacks that take advantage of converged networks. Any social engineering attack is less likely to succeed in an organization where employees are well informed and empowered by well-designed security policies. Education becomes more important on converged networks, to account for the heightened threat level and to allow users to take advantage of the available converged tools that may help prevent attacks.

CONCLUSION

Despite the negative press and despite the negative trends we discussed in this chapter, the good news is that the outlook is positive (Top myths, 2006a). The media is often portraying the situation as "dire" and reporting on a seemingly alarming increase in the number of attacks. For one, the number of users and the number and usage of information systems is increasing steadily. That in itself accounts for a staggering increase in the number of incidents reported. Additionally, the awareness of the general population with respect to information security issues in general and with respect to social engineering in particular is also increasing. The media is responding to this increased interest by focusing more attention on such topics. Surveys indicate that in fact the rate of occurrence of computer crime is actually steady or even decreasing, and that only the public perception and increased usage make computer crime seem to increase. A typical analogy is the seemingly daunting vulnerabilities in Microsoft operating systems, which are in fact only a perceived outcome of the increased usage base and increased attractiveness for attackers (Top myths, 2006b).

Whether the rate of computer crime is increasing or not, social engineering remains a real problem that needs to be continually addressed. Convergence in telecommunications makes it easier for users to access several information channels through a unified interface on one or a small number of productivity devices. This same trend makes it easier for attackers to deploy blended attacks using several information channels to a potential victim, and makes it easier to reach the user through the same converged interface or productivity device. By its nature, convergence means putting all one's eggs in one basket. The only rational security response is to guard the basket really well.

If there is one point we have tried hard to make painfully clear in this chapter, education, rather than technological solutions, appears to be the best answer to the social engineering problem. Users who are aware of attack techniques, who are trained in following safe usage policies, and who are supported by adequate technological safeguards are much more likely to recognize and deflect social engineering attacks than users who rely only on technology for protection.

REFERENCES

Antonopoulos, A. M., & Knape, J. D. (2002). Security in converged networks (featured article). *Internet Telephony, August.* Retrieved April 15, 2007, from http://www.tmcnet.com/it/0802/0802gr.htm

Applekid. (author's name). (2007). *The life of a social engineer.* Retrieved April 15, 2007, from http://www.protokulture.net/?p=79

APWG. (2007). *Phishing activity trends report for the month of February, 2007.* Retrieved April 15, 2007, from http://www.antiphishing.org/reports/apwg_report_february_2007.pdf

Argonne (2006). *Simulated 'social engineering' attack shows need for awareness.* Retrieved April 15, 2007, from http://www.anl.gov/Media_Center/Argonne_News/2006/an061113.htm#story4

bernz (author's name). (n.d.). *The complete social engineering FAQ.* Retrieved April 15, 2007, from http://www.morehouse.org/hin/blckcrwl/hack/soceng.txt

CERT. (2002). *Social engineering attacks via IRC and instant messaging* (CERT® Incident Note IN-2002-03). Retrieved April 15, 2007, from http://www.cert.org/incident_notes/IN-2002-03.html

Cobb, M. (2006). *Latest IM attacks still rely on social engineering.* Retrieved April 15, 2007, from http://searchsecurity.techtarget.com/tip/0,289483,sid14_gci1220612,00.html

CoreImpact. (n.d.). *Core impact overview.* Retrieved April 15, 2007, from http://www.coresecurity.com/?module=ContentMod&action=item&id=32

Crawford, M. (2006). Social engineering replaces guns in today's biggest bank heists. *Computer-World (Australia), May.* Retrieved April 15, 2007, from http://www.computerworld.com.au/index.php/id;736453614

Damle, P. (2002). Social engineering: A tip of the iceberg. *Information Systems Control Journal, 2.* Retrieved April 15, 2007, from http://www.isaca.org/Template.cfm?Section=Home&CONTENTID=17032&TEMPLATE=/ContentManagement/ContentDisplay.cfm

Espiner, T. (2006). Microsoft denies flaw in Vista. *ZDNet UK, December 5.* Retrieved April 15, 2007, from http://www.builderau.com.au/news/soa/Microsoft_denies_flaw_in_Vista/0,339028227,339272533,00.htm?feed=rss

Gaudin, S. (2007). Hackers use Middle East fears to push Trojan attack. *Information Week, April 9*. Retrieved April 15, 2007, from http://www.informationweek.com/windows/showArticle.jhtml?articleID=198900155

Gragg, D. (2003). A multi-level defense against social engineering. *SANS Institute Information Security Reading Room*. Retrieved April 15, 2007, from http://www.sans.org/reading_room/papers/51/920.pdf

Hollows, P. (2005). Hackers are real-time. Are you? *Sarbanes-Oxley Compliance Journal, February 28*. Retrieved April 15, 2007, from http://www.s-ox.com/Feature/detail.cfm?ArticleID=623

Holz, T., & Raynal, F. (2006). Malicious malware: attacking the attackers (part 1), *Security Focus, January 31*. Retrieved April 15, 2007, from http://www.securityfocus.com/print/infocus/1856

Jackson Higgins, K. (2006a). *Phishing your own users*. Retrieved April 26, 2007, from http://www.darkreading.com/document.asp?doc_id=113055

Jackson Higgins, K. (2006b). *Social engineering gets smarter*. Retrieved April 26, 2007, from http://www.darkreading.com/document.asp?doc_id=97382

Jaques, R. (2007). *UK smoking ban opens doors for hackers*. Retrieved April 26, 2007, from http://www.vnunet.com/vnunet/news/2183215/uk-smoking-ban-opens-doors

Kelly, M. (2007). Chocolate the key to uncovering PC passwords. *The Register, April 17*. Retrieved April 26, 2007, from http://www.theregister.co.uk/2007/04/17/chocolate_password_survey/

Leyden, J. (2007). Data theft replaces malware as top security concern. *The Register, April 19*. Retrieved April 19, 2007, from http://www.theregister.co.uk/2007/04/19/security_fears_poll/

McMillan, R. (2006). *Third word exploit released, IDG news service*. Retrieved April 15, 2007, from http://www.techworld.com/applications/news/index.cfm?newsID=7577&pagtype=samechan

Mitnick, K. D., & Simon, W. L. (2002). *The art of deception: Controlling the human element of security*. Indiana: Wiley Publishing, Inc..

Mohney, D. (2006). Defeating social engineering with voice analytics. *Black Hat Briefings*, Las Vegas, August 2-3, 2006. Retrieved April 25, 2007, from http://www.blackhat.com/presentations/bh-usa-06/BH-US-06-Mohney.pdf

Naraine, R. (2006a). Voice phishers dialing for PayPal dollars. *eWeek, July 7*. Retrieved April 15, 2007, from http://www.eweek.com/article2/0,1895,1985966,00.asp

Naraine, R. (2006b). Hackers use BBC news as IE attack lure. *eWeek, March 30*. Retrieved April 15, 2007, from http://www.eweek.com/article2/0,1895,1944579,00.asp

Naraine, R. (2006c). Drive-by IE attacks subside; threat remains. *eWeek, March 27*. Retrieved April 15, 2007, from http://www.eweek.com/article2/0,1895,1943450,00.asp

Online Safety Study. (2004, October). *AOL/NCSA online safety study, conducted by America Online and the National Cyber Security Alliance*. Retrieved April 15, 2007, from http://www.staysafeonline.info/pdf/safety_study_v04.pdf

Orgill, G. L., Romney, G. W., Bailey, M. G., & Orgill, P. M. (2004, October 28-30). The urgency for effective user privacy-education to counter social engineering attacks on secure computer systems. In *Proceedings of the 5th Conference on Information Technology Education CITC5 '04*, Salt Lake City, UT, USA, (pp. 177-181). New York: ACM Press.

Palmer, C. C. (2001). Ethical hacking. *IBM Systems Journal, 40*(3). Retrieved April 15, 2007, from http://www.research.ibm.com/journal/sj/403/palmer.html

Parizo, E. B. (2005). *New bots, worm threaten AIM network*. Retrieved April 25, 2007, from http://searchsecurity.techtarget.com/originalContent/0,289142,sid14_gci1150477,00.html

Parno, B., Kuo, C, & Perrig, A. (2006, February 27-March 2). Phoolproof phishing prevention. In *Proceedings of the 10th International Conference on Financial Cryptography and Data Security*. Anguilla, British West Indies.

Phishers raise their game. (2006). Retrieved April 25, 2007, from http://software.silicon.com/security/0,39024655,39164058,00.htm

Plewes, A. (2007, March). *VoIP threats to watch out for—a primer for all IP telephony users*. Retrieved April 18, 2007, from http://www.silicon.com/silicon/networks/telecoms/0,39024659,39166244,00.htm

Ross, B., Jackson, C., Miyake, N., Boneh, D., & Mitchell, J. C. (2005). Stronger password authentication using browser extensions. In *Proceedings of the 14th Usenix Security Symposium, 2005*.

Ryst, S. (2006, July 11). The phone is the latest phishing rod. *BusinessWeek*.

Schneier, B. (2000). *Secrets and lies*. John Wiley and Sons.

Sobrado, L., & Birget, J.-C. (2005). *Shoulder surfing resistant graphical passwords*. Retrieved April 15, 2007, from http://clam.rutgers.edu/~birget/grPssw/srgp.pdf

Stasiukonis, S. (2006a). *Social engineering, the USB way*. Retrieved April 15, 2007, from http://www.darkreading.com/document.asp?doc_id=95556&WT.svl=column1_1

Stasiukonis, S. (2006b). *How identity theft works*. Retrieved April 15, 2007, from http://www.darkreading.com/document.asp?doc_id=102595

Stasiukonis, S. (2006c). *Banking on security*. Retrieved April 15, 2007, from http://www.darkreading.com/document.asp?doc_id=111503

Stasiukonis, S. (2006d). *Social engineering, the shoppers' way*. Retrieved April 15, 2007, from http://www.darkreading.com/document.asp?doc_id=99347

Stasiukonis, S. (2007). *By hook or by crook*. Retrieved April 15, 2007, from http://www.darkreading.com/document.asp?doc_id=119938

TechNET. (2006). *How to protect insiders from social engineering threats*. Retrieved April 15, 2007, from http://www.microsoft.com/technet/security/midsizebusiness/topics/complianceandpolicies/socialengineeringthreats.mspx

Thomson, I. (2006). 'Evil twin' Wi-Fi hacks target the rich. *iTnews.com.au, November*. Retrieved April 15, 2007, from http://www.itnews.com.au/newsstory.aspx?CIaNID=42673&r=rss

Top myths. (2006a). *The 10 biggest myths of IT security: Myth #1: 'Epidemic' data losses*. Retrieved April 15, 2007, from http://www.darkreading.com/document.asp?doc_id=99291&page_number=2

Top myths. (2006b). *The 10 biggest myths of IT security: Myth #2: Anything but Microsoft*. Retrieved April 15, 2007, from http://www.darkreading.com/document.asp?doc_id=99291&page_number=3

Treasury Inspector General for Tax Administration. (2007). *Employees continue to be susceptible to social engineering attempts that could be used by hackers* (TR 2007-20-107). Retrieved August 18, 2007, from http://www.ustreas.gov/tigta/auditreports/2007reports/200720107fr.pdf

Vishing. (2006). *Secure computing warns of vishing*. Retrieved April 15, 2007, from http://www.darkreading.com/document.asp?doc_id=98732

Wiedenbeck, S., Waters, J., Sobrado, L., & Birget, J. (2006, May 23-26). Design and evaluation of a shoulder-surfing resistant graphical password scheme. In *Proceedings of the Working Conference on Advanced Visual interfaces AVI '06*, Venezia, Italy,(pp. 177-184). ACM Press, New York: ACM Press. http://doi.acm.org/10.1145/11 33265.1133303

Wilson, T. (2007). *Five myths about black hats.* Retrieved April 15, 2007, from http://www.dark-reading.com/document.asp?doc_id=118169

Chapter X
A Social Ontology for Integrating Security and Software Engineering

E. Yu
University of Toronto, Canada

L. Liu
Tsinghua University, China

J. Mylopoulos
University of Toronto, Canada

ABSTRACT

As software becomes more and more entrenched in everyday life in today's society, security looms large as an unsolved problem. Despite advances in security mechanisms and technologies, most software systems in the world remain precarious and vulnerable. There is now widespread recognition that security cannot be achieved by technology alone. All software systems are ultimately embedded in some human social environment. The effectiveness of the system depends very much on the forces in that environment. Yet there are few systematic techniques for treating the social context of security together with technical system design in an integral way. In this chapter, we argue that a social ontology at the core of a requirements engineering process can be the basis for integrating security into a requirements driven software engineering process. We describe the i* agent-oriented modelling framework and show how it can be used to model and reason about security concerns and responses. A smart card example is used to illustrate. Future directions for a social paradigm for security and software engineering are discussed.

INTRODUCTION

It is now widely acknowledged that security cannot be achieved by technological means alone. As more and more of our everyday activities rely on software, we are increasingly vulnerable to lapses in security and deliberate attacks. Despite ongoing advances in security mechanisms and technologies, new attack schemes and exploits continue to emerge and proliferate.

Security is ultimately about relationships among social actors — stakeholders, system users, potential attackers — and the software that are instruments of their actions. Nevertheless, there are few systematic methods and techniques for analyzing and designing social relationships as technical systems alternatives are explored.

Currently, most of the research on secure software engineering methods focuses on the technology level. Yet, to be effective, software security must be treated as originating from high-level business goals that are taken seriously by stakeholders and decision makers making strategic choices about the direction of an organisation. Security interacts with other high-level business goals such as quality of service, costs, time-to-market, evolvability and responsiveness, reputation and competitiveness, and the viability of business models. What is needed is a systematic linkage between the analysis of technical systems design alternatives and an understanding of their implications at the organisational, social level. From an analysis of the goals and relationships among stakeholders, one seeks technical systems solutions that meet stakeholder goals.

In this chapter, we describe the *i** agent-oriented modelling framework and how it can be used to treat security as an integral part of software system requirements engineering. The world is viewed as a network of social actors depending on each other for goals to be achieved, tasks to be performed, and resources to be furnished. Each actor reasons strategically about alternate means for achieving goals, often through relationships with other actors. Security is treated as a high-level goal held by (some) stakeholders that need to be addressed from the earliest stages of system conception. Actors make tradeoffs among competing goals such as functionality, cost, time-to-market, quality of service, as well as security.

The framework offers a set of security requirements analysis facilities to help users, administrators, and designers better understand the various threats and vulnerabilities they face, the countermeasures they can take, and how these can be combined to achieve the desired security results within the broader picture of system design and the business environment. The security analysis process is integrated into the main requirements process, so that security is taken into account from the earliest moment. The technology of smart cards and the environment surrounding its usage provides a good example to illustrate the social ontology of *i**.

In the next section, we review the current challenges in achieving security in software systems, motivating the need for a social ontology. Given that a social modelling and analysis approach is needed, what characteristics should it have? We consider this in the following section. The two subsequent sections describe the ontology of the *i** strategic actors modelling framework and outline a process for analyzing the security issues surrounding a smart card application. The last section reviews several areas of related work and discusses how a social ontology framework can be complementary to these approaches.

BACKGROUND

Despite ongoing advances in security technologies and software quality, new vulnerabilities continue to emerge. It is clear that there can be no perfect security. Security inevitability involves tradeoffs (Schneier, 2003). In practicc, therefore, all one can hope for is "good enough" security (Sandhu, 2003).

But how does one determine what is good enough? Who decides what is good enough? These questions suggest that software and information security cannot be addressed by technical specialists alone. Decisions about security are made ultimately by stakeholders — people who are affected by the outcomes — users, investors, the general public, etc. — because the tradeoffs are about how their lives would be affected. In electronic commerce, consumers decide whether to purchase from a vendor based on the trustworthiness of the vendor's business and security practices. Businesses decide how much and where to invest on security to reduce exposure to a tolerable level. In healthcare, computerized information management can streamline many processes. But e-health will become a reality only if patients and the general public are satisfied that their medical records are protected and secure. Healthcare providers will participate only if liability concerns can be adequately addressed.

Tradeoffs are being made by participants regarding competing interests and priorities. Customers and businesses make judgments about what is adequate security for each type of business, in relation to the benefits derived from online transactions. Patients want their personal and medical information to be kept private, but do not want privacy mechanisms to interfere with the quality of care. In national defense, secrecy is paramount, but can also lead to communication breakdown. In each case, security needs to be interpreted within the context of the social setting, by each stakeholder from his/her viewpoint.

Current approaches to security do not allow these kinds of tradeoffs to be conveyed to system developers to guide design. For example, UML extensions for addressing security (see Chapter I for a review) do not lend themselves well to the modelling of social actors and their concerns about alternate security arrangements, and how they reason about tradeoffs. Access control models can specify policies, but cannot support reasoning about which policies are good for whom and

what alternate policies might be more workable. They cannot explain why certain policies meet with resistance and non-compliance.

Each of the common approaches in security modelling and analysis focuses on selective aspects of security, which are important in their own right, but cannot provide the guidance needed to achieve "good enough" overall security. Most approaches focus on technical aspects, neglecting the social context, which is crucial for achieving effective security in practice. The technical focus is well served by mechanistic ontology (i.e., concepts that are suitable for describing and reasoning about automated machinery — objects, operations, state transitions, etc.). The importance of social context in security suggests that a different set of concepts is needed. From the previous discussion, we propose that the following questions are important for guiding system development in the face of security challenges:

- Who are the players who have an interest in the intended system and its surrounding context? Who would be affected by a change?
- What are their strategic interests? What are their business and personal objectives? What do they want from the system and the other players?
- What are the different ways in which they can achieve what they want?
- How do their interests complement or interfere with each other? How can players achieve what they want despite competing or conflicting interests?
- What opportunities exist for one player to advance its interests at the expense of others? What vulnerabilities exist in the way that each actor envisions achieving its objectives?
- How can one player avoid or prevent its interests from being compromised by others?

These are the kind of questions that can directly engage stakeholders, helping them uncover issues and concerns. Stakeholders need the help of technical specialists to think through these questions, because most strategic objectives are accomplished through technological systems. Stakeholders typically do not know enough about technology possibilities or their implications. Technologists do not know enough about stakeholder interests to make choices for them. In order that stakeholder interests can be clarified, deliberated upon, and conveyed effectively to system developers, a suitable modelling method is needed to enable stakeholders and technologists to jointly explore these questions. The answers to these questions will have direct impact on system development, as they set requirements and guide technical design decisions.

We argue therefore that a social ontology is needed to enable security concerns to become a driving force in software system development. In the next section, we explore the requirements for such a social ontology.

APPROACH

If a treatment of security requires attention to the social context of software systems, can the social analysis be given full weight in a software engineering methodology that is typically dominated by a mechanistic worldview? How can the social modelling be reconciled and integrated with mainstream software modelling?

It turns out that a social paradigm for software system analysis is motivated not only by security concerns, but is consistent with a general shift in the context of software and information systems. The analysis of computers and information systems used to be machine-centric when hardware was the precious resource. The machine was at the centre, defining the human procedures and structures needed to support its proper functioning. Today, hardware and software are commoditized and distributed everywhere. Human practices and imagination determine how hardware and software are put to use, not the other way round. Pervasive networking, wired and wireless, has also contributed to blurring the notion of "system." Computational resources can be dynamically harnessed in ad hoc configurations (e.g., through Web services protocols in service-oriented architectures) to provide end-to-end services for a few moments, then dissolved and reconfigured for another ad hoc engagement. Even computational entities, in today's networked environment, are better viewed as participants in social networks than as fixed components in a system with predefined structure and boundary. Increasingly, the computational services that we desire will not be offered as a single pre-constructed system, but by a conglomeration of interacting services operated by different organisations, possibly drawing on content owned by yet other providers.

The questions raised in the previous section arise naturally from today's open networked environments, even if one were not focusing on security concerns. The relevance of a social ontology is therefore not unique to security. Competing interests and negative forces that interfere with one's objectives are ever present in every organisation and social setting. They are accentuated in an open network environment. In security scenarios, the negative forces are further accentuated as they materialize into full-fledged social structures, involving malicious actors collaborating with other actors, engaging in deliberate attacks, possibly violating conventions, rules, and laws. Security can therefore be seen as covering the more severe forms of a general phenomenon. Competing and conflicting interests are inherent in social worlds. Negative forces do not come only from well identified malicious external agents, but can be present legitimately within one's organisation, among one's associates, and even among the multiple roles that one person may play. It may not be possible to clearly separate security analysis from the analysis of "normal" business. We conclude, therefore, that a social ontology would serve well for "normal" business analysis, recognizing the increasingly "social" nature of software systems and their environments. A social ontology offers a smooth integration of the treatment of normal and security scenarios, as the latter merely refer to one end of a continuum covering positive and negative forces from various actors.

Given this understanding, the social ontology should not be preoccupied with those concepts conventionally associated with security. For example, the concepts of asset, threat, attack, counter-measure are key concepts for security management. In the social ontology we aim to construct, we do not necessarily adopt these as primitive concepts. Instead, the social ontology should aim to be as general as possible, so that the concepts may be equally applicable to positive as well as negative scenarios. The general ontology is then *applied* to security. Special constructs unique to security would be introduced only if the expressiveness of the general constructs is found to be inadequate. The principle of Occam's razor should be applied to minimize the complexity of the ontology. If desired, shorthand notations for common recurring patterns can be defined in terms of the primitives. The premises behind a social ontology are further discussed in Yu (2001a, 2001b).

BASIC CONCEPTS OF THE *i** STRATEGIC MODELLING FRAMEWORK

The *i** framework (Yu, 1993, 1997) proposes an agent oriented approach to requirements engineering centering on the intentional characteristics of the agent. Agents attribute intentional properties such as goals, beliefs, abilities, commitments to each other and reason about strategic relationships. Dependencies give rise to opportunities as well as vulnerabilities. Networks of dependencies are analyzed using a qualitative reasoning approach.

Agents consider alternative configurations of dependencies to assess their strategic positioning in a social context. The name *i** (pronounced eye-star) refers to the concept of multiple, distributed "intentionality."

The framework is used in contexts in which there are multiple parties (or autonomous units) with strategic interests, which may be reinforcing or conflicting in relation to each other. The *i** framework has been applied to business process modelling (Yu, 1993), business redesign (van der Raadt, Gordijn, & Yu, 2005; Yu et al., 2001), requirements engineering (Yu, 1997), architecture modelling (Gross & Yu, 2001), COTS selection (Franch & Maiden, 2003), as well as to information systems security.

There are three main categories of concepts: actors, intentional elements, and intentional links. The framework includes a strategic dependency (SD) model — for describing the network of relationships among actors, and a strategic rationale (SR) model — for describing and supporting the reasoning that each actor has about its relationships with other actors.

Actor

In *i**, an *actor* (◯) is used to refer generically to any unit to which intentional dependencies can be ascribed. An actor is an active entity that carries out actions to achieve its goals by exercising means-ends knowledge. It is an encapsulation of intentionally, rationality and autonomy. Graphically, an actor is represented as a circle, and may optionally have a dotted boundary, with intentional elements inside.

Intentional Elements: Goal, Softgoal, Task, Resource and Belief

The intentional elements in *i** are goal, task, softgoal, resource and belief. A goal (⬭) is a condition or state of affairs in the world that the stakeholders would like to achieve. A goal can be achieved in different ways, prompting alternatives to be considered. A goal can be a business goal or a system goal. Business goals are about the business or state of the affairs the individual or organisation wishes to achieve in the world. System goals are about what the target system should achieve, which, generally, describe the functional requirements of the target system. In the *i** graphical representation, goals are represented as a rounded rectangle with the goal name inside.

A *softgoal* (⬭) is typically a quality (or non-functional) attribute on one of the other intentional elements. A softgoal is similar to a (hard) goal except that the criteria for whether a softgoal is achieved are not clear-cut and *a priori*. It is up to the developer to judge whether a particular state of affairs in fact sufficiently achieves the stated softgoal. Non-functional requirements, such as performance, security, accuracy, reusability, interoperability, time to market and cost are often crucial for the success of a system. In *i**, non-functional requirements are represented as softgoals and addressed as early as possible in the software lifecycle. They should be properly modelled and addressed in design reasoning before a commitment is made to a specific design choice. In the *i** graphical representation, a softgoal is shown as an irregular curvilinear shape.

*Task*s (⬡) are used to represent the specific procedures to be performed by agents, which specifies a particular way of doing something. It may be decomposed into a combination of sub-goals, subtasks, resources, and softgoals. These sub-components specify a particular course of action while still allowing some freedom. Tasks are used to incrementally specify and refine solutions in the target system. They are used to achieve goals or to "operationalize" softgoals. These solutions provide operations, processes, data representations, structuring, constraints, and agents in the target system to meet the needs stated in the goals and softgoals. Tasks are represented graphically as a hexagon.

A *resource* (▭) is a physical or informational entity, which may serve some purpose. From the viewpoint of intentional analysis, the main concern with a resource is whether it is available. Resources are shown graphically as rectangles.

The *belief* (◯) construct is used to represent domain characteristics, design assumptions and relevant environmental conditions. It allows domain characteristics to be considered and properly reflected in the decision making process, hence facilitating later review, justification, and change of the system, as well as enhancing traceability. Beliefs are shown as ellipses in *i** graphical notation.

Strategic Dependency Model

A strategic dependency (SD) model consists of a set of nodes and links. Each node represents an actor, and each link between two actors indicates that one actor depends on the other for something in order that the former may attain some goal. We call the depending actor the *depender*, and the actor who is depended upon the *dependee*. The object around which the dependency relationship centers is called the *dependum*. By depending on another actor for a dependum, an actor (the depender) is able to achieve goals that it was not able to without the dependency, or not as easily or as well. At the same time, the depender becomes vulnerable. If the dependee fails to deliver the dependum, the depender would be adversely affected in its ability to achieve its goals. A *dependency* link (——Đ——) is used to describe such an inter-actor relationship. Dependency types are used to differentiate the kinds of freedom allowed in a relationship.

In a *goal dependency*, an actor depends on another to make a condition in the world come true. Because only an end state or outcome is specified, the dependee is given the freedom to choose how to achieve it.

In a *task dependency*, an actor depends on another to perform an activity. The depender's goal for having the activity performed is not given. The activity description specifies a particular course of action. A task dependency specifies standard procedures, indicates the steps to be taken by the dependee.

In a *resource dependency*, an actor depends on another for the availability of an entity. The depender takes the availability of the resource to be unproblematic.

The fourth type of dependency, *softgoal dependency*, is a variant of the goal dependency. It is different in that there are no *a priori*, cut-and-dry criteria for what constitutes meeting the goal. The meaning of a softgoal is elaborated in terms of the methods that are chosen in the course of pursuing the goal. The dependee contributes to the identification of alternatives, but the decision is taken by the depender. The notion of the softgoal allows the model to deal with many of the usually informal concepts. For example, a service provider's dependency on his customer for continued business can be achieved in different ways. The desired style of continued business is ultimately decided by the depender. The customer's softgoal dependency on the service provider for "keep personal information confidential" indicates that there is not a clear-cut criterion for the achievement of confidentiality.

The four types of dependencies reflect different levels of freedom that is allowed in the relationship between depender and dependee.

Figure 1 shows a SD model for a generic smart card-based payment system involving six actors. This example is adapted from Yu and Liu (2001). A Card Holder depends on a Card Issuer to be allocated a smart card. The Terminal Owner depends on Card Holder to present the card for each transaction. The Card Issuer in turn depends on the Card Manufacturer and Software Manufacturer to provide cards, devices, and software. The Data Owner is the one who has control of the data within the card. He depends on the Terminal Owner to submit transaction information to the central database. In each case, the dependency means that the depender actor depends on the dependee actor for something in order to achieve some (internal) goal.

The goal dependency New Account Be Created from the Card Issuer to the Data Owner means that it is up to the Data Owner to decide how to create a new account. The Card Issuer does not care how a new account is created; what matters is that, for each card, an account should be created. The Card Issuer depends on the Card Holder to apply for a card via a task dependency by specifying standard application procedures.

Figure 1. Strategic dependency model of a generic smart card system

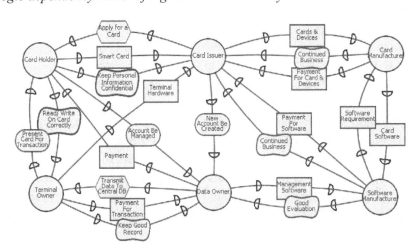

If the Card Issuer were to indicate the steps for the Data Owner to create a new account, then the Data Owner would be related to the Card Issuer by a task dependency instead.

The Card Issuer's dependencies on the Card Manufacturer for cards and devices, the manufacturer's dependencies on Card Issuer for payment are modelled as resource dependencies. Here the depender takes the availability of the resource to be unproblematic.

The Card Holder's softgoal dependency on the Card Issuer for Keep Personal Information Confidential indicates that there is not a clear-cut criterion for the achievement of confidentiality. In the Manufacturer's softgoal dependency on Card Issuer, Continued Business could be achieved in different ways. The desired style of continued business is ultimately decided by the depender.

The strategic dependency model of Figure 1 is not meant to be a complete and accurate description of any particular smart card system. It is intended only for illustrating the modelling features of *i**.

In conventional software systems modelling, the focus is on information flows and exchanges — what messages actors or system components send to each other. With the social ontology of *i**, the focus is on intentional relationships — what are the actors' expectations and constraints on each other. Since actors are intentional, strategic, and have autonomy, they reflect on their relationships with other actors. If these relationships are unsatisfactory, they will seek alternative ways of associating with others.

Security concerns arise naturally from this perspective. A social ontology therefore provides a way to integrate security into software system engineering from the earliest stages of conception, and at a high level of abstraction.

Intentional Links

Dependencies are intentional relationships between actors. Within each actor, we model intentional relationships in terms of means-ends, decomposition, contribution, and correlation links.

- **Means-ends** links (—▷—) are used to describe how goals can be achieved. Each task connected to a goal by a means-ends link is one possible way of achieving the goal.
- **Decomposition** links (——┼) define the sub-elements of a task, which can include sub-tasks, sub-goals, resources, and softgoals. The softgoals indicate the desired qualities that are considered to be part of the task. The sub-tasks may in turn have decomposition links that lead to further sub-elements. Sub-goals indicate the possibility of alternate means of achievement, with means-ends links leading to tasks.
- A **contribution** link (→) describes the qualitative impact that one element has on another. A contribution can be negative or positive. The extent of contribution is judged to be partial or sufficient based on Simon's concept of satisficing (Simon, 1996), as in the NFR framework (Chung, Nixon, Yu, & Mylopoulos, 2000). Accordingly, contribution link types include: *help* (positive and partial), *make* (positive and sufficient), *hurt* (negative and partial), *break* (negative and sufficient), *some+* (positive of unknown extent), *some-* (negative of unknown extent). *Correlation* links (dashed arrows) are used to express contributions from one element to other elements that are not explicitly sought, but are side effects.

Strategic Rationale Model

The strategic rationale (SR) model provides a detailed level of modelling by looking "inside" actors to model internal intentional relationships. Intentional elements (goals, tasks, resources, and softgoals) appear in SR models not only as external dependencies, but also as internal ele-

Figure 2. Strategic rationale model of card manufacturer

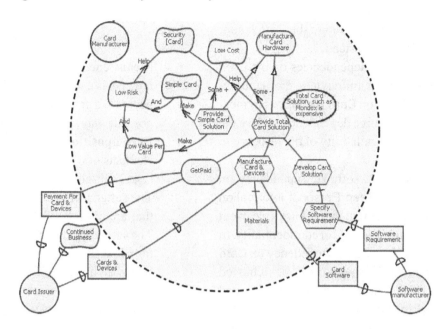

ments arranged into a predominantly hierarchical structure of means-ends, task-decompositions and contribution relationships.

The SR model in Figure 2 elaborates on the rationale of a Card Manufacturer. The Card Manufacturer's business objective Manufacture Card Hardware is modeled as a "hard" functional goal (top right corner). Quality requirements such as Security and Low Cost are represented as softgoals. The different means for accomplishing the goal are modeled as tasks. The task Provide Total Card Solution can be further decomposed into three sub-components (connected with task-decomposition links): sub-goal of Get Paid, sub-task Develop Card Solution, and sub-task Manufacture Card & Devices. To perform the task Manufacture Card & Devices, the availability of Materials need to be taken into consideration, which is modeled as a resource.

In the model, task node Provide Simple Card Solution (such as the Millicent solution), and Provide Total Card Solution (such as the Mondex solution) are connected to the goal with means-ends links. This goal will be satisfied if any of these tasks is satisfied. Provide Total Card Solution will help the Security of the system (represented with a *Help* contribution link to *Security*), while Provide Simple Card Solution is considered to have no significant impact on security if it is applied to cards with small monetary value. The Simple Card Solution is good for the goal of Low Cost whereas the Total Card Solution is bad. This is supported by the belief that "Total Card Solution, such as Mondex, is expensive." Beliefs are usually used to represent such domain properties, or design assumption or environmental condition, so that traceability of evidence of design decision could be explicitly maintained with the model.

During system analysis and design, softgoals such as Low Cost and Security [card] are systematically refined until they can be operationalized and implemented. Unlike functional goals, nonfunctional qualities represented as softgoals frequently interact or interfere with each other, so the graph of contributions is usually not a strict tree structure (Chung et al., 2000).

Agents, Roles, and Positions

To model complex relationships among social actors, we further define the concepts of agents, roles, and positions, each of which is an actor, but in a more specialized sense.

A *role* ( ) is an abstract actor embodying expectations and responsibilities. It is an abstract characterization of the behavior of a social actor within some specialized context or domain of endeavor. An *agent* ( ) is a concrete actor with physical manifestations, human or machine, with specific capabilities and functionalities. A set of roles packaged together to be assigned to an agent is called a position. A *position* ( ) is intermediate in abstraction between a role and an agent, which often has an organisational flavor. Positions can COVER roles. Agents can OCCUPY positions. An agent can PLAY one or more roles directly. The INS construct is used to represent the instance-and-class relation. The ISA construct is used to express conceptual generalization/specialization. Initially, human actors representing stakeholders in the domain are identified together with existing machine actors. As the analysis proceeds, more actors are identified, including new system agents, when certain design choices have been made, and new functional entities are added.

Figure 3 shows some actors in the domain. At the top, six generic abstract roles are identified, including the Card Holder, the Terminal Owner, the Data Owner, the Card Issuer, the Card Manufac-turer, and the Software Manufacturer. These actors are modeled as roles since they represent abstractions of responsibilities and functional units of the business model. Then concrete agents in smart card systems are identified. For instance, actors in a Digital Stored Value Card system include Customer, Merchant, Subcontractor Company, and their instances. These agents can play one or more roles in different smart card systems. Here, Financial Institution is modeled as a position that bridges the multiple abstract roles it covers, and the real world agents occupying it. Initially, human/organisational actors are identified together with existing machine actors. As the requirements analysis proceeds, more actors could be added in, including new system agents such as security monitoring system, counter-forgery system, etc., when certain design choices have been made, and new functional entities are added.

An *agent* is an actor with concrete, physical manifestations, such as a human individual. An agent has dependencies that apply regardless of what role he/she/it happens to be playing. For example, in Figure 3, if Jerry, a Card Holder desires a good credit record, he wants the credit record to go towards his personal self, not to the positions and abstract roles that Jerry might occupy or play. We use the term agent instead of person for generality, so that it can be used to refer to human as well as artificial (hardware, software, or organisational) agents. Customer and Merchant are represented as agent classes and groups. De-

Figure 3. Actor hierarchy (roles, positions, and agents) in a smart card system

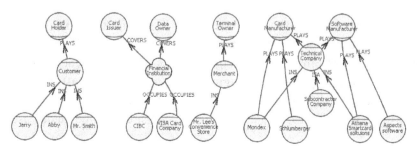

pendencies are associated with a role when these dependencies apply regardless of who plays the role. For example, we consider Card Holder an abstract role that agents can play. The objective of obtaining possession of the card, and deciding when and whether to use it, are associated with the role, no matter who plays the role.

The INS construct represents the instance-and-class relation. For example, Mr. Lee's Convenience Store is an instance of Merchant, and Jerry is an instance of Customer. The ISA construct expresses conceptual generalization/ specialization. For example, a Subcontractor Company is a kind of Technical Company. These constructs are used to simplify the presentation of strategic models with roles, positions, and agents. There can be dependencies from an agent to the role it plays. For example, a Merchant who plays the role of Terminal owner may depend on that role to attract more customers. Otherwise, he may choose not to play that role.

Roles, positions, and agents can each have subparts. In general, aggregate actors are not compositional with respect to intentional properties. Each actor, regardless of whether it has parts, or is part of a larger whole, is taken to be intentional. Each actor has inherent freedom and is therefore ultimately unpredictable. There can be intentional dependencies between the whole and its parts (e.g., a dependency by the whole on its parts to maintain unity).

DOMAIN REQUIREMENTS ANALYSIS WITH *i**

We now illustrate how the social ontology of *i** allows security issues to be identified and addressed early in the requirements process. We continue with the example of smart card systems design. Security in smart card systems is a challenging task due to the fact that different aspects of the system are not under a single trust boundary. Re-

sponsibilities are split among multiple parties. The processor, I/O, data, programs, and network may be controlled by different, and potentially hostile, parties. By discussing the security ramifications of different ways of splitting responsibilities, we aim to show how the proposed modelling framework can help produce a proper understanding of the security systems that employ smart cards. Figure 4 shows the basic steps to take during the process of domain requirements analysis with *i**, before we consider security. The process can be organised into the following iterative steps.

Actor Identification

In step (1), the question "who is involved in the system?" will be answered. According to the definition given above, we know that all intentional units may be represented as actors. For example, in any smart card based systems, there are many parties involved. An actor hierarchy composed of roles, positions, and agents such as the ones in Figure 3 is created.

Goal/Task Identification

In the step (2) of the requirements analysis process, the question "what does the actor want to achieve?" will be answered. As shown in the strategic rationale (SR) model of Figure 2, answers to this question can be represented as goals capturing the high-level objectives of agents. During system analysis and design, softgoals such as low cost and security are systematically refined until they can be operationalized and implemented. Using the SR model, we can reason about each alternative's contributions to high-level non-functional quality requirements including security, and possible tradeoffs.

The refinements of goals, tasks and softgoals (step (3) in Figure 4) are considered to have reached an adequate level once all the necessary design decisions can be made based on the existing in-

Figure 4. Requirements elicitation process with i*

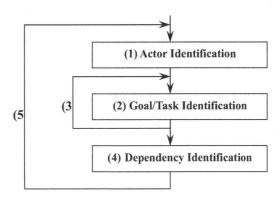

formation in the model. The SR model in Figure 3 was created by running through steps (1), (2), (3) in Figure 4 iteratively.

Strategic Dependency Identification

In the step (4) of the requirements analysis process, the question "how do the actors relate to each other?" will be answered. Figure 1 shows the SD model for a generic smart card-based payment system. By analyzing the dependency network in a Strategic Dependency model, we can reason about opportunities and vulnerabilities. A Strategic Dependency model can be obtained by hiding the internal rationales of actors in a Strategic Rationale model. Thus, the goal, task, resource, softgoal dependencies in a Strategic Dependency model can be seen as originating from SR models.

The kinds of analysis shown above answers questions such as "who is involved in the system? What do they want? How can their expectations be fulfilled? And what are the inter-dependencies between them?" These answers initially provide a sketch of the social setting of the future system, and eventually result in a fairly elaborate behavioral model where certain design choices have already been made. However, another set of very

important questions has yet to be answered (i.e., what if things go wrong)? What if some party involved in the smart card system does not behave as expected? How bad can things get? What prevention tactics can be considered?" These are exactly the questions we want to answer in the security requirements analysis.

SECURITY REQUIREMENTS ANALYSIS WITH *i**

We now extend the process to include attacker analysis, vulnerability analysis, and countermeasure analysis. The dashed lines and boxes on the right hand side of Figure 5 indicate a series of analysis steps to deal with security. These steps are integrated into the basic domain requirements engineering process, such that threats from potential attackers are anticipated and countermeasures for system protection are sought and equipped wherever necessary. Each of the security related analysis steps (step [1] to [7]) will be discussed in detail in the following subsections.

Figure 5. Security requirements elicitation process with **i***

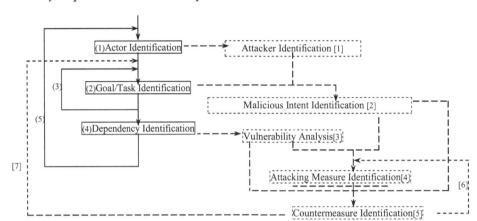

Figure 6. Modelling attackers in strategic actors model

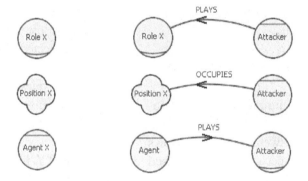

Attacker Analysis

The attacker analysis steps aim to identify potential system abusers and their malicious intents. The basic premise here is that all the actors are assumed "guilty until proven innocent." In other words, given the result of the basic *i** requirements modelling process, we now consider any one of the actors (roles, positions, or agents) identified so far can be a potential attacker to the system or to other actors. For example, we want to ask, "In what ways can a terminal owner attack the system? How will he benefit from inappropriate manipulation of the card reader, or transaction data?"

In this analysis, each actor is considered in turn as an attacker. This attacker inherits the intentions, capabilities, and social relationships of the corresponding legitimate actor (i.e., the internal goal hierarchy and external dependency relationships in the model). This may serve as a starting point of a forward direction security analysis (step [1] in Figure 5). A backward analysis starting from identifying possible malicious intents and valuable business assets can also be done.

Proceeding to step [2] of the process, for each attacker identified, we combine the capabilities and interests of the attacker with those of the legitimate actor. For simplicity, we assume that an attacker may be modeled as a role or an agent.

To perform the attacker analysis, we consider that each role may be played by an attacker agent, each position may be occupied by an attacker agent, and that each agent may play an attacker role (Figure 6). The analysis would then reveal the commandeering of legitimate resources and capabilities for illicit use. The intents and strategies of the attackers are explicitly represented and reasoned about in the models.

This approach treats all attackers as insider attackers, as attacks are via associations with normal actors. We set a system boundary, then exhaustively search for possible attackers. Random attackers such as Internet hackers/crackers, or attackers breaking into a building can also be dealt with by being represented as sharing the same territory with their victim. By conducting analysis on the infrastructure of the Internet, we may identify attackers by treating Internet resources as resources in the *i** model. By conducting building security analysis, break-in attackers, or attackers sharing the same workspace can be identified. Alternatively, we could adopt an opposite assumption, i.e., assume there is a trusted perimeter for each agent, all the potential threat sources within this trusted perimeter are ignored, measures will only be taken to deal with threats from outside of the perimeter.

As shown in the Strategic Rationale model in Figure 7, the motives of Attacker in the smart card system may be modeled as intentional elements

in an i* model. An attacker may be motivated by financial incentives (softgoal Be Profitable), or by non-financial ones (e.g., Desire for Notoriety). These malicious intents may lead to various attack strategies, such as Financial Theft, Impersonation Attack, Gain Unauthorized Access, Attack on Privacy, and Publicity Attack.

Dependency Vulnerability Analysis

Dependency vulnerability analysis aims at identifying the vulnerable points in the dependency network (step [3] in Figure 5). A dependency relationship makes the depender inherently vulnerable. Potential attackers may exploit these vulnerabilities to actually attack the system, so that their malicious intents can be served. *i** dependency modelling allows a more specific vulnerability analysis because the potential failure of each dependency can be traced to a depender and to *its* dependers. The questions we want to answer here are "which dependency relationships are vulnerable to attack?", "What are the chain effects if one dependency link is compromised?" The analysis of dependency vulnerabilities does not end with the identification of potential vulnerable points. We need to trace upstream in the dependency network, and see whether the attacked dependency relationship impacts other actors in the network.

Figure 7. Motives of attacker in a smart card system

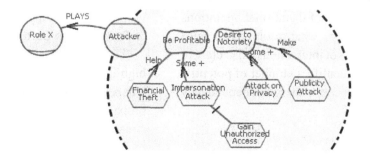

Figure 8. Dependencies (in other words, vulnerable points) in a smart card system

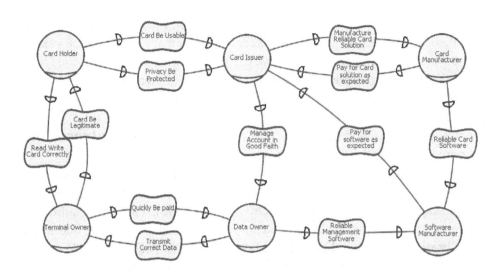

Figure 8 is a simplified version of the SD model of Figure 4, showing only the softgoal dependencies. We assume that each of the actors in the SD model can be a potential attacker. And as an attacker, an actor will fail to deliver the expected dependencies directed to it, of whom it is the dependee.

For instance, the Card Holder depends on the Terminal Owner to Read/Write Card Correctly. To analyze the vulnerability arising from this dependency, we consider the case where the terminal owner is not trustworthy. And we try to identify the potential attacks by answering question of "In what possible ways could the attacker break this dependency relationship?" To do this, we elaborate on the agent Attacker Playing Terminal Owner. Starting from attacker's potential motivations, we refine the high-level goals of the attackers (and possible attack routes) based on analysis of the SD and SR models of the normal operations of the smart card (e.g., what resources an actor accesses, what types of interactions exist, etc.). In this way, we may identify a number of potential attacks that are sufficient to make this dependency not viable (*Break*).

Proceeding to step [4], we now focus on how an attacker may attack the vulnerable points identified above by exploring the attacker's capacities. We model potential attacks (including fraud) as negative contributions from the attackers (from their specific methods of attack) toward the dependee-side dependency link. A *Break* contribution indicates that the attack is sufficient to make the softgoal unviable. For clarity of analysis, we place the attack-related intentional elements into agents called "Attacker Playing Role X." Details of the attack methods (e.g., Steal Card Information, Send Falsified Records) can be elaborated by further means-ends and decomposition analysis. Thus, the steps and methods of the attack can be modeled and analyzed. Other internal details of the Terminal Owner are not relevant and are thus not included in the model. Negative contribution links are used to show attacks on more specific vulnerabilities of the depender (e.g., refinements of Transact with Card).

The dependencies that could be broken are highlighted with a small square in Figure 9. When a dependency is compromised, the effect could propagate through the dependency network upstream along the dependency links. For example,

Figure 9. Attacks directed to vulnerable dependencies in a smart card system

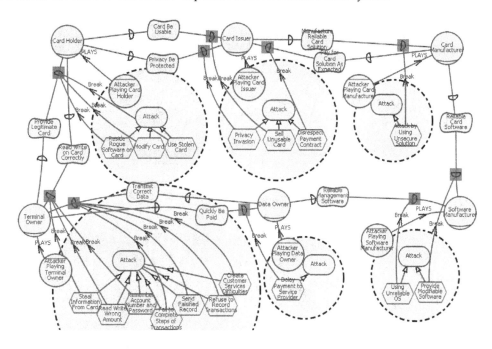

if the Terminal Owner is not Quickly Be Paid, he may stop accepting card as a payment option.

Countermeasure Analysis

During countermeasure analysis, system designers make decisions on how to mitigate vulnerabilities and set up defenses against potential attackers. This type of analysis covers general types of attacks, and formulates solutions by selectively applying, combining, or instantiating prototypical solutions to address the specific needs of various stakeholders. The general types of attacks and the prototypical solutions can be retrieved from a taxonomy or knowledge repository.

Necessary factors for the success of an attack are attacker's motivations, vulnerabilities of the system, and attacker's capabilities to carry out the attack. Thus, to counteract a hypothetical attack, we seek measures that will sufficiently negate these factors. Based on the above analysis, we already understand the attackers' possible malicious intents and system vulnerabilities. As shown in

Figure 5, countermeasure analysis is an iterative process. Adding protective measures may bring new vulnerabilities to the system, so a new round of vulnerability analysis and countermeasure analysis will be triggered (step [6]).

With the knowledge of some potential attacks and frauds, the depender may first look for trustworthy partners, or change their methods of operation, or add control mechanisms (countermeasures) to protect their interests. A countermeasure may prevent the attack from happening by either making it technically impossible, or by eliminating the attacker's intent of attack.

Figure 10 shows a SR model with defensive actions as well as attacks. Protection mechanisms are adopted to counteract specific attacks. In some cases, the protections are sufficient to defeat a strong attack (defense *Break* link (dotted arrow) pointing to an attack *Break* link). In other cases, countermeasures are only partially effective in defending against their respective attacks (through the *Hurt* or *Some-* contribution types).

Figure 10. Resistance models defeating hypothetical attacks

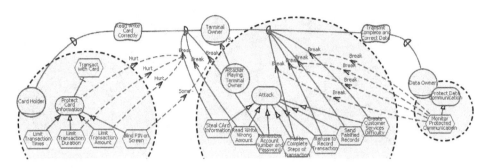

Figure 11. Countermeasure effectiveness evaluation model

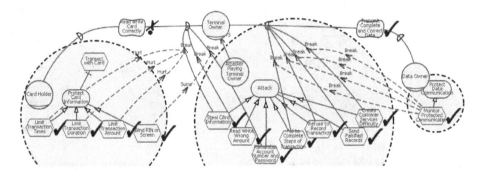

Qualitative Goal-Reasoning Mechanism

A qualitative goal-reasoning process is used to propagates a series of labels through the models. A label (or satisficing status) on a node is used to indicate whether that intentional element (goal, task, resource, or softgoal) is viable or not (e.g., whether a softgoal is sufficiently met). Labels can have values such as Satisfied "✓," Denied " ✗ ," Weakly Satisfied "✓• " and Weakly Denied "✗," Undecided "?," etc. (Liu et al., 2003). Leaf nodes (those with no incoming contributions) are given labels by the analyst based on judgment of their independent viability. These values are then propagated "upwards" through the contribution network (following the direction of the contribution links, and from dependee to depender). The viability of the overall system appears in the high level nodes of the various stakeholders. The pro-

cess is an interactive one, requiring the analyst to make judgments whenever the outcome is inconclusive given the combination of potentially conflicting contributions.

To begin, the analyst labels all the attack leaf nodes as Satisficed since they are all judged to be possible (Figure 11). Similarly, all the defense leaf nodes are judged to be viable, thus labelled Satisfied. The values are then propagated along contribution links. Before adding defense nodes, the Card Holder's dependency on the Terminal Owner for Read Write Card Correctly softgoal was labelled as Denied, because of the potentially strong attacks from Terminal Owner. However, as countermeasures are added, the influences of the attacks will be correspondingly weakened.

Regarding Read Write Card Correctly, three possible attacks are identified. One of them Steal Card Info is counteracted by three defense measures, though each one is partial (Hurt). Another attack Remember Account Number & Password has a defense of unknown strength (*Some-*). The third attack has no defensive measure. The softgoal dependency Read Write Card Correctly is thus judged to be weakly unviable (✗). On the other side, as the Data Owner's protection mechanism could sufficiently defeat the four possible attacks, the Transmit Complete and Correct Data softgoal dependency is thus judged to be viable (✓). Potential attacks lead to the erosion of viability of the smart card system. Incorporating sufficient countermeasures restores viability.

A prototype knowledge-based tool is being constructed to support this framework for analyzing information systems security.

Trust Analysis Based on System Configuration

In the models previously given, the various participants in a smart card system were modelled as abstract roles and analyzed generally. However, in real world smart card systems, various concrete physical or organisational parties play or occupy these roles. These are shown in Table 1. Thus, to actually understand their trust and security situations, we have to apply the generic model to the real world configurations. We consider two representative kinds of smart card based systems. One is the Digital Stored Value Card, the other is the Prepaid Phone Card (Schneier & Shostack, 1998).

Digital Stored Value Card System

These are payment cards intended to be substitutes for cash. Both Mondex and VisaCash are examples of this type of system. The Customer is the Card Holder. The Merchant is the Terminal Owner. The Financial Institution that supports the system is both the Data Owner and the Card Issuer. The Smart Card Technology Company, such as Mondex, is both the Card Manufacturer and the Software Manufacturer.

Table 1. Actors (roles, positions, and agents) in various smart card system configurations

Generic Smart Card Model	Card Holder	Terminal Owner	Card Issuer	Data Owner	Card Manufacturer	Software Manufacturer
Digital Stored Value card	Customer	Merchant	Financial Institution		Technology Company	
Digital Check Card	Customer	Merchant	Financial Institution	Customer	Technology Company	
Prepaid Phone Card	Customer	Phone Company				
Account-based Phone Card	Customer	Phone Company		Customer	Technology Company	
Key store card	User		Technology Company			
Employee Access Token	Employee	Employer				
Web browsing card	Customer		Financial Institution		Technology Company	

Figure 12. A threat model of digital stored value card system

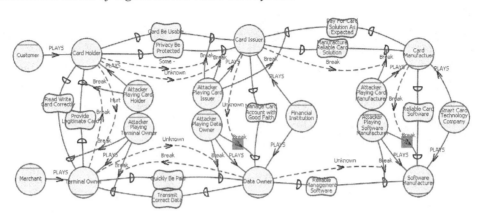

Figure 13. A threat model of prepaid phone card system

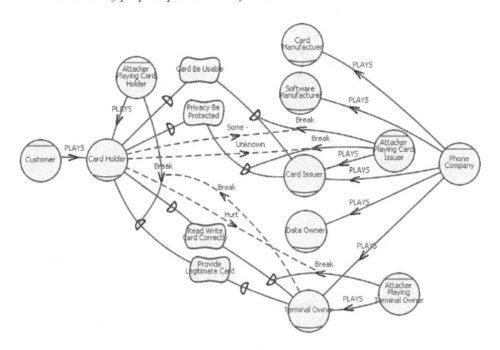

In such a configuration, the previously separated roles of Data Owner and Card Issuer are Played by the same physical agent, namely, Financial Institution. Similarly, Card Manufacturer and Software Manufacturer are combined into one physical agent — the Smart Card Technology Company. Figure 12 describes the threat model of a digital stored value card. Here the Software Manufacturer's attack on Card Manufacturer can be ignored since they belong to the same agent — the Smart Card Technology Company. Also

the attack from Data Owner to Card Issuer can be ignored since they both played by the Financial Institution. These two attacking-defending relationships are highlighted in Figure 11 with little squares.

Prepaid Phone Card System

These are special-use stored value cards. The Customer is the Card Holder. The Phone Company plays all the four roles of Terminal Owner, Data

Owner, Manufacturer, and Card Issuer. Figure 13 shows the threat model of a prepaid card system. Under such a system configuration, more attack-defense pairs disappear. Only four possible attacks need to be considered now. Three of them are from the phone company, which includes violating privacy, to issue unusable card, to read write card incorrectly. The other attack is from the Card Holder, who might use an illegitimate card.

Note that each time new roles are created, the possibility of new attacks arises. These models reflect Schneier's observation that the fewer splits we make, the more trustworthy the target system is likely to be (Schneier & Shostack, 1998).

RELATED WORK

This section is complementary to the review presented in Chapter I. Each approach to security and software engineering has an ontology, whether explicitly defined or implied. We expect that a social ontology can be complementary and beneficial to various approaches to integrating security and software engineering. We begin with work from the security community, followed by software engineering approaches that have paid special attention to security.

Security Models

Formal models have been an important part of computer security since mainframe computing (Samarati & Vimercati, 2001). Security policies originate from laws, regulations, or organisational practices, and are typically written in natural language. Security models using mathematical formalisms can provide a precise formulation of the policies for implementation. More importantly, formally specified policy models can be mathematically verified to guarantee security properties. As mathematical abstractions, they provide unambiguous specifications that are independent of implementation mechanisms. Some

concepts in security models include: subject, object, action, clearance level, user, group, role, task, principal, owner, etc.

Since security models are idealized abstractions, their application in real life requires a series of translations, involving interpretation and decision making at each stage. Organisational structures must be analyzed so as to select the appropriate models, or a combination of models. Policies need to be interpreted and codified properly to achieve the desired results. Real world entities and relationships are mapped to the model abstractions. Finally, the security model is mapped to security implementation mechanisms. The levels of abstractions used in security requirements, design, and implementation therefore mirror those in software system development and provide a basis for integration.

The social ontology outlined in this chapter can facilitate and augment an integrated security development process by enriching the reasoning support needed to arrive at decisions at each stage in the process. The ontology in existing security models are intended for the automated enforcement of specified security rules (e.g., to decide whether to give access). They do not support reasoning about why particular models or policies are appropriate for the target environment, especially when there are conflicting objectives and interpretations. Furthermore, many of the simplifying assumptions that formal models rely on do not hold in real life (Denning, 1999). The social ontology of strategic actors provides a framework for reasoning about the use of such models from a pragmatic, broader perspective.

In the development of new security models, there is a trend towards ontologies that are more closely aligned with the ontology of organisational work. For example, role based access control (RBAC) (Ferraiolo, Sandhu, Gavrila, Kuhn, & Chandramouli, 2001; Sandhu, Coyne, Feinstein, & Youman, 1996) allows privileges to be organised according to organisational roles such as loan officer or branch manager. These trends are consistent with the proposed social ontology approach, though RBAC models, like other access control models, are meant for enforcement, not strategic organisational reasoning.

Security Management Frameworks

While formal computer security models focus on policies built into the automated system, the overall security of information and software systems depends very much on organisational practices. Security practices have existed long before the computer age. Many of the principles continue to apply and have been adapted to software systems. Standards have been defined to promote best practices (e.g., ISO 17799, 1999).

OCTAVE (Alberts & Dorofee, 2002), CRAMM, and FRAP (Peltier, 2001), are oriented toward decision making from a business perspective, leading to management, operational, and technical requirements and procedures. Although few frameworks have explicit information models, they do have implicit ontologies revolving around key concepts such as asset, attack, threat, vulnerability, countermeasure, and risk.

The main focus of these frameworks is on prescriptive guidelines. Tables and charts are used to enumerate and cross-list vulnerabilities and threats. Potential countermeasures are suggested. Risks are computed from potential losses arising from estimated likelihood of threats. Since quantitative estimates are hard to come by, most assessments rely on ratings such as low, medium, high.

While formal computer security models attempt to guarantee security (requiring simplifying assumptions that may depart from reality), security management frameworks acknowledge that security breaches will occur, and suggest countermeasures to reduce risk. This pragmatic stance is very much in the spirit of the social ontology proposed in this chapter. Security management frameworks can be augmented by the modelling of strategic actor relationships and reasoning about how their goals may be achieved or hindered.

Another drawback of checklists and guidelines is that they tend to be too generic. Experience and expert judgment are needed to properly apply them to specific systems and organisational settings. Such judgments are hard to trace or maintain over time as the systems evolve.

The explicit modelling of strategic relationships can provide a more specific analysis of sources of vulnerabilities and failures, thus also allowing countermeasures to be targeted appropriately. Using the strategic dependencies and rationales, one can trace the impact of threats along the paths to determine which business goals are affected. The impact on goals other than security can also be determined through the model since they appear in the same model. One can see how security goals might compete with or are synergistic with non-security goals, thus leading to decisions that take the overall set of goals into account. Using an agent-oriented ontology, one can determine which actors are most affected by which security threats, and are therefore likely to be most motivated to take measures. Tradeoffs are done from the viewpoint of each stakeholder. This approach provides a good basis for an ontology of security, which can mediate between business reasoning from an organisational perspective and system design reasoning from a technical perspective.

Some preliminary work have been done to integrate the *i** modelling ontology with risk-based security management approaches (Gaunard & Dubois, 2003; Mayer, Rifaut, & Dubois, 2005). Further extensions could incorporate economic theories and reasoning (e.g., Anderson, 2001; Camp & Lewis, 2004). The ontology of *i** can provide the structure representation of social relationships on which to do economic reasoning.

Software Systems Design Frameworks

Having considered work originating from the security side, we now turn to contributions from the software engineering and system development perspective.

Extensions to UML (see Chapter I for information of such approaches).The ontology of UML, consisting of objects and classes, activities, states, interactions, and so forth, with its security-oriented extensions, are useful for specifying the technical design of security features and functionalities, but does not support the reasoning that lead up to those requirements and designs. As indicated in the second section of this chapter, technical design notations are useful for recording the results of decisions, but do not offer support for arriving at those decisions. The social ontology proposed in this chapter can therefore complement UML-based approaches, such as the one presented in Chapter IX, by supporting the early-stage requirements modelling and reasoning that can then be propagated to the technical design stage, resulting in design choices expressed in UML-like design notations. Stakeholder deliberations and tradeoffs therefore are effectively conveyed to technical designers. Conversely, the effect of technical choices can be propagated upstream to enable stakeholders to appreciate the consequences as they appear in the stakeholders' world.

Extensions to information systems modelling and design. In the information systems area, Pernul (1992) proposes secure data schemas (extension of entity-relationship diagrams) and secure function schemas (extension of data flow diagrams). In Herrmann and Pernul (1999) and Röhm and Pernul (1999), these models are extended to include a business process schema, with tasks, data/material, humans, legal bindings and information flow, and an organisational schema with role models and organisation diagrams to describe which activities are done where and by whom. Other information systems security approaches include the automated secure system development method (Booysen & Eloff, 1995) and the logical controls specification approach (Baskerville, 1993; Siponen & Baskerville, 2001).

These approaches illustrate the extension of conventional information systems ontologies to incorporate security-specific ontologies. Different concepts are added to each level of modelling (e.g., database schemas, process or function schemas, workflow schemas, and organisation diagrams). As with UML extensions, these approaches tend to emphasize the notation needed to express security features in the requirements specification or design descriptions and how those features can be analyzed. However, the notations (and the implied ontology) do not provide support for the deliberations that lead up to the security requirements and design. A social ontology that supports explicit reasoning about relationships among strategic actors, as outlined in this chapter, can be a helpful extension to these approaches.

Responsibility modelling. A number of approaches center around the notion of responsibility. In Strens and Dobson (1994), when an agent delegates an obligation, the agent becomes a responsibility principal, and the receiver of the delegation process is a responsibility holder. An obligation is a high-level mission that the agent can fulfill by carrying out activities. Agents cannot transfer their responsibilities, only their obligations. Three kinds of requirements are derived from responsibilities: need-to-do, need-to-know and need-for-audit. The need-to-know requirements relate to security policies — which subjects (e.g., users) should be allowed to access which objects (e.g., files, etc.) so that they are able to fulfill their responsibilities.

Backhouse and Dhillon (1996) also adopt a responsibilities analysis approach, incorporating speech acts theory. The model for automated profile specification (MAPS) approach (Pottas

& Solms, 1995) uses responsibilities and role models to generate information security profiles (such as access control) from job descriptions and organisational policies.

This group of work has a more explicit ontology of social organisation. The emphasis is on the mappings between organisational actors and the tasks or activities they have to perform. While actors or agents have responsibilities, they are not viewed as having strategic interests, and do not seek alternate configurations of social relationships that favor those interests. The focus of attention is on functional behaviors and responsibilities. Security is treated as additional functions to be incorporated, and there are no attempts to deal with interactions and tradeoffs between security and other non-functional objectives such as usability or maintainability. The social ontology of *i** can therefore be quite complementary to these approaches. Other socio-organisational approaches are reviewed in Dhillon and Backhouse (2001).

Requirements Engineering Approaches to Security

While security needs to be integrated into all stages of software engineering, there is general agreement that integration starting from the earliest stages is essential. It is well known that mistakes early in the software process can have far reaching consequences in subsequent stages that are difficult and costly to remedy. Fred Brooks (1995) had noted that the requirements stage is the most difficult, and suggested that software engineering should focus more on "building the right system," and not just on "building the system right."

In requirements engineering research, a large part of the effort has been devoted to verifying that the requirements statements are precise, unambiguous, consistent, and complete. Recently, more attention has been given to the challenge of understanding the environment and context of the intended system so that the requirements will truly reflect what stakeholders want.

Goal-oriented requirements engineering. Traditional requirements languages for software specification focus on structure and behavior, with ontologies that center around entities, activities, states, constraints, and their variants. A goal-oriented ontology allows systems to be placed within the intentional setting of the usage environment. Typically, goal-oriented requirements engineering frameworks employ AND/OR tree structures (or variants) to analyze and explore alternate system definitions that will contribute to stakeholder goals in different ways. Security can be readily integrated into such a framework since attacks and threats interfere with the normal achievement of stakeholder goals. Security controls and countermeasures can be derived from defensive goals to counteract malicious actions and intents.

The NFR framework: Security as softgoal. The NFR framework (Chung, 1993; Chung et al., 2000) is distinctive from most of the above cited approaches to security in that it does not start with vulnerabilities and risks, nor from security features and functions. It starts by treating security as one among many non-functional requirements. As with many other non-functional requirements such as usability, performance, or information accuracy, security is viewed as a goal whose operational meaning needs to be interpreted according to the needs of the specific application setting. This interpretation is done by a series of refinements in a goal graph until the point (called operationalization) where subgoals are sufficiently concrete as to be accomplishable by implementable actions and mechanisms, such as access control mechanisms or protocols. At each stage in the refinement, subgoals are judged to be contributing qualitatively to the parent goals in different ways. Because the nature and extent of the contribution requires judgement from experience and possibly domain expertise, the term softgoal is used, drawing on Simon's notion of satisficing (Simon, 1996).

The NFR framework thus offers a systematic approach for achieving "good enough" security — a practical objective in real life (Sandhu, 2003; Schneier, 2003) that have been hard to achieve in conventional mathematical formalisms. A formal treatment of the satisficing semantics of softgoals is offered in Chung et al. (2000).

The NFR framework is also distinctive in that it allows security goals to be analyzed and understood at the same time as other potentially competing requirements, for example, usability, performance, maintainability, and evolvability. In the past, it has been difficult to deal with these non-functional requirements early in the development life cycle. Typically functional requirements dominate the design process. Experienced and expert designers take non-functional requirement into account intuitively and implicitly, but without support from systematic frameworks, languages, or tools. The softgoal graph approach acknowledges that security needs to compete with other goals during requirements analysis and during design. Different aspects of security may also compete with each other. The NFR goal-oriented approach supports reasoning about tradeoffs among these competing goals and how they can be achieved.

Beyond clarifying requirements, the NFR softgoals are used to drive subsequent stages in system design and implementation, thus offering a deep integration of security into the software engineering process.

A related body of work is in quality attributes of software architecture, for example, the ATAM approach (Kazman, Klein, & Clements, 2000) for architectural evaluation. Many of the basic elements are similar to the NFR framework. The classification of quality attributes and mechanisms (for security and other attributes), however, are viewed from an evaluation viewpoint. The taxonomy structure of quality attribute is not seen

as goals to be elaborated based on tradeoffs encountered in the particular system. Quality attributes are concretized in terms of metrics, which are different for each quality, so trade-offs are difficult across different metrics.

The KAOS framework: Goals, obstacles, and anti-goals. KAOS (Dardenne, van Lamsweerde, & Fickas, 1993; van Lamsweerde, 2001, 2004; van Lamsweerde, Brohez, Landtsheer, & Janssens, 2003) is a goal-oriented requirements engineering framework that focuses on systematic derivation of requirements from goals. It includes an outer layer of informally specified goals, and an inner layer of formalized goal representation and operations using temporal logic. It is therefore especially suitable for real-time and safety critical systems. Refinement patterns are developed making use of temporal logic relationships.

The KAOS ontology includes obstacles, which impede goal achievement. The methodology provides techniques for identifying and resolving obstacles. To incorporate security analysis, attackers present obstacles to security goals. New security requirements are derived from attack generation and resolution.

Tree structures have been used in the security community for analyzing the structure of threats (Schneier, 1999), and in the safety community for the analysis of faults and hazards (Helmer et al., 2002). Experiences from these approaches can be incorporated into goal-oriented frameworks.

Agent-Oriented Requirements Engineering

The agent-oriented approach adopts goal-oriented concepts and techniques, but treats goals as originating from different actors. The *i** modelling framework views actors as having strategic interests. Each actor aims to further its own interests in exploring alternative conceptions of the future system and how the system will affect its relationships to other actors. This may be contrasted with other frameworks which may include some notion of actor which are non-intentional (e.g., in use case diagrams in UML) or non-strategic (e.g., in KAOS, where agents are passive recipients of responsibility assignments at the end of a goal refinement process).

i* adopts the notion of softgoal from the NFR framework, but makes further distinctions with goal, task, and resource. Softgoals are operationalized into tasks, which may in turn contain decompositions that include softgoals.

Security issues are traced to antagonistic goals and dependencies among attackers and defenders. As in the NFR framework, security is treated as much as possible within the same notational and reasoning framework as for other non-functional requirements (as softgoals), but extended to include functional elements (as goals, tasks, and resources). Security is therefore not treated in isolation, but interacts with other concerns at all steps throughout the process. The illustration of *i** in this chapter is based on the example in Yu and Liu (2000, 2001). Further illustrations are in Liu et al. (2002), Yu and Cysneiros (2001), Liu et al. (2003), Liu and Yu (2003, 2004).

The *i** approach has been adopted and extended in a number of directions. The Tropos framework (Bresciani, Perini, Giorgini, Giunchiglia, & Mylopoulos, 2004; Castro, Kolp, & Mylopoulos, 2002) further develops the *i** approach into a full-fledged software engineering methodology, using the agent-oriented social ontology originating from requirements modelling to drive architectural design, detailed design, and eventual implementation on agent-based software platforms. Formal Tropos incorporates formalization techniques similar to KAOS, so that automated tools such as model checking can be applied to verify security properties (Liu et al., 2003).

A number of extensions to *i** have been developed to address specific needs of security modelling and analysis. Mouratidis et al. (2003a, 2003b, 2004, 2005, also Chapter VIII) introduced the concepts of security reference diagram and security constraints. Common security concepts such as secure entities, secure dependencies, and secure capabilities are reinterpreted within the *i** ontology. The security constraint concept attaches a security-related strategic dependency to the dependency that it applies to. An intuitive benefit of this concept is that the association between the two is indicated without having to refer to the internal rationale structures of actors. An attack scenarios representation structure that aims to support the analysis of specific attacking and protecting situations at a more detailed design stage is developed. New language structures developed include secure capability, and attacking link.

Giorgini et al. (2003, 2005; also Chapter VIII) introduced four new primitive relationships related to security requirements: trust, delegation, offer and owner relation. These new primitives offer an explicit treatment of security concepts such as permission, ownership, and authority, which allows a more detailed analysis.

In Crook, Ince, and Nuseibeh (2005), the problem of modelling access policies is addressed by extending the Tropos approach (Liu et al., 2003), to ensure that security goals can be achieved and that operational requirements are consistent with access policies.

Misuse/Abuse Cases

Misuse and abuse cases techniques (Alexander, 2001; Sindre & Opdahl, 2000, 2001; see also Review in Chapter I) are complementary to goal-oriented techniques as they offer different ways of structuring requirements knowledge (Rolland, Grosz, & Kla, 1999). Use cases are action-oriented and include sequence and conditionals. Goal refinements are (mostly) hierarchical covering multiple levels of abstraction. In addressing security requirements, the development of misuse/abuse cases can be assisted by using goal analysis. Conversely, goal analysis can be made concrete by considering positive and negative use cases and scenarios. Note that use cases are better suited to later stages in requirements analysis since they assume that the system boundary is already defined. Unlike the strategic actors in *i**, actors in use cases are non-intentional and serve to delineate the boundary of the automated system.

CONCLUSION

In this chapter, we have argued that a social ontology can provide the basis for integrating security and software engineering. We presented the social ontology of *i** and illustrated how it can be used to include security goals when designing a smart card system. We have outlined how a social ontology is complementary to a number of techniques in security engineering and in software engineering, thus building common ground between the two areas.

ACKNOWLEDGMENT

The authors (1 & 3) gratefully acknowledge financial support from the Natural Sciences and Engineering Research Council of Canada, Bell University Laboratories, and author (2) the National Key Research and Development Plan (973, no.2002CB312004) and NSF China (no. 60503030).

REFERENCES

Alberts, C., & Dorofee, A. (2002, July). *Managing information security risks: The OCTAVE (SM) approach*. Boston: Addison Wesley.

Alexander, I. (2002, September). Modelling the interplay of conflicting goals with use and misuse cases. *Proceedings of the 8ᵗʰ International Workshop on Requirements Engineering: Foundation for Software Quality (REFSQ-02)*, Essen, Germany (pp. 9-10).

Alexander, I. (2003, January). Misuse cases: Use cases with hostile intent. *IEEE Software, 20*(1), 58-66.

Anderson, R. (2001). *Security engineering: A guide to building dependable distributed systems*. New York: Wiley.

Backhouse, J., & Dhillon, G. (1996). Structures of responsibilities and security of information systems. *European Journal of Information Systems, 5*(1), 2-10.

Baskerville, R. (1993). Information systems security design methods: Implications for information systems development. *Computing Surveys, 25*(4), 375-414.

Boehm, B. W. (1988). A spiral model of software development and enhancement. *IEEE Computer, 21*(5), 61-72.

Booysen, H. A. S., & Eloff, J. H. P. (1995). A methodology for the development of secure application systems. *Proceeding of the 11ᵗʰ IFIP TC11 International Conference on Information Security.*

Bresciani, P., Perini, A., Giorgini, P., Giunchiglia, F., & Mylopoulos, J. (2004) Tropos: An agent-oriented software development methodology. *Autonomous Agents and Multi-Agent Systems, 8*(3), 203-236.

Brooks, F. (1995, August). *The mythical man-month: Essays on software engineering, 20th Anniversary Edition* (1ˢᵗ ed.). Boston: Addison-Wesley.

Castro, J., Kolp, M., & Mylopoulos, J. (2002). Towards requirements driven information systems engineering: The Tropos project. *Information Systems, 27*(6), 365-389.

Chung, L. (1993). Dealing with security requirements during the development of information systems. In C. Rolland, F. Bodart, & C. Cauvet (Eds.), *Proceedings of the 5ᵗʰ International Confer-*

ence Advanced Information Systems Engineering, CAiSE '93 (pp. 234-251). Springer.

Chung L., Nixon, B. A., Yu, E., & Mylopoulos, J. (2000). *Non-functional requirements in software engineering.* Kluwer Academic Publishers.

CRAMM – CCTA (Central Computer and Tele-communications Agency, UK). *Risk analysis and management method.* Retrieved from http://www. cramm.com/cramm.htm

Crook, R., Ince, D., & Nuseibeh, B. (2005, August 29-September 2). On Modelling access policies: Relating roles to their organisational context. *Proceedings of the 13ᵗʰ IEEE International Requirements Engineering Conference (RE'05),* Paris (pp. 157-166).

Dardenne, A., van Lamsweerde, A., & Fickas, S. (1993). Goal-directed requirements acquisition. *Science of Computer Programming, 20*(1-2), 3-50.

Denning, D. E. (1998). *The limits of formal security models.* National Computer Systems Security Award Acceptance Speech. Retrieved October 18, 1999, from www.cs.georgetown.edu/~denning/ infosec/award.html

Dhillon, G., & Backhouse, J. (2001) Current directions in IS security research: Toward socio-organizational perspectives. *Information Systems Journal, 11*(2), 127-154.

Ferraiolo, D., Sandhu, R., Gavrila, S., Kuhn, R., & Chandramouli, R. (2001, August). Proposed NIST standard for role-based access control. *ACM Transactions on Information and Systems Security, 4*(3), 224-74.

Franch, X., & Maiden, N. A. M. (2003, February 10-13). Modelling component dependencies to inform their selection. *COTS-Based Software Systems, 2ⁿᵈ International Conference, (ICCBSS 2003)* (pp. 81-91). Lecture Notes in Computer Science 2580. Ottawa, Canada: Springer.

Gaunard, P., & Dubois, E. (2003, May 26-28). Bridging the gap between risk analysis and security policies: Security and privacy in the age of uncertainty. *IFIP TC11 18ᵗʰ International Conference on Information Security (SEC2003)* (pp. 409-412). Athens, Greece. Kluwer.

Giorgini, P., Massacci, F., & Mylopoulos, J. (2003, October 13-16). Requirement engineering meets security: A case study on modelling secure electronic transactions by VISA and Mastercard. *The 22ⁿᵈ International Conference on Conceptual Modelling (ER'03)* (LNCS 2813, pp. 263-276). Chicago: Springer.

Giorgini, P., Massacci, F., Mylopoulos, J., & Zannone, N. (2005). Modelling social and individual trust in requirements engineering methodologies. *Proceedings of the 3ʳᵈ International Conference on Trust Management (iTrust 2005).* LNCS 3477. Heidelberg: Springer-Verlag.

Gross, D., & Yu, E. (2001, August 27-31). Evolving system architecture to meet changing business goals: An agent and goal-oriented approach. The *5ᵗʰ IEEE International Symposium on Requirements Engineering (RE 2001)* (pp. 316-317). Toronto, Canada.

Helmer, G., Wong, J., Slagell, M., Honavar, V., Miller, L., & Lutz, R. (2002). A software fault tree approach to requirements analysis of an intrusion detection system. In P. Loucopoulos & J. Mylopoulos (Ed.), *Special Issue on Requirements Engineering for Information Security. Requirements Engineering* (Vol. 7, No. 4, pp. 177-220).

Herrmann, G., & Pernul, G. (1999). Viewing business-process security from different perspectives. *International Journal of Electronic Commerce, 3*(3), 89-103.

ISO 17799. (1999). *Information security management — Part 1: Code of practice for information security.* London: British Standards Institution.

Kazman, R., Klein, M., & Clements, P. (2000). *ATAM: Method for architectural evaluation (CMU/SEI-2000-TR-004).* Pittsburgh, PA: Software Engineering Institute, Carnegie Mellon University.

Liu, L., & Yu, E. (2003). Designing information systems in social context: A goal and scenario modelling approach. *Information Systems, 29*(2), 187-203.

Liu, L., & Yu, E. (2004). Intentional modelling to support identity management. In P. Atzeni et al. (Eds.), *Proceedings of the 23rd International Conference on Conceptual Modelling (ER 2004)* (pp. 555-566). LNCS 3288. Berlin, Heidelberg: Springer-Verlag.

Liu, L., Yu, E., & Mylopoulos, J. (2002, October 16). Analyzing security requirements as relationships among strategic actors. The *2nd Symposium on Requirements Engineering for Information Security (SREIS'02).* Raleigh, NC.

Liu, L., Yu, E., & Mylopoulos, J. (2003, September). Security and privacy requirements analysis within a social setting. *Proceedings of International Conference on Requirements Engineering (RE'03)* (pp. 151-161). Monterey, CA.

Lodderstedt, T., Basin, D. A., J, & Doser, R. (2002). SecureUML: A UML-based modelling language for model-driven security. *Proceedings of UML '02: Proceedings of the 5th International Conference on The Unified Modelling Language,* Dresden, Germany (pp. 426-441).

Mayer, N., Rifaut, A., & Dubois, E. (2005). Towards a risk-based security requirements engineering framework. *Workshop on Requirements Engineering For Software Quality (REFSQ'05), at the Conference for Advanced Information Systems Engineering (CAiSE),* Porto, Portugal.

McDermott, J., & Fox, C. (1999). Using abuse case models for security requirements analysis. *Proceedings 15th IEEE Annual Computer Security Applications Conference,* Scottsdale, USA (pp. 55-67).

Mouratidis, H., Giorgini, P., & Manson, G. A. (2003a). Integrating security and systems engineering: Towards the modelling of secure information systems. *Proceedings of the 15th Conference on Advanced Information Systems Engineering (CAiSE 03)* (Vol . LNCS 2681, pp. 63-78). Klagenfurt, Austria: Springer.

Mouratidis, H., Giorgini, P., & Manson, G. (2004, April 13-17). Using security attack scenarios to analyse security during information systems design. *Proceedings of the 6th International Conference on Enterprise Information Systems,* Porto, Portugal.

Mouratidis, H., Giorgini, P., & Schumacher, M. (2003b). Security patterns for agent systems. *Proceedings of the 8th European Conference on Pattern Languages of Programs,* Irsee, Germany.

Mouratidis, H., Kolp, M., Faulkner, S., & Giorgini. P. (2005, July). A secure architectural description language for agent systems. *Proceedings of the 4th International Joint Conference on Autonomous Agents and Multiagent Systems (AAMAS05).* Utrecht, The Netherlands: ACM Press.

Peltier, T. R. (2001, January). *Information security risk analysis.* Boca Raton, FL: Auerbach Publications.

Pernul, G. (1992, November 23-25). Security constraint processing in multilevel secure AMAC schemata. The *2nd European Symposium on Research in Computer Security (ESORICS 1992)* (pp. 349-370). Toulouse, France. Lecture Notes in Computer Science 648. Springer.

Pottas, D., & Solms, S. H. (1995). Aligning information security profiles with organizational policies. *Proceedings of the IFIP TC11 11th International Conference on Information Security.*

Röhm, A. W., & Pernul, G. (1999). COPS: A model and infrastructure for secure and fair electronic markets. *Proceedings of the 32ⁿᵈ Annual Hawaii International Conference on Systems Sciences.*

Rolland, C., Grosz, G., & Kla, R. (1999, June). Experience with goal-scenario coupling in requirements engineering. *Proceedings of the IEEE International Symposium on Requirements Engineering*, Limerick, Ireland.

Samarati, P., & Vimercati, S. (2001). Access control: Policies, models, and mechanisms. In R. Focardi & R. Gorrieri (Eds.), *Foundations of security analysis and design: Tutorial lectures* (pp. 137-196). LNCS 2171.

Sandhu, R. (2003, January/February). Good enough security: Towards a business driven discipline. *IEEE Internet Computing, 7*(1), 66-68.

Sandhu, R. S., Coyne, E. J., Feinstein, H. L., & Youman, C. E. (1996, February). Role-based access control models. *IEEE Computer, 29*(2), 38-47.

Schneier, B. (1999). *Attack trees modelling security threats.* Dr. Dobb's Journal, December. Retrieved from http://www.counterpane.com/attacktrees-ddj-ft.html

Schneier, B. (2003). *Beyond fear: Thinking sensibly about security in an uncertain world.* New York: Copernicus Books, an imprint of Springer-Verlag.

Schneier, B., & Shostack, A. (1998). *Breaking up is hard to do: Modelling security threats for smartcards.* First USENIX Symposium on Smart-Cards, USENIX Press. Retrieved from http://www.counterpane.com/smart-card-threats.html

Simon, H. (1996). *The sciences of the artificial* (3ʳᵈ ed.). MIT Press.

Sindre, G., & Opdahl, A. L. (2000). Eliciting security requirements by misuse cases. *Proceedings of the 37ᵗʰ Conference on Techniques of Object-Oriented Languages and Systems* (pp. 120-131). TOOLS Pacific 2000.

Sindre, G., & Opdahl, A. L. (2001, June 4-5). Templates for misuse case description. *Proceedings of the 7ᵗʰ International Workshop on Requirements Engineering, Foundation for Software Quality (REFSQ2001)*, Switzerland.

Siponen, M. T., & Baskerville, R. (2001). A new paradigm for adding security into IS development methods. In J. Eloff, L. Labuschagne, R. von Solms, & G. Dhillon (Eds.), *Advances in information security management & small systems security* (pp. 99-111). Boston: Kluwer Academic Publishers.

Strens, M. R., & Dobson, J. E. (1994). Responsibility modelling as a technique for requirements definition. *IEEE, 3*(1), 20-26.

van der Raadt, B., Gordijn, J., & Yu, E. (2005). Exploring Web services from a business value perspective. To appear in *Proceedings of the 13ᵗʰ International Requirements Engineering Conference (RE'05)*, Paris (pp. 53-62).

van Lamsweerde, A. (2001, August 27-31). Goal-oriented requirements engineering: A guided tour. The *5ᵗʰ IEEE International Symposium on Requirements Engineering (RE 2001)* (p. 249). Toronto, Canada.

van Lamsweerde, A. (2004, May). Elaborating security requirements by construction of intentional anti-models. *Proceedings of ICSE'04, 26ᵗʰ International Conference on Software Engineering* (pp. 148-157). Edinburgh: ACM-IEEE.

van Lamsweerde, A., Brohez, S., Landtsheer, R., & Janssens, D. (2003, September). From system goals to intruder anti-goals: Attack generation and resolution for security requirements engineering. *Proceedings of the RE'03 Workshop on Requirements for High Assurance Systems (RHAS'03)* (pp. 49-56). Monterey, CA.

Yu, E. (1993, January). Modelling organizations for information systems requirements engineering. *Proceedings of the 1ˢᵗ IEEE International*

Symposium on Requirements Engineering (pp. 34-41). San Diego, CA.

Yu, E. (1997, January 6-8). Towards modelling and reasoning support for early-phase requirements engineering. *Proceedings of the 3ʳᵈ IEEE International Symposium on Requirements Engineering (RE'97)* (pp. 226-235). Washington, DC.

Yu, E. (2001a, April). Agent orientation as a modelling paradigm. *Wirtschaftsinformatik*, *43*(2), 123-132.

Yu, E. (2001b). Agent-oriented modelling: Software versus the world. *Agent-Oriented Software Engineering AOSE-2001 Workshop Proceedings* (LNCS 222, pp. 206-225). Springer Verlag.

Yu, E., & Cysneiros, L. (2002, October 16). Designing for privacy and other competing requirements. *The 2ⁿᵈ Symposium on Requirements Engineering for Information Security (SREIS'02)*. Raleigh, NC.

Yu, E., & Liu, L. (2000, June 3-4). Modelling trust in the i* strategic actors framework. *Proceedings of the 3ʳᵈ Workshop on Deception, Fraud and Trust in Agent Societies,* Barcelona, Catalonia, Spain (at Agents2000).

Yu, E., & Liu, L. (2001). Modelling trust for system design using the *i** strategic actors framework. In R. Falcone, M. Singh, & Y. H. Tan (Eds.), *Trust in cyber-societies--integrating the human and artificial perspectives* (pp. 175-194). LNAI-2246. Springer.

Yu, E., Liu, L., & Li, Y. (2001, November 27-30). Modelling strategic actor relationships to support intellectual property management. *The 20ᵗʰ International Conference on Conceptual Modelling (ER-2001)* (LNCS 2224, pp. 164-178). Yokohama, Japan: Spring Verlag.

Section III
Usability Issues

Chapter XI
Security Configuration for Non-Experts:
A Case Study in Wireless Network Configuration

Cynthia Kuo
Carnegie Mellon University, USA

Adrian Perrig
Carnegie Mellon University, USA

Jesse Walker
Intel Corporation, USA

ABSTRACT

End users often find that security configuration interfaces are difficult to use. In this chapter, we explore how application designers can improve the design and evaluation of security configuration interfaces. We use IEEE 802.11 network configuration as a case study. First, we design and implement a configuration interface that guides users through secure network configuration. The key insight is that users have a difficult time translating their security goals into specific feature configurations. Our interface automates the translation from users' high-level goals to low-level feature configurations. Second, we develop and conduct a user study to compare our interface design with commercially available products. We adapt existing user research methods to sidestep common difficulties in evaluating security applications. Using our configuration interface, non-expert users are able to secure their networks as well as expert users. In general, our research addresses prevalent issues in the design and evaluation of consumer-configured security applications.

INTRODUCTION

For home consumers, the setup and configuration of new technologies is a daunting experience. The most intimidating configuration interfaces are often feature-based. They list the different technical features that end users can configure. Users select the appropriate radio button or drop-down box option and the product changes its behavior accordingly. This approach is effective — if users know what they are doing. For users unfamiliar with the technology, the obstacles are formidable. First, users must articulate their goals for the configuration. Second, they must map these goals to the product's features. Last, users must configure the product features correctly.

Feature-based configuration interfaces fail to consider how people interact with technology. Reeves and Nass (1996) show that we apply the same social norms that we use for human beings to our "conversations" with computers. Now consider the typical interaction between a person and a security product. It is a dysfunctional conversation. The user states, "I would like to achieve goals 1, 2, and 3." The product declares, "I have features A through Z!" Unfortunately, user goals and product features may not map easily to one another. As a result, many users struggle or give up entirely. For security professionals, we argue these interfaces are psychologically *un*acceptable (Saltzer & Schroeder, 1975).[1]

In the early days of computing, security configuration was a lesser problem. Systems were configured by early adopters, who tend to be expert users. Experts have the ability and the willingness to master psychologically unacceptable configuration schemes. However, the recent explosion of personal computers and mobile devices changes the nature of the problem; home systems are now regularly managed by non-expert users. Today, security configuration is required for each system, in each home. We are beginning to see the consequences of difficult configuration schemes: very few users enable available security features. This problem will only grow as devices proliferate.

Among IEEE 802.11 wireless networks in the home, only 20% to 30% enable some type of security feature (Cohen, 2004). Some security experts interpret this statistic as evidence that home users are too ignorant or too unconcerned about security to enable security measures. However, the problem is more fundamental: the user experience of consumer 802.11 (also known as "Wi-Fi") products is flawed. For approximately every 10 products sold, one consumer calls technical support. Most calls address basic setup issues, such as establishing Internet connectivity. Moreover, representatives of the Wi-Fi Alliance report that up to 30% of all 802.11 equipment purchased for the home is returned (Gefrides, 2004). This is an order of magnitude higher than other electronics products, such as VCRs. Furthermore, the vast majority of returned products—an estimated 90%—is *not* defective. For many home consumers, basic network setup is too difficult—even without considering secure network setup.

In this chapter, we present our design, implementation, and evaluation of a configuration interface for 802.11 access points. The interface enables home consumers to configure their wireless networks securely. Our system acts as an "expert friend," asking simple, high-level questions to elicit users' needs and goals. This information is automatically translated into a security policy for users. By avoiding feature-based questions, our system empowers end users—even novices—to make configuration decisions appropriate to their situation. With existing interfaces, more knowledgeable users are better able to configure secure networks than novice users. Our system levels the playing field, enabling non-experts to perform as well as experts. The lessons that we learned in this domain will apply to other security configuration interfaces.

Outline

First, we explore the challenges in designing and evaluating good security applications. Next, we define our problem space and our design principles. The design principles were used to implement our configuration interface, which is described in the design and implementation section. We tested our implementation against two commercially available access points. The evaluation method and experimental results are briefly summarized in their respective sections. Finally, we discuss how this work may be applied to other domains.

BACKGROUND

In recent years, application designers have discovered that the design guidelines that work for most consumer applications fail for security applications. Intuitively, the explanation is simple: users' mental models of the world do not match the assumptions underlying the technical implementations.

Whitten and Tygar (1999) delineated five properties that make designing user interfaces for security applications challenging:

- The *unmotivated user* property, which signifies that security is usually a secondary goal for users;
- The *abstraction* property, which highlights how users have difficulty conceptualizing security concepts;
- The *lack of feedback* property, which speaks to application designers' difficulty in providing adequate feedback for users;
- The *barn door* property, which states that an error cannot be undone once information has been (potentially) compromised; and
- The *weakest link* property, which reminds us that the security of a system is only as strong as its weakest link.

For these reasons, the design rules that work for most consumer applications often fall short for security applications.

Furthermore, the effectiveness of security applications is difficult to evaluate. Textbook user study methods make assumptions that may *not* hold when researchers evaluate security applications. We identify five assumptions in Kuo, Perrig, and Walker (2006):

- *There are clear-cut criteria for success.* Computer security is a risk management process. Each user may be exposed to different risks, and as a result, may require a different configuration. One security configuration may not fit all.
- *Applications should tolerate variation in user behavior and user error.* In many applications, users can take multiple paths through the user interface to reach the same end state. Mistakes can be made and corrected. In security applications, some mistakes are critical errors: once these mistakes have been made, there is no way to recover.
- *Users are familiar with the underlying concepts.* Users may be unfamiliar with the security concepts tested in a study. The very act of providing evaluation tasks during a user study may introduce a bias—by giving users information they did not previously have.
- *Users' tasks are their primary goals.* Study designs need to account for the secondary nature of security-related goals.
- *Users respond in socially acceptable ways.* Study participants sometimes try to please the experimenter by saying what they think the experimenter wants to hear. Many users think they should be more security-conscious than they are; this may cause them to exaggerate their responses.

These assumptions must be considered when evaluating security applications. Often, this means adapting traditional user study methods to avoid the introduction of biases.

The five properties of security applications are problematic for designers of security user interfaces. The five assumptions underlying traditional user study methods challenge evaluators of security user interfaces. Together, these factors frustrate many attempts to improve security applications. This chapter documents the design and evaluation of one successful project.

Related Work

Recently, several industry groups have been developing specifications for user-friendly setup. Specifications include Wi-Fi Protected Setup, Bluetooth Simple Pairing, and setup in HomePlug AV (Lortz et al., 2006; Linsky et al., 2006; Newman, Gavette, Yonge, & Anderson, 2006). These specifications deal mainly with the exchange of authentication credentials. In comparison, this chapter focuses on the selection and implementation of a security policy (which may or may not include the exchange of authentication credentials).

In the academic world, the most closely related work is network-in-a-box (NiaB) by Balfanz, Durfee, Grinter, Smetters, and Stewart (2004). NiaB is a user-friendly method for setting up a secure wireless network. The scheme uses a custom-built access point. The access point supports a *location-limited channel,* such as infrared. The location-limited channel ensures that communication occurs between the wireless client and the correct access point. NiaB assumes that the access point can automatically configure itself and that the same security policy can be applied for all users. Automatic configuration is ideal in environments which use a common security policy.

Other technologies for intuitive and secure key establishment include work by Balfanz, Smetters, Stewart, and Wong (2002); Gutmann (2003); McCune, Perrig, and Reiter (2005); Perrig and Song

(1999); and Stajano and Anderson (1999).

Rather than developing new technology, our research tackles a different challenge: empowering users to enable a security policy of their choice. Applications that require user input in a security policy will need to leverage the approaches we present here.

The design of our system draws on several concepts which are used in the field and documented in the literature. For example, Alan Cooper's *The Inmates are Running the Asylum* (1999) drives home the benefit of goal-directed design. Cooper dissects the differences between users' goals and tasks. He argues that products should be designed to accommodate users' goals (not tasks). Security may be a secondary goal for most users, but we believe that this makes goal-based design even more effective.

In addition, Friedman et al. have explored how to design systems that take human values into account (Friedman, Kahn, & Borning, 2006; Friedman, Lin, & Miller, 2005; Friedman & Nissenbaum, 1997). This project could be considered an implementation of value-sensitive design.

On the evaluation side, Uzun, Karvonen, and Asokan (2007) show that user interface design can dramatically affect user error rates. Also, Friedman, Hurley, Howe, Felten, and Nissenbaum (2002) use a semi-structured interview to elicit users' understanding of Web security.

PROBLEM DEFINITION

In the previous section, we examined the application designer's problem; we introduced the factors that make designing and evaluating a configuration interface difficult. In this section, we delve into the user's predicament.

We begin with a networking or security expert's mental model. Figure 1 illustrates how an expert might evaluate her own wireless network. A secure configuration depends on the

Figure 1. Expert's mental model for configuring a secure wireless network

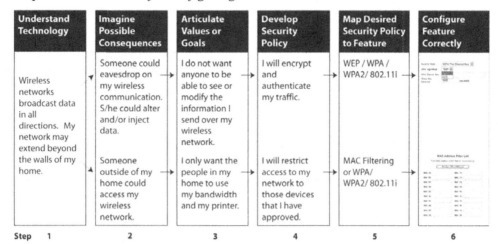

Understand Technology	Imagine Possible Consequences	Articulate Values or Goals	Develop Security Policy	Map Desired Security Policy to Feature	Configure Feature Correctly
Wireless networks broadcast data in all directions. My network may extend beyond the walls of my home.	Someone could eavesdrop on my wireless communication. S/he could alter and/or inject data.	I do not want anyone to be able to see or modify the information I send over my wireless network.	I will encrypt and authenticate my traffic.	WEP / WPA / WPA2/ 802.11i	
	Someone outside of my home could access my wireless network.	I only want the people in my home to use my bandwidth and my printer.	I will restrict access to my network to those devices that I have approved.	MAC Filtering or WPA/ WPA2/ 802.11i	
Step 1	2	3	4	5	6

successful completion of each step in Figure 1. In other words, each step represents a potential point of failure.

Existing configuration interfaces are often organized around the *features* of a wireless network—not the problems that the user wants to solve. Currently, consumers will reach the configuration step (Step 6 in Figure 1) only if they want to enable a certain feature (Step 5 in Figure 1). Thus, unless consumers *know* that they want encryption (Step 4 in Figure 1), the likelihood of enabling it is small.

Now suppose that average consumers do not have tech-savvy friends or relatives. In this case, consumers only know that they want encryption if they can articulate their goals or values regarding wireless network security (Step 3 in Figure 1). Articulation relies on the consumer's knowledge of security vulnerabilities and their possible consequences (Step 2 in Figure 1). Evaluating the consequences requires a working knowledge of wireless networks and radio signals (Step 1 in Figure 1).

Without a fairly sophisticated level of technical understanding, it is unlikely that today's consumers will be able to effectively reason about their security needs. Users may be unaware that the broadcasting of their data leads to security

vulnerabilities; that these vulnerabilities may warrant concern; and that if security is important, steps must be taken to protect their data.

Note how the configuration process illustrated in Figure 1 is extremely delicate. If the user fails to negotiate any of the six steps, the outcome will tend towards an insecure network.

Existing Configuration Interfaces

We conducted a series of preliminary studies to gain first-hand experience observing users' difficulties with network setup. We used two kinds of user study techniques: contextual inquiry and usability study. Contextual inquiry is a technique in which researchers select a few representative individuals, visit the individuals in their workplace or home, and observe their behavior. We conducted several contextual inquiries in people's homes, watching users setup and configure secure wireless networks. Each study lasted anywhere from one to 4 hours. The usability study is probably the best-known user study technique. In a usability study, experimenters observe participants while they try to complete a list of pre-determined tasks. We conducted a handful of usability studies, using the same tasks that we will describe.

Typically, when a home consumer opens an access point package, she will find a paper "quick start" guide that illustrates how to connect the access point correctly. Next, the guide will direct the user to pop in an installation CD or go to the URL of the configuration interface (e.g., http://192.168.1.1). We observed many users who struggled with network configuration. During network setup, several users had difficulty establishing an Internet connection and configuring the Windows networking dialogs. In addition, many users failed to secure their networks for a variety of reasons. Some users were unaware of the vulnerabilities in unsecured wireless networks. Others did not know what features needed to be configured.

These preliminary studies led us to develop the model in Figure 1. We found that users stumbled at each step. In general, users had more difficulty completing Steps 4 through 6, compared to Steps 1 through 3.

It is important to note that earlier configuration interfaces were organized by technical functionality. Commercial access point interfaces exposed on the order of 50 distinct, configurable features. The different features were grouped by similarity in the underlying engineering implementation, which was often unrelated to users' high-level goals. Users often visited several different pages in order to accomplish one goal. However, as more and more users have adopted wireless technology—and called vendors' technical support lines—the configuration interfaces have improved. Recently, vendors have shifted towards user-friendly configuration wizards. This is good news for both consumers, who appear to be struggling less with network setup, and vendors, who have reduced the volume of technical support calls.

Issues Addressed

The work we describe addresses three main issues:

Empowering Users to make their own Choices

A one-size-fits-all approach to system configuration cannot work in all circumstances. For example, there may be different categories of users who run 802.11 networks in their home. Some households may use wireless networks to transmit confidential information and desire a high level of security. Other households, such as those full of college students, may have many transient users, so that only the most basic access control measures are practical. Still others may choose to run an open wireless network on principle, allowing anyone within range to use their network. On a practical level, a single default cannot work for everyone. On a philosophical level, we believe technology users should have the right to configure and change their technology's behavior as desired.

Leveling the Playing Field: Making Security more Accessible to End Users

Currently, experts are able to configure products more successfully and more quickly than non-experts. However, expertise need not function as a barrier. Novices should be able to setup and configure secure technologies as well as the experts.

Maintaining Flexibility for Application Designers and Vendors

People often use products in unexpected ways. Keeping changes in software allows vendors to make quick modifications. This is particularly useful for initial product generations, as application designers figure out who is buying their products and what they will be used for. Once usage models have been more clearly delineated, the software can be easily customized for different audiences or uses.

DESIGN PRINCIPLES

Based on our preliminary user study observations, we define the following set of design principles for developing user-friendly security applications.

1. **Assume no prior technical knowledge or expertise on the part of users.** Making security accessible means that we must allow people of *all* expertise levels to perform equally well.
2. **Minimize human effort: maximize application work.** Lighten users' cognitive loads by automating as much of the configuration work as possible. Also, present only as much information as users need, and make that information available when users need it.
3. **Maintain a positive user experience.** Small details make a big difference. For example, we noticed in our preliminary studies that users strongly preferred setup directions on paper. As a result, we made a point to provide information via users' preferred medium. Also, we observed that people have little patience for configuration. At 30–45 minutes, users expressed their displeasure. At 60–70 minutes, users were visibly frustrated. We set a goal of a maximum of 45 minutes for our configuration process.
4. **Anticipate error states.** Users will get lost and make mistakes. A good design needs to anticipate what issues require troubleshooting. It should handle errors gracefully. It should provide useful feedback: Were the configuration settings successfully applied? Do they make sense? Do they do what the user thinks they should do?
5. **Separate distinct concepts.** Conflating different concepts leads to confusion. First, separate users' values and goals from security policies. Novice users are comfortable stating their values, but they are not experts in designing security policies. A better design elicits users' values and de-

rives consistent security policies from the values. Second, separate security policies from their underlying mechanisms. This concept is well known in many disciplines, such as operating system design (Grimm & Bershad, 2001). Existing configuration applications require users to become experts in security mechanisms before they can realize their preferred policies. Automating the policy–mechanism translation removes a substantial barrier to configuration.

Although these principles may appear obvious, the access point interfaces that we studied violate several of these principles. In the following sections, we show that applying these principles can improve the configuration experience a great deal—particularly for novice users.

DESIGN AND IMPLEMENTATION

We developed a configuration interface that helps users articulate and implement a security policy using existing tools and technology. This was accomplished using a Linksys WRT54G access point and source code. The source code was downloaded off Linksys' Web site (firmware version 3.01.3). It was compiled on Red Hat Linux 2.4.20-8 using gcc 3.2.2.

We modified the source code and compiled a new version of the firmware. The new firmware includes our configuration interface, which co-exists with the original vendor user interface. Users access the configuration interface just as they would access the vendor user interface. Once they connect the access point to a DSL/cable modem and a computer, they open a Web browser and direct their browser to http://192.168.1.1. This opens the home page of our configuration interface.

The dual-interface design shown in Figure 2 was created so that both our design and the original vendor interface could be used. This was achieved by creating an HTML frame that

Figure 2. Example prototype screen (usually the most advanced question users will encounter)

contained two tabs. The Easy tab switches to our prototype, and the advanced tab switches to the original vendor interface.

Our configuration interface mirrors an online checkout process: the changes are not applied until the entire configuration has been reviewed. The wizard attempts to elicit a user's goals and values by asking general questions. (See the flowchart in Figure 3.) The questions were crafted so that they would include information about the consequences of making a particular choice. This was done to address the *abstraction* property of security.

The system automatically maps the user's preferences to the system's technical features. Any decisions that can be made for the user—and still reflect the user's preferences—are automated. This addresses the *unmotivated user* property, as well as our design principle to *minimize human work*.

The mapping produces a recommended configuration for the user, which can be changed if desired. The recommendation clearly states the implications of adopting a particular configuration. For example, the recommendation articulates what actions the user must take to add or remove devices from the network. If the user's preferences

produce a set of feature settings that conflict with one another, the wizard asks the user to resolve the conflict. This addresses the *lack of feedback* and *barn door* properties, as well as the principles of *anticipating error states* and *separating distinct concepts*.

Each time users access the configuration application, they are taken to the home page. The wizard is always available on the home page. On the home page, we grouped possible actions by goals. The list of actions includes the common actions that we expected consumers to take, and the items in the list change by context. For example, if no security settings have been enabled, the menu offers the option to turn on access control or encryption. Otherwise, it shows options for giving and revoking network access. The context-sensitive menu fulfills the design principle of *maximizing application work*.

The goal is for designers to craft a system where the target audience understands the questions, and the system provides the desired configuration. We believe the best way to accomplish this is by automating the knowledge required in Steps 4 to 6 in Figure 1. In other words, configuration interfaces should automate the translation from

Figure 3. Flowchart of application logic

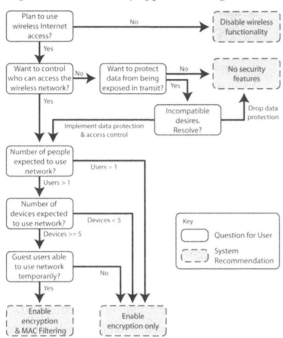

human goals to technical features—a process that taxes users' abilities.

The set of configuration questions shown in Figure 3 balances the needs of our users with the simplicity necessary for a positive user experience. However, this design is *not* a definitive design for 802.11 configuration. The questions and the application flow should be tailored to specific groups of users. *As the target population changes—as users' needs change and their level of technical understanding changes—the questions should also change.*

EVALUATION

To test the effectiveness of our design, we developed a methodology for assessing security interfaces. We then tested our configuration interface against the two best-selling commercial access points.

Target Population

We define the target population for 802.11 products as someone who:

1. Uses wireless Internet access at home, school, or work place on a daily basis (5+ days per week);
2. Has broadband access at home; and
3. Uses a laptop as his or her primary computer.

We included individuals who already had wireless networks at home, as well as individuals who did not.

Eighteen participants were recruited from a broad university population, drawing from both humanities and technology backgrounds. We recruited participants by posting paper flyers on bulletin boards throughout campus and by posting messages on electronic bulletin boards. Interested individuals were directed to a Web-based survey form. We selected participants based on their level of computer networking expertise. This was computed using: a self-assessment of their network troubleshooting abilities; whether they had ever managed a wired network; and whether they had ever managed a wireless network. The age of the participants ranged between 18 and 32. Seven participants were female.

Participants were randomly assigned an access point: the Linksys WRT54G, the Netgear WGT624, or our prototype (see Table 1).

Table 1. Participant assignment

Access Point	Low Expertise	High Expertise
Linksys WRT54G	3	3
Netgear WGT624	3	3
Prototype	3	3

Tasks Tested

We define the ideal secure wireless network as one where the consumer has:

1. Changed the default password;
2. Changed the SSID;
3. Generated or entered an encryption key on the access point;
4. Entered the encryption key on a client; and
5. Enabled MAC filtering.

We felt these five measures could provide a basic level of security for the average home user. (Note that MAC filtering becomes unnecessary when WPA or WPA2 is enabled. With WPA/WPA2, each received frame is authenticated by a session key instead of a hardware address. Many access points are now equipped with WPA, but the basic principles that motivate our study remain equally effective). They address the security requirements (i.e., secrecy and authenticity) that commercial technology is equipped to handle. These measures by themselves may be insufficient; for example, attackers may guess a key based on a password. However, such issues are outside the scope of our study.

Evaluation Method

To compare the effectiveness of different 802.11 configuration interfaces, we developed a technique that combines elements from several different methodologies: mental models interviews, contextual inquiries, usability studies, and surveys.

Mental models interviews are used to understand how interviewees conceptualize certain ideas (Morgan, Fischhoff, Bostrom, & Atman, 2002). Generally, the interviewer will start with a neutral statement, such as, "Tell me about X." The interviewee is allowed to respond with whatever thoughts come to her mind. The interviewer may ask her to talk more about an idea, and if there are other topics that the interviewer wants to cover, he may ask more specific follow-up questions.

Inspired by the mental models technique, we designed our evaluation method around the concept of *gradual revelation*. Participants were given no indication that the study was focused on wireless security; they were told we were studying wireless network setup. The questions we asked and the activities we planned were ordered such that no information about our study focus was revealed before we first evaluated participants' knowledge of it. For example, we did not mention "encryption" (1) unless participants brought up the concept themselves or (2) until participants had an opportunity to configure the network and failed to bring up the concept.

When participants arrived for the study, we interviewed them briefly to understand how they conceptualize wireless technology. We then asked participants to fill out a questionnaire. The questionnaire gathered participants' attitudes towards various aspects of wireless networks, including availability, reliability, ease of use, use of open wireless networks, security, privacy, and health. Many of these topics are unrelated to security so that participants would not suspect the focus of our study.

Next, participants were handed an access point. The access point was packaged in the box, as if it had been recently purchased. Experimenters presented participants with an open-ended scenario:

Okay, let's pretend you just received an 802.11 access point as a gift. You would like to set up and use the wireless connection today. Your laptop is already configured to use wireless—you just need to worry about the access point. Just set up the access point as you would if you were at home.

We provided participants with resources that they would have on their own, such as product manuals and access to the Internet. However, we refrained from giving participants a list of tasks to complete to avoid giving indications of our study focus. We observed participants while they set up and configured the access point as they deemed appropriate. During this phase, the experimenter treated the study like a contextual inquiry. Contextual inquiries are generally non-directed observations that allow researchers to observe what users actually do. We incorporated this element of qualitative analysis to evaluate what tasks we would expect participants to attempt on their own.

Since participants were not directed to complete any set of tasks, they may not have completed the tasks we had in mind. The experimenter first waited until the participant declared that the configuration was complete. Then the experimenter asked a series of follow-up questions to help guide the participant to the security tasks. For example, if the participant neglected to change the default administrative password, the experimenter would ask:

With your current configuration, did you know that anyone who knows the default password can log in to your access point? That means they could change any of your configuration settings without your permission. They could even lock you out from your own network if they wanted to. Did you know that could happen?

We then asked participants to complete the task. At this point, the study was more similar to a usability study. A usability study allows researchers to gather quantitative data about people's actions in a limited amount of time. We evaluated participants on their ability to complete the set of five tasks listed above.

Once the tasks were completed or participants ran out of time, we asked participants to complete the questionnaire again. Surveys allow researchers to gather quantitative data about people's attitudes quickly. However, because attitude ratings are highly subjective, we only used this data to measure within-subject changes in attitude.

In combining the different evaluation methods together, we believe our technique was able to capitalize on the strengths of each method and minimize its respective shortcomings.

EXPERIMENTAL RESULTS

We used the data that we collected to assess how well we expect users will be able to navigate each step in Figure 1. In this section, we highlight the points that are most relevant to the design of security configuration interfaces. First, we discuss users' understanding of wireless technology. This corresponds to Step 1 in Figure 1. Second, we show that on commercial access points, low expertise users have more problems configuring the security of wireless networks than high expertise users. In contrast, users perform comparably using our system, which automates Steps 4 through 6 in Figure 1.

Understanding of Wireless Technology

As mentioned, we first interviewed participants to understand how they conceptualize wireless technologies. For example, participants were asked to draw a picture illustrating how data travels from a wireless device to the Internet, and vice versa. As a follow-up question, the experimenter asked participants to choose the diagram in Figure 4 that most closely matches their ideas.

No participant selected Figure 4a, a scenario illustrating the access point and client communicating directly with one another across an "invisible wire." Two participants (11%) selected Figure 4b, which shows both sides using directional broadcast. We expected more people to select this diagram; it is commonly seen on access point packaging as a stylistic simplification. Interestingly, six participants (33%) selected Figure 4c. Figure 4c shows the access point broadcasting in all directions, while the client sends a directed "beam" of data back to the access point. Last, 10 participants (56%) selected Figure 4d, which shows both the laptop and client broadcasting data in all directions. Happily, all users selected a diagram that visualizes some element of broadcasting, and over half of the participants recognized that both the access point and the client broadcast in all directions.

Unfortunately, the half who selected the wrong figure holds beliefs that may lead them to underestimate the risks of wireless technologies. What if these users are not concerned about eavesdropping because they mistakenly believe the attacker must be physically located between their wireless device and the access point? We did not establish a link between conceptualization and risk perception in this study, but we believe it may warrant future work.

Configuration Interface Design

Our studies reveal that the design of a configuration interface substantially impacts users' behav-

ior. In this section, we present three fundamental observations. First, in contrast to commercial systems, low expertise users will attempt to configure the same security settings as high expertise users using our goal-oriented design. Second, our design enables users to configure the same level of security, regardless of expertise level. Finally, low expertise users react more positively to our prototype, in contrast to the commercial systems.

In our user study, the experimenter first asked study participants to configure the access point without providing any directions or tasks. There are two interesting points illustrated in Figure 5. First, on the commercial access points (Linksys and Netgear), high expertise users attempted to complete more of the five tasks than low expertise users. While disappointing, this is hardly surprising. However, the extent may be surprising: using the Netgear access point, low expertise users did not attempt any of the security-related tasks—not even changing the default password! With the Linksys access point, low expertise users attempted one task each. Two tried to change the default password; the other tried to change the SSID.

Figure 4. Follow-up exercise to assess users' notions of wireless broadcasting

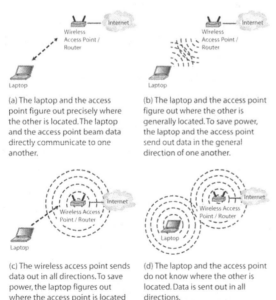

(a) The laptop and the access point figure out precisely where the other is located. The laptop and the access point beam data directly communicate to one another.

(b) The laptop and the access point figure out where the other is generally located. To save power, the laptop and the access point send out data in the general direction of one another.

(c) The wireless access point sends data out in all directions. To save power, the laptop figures out where the access point is located and beams data directly to the access point.

(d) The laptop and the access point do not know where the other is located. Data is sent out in all directions.

Figure 5. Average number of security tasks attempted without experimenter prompting* (*In the bar graphs, vertical lines represent the standard error of the mean. The absence of a bar indicates the standard error is zero.)

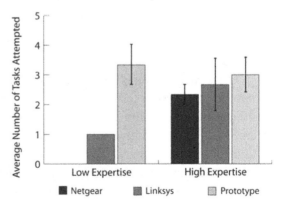

The second lesson in Figure 5 is that low expertise users would try to configure the same level of security as high expertise users, if given the opportunity. In contrast to the commercial access points, all users on our prototype, both low and high expertise, attempted to change the default password, enable MAC filtering, and enable encryption. By eliciting users' goals, our prototype interface indicates that users have similar needs to one another, regardless of technical expertise. In feature-based interfaces, however, technical experience and knowledge may serve as a barrier for less savvy users.

Once we began prompting users to complete the tasks, we found that the barrier of technical expertise remained for the commercial access points. This is illustrated in Figure 6. We consider the results in Figure 6 to be more representative of what would happen in the real world. However, a significant difference between the lab and home environments is that participants did not have access to a technically-savvy friend. At home, users would not be told to complete tasks as they were in our study. It is more likely that users would struggle with the configuration on

their own and/or ask a technically-savvy friend to configure the network for them.

Finally, we evaluated the general user experience of the prototype, compared to the commercial access points. We captured this in the questionnaire with a series of questions assessing how positively the user feels about wireless network setup.

Recall that the questionnaire was administered once before the participants handled the access point and once afterwards. We used participants' change in attitude (measured on a 7-point Likert scale) as a rough indicator of their experience, relative to their prior expectations. A positive change reflects a positive user experience, and vice versa.

Figure 7 suggests that low expertise users were pleasantly surprised by the prototype. In contrast, low expertise users showed negative shifts in attitude for the commercial access points. We expect this reflects the frustration participants often expressed during the user study. It is also interesting to note that high expertise users may have been less happy with the prototype than with the commercial access points. We speculate that

Figure 6. Average number of security tasks completed (ability to configure security features)* (* In the bar graphs, vertical lines represent the standard error of the mean. The absence of a bar indicates the standard error is zero.)

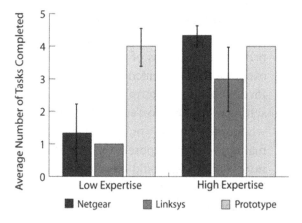

Figure 7. Average change in ease of use rating per question (user experience)* (* In the bar graphs, vertical lines represent the standard error of the mean. The absence of a bar indicates the standard error is zero.)

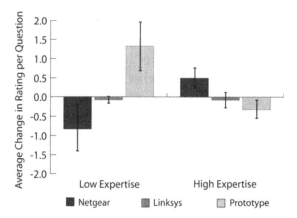

this is a result of prior expectations: many of the high expertise users managed wireless networks at home, and our prototype did not match their expectations of how a configuration interface should behave.

Due to the high costs of technical support calls and product returns, access point vendors have large economic incentives to improve their configuration interfaces. Vendors have made numerous attempts to remedy the situation in recent years. Thus, it is even more surprising that our goal-oriented design so clearly enhanced users' inclination and ability to configure security features. These results demonstrate that vendors could improve their products dramatically without incurring major costs. This would reduce user frustration and increase technology adoption.

DISCUSSION AND FUTURE TRENDS

Many system designers may wonder why we even give users a choice in their security configuration. It benefits the engineers and designers to make the product more "flexible" and "general," but does it benefit the users? Would it not be simpler to enforce a secure default setting? Many of the choices that users can make in today's software are choices for which the users cannot make informed decisions. A pre-configured, easy-to-use, easy-to-secure access point (such as NiaB) would certainly be desirable to many consumers. However, there are several reasons why it is important for users to have a choice. On a practical level, there may be different types of users. Some households have a small number of users and devices, so a high level of security may be easily implemented. Others may have large numbers of transient users, so only the most basic access control measures are practical. Still others may choose to run an open access point, allowing anyone within range to use their network. A single default can never work for everyone.

On a more fundamental level, choice is also viewed as a desirable feature. In the language of value-sensitive design, users should be autonomous. Users should "construct their own goals and values, and [be] able to decide, plan, and act in ways they believe will help them achieve their goals and promote their values" (Friedman & Nissenbaum, 1997). If users are autonomous, they take responsibility for the decisions they make and the actions they take. According to Friedman et al. (1997), autonomy is "fundamental to human flourishing and self-development." Without autonomy, individuals are not morally responsible for their actions. Without user interfaces to support the choices they make, users cannot be autonomous.

As a community, the challenge is to design a system that enables users to successfully configure options with which they may be unfamiliar. Our configuration interface is purely software-based, which means that system designers can iterate through software designs quickly, since no hardware changes are required. It does, however, mean that software development teams need to research their target users in order to formulate the right questions. Determining the right questions to ask target users is time-consuming, and the questions may change as the audience shifts.

Goal-based questions can be used for anything from configuring location-based applications to Bluetooth security. For example, take a location-based application where users can choose to reveal their location to family members, friends, or other acquaintances. Since the technology is new to most people, users may not fully understand the privacy implications of revealing their location over time. Goal-oriented questions may be useful for helping users determine what kind of privacy settings would be most suitable for their needs: to whom information would be given; what information would be exposed; the granularity of the information that would be available; and so on. Users may not initially realize what options are available to them. A well-crafted configuration interface will make them aware of the implications of the technology, as well as match the configuration with their comfort level.

The lessons we have learned in our 802.11 case study can help designers improve the user experience of new technologies. For new technologies to succeed, they must be both easy-to-use and trustworthy. Ease of use and trustworthiness imply that users need to understand what the technology is doing—at least to the level where they can form correct expectations of how the technology should behave. Users who understand the implications and limitations of a technology will ultimately be satisfied because the technology meets—or exceeds—their expectations.

Unpredictability breeds intimidation in users' relationships with technology. Without a basic level of understanding, users will be unhappy and bewildered when something does not behave as they anticipate. Inevitably, this will happen if they form the wrong mental models of the technology.

CONCLUSION

Home consumers are now responsible for configuring the security settings of their devices. While configuration interfaces have improved since the days of inscrutable VCR recording menus, they still terrorize many end users. Configuration interfaces are often feature-based, listing options available for different technical features. People, on the other hand, are goal-based. Users may not have a deep understanding of the technology—and they probably never want to. This lack of understanding makes it hard for users to properly assess their security and privacy risks. It also makes it hard for users to configure product features. Very few consumers truly understand wireless or cryptographic technology, and as a result, very few consumers are willing to configure security in their wireless devices.

Assisting users with the translation from high-level security goal to low-level product feature is a simple but powerful method for building easy-to-use security configuration applications. We developed a prototype using this strategy. We also adapted traditional user study methods to evaluate security applications. We conducted a user study to compare the effectiveness of our prototype to two commercially available access points. Our study demonstrated that the prototype allowed non-expert users to securely configure their networks as well as expert users.

Our work generalizes to other security configuration problems, and we hope that the community will explore this aspect of application design. Making systems easy-to-use and secure is critical to the adoption of new technologies. After all, new technologies only succeed if they satisfy the people who use them.

ACKNOWLEDGMENT

This research was supported by a gift from Intel. The views and conclusions contained here are those of the authors and should not be interpreted as necessarily representing the official policies or endorsements, either express or implied, of Carnegie Mellon University or Intel Corporation.

We would like to thank Vincent Goh and Adrian Tang for their exceptional work with the implementation and the user studies.

REFERENCES

Balfanz, D., Durfee, G., Grinter, R., Smetters, D., & Stewart, P. (2004). Network-in-a-box: How to set up a secure wireless network in under a minute. In *Proceedings of the 13th Conference on USENIX Security Symposium* (pp. 207–222). Berkeley: USENIX Association.

Balfanz, D., Smetters, D., Stewart, P., & Wong, H. C. (2002). Talking to strangers: Authentication in ad-hoc wireless networks. In *Proceedings of Symposium on Network and Distributed Systems Security (NDSS)*.

Cohen, D. (2004). *Consumer front-end to WPA.* Wi-Fi Alliance.

Cooper, A. (1999). *The inmates are running the asylum: Why high-tech products drive us crazy and how to restore the sanity.* Sams Publishing.

Friedman, B., Hurley, D., Howe, D. C., Felten, E., & Nissenbaum, H. (2002). Users' conceptions of Web security: a comparative study. *Extended Abstracts of the CHI 2002 Conference on Human Factors in Computing Systems* (pp. 746-747). New York: Association for Computing Machinery.

Friedman, B., Kahn, P., & Borning, A. (2006). Value sensitive design and information systems. In P. Zhang, & D. Galletta (Eds.), *Human-computer interaction in management information systems: Foundations* (Vol. 4).

Friedman, B., Lin, P., & Miller, J. K. (2005). Informed consent by design. In L. F. Cranor, & S. Garfinkel (Eds.), *Security and usability* (Chap. 24, pp. 495-521). O'Reilly Media, Inc.

Friedman, B., & Nissenbaum, H. (1997). Software agents and user autonomy. In *Proceedings of the First International Conference on Autonomous Agents* (pp. 466–469).

Grimm, R., & Bershad, B. (2001). Separating access control policy, enforcement, and functionality in extensible systems. *ACM Transactions on Computer Systems, 19*(1), 36-70.

Gutmann, P. (2003). Plug-and-play PKI: A PKI your mother can use. In *Proceedings of the 12th USENIX Security Symposium* (pp. 45–58). Berkeley: USENIX Association.

Kuo, C., Perrig, A. & Walker, J. (2006). Designing an evaluation method for security user interfaces: Lessons from studying secure wireless network configuration. *ACM Interactions, 13*(3), 28-31.

Linsky, J., Bourk, T., Findikli, A., Hulvey, R., Ding, S., Heydon, R., et al. (2006, August). *Simple pairing* (Whitepaper, revision v10r00).

Lortz, V., Roberts, D., Erdmann, B., Dawidowsky, F., Hayes, K., Yee, J. C., et al. (2006). *Wi-Fi simple config specification* (version 1.0a).

McCune, J. M., Perrig, A., & Reiter, M. K. (2005). Seeing-is-believing: Using camera phones for human-verifiable authentication. In *Proceedings of IEEE Symposium on Security and Privacy.*

Morgan, G., Fischhoff, B., Bostrom, A., & Atman, C. (2002). *Risk communication: A mental models approach.* New York: Cambridge University Press.

Newman, R., Gavette, S., Yonge, L., & Anderson, R. (2006). Protecting domestic power-line communications. In *Proceedings of Symposium on Usable Privacy and Security (SOUPS)*.

Perrig, A., & Song, D. (1999). Hash visualization: A new technique to improve real-world security. In *Proceedings of International Workshop on Cryptographic Techniques and E-Commerce (CrypTEC)*.

Reeves, B., & Nass, C. (1996). *The media equation: How people treat computers, televisions and new media like real people and places.* Cambridge University Press.

Saltzer, J. H., & Schroeder, M. D. (1975). The protection of information in computer systems. In *Proceedings of the IEEE, 63*(9), 1278-1308.

Stajano, F., & Anderson, R. (1999). *The resurrecting duckling: Security issues for ad-hoc wireless networks.* Security Protocols, 7th International Workshop.

Uzun, E., Karvonen, K., & Asokan, N. (2007). Usability analysis of secure pairing methods. *Usable Security (USEC)*.

Whitten, A., & Tygar, J. D. (1999). Why Johnny can't encrypt: A usability evaluation of PGP 5.0. In *Proceedings of the 8th USENIX Security Symposium*. USENIX, Washington, D.C., USA.

ENDNOTE

[1]   Saltzer and Schroeder (1975) outlined eight design principles for minimizing application security flaws. The eighth principle is psychological acceptability: *Psychological acceptability*: It is essential that the human interface be designed for ease of use, so that users routinely and automatically apply the protection mechanisms correctly. Also, to the extent that the user's mental image of his protection goals matches the mechanisms he must use, mistakes will be minimized. If he must translate his image of his protection needs into a radically different specification language, he will make errors.

Chapter XII
Security Usability
Challenges for End–Users

Steven Furnell

Centre for Information Security & Network Research, University of Plymouth, UK

ABSTRACT

This chapter highlights the need for security solutions to be usable by their target audience, and examines the problems that can be faced when attempting to understand and use security features in typical applications. Challenges may arise from system-initiated events, as well as in relation to security tasks that users wish to perform for themselves, and can occur for a variety of reasons. This is illustrated by examining problems that arise as a result of reliance upon technical terminology, unclear or confusing functionality, lack of visible status and informative feedback to users, forcing users to make uninformed decisions, and a lack of integration amongst the different elements of security software themselves. The discussion draws upon a number of practical examples from popular applications, as well as results from survey and user trial activities that were conducted in order to assess the potential problems at first hand. The findings are used as the basis for recommending a series of top-level guidelines that may be used to improve the situation, and these are used as the basis assessing further examples of existing software to determine the degree of compliance.

INTRODUCTION

End-users are faced with an increasing requirement to use security, with recent years witnessing a significant surge in the range and volume of security threats that can affect their IT systems. Highly publicized incidents involving malware, spyware, phishing, and denial of service have all served to heighten general awareness of Internet threats, with the consequence that users at all levels (be they at work or at home) are likely to have at least some appreciation of the need to keep their systems secure. However, adequate protection will rarely be achieved by default, and here we often find that even the security technologies that *are* used are often used badly (classic examples being bad practice with passwords, and poorly maintained anti-virus protection). In some cases, the blame for this clearly resides with careless or irresponsible end-users. However, it is important to realize that another significant factor is often the underlying unfriendly nature of the technology.

Security-related functionality can be found in both specific tools and embedded within general applications, and users will frequently encounter the requirement to make security-related decisions during routine use of their system. However, provision of security functionality is only of value if the target audience can understand and use it. Unfortunately, the manner of presentation, and the implicit assumptions about users' abilities, can often hamper usage in practice. This can represent a particular problem in contexts where users are required to fend for themselves, and may result in necessary protection being under-utilized or misapplied.

Although much security-related functionality is now presented via the ostensibly friendly context of a graphical user interface, if we look beyond the surface, the user-friendliness can quickly disappear. For example, a series of apparently simple check boxes or low-medium-high settings can soon become more complex if you have to understand the actual functionality that they control (Furnell, 2004). As a result, many users will ultimately remain as baffled as they would have been by a command line interface. Those most likely to suffer are non-technical users, who lack the knowledge to help themselves, or any formal support to call upon. Should they be implicitly denied the level of protection that they desire simply because they are not technology experts? Clearly, the answer is no. As such, the usability of security is a crucial factor in ensuring that it is able to serve its intended purpose. Although this requirement is now beginning to achieve much more widespread recognition (CRA, 2003; Cranor & Garfinkel, 2005), usable security remains an area in which current software is often notably lacking.

This chapter examines the nature of the usability problem, presenting examples from standard end-user applications, as well as supporting evidence from current research. Having established the existence and nature of the problem, the discussion proceeds to consider specific issues that can present obstacles from the usability perspective. Particular consideration is given to problems at the user interface level, and how we may consequently find our attempts to use security being impeded (or entirely prevented) as a result of inadequate attention to human-computer interaction (HCI) aspects. The discussion then proceeds to present a brief examination of means by which the situation can be improved, and the chapter concludes with a summation of the main issues.

BACKGROUND

If we consider the factors that may prevent users from securing their systems then, perhaps unsurprisingly, lack of knowledge and inability to use the software concerned are amongst the prominent reasons, particularly for the novice community. Evidence here can be cited from a study of security perceptions amongst 415 personal Internet users who were asked to identify the factors that prevented them from carrying out security practices (Furnell, Bryant, & Phippen, 2007). The overall findings are illustrated in Figure 1, and although 41% considered that they devoted sufficient attention to security, a variety of reasons were seen to be impeding the remainder. Although there is no single issue that stands out as an obstacle to all users, there are clearly some reasons that can be related to the users' knowledge and the usability of the software (e.g., "I don't understand how to use security packages" clearly shows that some users find the protection challenging to use, whereas "Security impedes the use of my computer" illustrates a usability constraint from a different perspective). When specifically considering the main reasons cited by respondents that classed themselves as novices (as opposed to intermediate or advanced users), it is revealed that factors relating to lack of knowledge and understanding are the most prominent constraints (e.g., 43% claimed not to understand the threats, 38% claimed they did not know how to use security packages, 35% indicated that they did not know how to secure their computer, and 32% indicating that they did not know about the threats).

When considering the inclusion of security functionality within end-user software, a number of desirable criteria can be identified that will influence the overall usability of the resulting protection. Some key points include the following (Furnell, Jusoh, & Katsabas, 2006):

- **Understandable**—options and descriptions should be presented in a manner that is meaningful to the intended user population. Security offers a great deal of potential for the use of technical terminology and other jargon, but this could easily come at the cost

of excluding a proportion of the users. Sufficient help and support should be available to assist novices to achieve the level of security that they need.

- **Locatable**—users need to be able to find the features they need. If casual users have to spend too long looking for security, it increases the chances that they will give up and remain unprotected.

- **Visible**—the system should give a clear indication of whether security is being applied. Appropriate use of status indicators and warnings will help to remind users in cases where they may have forgotten to enable appropriate safeguards.

- **Convenient**—although visibility is important, the provision of security should not become so prominent that it is considered inconvenient or intrusive. Users are likely to disable features that become too much of an impediment to legitimate use.

Figure 1. Factors preventing security practices being carried out

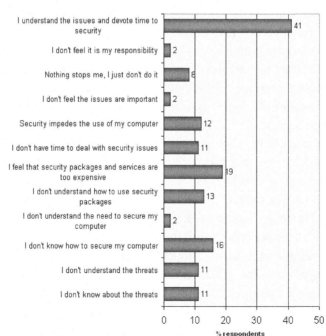

Examining current implementations of security can reveal deficiencies in these regards. Indeed, it often appears that security features have been included without a great deal of thought about how (and by whom) they will actually be used. There often seems to be an implicit assumption that users who have an interest in security and wish to protect themselves will be determined enough to work out how to do it. However, the situation will very often be the exact opposite, with users needing little excuse to avoid security unless they have no other choice. As a result, while the features enable developers to tick the box to say that security has been addressed (and avoid consequent accusations of negligence), it does not yield a very positive result for the users.

Some clear awareness issues still need to be overcome, and there is unfortunately ample evidence to show that users do not actually understand security very well in the first place. In other cases, users think that they understand it, but often find it very difficult to use correctly. For example, in the United States, the 2005 Online Safety Study conducted by AOL and the National Cyber Security Alliance interviewed a sample of 354 home users while also performing a technical scan and analysis of their machines. The survey concluded that 81% of home computers analyzed lacked core protection (i.e., recently-updated anti-virus software, a properly-configured firewall, and/or spyware protection) (AOL/NCSA, 2005). As a result, 12% currently had a virus on their computer, 61% of machines had known spyware or adware installed, and 44% did not have their firewall setup correctly. Such evidence clearly suggests that if users cannot understand the technologies they may not protect themselves properly.

The difficulty of using security options has a tendency to mirror the complexity of the security concepts involved. For example, using a tool such as PGP (pretty good privacy) to send and receive secure e-mail requires the user to have some appreciation of concepts such as encryption, keys, and digital signatures. Indeed, a widely cited paper by Whitten and Tygar (1999) specifically considered the usability and friendliness of the PGP utility, and conducted a laboratory test with 12 participants to investigate the ease with which they could use the tool to sign and encrypt a message. The study determined that only a third were able to do so within the 90 minutes allocated for the task, with problems arising from the user interface design and the complexity of the underlying concepts that participants needed to understand. However, such problems are by no means restricted to features such as cryptography. A more recent study from Johnston, Eloff, and Labuschagne (2003) considered the HCI aspects of the Internet Connection Firewall (since rechristened as the Windows Firewall) within Windows XP. This again found the presentation of the security functionality to be less than ideal, with the consequence that users would have likely difficulties in getting the most out of it.

A common factor in both of the aforementioned studies was that the target was a security-oriented tool. However, security features also exist within more general end-user applications. For example, word processors, Web browsers, e-mail clients, and databases can all be expected to have some security functionality. However, here too there can be significant barriers to effective use, and the following quote from Schultz (2002) sums things up fairly well:

"The overwhelming majority of software that supports security is also defective as far as usability goes. If software vendors would make software functions used in providing security more user-friendly, people would be more receptive to security."

This is very often the fundamental nature of the problem—the protection we need is often available, but provides no benefit because we cannot work out how to use it. Security functionality has to be conveyed in a meaningful manner, and the interface through which the user is expected to control and configure it must be appropriate to the audience that it intends to address.

Usability Problems in Practice

Broadly speaking, end-users are likely to face two categories of security event during their use of a system—those that they initiate for themselves and those initiated by the system.

- **System-initiated events:** These types of events occur with intention to inform the end-user about security issues and/or require related decisions. Thus, this type of event is initiated by the system and targets the end user. For example, many users will be familiar with seeing pop-up dialogs in their Web browser asking them whether or not they wish to allow an event, such as that depicted later in Figure 11.
- **User-initiated events:** These types of events differ from the system-initiated events because this time the user intends to deal with security. More specifically, this applies when an end-user actively seeks to invoke an element of security (e.g., encrypting a message) or perform a security-related task (e.g., controlling or configuring security-related features within applications and tools).

Unfortunately, both cases can pose problems from the usability perspective. Evidence for this comes from a study conducted by the author's research group. This work involved 26 users who were asked to record details of system- and user-initiated events that they encountered over a 2 week period, as well as any usability problems that resulted. Amongst the findings was the fact that users are frequently confused when they are asked to make security-related decisions. For example, two thirds of the system-initiated events required users to do this, and (as Figure 2 illustrates) although the majority were clearly comfortable, this still left more than a third of

instances in which participants were confused. Prior work from DeWitt and Kuljis (2005) has observed that, when faced with a requirement to make security-related decisions, users will often take whatever path seems quickest in order to get their work done—even if this means compromising their security. As such, encountering events that are unclear in the first place will add further incentive for security to be sidelined.

Although some of the confusion surrounding system-initiated events could be explained by the fact that they occurred unexpectedly, the problems also extend to the user-initiated context. In the aforementioned study, the majority of these events (59%) again required participants to make some decision, and again the extent to which they felt able to do so was variable (see Figure 3). Although a greater proportion felt "totally clear" in this context (possibly reflecting the fact that the

Figure 2. Users' understanding of how to respond to decisions required by system-initiated events

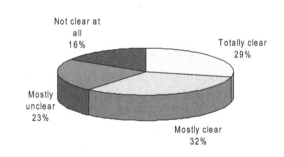

Figure 3. Users' understanding of how to perform user-initiated events

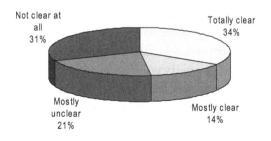

users themselves were in control of the situation when initiating events), there was also a far greater proportion that were 'not clear at all'.

The remainder of this section highlights a number of examples of common failings that are apparent in programs that target end-users. For the purposes of discussion, five key themes are used to group the problem issues. However, it should be noted that several of the points are inter-related, and the practical examples used to illustrate them can certainly be seen to be suffering from more than one of the problems. It should also be noted that the occurrence of these issues is not restricted to the implementation of security functionality, and indeed the themes identified here are closely related to usability heuristics proposed by Nielsen (1994) for systems in general.

In addition to practical examples, the discussion draws upon the results from related studies that have been conducted in order to assess users' understanding of application-level security features, and their ability to use them in practice.

End-User Survey

The aim of the survey was to assess users' understanding, and hence the potential usability of security-related interfaces within a number of well-known software packages. An online questionnaire presented respondents with screenshots relating to the security functionality within a number of popular end-user applications and attempted to determine whether they were meaningful (e.g., in relation to the terminology used) and correctly interpreted (i.e., whether the intention of the functionality was properly understood). A total of 342 responses were received, and the main characteristics of the respondent group were as follows:

- Almost equally split between male and female
- Over 80% in the 17-29 age group
- Over 80% have university-level education

- Over 96% are regularly use a computer at home and/or at work
- Almost 90% rated themselves as intermediate or advanced users

These factors suggest that the respondents as a whole were likely to have a high level of IT literacy, making them well-placed to provide relevant comments about the usability of security features within the targeted applications. Some of the significant findings from the survey are therefore used to support the discussion presented here. For readers interested obtaining further information, the full details of the survey and the associated results can be found in Furnell et al. (2006).

End-User Trials

While the survey allowed a large-scale assessment of the extent to which users understood the information before them, it was not able to reveal deeper insights into the extent to which the programs could actually be used. As such, the findings were supplemented by a series of hands-on trial activities, in which users were required to make practical use of the security features within a range of applications. The trials involved 15 participants, eight of whom were general users and seven of whom were advanced. The general users were familiar with using IT (and some of the applications concerned) on a regular basis, but had no specific knowledge about the detail of the technology. By contrast, the advanced users all held academic qualifications relating to IT and had some prior knowledge in relation to security. The required tasks were presented in writing and explained to the participants. Note that they were told *what* they needed to achieve, but not *how* to do it, and the aim of the trial was to determine whether they could understand and use the security features within the application sufficiently well to achieve the objectives. Each trial session lasted between 1 and 2 hours, depending upon the ability of the participants and the ease with which they completed the tasks (Furnell, Katsabas, Dowland, & Reid, 2007).

Both the survey and the trials drew heavily upon Microsoft products as the basis for examples, and this is further reflected by the examples discussed in this chapter. However, it should be noted that this is not intended to imply that the usability of security features within Microsoft's software is specifically poor. The examples were actually chosen to reflect the widespread usage and popularity of the programs concerned—thus maximizing the chances of survey and trial participants also being end-users of the software (although this was not a prerequisite for either activity, it was considered that participants would feel more comfortable with programs they were familiar with).

Reliance upon Technical Terminology

One of the traditional barriers to newcomers into IT is the significant degree of technical terminology that accompanies the domain. Over time, efforts have been made to ease this burden, with increased use of pictures and plain language as a means of expressing concepts to novices. However, security is one area in which the message is still very likely to be unclear, with technical terms often being an intrinsic part of how features are conveyed. An example of this problem is illustrated in Figure 4, which shows the means by which users are able to control the security settings within Internet Explorer (IE) version 7. Provided as the standard browser within the most popular operating system, IE is consequently the means by which most users come into contact with the Web, and browsing is a context in which appropriate security is most definitely required. However, although the interface initially looks quite straightforward, with the use of a slider control to set the desired security level (which, for the "Internet" zone, has a three-point scale

of medium, medium-high, and high), it becomes somewhat less intuitive if users try to understand the descriptions of the settings. For example, one of the characteristics of the "medium-high" setting described in the Figure is that "unsigned ActiveX controls will not be downloaded." Although this would be unlikely to cause problems for users with a technology background, it has clear potential to confuse the average user (who might nonetheless have an interest in setting up their system securely, and so could certainly find themselves looking at the related options). As a result, while they will appreciate the idea of the medium-to-high scale, the descriptions may impede their ability to relate this to their browsing needs. As an aside, it should be noted that the slider used to control the level in the other three content zones shows a five-point scale (adding settings of low and medium-low to the list of options). This reflects the fact that the safer environment that is hopefully provided by the "local intranet" and "trusted sites" may allow the level of protection to be relaxed. Meanwhile, although a slider is displayed in the "restricted sites" zone, the level is permanently set to "high" and the user cannot alter it.

Respondents to the authors' survey were presented with the analogous interface from IE6 (which was the current version at the time of the study), and asked to indicate whether they understood various elements of it. One question specifically focused upon the content zone concept and showed the related part of the interface with the "trusted sites" and "restricted sites" highlighted. Respondents were then asked to indicate whether they knew the difference—revealing that 14% did not and a further 22% were not sure. Similarly, as part of the practical user trial, participants were asked to explain their understanding of the different zones, revealing that only two-thirds could do so adequately. However, a slightly greater proportion (12 out of 15 participants) was still able to use the functionality, and add sites to the trusted and restricted zones.

Figure 4. The security settings interface from Internet Explorer 7

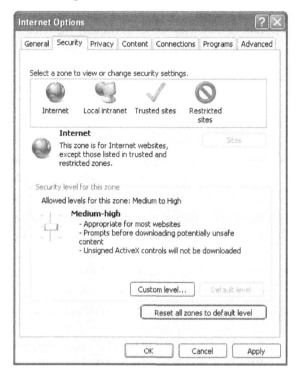

Proceeding to consider users' understanding of the actual security level, survey respondents were presented with description of the "medium" setting from IE6 (which is closely similar to that of the IE7 "medium-high" setting shown in Figure 4) and asked to indicate if they understood it—the results revealed that 34% did not. Although this is already a sizeable proportion of users to lose, the authors anticipated that some respondents would claim to understand the interface even though they did not actually understand all of the terminology. As such, the questionnaire proceeded to ask whether respondents had heard of ActiveX before, and if so, whether they actually knew what it meant. Although the initial finding here was mostly positive, with 65% claiming to have heard of the term, only 54% of these people (i.e., only 35% of the overall respondent group) knew the meaning. This puts a rather different interpretation upon the proportion of people who would fully

understand the setting in Figure 4, with almost two thirds of the overall respondent group unable to comprehend the complete description.

An even more significant terminology problem is likely to be encountered if users attempt to go beyond the three presets and select the "custom" setting. Doing so yields a new window offering 46 distinct settings (note that the number varies depending upon the version of IE in use); making things considerably more complicated than a 3-position slider. Some of these (relating to the security of ActiveX controls) are illustrated in Figure 5, and examples of others include the following:

- Loose XAML
- Run components signed with Authenticode
- Allow META REFRESH
- Launching programs and files in an IF-RAME
- Software channel permissions
- Active scripting

In most cases, the options available allow a user to completely enable or disable a particular setting, or have the system prompt them for a decision each time a relevant activity occurs. However, it is very unlikely that the majority of users would actually understand what they are being asked to enable or disable anyway (and so selecting the option for the system to prompt them each time would not improve things—it would simply oblige them to take a decision that they did not understand on multiple occasions). Moreover, the system offers no context-sensitive help to explain any of the settings, and even looking at the main help system reveals that only a subset of the terminology is actually explained (for example, while explanations can be found for "ActiveX" and "Authenticode," there is nothing to explain the meaning of "IFRAME," "META REFRESH," and "Software channel permissions"—although determined users can find definitions on Microsoft's Web site if they look there). With these observations in mind, it is perhaps not surprising to find that the majority of respondents to the usability survey were confused when presented with the IE6 version of the interface in Figure 5, with only 40% claiming to understand the options.

One of the further IE tasks required in the user trial was to customize the security settings in order to be prompted before running ActiveX content. Although 5 out of 7 of the advanced users were able to achieve this, only one of the general users was able to complete the task. The overall success rate for the trial group as a whole was 40%, and as such the trial activities confirmed the earlier findings from the survey in this regard.

Unclear and Confusing Functionality

If users are confronted with security features that they do not understand, then the first danger is that they will simply give up and not use it at all. However, if they are not put off (or, alternatively, have no choice but to use it), the next danger

is that it will increase their chances of making mistakes. In some cases, these mistakes will put their system or data at increased risk, whereas in others they may serve to impede the user's own use of the system. Confusion can often arise from the way in which features are presented, with the result that even the most straightforward and familiar security safeguards can become challenging to use.

As an example, we can consider the way in which password protection is used in several Microsoft Office applications. Excel, PowerPoint, and Word all allow two levels of password to be applied to user files—to control access to the file (i.e., in order to maintain confidentiality) or to restrict the ability to modify it (i.e., controlling integrity). Using the Word 2007 interface as an example, these are set via the dialog shown on the left side of Figure 6. However, an immediate observation here is that the route to actually finding and using this interface is rather curious. Whereas earlier versions of Word made security settings available from the "tools–options" menu, they are now only accessible via the "tools" button in the bottom left corner of the "save as" dialog box. Although this was also one of the routes available in earlier versions, it was arguably the more obscure one. Additionally, rather than being labeled "security" (and as had previously been the case), the option to select is now called "general"—even though the only options it contains are security-related. Another aspect that seems rather unintuitive is that, in addition to initially setting passwords via this route, users must also go to the "save as" dialog box in order to change or remove them. Finally, anyone expecting to get guidance on how to use the options will be rather disappointed—although the main help system does include an entry about passwords, using the context-sensitive help simply takes you to Word's top level help page and requires the user to enter a search term manually. This is in contrast to what happens when you use the context-based help feature in most other dialogs, with the system

Figure 5. IE7 custom security settings

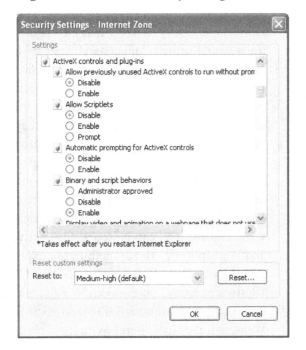

directing you to a specific themed page, or at least providing a series of suggested topics that might be followed.

Users who subsequently attempt to open a password-protected file are then presented with the dialogs on the right-hand side of Figure 6. However, whereas the prompt for opening an access-controlled file (the upper dialog) is relatively easy to understand (i.e., you need a password and cannot open the document without it), the dialog for files that are merely protected against modification is often misunderstood. Users who wish to simply view or print the file can select the "read only" option, in order to bypass the password request. However, the presentation of the interface causes confusion in practice, and many users are so distracted by the apparent requirement for a password that they believe they cannot do anything without it. Indeed, in the usability survey, respondents were presented with an example of the lower password dialog and asked to indicate which of three options they understood it to mean. Although the majority correctly indicated that it meant the document could not be modified without a password, 23% incorrectly believed that the file

could not be *opened* without a password, and a further 13% were not sure how to interpret it. As such, more than a third of users would not have been in a position to make the correct decision.

Whereas the survey focused upon the interpretation of the password prompts, the practical trial activities included the task of setting the passwords in the first place. Specifically, trialists were given a sample Word document and then instructed to make sure that a password was required to read it (which would require them to use the upper password box in Figure 6), and then later to use a password to prevent unauthorized changes (requiring the other password to be set). The overall success was low in both cases, with only five users (two general and three advanced) able to complete the first task, and six participants able to do the second one (with one more advanced user working it out this time). This clearly shows that even familiar security features (and the password is surely the most familiar security measure that we use) can be rendered unusable if they are not presented in an effective manner.

Looking at other aspects within the dialog box on the left of Figure 6, another element that has

Figure 6. Password options and the resulting prompts within Microsoft Word

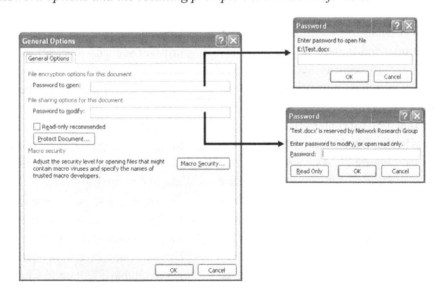

the potential to cause confusion is the "protect document" button. From the outset, the presence of such a button seems odd, given that selecting a password to open or modify a document could also be considered to be aspects of document protection. Although this observation could be perceived as overly picky, it is the type of issue that could easily confuse or impede beginners. Indeed, in this particular case, even Microsoft's own tutorial for the security features acknowledges the confusing nature of the situation (Microsoft, 2007):

*Some of the settings that appear on the **Security** tab, including some that sound like security features, do not actually secure documents . . . The **Document Protection** task pane and **Protect Document** features (available in Word) do not secure your documents against malicious interference either. They protect the format and content of your document when you collaborate with co–workers.*

Given such comments, it is surprising to find the "protect document" option remaining under the security tab, and not being renamed to something more meaningful (such as 'document editing restrictions").

Another relevant example of unclear and potentially confusing functionality within Office 2007 is provided by the "trust center." This interface is accessible from within most Office 2007 applications, and is used to configure aspects such as macro security settings, trusted publishers and locations, and privacy options. However, one potentially confusing aspect arises from the fact that the trust center's interface looks very similar when invoked from within different applications (see Figure 7). As such, users may be inclined to assume that it is a generic utility and that any changes will apply across all their Office applications and files. Although this is indeed true in some cases (e.g., changes to the "ActiveX Settings," "message bar," and "privacy options" affect these settings across all Office

applications), other options (such as "Trusted Locations," "add-ins," and "macro settings") only initiate changes within the current application. Unfortunately, with the exception of the ActiveX settings (where the window heading says "ActiveX settings for all Office applications"), the scope of the settings is not remotely obvious from the interface presented at the time. Moreover, even the help system does not provide clarity in some cases (e.g., while it indicates that macro settings are only applicable to the current application, it says nothing similar in the descriptions of trusted locations and add-ins).

Lack of Visible Status and Informative Feedback

Users ought to know when security is being applied and what level of protection they are being given. This not only provides a basis for increasing their confidence when using particular services, but can also remind them to configure the system correctly. Without such a reminder, users may proceed to perform sensitive tasks without adequate protection, or may inadvertently leave settings at a level that impedes their legitimate usage. As such, the lack of visible status information is another example of undesirable HCI. As an illustration of how this can cause problems, Figure 8 shows an attempt to reach Microsoft's Hotmail service via Internet Explorer, with the browser security level set to 'high'. The user receives no message at all, and there is no indication of what the problem might be. As such, they may conclude that the site is simply not operational. What the user should receive is a clear message to remind them that their browser security is set to 'high', and to indicate that this may cause the site to operate incorrectly.

Another good example from within Internet Explorer relates back to the use of the custom settings mentioned earlier in the discussion. If a user changes one of the many settings at this level, it has a notable effect upon what they subsequently

Figure 7. The trust center when accessed from (a) Word, (b) Excel, (c) PowerPoint, and (d) Access

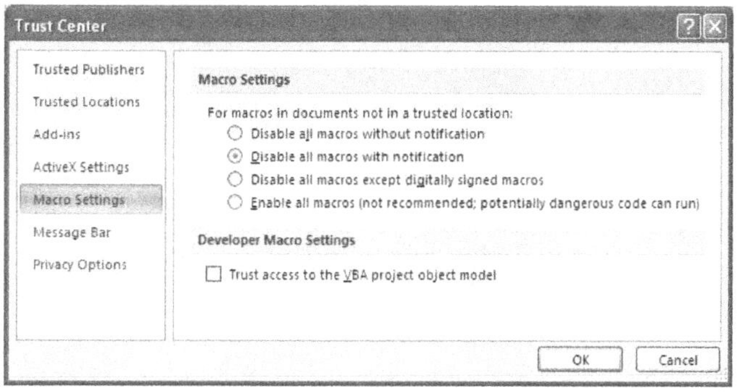

(a)

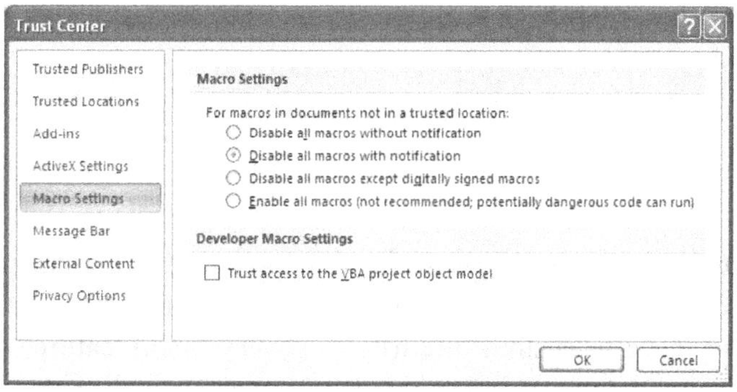

(b)

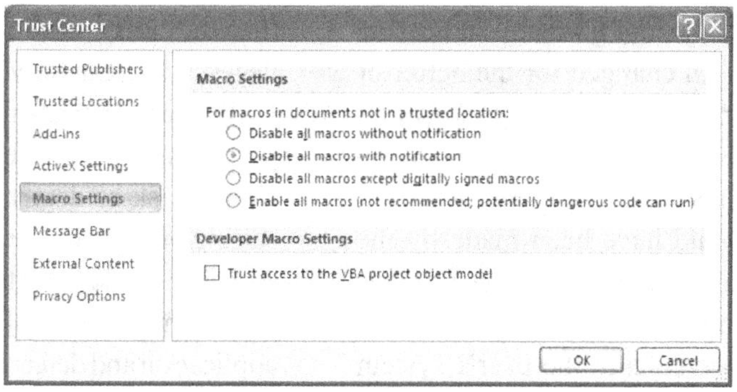

(c)

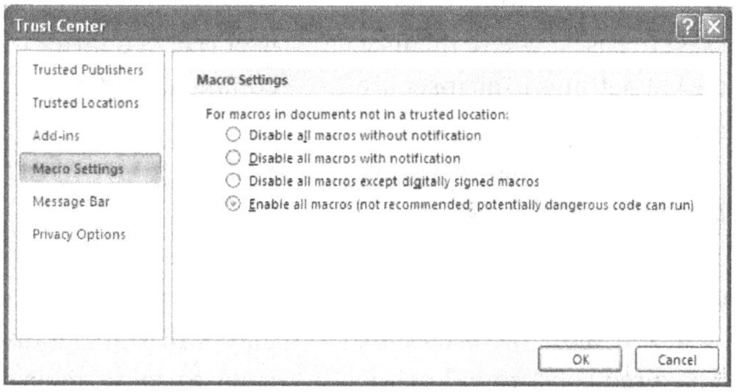

(d)

Figure 8. Attempts to access Hotmail with Internet Explorer security set to "high"

see in the main security settings window. Rather than getting the 3- or 5-point slider, the user now simply sees that they have a "custom" security level, as shown in Figure 9a. From an information perspective, all this tells you is that something has been changed —it does not give any indication of whether it has been changed for the better or worse, and the user no longer has any indication of where their protection resides in relation to the previous slider. This is fair enough if one assumes that any change would have been made by the user directly (i.e., assuming they had not forgotten, they would know what had been changed and why), but in some cases the user's system might have been initially configured by someone else (e.g., their supplier or system administrator). Having said this, in severe cases, where the user has moved some of the key settings to an insecure status, they *are* warned that they have placed the system at risk. This is illustrated in Figure 9b, which shows a change to the message in the security level area and warning symbols on the icons for the affected zone. In addition, going to the custom options list will show the offending settings highlighted on a red background, while returning to the main browser window yields a

warning banner as a reminder and the option to automatically fix the settings. This is clearly a very useful feature (which is a notable improvement since the previous version of the browser), but there is no analogous warning to tell the user that they may have made changes that are unnecessarily restrictive.

In the user trials involving Internet Explorer, participants were asked to perform the rather more simple task of determining the current security setting of the browser before any custom changes had been made (i.e., they simply needed to be able to find the location of the security settings in the application and determine the current setting of the slider). However, even this proved problematic for some with three general users and one advanced user (i.e., a quarter of the participants) unable to complete the task.

Forcing Uninformed Decisions

Even if users do not go looking for security-related options and attempt to change the settings, they may still find themselves confronted with the need to take security-related decisions during the course of their normal activities as a result of

Figure 9. The result of altering custom security settings

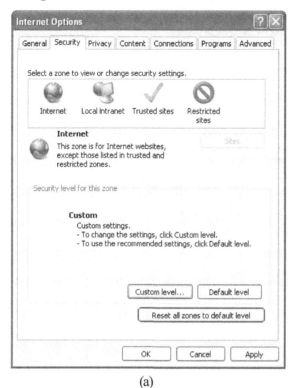

(a)

(b)

system-initiated events. In these contexts, it should be all the more important for the information to be conveyed to them in a meaningful fashion, with minimal assumptions of prior knowledge and maximum help available to ease the process. Unfortunately, however, users may again find themselves at a disadvantage in practice, with dialogs often being conveyed in a manner that only advanced participants would be comfortable with. To illustrate the point, Figure 10 and Figure 11 present two examples of dialogs that may be encountered by users during standard Web browsing activities. The first example illustrates the type of warning that a user would receive in Internet Explorer when a Web site's security certificate has been issued by a provider that is not specified as trusted in their security configuration. This does not, of course, mean that the certifying authority cannot be trusted, but the user is being asked to check in order to make a decision. The likely problem here is that most users will not know what a security certificate is, let alone be able to make a meaningful decision about one. Although the style of this warning has changed in the newer version of IE (see Figure 10b), appearing as part of the browser pane rather than a separate dialog box, the underlying information (and hence the potential to confuse users) remains the same. As an aside, and relating back to the comments in the previous section, the "more information" link shown in Figure 10b does not work if the browser security has been set to "high."

Meanwhile, the example in Figure 11 is warning the user that a Web page they are attempting to download contains active content that could potentially be harmful to their system. The difficulty for most users is again likely to be that they would not understand what they were being asked, with terms such as "active content" and "ActiveX" being more likely to confuse than explain. Of course, part of the problem in these examples relates to the earlier issue of using technical terminology. However, the problem here goes somewhat deeper, in the sense that both

Figure 10. Web site security certificate warning (a) IE6 version (b) IE7 version

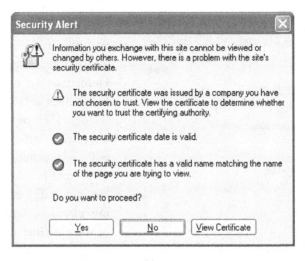

(a)

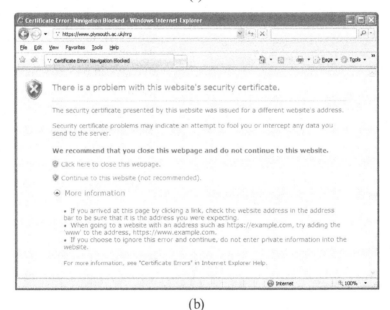

(b)

cases are obliging the user to make a decision without the option to seek further help from the system. As such, they would be forced to make a decision in the absence of sufficient information. As an indication of the scale of this problem, the example from Figure 11 was presented to the survey respondents, and 56% indicated that they would not know how to make a decision.

Returning to Word 2007, an interesting new addition to the application when compared to earlier versions is the "document inspector," which allows the user to audit their document to ensure that it is not inadvertently holding personal/private information. Although this is a potentially useful feature, the reports that it generates are less informative than one might hope. Considering, for example, the report in Figure 12, we can see that although three areas have

Figure 11. Active content warning

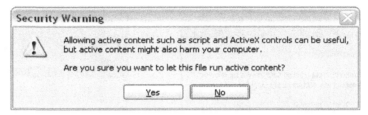

Figure 12. An example report from the document inspector

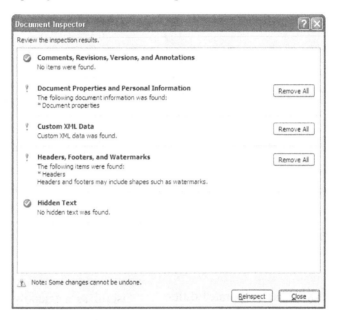

been flagged for concern, there is no indication of what was specifically found under each of the categories. Moreover, the interface offers no option to manually inspect the information—only to remove it. In some cases (such as with the headers highlighted in the Figure), this could result in the over-eager user removing something that they actually wanted to keep, while in other cases (such as the custom XML data), the average user may not know what is being referred to in the first place and may not appreciate the implications of retaining or removing the data.

Lack of Integration

Another way in which the presentation of security features may serve to confuse users is if different aspects do not integrate together in an appropriate manner. Although individual mechanisms are often provided in different software from different vendors, it would not be unreasonable for users to expect security features to work together in concert. Unfortunately, it is possible to identify examples in which this does not happen, and where integration and compatibility issues can instead cause users to receive incorrect and inappropriate advice. A good example here is provided by a widely reported case in which an upgrade to Windows AntiSpyware (Beta 1) caused it to falsely

Figure 13. Examples of misinformation due to lack of integration

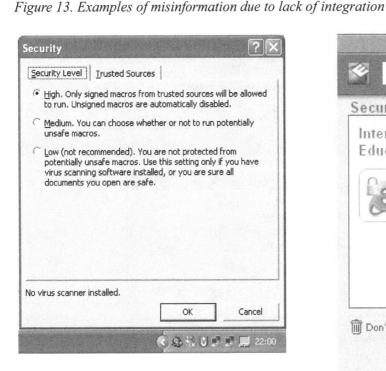

(a)   (b)

identify Symantec's AntiVirus Corporate Edition and Client Security packages as being instances of a password stealing Trojan. Any users who followed the consequent advice to remove certain registry keys found that they ended up disabling their antivirus solution (Leyden, 2006).

As a more visual example of an integration problem, Figure 13a shows the security settings for macro functions within Microsoft Word 2003. The significant part of the image is near the very bottom, with the indication that no virus scanner is installed. In actual fact, this screenshot was taken from a machine running McAfee VirusScan Enterprise 7 (the icon for which is visible as the third item in the system tray), and so receiving a message claiming that no virus protection is installed is hardly useful to the user. Meanwhile, Figure 13b presents an example of a pop-up message that appeared on a Dell PC during normal daily usage. Although this could be considered

useful as a friendly reminder to general users that they need to be concerned about security, the problem in this case was that the message popped up on a machine running Norton Internet Security—which meant it already had the firewall and anti-virus protection being referred to. Some users will interpret the wording of the message ("you should have a firewall...") to mean that the system is telling them that they are not adequately protected—which could cause obvious confusion and concern for users who considered they already had suitable safeguards. It would be preferable to offer more specific advice, tailored to user's actual circumstances (e.g., "You have a firewall and virus protection, but should also have anti-spyware protection installed"). Failing this (e.g., if it was not possible to determine existing protection status), the wording could still be adjusted to something that would pose a question rather than make an apparent statement (e.g.,

"Do you have a firewall?"), and therefore allow users who knew they were protected to pass by without concern.

Although the messages in both of these examples aimed to be helpful, by warning and reminding users that security needs to be considered, it could be argued that if the system is unable to give an accurate message that it would be preferable to say nothing at all.

In some cases, the lack of integration can cause security to conflict with things that other software is legitimately trying to do. As a result, users may actually be encouraged to ignore security warnings—as illustrated by the text at the bottom of Figure 14, which is from a prompt displayed when attempting to download Macromedia's Flash Player. The text clearly suggests that if a warning appears, users should simply tell the system to proceed or otherwise risk missing out on functionality. This is hardly helpful from a security awareness perspective, as it clearly sends out the wrong message. For example, novice users may use this experience as a basis for making future judgments in any similar scenarios. In fact, in a wider security context, this is exactly the sort of advice that users ought *not* to accept. If users

are receptive to instructions that tell them to ignore security, then it offers the ideal means for malicious code to find its way into their system (e.g., telling the user to ignore any warning that says the code may be harmful and allow it to be installed anyway).

Addressing the Problems

Having established that a range of problems may exist, this section considers some of the steps that may be taken in order to limit or remove them.

Recognizing that many users will not be inclined to look at security in the first place unless they are forced to do so, one important step is to ensure that the default settings are as appropriate as possible. It is certainly valuable to enable the necessary protection by default so that (in the first instance at least) the user does not have to worry about it, and in an extreme case the simplification can extend to hiding the existence of the security altogether. However, this relies upon the suitability of the default setting, and there is plenty of past evidence to show that this is not always effective. For example, until the arrival of XP Service Pack 2, the personal firewall and the

Figure 14. Encouragement to ignore security warnings

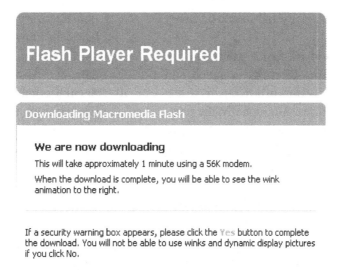

automatic software updates feature were switched off by default within Windows. Similarly, it was several years before data encryption was enabled by default on wireless access points, which led to a large-scale proliferation of unsecured networks by both personal and business users.

Unfortunately, however, simply relying upon defaults is not an adequate solution in scenarios where a single level of security cannot reasonably be expected to suffice for all users. In addition, there are many scenarios in which explicit choices and decisions need to be made. As such, it is still important to consider how things can be conveyed in a clear and meaningful manner.

In order to improve the situation, there are several guidelines that could usefully be followed in order to deliver a more appropriate HCI experience. A set of 10 such guidelines are presented, with content based upon an earlier set proposed by Johnston et al. (2003), along with additional considerations based upon the usability heuristics proposed by Nielsen (1994).

1. **Visible system state and security functions:** Applications should not expect that users will search in order to find the security features. Furthermore, the use of status mechanisms can keep users aware and informed about the state of the system. Status information should be periodically updated automatically and should be easily accessible.

2. **Security should be easily used:** The interface should be carefully designed and require minimal effort in order to make use of security features. Additionally, the security settings should not be placed in several different locations inside the application, because it will be hard for the user to locate each one of them.

3. **Suitable for advanced as well as first time users:** Show enough information for a first time user, while not too much information for an experienced user. Provide shortcuts or

other ways to enable advanced users to control the software more easily and quickly.

4. **Avoid heavy use of technical vocabulary or advanced terms:** Beginners will find it hard to use the security features in their application if technical vocabulary and advanced terms are used.

5. **Handle errors appropriately:** Plan the application carefully so that errors caused by the use of security features could be prevented and minimized as much as possible. However, when errors occur, the messages have to be meaningful and responsive to the problem.

6. **Allow customization without risk of being trapped:** Exit paths should be provided in case some functions are chosen by mistake, and the default values should be easily restored.

7. **Easy to setup security settings:** This way the user will feel more confident with changing and configuring the application according to their needs

8. **Suitable help and documentation for the available security:** Suitable help and documentation should be provided that would assist the users in the difficulties they may face.

9. **Make the user feel protected:** Assure that the user's work is protected by the application. Recovery from unexpected errors must be taken into account and the application should ensure that users will not lose their data.

10. **Security should not reduce performance:** By designing the application carefully and using efficient algorithms, it should be possible to use the security features with minimum impact on the efficiency of the application.

These guidelines were used by Katsabas, Furnell, and Dowland (2006) as the basis for evaluating the security provision within a number

Table 1. Grading for guideline compliance

Grade	Description
0	Application diverges completely from the guideline
1	Application significantly diverges from the guideline
2	Application has paid some attention to the guideline but still has major problems
3	Application has paid some attention to the guideline but still has minor problems
4	Application follows the guideline in some sections
5	Application completely follows the guideline in all possible sections

Table 2. Score summary for assessed applications against guidelines

	Firefox	McAfee	MS Word	Norton	Opera	Outpost	ZoneAlarm
Visible system state and security functions	2	4	3	2	3	3	5
Security should be easily used	4	3	3	4	3	3	4
Suitable for advanced as well as first time users	5	2	4	4	2	2	3
Avoid technical vocabulary or advanced terms	2	4	1	2	3	0	2
Handle errors appropriately	3	3	4	2	4	2	4
Allow customization without risk of being trapped	2	0	1	2	2	2	1
Easy to setup security settings	2	5	3	2	5	5	2
Suitable security help and documentation	0	1	4	5	5	1	2
Make the user feel protected	3	4	4	3	3	4	3
Security should not reduce performance	3	1	4	3	4	4	1
TOTAL (/50)	26	27	31	29	34	26	27

of established end-user tools and applications. Security-specific tools selected for assessment included Norton Antivirus, McAfee VirusScan, Outpost firewall, and ZoneAlarm firewall, while more general applications included Microsoft Word and the Opera and Mozilla Firefox browsers. Each application was tested according to the level of compliance with each of the 10 guidelines. A mark from zero to five could be achieved for each guideline (giving a maximum score of 50) based upon the scale in Table 1.

Table 2 shows a summary of the score that each application achieved for each of the 10 guidelines. It can be noted that there are no guidelines that seem to score uniformly well or uniformly badly across all applications. As such, no consistent pattern can be observed in terms of where applications are failing to present security appropriately.

In order to demonstrate the improvements that can be achieved by following the guidelines, the user interfaces of a subset of the applications

216

Figure 15. An example of applying interface guidelines

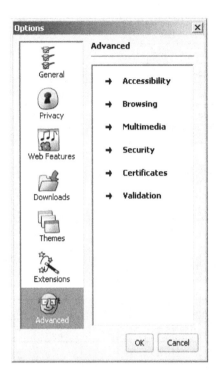
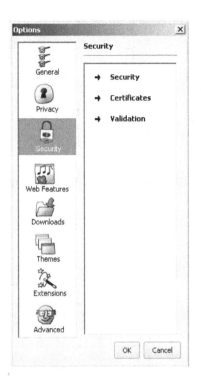

were modified in order to enhance their compliance with the visual aspects (Katsabas, 2004). Presentation of the full set of the modifications made is beyond the scope of this chapter, and so Figure 15 presents a specific example based upon a security-related interface from Firefox. In the original interface (on the left of the Figure), the security options were among options presented in an "advanced" tab. Studies in HCI have shown that options classified as "advanced" can scare many users, especially beginners. Therefore, locating the security settings here may result in a number of users never accessing them. In order to improve the accessibility of the security settings, a dedicated tab is added in the revised interface and moved higher up the list to increase the visibility and perceived priority.

Having identified a series of less desirable examples, it is also relevant to observe that many existing examples of stronger interface design can

be found. As an illustration, Figure 16 presents two screenshots taken from the Norton Internet Security package, which provides an integrated security solution (including firewall, anti-virus, anti-spam, and intrusion detection) for end-user systems. The tool, of course, differs from the earlier examples in the chapter, because it represents an example of software that has been specifically designed to fulfill a security role, rather than a wider application within which security is just one of the supporting functions. As such, it can be assumed that the designers and developers would have been in a position to devote more specific attention to the presentation and usability of the protection features. As a result, some of the positive observations arising from this particular interface are that:

- All of the top-level security options are visible and configurable from a single window;

Figure 16. Examples of more effective interface design

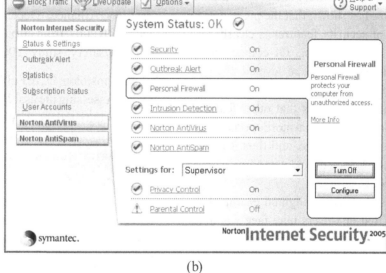

(a)

(b)

- The status of each option is clearly conveyed, along with the consequent security status of the overall tool; and
- Brief and clearly-worded explanations are provided to accompany each main option, and further help is easily accessible in each case.

In Figure 16a, the user receives a clear visual indication that things are amiss, with the "urgent attention" banner and the warning icon beside the aspect that is causing the concern (in addition, the background of the information area is shaded red). Meanwhile, the next dialog (Figure 16b) shows the system to be in the more desirable state of having all the critical elements working correctly (note that although the "parental control" option is disabled, it does not affect the overall security status, and the window is now shaded with a reassuring green background). Comparing this to the examples presented earlier in the chapter, it is apparent that none of the previous problems are immediately on show.

CONCLUSION

Doubtless, the most usable and friendly scenario from the end-user perspective would often be the one in which security is not used at all, in the sense that it inevitably incurs an additional level of complexity and effort. Unfortunately, however, the range of threats to which we are exposed if we operate without appropriate protection means that this is an increasingly unrealistic proposition.

This chapter has shown that the presentation and usability of security features is clearly less than optimal in some cases. Of course, many similar criticisms can also be leveled at other aspects of application functionality. However, the significant difference is that other features could be considered somewhat more optional than security in this day and age, and thus it is less important if users' lack of understanding causes them to neglect to use them.

The discussion has highlighted examples of the problems that end-users may face when attempting to understand and use security-related functionality within common software applications. Although some users will actively seek to overcome their lack of knowledge if the situation demands it, the more likely scenario for the majority is that security options will be unused or mis-configured.

The survey and trial findings have revealed clear problems in the understanding and use of security features. In considering these, it is worth remembering that both sets of findings were based upon overall groups of users with above-

average IT literacy. As such, it is likely that the usability difficulties they highlighted would be even more pronounced amongst a more general sample of users.

Finally, an important point to appreciate is that the challenge of end-user security will not be solved by HCI and usability improvements in isolation. The issue needs to be seen as part of a wider range of user-facing initiatives, including awareness-raising and education, so that users properly appreciate their need for security and the threats that they may face. Without this, we could simply have usable solutions that no-one recognizes the need to use.

REFERENCES

AOL/NCSA. (2005). *AOL/NCSA online safety study*. America Online and the National Cyber Security Alliance, December 2005. Retrieved March 21, 2007, from http://www.staysafeonline. info/pdf/safety_study_2005.pdf

Chatziapostolou, D., & Furnell, S. M. (2007, April 11-13). Assessing the usability of system-initiated and user-initiated security events. In *Proceedings of ISOneWorld 2007*, Las Vegas. Washington DC: The Information Institute.

CRA. (2003). *Grand research challenges in information systems*. Washington DC: Computing Research Association. Retrieved March 21, 2007, from http://www.cra.org/reports/gc.systems.pdf

Cranor, L. F., & Garfinkel, S. (Eds.). (2005). *Security and usability: Designing secure systems that people can use*. Sebastopol, CA: O'Reilly Media.

DeWitt, A. J., & Kuljis, J. (2006, July 12-14). Aligning usability and security: a usability study of Polaris. In *Proceedings of the Second Symposium on Usable Privacy and Security (SOUPS '06)* (pp. 1-7). Pittsburgh, Pennsylvania.

Furnell, S. M. (2004). Using security: easier said than done? *Computer Fraud & Security, April,* 6-10.

Furnell, S. M., Bryant, P., & Phippen, A. D. (2007). Assessing the security perceptions of personal Internet users. *Computers & Security, 26*(5), 410-417.

Furnell, S. M., Jusoh, A., & Katsabas, D. (2006). The challenges of understanding and using security: A survey of end-users. *Computers & Security, 25*(1), 27-35.

Furnell, S. M., Katsabas, D., Dowland, P. S., & Reid, F. (2007, May 14-16). A practical usability evaluation of security features in end-user applications. In *Proceedings of 22nd IFIP International Information Security Conference (IFIP SEC 2007)*, Sandton, South Africa. New York: Springer.

Johnston, J., Eloff, J. H. P., & Labuschagne, L. (2003). Security and human computer interfaces. *Computers & Security, 22*(8), 675-684.

Katsabas, D. (2004). *IT security: A human computer interaction perspective.* Master's thesis, University of Plymouth, UK.

Katsabas, D., Furnell, S. M., & Dowland, P. S. (2006, April). Evaluation of end-user application security from a usability perspective. In K. K. Dhanda & M. G. Hunter (Eds.), *Proceedings of 5th Annual ISOneWorld Conference and Convention*, Las Vegas, USA, (pp. 19-21). Washington DC: The Information Institute.

Leyden, J. (2006). MS anti-spyware labels Symantec as Trojan. *The Register, 14*. Retrieved March 21, 2007, from http://www.theregister.co.uk/2006/02/14/ms_anti-spyware_false_positive

Microsoft. (2007). *What's not secure. Help protect yourself: Security in Office tutorial.* Microsoft Office Online, Microsoft Corporation. Retrieved March 21, 2007, from http://office.microsoft.com/training/training.aspx?AssetID=RP010425901033&CTT=6&Origin=RP010425891033

Nielsen, J. (1994). Heuristic evaluation. In J. Nielsen & R.L. Mack (Eds.), *Usability inspection methods* (pp. 25-64). New York: John Wiley & Sons.

Schultz, E. (2002). Network associates drops PGP. *Computers & Security, 21*(3), 206-207.

Whitten, A., & Tygar, J. D. (1999, August 23-26). Why Johnny can't encrypt: A usability evaluation of PGP 5.0. In *Proceedings of the 8th USENIX Security Symposium*, Washington, DC, USA.

Chapter XIII
CAPTCHAs:
Differentiating
between Human and Bots

Deapesh Misra
VeriSign iDefense Security Intelligence Services, USA

ABSTRACT

The Internet has established firm deep roots in our day to day life. It has brought many revolutionary changes in the way we do things. One important consequence has been the way it has replaced human to human contact. This has also presented us with a new issue which is the requirement for differentiating between real humans and automated programs on the Internet. Such automated programs are usually written with a malicious intent. CAPTCHAs play an important role in solving this problem by presenting users with tests which only humans can solve. This chapter looks into the need, the history, and the different kinds of CAPTCHAs that researchers have come up with to deal with the security implications of automated bots pretending to be humans. Various schemes are compared and contrasted with each other, the impact of CAPTCHAs on Internet users is discussed, and to conclude, the various possible attacks are discussed. The author hopes that the chapter will not only introduce this interesting field to the reader in its entirety, but also simulate thought on new schemes.

INTRODUCTION

Human interactive proofs (HIPs) are schemes which require some kind of interaction from a human user that is tough for a program to simulate. "Completely automated public Turing test to tell computers and humans apart" (CAPTCHAs) are a class of HIPs which are tests that are so designed that humans can easily pass them while automated

programs have a very tough time in passing them. Thus, such tests try to prevent malicious automated programs from accessing Web services which are meant to be used by human users only.

Differences in the capabilities between humans and computer programs, which can be tested and evaluated over the Internet, are made use of to create a CAPTCHA. Generally, hard "artificial intelligence" (AI) problems are turned into

CAPTCHAs. Usually such tests utilize schemes which exploit the differences in the cognitive capabilities between humans and computers, for instance, exploiting the difference between humans and computer programs in understanding distorted text.

Necessity

As the Internet grows into our daily lives and removes human to human interaction by considerable leaps and bounds, the necessity to identify whether the entity on the other side of Internet is really a human being or an intelligent program has gained immense importance. Many e-commerce businesses which cater to such a growing population of human users on the Web have business models in which the primary assumption is that humans are the users of the service. Automated programs are increasingly able to perform many tasks on the Web just like a human user. In many cases, these automated bots are to be denied access to the service. In all such scenarios CAPTCHAs play the role of the guard which keeps the bots from accessing the services.

Some of the immediate scenarios wherein there is a necessity of segregating the human and the non-human user are as follows:

- Online polls
- Preventing spammers from getting free mail IDs
- Preventing chat bots from irritating people in chat rooms with advertisements
- Preventing automated dictionary attacks in password systems (Pinkas & Sander, 2002)
- Preventing unruly search engine bots from indexing sites
- Preventing unethical pricing practices in e-commerce
- Preventing inflating/deflating rankings in online recommender systems
- Preventing spam in blog comments

- Preventing game bots from playing online games
- Preventing DDoS attacks (Gligor, 2005)
- Preventing automated worm propagation (e.g., Santy Worm, Provos, McClain, & Wang, 2006)

While these were some of the current reasons for the deployment of CAPTCHAs, as e-commerce grows and as the Internet replaces human to human interaction, new scenarios requiring CAPTCHAs will emerge.

History

The earliest attempt and perhaps the longest continuing one, is a classic example of trying to fool the automated programs which try to harvest mail IDs on the Web. This is the custom of putting out mail IDs on the Web with the "@" symbol replaced by "at" and by other such variations. Some variants are:

- Mail_id(AT)mail_provider(DOT)com
- Mail_id@mail_providZr.nZt (Replace Z with E)

instead of mail_id@mail_provider.com. This practice called "address/mail munging" is still prevalent and has been able to withstand attacks from basic automated scripts which try to harvest mail IDs.

Moni Naor (Naor, 1996) and the researchers at Georgia Tech (Xu, Lipton, & Essa, 2000; Xu, Lipton, Essa, & Sung, 2001) were one of the earliest contributors to the field of CAPTCHAs. The earliest attempt of using a CAPTCHA on the Internet was by Altavista in 1997 and was to prevent Web-bots from abusing the free URL submission utility. This was a word based CAPTCHA in which the user had to recognize the distorted word. In 2000, Yahoo was in need of some mechanism to prevent bots from joining the chat rooms and directing the chat room users to advertisements.

The team at Carnegie Mellon University (CMU) came up with many new ideas (Ahn, 2005; Ahn, Blum, & Langford, 2004, 2002).

Turing Tests

The task of differentiating between a computer program and a human being is related to the concept of the "Turing test." In a classic paper (Turing, 1950), Turing suggested a simple game called "the imitation game." This went on to be called as the "Turing test." The test aims to determine if a machine is intelligent or not. Turing suggested that a parameter which could be conveniently used as a yardstick to determine if a computer program is intelligent or not, is the ability of a program to carry on a meaningful conversation with a human. If the program can do so for some stipulated amount of time, then it can be safely asserted that the program is intelligent. This is the famous Turing test.

The Turing test comprises of three parties, a human judge, a human participant, and a machine. The machine and the human are able to interact with the judge in a manner which does not give away their true identities. The interactions with the judge consist of answers to the questions asked by the judge. The judge tries to identify the machine by asking intelligent questions. The machine pretends to be a human while the human tries to prove that he/she is the real human. If the machine has been able to successfully pretend to be a human by means of conversation, then it can be stated that the machine is intelligent. The philosophical considerations of this test have been discussed widely (Anderson, 1964; Penrose, 1994, 1989; Oppy & Dowe, 2005; Crockett, 1994).

These tests are related to CAPTCHAs, since the CAPTCHA test also tries to differentiate between humans and machines.

The rest of this chapter is organized as follows. We start off with the various existing definitions for a CAPTCHA along with our own inputs for the definition in the second section. We then look at the existing CAPTCHA schemes in the third section. We also compare and analyze these existing schemes. Then in the fourth section we take a look at some new schemes that we have created. In the sixth section we look at the real world issues surrounding the use of CAPTCHAs. Here we look into acceptance issues, the use of CAPTCHA like schemes for sending out spam, and the problems faced by the online gaming industry from CAPTCHAs. To round up, we look at some of the attack mechanisms that have been proposed in the sixth section. We end with our conclusions in the seventh section and peek at what the future might have in store for CAPTCHAs.

CAPTCHA DEFINITION

Existing Definitions

A "completely automated public Turing test to tell computers and humans apart" (CAPTCHA) has been defined (CMU, 2000) as a program which generates a test which

- Most humans can pass
- Current computer programs can not pass

Additional requirements for a test to be called a CAPTCHA are as follows:

- Test generation code and data should be public
- The test should automatically be generated and graded by a machine

CAPTCHA tests should be such that an average computer user has no difficulty in passing it, and feels at ease while going through the test.

A more technical definition of CAPTCHA is provided in (Ahn, Blum, Hopper, & Langford, 2003) as: "A CAPTCHA is a cryptographic protocol whose underlying hardness assumption is based on an AI problem."

This definition suggests that what could be classified as a CAPTCHA currently, would loose that distinction if a computer program could pass that test sometime in the future with the growth of artificial intelligence (AI). The authors of (Ahn et al., 2003) state that CAPTCHAs have a two way effect. On one hand, they keep the malicious programs away and on the other hand they provide motivation to the growth of the field of AI.

Also to be noted is that the definition of the term "hardness" is not precise and is defined in terms of the consensus of a community: an AI problem is said to be hard if the people working on it agree that it is hard.

Revised Definition

We have revised the definition of a CAPTCHA and also provided some features that are desirable for the CAPTCHA to have. These new guidelines are an amalgamation of the original definitions and desired properties with the guidelines from the Microsoft CAPTCHA team (Rui & Liu, 2003a) and our own inputs.

CAPTCHA is a test which:

- Most humans can easily pass
- Computers can not pass (unless they randomly guess)
- Is generated and graded by a machine
- Does not base its strength on secrecy

CAPTCHAs have the following desirable properties:

- They can be quickly taken by a user
- They can be quickly generated and evaluated
- The probability of guessing the right answer is small
- They are intuitive to understand and to solve for humans
- They are independent of the language and culture—universal in nature

- The strength of the scheme is well understood

A desirable property is that the problem is well understood. We do not intend to suggest that a CAPTCHA necessarily make use of well researched hard problems, though we point out that to remain robust for a long time, the problem that the CAPTCHA is exploiting better be a well known hard problem. If CAPTCHAs are to contribute to the development of AI, then it might be better that they also try to exploit relatively obscure AI problems and in that process increase the understanding of areas that are not well researched yet.

CAPTCHA Names

CAPTCHAs have been called by different names. The different names used for them are "human interaction proofs" (HIP), "reverse Turing tests" (RTT), "mandatory human participation scheme," "human-in-the-loop protocols," and "automated Turing tests" (ATTs).

The researchers who were responsible for coining the name "CAPTCHA" and "HIP" maintain that CAPTCHAs are a class of HIPs. HIPs are much broader in the sense that they could be protocols to distinguish a particular human or a class of humans (like identifying humans based on gender or age, etc.).

Reverse Turing Tests

It has been suggested that the CAPTCHA is a "reverse Turing test" (RTT) since the judge is a machine which tries to identify the human. In the original Turing test, the judge was a human trying to identify the machine.

Another reason for calling it so is the fact that these tests have a goal which is the reverse of the original Turing test. The Turing test assumes that a computer program can be intelligent and goes on to determine if such a claim of a computer program is true or not. The CAPTCHA test starts off with the assumption that the computer program is not as intelligent as the human and exploits this difference.

It is important to note that Turing tests do not aim to differentiate between humans and computers while CAPTCHAs do. CAPTCHAs and Turing tests are related to each other only because most CAPTCHAs use the test for intelligence as a way to differentiate between these two classes of entities.

Dr. Luis von Ahn (Carnegie Mellon University) suggests that the term RTT has already been reserved for a different scenario (*personal communication*). It was first used in the context of denoting that the human player reversed his/her objective and instead of trying to prove he/she to be human, would try to prove to be a computer.

EXISTING CAPTCHA SCHEMES

Published Schemes

Many research teams have created new CAPTCHA schemes. Current CAPTCHA schemes can be subdivided largely into:

- Character based CAPTCHA schemes
- Image based CAPTCHA schemes
- Audio based CAPTCHA schemes
- Miscellaneous CAPTCHA schemes

Character Based CAPTCHA Schemes

Gimpy

The Carnegie Mellon University team came up with many CAPTCHA schemes. Their character based CAPTCHA scheme was called "Gimpy" (CMU, 2000).

Gimpy bases its strength on the assumption that humans can read extremely distorted and corrupted text while the current computer programs

are not very efficient in doing the same. The test chooses a few words randomly from a dictionary and then displays the corrupted and distorted version of these words to the user as an image. The user is expected to recognize the word/s and type them in order to pass the test.

Another version called ez-Gimpy is a simpler test in which, instead of multiple words, a single word is displayed to the user.

The test is not universal in nature since it assumes that the user is comfortable with a particular language.

Georgia Tech's Contributions

The team at Georgia Tech also came up independently with their CAPTCHA scheme (Xu et al., 2000; Xu et al., 2001). They suggested the use of a new type of trapdoor one-way hash function to convert a character string into an image. They came up with the idea of such a CAPTCHA while trying to solve the issue of "screenscrapers" in the context of Web commerce pricing wars. Apart from this problem, they proposed that their CAPTCHA scheme would also prevent online dictionary attacks and denial of service attacks. The

Figure 1. Gimpy

protocol that delivered the CAPTCHA was called a "humanizer." Instead of storing the answer to the puzzle, they recommended the use of message authentication codes (MAC) which would hash the right answer for later comparison purposes. They did not propose any specific schemes.

Pessimal Print

In this scheme (Coates, 2001), low quality images of text are used as a way to differentiate between computer programs and human users. The test taker has to recognize the word and type it in. The assumptions of the test are that the readers are well versed with the English language's alphabet and have some years of reading experience and familiarity with the English language.

The test uses English dictionary words. Thus, the test assumes that the user is comfortable with English language. The test is thus not universal in nature. The database has to be kept a secret, since an attacker who knows all the words and the distortions can either create a database of all possible distorted words or when presented with a test, use the word database to increase the chances of guessing what the distorted word is.

Baffle Text

Utilizing ideas of psychophysics of human reading, this CAPTCHA scheme (Chew & Baird, 2003) distorts non-dictionary, but pronounceable words and asks the user to recognize the letters.

The words chosen are not close to dictionary words.

Some amount of familiarity with the English language is assumed.

ScatterType

The aim of this CAPTCHA scheme (Baird & Riopka, 2004) is to form images of English-like words which can resist character segmentation attacks. Each letter is subjected to cutting and scattering and then combined to form the word image. Each character is fragmented using either horizontal or vertical cuts and these fragments are scattered by vertical or horizontal displacements. Thus, the letters are now not prone to segmentation attacks. The segmented letters are then combined to form the word image.

This test also assumes that the test taker is familiar with the English language and is thus not universal in nature.

Microsoft CAPTCHAs

The Microsoft team came up with a few ideas for word based CAPTCHAs (Patrice, 2003; Chellapilla, Larson, Simard, & Czerwinski, 2005b). Their HIPs are claimed to be robust against segmentation attacks. The test uses local warps at the character level and uses word warps at the word

Figure 3. Baffle text

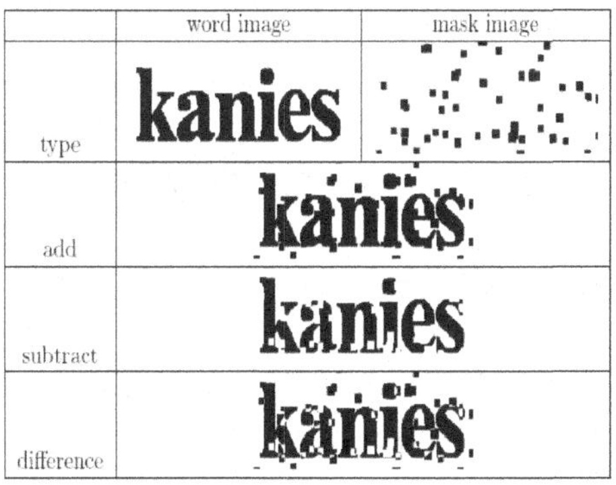

	word image	mask image
type	kanies	
add	kanies	
subtract	kanies	
difference	kanies	

Figure 2. Pessimal print

Figure 4. Scatter type

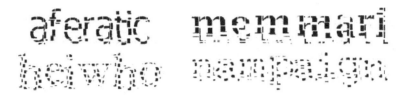

Figure 5. Microsoft HIP

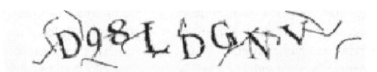

level. Words are intersected with arcs (thick and thin) to further prevent segmentation attacks.

The letter based CAPTCHA requires that the test taker is familiar with the set of alphabets. User complaints against this test have been that it is tough to differentiate between some letters and numbers, such as the digit "1" and the lowercase alphabet character "l." The scheme is dependent on the language.

Human Handwriting Based CAPTCHAs

This scheme (Rusu & Govindaraju, 2005) suggests that human handwriting can be used as a CAPTCHA. Gestalt laws are applied to handwritten samples so as to make it tough for the computers to recognize the text while keeping it possible for humans to recognize the text. The scheme assumes familiarity with the handwritten words and the language. Automatic generation and grading would be a problem.

Image Based CAPTCHA Schemes

Bongo and Pix

The CMU team came up with two image based CAPTCHA schemes—Bongo and Pix (CMU, 2000).

- **Bongo:** This CAPTCHA tests the visual recognition ability of the user. Two series of blocks, left and right are displayed to the user. The blocks in the left series differ from those in the right in a certain fixed way. The user is provided with four options which consist of four single blocks and the user is asked to determine if each of these options belongs to the right or to the left series. Bongard problems have been studied for some time now and this database is available on the Internet (Index of Bongard Problems, n.d.). Generating new puzzles require human intervention and since this is a test of intelligence, most users will find taking them stressful.
- **Pix:** This is a test in which the user is presented with four distorted images of a particular object and asked to recognize the name of the object. The test maintains a large database of labeled images. It randomly picks an object, then randomly finds images of this object, distorts them, and presents these to the user who has to recognize the theme/object to pass the test.

In order to label images, a parallel ongoing effort is a game which is played on the Internet. Playing this game results in the labeling of images (The ESP Game, n.d.; Ahn & Dabbish, 2004).

Figure 6. Pix

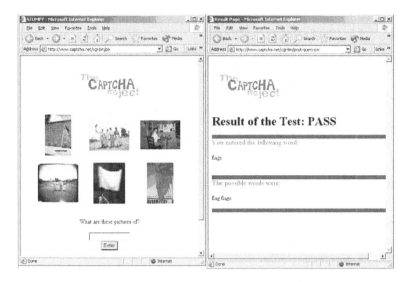

The game is called "The ESP Game." The idea of utilizing human cycles to do some useful work is being researched (Ahn, 2005).

The scheme requires a database of labeled images. This requires human intervention. Labels and images can be very specific and thus not universal. Also the database may need to be kept a secret.

Implicit CAPTCHA

These CAPTCHAs (Baird & Bentley, 2005) are completely different from the character based ones and the goal here is to reduce the irritation to the test taker. The tests are clever enough so that the user does not feel threatened by it and completes it with the least amount of stress.

In one of the suggested schemes, the user is supposed to interact with the given picture by clicking on some part of it and thus pass the test. The image in this scheme provides the background for the test, upon which an interaction based task is built.

Some ideas to perform this are as follows:

- Challenges are disguised as necessary browsing links

- Challenges can be answered with a single click while still providing several bits of confidence
- Challenges can be answered only through experience of the context of the particular Web site
- Challenges are so easy that failure indicates a failed bot attack

Automatic creation of such tests is not possible. A human has to design these tests. It can be expected that the instruction set would result in this test not being universal in nature.

Figure 7. Implicit CAPTCHA

ARTiFACIAL

This scheme (Rui & Liu, 2003b; Rui & Liu, 2003a) reasons that human faces are the most universally familiar object to humans thus making them a very good candidate for HIPs and particularly so, since programs are yet not as good as humans in detecting human faces. The researchers also came up with a more concrete set of desirable features for a CAPTCHA.

The test is to detect human faces in a cluttered background. The program called ARTiFACIAL generates a distorted face in a cluttered background for each test. The test taker has to detect the only complete human face.

For every user request, an image of a complete face and many incomplete faces on a cluttered background is presented and the user is asked to click on the six points (eye corners, mouth corners) of the only complete face and if this is done correctly then the user is deemed to be a human.

This CAPTCHA meets all the requirements and also possesses all the desirable features required in a CAPTCHA. But during user trials, some users complained that the distorted faces were disturbing and found the test to be repulsive (Rui, Liu, Kallin, Janke, & Paya, 2005).

Figure 8. ARTiFACIAL

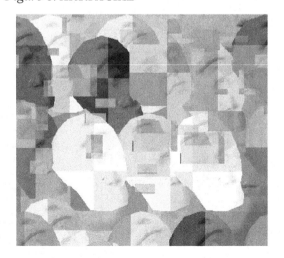

Image Recognition CAPTCHA

In the scheme "image recognition CAPTCHAs" (Chew & Tygar, 2004) the hardness of the problem is provided by the one way transformation between words and pictures. For a machine, it is easy to get pictures corresponding to a particular chosen word, but tough the other way around. Thus, given a set of pictures associated with a word, the human test taker can easily find the word while the machine will fail. This scheme plays around with a few possibilities of this mapping between words and their associated pictures.

- The three schemes discussed are:
- The naming images CAPTCHA
- The distinguishing images CAPTCHA

The Identity Anomalies CAPTCHA

In the naming CAPTCHA scheme, the user is presented with six images of a common term. The user has to type the common term associated with these images to pass the CAPTCHA.

In the distinguishing CAPTCHA, the user has to determine if two subsets of images are associated with the same word or not. In the identifying anomalies CAPTCHA, the test subject is shown a set of images where all but one image is associated with a word and the test taker has to identify the anomalous image.

The problem with these image schemes is that they need images which are labeled. The use of a search engine such as Google is suggested. But this has the problem of wrongly labeled images. The solution suggested to this problem is that the multiple rounds of the test need to be given to the user. This is not practical in the real world, wherein a single round of CAPTCHA in itself is considered to be annoying. Some of these schemes are susceptible to simple guessing attacks.

IMAGINATION CAPTCHA

The IMAGINATION (image generation for Internet authentication) CAPTCHA (Datta, Li, & Wang, 2005) is an image based CAPTCHA scheme. It is similar to the previously discussed "image recognition CAPTCHA" scheme. In this scheme the user is first provided with a composite image of many images and has to choose an image to annotate. Once the user chooses an image, a distorted version of that image is presented with a group of labels. The user now has to select the appropriate label for the image from this group.

The scheme requires an annotated database. It aims to reduce the number of rounds required to minimize the success rate of random guessing attacks. This is achieved by the added task of asking the user to click on the geometric center of the image.

Animation Based CAPTCHA

In this scheme (Athanasopoulos & Antonatos, 2006) the authors proposed the idea of using animated tests as CAPTCHAs. One of the major goals of this work was to prevent "replay-attacks." To do so, the authors used animation in their CAPTCHA tests, so that the test is not a static image which can be easily forwarded.

Audio Based CAPTCHA Schemes

Existing CAPTCHA schemes are unfair towards the visually disabled people. The basic assumption in almost all schemes has been that the test taker can see. An attempt to make the CAPTCHAs suitable for the visually impaired was made by the CMU team with their "sounds CAPTCHA" (CMU, 2000), while other attempts at audio CAPTCHAs also exist (Kochanski, Lopresti, & Shih, 2002; Google's Audio CAPTCHA, 2006).

Sounds CAPTCHA

This audio based CAPTCHA was developed by the CMU research team (CMU, 2000). This is an attempt to use audio as a way to distinguish between the human and the computer program. This is similar to the picture based Gimpy. A word or a sequence of numbers are picked up at random, they are combined into a sound clip and distorted. This distorted clip is presented the user who is asked to recognize the word/numbers. The test has to be specific to each test taker, since this depends on the languages that the test taker knows.

Miscellaneous CAPTCHA Schemes

Here we describe general CAPTCHA schemes.

Collaborative CAPTCHAs

Collaborative filtering CAPTCHAs (Chew & Tygar, 2005) try to extract complex patterns that reflect human choices. Thus, for a particular question which has a set of choices as an answer, it is suggested that computer programs would not know the most popular choice of humans. The right choice among the answer choices depends upon the answers of a group of human users and the response of the test taker to a set of control questions. Thus, the questions asked in this CAPTCHA test do not have an absolutely right answer. The correct answer is measured from different human opinions and is a reflection of human choices. For example, a set of jokes can be given and the user could be asked to rate them.

The CAPTCHA consists of multiple rounds. The test instructions are long and complicated. New CAPTCHA tests need to be rated thus quick production of a large number of tests is not possible. Creation of new sources of data that can be rated is itself a problem. Also answers to such kind of

CAPTCHAs are very specific to culture and thus not international in nature. There could be also an attack by motivated large groups of malicious people who would answer incorrectly so as to skew the results of the collaborative filter.

Other Ideas

Moni Naor had the first nascent CAPTCHA ideas which are wide and general in nature (Naor, 1996). Some of the ideas are:

- Gender recognition—given a face, decide if it is male or female
- Facial expression—given a face, decide its emotion
- Body part recognition—"click on the left eye"
- Deciding undressed-ness—given a few photos, decide which has the most/least clothes
- Naive drawings—look and recognize the object
- Handwriting recognition
- Speech recognition
- Fill in the blanks or reorder to make meaningful sentences

A way to detect Web robots is detailed in Tan, Steinbach, and Kumar (2005). This idea tries to extract useful patterns from Web access logs. The basis of differentiating between a human Web surfer and a bot is based on the characteristics of Web surfing. For instance, access by Web robots would be broad but shallow, while human user access to a particular site would tend to be more focused. Using such assumptions and Web browser logs, a decision tree classifier could be made, which could detect the presence of Web robot surfing. Since the Web access logs are used to make the decision, the identification can be made only after the Web bot or the human user has finished surfing the site.

Unpublished Schemes

Many schemes have been created by people interested in CAPTCHAS and released on the Internet. The use of Google as a search engine and a labeler of images is one such idea. A few tools created for fun could be used for creating CAPTCHAs (Guess the Google, n.d.; Montage a Google, n.d.). Related to it is the idea of using photos in online photo databases such as Flickr for CAPTCHA tests. Though with any public image database, there are always problems of wrongly labeled images, offensive images, and so forth.

One CAPTCHA scheme uses photos of kittens and challenges the user to identify all the kitten photographs (KittenAuth, n.d.). Another scheme presents photographs of humans and asks the test taker to rank the photos in terms of "hotness" (HotCaptcha).

Microsoft recently came up with an image based CAPTCHA scheme called "Asirra" (animal species image recognition for restricting access). The test taker is presented with photographs of dogs and cats and has to identify the cats in these photographs.

Our New CAPTCHA Schemes

Our attempt was to try to come up with new CAPTCHA schemes which are more human friendly than current schemes.

The Problem with Existing Schemes

Most of the CAPTCHA schemes in use as of now are text based CAPTCHAs. Distorted letters are given to the test taker and the test taker has to recognize these letters. Text based CAPTCHAs assume that the user is familiar with the English language. International users might not be very familiar with the English language character set.

To keep up with the development of OCR systems and character recognition schemes, these tests will have to get tougher with passing time.

As of now, already they are quite tough to solve sometimes. Thus, new ideas for CAPTCHAs would be soon required.

CAPTCHA schemes which can be easily modified with every new attack or progress in AI, have to be rather thought of. Such schemes can be deployed for a longer time without the fear of having to redeploy a completely new scheme of CAPTCHA after every new successful attack.

Since it is tough to measure distortion per-se, various Web service providers have used their own measure of what they think is considerable distortion to create distorted letter CAPTCHAs. Thus, these CAPTCHAs range from being very easy for the machine to break to very tough for the human user to pass. Both the extremes are of no use at all.

Moreover, the Internet is full of complaints against text based CAPTCHAs, as users have generally found them to be irritating and at times, tough. Since the current user ease with these CAPTCHAs seems to be low, human friendly CAPTCHAs need to be thought of.

Face Recognition CAPTCHA

Your brain is very weak compared to a computer. I will give you a series of numbers, one, three, seven... Or rather, ichi, san, shichi, san, ni, go, ni, go, ichi, hachi, ichi, ni, ku, san, go. Now I want you to repeat them back to me.

A computer can take tens of thousands of numbers and give them back in reverse, or sum them or do lots of things that we cannot do. On the other hand, if I look at a face, in a glance I can tell you who it is if I know that person, or that I don't know that person. We do not yet know how to make a computer system so that if we give it a pattern of a face it can tell us such information, even if it has seen many faces and you have tried to teach it.

- Richard P. Feynman. (Feynman, 2001)

Our proposed scheme (Misra & Gaj, 2006a) utilizes the fact that humans are better than computers at recognizing human faces. For a machine, this task is still very tough (Zhao, Chellappa, & Phillips, 2003) and there is a good understanding of how hard the problem is. These properties are well exploited to create a CAPTCHA.

Our scheme is an image based CAPTCHA. The scheme is similar to "ARTiFACIAL" (Rui & Liu, 2003a), the difference being that ARTiFACIAL is a face detection problem while ours is a face recognition problem. In our scheme, we move away from making any assumption about the language familiarity of the Web service user. We use image based CAPTCHAs to make our tests universal and to increase the comfort level of the user.

The property that we exploit to create our CAPTCHA is that given two distorted images of a human face, the human user can match these two images as being of the same person quickly, while for a computer program it is very tough to match these two distorted images. The test taker is presented with two sets of distorted human face images. Each set has the distorted images of the same group of people. Each set could have four to five images though the exact number of faces is something that is yet to be determined. The user is expected to match the same person's faces in these two sets, to pass the tests.

The images are chosen from any one of the publicly available face databases. Image processing tools such as the Gimp (Gimp 2.2, n.d.) can be easily automated to create the distortions and apply them to the photographs. The distortions applied to the faces are cleverly chosen so as to be able to defeat the face recognition algorithms.

Test Generation Scheme

The generation of the CAPTCHA requires a database of human face images. Distortion of the images, creation of the CAPTCHA test, and evaluation are automated tasks.

Image Databases

Our scheme makes use of human face photograph databases that are public and there is no need for the database to be secret. We chose the UMIST face database (Graham & Allinson, 1998). The frontal face shots of the people in the database were distorted to create the test.

Image Processing Tools

The use of commonly available image processing tools was looked into. Successful results were obtained with the use of the open source tool "Gimp 2.2." This tool is particularly suitable for this task since it has a scripting language called "script-fu," which allows automatic creation of the CAPTCHAs.

The tool comes with built in image manipulation effects called "filters." These basic built-in filters were used to create the distortion effects. The image distortion effects can be easily extended to create new effects as and when the attackers are able to successfully attack a distortion scheme that is being currently used.

For human faces, we cannot use any random distortion since the output should be acceptable aesthetically. Extreme distortions to the human face would make the CAPTCHA disgusting. While on the other hand, when choosing the parameters for the distortions, we have to ensure that the distorted output is not too simple for an image recognition scheme applied by a machine. Acceptable parameter bounds for the distortions have to be decided by a human being. Once these bounds are set for the various distortions, at run time, random values for the parameters are chosen for the distortion.

Using Human Faces in Image Recognition: Scheme One

This CAPTCHA scheme requires the user to recognize the same image of a subject with two different and random distortions applied to it. Thus, in effect, the human user is performing an image recognition task, the image being a human face.

The two distortions can be chosen such that one distortion makes it tough for holistic feature matching face recognition schemes while the other makes it tough for feature matching face recognition schemes.

Recognizing Human Faces: Scheme Two

An extension to our basic idea is to use different photos of the same individual (in two different poses for instance) to which different distortions are applied respectively.

User Trials

Methodology

The CAPTCHA test was taken by a few volunteers. The UI for the tests consisted of a simple Web page as shown.

Figure 9. Example—CAPTCHA test for scheme 1

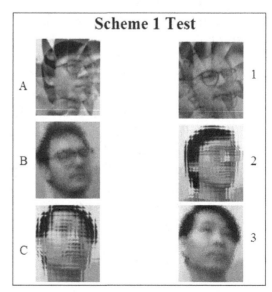

232

Figure 10. Example—CAPTCHA test for scheme 2

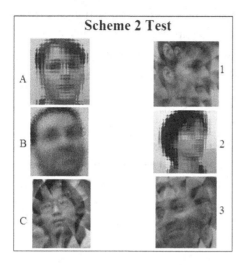

Figure 11. User interface—test 1

Figure 12. User interface—test 2

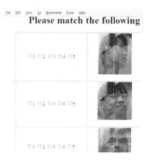

Figure 13. Example 1—image based CAPTCHA

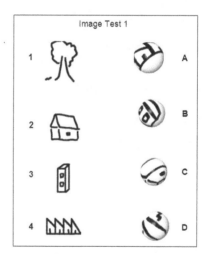

Extension

There has been a renewed interest in face recognition in the recent years. Thus, though we understand its current limitations and exploit them to create CAPTCHAs, there has and will be progress in this area. To make the CAPTCHA tougher against human face recognition programs, this scheme could be extended to distortions of general images rather than only human face images. The advantage being that it is tougher to recognize general random images in comparison to recognizing human faces, since all human faces share common features.

Improvements

The obvious disadvantage in such a "multiple choice test" is that it is susceptible to guessing

Figure 14. Example 2—image based CAPT-CHA

Figure 15. Modified UI to accept the input

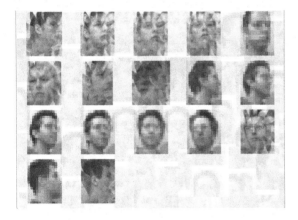

attacks. Existing word based CAPTCHAs have a much higher probable answer space, but at the same time are much more inconvenient for international users. A conflict between "security" and "usability" exists.

The current UI scheme suffers from being susceptible to "no effort" guessing attacks. Thus, we claim that the scheme is "somewhat" susceptible to a random guessing attack, since this susceptibility depends on the UI scheme to take in the input.

A method to increase the answer space makes use of a different UI scheme to take the inputs. In this scheme there are no radio buttons and instead the test taker has to click on the correct matching

photo which is a part of a larger image consisting of all possible answers. The probability of a random attack being successful reduces in this way when compared to the previous scheme. Automatic generation of such a UI is possible through the use of ImageMagick (ImageMagick 6.2.8, n.d.).

Analysis and Conclusions

Our new human face recognition scheme makes use of an area that is well researched and understood. Human face detection and recognition are still hard problems for machines to solve and this is made even harder by the application of distortions to the images. The distortions also serve to break the existing face recognition schemes. Easy extensibility of these distortions due to the use of the tool, "Gimp," ensures that as the face recognition schemes get better, new distortions can be easily created, thus keeping this idea in vogue for a long time.

Existing human face photo databases generally consist of photographs which are taken in constrained environments. Particularly, the lighting, expression, and pose are very constrained (Howell, 1999). The creation of an image database with CAPTCHA like tests in mind (with large variations in pose, facial expressions, and lighting) will result in images which are tougher to break by computer systems. This is particularly true for our second scheme.

The development of image distortion effects specifically to defeat human face recognition schemes (for instance Fischerfaces and Eigenfaces) would be the way ahead. As new schemes are developed to recognize human faces, new image distortion effects will have to be developed. Also, what needs to be looked into is a way to prevent guessing attacks.

Simple Games CAPTCHA

We propose a new idea for a CAPTCHA which is more universal than existing character based tests and also is easier and fun for humans to take (Misra & Gaj, 2006b). The proposed CAPTCHA relies on the user being able to successfully play a simple game and is thus visual in nature. The test taker plays a simple game using the mouse/touchpad (or keyboard) as the input device.

A very simple game is presented to the user which is chosen randomly from a large pool of games. If the user is able to complete the game successfully, then the user is judged to be a hu-

man, else the user is judged to be a machine. Playing this simple game provides the hardness to the CAPTCHA. A machine would be unable to play this game while a human user can play this simple game very well.

We propose the use of "Macromedia Flash" (Macromedia Web site, n.d.) based games for such simple CAPTCHAs, as such games are already widely spread over the Internet. Screen shots of a few of these simple games are as shown. We propose the use of such simple games as CAPTCHAs. For instance, with reference to Fig. 17, a CAPTCHA could ask the user to make the frog eat a certain number of flies, for instance, four flies.

The best games for our scheme would be those which can be played with either the mouse or the keyboard.

Online Games and Bots

Online games are plagued with the problem of game bots playing the games and winning prize monies. Although the bots can play a few online games, it would need a large jump in AI capabili-

Figure 16. Simple "hitting the post" game

Figure 17. Simple "catching a fly" game and "shooting" game

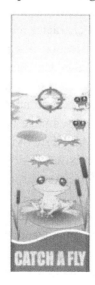

ties to have a bot which can play any game from the large random pool of games.

This scheme is new and differs from what was proposed and rejected in (Golle & Ducheneaut, 2005). It was proposed that well established popular games be used as a CAPTCHA. But the authors did not mean simple games which changed every time but rather thought of using well established games as CAPTCHA, for instance, some MMORPG (massively multiplayer online role playing games). One of the conclusions was that already, game bots exist to play such games and those game bots would be able to play the CAPTCHA games very well.

Analysis

A general discussion of our scheme follows.

Real World Existence

The kind of simple games that we propose to use in our scheme already exist in the real world, though they are being used with a different purpose in mind. A recent concept which has become popular on the Internet scene is that of "advergaming" (Advergaming, n.d.; Advergaming on the Blockdot Web site, n.d.; Advergaming on the Innoken Web site, n.d.) and this led to an exponential increase in the creation of such games. These are games that are used by advertisers to attract consumers, to help in brand awareness, and to increase brand recall.

So we can reuse a simple advergame as a CAPTCHA. This would perhaps keep both the Web service provider and the human test taker happy. This offers an extended capability to a CAPTCHA.

Usability

Playing games has always been considered as a "fun activity," more so if the game is simple enough. Thus, the user is not stressed at all in completing this CAPTCHA. Also, such simple games have neither complicated rules nor complicated instructions. They are intuitive enough that the user can start playing after just having read one line of instruction. These games are universal in nature and also are not restricted to any age group.

COMPARISON AND ANALYSIS OF CAPTCHA SCHEMES

The schemes are compared based on our definition and desirable properties of a CAPTCHA.

A CAPTCHA must have these properties:

- Most humans can easily pass—"humans pass easily"
- Computers can not pass, unless they randomly guess—"computers fail"
- Generated and graded by a machine—"automation"
- Does not base its strength on secrecy—"public scheme"

Humans pass easily: Most of the character distortion schemes are tough to pass easily. Since they are language dependent, native speakers of the English language experience lesser problems in passing them in contrast with non-native speakers. As OCR and character recognition systems get better, the distortion has to increase, thus making them tougher for humans to pass. The general complaint against these schemes is the confusion between certain numbers and certain lowercase characters. Image based CAPTCHA schemes such as ARTiFACIAL, implicit CAPTCHAs, animation based CAPTCHAs, and face recognition CAPTCHAs are some schemes which are relatively easy.

Computer fails: Most of the existing schemes are robust against computer attacks as of now. The only exception is Gimpy, which has been broken by computer programs.

Automation: Generating implicit CAPTCHAs automatically seems to be a tough task. Schemes like Pix, image recognition CAPTCHAs, and IMAGINATION CAPTCHAs are burdened with the requirement of a pre-labeled image database. This is a tough requirement to meet. There are ideas as to how one could obtain a large database of pictures with labels, but those schemes are not very robust. Obtaining non-offensive images automatically, with the correct label free from all contextual connotations is a tough task.

Public scheme: Schemes which rely on a database are susceptible to attacks if the database becomes public. The easy way to solve this problem is to use some kind of distortion on the images and then use them in CAPTCHA schemes.

CAPTCHA have the following desirable properties:

- They are intuitive to understand and to solve for humans—"human friendly"
- They can be quickly taken by a user—"human easy"
- The probability of guessing the right answer is small—"no effort attack resistant"
- They are independent of the language and culture—"universal"

- The strength of the scheme is well understood—"well understood problem"
- They can be quickly generated and evaluated—"quick generation & evaluation"

Human friendly: The schemes need to be easy to understand and intuitive to perform. This also means that the instructions to perform the test will be short and easy. Any CAPTCHA scheme with a long and complicated instruction will lead to greater irritation to the test taker. The fact that the CAPTCHA should be universal in nature implies that CAPTCHAs should be intuitive to a large population across the world. Tasks which involve recognizing a particular language are not as easy and intuitive as image recognition tasks. Matching images is intuitive and does not assume any level of skill. This is an activity which almost all humans can perform. Though implicit CAPTCHAs are easy to perform, the instruction set itself might be tough and unintuitive.

Human easy: A CAPTCHA test should be easy to perform. The user should be able to complete it quickly. Character distortion schemes might be fast to complete or not, depending on the amount of distortion that is applied. Image matching is much quicker than performing error correction

Table 1. Comparison of existing schemes based on the definition of a CAPTCHA

Definition Guidelines	Humans Pass Easily	Computers Fail	Automation	Public Scheme
Gimpy	Somewhat	No	Yes	Yes
Pix	Somewhat	Yes	No	No
Pessimal Print	Somewhat	Yes	Yes	Yes
Baffle Text	Somewhat	Yes	Yes	Yes
ARTiFACIAL	Yes	Yes	Yes	Yes
Scatter Type	Somewhat	Yes	Yes	Yes
Implicit CAPTCHA	Yes	Yes	No	Yes
Microsoft HIP	Somewhat	Yes	Yes	Yes
Image Recognition	Somewhat	Yes	Somewhat	Yes
Animation CAPTCHA	Yes	Yes	No	Yes
Face CAPTCHA	Yes	Yes	Yes	Yes

on distorted words. With regards to the input mechanism though, the character based schemes are the fastest, since using the keyboard is the fastest way to input the answer in comparison to the mouse or any other pointing device.

No effort attack resistant: The CAPTCHA tests must be resistant to random guessing attacks. Schemes such as the identifying anomalies image recognition CAPTCHA can be trivially broken by random guessing.

Universal: All the character distortion based schemes make an assumption of the language and thus are not universal. The image based schemes are universal (assuming that the instruction set is small and the test by nature is intuitive).

Well understood problem: To be successful as a valid CAPTCHA for a long time, it is imperative that the scheme is well understood. All the present CAPTCHA schemes are created out of known open problems in AI.

Quick generation and evaluation: Since the CAPTCHAs are to be used on the Internet and in all probability on high volume sites, it is necessary that the scheme be able to rapidly generate new CAPTCHA tests and also be able to evaluate them. Implicit CAPTCHAs for instance, need time for generation. The CAPTCHAs which rely on labeled image databases can also not be quickly generated as time and effort is required to label the images. Animation CAPTCHAs and simple game based CAPTCHAs need to be created beforehand.

CAPTCHA schemes are another example of the conflict between usability and security. The most secure schemes might not be popular while the most popular schemes might not be secure.

CAPTCHAs in the Real World

CAPTCHAs can be seen in action at many sites on the Web. A few being:

- http://www.yahoomail.com
- http://www.gmail.com
- http://www.hotmail.com
- http://www.blogger.com
- https://www.kiwibank.co.nz/banking/login.asp

Table 2. Comparison of existing schemes based on the desirable features in a CAPTCHA

Desirable Properties	Human Friendly	Human Easy	No Effort Attack Resistant	Universal	Quick Generation & Evaluation	Well Understood Problem
Gimpy	Somewhat	Yes	Yes	No	Yes	Yes
Pix	Yes	Yes	Yes	No	No	Yes
Pessimal Print	Somewhat	Yes	Yes	No	Yes	Yes
Baffle Text	Somewhat	Yes	Yes	No	No	Yes
ARTiFACIAL	Yes	Yes	Yes	Yes	Yes	Yes
Scatter Type	Somewhat	Yes	Yes	No	Yes	Yes
Implicit CAPTCHA	Somewhat	Yes	Somewhat	Yes	No	No
Microsoft HIP	Somewhat	Yes	Yes	Yes	Yes	Yes
Image Recognition	Yes	Yes	No	No	No	Yes
Animation CAPTCHA	Yes	Yes	Yes	Yes	No	Yes
Face CAPTCHA	Yes	Yes	Somewhat	Yes	Yes	Yes

Figure 18 Security vs. Usability Matrix

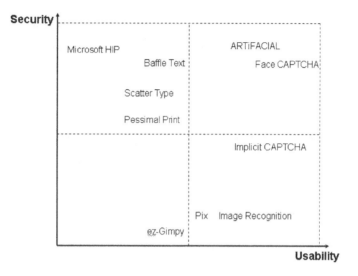

• http://www.register.com
• http://www.ticketmaster.com
• http://www.usps.com

Anti-spam products in the market based on CAPTCHAs:

• mailblocks
• www.spamarrest.com

It has been suggested (Lopresti, 2005) that CAPTCHA problems, instead of being artificial problems that need to be solved, should rather be problems from the real world. This would help research work, since answers got from the test takers can be used as a baseline for programs trying to advance AI. But a potential problem could be that groups of malicious users can skew the results of such an attempt. Also, since the correct answer to any such problem is not exactly known, multiple tests would be required.

Acceptance of CAPTCHAs by the Users

There are many users who get irritated when they have to pass a CAPTCHA and have voiced their resentment on various Internet forums. This is not surprising. Any new extra steps and especially those which need some work from the human are going to be viewed as irritating. Thus, it is necessary that these tests should not be too tough to be considered as a challenge by the users. An element of fun should be inbuilt in the CAPTCHA. Implicit CAPTCHAs (Baird & Bentley, 2005) was a first good attempt in making this process fun.

Real world schemes have had problems with negative user feedback. Gimpy was being used at Yahoo's site but then upon complaints that it was too tough, it was replaced by the easier version called ez-Gimpy. Artifacial uses an image consisting of distorted human faces. In user trials, these faces were deemed to be repulsive, disturbing, and unpleasant by human test takers (Rui et al., 2005).

Abuse of CAPTCHAs—Spam

There has been a recent wave of increase in spam mails (June, 2006). This has been because spammers are making use of a CAPTCHA concept: "Humans are good at understanding the information in images while machines can not decipher images." This CAPTCHA property is being used in sending spam which has images instead of text. Thus, the spam filters which are not able to understand the graphic information are unable to flag such mails as spam.

Online Games and Bots

Online games are a multi-billion dollar industry and are expected to grow. Online games are plagued with the problem of game bots playing the games and winning prize monies. This not only deters new comers from joining the online gaming sites, but also cheats the skilled human users of their prizes. Thus, the online multi-million dollar industry is extremely interested in seeing to it that the game bots are kept away.

With regards to poker for instance, powerful AI software exist which can play such online games very well (Brunker, 2004; Roarke, 2005). "Vexbot" and "Sparbot" are prime examples of bots which can be used to win a lot of online tournaments. Other online game business models are also severely affected by this problem. Some game sites resort to periodically updating the game and keeping a constant vigil for bots (Times, 2006). Also there has been a report of conviction of a game bot user who made money by auctioning the items that his Web bot got for him in games (service, 2005). The number of MMORPG game (massively multiplayer online role playing games) players and the money to be won, is increasing. Games such as "World of Warcraft" had around 8,000,000 gamers involved (Blizzard Entertainment Ltd., Press Release January 2007, n.d.) as of January 2007, according a press release by the company.

Thus, online game industry is a big multi-billion industry that is affected tremendously by Web bots. Better solutions to keep the bots away from playing will always be needed here.

Problems with CAPTCHAs

The biggest problem with the majority of the existing CAPTCHAs is that they are unfair to the visually impaired people. Most of the existing schemes and the newly proposed ones, assume that the test taker can see. This is a limitation and to ensure fairness, ways to allow visually impaired people to authenticate that they are human have to be thought of.

Various countries have introduced measures and laws to ensure that the Web sites remain accessible to all without any discrimination, specifically without any discrimination based on physical ability. Web sites which wish to remain compliant with various disability laws need to ensure that they do not discriminate against visually or physically challenged users. The World Wide Web Consortium (W3C) has set a series of standards for accessibility for Web sites, known as Web accessibility initiative (WAI) (WAI, n.d.).

Some existing schemes try to solve this problem by allowing the test taker to request for an audio CAPTCHA instead of a visual one, while some schemes allow the test taker to speak with a customer representative to authenticate themselves as humans. As an example of the first method is Google's introduction in April, 2006, of an audio CAPTCHA (Google's Audio CAPTCHA, 2006) scheme in which the test taker can choose to hear an audio clip. Yahoo provides the second method as an alternate way to authenticate oneself as a human.

ATTACKING CAPTCHAS

There has been a lot of interest in attacking CAPTCHAs. Generally, the attacks on a CAPTCHA scheme can be broadly subdivided into (Pinkas & Sander, 2002):

- Guessing attacks
- Technical AI attacks

- Relay attacks

Guessing attacks are trivial to implement and lead to no development of AI. The attacker randomly guesses the answer. These attacks are viable for schemes which have a few answer choices.

Technical AI Attacks

A team of researchers were able to break the ez-Gimpy with 92% success and the Gimpy scheme with 33% success rate (Mori & Malik, 2003). Another successful attempt was to break the clock face HIP (Zhang, Rui, Huang, & Paya, 2004). Thayananthan, Stenger, Torr, and Cipolla of the Cambridge vision group have written a program that can achieve 93% correct recognition rate against ez-Gimpy. Gabriel Moy, Nathan Jones, Curt Harkless, and Randy Potter of Arete Associates have written a program that can achieve 78% accuracy against gimpy-r (CMU, n.d.).

Schemes to break a few visual HIPs are detailed in Chellapilla and Simard (2005). The conclusion of this research work indicated that for character based CAPTCHAs, it is important that apart from the recognition problem, the segmentation problem (that it should not be able to trivially segment the individual letters) should also exist to make it very robust against attacks. One paper which studied the text recognition problem alone (assuming that segmentation had been performed successfully) concluded that computer programs were better or in the worst case as good as humans in recognizing distorted characters (Chellapilla, Larson, Simard, & Czerwinski, 2005a).

Apart from the research labs, interested individuals are also trying to break CAPTCHA schemes and various such attempts can be found on the Internet.

Relay Attacks

A possible attack against CAPTCHAs is the "relay attack" (Pinkas & Sander, 2002; Stubblebine & Oorschot, 2004). In this attack, when a malicious entity (usually an automated bot) is presented with a CAPTCHA, the test is relayed to a human being willing to solve it in exchange for something. The human user to whom the test is relayed participates in this activity either because the user is rewarded for doing so or is unaware of the relay. Relay attacks are tough to stop. An initial study to negate this kind of attack is in Stubblebine and Oorschot (2004). The imagination CAPTCHA (Datta et al., 2005) is the only CAPTCHA which attempted to address this issue in its design.

The scheme of the relay attack can be described as:

1. Entity 1 requests for the test
2. Entity 1 relays the test to Entity 2
3. Entity 2 solves the test and relays the answer to Entity 1
4. Entity 1 inputs the answer and passes the CAPTCHA

Here "Entity 1" is generally the malicious automated program while "Entity 2" is a human user. Generally it can be assumed that these two entities are physically apart.

Since the CAPTCHA test itself should be as simple as possible so as not to irritate the genuine human user, the malicious human also finds the test simple enough to devote resources to solve it. The malicious human users perform the test in return

Figure 19. Relay attacks

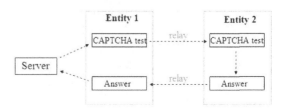

for an incentive (free service, financial incentives, etc.). The value they associate with the incentive decides what tests they will consider irritating to the point that they refuse to take it and what tests they will take. Thus, if the genuine human user places a considerably higher value on the service being accessed than the value the relay attacker places on the incentive got in return for performing the attack, the genuine human user of the service will continue to solve the CAPTCHA while the attacker would refuse to participate in the attack. In a Web service usability perspective, ways to ensure this need to be further looked into.

Online Relay Attacks

In online relay attacks, the human attacker solves the CAPTCHA in real time and this answer is used by the bot to overcome the CAPTCHA barrier in real time. While this attack is highly plausible and would be highly successful, there are no reports of an instance in which it was used.

The case of the bot pretending to be the server to an innocent and non-suspecting human user and thus getting it solved can be avoided by solutions which have been described (Stubblebine & Oorschot, 2004).

As per "implicit CAPTCHAs" (Baird & Bentley, 2005), if the CAPTCHA is a task that is intertwined with the actions to access a Web service, then relay attacks can be prevented. In character recognition schemes, a simpler idea for the creation of new login IDs would be to embed the login id and the password into the image CAPTCHA. Thus, the attacker would not want to send this private information to a third party. This kind of mechanism can be used in many scenarios wherein there is some confidential information or private information involved.

Detection of different IP addresses can lead to discovery of a relay attack (Athanasopoulos & Antonatos, 2006). The disadvantage in this counter-measure being that the server has to maintain state information.

Off-Line Relay Attacks

In off-line relay attacks, the human solves the CAPTCHA tests off-line. There are real world examples for this kind of an attack.

At George Mason University, one of the undergraduate students volunteered to inform that he had been a part of a relay attack. A friend of his supplied him with the distorted text CAPTCHAs and he was paid for solving them. He was paid $10 for every 1000 CAPTCHAs that were solved. On an average, it took him one and half hours to answer 1000 CAPTCHAs. Also, he informed that his friend had obtained a computer program which did the same task and so he was no longer employed to break CAPTCHAs. The exact reason for needing the CAPTCHAs solved is unknown.

On a free lancer recruitment Web site "www.getafreelancer.com" (getafreelancer.com Web site, 2006), a query was posted requesting a quote for solving CAPTCHAs for a 50 hour week period. The average asking price to solve CAPTCHAs in 50 hours was $57, which makes it almost a dollar for an hour. The least asking quote was $30 ($0.6 for an hour). The description for this job type was really vague, the number of CAPTCHAs to be solved was not given and it seemed that most of the bidders had no clue about what the task really entailed.

Audio CAPTCHAs have not yet become as widespread as their text based cousins, but once they are implemented they can also be attacked. Audio CAPTCHAs are not only language dependent but also depend on the accent used. To make it as general as possible, it can be assumed that only digits will be used in audio CAPTCHAs, as is the case with Google's present audio CAPTCHA scheme (Google's Audio CAPTCHA, 2006). Dr. Luis von Ahn (Carnegie Mellon University) tried to attack one of the digit based audio CAPTCHAs by feeding the audio stream to an automated speech recognition system of an U.S. airline company, through the phone. The automated speech recognition system was able to recognize the digits properly.

The view point that CAPTCHAs will also lead to the solutions of AI problems has not always been true. Relay attacks are very successful against CAPTCHAs and do not lead to any improvement in AI. It has also been argued that the development of programs which are able to break distorted characters is not helpful to solve real world problems (Lopresti, 2005). This is a consequence of the fact that the distorted letter CAPTCHAs are synthetic scenarios which are not letter recognition problems encountered in real world applications.

SUMMARY AND CONCLUSION

CAPTCHAs are finding more and more use on the Internet. Such a need can be attributed to the growing power of bots. For instance, DDoS attacks and spam mails largely originate from massive botnets. New online business models and the growing power of bots have resulted in the proliferation of CAPTCHAs in areas which were not thought of previously. And thus, CAPTCHAs have come a long way from way back in 1996, when they were used to prevent automated URL submission by AltaVista to the recent use of CAPTCHAs against the Slaty Worm by Google. In the future this growth in the use of CAPTCHAs to safeguard against the power of bots will continue.

With this increase in number, CAPTCHAs which do not rely on vision alone will have to be further developed so that Web sites can be accessed by all without any discrimination. Current schemes have generally been character distortion based schemes. With the advancement in deciphering distorted text, such schemes will have to get more and more garbled to the extent that users will not accept them. New CAPTCHA schemes will then have to be deployed.

Online users have so far grudgingly accepted CAPTCHAs. A shift to other user friendly schemes such as image based CAPTCHAs will decrease the online users' irritation. As it is with most new schemes, the initial resentment usually changes into a gradual acceptance. Similarly, with CAPTCHAs, Internet users will accept user friendly CAPTCHA schemes as a part and parcel of their online transactions.

Current CAPTCHA schemes have not faced a lot of attacks. Increasing attention from the cyber crime industry will result in standardized CAPTCHAs.

CAPTCHAs have played an important role in safeguarding the interests of various online businesses. They have also been used in preventing automated attacks. With the increasingly proliferation of the Internet and as we move towards an increasingly networked world, the role and significance of CAPTCHAs will increase.

REFERENCES

Advergaming on the blockdot Web site. (n. d.). Retrieved April 27, 2007, from http://games. blockdot.com/basics/index.cfm/.

Advergaming on the innoken Web site. (n.d.). Retrieved April 27, 2007, from http://www.innoken. com/ar_brandgames.html/.

Anderson, A. R. (Ed.). (1964). *Minds and machines*. Prentice Hall.

Athanasopoulos, E., & Antonatos, S. (2006). Enhanced captchas: Using animation to tell humans and computers apart. In H. Leitold & E. Leitold (Eds.), *Communications and multimedia security* (Vol. 4237, pp. 97-108). Springer.

Baird, H. S., & Bentley, J. L. (2005). Implicit captchas. In *Proceedings of Spie/IS&T Conference on Document Recognition and Retrieval Xii*.

Baird, H., & Riopka, T. (2004, Dec). ScatterType: a reading CAPTCHA resistant to segmentation attack. In L. L. J. M. D. M. W. A. Y (Ed.), *Vision geometry Xiii. Proceedings of the Spie* (Vol. 5676, pp. 197-207).

Blizzard entertainment ltd., press release January 2007. (n.d.). Retrieved April 27, 2007, from http://www.blizzard.com/press/070111.shtml

Brunker, M. (2004, September). *Are poker bots raking online pots*? Retrieved April 27, 2007, from http://www.msnbc.msn.com/id/6002298/

Chellapilla, K., Larson, K., Simard, P. Y., & Czerwinski, M. (2005a, July 21-22). Computers beat humans at single character recognition in reading based human interaction proofs (hips). In *Proceedings of Ceas 2005—Second Conference on E-mail and Anti-spam*. Stanford University, California, USA.

Chellapilla, K., Larson, K., Simard, P., & Czerwinski, M. (2005b). Designing human friendly human interaction proofs (hips). In *Chi '05: Proceedings of the Sigchi Conference on Human Factors in Computing Systems* (pp. 711-720). New York: ACM Press.

Chellapilla, K., & Simard, P. Y. (2005). Using machine learning to break visual human interaction proofs (hips). In L. K. Saul, Y. Weiss, & L. Bottou (Eds.), *Advances in neural information processing systems 17* (pp. 265-272). Cambridge, MA: MIT Press.

Chew, M., & Baird, H. S. (2003). Baffletext: a human interactive proof. In *Proceedings of the 10th IS&T/Spie Document Recognition & Retrieval Conference*.

Chew, M., & Tygar, J. D. (2004). Image recognition captchas. *Isc* (p. 268-279).

Chew, M., & Tygar, J. (2005, Jan). Collaborative filtering captchas. In H. S. Baird & D. P. Lopresti (Eds.), *Lecture notes in computer science* (pp. 66-81). Springer Verlag.

CMU. (2000). *The captcha project*. Retrieved April 26, 2007, from http://www.captcha.net

Coates, A. L. (2001). Pessimal print—a reverse Turing test. In *Proceedings of the Sixth International Conference on Document Analysis and Recognition (Icdar '01)* (p. 1154). Washington, DC: IEEE Computer Society.

Crockett, L. J. (1994). *The Turing test and the frame problem*. Ablex Publishing Corporation.

Datta, R., Li, J., & Wang, J. Z. (2005). Imagination: a robust image-based captcha generation system. In *Proceedings of the 13th annual ACM International Conference on Multimedia (Multimedia '05)* (pp. 331-334). New York: ACM Press.

The esp game. (n.d.). Retrieved April 26, 2007, from http://www.espgame.org/

Feynman, R. P. (2001). *The pleasure of finding things out*. Penguin Books.

getafreelancer.com Web site. (2006). Retrieved April 27, 2007, from http://www.getafreelancer. com/projects/Data-Processing-Data-Entry/Data-Entry-Solve-CAPTCHA.html

Gimp 2.2. (n.d.). Retrieved April 26, 2007, from http://www.gimp.org/

Gligor, V. D. (2005, Sep). Guaranteeing access in spite of distributed service-flooding attacks. In *Proceedings of the 12ᵗʰ ACM Conference on Computer and Communications Security* (pp. 80-96). *Lecture Notes in Computer Science, 3364*.

Golle, P., & Ducheneaut, N. (2005). Preventing bots from playing online games. *Computer Entertainment, 3*(3), 3.

Google's audio captcha. (2006, November). Retrieved April 29, 2007, from http://googleblog. blogspot.com/2006/11/audio-captchas-when-visual-images-are.html

Graham, D. B., & Allinson, N. M. (1998). *Characterizing virtual eigensignatures for general purpose face recognition*.

Guess the google. (n.d.). Retrieved April 27, 2007, from http://grant.robinson.name/projects/guess-the-google/

Howell, J. (1999). *Introduction to face recognition.* Boca Raton, FL: CRC Press, Inc.

Imagemagick 6.2.8. (n.d.). Retrieved April 26, 2007, from http://www.imagemagick.org/

Index of bongard problems. (n.d.). Retrieved April 26, 2007, from http://www.cs.indiana.edu/~hfoundal/res/bps/bpidx.htm

Kochanski, G., Lopresti, D., & Shih, C. (2002, September). A reverse Turing test using speech. In *Proceedings of the International Conferences on Spoken Language Processing (ICSLP).* Denver, Colorado.

Lopresti, D. (2005, May). Leveraging the captcha problem. In H. S. Baird & D. P. Lopresti (Eds.), *Human interactive proofs: Second international workshop (HIP 2005)* (Vol. 3517, p. 97). Springer Verlag.

Macromedia Web site. (n.d.). Retrieved April 27, 2007, from http://www.macromedia.com/

Misra, D., & Gaj, K. (2006a, February). Face recognition CAPTCHAs. In *Proceedings of the the Advanced Int'l Conference on Telecommunications and Int'l Conference on Internet and Web Applications and Services (AICT-ICIW '06).* (pp. 122). Washington, DC: IEEE Computer Society.

Misra, D., & Gaj, K. (2006b, July). *Human friendly CAPTCHAs—simple games* (Poster). Symposium on Usable Privacy and Security (SOUPS). Pittsburgh, Pennsylvania, USA.

Montage a google. (n.d.). Retrieved April 27, 2007, from http://grant.robinson.name/projects/montage-a-google/

Mori, G., & Malik, J. (2003). Recognizing objects in adversarial clutter: breaking a visual captcha. In *Proceedings of 2003 IEEE Computer Society Conference on Computer Vision and Pattern Recognition* (pp. I-134–I-141).

Naor, M. (1996). *Verification of a human in the loop or identification via the Turing test* [Unknown]. Retrieved April 27, 2007, from http://www.wisdom.weizmann.ac.il/%7Enaor/PAPERS/human_abs.html

Oppy, G., & Dowe, D. (2005). The Turing test. In E. N. Zalta (Ed.), The *Stanford encyclopedia of philosophy.* Retrieved April 27, 2007, from http://plato.stanford.edu/archives/sum2005/entries/turing-test/.

Patrice, J. B. J. C. I. C., Simard, Y., & Szeliski, R. (2003). Using character recognition and segmentation to tell computer from humans. In *Proceedings of the Seventh International Conference on Document Analysis and Recognition (ICDAR '03)* (p. 418). Washington, DC: IEEE Computer Society.

Penrose, R. (1989). *The emperor's new mind.* Oxford University Press.

Penrose, R. (1994). *Shadows of the mind.* Oxford University Press.

Pinkas, B., & Sander, T. (2002). Securing passwords against dictionary attacks. In Ccs '02: Proceedings of the 9th acm conference on computer and communications security (pp. 161–170). New York, NY, USA: ACM Press.

Provos, N., McClain, J., & Wang, K. (2006). Search worms. In *Proceedings of the 4th ACM Workshop on Recurring Malcode (WORM '06)* (pp. 1-8). Alexandria, VA: ACM Press.

Roarke, S. P. (2005, July). *Bots now battle humans for poker supremacy.* Retrieved April 27, 2007, from http://www.Foxsports.com

Rui, Y., & Liu, Z. (2003a). Artifacial: automated reverse Turing test using facial features. In *Proceedings of the Eleventh ACM International Conference on Multimedia (Multimedia '03)* (pp. 295-298). New York: ACM Press.

Rui, Y., & Liu, Z. (2003b). Excuse me, but are you human? In *Proceedings of the Eleventh ACM International Conference on Multimedia (Multimedia '03)* (pp. 462-463). New York: ACM Press.

Rui, Y., Liu, Z., Kallin, S., Janke, G., & Paya, C. (2005). Characters or faces: A user study on ease of use for hips. *Hip* (pp. 53–65).

Rusu, A., & Govindaraju, V. (2005, Jan). Visual captcha with handwritten image analysis. In H. S. Baird & D. P. Lopresti (Eds.), *Human interactive proofs: Second international workshop* (Vol. 3517). Bethlehem, PA: Springer Verlag.

service, N. S. news. (2005, August). *Computer characters mugged in virtual crime spree.* Retrieved April 27, 2007, from http://www.newscientist.com/article.ns?id=dn7865

Stubblebine, S., & van Oorschot, P. (2004, February). Addressing online dictionary attacks with login histories and humans-in-the-loop. In *Proceedings of Financial Cryptography.* Springer-Verlag.

Tan, P., Steinbach, M., & Kumar, V. (2005). *Introduction to data mining.* Addison-Wesley.

Times, T. (2006, May). *Computer game bot: Arch-nemesis of online games.* Retrieved August 1, 2006, from http://times.hankooki.com/lpage/culture/200605/kt2006052116201765520.htm

Turing, A. M. (1950). Computing machinery and intelligence. LIX (236).

von Ahn, L. (2005). *Utilizing the power of human cycles.* Unpublished doctoral dissertation, Carnegie Mellon University.

von Ahn, L., Blum, M., Hopper, N., & Langford, J. (2003). Captcha: Using hard AI problems for security. In *Proceedings of Eurocrypt* (pp. 294-311).

von Ahn, L., Blum, M., & Langford, J. (2002). *Telling humans and computers apart automatically or how lazy cryptographers do AI* (Tech. Rep. No. CMU-CS-02-117). Carnegie Mellon University.

von Ahn, L., Blum, M., & Langford, J. (2004). Telling humans and computers apart automatically. *Communications of the ACM, 47*(2), 56-60.

von Ahn, L., & Dabbish, L. (2004, April). Labeling images with a computer game. In *Proceedings of the SIGCHI Conference on Human Factors in Computing Systems (CHI '04)* (pp. 319-326). Vienna, Austria: ACM Press.

Web Accessibility Initiative. (n.d.). Retrieved April 29, 2007, from http://www.w3.org/WAI/

Xu, J., Lipton, R., & Essa, I. (2000, November). *Are you human?* (Tech. Rep. No. GIT-CC-00028). Georgia Institute of Technology: Georgia Institute of Technology.

Xu, J., Lipton, R., Essa, I., & Sung, M. (2001). *Mandatory human participation: A new scheme for building secure systems* (Tech. Rep. No. GIT-CC-01-09). Georgia Institute of Technology.

Zhang, Z., Rui, Y., Huang, T., & Paya, C. (2004). Breaking the clock face hip. *ICME* (pp. 2167-2170).

Zhao, W., Chellappa, R., Phillips, P.J., & Rosenfeld, A. (2003). Face recognition—a literature survey. *ACM Computer Survey, 35*(4), 399-458.

Chapter XIV
Privacy Concerns when Modeling Users in Collaborative Filtering Recommender Systems

Sylvain Castagnos
LORIA—Université Nancy 2, Campus Scientifique, France

Anne Boyer
LORIA—Université Nancy 2, Campus Scientifique, France

ABSTRACT

This chapter investigates ways to deal with privacy rules when modeling preferences of users in recommender systems based on collaborative filtering. It argues that it is possible to find a good compromise between quality of predictions and protection of personal data. Thus, it proposes a methodology that fulfills with strictest privacy laws for both centralized and distributed architectures. The authors hope that their attempts to provide a unified vision of privacy rules through the related works and a generic privacy-enhancing procedure will help researchers and practitioners to better take into account the ethical and juridical constraints as regards privacy protection when designing information systems.

INTRODUCTION

Do you remember the satirical paper from Zaslow (2002) in the Wall Street Journal? The problem was the following: a man suspects that his digital videorecorder named TiVo thought he was gay. Indeed, it inexplicably recorded programs with gay themes. This man decided to modify TiVo's gay fixation by recording war movies. Then the machine started giving him documentaries on Joseph Goebbels and Adolf Eichmann. He has overcompensated and the machine stopped thinking he was gay and decided he was a fan of the Third Reich. The general principle of TiVo is to record for its owner some programs it just assumes he will like, based on shows he has chosen to record. The recommendation process used what he did to predict what he likes. A major aspect related to recommender systems is to collect pertinent data about what you do in order to determine what you are. Such systems are very popular in many contexts, as for example e-commerce, papers online, or Internet access. Recommenders individualize their prediction which each user. Therefore, they need to collect and to utilize personal data. Fundamental issues arise such as how to ensure that user privacy will be guaranteed, particularly when individuals can be identifiable?

We have to keep in mind that many consumers appreciate having computers able to anticipate what they like, what they want to do or to read. Web personalization has been shown to be advantageous for both online customers and vendors. But for consumers shopping on the Internet, privacy is a major issue. Almost three-quarters of Internet users are concerned about having control over the release of their private information when shopping online (Source: U.S. Census Data on http://www.bbbonline.org/privacy/). This is also true in the Internet context of information retrieval. As the amount of data available on Internet is so huge, it becomes mandatory to assist the active user when searching or accessing Internet resources. Furthermore, the number of available resources is still exponentially growing: for example, the number of pages referenced by Google has increased from 1 to 8 trillion between June 2000 and August 2005.

Traditional search engines use to provide the active user with too many results to ensure that he/she will identify the most relevant items in a reasonable time. For instance, Google returns 5.4 billion links when the user asks for "news." There are still 768 million sites about news related to New York City. Moreover, searches may never end since new resources constantly appear. Confronted with this overload of data, the rationality of the active user is bounded to the set of choices that can be considered by human understanding. He/she tends to stop the search at the first choice which seems satisfying (Simon, 1982). This is the

reason why the relevancy of results is no longer guarantee in most of existing information providers. Furthermore, searching information by using keywords and logical operators seems not easy enough for the general audience. As a result, the scientific community is rethinking the existing services of search and access to information, under the designation "Web 2.0" (White, 2006).

There are several possible approaches to assist the active user: adaptive interfaces to facilitate the exploration and the searches on the Web, systems relying on social navigation, sites providing personalized content, statistical tools suggesting keywords for improving searches, and so forth. Another solution consists in providing each user with items likely to interest him/her. Contrary to the personalized content, this solution does not require to adapt resources to the potential readers. Each item has to be proposed to concerned persons by using push-and-pull techniques.

To supply the active user with his/her concerns, we first have to build his/her model of preferences by collecting data about his/her activities. This approach is based on an analysis of usage. Nevertheless, it is not always possible to collect quickly enough data about the active user. Collaborative filtering techniques (Goldberg, 1992) are a good way to cope with this difficulty. They amount to identifying the active user to a set of persons having the same tastes, based on his/her preferences and his/her past actions. This kind of algorithms considers that users who liked the same items have the same topics of interest. Thus, it becomes possible to predict the relevancy of data for the active user by taking advantage of experiences of a similar population.

There are several fundamental problems when implementing a collaborative filtering algorithm. Beyond technical questions such as quality of service or cold start, are ethical aspects such as intimacy preservation, privacy, or reglementary aspects. These questions are crucial since they are related to human rights and freedom and consequently will impact development and generalisation of recommenders in our everyday life.

This chapter focuses mainly on privacy aspects in recommenders, based on collaborative filtering algorithms. First we will provide an overview about privacy issues. Indeed, when modeling user actions and preferences in order to compute recommendations, intelligent systems access personal information about users. For ethical and legal reasons, we have to be careful to be as unintrusive as possible and at least to guarantee the anonymity of users.

As privacy laws are differing in countries all over the world, we first assume that a recommender system should be as strict and restrictive as the strictest law. Starting from this statement, the goal of this chapter is to discuss how and what kind of data may be collected, for how long time they can be stored, in which aim it is allowed to use them, and what data it is reasonable and acceptable to share. Indeed, laws use to lay out both organizational and technical requirements (in terms of data acquisition, purpose of use, transfer, processing, etc.) for information systems that store and/or process personal data in order to ensure their protection (see Wang, 2006 for an overview).

Because of the personal and confidential nature of some data, we secondly state that users must be aware of the prediction computation process. It is important that they can explicitly choose the part of their profile they agree to communicate and/or to share. Users have to know which data are stored about their activities, more especially when the system relies on implicit observations that are collected in a transparent way.

In the first section, we will introduce what means privacy in the context of collaborative filtering applications, based on a state-of-the-art of the most popular approaches. Then, we will present our perspectives on the issues related to this theme, and we will provide some recommendations in dealing with the issues. At last, we will discuss future trends, and we will conclude this chapter.

BACKGROUND

Statements

Due to the overload of data on the Internet, personalizing tools seem to be promising ways to provide users with the most relevant items. In this chapter, we will particularly focus on collaborative filtering techniques. It amounts to collect information about users' preferences. The latter are often represented under the form of rating vectors, called user profiles. These profiles are then aggregated in a global rating matrix or in several partial matrices, depending on the fact that computations are centralized or distributed. This aggregation allows the system to know the preferences of a population. Afterwards, communities of interests and/or clusters of similar items are inferred by computing distances between profiles and by selecting neighborhood in the user/item representation space. This process makes explicit the similarities between users. Similar user profiles are the most suitable for suggesting new interesting items to the active user.

This technology is sometimes perceived by the general audience as a kind of "big brother," since it requires collecting information about preferences of users. In order to promote this new approach of consultation and search on the Internet, it is consequently necessary to understand users' concerns and to provide privacy guarantees so that they are reassured.

A survey has been conducted by a provider of personalization called ChoiceStream[1] in 2005, among more than 900 American citizens. This study has shown that 80% of them come out in favour of personalizing processes. More than half of the interviewed persons are disposed to spend 2 minutes to fill a questionnaire in order to get a personalizing function. Nevertheless, less than 10% would accept spending 10 minutes or more. This survey has also highlighted the fact that the main obstacle remains the fear of diffusion of personal data and, generally speaking, the respect of privacy. However, they are ready to do some compromises as far as tolerance to surveillance is concerned, in exchange for a lower required effort to fill forms. In any case, Internet users want to keep the control on the settings of their personalization level and retrievable data.

Definition of Privacy

Westin (1967) has provided a definition which includes all these aspects by describing the privacy as the ability to determine for ourselves when, how, and to what extent information about us is communicated to others. Cranor (2005) has completed this definition by considering that the privacy enhancing process often relies on the way pieces of data are collected, stored, and used. In order to estimate the degree of privacy of a recommender system, she introduces four axes of personalization: the data collection method, the duration of data storage, the user involvement in the personalizing process, and the reliance on predictions.

The data collection method can be either explicit or implicit. In the first case, personalization relies on information explicitly provided by users, such as ratings or demographics. For example, users may rate a sample of items in order to receive suggestion of new items that may interest them. On the opposite, personalization based on implicit data collection infers unknown preferences of a user from his/her browsing history, purchase history, search queries, and so forth.

The duration of data storage can be task-focused or profile-based. On one hand, task-focused personalization keeps information about users for a limited duration. For example, it can be based on actions a user has taken while performing a task or during a session. On the other hand, Cranor defines profile-based approach as the fact to keep all preferences, whatever their form (implicit or explicit, numeric or symbolic), for an unlimited

duration. Cookies belong to this category by recognizing visitors automatically, even if they have not returned for a very long time.

The third axe of personalization distinguishes processes that are user-initiated from those which are system-initiated. In the first category, users can define their own settings. They can, for example, choose their level of personalization, the number of items to display, the preferences that are sharable, and so forth. In the second case, the system provides personalization for every user, even when they do not request customized features.

At last, Cranor compares reliance on predictions for both prediction-based and content-based systems. Prediction-based personalization compares the active user's preferences with other similar profiles in order to predict his/her future interests and supply recommendations based on the stated preferences of the others. This kind of personalization may have very good results, providing that there is enough data about compared users. But sometimes, the system can provide results that have been appreciated by similar users but are not related to the active user's preferences. On the contrary, content-based personalization favours similarities between items, rather than between users. For example, if a user buys a book on movie makers, this kind of systems may suggest other books on movie makers. However, this approach starts from the strong claim that items are persistent on the recommender platform.

Cranor assumes that an ideal privacy-enhanced system should be based on an explicit data collection method, transient profiles, user initiated involvement, and non-invasive predictions. Nevertheless, it is often necessary to find a compromise between quality of predictions and privacy. The next subsection provides a state-of-the-art of privacy-enhancing techniques in the field of collaborative filtering.

Related Work in Collaborative Filtering

Many researches have been conducted to make collaborative filtering algorithms as unintrusive as possible. We propose here an overview of main works dealing with privacy issues. Several approaches have been considered. The most popular are encryption of data, public aggregates, and alteration of profiles.

Canny (2002a, 2002b) concentrates on means to provide powerful privacy protection by computing a "public" aggregate for each community without disclosing individual users' data. He constructs probabilistic models of user behavior from observations and extrapolates user ratings from these observations for collaborative filtering. He has proved that collaborative filtering can be considered as a linear factor analysis problem, which generalizes SVD and linear regression. He chooses to use the EM algorithm (expectation maximization) for factor analysis, since it can handle missing data without requiring default values for them. Furthermore, the EM algorithm has a simple recursive definition which fits with his privacy method. His approach is based on homomorphic encryption to protect personal data. This property is used in several common encryption schemes, such as RSA protocol. Privacy protection is provided by a P2P protocol. Each user starts with his/her own preference data, and knowledge of who their peers are in his/her community. Users exchange various encrypted messages when running the protocol. The latter consists in multiplying several encodings of several messages to get the encoding of their sum which corresponds to the encryption of the community's preferences. The decryption process relies on key-sharing. The key needed to decrypt the total is not owned by anyone, but shared between several users. At the end, every user has an unencrypted copy of the community's preferences. Individuals can then compute their own personal recommendations and have not revealed their individual data.

However, he supposes that a reasonable number of clients are online at the same time, which is a strong requirement since the system needs to have enough users putting their shares together to see the whole decryption key.

In Polat and Du (2004), the authors also assume the fact that privacy concerns are closely related to security aspects. They define specific communication protocols to deal with these issues in SVD-based collaborative filtering. Their goal is to ensure users' privacy and to provide accurate predictions. However, they consider privacy and accuracy as conflicting goals and propose a technique to achieve a balance between them. Their model differs from Canny (2002b), since Canny was focusing on the P2P framework in which users participate in the collaborative filtering process. In Polat and Du (2004), users send their data to a server and they do not participate in the computing process. Randomized perturbation techniques are used during communication to achieve privacy. Randomization perturbs the data in such a way that the server can only know the range of the data. Thus, the server does not know the true ratings of each user. Random numbers are generated using uniform or Gaussian distribution and replace partially the true ratings.

Berkovsky, Eytani, Kuflik, and Ricci (2006) also deal with privacy concerns by using policies for modifying the contents of user profiles. They denote three techniques. The *uniform random obfuscation* allows the system to substitute real ratings by random values chosen uniformly in the range of possible ratings in the dataset. The bell curved random obfuscation replaces real votes by random values using a bell-curve distribution in the same way as in statistics, that is to say by paying attention to the average and standard deviation of the ratings. At last, the *default obfuscation(x)* uses a predefined constant value x for the replacement of real data.

In addition to these policies, the authors of Berkovsky et al. (2006) propose an aggregating method to enhance privacy in P2P recommender systems. They address the problem by electing super-peers whose role is to compute an average profile of a sub-population. In this model, only these super-peers can access profiles of other peers. We can, for example, consider that the provider of the service supplies some computers to play the role of super-peers. The network is configured to be hierarchical, which means that each peer is associated to a super-peer and that super-peers can only collect data about peers under their responsibility. Consequently, each super-peer manages a rating matrix containing a subset of user profiles. There is no common profile between these super-peer matrices. The union of these matrices would constitute the whole population rating matrix. Each super-peer computes the isobarycenter of its matrix, which is called *average profile*. In order to get predictions, standard peers have to contact all these super-peers and to exploit these average profiles to compute predictions. In this way, they never access the public profile of a particular user. Nevertheless, using these average profiles can reduce the accuracy of the system. The sub-populations have been constituted randomly and the preferences are smoothed, thus reducing the influence of neighbors.

Among other works related to privacy in collaborative filtering, we can cite the paper of Miller, Konstan, and Riedl (2004), which provides a method in accordance with the fourth axe of personalization of Cranor. They propose a P2P version of the item-item algorithm. Consequently, correlations are computed between items rather than between users. The recommender system gives content-based suggestions with a high accuracy, since it can determine the similarity with the items that have been appreciated by the active user without basing the predictions on a single neighbor. However, this approach works for recommender systems whose items are persistent: they are never removed from the platform and the system badly reacts to the introduction of new items. Their model can adapt to different P2P configurations. We can also mention the work of

Han, Xie, Yang, Wang, and Shen (2004), which addresses the problem of privacy protection in a distributed collaborative filtering algorithm called PipeCF. Both user database management and prediction computation are split between several devices. This approach has been implemented on peer-to-peer overlay networks through a distributed hash table method.

GENERIC PRIVACY ENHANCING PROCESS

In the previous section, we have introduced efficient privacy-enhancing methods. However, these techniques can suffer from limitations according to their context of use. Techniques based on alteration of data (such as random perturbation of profiles) have a lower accuracy than standard collaborative filtering methods. Techniques relying on encryption of data often need to share the decryption key, which requires an important number of simultaneous connections. At last, public aggregates can guarantee the privacy of users without reducing the quality of predictions, provided that these aggregates should highlight the preferences of virtual communities of interests rather than randomly chosen sub-populations. In the following, we propose to introduce a generic privacy-enhancing process which gathers the same advantages than the previously mentioned algorithms and works on various architectures.

User Modeling Process

The first step when modeling preferences of users consists in choosing a good manner to collect data. Proposing a series of questions to users is an efficient way to do accurate preference elicitation (Viappiani, Faltings, & Pu, 2006). However, it would be necessary to ask for hundreds of questions. People generally do not take time to carry through such a lengthy process. According to the constraints of the system, it could be preferable to let users explicitly rate for the items they want, without order constraints. Each user can always check the list of items that he/she shares or has consulted. He/she may explicitly rate each of these items on an arbitrary scale of values. We can also consider the case where the active user initializes his/her personal preference with a set of items[2] proposed to everyone in the system interface in order to partially face the cold start problem. This offers the advantage of completing the profile with more consistency and of finding similarities with other users more quickly, since everyone can fill the same criteria rating form.

However, an explicit data collection may be insufficient. Psychological studies (Payne, Bettman, & Johnson, 1993) have shown that people construct their preferences while learning about the available items. That means *a priori* ratings are not necessarily relevant. Unfortunately, few users provide a feedback about their consultations. We assume that, despite the explicit voluntary completion of profiles, there are a lot of missing data. A way to face this problem consists in adding a user modeling function based on implicit criteria (Castagnos & Boyer, 2006b). This function relies on an analysis of usages. It collects information about the active user's actions (such as frequency and duration of consultations for each item, etc.). This data collation method provides better user models, and consequently better predictions in collaborative filtering computations. However, this process is quite intrusive into privacy of users.

The following subsection is dedicated to the ways that we propose in order to guarantee privacy, despite this intrusive data collection method.

Generic Solution to Guarantee Privacy

In the previous subsection, we have seen that a useful way to collect preferences consists in analysing log files of the active user to retrieve useful data. These are pieces of information easily and legally retrievable in the Web browser of the client. As the collected usages constitute very sensitive data, all pieces of information retrieved in these log files must remain on the client side. However, collaborative filtering processes require sharing knowledge about the active user with neighbors. User models consequently have to be transformed in a less intrusive form in order to be usable. According to the first axe of personalization defined by Cranor, this implicit data collection has to be transformed in explicit ratings. The user modeling function can easily be modified to reach this objective. It amounts to estimate ratings that the user is likely to give to different items from implicit criteria. Only numerical votes which have been deduced from this process are sharable with other users. We propose to use the following formula adapted from Chan (1999), to achieve this transformation in numerical profiles (see Box 1).

This formula adapts itself to implicit pieces of information that are retrievable, according to

Box 1.

$$Interest(item) = 1 + 2 \times IsFavorite(item) + \mathrm{Re}\,cent(item) + 2 \times Frequency(item) \times Duration(item)$$
$$+ PercentVisitedLinks(item)$$

$$With: \mathrm{Re}\,cent(item) = \frac{date(last\ visit) - date(\log beginning)}{date(present) - date(\log beginning)}$$

$$And: Duration(item) = \max_{consultations} \left(\frac{time\ spent\ pages\ of\ item}{size\ of\ the\ item}\right)$$

the type of consulted items, the architecture of the system and the local settings defined by the active user. *Interest(item)* must be rounded up to the nearest integer and expresses the estimated rating for the selected "*item*." Here are some criteria that can be taken into account:

- *Log beginning* corresponds to the date of first execution of the recommender module;
- *IsFavorite(item)* equals 1 if the item has been explicitly and positively voted by the user and 0, otherwise. According to the interface of the system, this vote can take the form of a rating. In this case, a positive vote corresponds to a high rating. If the active user has not the possibility to rate items in the interface, we consider that adding the item among bookmarks in the Web browser constitutes an explicit positive vote;
- *Frequency(item) x Duration(item)* must be normalized so that the maximum is 1;
- *PercentVisitedLinks(item)* corresponds to the number of visited pages divided by the number of pages on the item; and
- It is possible to include new implicit criteria in the formula, such as the fact that the active user has printed the item, that he/she has sent it by e-mail, and so forth.

This estimation of ratings requires storing locally the implicit actions for a while. To be in accordance with the second axe of personalization of Cranor, we recommend periodically deleting the oldest actions in the implicit data collection. The ideal retention period for these actions depends on the habits of consultation of the active user.

By reference to the third axe of personalization previously mentioned, we argue that the exchange of the numerical profiles between neighbors must be initiated by the users rather than by the system. Moreover, to increase the trust of users into the system, it is important to grant them the right to access and modify the content of their own profiles at any time. They can change or delete ratings stored in their personal profiles. They can also define their public profiles which are the part of the personal profiles they accept to share with others.

Rather than deteriorating profiles as in Berkovsky et al. (2006), and thus potentially reducing the accuracy of the system, we recommend sending profiles anonymously. This approach also presents the advantage to comply with the strictest international privacy laws. However, single IDs associated to these profiles are required to avoid duplication of data. We have conceived the privacy enhancing procedure in such a way that anonymity of users is guaranteed, even if each of them has a unique ID. Users have to open a session with a login and a password before using the recommender system. In this way, several persons can use the same computer (for example, the different members of a family) without disrupting their respective profiles. To summarize, each user on a given computer has his/her own profile and a single ID. For each user, we use a hash function requiring the IP address and the login in order to generate his/her ID on his/her computer. The use of a hash function H is suitable, since it has the following features:

- Non-reversible: knowing "y," it is hard to find "x" such as $H(x)=y$;
- No collision: it is hard to find "x" and "y" such as $H(x)=H(y)$;
- Knowing "x" and "H," it is easy to compute $H(x)$; and
- $H(x)$ has a fixed size.

In this way, an ID does not allow identification of the name or IP address of the corresponding user. Thanks to this ID generator, the communication module can guarantee the anonymity of users by using an IP multicast address—shared by all the users of the personalizing service—to broadcast the packets containing the profiles, the sender's ID, and optionally the addressees' IDs.

At last, we pay attention to the fourth axe of personalization when making recommendations, by favouring when possible the items explicitly and positively rated by the active user, rather than those which could be interesting according to neighbors' experience.

In the following subsection, we will show on real industrial applications that it is possible to put this privacy enhancing procedure into practice, both for client/server and peer-to-peer architectures.

Examples of Applications with Different Architectures

Client/Server Architecture

We have implemented our work in the context of satellite Web site broadcasting (Castagnos & Boyer, 2006a). Our model has been integrated within the architecture of *Casablanca*, which is a product of the ASTRA company.[3] ASTRA, located in Luxembourg, conceived a service of satellite Web site broadcasting service called *Sat@once*. This service is sponsored by advertisement so that it is free for users, provided that they use a DVB receiver. The satellite bouquet holds hundreds of Web sites which are sent to several hundred thousands of persons through a high-bandwidth and one-way transmission.

Web sites are sent from the server to clients using satellites. Moreover, the users can send non-numerical votes. These votes appear as the list of favorite Web sites (cf. supra, *IsFavorite* in the Chan formula, 3.2 Generic Solution to Guarantee Privacy). However, we cannot describe these non-numerical votes as boolean. We cannot differentiate items in which the active user is not interested (negative votes) from those he/she does not know or has omitted. This kind of votes is not sufficient to do relevant predictions with collaborative filtering methods. The users can also suggest new contents into the server. The votes and the suggestions are used to make up the bouquet: only the most popular Web sites are sent per satellite.

In order to distribute the system, the server side part is separated from the client side. The function of user modeling, based on the Chan formula, determines estimated ratings for items according to user actions. These user actions are stored temporarily and remain on client side.

Then, users have the possibility to send anonymously the estimated ratings to the server, like the non-numerical votes. This is a user-initiated process and nothing is shared without the agreement

Figure 1. Architecture of the information filtering module in Casablanca

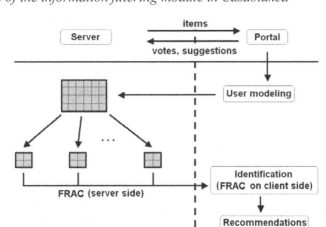

of the owners of these profiles. Each user profile containing estimated ratings is associated to a single ID to avoid duplication, as explained.

The server uses, as input parameters, the matrix of user votes and the database including sites and descriptors. Thanks to this privacy enhancing procedure, the server has no information about the population, except anonymous votes. User preferences are stored in the profile on clients. Thus, the privacy criterion is duly fulfilled.

Once the profiles of users have been sent to the server, the system has to build virtual communities of interests. In our model, this step is carried out by an improved hierarchical clustering algorithm, called *FRAC*. It allows, within the scope of our architecture, to limit the number of persons considered in the prediction computations. Thus, the results will be potentially more relevant, since observations will be based on a group closer to the active user. This process amounts to considering that the active user asks for the opinion of a group of persons having similar tastes to his/hers. It is obviously transparent for users.

In order to compute these groups of interests, the server extracts data from the profiles of users and aggregates the ratings in a global matrix. This matrix constitutes the root of the tree which is recursively built by *FRAC* (cf. Figure 2).

The set of users is then divided into two subgroups using the *k-means* method. In our case, the k equals 2, since our overall strategy is to recursively divide the population into binary sub-sets. Once this first subdivision has been completed, it is repeatedly applied to the new subgroups, and this until the selected depth of the tree has been reached. This means, the more one goes down in the structure of the tree, the more the clusters become specific to a certain group of similar users. Consequently, people belonging to a leaf of the tree share the same opinion concerning the assignment of a rating for a given item.

Once groups of persons have been formed as previously mentioned, the barycenter is calculated for each cluster. Each barycenter is a kind of typical user profile aggregating the preferences of a sub-population.

The profiles of typical users are then sent on client side, using the satellite connection. Subsequently, the system uses the Pearson correlation coefficient to compute distances between the active user and the typical users. We consider that the active user belongs to the community whose center is the closest to him/her. At last, we can predict the interests of the active user from the knowledge of his/her community.

This way, to proceed allows the system to provide the active user with interesting items, even when he/she does not want to share his/her profile. Indeed, the typical profiles are sent on client side, in any case. Consequently, it is always possible to compute distance between the active user's profile which is stored locally and these typical profiles. Once the system has selected a community, it can suggest items that have been the most liked by this group of persons, that is to say items with the highest ratings in the corresponding typical profile. This way, to proceed does not reduce the accuracy of the system, since typical profiles summarize the preferences of similar users, rather than randomly chosen users. The level of similarity within a community is a feature of the system and can be parameterised.

Figure 2. Communities of interests built with FRAC

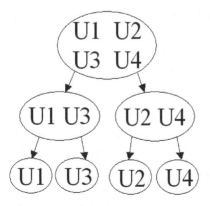

The privacy of users is guaranteed both on the client and server side. On the client side, the active user never has access to profiles of other users since he/she only knows preferences of his/her community. Moreover, he/she can choose if and what to share with other people at any time. On the server side, profiles are stored using single IDs which do not allow the system to retrieve the corresponding users.

Grid Computing

SofoS is our new document sharing platform (Castagnos & Boyer, 2007), using a recommender system to provide users with content. Once it is installed, users can share and/or search documents, as they do on P2P applications like *Napster*. We conceived it to be as open as possible to different existing kinds of data: hypertext files, documents, music, videos, and so forth. The goal of *SofoS* is also to assist users to find the most relevant sources of information in the most efficient way. In order to reach this objective, the platform exploits the *AURA* recommender module. Users can integrate in the platform a feedback about their preferences, by explicitly rating for items. Each item has a profile on the platform. The performance of this module crucially depends on the accuracy of the individual user preference models.

These personal preference-based profiles are used by our distributed collaborative filtering algorithm, in order to provide each user with the content that most likely interests him/her. *AURA* relies on a peer-to-peer architecture. We presume that each peer in *SofoS* corresponds to a single user on a given device, having a single ID generated by our privacy enhancing module (cf. 3.2 Generic Solution to Guarantee Privacy).

In addition to the available documents, each peer owns seven pieces of information: a personal profile, a public profile, a group profile and some lists of IDs (list "A" for IDs of peers belonging to its group, list "B" for those which exceed the minimum-correlation threshold as explained later, list "C" for the black-listed IDs, and list "O" for IDs of peers which have added the active user to their group profile).

The personal profile is the combination of the explicit ratings and of the ratings estimated from the actions of the active user on the platform for a limited duration. The estimation is based on the Chan formula. The public profile is the part of the personal profile that the active user accepts to share with others. The algorithm also has to build a group profile. It represents the preferences of a virtual community of interests, and has been especially designed to be as close as possible to the active user's expectations. In order to do that, the peer of the active user asks for the public profiles of all the peers it can reach through the platform. Then, for each of these profiles, it computes a similarity measure with the personal profile of the active user. The active user can define a minimum-correlation threshold which corresponds to the radius of his/her trust circle (cf. Figure 3).

If the similarity is lower than this fixed threshold, which is specific to each user, the ID of the peer is added to the list "A" and the corresponding profile is included in the group profile of the active

Figure 3. Minimum-correlation threshold defining the bounds of the trust circle

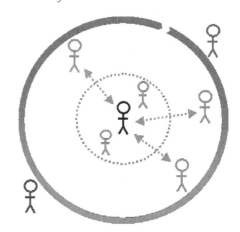

user. We used the Pearson correlation coefficient to establish the similarity measure, since the literature shows that it works well (Shardanand & Maes, 1995).

Of course, if this similarity measure is higher than the threshold, we add the ID of the peer to the list "B." The list "C" is used to systematically ignore some peers. It enables to improve trust—that is, confidence that users have in the recommendations—by identifying malicious users.

When his/her personal profile changes, the active user has the possibility to update his/her public profile p_a. In this case, the active peer has to contact every peer[4] whose ID is in the list "O." Each of these peers re-computes the similarity measure. If it exceeds the threshold, the profile p_a has to be removed from the group profile. Otherwise, p_a has to be updated in the group profile, that is to say the peer must remove the old profile and add the new one.

In order to provide recommendations, the system determines the most popular items in the group profile. This model provides more accurate results than methods based on public aggregates, since the group profile is built in order to be user-centric. This means that the active user is the gravity center of his/her community of interests. In this model, privacy is guaranteed by the fact that public profiles of other users are not kept on the peer. These public profiles are automatically and iteratively integrated in the group profile of the active user. At last, exchanges of profiles are made with anonymity which prevents hackers from identifying the owner of a profile by intercepting the packets over the network.

FUTURE TRENDS

Collaborative filtering techniques model the social process of asking friends for recommendations on unseen resources. It is not limited to recommending similar items to those already liked, but can offer surprising suggestions to the user.

Thus, despite their increasing success, collaborative filtering algorithms still suffer from some significant limitations. It becomes strongly crucial to improve the quality and the robustness of prediction in order to provide users with reliable and pertinent results.

For example, recommender systems could be targets for attacks from malicious users since there are political, economical, or many other motivations for influencing the promotion or the demotion of recommendable items. Recent works (O'Donovan & Smith, 2006; Weng, Miao, & Goh, 2006; Goldbeck, 2006) have shown that incorporating trust model into the recommendation process have a positive impact both on the accuracy of the predictions and the confidence the user has in the system. Trust is a social notion which provides information about with whom we should share information, from whom we should accept information and what consideration to give to information when filtering or aggregating data. So it seems that trust is a promising way to investigate also, in terms of privacy issues. Users could accept to share information with people they trust and could allow a system to collect information about their preferences if they know it is able to differentiate trusty and untrusty users.

CONCLUSION

In this chapter, we have provided definitions and compared different research works about privacy protection in recommender systems. We have highlighted the drawbacks and benefits of privacy-enhancing methods, according to the context. This overview has led to the definition of a generic procedure that is suitable for collaborative filtering techniques. We referred to the four axes of personalization defined by Cranor (2005), to define the degree of privacy of our method. Real industrial frameworks allowed us to illustrate the benefits of this new approach. We have explored both distributed and centralized approaches for collaborative filtering techniques, as the privacy problem is linked to the choice of architectures. In Castagnos and Boyer (2006a), we introduce a client/server algorithm which has been integrated in a satellite Web site broadcasting service used by 120,000 persons. Similar privacy-enhanced models have been designed for centralized architectures and grid computing, respectively in Boyer, Castagnos, Anneheim, Bertrand-Pierron, and Blanchard, (2006) and Castagnos and Boyer (2007).

Through these examples, the proposed chapter aimed at providing an unified definition of the term "privacy." Indeed, countries over the world have different laws about privacy. We have shown that it is possible to guarantee that pieces of software fulfill the national laws in these conditions. We have also shown that users have different expectations in the matter of privacy protection and we have conceived the generic privacy enhancing procedure in the goal of increasing the trust of users. At last, we have discussed the possibility to get good prediction quality—or, at least, to not alter this quality too much—while preserving privacy of users.

REFERENCES

Berkovsky, S., Eytani, Y., Kuflik, T., & Ricci, F. (2006, April). *Hierarchical neighborhood topology for privacy enhanced collaborative filtering*. Paper presented at CHI 2006 Workshop on Privacy-Enhanced Personalization (PEP2006), Montreal, Canada.

Boyer, A., Castagnos, S., Anneheim, J., Bertrand-Pierron, Y., & Blanchard, J-P. (2006, December). Le filtrage collaboratif : Pistes d'applications dans le domaine bancaire et présentation de la technologie. *Dossiers de la veille technologique du Crédit Agricole S.A.* : Number 27.

Canny, J. (2002a, May). Collaborative filtering with privacy. In *Proceedings of the IEEE Sym-*

posium on Security and Privacy (pp. 45-57). Oakland, CA.

Canny, J. (2002b, August). Collaborative filtering with privacy via factor analysis. In *Proceedings of the 25th Annual International ACM SIGIR Conference on Research and Development in Information Retrieval (SIGIR 2002)*. Tampere, Finland.

Castagnos, S., & Boyer, A. (2006a, April). *From implicit to explicit data: A way to enhance privacy*. Paper presented at CHI 2006 Workshop on Privacy-Enhanced Personalization (PEP 2006), Montreal, Canada.

Castagnos, S., & Boyer, A. (2006b, August). A client/server user-based collaborative filtering algorithm: Model and implementation. In *Proceedings of the 17th European Conference on Artificial Intelligence (ECAI2006)*. Riva del Garda, Italy.

Castagnos, S., & Boyer, A. (2007, April). Personalized communities in a distributed recommender system. In *Proceedings of the 29th European Conference on Information Retrieval (ECIR 2007)*. Rome, Italy.

Chan, P. (1999, August). A non-invasive learning approach to building Web user profiles. In *Proceedings of the Workshop on Web Usage Analysis and User Profiling, Fifth International Conference on Knowledge Discovery and Data Mining*, San Diego, California.

Cranor, L. F. (2005). *Hey, that's personal!* Invited talk at the International User Modeling Conference (UM05).

Golbeck, J. (2006). Generating predictive movie recommendations from trust in social networks. In *Proceedings of the Fourth International Conference on Trust Management*. USA.

Goldberg, D., Nichols, D., Oki, B., & Terry, D. (1992). Using collaborative filtering to weave an information tapestry [Special Issue]. *Communications of the ACM, 35*, 61-70.

Han, P., Xie, B., Yang, F., Wang, J., & Shen, R. (2004, May). A novel distributed collaborative filtering algorithm and its implementation on P2P overlay network. In *Proceedings of the Eighth Pacific-Asia Conference on Knowledge Discovery and Data Mining (PAKDD04)*. Sydney, Australia.

Miller, B. N., Konstan, J. A., & Riedl, J. (2004, July). PocketLens: Toward a personal recommender system. *ACM Transactions on Information Systems, 22*.

O'Donovan, J., & Smith, B. (2006, January). Is trust robust? An analysis of trust-bades recommendation. In *IUI 2006*. Sydney, Australia.

Payne, J. W., Bettman, J. R., & Johnson, E. J. (1993). *The adaptive decision maker*. Cambridge University Press.

Polat, H., & Du, W. (2004). SVD-based collaborative filtering with privacy. In *Proceedings of ACM Symposium on Applied Computing*. Cyprus.

Shardanand, U., & Maes, P. (1995). Social information filtering: Algorithms for automating "word of mouth." In *Proceedings of ACM CHI'95 Conference on Human Factors in Computing Systems* (Vol. 1, pp. 210-217).

Simon, H. A. (1982). Economic analysis and public policy. In *book "Models of Bounded Rationality"*: volume 1 and 2: MIT Press.

Viappiani, P., Faltings, B., & Pu, P. (2006, June). The lookahead principle for preference elicitation: Experimental results. In *Proceedings of the 7th International Conference on Flexible Query Answering Systems (FQAS 2006) Lecture Notes in Computer Science, 4027,* 378-389. Milan, Italy: Springer.

Wang, Y., & Kobsa, A. (2006, April). *Impacts of privacy laws and regulations on personalized systems*. Paper presented at the CHI 2006 Workshop on Privacy-Enhanced Personalization (PEP 2006), Montreal, Canada.

Weng, J., Miao, C., & Goh, A. (2006, April). Improving collaborative filtering with trust-based metrics. In *Proceedings of SAC'06*. Dijon, France.

Westin, A. (1967). *Privacy and freedom. Talk at the Atheneum*. New York.

White, B. (2006). *The implications of Web 2.0 on Web information systems*. Invited talk, Webist 2006.

Zaslow, J. (2002). If TiVo thinks you are gay, here's how to set it straight: What you buy affects recommendations on Amazon.com, too; why the cartoons? *The Wallstreet Journal,* Retrieved November 26, 2002, from http://online.wsj.com/article_email/0,,SB1038261936872356908,00.html

ENDNOTES

[1] http://www.choicestream.com/
[2] Ideally, this set of items should cover all the implicit categories that users can find on the platform.
[3] http://www.ses-astra.com/
[4] A packet is broadcasted with a heading containing peers' IDs, the old profile, and the new public profile.

Section IV
Organizational Aspects

Chapter XV
An Adaptive Threat–Vulnerability Model and the Economics of Protection

C. Warren Axelrod
US Trust, USA

ABSTRACT

Traditionally, the views of security professionals regarding responses to threats and the management of vulnerabilities have been biased towards technology and operational risks. The purpose of this chapter is to extend the legacy threat-vulnerability model to incorporate human and social factors. This is achieved by presenting the dynamics of threats and vulnerabilities in the human and social context. We examine costs and benefits as they relate to threats, exploits, vulnerabilities, defense measures, incidents, and recovery and restoration. We also compare the technical and human/social aspects of each of these areas. We then look at future work and how trends are pushing against prior formulations and forcing new thinking on the technical, operational risk, and human/social aspects. The reader will gain a broader view of threats, vulnerabilities and responses to them through incorporating human and social elements into their security models.

INTRODUCTION

Have you noticed that when you drive a particular make of car, it appears that virtually every second or third vehicle on the road is from the same manufacturer as yours, and often the same model, too? While it could be true, depending on the brand that you choose, it is mostly perception. It is just that you are more aware of and notice this particular brand. So it is with the subject of this book.

When the editors first suggested the topic in 2006, articles examining the impact of human and social aspects of information security, though they did exist, were few and far between. Suddenly, in the early months of 2007, the gurus of information security—such as Bruce Schneier—had "found religion" and seemed to be talking and writing about little else. In a report on the 2007 RSA Conference, Ellen Messmer reported that Bruce Schneier "casts light on psychology of security," where Schneier emphasizes the importance of human factors in the security equation (Messmer, 2007). Schneier has also drafted a paper on the topic (Schneier, 2007a).

With such a boost as this, I am sure that you will see a flood of quotations, articles, and books on the topic over the next several years. As a result of this, the face of information security practice will change forever.

Historically, the average security professional has been highly technical and operational, but many have recently become more risk-aware, and will be called upon to be a psychologist and behavioral scientist as well as a security expert. To quote John Kirkwood, chief security officer at Royal Ahold, the Dutch parent of the Stop & Shop supermarket chain, in regard to security assessments: "Do it from the way the hacker would think" (Scalet, 2007). Several Stop & Shop stores in New England were victims of a scam involving the substitution of card data skimming devices for regular point-of-sale readers. Kirkwood touts the importance of convergence between information security and physical security in order to provide more complete protection. As we delve into the subject, we will see how these differences in backgrounds, knowledge, and experience between "logical" and physical security personnel, many with law enforcement origins, can enrich the threat-vulnerability model.

It is gratifying to see that the human and social aspects of information security are finally getting the attention that they deserve. As with many innovative approaches, it might attract excessive interest, certainly more than warranted, and divert attention and resources from other critical technology and risk areas before it settles into its rightful place in security professionals' toolkits. The Gartner Group has developed a life-cycle model, primarily for IT-related products, called the "hype cycle."[1] In a graphical depiction, they show the visibility of a product varies with maturity of the product over time. The first phase is the called the "technology trigger." I believe that, if we adopt

Gartner's model for the social and human aspects of information security, we are currently in this first phase. Taking the Gartner model further, we can expect to go through subsequent phases named "peak of inflated expectations," "trough of disillusionment," "slope of enlightenment," and "plateau of productivity," respectively. This process is likely to take 2 to 5 years before we might reach the productivity plateau. But this can only be done with dispatch if we begin the journey. Perhaps by embarking early on this road, we can ultimately accelerate the process and achieve the desired goal of the full consideration of social and human factors more expeditiously.

In favor of giving the social and human side more consideration, one might argue that you can not know where most effectively to put your security funds without including the economic ramifications of these factors and how they affect security. This is somewhat similar to the need to include "social costs" into an economic justification of a power plant, say, that pollutes the air and raises the temperature of the adjacent river water, which it uses for cooling. The impact on society is of polluted air, which causes respiratory and other diseases, and heated and polluted water, which results in dead fish and other creatures. If these health and environmental factors are not considered, then there is little incentive for the builders of the power plant to install equipment to scrub the air before it is emitted, use less polluting fuels, and devise less damaging cooling methods, for example. Similarly, with information security, information security professionals and general business management must be persuaded to apply methods and use tools that are effective in minimizing the technical, human, and social vulnerabilities of the overall system.

Another related area, which should not be ignored but which is not addressed in detail here, is the impact of social and human factors on security systems themselves, particularly as they relate to security professionals. Mendell (2007) notes that many psychological factors, among them "information overload," serve to impair or degrade security professionals' performance and judgment.

In this chapter, we develop a practical adaptive model of the threat-vulnerability interaction by including human and social factors along with the traditional technology- and risk-related influences. We carry the process through to develop an economic model with which to determine the most appropriate allocation of security funds subject to technological and human constraints.

Some Definitions

Let us take a few minutes to develop and discuss some definitions using Figure 1 as a basis. Most of the definitions are gleaned from the glossary posted online by Symantec (2007).

Security begins with a threat, which may be defined as follows:

*A **threat** is a circumstance, event, or person with the potential to cause harm to a system in the form of destruction, disclosure, data modification, or denial of service (DoS).*

It should be noted that a threat is "potential" rather than "actual," and may only result in an incident if it meets up with a vulnerability.

As shown in Figure 1, threats might be known or unknown, and sometimes they might be partially known. For example, it was well known that terrorists highjack airplanes prior to 9-11, but it was not generally anticipated that they would cause them to be flown into specific buildings. Post 9-11, such threats were perceived as being not only possible but also likely.

Threats lose much of their uncertainty when an actual exploit is developed.

In the IT (information technology) security context, an **exploit** is a program or technique that takes advantage of a vulnerability in software and that can be used for breaking security, or otherwise attacking a host over a network.

Figure 1. A Threat-Vulnerability Flow Model

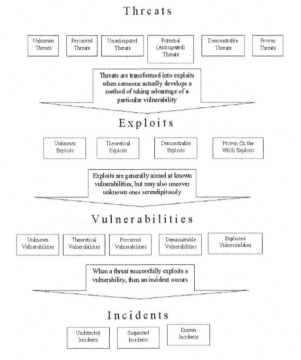

A further refinement of exploits is whether they are "in the zoo" or "in the wild." The former generally means that the exploit has been demonstrated in the laboratory of a security vendor or protection service provider, and the latter means that it has been released and may be spreading.

An exploit is effectively the demonstrable realization of a threat. However, it is not a danger unless it is used by someone for an attack and is able to take advantage of a vulnerability.

A **vulnerability** is a state in a computing system or set of systems and networks that allows an attacker to:

• Execute commands as another user;
• Access data that is contrary to specified access restrictions for the data;
• Pose as another entity; and/or
• Conduct a denial of service attack.

When an exploit is successful against a vulnerability, then an incident occurs.

Here Symantec (2007) defines an **incident** as "the actualization of a risk." This definition has semantic issues. It implies that a risk is the successful exploitation of a vulnerability. In fact, Symantec defines a risk in this way. However, when listing "types of risk," the Symantec glossary includes threats, such as adware, spyware, hack tools, viruses, worms, and Trojan horses, thereby confusing threat and risk. In regard to "risk impact," they suggest that the impact be on performance, privacy, and so forth, in this case confusing risk and incident.

Others provide formulae for calculating risk that combines value of an asset, the level of threat against that asset, and how vulnerable the asset is to given threats. While this is a reasonable construct, the analyst generally assigns points and/or levels (e.g., high, moderate, or low) to each of the three factors and somehow aggregates them via addition or multiplication. Such a methodology is highly subjective and the aggregation method has no real basis.

Risk is more appropriately defined in terms of the probability of loss and the estimated magnitude of the loss incurred. The probability of loss, which is based on threats and the chances of their being translated into exploits that are successful against vulnerabilities, is admittedly highly subjective but is more realistic than assigning arbitrary values to each component. Also, there are potentially many types of threat and exploit, which might be wielded against an asset. Furthermore, the risk is often a combination of expected losses from expected incidents against the asset.

Another aspect of these definitions and approaches is that they do not explicitly take human and social factors into account, a situation that we are about to rectify.

BACKGROUND

Human characteristics and social behavior are central and critical to the creation and evolution of threats and the exploitation of vulnerabilities. Information security professionals have generally given the human and social aspects of information security short shrift, since they most likely have been trained in technical and operational disciplines. While the same security professionals regularly purport to be sensitive to certain reactions of the "user community," security practitioners have been notorious in their implementing misguided technologies and procedures. This is evidenced by the many articles on the resistance to, and annoyance with, newly introduced security measures, such as complex passwords (Axelrod, 2005) and other supposedly strong authentication (Stone, 2007).

On the other hand, physical security specialists, frequently with law enforcement backgrounds, are usually much more knowledgeable about evil human motives and more sensitive to nefarious activities than are their computer-oriented counterparts. However, they often do not understand the nuances of information technology well enough.

A major difference between the attitudes of information security and physical security professionals is that the former are generally more focused on protecting information assets through preventing bad things from happening, whereas the latter tend to lean towards investigations, forensic analysis, and apprehending the perpetrators. While these goals are not mutually exclusive, they can lead to significantly different impacts on organizations and their employees.

The key is to find the "sweet spot" among the various disciplines. In Figure 2, we show roughly where the various job functions and background disciplines fall on a continuum from technical through to behavioral orientations. As we can see, the traditional computer security practitioners tend to have engineering and computer science backgrounds and to concentrate on the implementation and technical support of security tools. At the other extreme, we have psychology and behavioral experts who are focussed on how individuals interact with various technical interfaces and security measures and, in particular, how they might try to get around them. Between these two extremes, we have technically-oriented business staff (if such actually exist) and business-oriented technical staff, which is likely to be a more common situation. This view conforms with a particular set of graduate programs at the Stevens Institute of Technology in Hoboken, New Jersey. Stevens offers a graduate degree (the MSIS or masters of science in information systems) to those with technical backgrounds who want to learn "the business" in selected sectors, such as financial and health services. They also offer technical certifications to those with a more general business background, who want to augment their experience with a more in-depth understanding of technologies. The former has historically outpaced the latter by an order of magnitude. An increasing number of institutions of higher education are offering undergraduate and graduate degrees and certifications in these areas.

In this chapter, we bridge the gap between those who view themselves as defenders of the information "crown jewels" and those who are more interested in capturing and punishing the perpetrators. Both are important aspects of security and each has its place. It is, however, important

to balance both approaches. Sometimes it is well neigh impossible to bring criminals, who may be operating half way around the globe, to justice. On such occasions it is much more feasible to try to prevent damage. Conversely, it might be more effective to apprehend the criminal, particularly if the person is a "trusted" insider, since it is often difficult to apply defenses against insider abuse and still provide the access needed to do a particular job.

We develop an adaptive human-technical threat-vulnerability model, based on the model shown in Figure 3, in which we show how the impact of attack and defense mechanisms change dynamically, as individuals and groups interact with opportunities that they create or are presented to them. We examine how attackers and defenders might adapt to dynamic new technologies. We consider whether adverse actions are intentional or not. If intentional, we try to understand what the objectives and motivation of the attacker might be. If accidental, we consider how controls might be affected to avoid such occurrences from taking place.

We then take this model and apply cost-benefit and risk analysis to it in order to derive a new economic basis for selecting remediation approaches. It is shown how decisions will differ depending upon whether or not human and social aspects have been considered, and demonstrate why certain responses, which do not include the human element, exacerbate rather than alleviate the risks from threats.

BROADENING THE SECURITY CONCEPT

Because the academic disciplines of human behavior and sociology are generally held to be so different from technology, they are seldom linked to one another. However, it is worth defining relevant threats and vulnerabilities in terms of

Figure 2. The Technical/Human Continuum and Job Functions and Backgrounds

Figure 3. The Adaptive Threat-Vulnerability Model

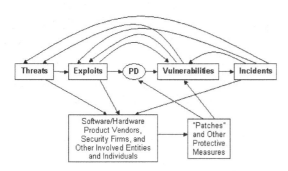

characteristics that are technical, behavioral, and cultural. We cannot treat human and technical aspects separately if we are truly to understand the interaction of threats and vulnerabilities. Nor can we exclude social and human factors when determining the most cost-effective approaches to protecting information assets. After all, the best-devised technical approaches can be readily undermined or sabotaged by individuals who consider a particular approach to be against their personal interests. Such interests may protect their position within the organization or society, or help decide which methods represent cultural compromises, that they are not willing to accept.

Furthermore, we must not separate the logical and physical aspects of a secure environment as they frequently work together to create an overall secure environment, where one aspect mitigates risks that remain untreated by the other.

To simplify matters, we offer the concept that technical security tools are one of the means of administering defenses, defending against exploits, discovering vulnerabilities, and mitigating them. However, technical tools are only part of the story and the different ways in which humans respond to vulnerabilities, as well as to threats and exploits, must be included. Individuals might support or undermine security measures, either intentionally or obliviously, depending upon circumstances.

If security requirements are complex and difficult to operate, subjects will seek and find means of circumventing them. If evildoers are capable and devious enough, they will come up with ways of persuading their victims of their own authenticity so that the objects of the onslaught will yield to the deceptions, often unaware that they are doing so. Thus, a defense measure is only as effective as the extent to which those responsible for its implementation are committed to ensuring the protection of the assets under attack and knowledgeable enough to recognize that an attack is underway.

Wrapped Exploits and Open Responses

One way of looking at this is to view exploits and vulnerabilities existing at the physical, technical, human, and societal levels.

As an example, consider a computer worm or virus. In the health field, many viruses develop, begin to spread, and then fizzle, whereas others proliferate wildly. So it is with computer viruses. Only a few of those released from the "zoo" to the "wild" are actually successful in their missions. Success is often contingent upon a particular human action or inaction. The inaction may be intended or not. For example, the inaction of not patching a particular system or of not closing off an unneeded service and/or port may be for one of many reasons. Perhaps those responsible are not aware, do not try to find out, know about it but think that the risk is low, or are unable to fix it in time. In regard to actions, the spreading of the virus might require that the potential victims perform some action, such as innocently clicking on a link or an attachment, visiting dubious Web sites, or otherwise responding to some implicit or explicit request for action.

Likewise, the evildoer does not usually present a raw exploit but frequently cloaks it in some sort of social-engineering disguise, much like the wolf donned Little Red Riding Hood's grandmother's clothing. Rather, he couches it in terms that might engender a response from the recipient. This might include an enticing subject line in an e-mail, or threatening or cajoling the recipient to link to a Web site and divulge personal information, or persuading someone to open an attachment or perform some other innocuous task while the hacker implants some malevolent code, or "malware," on the unsuspecting recipient's computer system.

The relationship between technology-related threats and vulnerabilities and the human players on each side of the fence are shown diagrammatically in Figure 4. In many cases, there is an initial human interaction (1), such as replying to an e-mail, opening an attachment, or clicking on a link. By responding to this initial probe, the responder effectively opens the door to his or her environment (2), allowing for the insertion of malware or extraction of identifying information, and so forth (3).

Sometimes malware self-activates without the victim actually having to do anything. However, in some of these cases, it is a matter of the victim **not** having done something that he or she should have done, such as installing the most recent antivirus software.

The attacks can be thwarted somewhat by such approaches as automating the patching process, installing antivirus and anti-malware software, and training personnel to be on the lookout for phishing, pharming, and other types of attack that involve social-engineering methods.

Figure 4. Human and Technical Elements of Threats and Vulnerabilities

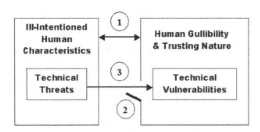

Another factor that greatly affects the success rates of the various criminal elements engaged in destructive and fraudulent activities is their ability to modify exploits in response to the defenses that have been created to protect against known threats and exploits. This adaptive mechanism, which evildoers are quick to adopt, is one of the keys to the increasing success of malware.

In some ways, the technical aspects of threat-vulnerability interactions are predictable in that technical exploits are built to perform a specific task, although they sometimes act in an unpredictable way. A famous example of this is the Morris worm, which, beginning on November 2, 1988, proliferated well beyond the expectations of its creator.[2]

The social and cultural aspects of the potential victims' reaction may also be predictable based on an understanding of the motivations and responses of a particular culture, although some exploits (such as the "ILOVEYOU" worm) cut across many cultures.[3]

The purely human aspects in regard to both attacks and defenses are generally much less predictable. Sometimes experience and training will make one person more suspicious of an unexpected and unusual e-mail, whereas others will be taken in by a more sophisticated version of the same exploit. Whereas a technical exploit can be expected to be effective whenever it gains access to a particular vulnerable system, the effectiveness of a social-engineering exploit is much less predictable, although if the attacker engages a very large number of subjects, then there is a strong likelihood that a small percentage, but a substantial number of recipients, will be fooled.

The Dynamics of Threats and Vulnerabilities

No sooner have defenses against particular types of attack been developed, than these former exploits change or morph into other forms, to get around previously available defenses. In other cases, entirely new attack vectors are created to circumvent the defenses. As a consequence, security professionals are always playing catch-up in an ever-escalating battle with evildoers. Both attackers and victims display particularly human motivations and social responses, such as perversity and gullibility respectively, which only adds to the difficulty in, and expense of, protection. There are numerous cases of knowledgeable individuals falling for new variants of social-engineering ploys, even if they should have known better. The attacker can keep changing his method until he finds one that works.

The speed at which technology is changing makes for the never-ending creation of new vulnerabilities. At the same time, these same technologies also facilitate better-crafted and more effective attacks. Typically, when new software is introduced, it contains significant numbers of errors (or "bugs") and vulnerabilities, which are often fixed soon after they are discovered. Consequently, we are likely to see a diminution of vulnerabilities over time. We then most often see a step-up in the number of errors and vulnerabilities with each new release, followed by a fall-off. This is illustrated in Figure 5.

As can be seen in Figure 5, the best policy is to ride the vulnerability curve down (as illustrated by the thick jagged line) by acquiring the new releases some time after their introduction so as to avoid the initial period of higher errors and vulnerabilities.

At the same time, as the software vendors are reducing the number of known vulnerabilities, hackers are improving their ability to exploit the remaining vulnerabilities, while simultaneously discovering new ones. This effort will tend to lag the software development and revision release cycles for the most part since vulnerabilities are generally discovered only after the targeted software is released. However, the exploiting technologies are also improving over time and are becoming easier to use and more generally available. This is illustrated in Figure 6.

Now let us consider that the software vendors are able to provide fixes, patches, or workarounds for many of the vulnerabilities, but that there remains a residue of vulnerabilities which cannot be mitigated or which would require unacceptable measures or a reduction in features. The remaining hard-core vulnerabilities, shown as the lower line in Figure 6, track the total number of vulnerabilities to some degree. If everyone were very diligent in their vulnerability mitigation efforts, they would track along this lower line. However, it often is not cost-effective to fix everything for which remedies are available, so that most organizations will lie somewhere between these lines depending upon their degree of diligence.

On the exploits side, there is an equivalent relationship between the number of exploits developed ("in the zoo"), the number released ("in

Figure 6. Interaction of Vulnerabilities and Exploits

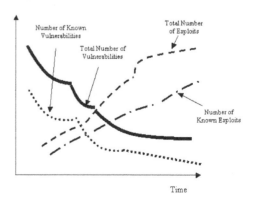

Figure 5. Variations in Number of Vulnerabilities with New Releases of Products

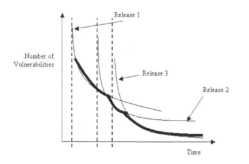

the wild"), and the number that are effective. This is also shown in Figure 6.

In reality, the threat of an incident affecting any particular asset is governed by the number of exploits in the wild and the number of vulnerabilities that exist on the organization's systems and networks.

Just how these major influences interact with each other will vary with characteristics of the software, with vendor, ubiquity, and market share being major factors taken into account by hackers. Thus, for example, vulnerabilities in software products manufactured by Microsoft have been more publicized and generally under greater attack than products from Apple Computer, say. While some contend that this is because Apple products are generally more secure, others believe that it is only because Apple has a much smaller market

share so that they are ignored by hackers. Hackers looking for notoriety will generally seek out the more popular systems to attack, but so will those looking for monetary gain or to disrupt operations. However, there are select groups, having very specific targets in their sights, which will go after particular systems that promise to yield significantly greater financial, strategic or military gains.

The Changing Threat Environment

It is increasingly being reported that the population of "bad guys" or "black hats" is changing. Most notably, the misguided teenager, who sought kudos and the admiration from his peers, has been largely replaced or augmented by those more interested in financial gain than publicity. Thus,

Table 1. Different views of various vulnerability disclosure/nondisclosure strategies

Discoverer's Strategy	Views of Discoverer of Vulnerability	Views of Vendors and Security Firms	Views of Targeted Victims
Do nothing	Will not gain any notoriety, money or satisfaction	Not aware	Not aware
Make public	Shame vendor into coming up with a quick fix before an exploit can be created	Aware—under pressure to come up with solution	Aware—nervous about creation of an exploit; pressuring vendor to fix it
Make available to vendor only at no charge for given period for vendor to fix problem	Good Samaritan	Good deed if deadline to fix is reasonable; otherwise, not good	May not be aware if done clandestinely. Good if fixed before going public. Bad if goes public before being fixed.
Sell to bad guys	Can be very profitable	Bad news	Bad news
Sell to good guys	Profitable, but may be less so than if sold to bad guys	May be beneficial if sold to security vendor on an exclusive basis as it creates competitive advantage. Good for software vendor if it can be fixed without anyone knowing.	Generally not aware
Sell to highest bidder	Most profitable if it initiates a bidding war, but may be dangerous for discoverer	Generally bad but depends on who wins bidding war	Neutral (not aware) or bad depending upon winner in bidding war
Use as the basis for a targeted attack, which is not generally known, so no defenses would have been created	Opportunity for fraud, destruction, blackmail	Not aware	Bad news—no protection available from vendors or security firms

Table 2. Different views of various exploit disclosure/nondisclosure strategies

Creator's Strategy	Views of Creator of Exploit	Views of Vendors and Security Firms	Views of Targeted Victims
Do nothing	Will not gain any notoriety, money or satisfaction	Not aware	Not aware
Make public	Shame vendor(s) into coming up with a quick fix before the exploit is activated	Aware—under greater pressure to come up with protective solution	Aware—nervous about activation of the exploit. Pressure vendor to protect against it. Pressure law enforcement to capture creator and deactivate exploit.
Make available to vendor only at no charge for given period for vendor to fix problem	Good Samaritan	Good deed if deadline to fix is reasonable, otherwise, not good	May not be aware if done clandestinely. Good if vulnerability fixed before going public with exploit. Bad if goes public before being fixed.
Sell to bad guys	Can be very profitable	Bad news	Bad news
Sell to good guys	Profitable, but may be less so than if sold to bad guys	May be beneficial if sold to security firm on an exclusive basis as it creates competitive advantage. Good for software vendor if it can be fixed without anyone knowing.	Generally not aware
Sell to highest bidder	Most profitable if it initiates a bidding war, but may be dangerous for creator	Generally bad but depends on who wins bidding war	Neutral (not aware) or bad depending upon the winner of the bidding war
Use as targeted attack, which is not generally known and for which no defenses have been created	Opportunity for fraud, destruction, blackmail	Not aware	Bad news—no protection available from vendors or security firms

vulnerabilities and exploits are being marketed for cash to security software companies, hackers, fraudsters, and governments, with prices commensurate with the risk of the vulnerability and the effectiveness of the exploits.

This is a particularly important change since, if publicity and peer recognition are removed as factors, the crime can be effected in secret, which can be far more dangerous. This is particularly true for targeted attacks, which may never be detected, and which certainly will not result in general defenses, such as common antivirus signatures.

One of the most disturbing aspects of this change in perpetrator is the appearance of well-organized groups that engage in carefully planned

exploits extending over long periods of time. This results in much more targeted and lucrative incidents. The greatest concern here is that the evildoers will eventually become well-funded nation states intent on much more insidious and damaging objectives.

The Changing Vulnerability Environment

The great debate these days is whether or not those discovering vulnerabilities in commercial software should publicize them to the world at large, or quietly disclose them to the manufacturer of the software. Bruce Schneier presented his ideas on this in a *CSO Magazine* column (Schneier, 2007b). Of course, the risk of exploitation is likely to be greater when the vulnerability is made public without the vendor or, in the case of open source software, the community having a mitigation plan in place. On the other hand, software makers may not be motivated to correct the problem if they believe it will not be generally known.

There are strong arguments on both sides as to whether a security vendor should buy information about a vulnerability in order to be the first to have a protective measure available.

This is a prime example of how the human factor can be the predominant force in determining whether the average computer user is protected or not. Table 1 lists various participants, whether they are intentionally participating or not, and where they stand in regard to the various strategies, assuming that someone external to the vendor discovers the vulnerability.

A similar set of scenarios is initiated if an exploit is in fact created. Sometimes purveyors of security solutions or the vendors of the particular software under attack are the ones who develop exploits in their own laboratories. Security firms might just make public the fact that it is possible to develop such an exploit without describing it. Fearful customers have accused such firms of publicizing the existence of viable exploits in order to encourage the purchase of their products and services. Conversely, evildoers may be encouraged to move quickly to develop specific exploits as they already have a measure of assurance that it is achievable.

THREATS AND VULNERABILITIES IN THE HUMAN CONTEXT

We now examine how threats, exploits, vulnerabilities, and incidents interact within a typical human context. On one side we have the hacker. He (and the person is usually male) is looking to take advantage of weaknesses in the computer-

network-people complex for personal aggrandizement, financial gain, or other insidious objectives. On the other side are the defense mechanisms, also made up of systems, networks, and people, all of which can be compromised by the nefarious actions of the predators. To the extent that the sides are uneven, with highly motivated attackers, who are often very skilled, and predominantly naïve and gullible victims, so do many of the attacks meet with success. Perhaps the all-time most successful exploit was the previously mentioned "ILOVEYOU" worm, which immediately appealed to millions of computer users as it struck an irresistible chord. The worm appeared on May 3, 2000 and rapidly spread to cause an estimated $5.5 billion in damage globally.

The human and social components of today's attack-defense mechanisms are often so significant as to dwarf other factors. Yet security professionals have often ignored them, preferring to address all threats with technical solutions, rather than taking a holistic view. Could it be because those addressing defense measures are technicians who may have little interest or understanding of the human interactions? Or are the attackers just so much smarter and more incisive in regard to human behavior that they are able to overwhelm or fool individuals' regular abilities to defend and resist? Or should we consider that it might be the attackers' ability to adapt that leads to their eventual successes?

Mendell (2007) advises information security professionals to add psychological insights to their toolkits and he specifically recommends the following actions in order to minimize information overload and still ingest the knowledge required to maintain currency and remain effective:

- Develop an intelligence gathering plan, particularly to learn about "the mindset of potential threat agents"
- Develop a focus plan so as to absorb as much relevant knowledge as possible
- Maintain a library of articles on specific topics for later reference

- Acquire automated tools to assist in the analysis of security logs and alerting
- With regard to security operations centers, involve end users in their design and have a human-factors expert ensure that the user interface promotes good decisions
- Have data owners work on the security classification process
- Develop a plan for protecting against electronic impersonation, such as "pretexting"

While these tips are very valuable, they still beg the fundamental question as to whether investing in protecting against attacks is cost-effective as each security measure appears to beget a new attack, often requiring even more costly defenses, not to mention the direct costs of successful attacks and breaches themselves. After all, the attacker only needs to be successful one time, whereas the defender must protect against a myriad of attacks.

Here we will show how the relationship between attacker and victim is complex as each tries to outwit the other and how the defender is always at a disadvantage.

The Technical Viewpoint

On the technical side, the trend of vulnerabilities will likely follow a familiar downward sloping curve, as is common for depicting the number of "bugs" remaining in a software product. Such a curve is shown in Figure 5. As with computer program bugs, the number of outstanding errors or vulnerabilities will jump when a new version of the product is introduced and then begin to fall again. However, while there are arguably a fixed number of bugs to be corrected, and many of them might be security related, the concern is that new exploits will uncover vulnerabilities not previously known to exist. While this is also true of bugs in general in that new ways of using the product may uncover new bugs, for security vulnerabilities the consequences can be much more serious. This becomes particularly significant

when a vendor decides to discontinue support of an obsolete product, such as Microsoft did with Windows NT 4.0. While a licensee of a software product might feel more at risk when support is pulled, hackers might lose interest in trying to penetrate and cause damage through an obsolete product since the absolute number of operational systems falls as it is being phased out. This calls into question the need to contract for expensive end-of-life product support. For example, the cost of custom support following discontinuance of Microsoft Windows NT 4.0 was very high for companies, and I am not aware of a single critical vulnerability and consequent security patch required from when support was officially pulled a couple of years ago.

The technical approach is inherently reactive and more generally used to protect against future occurrences of events that have already happened. This is because it is difficult to sell technical measures that are meant to address anticipated threats and exploits, particularly if a specific vulnerability has not yet been identified. This view extends to a national and global level, where little support is given to those who rant and rave about something that the populace believes will either never happen or, if it were to occur, someone will surely be able to resolve it. This was somewhat true with the Y2K "millennium bug" for which the remediation was high and the resulting impact small, whereas the change in date of Daylight Savings Time to March 11 from April 1 was mostly ignored or treated cavalierly until right before the event, with a resulting significant negative impact, particularly with electronic calendaring systems.

A significant reason why security is directed by those looking into the rear-view mirror, rather than through the windshield, is that known problems are easier to solve than unknown ones, and technical problems are easier to deal with than non-technical ones. But to really address the issues at hand, the human element must be incorporated along with technical considerations.

The Interaction of Metrics and Behavior

We have all heard the expression that "you can only manage what you can measure." This can be deceptive and is not always true (Hinson, 2006). In her weighty book on security and privacy metrics, Debra Herrmann (2007) begins with the following quotation from S.H. Kan (1995): "It is an undisputed statement that measurement is crucial to the progress of all societies."

I prefer the statement by Jerry Gregoire (2007) that "The ability to measure things begets new behaviors." That allows for inappropriate metrics leading to adverse behavior or responses, which may be the single most important reason why information security professionals might suffer from a lack of credibility.

That is why, in my opinion, it is crucial to include not only technical aspects of security but also human responses and social interactions.

The Human Component

If one were to introduce human and social aspects, security takes on a whole new form. It goes from backward looking and reactive, to forward looking and proactive. Rather than trying to see how to defend against a current exploit (which must be done anyway as a baseline practice), the analyst tries to predict how both the attacker and the victim will behave in response to changing circumstances. Ideally, we are able to identify, develop, and analyze a set of scenarios relating to the likelihood of a particular event occurring and how the other party might respond to it.

Thus, for example, even before the strong authentication measures in U.S. banking, which were mandated by the FFIEC, went into effect, the OCC (2007) was warning that evildoers will likely take advantage of the transition by pretending to represent those banks introducing the measures and pilfering identity information. This illustrates a key aspect of the human-system interaction, namely, that the bad guys will even exploit bona fide attempts at strengthening the commercial environment by taking advantage of customer confusion.

Unfortunately, the implication is that one cannot fully trust any system at any particular time, even if the interaction is one purportedly intended to improve or safeguard your identity and your assets. A very common ploy of phishing scams is to imply that your security or assets are at risk. This results in even the most innocuous of interactions becoming suspect. As customers increasingly sense that no unsolicited and unexpected electronic communications can be trusted, so are efficient and lower-cost methods reduced as effective means of doing business. This has a major cost impact as will be discussed later.

At the same time, the hackers and fraudsters are evolving their attacks so that the victims are not suspicious and respond as desired. This is particularly the case for new technologies about which the victims are unfamiliar. Innovative technologies, such as RSS (really simple syndication), whereby feeds are used to update content in real time, have become the latest vector for injecting malware into users' computers.

However, it is important, from the evildoers' perspective, not to close off mechanisms which they themselves use for practicing their criminal activities. To some extent, those organizations hosting online services, particularly financial firms, are playing into the hands of the evildoers by developing stronger security measures. Despite this, defending organizations have little choice if they are to retain certain lucrative channels of communication. There is a degree of symbiosis among evildoers, defending entity and individual victims, which significantly contributes to the continuation of an environment in which the cost of the crime is balanced against the financial benefits of maintaining the channel. When costs and liabilities are limited, there is little incentive to change much. However, legal and regulatory environments are changing the liability picture and victims, or potential victims, eschewing business methods that they consider to be a threat to their privacy, themselves change the equation radically.

The argument that evildoers do not wish to destroy the mechanisms that support their activities is also applicable to terrorists, where it is considered to be in their interest not to bring down the Internet because it is an important communication vehicle for them.

An analogy is the road to success for a virus in the physical world, where, in order to survive and proliferate, a virus must not kill its victim until it has had the opportunity to reproduce and spread to others.

Of course, misjudgment by the evildoer, victim, and hosting organization can lead to unintended consequences. For the perpetrators, avoiding negative consequences means restricting their criminal activities in order to maintain the means of continuing those activities. For the victim, it is to avoid being victimized while enjoying the convenience and lower cost of performing their desired business or pleasure activities. For the hosting organization, it is to keep the customers happy by safeguarding their personal information and continuing to operate lower cost channels.

Cost-Benefit Aspects

In the end it really comes down to determining how best to apply security and privacy funding. Security budgeting and spending tends to be skewed towards technical solutions, which are in many cases yielding diminishing returns. Greater emphasis needs to be placed on examining and analyzing the human and social aspects, and putting money into research of the human-machine interaction. It is commonly held that the biggest bang for the buck is often achieved from training and awareness programs, which are generally inexpensive to implement, yet can have a considerable impact, especially when ac-

companied by deterrence in the form of threats of serious consequences for not following policy. However, despite extensive education and training programs, we still see unsuspecting or unthinking individuals responding inappropriately to the latest social-engineering gimmicks. Does this mean that training is ineffective, or is it a matter of not using the right training methods and materials, or not applying the training often enough? Or is it that the attackers and fraudsters are just that much smarter and are able to fool even those alert individuals who know better?

And then there is a whole raft of incidents that slip through the cracks and occur "inadvertently." These need to be addressed using preventative measures that are effective and easy to use, with procedures that can be readily followed, preferably, without human intervention. The value of such systems, in terms of avoiding unintentional slips or errors, requires a different type of analysis; one that accounts for anticipated human and social behavior.

Some behaviors are universal, whereas other are limited to particular countries, cultures, ethnic groups, and so on. These similarities and differences greatly affect the outcome, particularly in countries where deterrence might be less effective.

Costs of Threats

Most threats aimed at information systems have some level of technology built into them. Even those threats that predominantly use social-engineering usually have some technical basis, if only in regard to the delivery system. While the technology for use by "amateurs" or "script kiddies" may have been costly in time and effort for someone to develop, many such malware developers make their software available at little or no charge to anyone accessing their nefarious Web sites. "Professionals," who are usually more interested in financial gain than kudos, tend to keep the techniques and technology, which they and others develop, to themselves for their own use. It was recently reported (Vijayan, 2007) that several Web sites have sprung up to cater to the professionals, such as organized gangs.

Costs are also incurred by potential individual and organizational victims since a significant number of protective and defensive measures, such as blocking certain traffic or closing off specific services, are taken on the basis of possible exploits that have not yet been developed and/or released. These measures can be expensive.

Benefits of Threats

Strange as it may seem, there are real benefits to threats. Threats perform a service to potential victims, even if the threats never become exploits. They serve to encourage individuals and organizations to maintain a high level of vigilance and apply patches and other measures sufficiently in advance.

The value of the threat is measured in terms of the down-the-line costs of not having put in protective measures and being subject to an exploit derived from the threat.

The main issue here is in determining whether a particular threat can and will become an exploit.

Comparisons of Technical and Human/Social Threats

One usually addresses threats to the technical infrastructure and applications by means of specific tools and measures. These are designed to avoid or prevent a potential exploit from doing damage. Threats to people and their general and financial well-being are more along the lines of the possibility for identity theft, which may or may not be engaged in by the perpetrator when an attack is launched. However, the mere threat of identity theft raises significant reaction from the public, from lawmakers, regulators, and auditors, and from management. The resulting requirements can be very costly to implement and operate.

Costs of Exploits

The costs of exploits are similar to those of threats, only more so. When a threat transitions to an exploit, particularly an exploit that has been shown to have been used effectively "in the wild," then clearly the expectation that one's systems or networks might be attacked increases significantly. Also, for the developers of the malware, success will likely lead to renewed enthusiasm and a possible increase in related activities.

From the victims' perspective, costs go up when a threat becomes an exploit. Typically, a relatively very small number of threats are actually realized as exploits. Analysts, who thought that a particular exploit would not be developed and successful, must revise the assessment of the probability of attack. They must also estimate the cost of damage incurred. With a new higher estimate of expected loss, additional funds will normally have to be released for emergency patching of the systems or other means of quickly reducing exposure.

On balance, it may not be a bad strategy to at least wait until notified that a real exploit is developed before doing the remediation work. Since few threats materialize, one must use judgment to determine the risk to the organization. There are a couple of downside aspects, however. If one waits for a proven exploit to appear, it may already be too late to avoid damage. Secondly, one might not know whether or not one's organization is indeed vulnerable to a particular exploit until an incident happens. This was true of the SQL Slammer worm, when many organizations did not realize that they even had the vulnerable code within certain applications.

Benefits of Exploits

While similar to the limited benefits of threats, benefits of exploits will generally be much less since there is less time to prepare defenses. It is generally more difficult and costly to try to install defense mechanisms when subject to the relative immediacy of an active exploit. Also, by the time the fixes are completed, some damage may have been incurred already.

Some see a real benefit from hackers attempting to invade one's environment. In a published interview (Cone, 2007), Edward Amoroso, the chief information security officer at AT&T, states that he believes that hackers perform a positive service to organizations by pointing out weaknesses, which can then be fixed.

Comparisons of Technical and Human/Social Exploits

Technical exploits often attack without the victims even being aware of them. Conversely, those exploits that depend upon deceiving victims into taking particular actions to activate the exploit or to disclose personal information to a suspect Web site, for example, may be ameliorated by technical means, such as SPAM filters. However, with the nature of the exploit likely to mutate or morph into another form, the human aspect becomes important. In many cases, the last line of defense is the person being subject to the attack, so that training them on an appropriate behavior and response is paramount.

Costs of Vulnerabilities

Many vulnerabilities exist because software manufacturers have not taken enough care in ensuring program code follows secure practices and have not thoroughly tested the software for security vulnerabilities. In one sense, the manufacturers have saved money with this practice and presumably pass some of the savings to the purchaser. However, it is unlikely that net savings on the licensing costs of the software products offset the burden and cost of patching the software after it has been distributed, installed and is in use.

Costs occur mostly in two areas: one is the cost of the patching efforts themselves and the other is

the cost of having vulnerable systems, which have not been patched, attacked successfully.

Not only is there an illicit market for threats and exploits, as mentioned previously, but there is also a similar market for vulnerabilities, including those for which exploits do not yet exist.

Benefits of Vulnerabilities

There is really very little tangible benefit of having vulnerabilities as far as those who acquire the vulnerable products are concerned.

It is ironic that the same vendors who license software products with inherent vulnerabilities may also profit from the patching of those vulnerabilities, since the presence of vulnerabilities helps to justify spending on maintenance and support services.

From the perspective of those who exploit vulnerabilities for fame and/or fortune, they may well provide a livelihood in terms of the ill-gotten gains of either blackmailing potential victims or exploiting the vulnerability directly.

Comparisons of Technical and Human/Social Vulnerabilities

Technical vulnerabilities are generally fairly well defined and understood once they have been discovered. There are also a finite number of vulnerabilities, although that number can only be guessed at. The real challenge is in finding them, and doing so before the attackers do.

On the other hand, human and social vulnerabilities are both difficult to identify, and even if they are defined, they are likely to change rapidly over time. There is effectively no limit on the number of ways a person can be fooled and exploited. There are also many more potential chinks in the armor when it comes to compromising individuals. One can fool, cajole, or threaten an individual into exposing vulnerabilities.

Costs of Defense Measures

A huge business has evolved to protect systems, networks, and the human beings who interface with them against potential and real attacks. The more protection that is implemented, the costlier it will be. Some measures are much more effective than others, so that the key is to select the right combination of measures as it relates to technology and human and social environments. The goal here is to produce the most security for the least cost. A portfolio approach, as described by Axelrod (2007), can assist with such a decision.

Many information security professionals look to technical solutions for their security requirements and too few place much faith in the human and social aspects. This will tend to produce relatively more expensive approaches than would a more holistic approach that takes into account the human and social environment in which the systems operate and at some point will reach diminishing returns, without having benefited from more cost-effective lower tech approaches.

Benefits of Defense Measures

It goes without question that major benefits can be derived from the right set of defense mechanisms. Costs and benefits do not always align, however. And sometimes the same amount of money spent on different types of measure can yield very different returns.

Comparisons of Technical and Human/Social Defense Measures

For illustrative purposes, let us consider two cases—one in which greater reliance is placed on technical defenses and protective measures, and the other where the main line of defense is the human being rather than a machine.

Let us consider an illustrative example where the initial exploits are predominantly technical. We will assume an arbitrary measure of 50 "units"

for the human-social exploits, such as phishing, aimed at a particular system and 150 units for the technical exploits, such as self-activating targeted viruses, worms, and Trojan horse malware. We now apply protective measures to each category of exploit. Let us assume that we install e-mail filtering, for example, at a cost of $20,000, and reduce the number of suspect e-mails by 50% to 25 units. In regard to technical exploits, let us assume that we install an IPS (intrusion prevention system) at a cost of $80,000, with a resulting reduction of 20% in the number of exploits getting through the defenses to 120 units.

The net result is that we have reduced the total exploits from 200 units to 145 units, or by 55 units, at a cost of $100,000, which produces 0.55 units of exploit reduction per $1,000 of cost.

Now, we will look at another example with the same level of initial exploits, namely, 50 units of human exploits and 150 units of technical exploits and the same total expenditure of $100,000 units. We now spend $10,000 on human protection measures, and see a resulting reduction in exploits of 20%, or 10 exploit units. We also spend $90,000 on measures to reduce the technical exploits and cut them by 35 units. Now, for same total cost of $100,000, we have reduced the exploit level by 45 units. This is a reduction of 0.45 exploit units per $1,000 of cost, indicating that spending more on the technical side versus the human side, with the same total budget, actually reduces the effectiveness of the protection in this example.

Now let us assume that, in the first example, the attacker responds to the filtering program by coming up with more sophisticated attacks that manage to get through the filters and that the available technology is not able to defend against the new version of the attack.. The victim organization then responds by instituting a training program for users so that they will recognize the new attack and avoid it. If the cost of training is $5,000, and the result is to get back to the former level of protection, then the exploit reduction of

55 units now cost $105,000, leading to an exploit reduction of 0.52 units per $1,000.

We can see, therefore, that reducing the effectiveness of exploits is an ongoing iterative process and requires the fine tuning over time of protective measures, between those affecting human and technical victims, in response to the attackers modification of their exploits.

Costs of Incidents

The whole purpose of security measures, whether they be human, technical, or blended, is to avoid incidents or, if they are not avoided or avoidable, to minimize their impact. The impact can be measured in terms of the total costs of incidents to the organization and its stakeholders (shareholders, employees, customers, competitors), as well as indirect costs borne by other organizations and individuals.

We see many estimates of the cost of incidents in the press based on surveys (FBI/CSI, 2006) and reported incidents. They run the whole gamut from, at one extreme, the direct costs of stemming the breach, shoring up the systems, and getting back to normal business, and at the other, determining the intangibles such as loss of reputation. In between, there are such costs as the opportunity costs of lost customers, if the breach is made public.

Benefits of Incidents

Incidents can be beneficial to the organizations that sustain them, but produce even greater benefits to those that are not directly impacted. This is because, perhaps more than anything else, incidents promote action in terms of implementing security measures. For the organization sustaining the incident, there are all the costs associated with it, which must be subtracted from the benefits of taking appropriate risk mitigating actions. For those less affected observers of the incident, the lesson is learned without incurring the direct costs, so that the net benefits are that much greater.

While many fixes may be technical, the human and social aspects come to the fore when an incident is reported. Often the message is conveyed to senior management by employees, their peers, or through the press, and management responds by mandating action to protect against a like incident occurring in their organization. The degree to which senior management and, where appropriate, the Board of Directors, take personal responsibility for fixing the vulnerability depends on the laws, regulations, and culture of the organization and its country of residence.

Comparisons of Technical and Human/Social Incidents

The resolution of an incident will depend heavily upon whether it was predominantly technical or human. For example, a large proportion of reported data breaches are low-tech human errors or events, such as those involving lost or stolen laptop computers, computer tapes, and other storage devices. Here the remedy might be procedural and physical, such as put tapes in locked cases, but may also be technical, such as encrypting the data on the hard disks of laptop computers.

In other cases, the attack might be technical, such as gaining access to data files containing customers' personal information. For the most part, fixing these vulnerabilities requires technical means, but will likely also have a human component, such as in verifying the identity of someone requesting access.

Costs of Recovery and Restoration

Often forgotten in the overall equation are the costs of recovering from an incident and, depending on the nature of the incident, restoring the operation back to its original standing. In a real sense, these costs depend upon how much preparation has been done beforehand and whether sufficient redundancy and resiliency has been built into the system. Usually, the more planning and testing, the lower the costs when an actual incident occurs. The tradeoff here is between security, which serves to protect the system and network environment and prevent incidents, and survivability, the aim of which is to ensure that the environment can be reestablished and reconstituted after an incident has taken place. Axelrod (2007) provides a more detailed analysis of the balance between security and survivability.

Interestingly, human intervention and control may be the more critical in the recovery process than technical prowess, as often judgment is required beyond which an automated solution might be capable. This is particularly the case when a particular incident does not follow a previously established script. In my experience, the complexity of most systems and networks requires, in addition to technical tools, the personal knowledge and experience of the operational staff as resolutions to all possible permutations and combinations of events are not built into the written procedures.

Benefits of Recovery and Restoration

Clearly, the benefits of an effective recovery and restoration come from the ability to survive an incident or series of incidents and restore viable operations. However, whether an incident response exercise is a test or in response to an actual event, there are always lessons to be learned. It is hoped that the observed deficiencies in the process will result in improvements to the procedures so that, should a similar event occur in the future, the recovery will flow better.

Comparisons of Technical and Human/Social Recovery and Restoration

As has been mentioned, human participation often dominates the recovery and restoration phases since the automated tools for these procedures have not been sufficiently developed to allow for

a completely automated process. More likely, the process will be computer assisted. There have been attempts at instilling learning and adaptation into tools for failures that are more limited in scope, in that the tools recognize a failure, or potential failure, from the system and network behavior and respond according to predetermined scripts. In a sense, this is what IPS (intrusion prevention systems) do. Perhaps we will develop FPS (failure prevention tools), much as existed with Tandem and Stratus Technologies high-availability computers, which contained many processors and failed over from one that was broken to other hot standby computers. Tandem favored hardware fail-over, whereas Stratus used a software approach. The same fail-over concept can be employed in RAID (redundant array of independent—or inexpensive—disks) systems.

FUTURE WORK ON SUCCESSIVE ITERATIONS

While we have mostly focussed on a linear one-time process, mention was made of processes that involved action and reaction behaviors. These latter processes are more realistic but more difficult to model and follow. They call for computer simulation models wherein the feedback from attacker to victim and vice versa with consequent modifications of attacks and defenses, much as a game would involve strong and rapid interactions between and among players.

Most academic and commercial models to date have focused on the technical aspects, and behavior monitoring methods have addressed behavior as depicted through the monitoring of, say, traffic flowing over a network. What is needed is a more macro-level view of how attackers might develop an exploit upon learning of a vulnerability, how the victims might attempt to shore up the vulnerability, and how the attacker then modifies his exploit to get around the new protective measures, and so on.

One might then consider whether the iterative model will eventually converge to equilibrium or whether instability will increase over time. Axelrod (1979) developed such a model with respect to the interaction of users to different pricing models for computer resources.

This is clearly an area that could benefit from applied research.

Future Trends

The IT industry is abuzz with the rapid evolution of the Web and ways in which applications and services can be delivered as Web services or service orientations. Common terms are SOA (service-oriented architecture), SaaS (systems as a service), grid computing, Web 2.0, and Web 3.0.

Much of these leading-edge technologies involve a different set of user-vendor models, where applications, processing, data handling, and storage are provided on a pay-per-use basis and security depends on the provider and other participants. As applications are pushed out to the end user, the latter must be able to trust that the applications thus distributed are secure and protect data entrusted to the applications and the infrastructure on which the applications run. As collaborative work groups and social structures evolve, there needs to be ways to ensure the confidentiality and integrity of information and its sources. As the collaborative, sharing model of Web 2.0 evolves into the adaptive, intelligent "semantic" Web 3.0, there is an even greater need to understand the technical and human threats, exploits, and vulnerabilities that will abound. In fact, as dependency on systems increases and the systems themselves will take on many human elements in regard to judging authenticity and recognizing the appropriateness of results of inquiries. In addition, there will be a need to and validate the security of all the many integrated environments and verify the accuracy of the data and processes that will have been aggregated into the user interfaces.

Future environments and models will make those being worked on today appear to be very primitive. It is important to develop the right effective tools today for today's and tomorrow's worlds in order to stand any chance at all of maintaining control over the human, social, and technical factors that are evolving rapidly.

SUMMARY AND CONCLUSION

Perhaps the most neglected aspects of securing computer systems and networks against malevolent attacks or unintended breaches are those related to human behavior and social practices. By including them in a model of threats and vulnerabilities, the economics of protection change. The intention is to channel information security funds into more appropriate security measures than would have been applied had the human and social factors been ignored.

It is recognized that models that account for all aspects of behavior along with technical realities are complex and difficult today, but will become even more of a challenge as new technologies burst forth.

REFERENCES

Axelrod, C.W. (1979). *Computer effectiveness: Bridging the management-technology gap.* Washington, D.C.: Information Resources Press.

Axelrod, C. W. (2005). The demise of passwords: Have rumors been exaggerated? *The ISSA Journal, May*, 6-13.

Axelrod, C. W. (2007a). The dynamics of privacy risk. *Information Systems Control Journal, 1*, 51-56.

Axelrod, C. W. (2007b). Analyzing risks to determine a new return on security investment: Optimizing security in an escalating threat environment. In H.R. Rao, M. Gupta, & S. Upadhyaya (Eds.), *Managing information assurance in financial services* (pp. 1-25). Hershey, PA: IGI Global.

Cone, E. (2007). Hacking's gift to IT. *CIO Insight, March 7*. Retrieved August 15, 2007, from www.cioinsight.com/article2/0,1397,21087886,00.asp

CSI/FBI. (2006). *Eleventh annual CSI/FBI computer crime and security survey.* Retrieved August 15, 2007, from http://i.cmpnet.com/gocsi/db_area/pdfs/fbi/FBI2006.pdf

Gartner (2005). Retrieved April 1, 2007 from http://www.gartner.com/130100/130115/gartners_hyp_f2.gif

Gregoire, J., Jr. (2007). CIO confidential: The Manhattan effect. *CIO Magazine, 20*(9), 30-34.

Herrmann, D. (2007). *Complete guide to security and privacy metrics.* Boca Raton, FL: Auerbach Publications.

Hinson, G. (2006). Seven myths about information security metrics. *The ISSA Journal, July*, 43-48.

Kan, S. H. (1995). *Metrics and models in software quality engineering.* Boston: Addison-Wesley.

Mendell, R. L. (2007). The psychology of information security. *The ISSA Journal, March*, 8-11.

Messmer, E. (2007). RSA '07: Bruce Schneier casts light on psychology of security. *CSO Online, February 7*. Retrieved August 15, from http://www.networkworld.com/news/2007/020707-rsa-schneier.html

OCC. (2006). Customer authentication and internet banking alert (OCC Alert 2006-50). Retrieved April 1, 2007, from http://www.occ.treas.gov/ftp/alert/2006-50.html

Scalet, S. D. (2007). Alarmed: Bolting on security at Stop & Shop. *CIO Online, March 9*. Retrieved on August 15, 2007, from www.csoonline.com/alarmed/03092007.html

Schneier B. (2007a) The psychology of security. *DRAFT, February 28*. Retrieved August 15, 2007, from www.schneier.com/essay_155.html

Schneier, B. (2007b). All or nothing: Why full disclosure—or the threat of it—forces vendors to patch flaws, *CSO Magazine, 6*(2), 20.

Stone, B. (2007). Study finds web antifraud measure ineffective. *The New York Times, Feb 5.*

Symantec. (2007). Symantec security response—glossary. Retrieved August 15, 2007, from www.symantec.com/avcenter/refa.html

Vijayan, J. (2007). Hackers now offer subscription services, support for their malware. *Computerworld, April 4*. Retrieved August 15, 2007, from www.computerworld.com/action/article.do?command=viewArticleBasic&taxonomyName=security&articleId=9015588

ENDNOTES

[1]   A document "Understanding Gartner's Hype Cycles, 2007," which describes the proprietary hype cycle in greater detail, may be ordered from the Gartner Web site at www.gartner.com/Display/Document?id-509085&ref=g_SiteLink

[2]   For more details about the Morris worm, see http://en.wikipedia.org/wiki/Morris_worm retrieved August 15, 2007.

[3]   For more details about the ILOVEYOU worm see http://en.wikipedia.org/wiki/ILOVEYOU retrieved August 15, 2007.

Chapter XVI
Bridging the Gap between Employee Surveillance and Privacy Protection

Lilian Mitrou
University of the Aegean, Greece

Maria Karyda
University of the Aegean, Greece

ABSTRACT

This chapter addresses the issue of electronic workplace monitoring and its implications for employees' privacy. Organisations increasingly use a variety of electronic surveillance methods to mitigate threats to their information systems. Monitoring technology spans different aspects of organisational life, including communications, desktop and physical monitoring, collecting employees' personal data, and locating employees through active badges. The application of these technologies raises privacy protection concerns. Throughout this chapter, we describe different approaches to privacy protection followed by different jurisdictions. We also highlight privacy issues with regard to new trends and practices, such as teleworking and use of RFID technology for identifying the location of employees. Emphasis is also placed on the reorganisation of work facilitated by information technology, since frontiers between the private and the public sphere are becoming blurred. The aim of this chapter is twofold: we discuss privacy concerns and the implications of implementing employee surveillance technologies and we suggest a framework of fair practices which can be used for bridging the gap between the need to provide adequate protection for information systems, while preserving employees' rights to privacy.

INTRODUCTION

Employee monitoring is not a new phenomenon. Employers have always monitored their employees for reasons of efficiency, security, or legal obligation. Nowadays, however, information technology (IT) has significantly reduced the cost and time needed for information processing, storage, and retrieval, thus making monitoring easier. Moreover, new technologies allow for the creation of increasingly more sophisticated information sources on employees. At the same time, companies and their information systems face increased threats originating from their interior. To address this so-called *insider threat*, companies adopt a wide range of monitoring tools provided by the IT industry. The use of these tools, however, has been reported as threatening employees' privacy. As monitoring and surveillance devices is steadily becoming easier to use as well as cheaper, it is to be expected that monitoring and surveillance technologies will be used even more intensively in the near future.

Is the workplace to be considered as a public domain where the notion of privacy is out of place? Do employers' property rights prevail over employees' right to privacy? This chapter aims to provide answers to these questions and to analyze privacy implications of the use of monitoring technologies, with regard to lawful monitoring principles.

BACKGROUND

Employee monitoring or *employee surveillance* denotes employer-controlled observation of employees in order to ascertain the performance, behavior, and other characteristics of employees. Traditionally, frontline supervisors had the duty to perform employee surveillance as a means of managing their workforce and protecting the workplace. Surveillance nowadays is, in most cases, automatically performed through the use of technologies such as video and monitoring software. Electronic monitoring entails the following actions:

- An employer's use of electronic devices to review and evaluate the performance of employees;
- An employer's use of electronic devices to observe actions of employees while employees are not directly performing work tasks, or for a reason other than measuring work performance;
- An employer's use of computer forensics, the recovery and reconstruction of electronic data after their deletion, concealment, or attempted destruction (Lasprogata, King, & Pillay, 2004).

Why Do Companies Conduct Surveillance?

Typically, employment terms entail collecting a considerable amount of information about employees, as these data are necessary for basic management activities (Mitrou & Karyda, 2006). Electronic monitoring in the past was mainly used to measure and evaluate employee performance (for instance, through keystroke analysis). Employers tend to regard control of the workplace as their prerogative, including the right to protect and control their property, and the right to manage employee performance in terms of productivity, quality, training, and the recording of customer interactions (Findlay & McKinlay, 2003).

Lately, however, the stakes of security and liability have altered the rationale of employee monitoring. One of the reasons most commonly cited by enterprises employing monitoring technologies is the endeavor to protect the interests of the company and its stakeholders. The following paragraphs illustrate the main reasons used for justifying employee surveillance.

Productivity, Cost Control, and Allocation

Employers have legitimate rights and interests to run their business efficiently, evaluating and assessing the workforce and also have the right to protect themselves from the liability or the harm that employees' actions may cause (DPWP, 2001). Monitoring methods are implemented for reasons such as controlling and allocating costs of different performances and communications and measuring and improving productivity. As computer systems have become an integral component of work, process monitoring aims at maximizing productive use of these systems. Reportedly, U.S. corporations lose more than $54 billion a year because of non-work related employee use of the web (Conry-Murray, 2001). Other cost related reasons used for justifying employee monitoring include the cost and downgrade of the company's network bandwidth when employees use the Web and e-mail for non-work related activities.

Security

Employers also use surveillance methods to discover theft and pilferage, to investigate suspected theft, and to identify possible culprits. They have also to deal with additional security problems caused or intensified through the use of information and communication technologies.

A major purpose of monitoring employees, under this perspective, is to discover and deter activities adverse to company interests such as theft of tangible and intangible property (e.g., trade secrets). Employers monitor the use of computer and communication systems in order to prevent or respond to unauthorized access to computer systems, including access by computer hackers and to protect computer networks from becoming overloaded by large downloadable files.

Moreover, employers often need to verify breaches of confidentiality or monitor compliance with security rules and to prevent security breaches which are caused, for example, when an employee, intentionally or unintentionally, downloads a virus or opens an e-mail that contains a Trojan horse program as an attachment. Other objectives pursued through employee's surveillance include the prevention or detection of industrial espionage and copyright, patent, or trademark infringement by employees and third parties.

Insider threats have been identified to pose a significantly high level of risk and to have a heavier cost for organisations (Schultz, 2002). Security controls used for protecting information systems from externally initiated attacks (e.g., firewalls and intrusion detection systems) are considered to be ineffective in detaining insider threats, since these require a different approach (Porter, 2003; Lee & Lee, 2002; Schultz, 2002). The main risks connected to the insider threat include the intentional or unintentional leak of confidential or proprietary company information, contamination from viruses, Trojans and other types of malicious code, unauthorized access to information, degrade of Internet connection/network service as a result of abusive use, financial fraud, and adverse actions or sabotage from disgruntled employees. It is also important to note that the cost associated to such threats is not negligible. Forty-two percent of the companies that took part in the 2006 Computer Crime and Security Survey reported that their employees had abused Internet privileges, by downloading, for instance, pornography or pirated software. Losses from this type of abuse alone were estimated over $1.800.000 (CSI/FBI, 2006).

Protection of Own or Third Persons' Interests

Employers are confronted with the obligation to prevent or detect unauthorized utilization of the employers' computer systems for criminal activities and terrorism (Bloom, Schachter, & Steelman, 2003). For instance, the widespread use of e-mail can entail a number of severe problems for organisations. The dissemination of illegal or offensive material via e-mail by employees, or the distribution of confidential information, can cause bad reputation or even result to legal prosecution for companies. Controlling employer's compliance with workplace policies on the use of computer systems, e-mail accounts, and Internet access is a means to prevent and to investigate complaints of employee misconduct, including harassment and discrimination complaints. Lately, with the rise of the "*blogosphere*," employers are also interested in protecting themselves from defamation: employees' Internet activities are checked for offensive or libelous content. Blogging about the employer, even with comments posted on private servers outside company time, has already led to dismissals (Ball, 2006).

As organisations are becoming, through the use of IT, decentralized, accountability becomes inevitably localized (Findlay & McKinlay, 2003). Monitoring helps employers to prepare their defense to lawsuits or administrative complaints, such as those brought by employees-victims of discrimination or harassment, or in case of discipline measures and/or termination of employment. In some cases, monitoring proved to be useful in responding to discovery requests in litigation related to electronic evidence (Lasprogata et al., 2004). Employee monitoring technologies are also used for collecting evidence for auditing and judicial purposes after an incident has occurred.

Finally, other factors driving the growing numbers of employers monitoring their employees' activities are the low cost of monitoring technologies and the increase in employees using the company's IT resources for personal reasons.

WORKPLACE SURVEILLANCE: TOOLS AND TECHNIQUES

As computer software enabling workplace surveillance drops in price and increases in sophistica-

tion, more employers are using electronic means of monitoring. The business of surveillance and monitoring software is rapidly augmenting in the recent years and increasingly more companies obtain them. The main reasons for that have been attributed to the lowering costs of the technology, as well as to the increasing need companies have to protect their infrastructure, especially after 9/11. Widely employed surveillance technologies can be categorised as follows: communications monitoring; video surveillance; desktop monitoring; location monitoring; and biometrics.

Communications monitoring entails surveillance of e-mails, Web sites that have been visited, phone calls, and intranet and Internet traffic. The technology used to support this type of monitoring includes software monitoring, firewalls, intrusion detection systems that monitor all network traffic, sniffers, passive listeners to intercept Internet communications, and antivirus programs. The percentage of employers in the U.S. who use video monitoring to detect theft, violence, sabotage, and other employee misconduct was raised from 33 % in 2001 to 51 % in 2005 (AMA, 2005). Remote control programs which are installed on employees' computers allow control of a remote host for surveillance purposes, redirecting the video display of the remote host to another host. In this way, an employer can view in real time a copy of what the employee is viewing. Desktop monitoring also includes files content monitoring. In many companies, employees are equipped with *smart* ID cards which can track their location while they move through the workplace. New employee ID cards can even determine the direction the worker is facing at any given time. Global positioning technology (GPS systems) is also used to monitor employee cell phones, to keep track of company vehicles, and to monitor employee ID cards. The latter are also widely used for controlling physical security and access to buildings and data centers. However, RFID cards are also used for gathering and retaining personally identifiable data regarding employee movement. Finally, fingerprint scans, facial recognition technology, and iris scans are also used by a few companies for employee monitoring.

Generally, monitoring software provides a variety of capabilities, including the following:

- **Preventing access:** This type of software entirely blocks access to any Web site which has been previously characterized as inappropriate by employers.
- **Alerting:** Monitoring software can be set to alert employers (or the person appointed by them) when employees visit Web sites they ought not to.
- **Direct surveillance:** Of employee's computer.
- **Flagging:** Employees' e-mails are screened for containing predefined keywords.
- **Keystroke logging:** Keystrokes, as well as idle time, are recorded, thus allowing for the recreation of employees actions. In this way information can be recorded, even after it has been deleted.
- **Instant messaging monitoring:** Software that allows monitoring the messages exchanged by employees.

Current Use of Monitoring Technologies

According to the Information Security Breaches Survey (DTI, 2006), 80% of UK large businesses with Internet access log and monitor their employees' Web access, while 90% of them filter incoming mail for spam. The same survey reports the case of a UK publishing company that logs all Internet access by its staff and has line managers monitoring it (DTI 2006). Moreover, 52% of large businesses attribute the worst security incident they suffered to internal causes while 65% reported staff misuse of the company's information systems. Misuse of Web access (including access to inappropriate Web sites and excessive Web surfing) was reported as the most common form

of misuse; other types of staff misuse cited were misuse of e-mail access, unauthorized access to data, breaches of data protection laws or regulations, and misuse of confidential information. It should also not go without mention that 22% of the companies needed two to ten man days to recover from the worst security incident caused by Internet misuse.

According to the Forrester Research reports (Forrester, 2006), 38% of respondents in the U.S. and UK said they employed staff to read or otherwise analyze outbound e-mail. Responding to the same research, 44% of U.S. companies with more than 20,000 employees said they hire workers to snoop on workers' e-mail. Nearly one in three U.S. companies also said they had fired an employee for violating e-mail policies in the past 12 months and estimated that about 20% of outgoing e-mails contain content that poses a legal, financial, or regulatory risk.

Finally, 58% of the companies that responded to the CSI/FBI Computer Crime and Security Survey (CSI/FBI, 2006) use special software to monitor Web activity and 62% of them use e-mail monitoring software. Moreover, many companies use packet-sniffing software that can intercept, analyze, and archive all communications on their intranet.

Discussion

Apart from using software for monitoring their employees e-mails and the content of the Web sites they visit, companies also apply a variety of means for controlling the use of e-mail accounts and Internet access, including firewalls (in this case to monitor outbound and not only inbound traffic), restriction of Internet access, limitation of the space of employee e-mail accounts, enforcement of code of conduct and performance management systems, and provision of right to read e-mail content to security personnel. Companies also apply random checks to their employees' e-mails (White & Pearson, 2001). It is interesting to note, at this point, that though e-mail monitoring is widely adopted, at the same time employers seldom open postal mail received by their employees.

PRIVACY IMPLICATIONS OF WORKPLACE SURVEILLANCE TECHNOLOGIES

A Changing Work Environment

Traditionally, workplace monitoring involved some type of human intervention (for instance, in the form of foreman's surveillance, access or physical/body controls) and either the consent, or at least the knowledge, of employees (EPIC, 2002). In this way, monitoring was, at least in most cases, visible by the persons who were monitored. Technological progress, however, has not only facilitated surveillance through the use of automated means. It has also radically altered the nature and structure of workplace and has increased the risks an employer has to face. Furthermore, it has extended and intensified employees' monitoring and has changed its nature. These profound changes are strictly interrelated and interdependent with each other and their impact needs to be thoroughly explored.

The evolution of information technologies has changed both day-to-day working conditions and also the individual and group relationships forged within the work environment (Lasprogata et al., 2004). Apart from the socio-economic developments, a critical change concerns the "*genuine migration of the technologies from the periphery to the very center of the work process*" (CNIL, 2002). Means used for working, like the PC or an intranet, are now becoming means and space for communication. When e-mail replaced the telephone as a communication means it became easier for employees to feel a sense of privacy (Selmi, 2006). Intranets offered new types of social spaces inimical to managerial control.

Communication means are, at the same time, object and instrument of surveillance.

The changing structure and nature of the workplace has led to more invasive and often covert monitoring practices. Recently, much of the focus has been on electronic monitoring, as technology has enabled employers to engage in constant supervision of employees at work and access to employees' electronic communications (Hodges, 2006). Advances in science have also pushed the boundaries of what information and personal details an employer can acquire from an employee (Privacy International, 2006). With the rise of team working, peer surveillance (watching colleague' performance, behaviors or characteristics) is growing, reinforced through social norms and culture (Ball, 2006). Developments in the nature of work and the structure of organisations has made difficult to distinguish clear and unambiguous boundaries between work and private life as people work longer hours, work from home on computers owned by their employer, and work on call (Findlay & McKinlay, 2003; DPWP, 2004). As the once clear lines between an employee's personal and professional life are blurring, monitoring may nowadays extent to private spaces, activities, and time.

The legitimization of employers' monitoring activities is closely related to the actual perception of the individual that is monitored. It seems to be justifiable that if a probable cause exists that an employee is involved in an illegal or harmful activity that person's rights may be restricted to a greater extent than would have been normally allowed (Nouwt, de Vries, & Loermans, 2005). However, surveillance affects the rights and interests of every person in the workplace. As monitoring technologies are increasingly modular and self perpetuating, surveillance becomes a "mundane, ubiquitous and inescapable fact of everyday (working) life" (Findlay & McKinlay, 2003).

Employees' Privacy

In recent years, privacy has emerged as one of the central issues. What is included in the right to privacy is, however, highly debatable. The quest for the concept of privacy focuses on the search for a means to establish an identifiable and sustainable interface between the public and the private sphere of human life. The concept of privacy can only be defined in terms of the cultural norms of a particular society and the position of the individual within this society.

Privacy represents primarily a sphere where it is possible to remain separate from others, anonymous and unobserved. The public sphere offers no such guarantee. Similarly, the concept of private represents an aspect of freedom and, more specifically, freedom from interference. However, the need for privacy emerges from within the society, from the various social relationships that people form with each other, with private sector institutions and with the government. Thus, privacy is not merely a right possessed by an individual but it is a form of freedom built into the social structure (Solove, 2004). In this respect, privacy aims to protect life choices from public control so that everyone can preserve an underlying capacity for autonomous decision-making. Privacy represents a social ability or capacity of the individual and is a characteristic of relation with others. It is a claim from being simplified, objectified, and judged out of context (Simitis, 1987; Schwartz & Reidenberg, 1996).

The right to privacy is often treated as akin to property. Under this perspective, privacy is *bargainable*. Consequently, it can be exchanged with other rights and privileges: in the employment context privacy, if any, may be exchanged for something of commensurate value, like taking or keeping a job (Lasprogata et al., 2004). However, this approach underlines the freedom to alienate privacy rights and ignores the dignity element, which is inherent in the notion of privacy: as related to privacy, dignity summarizes, among other principles, the recognition of an individual's personality, respect for other people, non-interference with another's life choices, and the possibility to act freely in society (Rodota, 2004). The protection of privacy is built into society's structure in order to shape the quality of life in the public sphere (Solove, 2006). Human dignity, as a source and expression of privacy, is not generated by the individual (it) "is instead created by one's community and bestowed upon the individual. It cannot therefore be bartered away or exchanged" (Lasprogata et al., 2004). Furthermore, privacy is a fundamental component of *equality*, in order to prevent monitoring from turning into a tool that is used to discriminate against certain individuals.

The issues surrounding employees' privacy are representative of the broader transformation that has occurred in the workplace over the last decades: in stable workplaces and lifetime employment relationships there was a stronger element of trust between employers and employees, which rendered privacy less significant. "Once the workplace was dismantled…privacy became of greater importance for employees and on the flipside, a greater threat to employers" (Selmi, 2006). The discussion about employees' privacy rights mirrors also a recent and fundamental realignment of the guiding principles of labor law, at least in Europe: the emphasis is redirected upon the rights and the empowerment of the individual employee rather than the paradigm of *"collective laissez faire"* and the representative function of employees' representatives (Simitis, 1999).

The lack of clarity in relation to the notion of privacy creates difficulties when elaborating a policy or resolving a case. While the interests on the employer's side (e.g., property, efficiency, security) are often readily articulated it is, sometimes, difficult to define the privacy harm. In the employment context, privacy violations involve a variety of types of harmful or problematic activities.

The communication with others as well as the use of communication services falls within the zone of (communicational) privacy (Mitrou & Karyda, 2006). The collection and storage of personal information relating to telephone use, as well as to e-mail and Internet use, regardless the knowledge of the monitored employee, amounts to an interference with the right to respect for private life and freedom of communication. The French Cour de Cassation (*Onof v. Nikon*) ruled than an employer cannot read personal messages sent or received by employees, without violating the right to privacy and infringing the fundamental liberty of confidentiality of correspondence, even if the employer has prohibited non-work related use of the computer (Lasprogata et al., 2004; Delbar, Mormont, & Schots, 2003). The increasing number of computer users, applications, and system interconnections along with the increased complexity of overall technological capabilities entails a greater chance that e-mail privacy is compromised. Additional concerns emerge when internal email monitoring is used to track employee performance. In this case it is not just "suspected employees" whose e-mail is read (Sipior & Ward, 1995) and the secrecy of communications that is affected, but also employees' *dignity* (*Austrian Supreme Court (Oberster Gerichtshof)*, 2002).

Increased employee monitoring raises the risk that false inferences can be drawn about employees conduct: what if an employee is sent an "offensive" e-mail accidentally or, even, maliciously? What if an employee accidentally visits a pornographic site upon opening a spam e-mail that links to such a site or when such a site is displayed as a "hit" in response to a perfectly innocent search query? Even if Internet use surveillance has common elements with traditional searches for hard copy pornography, there are significant additional dangers for the individuals who are monitored. As underlined in the Report of Privacy International, "surveillance technology cannot distinguish between an innocent mistake and an intentional visit" (Privacy International, 2006). In any case, electronic surveillance extends beyond searching, for it records behavior and social interaction (Solove, 2004).

Implications of Video Surveillance and Location Monitoring Techniques

Several privacy invasions arise from video and location surveillance techniques. Pervasive video surveillance and image digitalization allows tracking of movements. Surveillance rigidifies one's past: it is a means of creating a trail of information about a person and in this perspective makes the past "*visible*" (Rodota, 2004) and "*present*." Surveillance inhibits freedom of choice, impinging upon self-determination.

Video surveillance interferes with the principle of "*free development of personality*," a principle that is embedded in most European constitutions: Video surveillance seems to be accepted only for the protection of goods and persons. More specifically, case law states that permanent video surveillance is an infringement of the "*right pertaining to one's own picture*". The German Federal Labour Court recently accepted that privacy and informational self-determination are seriously affected through permanent surveillance and the "surveillance pressure" created thereby. The court emphasized that "innocent" employees would face a serious and disproportionate interference into their right of personality (Bundesarbeitsgericht, Beschluß vol 14. December 2004, RDV 5-2005). Solove (2004) points out the Justice Cohen's remark that "pervasive monitoring of every first move or false start will, at the margin, incline choices toward the bland and the mainstream."

Essential privacy concerns are also raised through the use of location techniques. The aggregate information collected over several days or months through active-badge systems can reveal movement profiles and behavior patterns. "*Traffic analysis*" can be aggregated or combined with other sources of information to reveal data, potentially discriminating or damaging the monitored person. Although it can be a highly effective security system, a common perception for active badges is that employers can use them to spy on employees or monitor their activities such as time spent in the restroom or the length of coffee breaks (Starner, 2001). As trade unions argue, employees' privacy may also be inhibited by RFID tracking technology (OECD, 2006). The introduction of global positioning devices in vehicles and occasionally on individuals, providing locational information of employees, has often proved controversial, with many claiming that they infringe on employee privacy interests while demonstrating a lack of respect for employees (Selmi, 2006). A violation of human dignity is also assumed if video surveillance or other tracking methods are used in order to monitor working speed or if restrooms are monitored to prevent people reading newspapers in secret (Hoeren & Eusterling, 2005). Finally, video surveillance and location techniques jeopardize another historically fundamental freedom right, that is, the freedom of movement (DPWP, 2004).

Besides challenging employees' privacy rights, electronic surveillance practices also challenge rights concerning the *freedom of expression* and the *freedom of association*. Unrestricted access to and use of personal data imperils virtually every constitutionally guaranteed right: neither freedom of speech, nor freedom of association nor freedom of assembly can be fully exercised as long as it remains uncertain whether, under what circumstances and for what purposes, personal information is collected and processed (*German Federal Constitutional Court, Census case,* 1983). Slobogin argues that being placed under surveillance impedes one's anonymity, inhibits one's freedom to associate with others, makes one's behaviour less spontaneous, and alters one's freedom of movement (Solove, 2006).

As the use of surveillance technologies may lead to the so called *function creep*, the information gathered may be linked with other personally identifiable data (for example, personnel records), it may be used for other purposes and may become an instrument for monitoring performance. In this case, strictly legal justifications for surveillance are replaced by organisational justifications. Finally, electronic surveillance practices may have an impact on the relative distribution of reward, undermining existing processes of consultation and altering the concepts of distributive justice (Ball, 2006).

RELEVANT REGULATORY FRAMEWORK

Undoubtedly, privacy and other fundamental rights are affected by monitoring in the context of employment relationships. Although several aspects of privacy can be defined, there is no absolute or uniform concept of privacy or personal data protection. The issue of workplace privacy can be summarised in the dilemma between a property-based and a rights-based approach (Ball, 2006; Lasprograta et al., 2004).

Privacy in Private Contexts and Relationships

A first critical difference between the presented (and—to the extent possible—compared) approaches and the respective legal systems (U.S. and European Union) pertains to the scope of constitutional protection of privacy rights: The U.S. Constitution does not contain an expressed right to privacy; furthermore, there is no comprehensive legal framework providing for the protection of privacy in the U.S. However, in certain situations, the Supreme Court has interpreted the constitution to protect the privacy of the individuals: The Fourth Amendment protects against unlawful searches and seizures (*U.S. Supreme Court, Katz v. U.S.*) and applies to federal, state, and local government employees, where employers conducted the searches (*U.S. Supreme*

Court, O'Connor v. Ortega). Employees' privacy expectation and, consequently, privacy protection, are hardly founded on constitutional texts, since they have been found to restrict only government intrusions into privacy, and are therefore inapplicable to workplace privacy intrusions by private employers (Lasprogata et al., 2004; Phillips, 2005; Bloom et al., 2003).

The U.S. approach to privacy seems diametrically opposite to that in the European Union (EU): Article 8 of the European Convention for the Protection of Human Rights and Fundamental Freedoms (ECHR) states: "Everyone has the right to respect for his private and family life, his home and his correspondence" and the more recent Charter of Fundamental Rights of the European Union affirms that "everyone has the right to respect for his or her private and family life, home and communications" (Art.7) as well as "to the protection of personal data" (Art.8). Although the jurisprudence of the European Court of Human Rights (*Niemitz, Halford, Copland,* and other similar cases) concerns government action, it appears that in the EU the opinion that Article 8 of the Convention is relevant also in private context has gained a strong support. In the European approach, constitutional rights cease to be mere means of defence against state activities and become structural components of the employment relationship. As the employer's opportunities to monitor the employees, "the citizens of the enterprise" (France—Rapport Auroux, 1981), augments the chances to influence their behaviour and thus increases their dependence on the employer (*Federal German Labour Court,* 1984), rights and freedoms penetrate the employer-employee relationship and question a system of "*indisputable prerogatives*" of the employer (Simitis, 1999). The horizontal effect of the provisions of Article 8 of the European Convention is generally accepted by the jurisprudence in European states (for example, *French Cour de Cassation, the case Onof, Belgian Supreme Court,* 2001).

The U.S. Doctrine of "Reasonable Expectation of Privacy"

The so-called "*Katz test*" has to be applied to determine the "reasonableness" of the employees' "privacy expectations" in light of the totality of circumstances as well as the "realities of the workplace" (Supreme Court, *O'Connor v Ortega*). Case studies show that courts have held that the reasonableness of privacy expectations varies considerably with the norms and circumstances surrounding the specific activity and that the workplace reasonably entails very low privacy expectations, as other public or private interests may override privacy expectations, thus making intrusions through monitoring reasonable.

Given the, per definition, public nature of the workplace and its purposes, many argue that employees, who are hired to attend company business, cannot have a "reasonable expectation of privacy" (Fazekas, 2004). In some jurisdictions, law and courts have recognized only a "*minimal right to privacy*" which is limited to those instances where the matter or area intruded upon is "intensely private." There must be solitude or seclusion to be intruded upon, that is, monitoring in public places does not constitute an invasion (Phillips, 2005).

Under the "content approach" courts "decide the legitimacy of the employer's interest…by analysing the purposes behind the monitoring and whether the content of the communication is reasonably related to the proffered purposes." Under the "*context approach*," courts "determine the reasonableness of the employee's expectations by analysing the employer's notification procedures" (Kesan, 2002). In this approach, a policy posted in a company bulletin or site or a "surveillance clause" included in a contract, are likely to diminish or extinguish privacy expectations in the workplace. However, in Smyth v. Pillsbury the judge noted that the plaintiff had no reasonable expectation of privacy notwithstanding his employer's assurance about the confidentiality of the messages" (Desprocher & Roussos, 2001; Phillips, 2005). Consent may destroy such an expectation: It is the alienability of privacy that allows an employer to receive (in most cases even "implied") consent of the employee or to virtually eliminate any reasonable expectation of privacy by notifying its employees of a monitoring policy.

Furthermore, many justify the lack of privacy, by referring to the fact that monitored communications are voluntarily transmitted on an employer's network, using equipment designated to serve business objectives (Fazekas, 2004). The *"property argument"* has been proved a decisive one (Lasprogata et al., 2004): Courts have insisted on property rights, affirming the principle that employers may monitor communications taking place inside their premises with the use of their equipment. In McLaren v. Microsoft, the Texas Court of Appeals expressed the opinion that McLaren did not have a reasonable expectation of privacy since the emails were transmitted over the company's network and were "at some point accessible to a third-party." The judges noted that notwithstanding the personal password he used to access his messages and the fact he stored them in his *"personal folder,"* the messages "were not McLaren's personal property, but were merely an inherent part of the office environment" (Desprocher & Roussos, 2001).

The European Approach to Privacy Rights in the Workplace

Electronic employee monitoring is currently at the forefront of legal and public debate in Europe. Since the 1992 Niemitz decision, the European Court of Human Rights has recognised that the right to privacy extends to workplace (Findlay & McKinlay, 2003). The court rejected the distinction between private life and professional life exactly because the workplace is especially suited for social intercourse and "it is after all in the course of their working lives that the majority of people have a significant opportunity of developing relationships with the outside world" (ECHR, *Niemitz v. Germany*). A decisive criterion is the difficulty to "distinguish clearly which of an individual's activities form part of its professional life and which not" (*Niemitz v. Germany*).

The case *Halford v. the United Kingdom* was insightful for the extension of the protection of privacy in correspondence to electronic communications: The court decided that interception of workers phone calls in the workplace constituted a violation of Art. 8 of the European Convention and rejected the argument of United Kingdom that the plaintiff had no reasonable expectation of privacy in those calls, as they were made using telephones provided by the employer. The court has recently (April 2007) confirmed this approach: in *Copland v. the United Kingdom*, it stated that the reasonable expectation as to the privacy of calls "should apply in relation to the applicant's e-mail and Internet usage." The court recalled explicitly that the use of information relating to the date and length of telephone conversations and in particular the numbers dialed, as "integral element of the communications made by telephone" (*Malone v. the United Kingdom),* can give rise to an issue under Article 8 of the Convention. Accordingly, the court considered that the collection and storage of personal information relating to the applicant's telephone, as well as to her e-mail and Internet usage, without her knowledge, amounted to an interference with her right to respect for her private life and correspondence.

The concept of "reasonable expectation of privacy" is also present in the European approach. In *Halford v. United Kingdom*, the court considered that the failure to inform Mrs. Halford that her calls might be monitored created a "reasonable expectation of privacy." This consideration is given the interpretation that the court's ruling suggested that the extent of employees' privacy can be determined largely by the employer (Findlay & McKinlay, 2003). However, in the case *P.G. and J.H. v. the United Kingdom* (2004) the court concluded that a reasonable expectation of privacy is only one criterion to determine whether an interference with the right to privacy exists. The concept of Article 8 of the European convention recognizes the mere existence of privacy expectations in a free and democratic society. The protection afforded by the convention is also stronger from the employees' perspective as they would not have to prove the reasonableness of their expectations.

Privacy and Data Protection Principles

The Data Protection Working Party extracts three principles from the Article 8 jurisprudence that apply to public and private workplaces:

a) Employees have a legitimate expectation of privacy in the workplace, which is not overridden by the location and ownership of the electronic communications means used;

b) Respect for private life includes, to a certain degree, the right to establish and develop relationships with other human beings. The fact that such relationships, to a great extent, take place at the workplace puts limits to employer's legitimate need for surveillance measures;

c) The general principle of secrecy of correspondence covers communications at the workplace (DPWP, 2002). A number of cases judged by courts in European states, confirms this approach (Delbar et al., 2003).

The fundamental rights of privacy and secrecy of communications of employees are, however, subject to derogations and limitations, in particular when they are confronted with rights and freedoms of others similarly protected by the law, for example, the legitimate interests of the employers. More specifically, employees' rights are balanced against the interests of employers when validating the processing of employees' communications and their personal data (Mitrou & Karyda, 2006). Can

employers shape expectations of privacy or define the protection level through contractual provisions or simply organisational policies?

In the U.S., the reasonable expectation of workplace privacy is often reduced by the use of consent from employees: employers demand such consent as a "standard business procedure" (Phillips, 2005). As a result, consent to monitoring is becoming implicitly acknowledged in the employment relationship. It is noteworthy that the concept of consent as a way to legitimize monitoring practices under the European Union law is not quite straightforward as under U.S. law, particularly in the employment context, where withholding consent can have immediate negative jobs consequences.

According to the EU Data Protection Directive (*Directive 95/46/EC*), which has a direct and immediate effect on the human resource operations of employers, consent must be explicit, freely given and fully informed. The European Commission has expressed the opinion that "employers should avoid relying on the worker's consent as a means that legitimises by itself processing of personal data" (European Commission, 2002), while the International Labour Organisation accepts, under conditions, employee's consent as legitimate basis for the collection of data (ILO, 1997). The Data Protection Working Party has taken the view that when an employer has to process personal data, as a necessary and unavoidable consequence of the employment relationship; it is misleading to seek to legitimize this processing through consent (DPWP, 2001). Due to the nature of the employment relationship, in which there is an inherent asymmetry of power and the employee is subordinate and dependent, reliance on consent should be confined only to, the very few, cases where the employee has a genuine free choice and is subsequently able to withdraw the consent without detriment (Mitrou & Karyda, 2006).

International and national regulations as well as other non-legally binding texts, such as the International Labour Organisation's Code of Conduct

(1997) or the OECD Privacy Guidelines (1980), allow us outline the core principles pertaining to lawful and legitimized monitoring of employees. These principles are: *legitimacy, finality, necessity, proportionality*, and *transparency*.

- **Legitimacy:** Legitimate employee monitoring and processing of the derived data includes data that are necessary: (a) for compliance with a legal obligation of the employer; (b) for the performance of the work contract; (c) for the purposes of a legitimate interest pursued by the employer; or (d) for the performance of a task carried out in the public interest (DPWP, 2001). The legitimate purpose, which is pursued through monitoring, should be set in advance of a measure's application and be readily demonstrable to employees (Charlesworth, 2003).

- **Finality:** Employers must distinguish between the various aspects of the employment relationship and specify the aims for which monitoring is required. Information processing must be strictly confined to the data necessary in relation to the particular employment relationship. Both the amount and the type of data vary according to the individual employee's tasks or the context of the employer's decisions (Simitis, 1999). Monitoring should be carried out for a specific, explicit, and legitimate purpose and the derived information should not be further processed in any way that is incompatible with that purpose. For instance, personal data collected in order to ensure the security or the proper operation of processing systems should not be processed to control the behavior of individual employees, except where the latter is linked to the operation of these systems (European Commission, 2002; ILO, 1997). Furthermore, personal data collected by electronic monitoring should not be "the only factors in evaluating worker performance" (ILO, 1997).

- **Necessity** and **proportionality:** The level of tolerated privacy intrusion depends on the nature of the employment as well as on the specific circumstances surrounding and interacting with the employment relationship (DPWP, 2001). The employer's monitoring policy should be tailored to the type and degree of risk the employer faces. Monitoring must, in all cases, be *necessary, appropriate, relevant*, and *proportionate* with regard to the aims that it is pursuing. The employer may carry out monitoring of electronic online communications data as long as it is pursuing the following: the *prevention of illegal or defamatory acts*; acts that are contrary to good ethics or which can damage the dignity of another person; the protection of the economic, commercial, and financial interests of the organisation; the security and good operation of its information and communication systems; and the observance of the principles and rules applicable in the company for the use of online technologies (Mitrou & Karyda, 2006). Employers must check if any form of monitoring is absolutely necessary for a legitimate and specified purpose before proceeding to such activities. The UK information commissioner proposes to carry out a formal or informal "*impact assessment*" to decide if and how to carry out monitoring. This assessment involves the identification of purposes and benefits, the identification of "*adverse impacts*" on workers, and possibly on third parties, such as customers and the consideration of possible alternatives (for example, limitation of monitoring to high risk workers or areas) (UK Information Commissioner, 2003). The proportionality principle rules out routine monitoring of all staff, notwithstanding particular cases such as automated monitoring for purposes of security and proper operation of the system (e.g., viruses) (DPWP, 2002; European Commission, 2002). The most important of the effects of the proportionality principle is that the employers should always monitor employees "in the least-intrusive way" (ILO, 1997).

- **Transparency:** The transparency requirement seems to be the commonly accepted *minimum component of a workplace privacy policy*. The transparency principle requires that employers' monitoring practices be fully and clearly *disclosed* to all employees subject to the policy, along with the *reasons* for the monitoring and, ideally, upon hiring. Notably, courts in Denmark, the Netherlands, the UK, and Germany, have established the necessity for employers to have issued a clear use policy or instructions on Internet and e-mail use before it is legitimate for them to dismiss or discipline employees on grounds of misuse (Delbar et al., 2003). Employers should also inform their employees about the principal and secondary uses to which personal data generated by such systems are being put (IWGDPT, 1996). The so-called *secret or covert monitoring* can only be justified in exceptional circumstances. This requires that there is suspicion on reasonable grounds that a grievous criminal activity has been or will be committed (IWGDPT, 1996; ILO, 1997). Finally, according to ILO's code of practice, secret monitoring should be permitted only if "it is in conformity with national legislation."

FAIR PRACTICES

This section describes a set of *fair practices* which, when adopted, could enable bridge the gap between privacy and the countervailing interests of security. These suggestions have been based on the previous analysis and follow the lawful monitoring principles identified in the legal framework.

First, it is important that all monitoring activities are compliant with the legal and regulatory framework and that they are in line with business ethics. The main concerns with regard to this include the lack of specific policy provision by employers, lack of audit or review as to how employee information is used, and a subsequent lack of awareness of monitoring practice and police on the part of employees (Ball, 2006). For these reasons, compliance with the legal requirements and business ethics should be demonstrated and illustrated in the monitoring policy adopted and properly communicated to employees of companies, who apply surveillance techniques.

Second, companies should provide clear, well-defined, written policies concerning the use of their IT resources (e.g., use of e-mail, Internet access, etc.) (Mitrou & Karyda, 2006). Monitoring policies should describe in detail the types of employee monitoring techniques used, the reasons for the monitoring, who will have access to the information collected, those to whom the information may be disclosed, and should also make explicit which e-mail or Internet usage is allowed and which is not. Information should also be provided with regard to the nature and duration of the surveillance, the features of technology used and the type of information compiled, the details of any enforcement procedures outlining the notification of breaches of internal policies, and finally their rights to have access to the data processed about him and to correct errors (DPWP, 2002 ; IWGDPT, 1996). In this way, employees can have a clear understanding as to what is considered permitted, responsible, and ethical use of the technological infrastructure.

Third, a critical principle laid down in international and national legal texts requires that employers minimize the intrusion on the privacy of their employees and workers. For instance, the UK Employment Practices Data Protection Code suggests "impact assessment" as the best way to approach workplace monitoring (Nouwt et al., 2005). Generally, most of the risks directing the application of monitoring tools can be confronted using a combination of security controls which are less intrusive with regard to employees' privacy. For example, the risks of unintentional leakage of confidential information or the spread of a virus after opening an e-mail attachment could be avoided if employees were properly trained and received information on security issues such as the risks of opening attachments e-mailed from unknown senders or the practices of social engineering.

Fourth, implementing filtering tools against non-authorized sites, in association with firewalls for monitoring Internet connections, are prevention measures that do not necessitate informing employees. A posteriori control of Internet connection data, for instance, by department or by user, or a statistical control, should in most cases be sufficient without it being necessary to carry out an individualized, personal control of the accessed sites (CNIL, 2004). Furthermore, e-mail monitoring should be performed through automated means, searching for key words instead of viewing the content of the e-mail. Specific procedures for managing the content of e-mail (e.g., storing, deleting, etc.) should also be followed. As far as location monitoring is concerned, an alternative to active badges is to design systems in which the user solely controls the resultant information. In other words, the user's wearable computer would gather, process, and filter any data collected or distributed about the user (Starner, 2001).

Fifth, another issue to keep in mind when designing a monitoring policy, is granting employees with explicit control over their personal information. In this way, an employer shows respect and confidence in employees' use of the technology and the employee-employer relation is positioned on a trust basis (Starner, 2001). Involving employees in the design and implementation of monitoring systems will ensure that these systems have a better chance of being accepted, and that employees are informed about where monitoring information goes and how long it is kept (ILO, 1997; Hodges, 2006).

It should also be noted that privacy, in general, has not yet entered the domain of collective bargaining at the level of formal agreements. Surveillance and disclosure remain emergent issues in which the scope and depth of joint regulation of surveillance practices is settled at the enterprise level. In non-union firms, surveillance is regarded exclusively as a managerial prerogative, tempered by corporate human resources philosophies and practices (Findlay & McKinlay, 2003). However, in many European states like Germany, France, Sweden, Netherlands, and Belgium, there are stringent requirements for consultation with employees' representatives and collective agreements or model codes of conducts at place as instruments to regulate the use of IT-infrastructure as well as the use of surveillance means (Nouwt et al., 2005). Regulating workplace monitoring and privacy should not focus on the "physical artifacts or techniques" but on the "social relationship between employer and employees" (Phillips, 2005).

CONCLUSION AND OPEN ISSUES

Monitoring has negative side effects that affect both the observed and the observers: the panoptic effect of being constantly monitored, achieved through electronic surveillance, has negative impacts on the relationship of mutual trust and confidence that should exist between employees and employer (UK Information Commissioner, 2003; Desprocher & Roussos, 2001). Fazekas (2004) reports that workers whose communications were monitored, suffered from higher rates of depression, anxiety, and fatigue than those not subject to monitoring at the same business. More specifically, monitoring technologies affect employees' feelings towards their work and the workplace, their attitudes, emotions, beliefs, norms, and so forth. Stanton (2000) proposed a framework in which perceptions of fairness, satisfaction with monitoring, and monitoring invasiveness were interrelated attitudinal outcomes.

Fairness is defined as the degree to which workers evaluate monitoring practices affecting them as reasonable and appropriate. Finally, the notion of *invasiveness* is used to describe the extent to which employees perceive monitoring practices as an invasion of privacy.

It is also important to note that monitoring tools aim to address an inherent controversy: Companies provide their employees with Internet access and e-mail accounts mainly for increasing productivity and lowering transaction costs. Restricting these privileges may, up to a certain point, provide a level of protection against risks resulting of the so-called insider threat, but, at the same time the much anticipated benefits of the IT technology are undermined. Moreover, new types of employment, such as teleworking, can be rendered unfeasible, by employing such restrictions. At the same time, teleworking entails a set of new privacy challenges. For example, how can an employee's home be monitored without impinging upon non-work-related activities? How can employee surveillance during off-hours be prevented?

On the other hand, however, technology benefits can be negated by inappropriate use of information technology. It seems therefore, that a balance between the employees' right to privacy and the need to ensure employers' benefits is not very easily attainable. The guidelines for fair practices that have been previously described can help limit this discrepancy.

Conflicting laws and jurisdictional approaches reflect not only the contrasting philosophical assumptions underlying different legal systems, but also the inherently ambiguous relationship between property and privacy rights in the contemporary workplace (Findlay & McKinlay, 2003). Privacy protection requires careful balancing, as neither privacy nor its countervailing interests are absolute values. Due to conceptual confusions, courts and legislatures often fail to recognize privacy problems and thus no balancing is possible. This does not mean that privacy

should always win in the balance, but it should not be dismissed just because it is ignored or misconstrued. Maintaining employees' privacy can contribute to individual self-esteem and the development of workplace relations on a trust basis, which can be for the mutual benefit of both the employees and the employers' side.

REFERENCES

American Management Association. (2005). *Workplace e-mail and instant messaging survey.* Retrieved March 2006, from http://www.amanet.org/research/

Ball, K. (2006). Expert report: Workplace. In D. M. Wood (Ed.), *Surveillance studies network, a report on the surveillance society for the information commissioner (UK), appendices* (pp. 94-105). London.

Bloom, E., Schachter, M., & Steelman E. H. (2003). Competing interests in the post 9-11 workplace: the new line between privacy and safety. *William Mitchell Law Review, 29,* 897-920.

Charlesworth, A. (2003). Privacy, personal information and employment. *Surveillance and Society, 1*(2), 217-ff.

Commission Nationale de l'Informatique et des Libertés (CNIL). (2002). *La cybersurveillance sur les lieux de travail.* Paris.

Conry-Murray, A. (2001). The pros and cons of employee surveillance. *Network Magazine, 12*(2), 62-66.

CSI/FBI. (2006). *Computer crime and security survey.* Retrieved February 2007, from http://www.gocsi.com

Data Protection Working Party—DPWP. (2004). *Opinion 4/2004 on the processing of personal data and video surveillance* (11750/02/Final).

Data Protection Working Party—DPWP. (2001). *Opinion 8/2001 on the processing of personal data in the employment context* (5062/01/Final).

Data Protection Working Party—DPWP. (2002). *Working document on the surveillance of electronic communications in the workplace* (5401/01/Final).

Delbar, C., Mormont, M., & Schots, M. (2003). New technology and respect for privacy at the workplace. *European Industrial Relations Observatory*. Retrieved January 2006, from http://www.eiro.eurofound.eu.int/print/2003/07/study/TN0307101S.html

Desprocher, S., & Roussos, A. (2001). The jurisprudence of surveillance: a critical look at the laws of intimacy (Working Paper), *Lex Electronica*, 6(2). Retrieved March 2006, from http://www.lex-electronica.org/articles/v6-2/

DTI. (2006). *Information security breaches survey 2006*. Retrieved March 2006, from www.dti.gov.uk

Electronic Privacy Information Center (EPIC). (2002). Possible content of a European framework on protection of workers' personal data. *Workplace Privacy*, European Commission. Retrieved October 2005, from //www.epic.org/privacy/workplace

Fazekas, C. P. (2004). 1984 is still fiction: Electronic monitoring in the workplace and U.S. privacy. *Duke Law & Technology Review, 15*. Retrieved January 2006, from http://www.law.duke.edu/journals/dltr/articles/PDF/2004DLTR0015.pdf

Findlay, P., & McKinlay, A. (2003). Surveillance, electronic communications technologies and regulation. *Industrial Relations Journal, 34*(4), 305-314.

Forrester. (2006). *Forrester research reports*. Retrieved March 2006, from http://www.forrester.com

Hodges, A. C. (2006). Bargaining for privacy in the unionized workplace. *The International Journal of Comparative Labour Law and Industrial Relations, 22*(2), 147-182.

Hoeren, T., & Eustergerling, S. (2005). Privacy and data protection at the workplace in Germany. In S. Nouwt, B. R. de Vries, & C. Prins (Eds.), *Reasonable expectations of privacy* (pp. 211-244). The Hague, PA: TMC Asser Press.

International Labour Office—ILO. (1997). *Protection of workers' personal data*. Geneva.

International Working Group on Data Protection in Telecommunications—IWGDPT. (1996). *Report and recommendations on telecommunications and privacy in labour relationships*. Retrieved January 2006, from http://www.datenschutz-brlin.de/doc/int/iwgdpt/dsarb_en.htm

Kesan, J. P. (2002). Cyber-working or cyber-shirking?: a first principles examination of electronic privacy in the workplace. *Florida Law Review*, 289ff.

Lasprogata, G., King, N., & Pillay, S. (2004). Regulation of electronic employee monitoring: Identifying fundamental principles of employee privacy through a comparative study of data privacy legislation in the European Union, United States and Canada. *Stanford Technology Law Review, 4*. Retrieved March 2006, from http://stlr.stanford.edu/STLR/Article?04_STLR_4

Lee, J., & Lee, Y. (2002). A holistic model of computer abuse within organisations. *Information Management & Computer Security, 10*(2), 57-63.

Mitrou, E., & Karyda, M. (2006). Employees' privacy vs. employers' security: Can they be balanced. *Telematics and Informatics Journal, 23*(3), 164-178.

Nouwt, S., de Vries, B. R., & Loermans, R. (2005). Analysis of the country reports. In S. Nouwt, B. R. de Vries, & C. Prins (Eds.), *Reasonable ex-*

pectations of privacy (pp. 323-357). The Hague, PA: TMC Asser Press.

Organisation for Economic Co-Operation and Development—OECD. (2006). *RFID: Drivers, challenges and public policy considerations* (DSTI/ICCP (2005)19/FINAL).

Phillips, J. D. (2005). Privacy and data protection in the workplace: the US case. In S. Nouwt, B. R. de Vries, & C. Prins (Eds.), *Reasonable expectations of privacy* (pp. 39-59). The Hague, PA: TMC Asser Press.

Porter, D. (2003). Insider fraud: Spotting the wolf in sheep's clothing. *Computer Fraud & Security, 4,* 12-15.

Privacy International. (2006). *PHR2005—threats to privacy* (28/10/2006). Retrieved March 2006, from http://www.privacyinternational.org/

Rodota, S. (2004, September 16). Privacy, freedom and dignity. *Closing remarks at the 26th International Conference on Privacy and Personal Data Protection*, Wroclaw.

Schultz, E. E. (2002). A framework for understanding and predicting insider attacks. *Computers and Security, 21*(6), 526-531.

Schwartz, P., & Reidenberg, J. (1996). *Data privacy law.* Charlottesville, VA: Mitchie Law Publishers.

Selmi, M. (2006). *Privacy for the working class: public work and private lives* (Public law and legal theory working paper No 222). The George Washington University Law School.

Simitis, S. (1987). Reviewing privacy in an information society. *University of Pennsylvania Law Review, 135,* 707-728.

Simitis, S. (1999). Reconsidering the premises of labour law: Prolegomena to an EU refulation on the protection of employees' personal data. *European Law Journal, 5,* 45-62.

Sipior, C. J., & Ward, T. B. (1995). The ethical and legal quandary of email privacy. *Communications of the ACM, 38*(12), 48-54.

Solove, D. J. (2004). Reconstructing electronic surveillance law. *The George Washington Law Review, 72,* 1701-1747.

Solove D. J. (2006). A taxonomy of privacy. *University of Pennsylvania Law Review, 154*(3), 477-564.

Stanton, J. M. (2000). Reactions to employee performance monitoring: framework, review, and research directions. *Human Performance, 13,* 85-113.

Starner, T. (2001). The challenges of wearable computing: Part 2. *IEEE Micro,* 54-67.

UK Information Commissioner. (2003). *The employment practices data protection code.*

White, G. W., & Pearson, S. J. (2001). Controlling corporate e-mail, PC use and computer security. *Information Management and Computer Security, 9*(2), 88-92.

Chapter XVII
Aligning IT Teams' Risk Management to Business Requirements

Corey Hirsch
LeCroy Corporation, USA

Jean-Noel Ezingeard
Kingston University, UK

ABSTRACT

Achieving alignment of risk perception, assessment, and tolerance among and between management teams within an organisation is an important foundation upon which an effective enterprise information security management strategy can be built .We argue the importance of such alignment based on information security and risk assessment literature. Too often lack of alignment dampens clean execution of strategy, eroding support during development and implementation of information security programs . We argue that alignment can be achieved by developing an understanding of enterprise risk management plans and actions, risk perceptions and risk culture. This is done by examining context, context and process. We illustrate this through the case of LeCroy Corp., illustrating how LeCroy managers perceive risk in practice, and how LeCroy fosters alignment in risk perception and execution of risk management strategy as part of an overall information security program. We show that in some circumstances diversity of risk tolerance profiles aide a management teams' function. In other circumstances, variances lead to dysfunction. We have uncovered and quantified nonlinearities and special cases in LeCroy executive management's risk tolerance profiles.

INTRODUCTION

A sociological understanding of risk perception as an input to information security development is becoming a necessity. We know this from two strands of literature: the first is the literature in risk assessment in fields other than information security. The second is the information security literature. In particular, understanding how management and functional teams perceive risk, and decide and act in managing risk, is one cornerstone of an effective enterprise information security management strategy. If managers do not understand the reasons behind an information security policy, or do not fully support the rationale behind it, they are unlikely to engage in its development or adhere to it later. Furthermore, divergent information security decisions and actions may have the effect of canceling out each other, and render the enterprise risk management strategy less effective. In addition, events such as mergers, security breaches, or regulatory changes may cause managers' perceptions of risk to evolve.

How, then, do managers perceive risk in practice? And how might an enterprise foster an aligned approach to risk management? This chapter presents such a methodology. We will use a medium sized manufacturer of test and measurement equipment, LeCroy Corp., to illustrate.

We will show that whilst there are areas where perceptions toward and tolerance of risk are shared within a department or work team, there can be substantial variations between different groups of managers. Groups which routinely work together on information security and risk management related tasks, however, have lower standard deviations in their risk judgments than teams which do not share this working experience. Yet this second group may have responsibilities that are critical to enterprise risk management.

Individuals in a population display variation in their tolerance for risk. A retired widower for example, might choose an investment known to

offer lower returns than other investments available, because it also presented a lower likelihood of variations in return. A young entrepreneur on the other hand, might be willing to accept a high probability of surprises, as long as she felt the upside was commensurate with the downside. Willingness to accept a reduction in return, in order to reduce expected variation in return, is *intolerance to risk*. Willingness to accept high expected variation in return, in order to maximize expected return is *tolerance for risk*. This chapter will illustrate how top executives are mathematical in their risk appetite at low and medium stakes, yet highly risk-averse when the stakes are higher, such as when complete business success or failure are potential outcomes. The chapter will also demonstrate how to quantify an organization's level of risk tolerance, which will in turn enable a reader to align IT risk management strategy to an organization's risk culture.

BACKGROUND

A good understanding of both intolerance and tolerance to risk is at the core of any successful information security policy, usually developed in three stages. The first stage typically entails risk identification and assessment. This is usually followed by stages looking at how risks can be monitored and controlled, with a third and final stage concerned with risk avoidance and mitigation. For instance, COBIT 4.0 (ITGI, 2005) proposes that the "assess and manage IT risks" high level control objective should be met through a series of 10 activities culminating in the maintenance and monitoring of a risk action plan. Similarly, in ISO 17799:2005 (ISO, 2005a), the first section describing best practice is one on "risk assessment and treatment."

Sources of information security risk are usually documented in taxonomies of risks. They tend to list broad categories of risk sources (Backhouse & Dhillon, 1996) that can be used to ensure that all sources of potential risks have been surveyed. For instance, Loch, Carr, and Warkentin (1992) classify sources of information security risks as internal versus external, human versus non-human, and accidental versus intentional. Similar classifications exist in the ISO 27001 control objectives (ISO, 2005b) and in most text relating to information security (see for instance, Whitman & Mattord, 2003)

Such taxonomies and classifications have been criticized by Dhillon and Backhouse (2001). They remark that checklists and taxonomies of threat tend to leave out the social nature of information security problems. This makes it difficult to get a clear picture of management's appetite for risk as an input to the information security strategy and subsequently ensure that the expectations and actions of various stakeholders are aligned. Yet, recent research suggests that understanding an organization's appetite for risk (and subsequently ensuring a good alignment between the stakeholders' attitudes to risk and its management) is perhaps as important to the success of an information security policy as is understanding risks clearly (Ashenden & Ezingeard, 2005; Ezingeard, Mcfadzean, Howlin, Ashenden, & Birchall, 2004). This is now understood in professional standards. COBIT 4.0 for instance, firmly reinforces the need to understand an enterprise's appetite for risk as part of the IT risk management process.

A key question therefore, seems to be how to measure (or estimate) the appetite for risk of an organization and use this estimate as an input to an information security strategy? Further, how can we ensure a good degree of alignment of attitudes to risk across an organization? The answers rely first of all on understanding the basis of risk management and alignment.

RISK MANAGEMENT AND ALIGNMENT

Alignment

The notion of alignment (strategic fit) is crucial in many other areas of business. It has its origins in the concept of strategic fit, popularised by Tom Peters in the 1980s, who argued that congruence among seven elements—strategy, structure, systems, style, staff, shared values, and skills—is necessary for success (Peters & Waterman, 1982). Strategic fit is important, because it leads to superior performance (Gietzmann & Selby, 1994).

Defining "fit" is, however, difficult as fit goes beyond knowing what needs to be aligned, to include how alignment should be achieved. This led Venkatraman and Camillus (1984) to define fit as *process* (how to achieve fit) and *content* (what fit looks like). The importance of process is also highlighted by Reich and Bensabat (1996) who argue that two aspects need to be considered. They highlight the importance of understanding how the *planning process* itself can help achieve alignment (in the case of enterprise risk management, this would involve an examination of the enterprise risk strategy). They also take this further by suggesting the importance of looking at *social relationships* in the organisation.

The idea behind the argument that social relationships need to be looked at is that alignment is not only a strategic, logical process, but also a social process. Therefore, good communication between business and the function to be aligned (for instance, IT executives) is often quoted as necessary for strategic fit (Reich & Benbasat, 1996; Reich & Benbasat, 2000). Alignment is also thought to be easier to achieve if business executives have a good knowledge of the functional areas where alignment is sought (Hussin, King, & Cragg, 2002).

The First Link between Strategic Processes and Social Processes: Risk Perceptions

Information security has been implemented as a process in many organizations for almost two decades now. It follows a sequence of risk identification, risk classification (for instance in terms of impact and probability), and risk mitigation or avoidance. The approach has been at the basis of some of the most common information security best practice approaches such as the ISO 27000 series (ISO, 2005b) at a management system level as well as the common criteria evaluation and validation scheme (CCEVS, 2005) at a lower technical level since their inceptions. Whilst treating information security as a process is now seen as good practice, there have been many calls to ensure that the process should not be treated solely as a *mechanistic* one and should be capable of continuously adapting to its context. This approach is very "functionalist" (McFadzean, Ezingeard, & Birchall, 2004) and can easily be seen as lacking completeness because its comprehension of the context of risk is limited. For instance, both Beck (1992) and Baskerville (1991) argue that much work on risk analysis for information security is too functionalist. They suggest that practitioners have become over-reliant on predictive models for developing a secure information system thus ignoring important issues such as employee understanding, motivation, and behaviour.

Adams (2005) outlines three types of risk: those that are perceived directly, those that are perceived through science, and virtual risk. He suggests that risks that are perceived directly are dealt with using judgment (this refers to risks such as crossing the road, for example). Virtual risks are culturally constructed because science is inconclusive, which means that "*whom we believe depends on whom we trust*." Those risks that are perceived through science are relatively objective in nature. Information security risk assessment has come from a scientific background and has

worked on the assumption that information security risks can be perceived through hard science. It now seems the case that many of the facets of information security fall into the category of virtual risk and if we are to address them from this perspective then we need a better understanding of how they are culturally constructed. There is therefore a need to "understand the relationships between human factors and risk and trust if a relatively secure cyberspace is to develop in the future" (OST, 2004).

In addition to the need to understand how risk is perceived because it can help employee motivation and behavior, and the need to understand how risk is culturally constructed, another reason why understanding how risk is perceived is important is the social complexity of risk itself. Willcocks and Margetts (1994) point out that recent research, "supports generally the finding that the major risks and reasons for failure tend to be through organizational, social and political, rather than technical factors." Although this is referring to risk in the broad information system environment rather than information security specifically, the same assertion still applies. They go on to recommend that risk should be assessed as, "a result of distinctive human and organizational practices and patterns of belief and action."

The Second Link between Strategic Processes and Social Processes: Risk Culture

Information security risk is only one category of risk organizations are exposed to and many organizations find it difficult to align their IT risk management efforts with those of the rest of the organization in other areas such as financial or business continuity risks (Birchall, Ezingeard, Mcfadzean, Howlin, & Yoxall, 2004). Often this is because risk management strategies, and more specifically information security strategies are not grounded in organizational values (Dhillon & Torkzadeh, 2006). Yet, legislative and regulatory requirements—for instance, in the corporate governance arena, requiring organizations to think of information security within their overall risk management frameworks (ITGI, 2003) make this a requirement. This means that not only do risk management processes need to be aligned across functional areas in the organization, but also that attitudes towards risk need to be aligned.

In order to address this need for alignment, Jahner and Krcmar (2005) propose a model of risk culture. The model has three dimensions (identify, communicate, and act). Whilst the "identify" and "act" dimensions are often clearly embedded in many information security processes, Jahner and Krcmar argue that an organization's information security efforts can only be successful if a shared understanding of possible threats is achieved and if a shared understanding of how to act consistently is reached. How people act in risk management is, according to Ciborra (2004), "intertwined in social processes and networks of relationships."

Whilst Jahner and Krcmar's model of risk culture is useful as a basis for understanding the social processes around risk in an organization, it does not discuss the importance of a shared understanding of the risk/reward equation in any of its three phases. Yet, this is likely to be crucial to the success of any risk management process. Whilst the IT risk management literature is often coy about making this explicit, the purpose of risk management is not solely the avoidance of risk to minimise losses, but in fact the need to take risks to reap rewards. The financial risk management community is by and large more explicit about this since the risk/reward equation is one of the fundamental rules of business. As pointed out in the Turnbull report "Since profits are, in part, the reward for successful risk-taking in business, the purpose of internal control is to help manage and control risk appropriately rather than to eliminate it" (Turnbull, 1999).

There is a growing body of literature that suggests that this risk-reward equation is an integral part of an organization's risk culture. For instance, according to Adams and Thompson (2002), the assessment of reward is a key aspect of the "risk thermostat" that is at play both at an institutional and individual level during risk assessment. In Adams' model, the "risk thermostat" includes perceptual filters (Adams, 1999) whose influence depends on the attitude of people to risk. Similarly, attitude to risks have been found to have a significant impact of the way boards of directors address information security in their organisation (Ezingeard, Mcfadzean, & Birchall, 2003). We therefore need to augment Jahner and Krcmar's model of risk culture by adding assessment of reward and assessment of the risk/reward equation in the "identify" and "communicate" dimensions of risk culture.

A Methodology to Understand Risk Culture and Alignment

Three Dimensions

In order to understand the interactions and dependencies between risk management, perception and culture, three dimensions need to be looked at: context, content, and process.

Context is about understanding the influence of four key communities on the enterprise risk strategy: customers, employees, owners, and competitors. In the case of for profit firms, understanding owner's views is critical. The influence of the environment, including regulatory, political, and economic also needs to be understood.

Content and process help us understand the two conceptual links we discussed earlier, namely the need to understand how risk perceptions and risk culture influence the alignment between enterprise risk management and business strategy.

The suggested framework is shown in Table 1.

Populating the framework can be done from on-the-job experience, interviews (ideally including the operational management and governance

Table 1. Analysis framework

	Enterprise Risk Management (ERM) Plans and Actions	Risk Perception	Risk Culture
Context	How the business context influences ERM	How the business context influences risk perceptions in the organisation	How the business context influences risk culture in the organisation
Content	What are the enterprise risk management mechanisms in place	How risk perceptions influence the ERM mechanisms in place (and vice versa)	How the risk culture influences ERM mechanisms (and vice versa)
Process	What are the processes in place to achieve and maintain alignment between business strategy and ERM	How risk perceptions impact on the alignment process	How risk culture impacts on the alignment process

executives), surveys, and examination of documentary evidence, such as:

- Policies
- Risk management spread-sheets
- Audit reports and audit recommendations

An Example

Company Background

LeCroy Corp. (Nasdaq LCRY, FY2006 Sales $U.S.168M) was founded by Walter O. LeCroy in 1964 in Irvington, New York. It operates in the test and measurement business, with the tag line "Innovators in Instrumentation." This illustrates a dilemma in so far as the business area the company works in is one where products must be trustworthy and innovation must therefore not get in the way of an equally important reputation for stability and robustness. Consequently, whilst innovations are required and can be significant source of competitive advantage, they cannot be allowed to be synonymous with surprises for the customer. Thus, instrumentation makers tend to test innovations heavily before introducing them into production. They are generally willing to spend heavily to avoid surprises. We can therefore, from the outset, categorise the organisation's strategic environment as "risk averse."

LeCroy's products are software intensive. Most are designed to be used connected to local area networks. It is therefore important that they should be patchable and upgradeable. When LeCroy's products began to be designed with embedded x86 architecture processors running Windows™ operating systems, a rigorous information security regimen became a requirement (Hirsch, 2005), in order to prevent malware contagion incidents that could affect the company, and possibly thereafter, its customers (Oshri, Kotlarsky, & Hirsch, 2005). At that time, the CEO chartered a new change initiative to elevate the information security culture. Two years later, when the security team had taken solid hold and the information security culture had clearly moved in the desired direction, the CEO further chartered a new supplemental change initiative to institute enterprise risk management at LeCroy. This is viewed as a completing element of the information security project.

Our example operates in a niche business area, characterised by complex products and few competitors. The two main competitors are much larger public companies. Instrumentation design and production is a high fixed cost business, hence there is a substantial advantage conferred by size. LeCroy must compete with these larger companies for relationships with customers, employees, and investors. LeCroy therefore has a strategy of fostering longer than average relationships with its partners in each of the mentioned three communities. "No surprises" is an element of the strategy.

Context

The first aspect of LeCroy's information security and risk management programme is how it is influenced by its environment and business area. In particular, its policies and procedures are designed to enable enterprise management of risk, such that customers, employees, and owners experience a coherent risk profile. The key influences are represented in Table 2.

Influence of Context of Perceptions of Risk (and Risk Tolerance)

The context LeCroy operates in recognizes "controllable risks" as those for which the probability of occurrence can be viably decreased or increased based on management's decisions to invest or withhold investment in mitigation strategies. Examples of such risks include data loss or corruption. Conversely, "uncontrollable risks" are those for which the probability of occurrence cannot be changed by management action (although the impact of occurrence may be influenced). Examples of such risk include the arrival of an Avian Flu pandemic.

Most managers at LeCroy are intolerant of controllable risks. On the other hand, most managers are comfortable to operate in a business environment and context where they know many risks are uncontrollable and only their consequences can be mitigated. For example, instrumentation makers must be one step ahead of their customers in terms of technology. If an oscilloscope is going to help a designer working on a 10gbit design, the oscilloscope itself must be significantly faster internally. Oscilloscope design activities therefore carry significant risk. Which technologies to "bet on?" Which vendors can supply needed components within the tight specifications required? One chipset (processor, memory) may offer a longer

Table 2. Key stakeholder influences

	Customer	**Employees**	**Owners**
Context	o Long warranties and product support o Easy and cheap software upgrades o Minimized risk of malware contagion o Information security policy is significantly influenced by the high software content of products	o Employee benefits offerings are designed to reduce risks for employees o Relatively comprehensive insurance coverage and support packages o Facilities investments and procedures designed to help employees manage risk o Health and safety policy based on halving exposure every year	o Expanding number of institutional shareholders (2006)
Implications	Low tolerance of risks that could influence customer relationships Decision to implement ISO9000, receiving the first certification issued under the ISO9000:2000 program	Low tolerance of risks that could influence employee relationships Risks to health and safety on the job are managed in a different paradigm than information security risks	High tolerance of market risks Management's strategy is to aggressively mitigate controllable risks, while managing the consequences of unavoidable risks
Key Performance Indicators	Higher than typical values for customer retention and repurchase	Average length of service at LeCroy is 8 years, double peer group average (2006)	8.2% of total shares outstanding are held by institutional holders with at least four quarters of ownership (2006)

period of stability while another may introduce the latest feature—which chipsets should be selected? Which development project is likely to succeed, and which is likely to fail?

Influence of Context on Risk Culture

LeCroy's early years were spent in the high-energy physics instrumentation market. This market had two main participant segments: academia and military. From an information security and risk management perspective, these segments presented a dichotomy. The bias for information sharing, typical of the "un-caged information" culture of the university, stood in stark contrast to the "need-to-know" information culture of the military and national research labs. For this reason, the information security culture at LeCroy is nuanced and complex. Traditionally, the collegial atmosphere at LeCroy had been characteristic of a relaxed information security culture with a bias toward knowledge management benefits obtained through easy and widespread access to information.

Content of the Risk Management Framework

The company bases its enterprise risk management methodology on a cycle of measurement and education. A significant element of the risk management framework is data driven—with the overarching philosophy that employees and managers are responsible and empowered to align their risk management decisions to the company risk management strategy, and only require data and understanding in order to carry this out.

A risk management team comprising executives, managers, and employees has been formed and charged with developing and implementing an enterprise risk management program. The programme differentiates between those risks for which a return on investment figure can be calculated should the company decide to mitigate the risk, and those risks for which a purely ROI basis for investment decision-making would be inappropriate (for instance, relating to employee health and safety).

For those risks where mitigation ROI can be calculated, LeCroy uses a spreadsheet whose key columns labelled as shown in Table 3. Each of these factors figures into an algebraic expression, whose value indicates an estimated ROI on mitigation, and a confidence level in the estimate. The spreadsheet gives management a first indication of which mitigation decisions to consider, based on expectation of financial return. This is well aligned to the company's willingness to spend to reduce uncertainty, its model of risk management.

All areas of risk are viewed as objective and treated in the same fashion, except those relating to the comfort, health, and safety of employees and visitors/partners of LeCroy. These health and safety risks are considered not suitable for a purely ROI based analytical approach, and instead are managed using an annual risk exposure halv-

Table 3. Headings of objective risks spreadsheet

Estimated Probability FY08 Event in %, as of May 1 2007	Estimated Severity of Consequences of Event in $	Estimated Seriousness of Threat (B*C)	Confidence Level in Estimate (0 low; 1 high)	Comments	External Cost to Mitigate ($)	Extent of Mitigation in %	Expected ROI	Action Plan	Estimated Seriousness of Threat Following Action Plan

ing process. The key columns of the associated spreadsheet are shown in Table 4. The management process is similar to that for objective risk, however, the scales used and the algebraic expressions are changed. The company could not and does not want to assign a specific dollar value, for example, to an employee's or customer's injury avoidance. The philosophy applied in this area is one of continuous improvement, hence the goal is to halve the summation of exposure (multiplication product of columns 1 and 2) each year.

Influence of Risk Perceptions on the Risk Management Framework

As explained earlier, the basis of the risk management framework is numerical. This means that perceptions of probability, severity, seriousness of threat, as well as costs to mitigate inevitably influence the robustness of the framework and its ability to deliver strategic objectives. For instance, we asked members of the company's executive team how much they would be prepared to spend to halve the probability of:

- 2 day building closure
- The loss of 2 days of BaaN (ERP) data
- Bodily injury to 2 employees
- The 2 most important LeCroy patents become invalidated
- A large bin of confidential documents intended for shredding is accidentally released into the insecure dumpster
- The Web site being attacked and defaced for 2 days

- A malware infestation of the network and 200 infected products are shipped to customers

The responses we got varied significantly. Interestingly, no significant pattern seemed to emerge based on the function of the respondent. When pressed for an explanation it became apparent that the *perceived severity* of such events was the cause of the variation.

Influence of the Risk Culture on the Risk Management Framework

We have so far characterised the company's risk culture as one that prefers to give priority to knowledge sharing and collegiality, and one that historically had a "relaxed" attitude towards information security. Yet we have also described how the "risk thermostats" are set low for controllable risks and higher for uncontrollable risks. The need to resolve this apparent tension influences the risk management framework at two levels:

- Risk management structures: A high profile is given to risk management, with two committees (the information security team and the risk management team) dealing with risk company-wide. These teams meet regularly. The chief information officer sits on both teams. The teams regularly seek (and get) input from members of the company's executive team and annually from the board.
- A strong sense that the company's efforts towards risk avoidance where made necessary by the market are appropriate. This is illustrated for instance, by the views of the

Table 4. Headings of the non-quantifiable risks spreadsheet

Estimated Probability FY08 Event in %, as of May 1, 2007	Estimated Severity of Consequences of Event (1 low, 10 high)	Estimated Seriousness of Threat (B*C)	Confidence Level in Estimate (0 low; 1 high)	External Cost to Mitigate	Extent of Mitigation in %	Action Plan	Estimated Seriousness of Threat Following Mitigation

sales force about whether LeCroy should be more risk tolerant than it is. Out of seven senior sales employees we questioned, only one thought LeCroy should be more risk tolerant, yet three described the company's culture as risk intolerant. Similarly, only one member of the executive team thought that LeCroy should be more risk tolerant.

Formal Alignment Process

It is assumed that each manager or employee, who was hired for their job expertise, is the most capable person to estimate the probability and consequences of unexpected outcomes in their area of activity (first two columns of the spreadsheet tool). However, attention is paid to alignment between the risk-management actions of individual managers and the company's desired risk profile. For information risks (generally viewed as not employee health or safety related), assessments are made of likelihood of an unexpected outcome during the coming fiscal year, and of the expected cost should such an event occur. Whenever possible, this is done based on LeCroy or peer company data. Then alternative mitigation actions/strategies are listed, as are the extent of estimated mitigation for each. Costs are listed as well, and from these factors an estimated ROI can be computed. In general, for information related risk mitigation, strategies are selected using this method and the current year's hurdle rate is applied. The first alignment mechanism is therefore *project finance*.

The second routine alignment process in place in the company is the participation of the chief information officer in three key forums with a significant stake in the company's enterprise risk management: The information security team, the risk management team, and the executive team. This is seen to be an effective alignment mechanism in so far as both the information security team and the risk management team are responsible for overseeing all planning related to ERM.

This is supplemented by two other mechanisms, which whilst not designed with the sole purpose of alignment in mind are widely seen in the organisation as important vehicles for validating the alignment of the ERM strategy. The first such mechanism consists of board agenda items where the ERM strategy and its information security components are discussed. The second such mechanism is company-wide (driven by IS and finance) participation in debates and preparations for risk related audits (ISO, Sarbanes-Oxley).

The company does not generally screen recruitment candidates using risk tolerance filters. The company therefore expects its employees and managers, in the absence of an enterprise risk management program, would represent a spectrum of individual risk cultures similar to the general population at large from which these groups are drawn. Therefore, the company seeks to actively define and communicate vocabulary, concepts, and methods in its risk management program, that will allow functions as diverse as sales, facilities, marketing, production, logistics, finance, and engineering, to achieve alignment in their approach to their diverse risk management tasks. These functions also need to be able to adjust risk management calibration quickly when company circumstances require an adjustment. In order to ensure that this is done in a fashion that accounts for the varying spectrums of risk perceptions, these are discussed regularly. This is explained.

Managing the Inter-Dependence between Risk Perceptions and ERM Alignment

Each year managers and selected employees fill in a risk profiling survey. These reflect a range of working groups, including the executive team, the security team, the risk management team, sales teams, the Board of Directors, and others. An example of a question asked in the survey is:

I would accept a business proposition that has n% chance of doubling LeCroy's size, enterprise value, and EPS over a one year period, however it also carries a y% chance of bankrupting the company.., with sets of [n,y] as follows:

[5%;95%], [25%;75%], [45%;55%], [50%;50%], [55%;45%], [75%;25], [95%;5%]

The results for the executive team are shown in Figure 1, on a 1-5 scale (strongly agree =1 ; strongly disagree = 5).

Results are presented to various stakeholders; executive team, board, information security team, and risk management team. The resulting discussions are seen as a valuable mechanism to achieve a common understanding, and convergence. Each participant is given insight into their risk perception and tolerance characteristics as well as those of the other members of their work group, and of

work groups adjacent in the value chain. Providing this periodic reminder of company vocabulary and methodology drives enterprise risk management behaviour toward convergence.

Managing the Influence of Culture on Alignment

We have so far highlighted the potential tensions between the low tolerance of customer and employee related risks and the collegiate, knowledge sharing culture. We have also highlighted the high tolerance for market related risks. Further culture-related complexity arises out of the confluence of all these daily risk management activities. Two key questions remain therefore:

• Does each actor know what the overall enterprise risk objectives are at the time?

Figure 1. Example results of risk tolerance survey, interviewees 1-7, risk neutral boundary, and 3 work teams

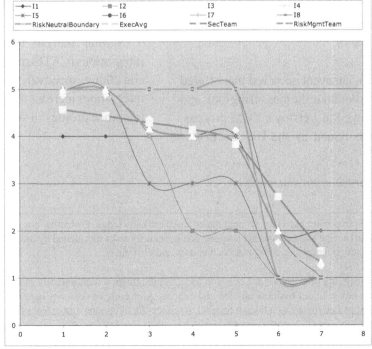

- Does each actor know the risk management practices (and potentially) biases of the other actors up and down the value chain to with whom they work?

In order to help all employees in the company answer these questions each year, the company conducts a Security Fair for all employees, up to and including the Board of Directors. The fair is comprised of five to eight booths, including at least one staffed by outside experts in the field. Each employee must take a test and/or sign a declaration at the end, establishing metrics for the company as to the state of "education" of its "human firewall." The human firewall is a stated part of the overall defense in depth strategy, summarized in the Security Mission Statement (see Figure 2) that is posted prominently at the company.

Top management further expresses its commitment to security through an annual facilities survey that captures employee concerns regarding physical safety and security. Investments such as upgraded outdoor lighting, traffic calming schemes, and security cameras have arisen from this process.

'Unusual Eevents Offer Chance to Validate Process'

In February 2007 an event occurred that offered an opportunity to validate the measuring tools and processes employed in LeCroy's ERM process. A subpoena was issued by the U.S. Securities and Exchange Commission (SEC) to LeCroy, as a witness in an action being brought against an organization being charged with manipulative stock trading. Twelve firms' shares were alleged to have been improperly traded, based on advance knowledge of the contents of company press releases. LeCroy's shares, among the 12 firms, represented only a minute fraction (total alleged improper profit U.S.D $18,000) of the total, however presented a potential "wake up call" at the company. A thorough investigation in support of the SEC inquiry led management to the conclusion that the e-mail system of a business partner downstream in the public relations/press release processing chain had been compromised, and a copy of the company's FY2007 Q2 public press release had been viewed on the day prior to its release by a stock manipulator. Would such an event have the effect of significantly re-calibrating the risk tolerance responses of senior managers or the Board of Directors?

Following this event a new measurement round was conducted, with findings that the profiles of non-involved business managers and the board members were unchanged. This stability, despite a high profile event, supports the underlying validity of the measurement process.

Similar analysis following acquisitions and integrations (CATC and Catalyst in October 2004 and 2006 respectively) informed the authors that integrations increase the standard deviation of risk tolerance profiles in the successor organization.

Figure 2. Security mission statement

LeCroy's most important assets are its employees and their knowledge. Protecting our assets preserves a competitive advantage and helps us achieve our goals. Security risks introduced by individuals' decisions affect the entire LeCroy community, including visitors, vendors and customers.

It is the responsibility of everyone at LeCroy to use good judgment to continuously manage security risks in a manner consistent with our business mission and culture. Alongside our security hardware, software and systems, the employees of LeCroy act as a human firewall to reduce the likelihood and extent of loss or harm.

CONCLUSION

Business is an endeavour which rewards effective management of risk. Wise and consistent acceptance of risk may be rewarded, proportionally, with profit. As all managers are financial managers, people managers, and information security managers, so too do all managers manage risk.

But should managers operate in organizations where each department makes diverse financial decisions? For example, if the CFO had arranged a line of credit at 5% pa, should a facilities manager be leasing copy machines on a discount rate of 22%? Or should a procurement team be paying a 15% premium for a JIT inventory consignment scheme? Likewise, in the area of risk management, alignment and convergence pay large dividends and enable clean execution of strategy.

The case of LeCroy offers an illustration of the effective use of mixed formal and informal ERM culture alignment mechanisms, ranging from committee structures to security fairs, surveys, to spreadsheet tools. The methodology is partly data-driven and partly a qualitative cycle of education and training. An interesting aspect of the methodology is that it encourages *discussion* to bring about a shared understanding of the appetite for risk of the organization. Recent work on aligning information assurance with business strategy (Birchall et al., 2004) has shown that an essential element of alignment is communication between the stakeholders and managers accountable for information assurance in the organisation. The case presented here suggests that this communication around risk and risk perceptions can be an important component of ensuring that alignment is achieved. This need for communication is implemented through a variety of mechanisms that encourage alignment (rather than prescribe it).

Communication regarding ERM with business partners offers tangible rewards. Insurance premiums, for example, at LeCroy have declined in each of the 6 years since the CEO's informa-

tion security and subsequent risk management charter was issued. During the negotiations with insurance brokers and underwriters, ERM events and progress of the prior year are brought to bear, with a resulting premium savings over the life of the initiative, so far, exceeding $1M. In the 2008 annual renewal cycle, there have been no (zero) insurance claims at LeCroy, a remarkable outcome for an organization of 500 employees in a dozen countries shipping thousands of units each quarter.

The massive power outage in the North Eastern USA during August 2005 did not bring LeCroy systems off the air, and LeCroy has enjoyed the most favourable Sarbanes-Oxley opinions each year. These and other favourable outcomes are attributed by the management team in part to the ERM and information security frameworks at the company.

The case raises interesting questions about the link between enterprise risk management and other forms of risk management in the company. At LeCroy, three committees have an important risk management function: The executive team, the risk management committee, and the information security committee. Because the risk management committee and the information security committee are at the same organizational level, this raises possibilities of duplication of activity between the two committees and accountability. Furthermore, the recommendations of the two committees may potentially overlap. There is therefore the need for coordination between them, as well as appropriate oversight by the executive team. At LeCroy, this is achieved by the role of the CIO (who is also a member of the executive team).

NOTE

An earlier version of this paper entitled Perceptual and Cultural Aspects of Risk Management Alignment: A Case Study, appears in the *Journal of Information Security, 4*(1), 2008.

REFERENCES

Adams, J. (1999). *Risk-benefit analysis: Who wants it? Who needs it?* Paper presented at the Cost-Benefit Analysis Conference, Yale University.

Adams, J. (2005). *Risk management, it's not rocket science: it's more complicated* draft paper available from http://www.geog.ucl.ac.uk/~jadams/publish.htm

Adams, J., & Thompson, M. (2002). *Taking account of societal concerns about risk. Framing the problem* (Research Rep. 035). London: Health and Safety Executive,

Ashenden, D., & Ezingeard, J.-N. (2005). *The need for a sociological approach to information security risk management.* Paper presented at the 4th Annual Security Conference. Las Vegas, Nevada, USA.

Backhouse, J., & Dhillon, G. (1996). Structures of responsibility and security of information systems. *European Journal of Information Systems, 5*, 2-9.

Baskerville, R. (1991). Risk analysis: An interpretive feasibility tool in justifying information systems security. *European Journal of Information Systems, 1*(2), 121-130

Beck, U. (1992). *Risk society.* London: Sage Publishers.

Birchall, D., Ezingeard, J.-N., Mcfadzean, E., Howlin, N., & Yoxall, D. (2004). *Information assurance: Strategic alignment and competitive advantage.* London: GRIST.

CCEVS. (2005). *Common criteria—Part 1: Introduction and general model* (Draft v3.0, Rev 2). Common Criteria Evaluation and Validation Scheme.

Ciborra, C. (2004). *Digital technologies and the duality of risk* (Discussion Paper). Centre for Analysis of Risk and Regulation, London School of Economics.

Dhillon, G., & Backhouse, J. (2001). Current directions in IS security research: toward socio-organizational perspectives. *Information Systems Journal, 11*, 127-153.

Dhillon, G., & Torkzadeh, G. (2006). Value-focused assessment of information system security in organizations. *Information Systems Journal, 16*, 293-314.

Ezingeard, J.-N., Mcfadzean, E., & Birchall, D. W. (2003). Board of directors and information security: A perception grid. In S. Parkinson & J. Stutt (Eds.), *Paper 222 presented at British Academy of Management Conference,* Harrogate.

Ezingeard, J.-N., Mcfadzean, E., Howlin, N., Ashenden, D., & Birchall, D. (2004). *Mastering alignment: bringing information assurance and corporate strategy together.* Paper presented at the European and Mediterranean Conference on Information Systems, Carthage.

Gietzmann, M. B., & Selby, M. J. P. (1994). Assessment of innovative software technology: Developing an end-user-initiated interface sesign strategy. *Technology Analysis & Strategic Management, 6*, 473-483.

Hirsch, C. (2005). Do not ship trojan horses. In P. Dowland, S. Furnell, & B. Thuraisingham (Eds.), *Security management, integrity, and internal control in information systems.* Fairfax, VA: Springer.

Hussin, H., King, M., & Cragg, P. (2002). IT alignment in small firms. *European Journal of Information Systems, 11*, 108-127.

ISO. (2005a). *Information technology—security techniques—code of practice for information security management* (ISO/IEC 17799:2005). London: BSI.

ISO. (2005b). *Information technology—security techniques —information security management systems—requirements* (ISO/IEC 27001:2005(E)). London: BSI.

ITGI (2003). *IT control objectives for Sarbanes-Oxley.* Rolling Meadows, IL: IT Governance Institute.

ITGI. (2005). *COBIT 4.0: control objectives and management guidelines.* Rolling Meadows, IL: Information Technology Governance Institute.

Jahner, S., & Krcmar, H. (2005). *Beyond technical aspects of information security: Risk culture as a success factor for IT risk management.* Paper presented at Americas Conference on Information Systems 2005.

Loch, K. D., Carr, H. H., & Warkentin, M. E. (1992). Threats to information systems: Today's reality, Yesterday's understanding. *MIS Quarterly, 16*, 173.

Mcfadzean, E., Ezingeard, J.-N., & Birchall, D. (2004). Anchoring information security governance research. In G. Dhillon & S. Furnell (Eds.), *Proceedings of the Third Security Conference.* Las Vegas, Nevada, USA.

Oshri, I., Kotlarsky, J., & Hirsch, C. (2005). *Security in networkable windows-based operating system devices.* Paper presented at Softwares Conference, Las Vegas, Nevada, USA

OST. (2004). *Cyber trust and crime prevention.* London: Office of Science & Technology—UK Department of Trade and Industry. HMSO.

Peters, T. J., & Waterman, R. H. (1982). *In search Of excellence: Lessons from America's best run companies.* New York: Harper and Row.

Reich, B. H. & Benbasat, I. (1996). Measuring the linkage between business and information technology objectives. *MIS Quarterly, 20*, 55-81.

Reich, B. H., & Benbasat, I. (2000). Factors that influence the social dimension of alignment between business and information technology objectives. *MIS Quarterly, 24*, 81-113.

Turnbull, N. (1999). *Internal control: Guidance for directors on the combined code:* The Turnbull report. London: The Institute of Chartered Accountants in England & Wales.

Venkatraman, N., & Camillus, J. C. (1984). Exploring the concept of 'fit' in strategic management. *Academy of Management Review, 9*, 513-525.

Whitman, M. E., & Mattord, H. J. (2003). *Principles of information security.* Boston, London: Thomson Course Technology.

Willcocks, L., & Margetts, H. (1994). Risk assessment and information systems. *European Journal of Information Systems, 3*, 127-138.

Chapter XVIII
Security Requirements Elicitation:
An Agenda for Acquisition of Human Factors

Manish Gupta
State University of New York, Buffalo, USA

Raj Sharman
State University of New York, Buffalo, USA

Lawrence Sanders
State University of New York, Buffalo, USA

ABSTRACT

Information security is becoming increasingly important and more complex as organizations are increasingly adopting electronic channels for managing and conducting business. However, state-of-the-art systems design methods have ignored several aspects of security that arise from human involvement or due to human factors. The chapter aims to highlight issues arising from coalescence of fields of systems requirements elicitation, information security, and human factors. The objective of the chapter is to investigate and suggest an agenda for state of human factors in information assurance requirements elicitation from perspectives of both organizations and researchers. Much research has been done in the area of requirements elicitation, both systems and security, but, invariably, human factors are not been taken into account during information assurance requirements elicitation. The chapter aims to find clues and insights into acquisition behavior of human factors in information assurance requirements elicitation and to illustrate current state of affairs in information assurance and requirements elicitation and why inclusion of human factors is required.

INTRODUCTION

In last few years, information security has attained a very important position in organizations and personal lives. A decade ago, it was very uncommon for colleges to offer any course in information security, privacy, or information assurance. In 2005, the U.S. National Security Agency certified 67 academic institutions as Centers of Academic Excellence in Information Assurance Education, which evidently underscores the importance of security of information in everyone's lives as corporate citizens and as individuals. However this has arisen to another interesting assumption that computer security is primarily a technical subject. This ignores the fact that computer security's technical aspects are only as effective as people designing, using, attacking, and protecting information systems. People are the cornerstone of information security and privacy. Security solutions that fail to take human factors into account are not going to be effective in protecting information systems or providing any assurance thereof. Schwartz (2005) quoted a survey finding that "89% of respondents believe major security breaches have been reduced as a result of IT security training and certification." According to the survey, the perceived benefits of training include "improved potential risk identification, increased awareness, improved security measures, and an ability to respond more rapidly to problems."

The chapter aims to investigate and suggest an agenda for state of human factors in information assurance requirements elicitation from perspectives of both organizations and researchers. For any project or information system implementation, requirements elicitation is one of the most important steps. Information security requirements have been long introduced as a vital component of overall requirements elicitation. Much research has been done in that area, as is also discussed in a following section. But, invariably, human factors are not been taken into account during

information assurance requirements elicitation. The chapter aims to find clues and insights into *acquisition behavior of human factors in information assurance requirements elicitation and to illustrate current state of affairs and importance of human factors of information assurance and requirements elicitation.* This chapter, based on survey and synthesis of existing literature, aims to bring out the current state of affairs in that area and also suggests why this is vitally critical for success of the information systems usage, more so, in light of growth of exploitation of human factors to manipulate and invalidate information systems.

SYSTEMS AND SECURITY REQUIREMENTS ELICITATION: HUMAN FACTORS

More often than not, it is becoming increasingly evident that the weakest links in an information-security chain are the people, because human nature and social interactions are much easier to manipulate than targeting the complex technological protections of information systems. Concerns and threats regarding human and social factors in organizational security are increasing at an exponential rate and shifting the informa-

Figure 1. Research coverage and areas

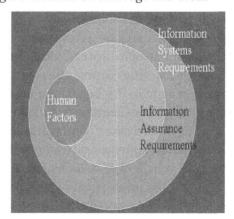

tion security paradigm. The growing number of instances of breaches in information security in the last few years has created a compelling case for efforts towards secure electronic systems. Security has been the subject of intensive research in the areas of cryptography, hardware, and networking. However, despite these efforts, designers often understand security as only the hardware or software implementation of specific cryptographic algorithms and security protocols. However, human factors are as important. Their non-functional nature imposes complex constraints on the emergent behavior of software-intensive systems, making them hard to understand, predict, and control. Figure 1 shows information systems requirements that have been amply researched, including human elements of it, though the concentric circle representing the information assurance requirements with the overlap with circle representing human factors is understudied.

Requirements engineering, a vital component in successful project development, often neglects sufficient attention to security concerns. Further, industry lacks a useful model for incorporating security requirements into project development. Studies show that upfront attention to security saves the economy billions of dollars. Industry is thus in need of a model to examine security and quality requirements in the development stages of the production lifecycle. Traditionally, security requirements have been derived in an *ad hoc* manner. Recently, commercial software development organizations have been looking for ways to produce effective security requirements. It is generally accepted that early determination of the stakeholder requirements assists in the development of systems that better meet the needs of those stakeholders. General security requirements defeat this goal because it is difficult to determine how they affect the functional requirements of the system. A benefit of considering human factors is also that the involvement of stakeholders in the high-level security analysis improves their

understanding of security and increases their motivation to comply with policies. Furthermore, the assessments of completeness, accuracy, and reliability of the requirements hinge on the analyst's ability to conduct effective inquiry (Waldron, 1986). Experimental results indicate that humans do not balance information costs and benefits well (Connolly & Gilani, 1982; Connolly & Thorn, 1987).

Analysts select a particular elicitation technique for any combination of four reasons (Hickey & Davis, 2004): (1) it is the only technique that the analyst knows; (2) it is the analyst's favorite technique for all situations; (3) the analyst is following some explicit methodology, and that methodology prescribes a particular technique at the particular time; and (4) the analyst understands intuitively that the technique is effective in the current circumstances (Hickey & Davis, 2004). Clearly, the fourth reason demonstrates the most sophistication by the analyst. We hypothesize that such maturity leads to improved understanding of stakeholders' needs, and thus a higher likelihood that a resulting system will satisfy those needs. Unfortunately, novice and expert systems analysts differ significantly in ability and maturity (Schenk, 1998). Most practicing analysts simply do not have the insight necessary to make such an informed decision, and therefore rely on one of the first three reasons. Note that the elicitation

Figure 2. The IS design motivations and components

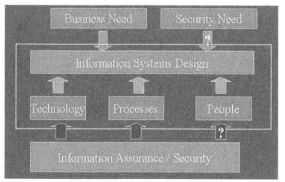

technique selection process is driven by problem, solution, and project domain characteristics as well as the state of the requirements. Figure 2 lays out different processes and motivations behind system design. The research focus arrow shown as a question mark is the primary focus of this study.

With the abundance of confidential information that organizations must protect, and with consumer fraud and identity theft at an all time high, security has never been as important as it is today for businesses and individuals alike. An attacker can bypass millions of dollars invested in technical and non-technical protection mechanisms by exploiting the human and social aspects of information security. While information systems deal with human interactions and communications through use of technology, it is often difficult to separate the human elements from the technological ones. In this chapter, we investigate the phenomena of under-acquisition of human factors during information assurance requirements elicitation. The importance of research of this study can be summarized as following salient points:

- *The weakest links in an information-security chain are the people and social networks*
- *Human nature and social interactions are much easier to manipulate than targeting the complex technological protections of information systems*
- *Security has been the subject of intensive research in the areas of technology and regulations*
- *While information systems deal with human interactions and communications through use of technology, it is impossible to separate the human elements from the technological ones*
- *Requirements engineering, a vital component in successful project development, often neglects sufficient attention to security concerns*

- *Industry lacks a useful model for incorporating security requirements into project development*
- *Upfront attention to security saves the economy billions of dollars*
- *Traditionally, security requirements have been derived in an ad hoc manner*
- *A benefit of considering human factors is also that the involvement of stakeholders in the high-level security analysis improves their understanding of security, and increases their motivation to comply with policies*
- *Insider threats are the greatest threat to individual and corporate privacy*
- *Insecure work practices and low security motivation have been identified by research on information security as major problems that must be addressed*

BACKGROUND AND DISCUSSIONS

Significant research has been done in the area of understanding and evaluating security requirements of information systems and processes from technical and procedural standpoints. No research, to the best of my knowledge, based on extensive literature survey, has focused on implications and role of human elements during requirements elicitation. While importance of information security is growing at an exponential rate in context of information systems and artifacts thereof, understanding the role of human factors in information security is equally critical.

Some of the existing research on security requirements based on technical and functional requirements of systems is discussed next. But none of them explicitly take into account human factors during security requirements elicitation. The common criteria for information technology security evaluation (CCITSE), usually referred to as the common criteria (CC), establishes a level of trustworthiness and confidence that should be placed in the security functions of products or systems and the assurance measures applied to them (Yavagal, Lee, Ahn, & Gandhi, 2005). CC achieves this by evaluating the product or system conformance with a common set of requirements set forth by it. Establishing secure systems assurance based on certification and accreditation (C&A) activities requires effective ways to understand the enforced security requirements, gather relevant evidences, perceive related risks in the operational environment, and reveal their causal relationships with other domain concepts (Lee, Gandhi, Muthurajan, Yavagal, & Ahn, 2006). Haley et al. present a framework for security requirements elicitation and analysis based upon the construction of a context for the system and satisfaction arguments for the security of the system (Haley et al., 2006). Mead and Stehney (2005) examine a methodology for both eliciting and prioritizing security requirements on a development project within an organization based on a model developed by the Software Engineering Institute's networked systems survivability (NSS) program. Haley, Laney, and Bashar (2004) illustrate how representing threats as crosscutting concerns aids in determining the effect of security requirements on the functional requirements. A lot of attention has been devoted to metrics focusing on operational security of deployed systems, analyzing defect rates, known and un-patched vulnerabilities, and configuration of systems (Dacier, 1994; Noel, Jajodia, O'Berry, & Jacobs, 2003). The TCSEC (TCSEC, 1985) ranks systems based on the number of security mechanisms, the scope of security mechanisms, and the granularity of security mechanisms. The activities and documents from the common criteria are tightly intertwined with the system development, which improves the quality of the developed system and reduces the additional cost and effort due to high security requirements (Vetterling, Wimmel, & Wisspeintner, 2002). This chapter reports on our experiences eliciting confidentiality requirements in a real world project in the health care area (Gürses, 2005). Sasse et al. argue that cur-

rent development practice suffers from two key problems: (1) Security requirements tend to be kept separate from other system requirements and not integrated into any overall strategy and (2) The impact of security measures on users and the operational cost of these measures on a day-to-day basis are usually not considered (Flechais, 2003).

Since software project failures are so rampant (Standish, 1995), it is quite likely that improving how the industry performs elicitation could have a dramatic effect on the success record of the industry (Hoffman & Lehner, 2001). Improving requirements elicitation requires us to first understand it (Hickey & Davis, 2004). Although many papers have been written that define elicitation, or prescribe a specific technique to perform during elicitation, none have yet defined a unified model of the elicitation process that emphasizes the knowledge needed to effectively elicit requirements from stakeholders. Better understanding of elicitation and the factors that should be considered during elicitation technique selection will improve the quality of the requirements elicitation process and, ultimately, increase the success of software development projects (Hickey & Davis, 2002). Most requirements models include a requirements elicitation activity, either as a separate activity or as part of another requirements activity (Hickey & Davis, 2004).

Requirements elicitation is all about determining needs of stakeholders. Most models of requirements elicitation focus on specific methodologies or techniques. Several researchers (Holbrook, 1990; Hsia et al., 1994) have developed specific models that define how to use scenarios for requirements elicitation. The state of the requirements drives technique selection because techniques vary significantly in their ability to elicit different types of requirements (Gottesdiener, 2002; Davis, 1993; Davis, 1998; Lauesen, 2002). The focus of this chapter is to highlight all techniques and investigate to what extent human factors are considered during information assurance requirements elicitation. Generally, decision-makers fall victim to two types of acquisition errors: over-acquiring and under-acquiring (Pitts & Browne, 2004). In IRD, over-acquisition involves the gathering of more information than is needed and results in wasted time and resources in the elicitation and analysis of requirements (Pitts & Browne, 2004). Under-acquisition, on the other hand, generates an incomplete view of the goals and functionality of the proposed system, leading to potential design problems, iterative redesign, implementation and maintenance difficulties, and possible system failure (Pitts & Browne, 2004).

There have been several studies on design methods for creating secure information systems. Some of them have utilized sociological and philosophical tenets of design paradigms (Backhouse, 1988, 1992; Dhillon & Backhouse, 2001; Siponen, 2005a; Siponen, 2005b). However, a direct link between specifically to highlight importance of human factors is lacking. There are several requirements elicitation methodologies employed by organizations driven by necessities that propose secure information systems design. Some security design methods emphasize more on conceptual level modeling, focusing more on the system features and environment. These methods tend to follow a strict structure for every system and use constraints as a basic tenet (Ellmer, Pernul, & Kappel, 1995; Pernul, 1992). There are models that view the key design entities, including humans, as organization-oriented. The business process paradigms consist of a secure information system design method suggested by Herrmann and Pernul (1998), and the fair and secure electronic markets method proposed by Ro¨hm and Pernul (2000). Common to these methods is an attempt to construct a modeling notation for describing security constraints in business process models (Siponen & Heikka, 2007). Siponen and Heikka's main finding was that secure information systems design methods provide modeling support only from particular perspectives, and therefore lack the comprehensiveness that may be needed in IS

development. As the design methods do not offer comprehensive modeling support, practitioners need to combine several design methods (Siponen & Heikka, 2007). As a result, future SIS design methods should provide modeling support at the organizational, conceptual, and technical levels (Siponen & Heikka, 2007).

One such paradigm analyzed by Siponen and Heikka (2007) was the responsibility modeling paradigm that includes secure information system design methods, representing the view that IS security requirements can be found by scrutinizing the job responsibilities in organizations (Siponen & Heikka, 2007). Siponen and Heikka (2007) analyzed several methods for their paper and suggest that the methods within this paradigm include a method by Strens and Dobson (1993), the semantic responsibility analysis method suggested by Backhouse and Dhillon (1996), the abuse case method suggested by McDermott and Fox (1999), McDermott (2001) and Sindre and Opdahl (2005), the task-based authorization method suggested by Thomas and Sandhu (1994). Strens and Dobson (1993) state that the context in which IS security requirements arises is poorly understood, and that understanding of users' responsibilities is the way to solve this problem. There are several methods in use today and are used based on specific methodology instructions or motivations. There is a severe lack of empirical and analytical research suggesting effects and influences of presence or absence of consideration of human factors from studying secure information systems design.

CONCLUSION AND FUTURE DIRECTIONS

Studies have consistently found that greater percentage of security defects in e-business applications are due to design-related flaws, which could be detected and corrected during applications development. Traditional methods of managing security vulnerabilities have often been ad hoc and inadequate, where most of the times human factors are not explicitly considered. Thus the designs are exposed to errors arising from two major facets: 1). humans designing the system and 2). the ones using it. A recent approach that includes understanding and incorporation of human and social factors promises to induce more effective security requirements as part of the application development cycle.

Security requirements engineering for effective information systems is mainly concerned with methods providing efficient systems that are economical and provide operationally effective protection from undesirable events (Lane, 1985), and as Anderson claims (Anderson, 2001), security engineering is about building systems to remain dependable in the face of malice, error, or mischance. It has been widely accepted that in order to effectively design secure systems, it is necessary to integrate security engineering principles into development techniques and introduce a development methodology that will consider security as an integral part of the whole development process (Devanbu & Stubblebine, 2000; Michailova, Doche, & Butler, 2002; Lamsweerde, 2004; Viega & McGraw, 2004). However, there is limited practice of secure development of applications and lack of research investigating the phenomenon of interaction human and social actors with the system and resulting influences. Security requirements engineering should provide techniques, methods, and standards for incorporating all the agents and actors while using repeatable and systematic procedures to ensure that the set of requirements obtained is complete, consistent and easy to understand, and analyzable by the different actors involved in the development of the system (Yu, 1995). Research is needed in employing and using the concepts of actors, goals, tasks, resources, and social dependencies for defining the interaction amongst actors and their intentions and motivations for interacting with the system or the organization where the system is deployed. So it is highly critical for

organizations and researchers to emphasize role and importance of human factors in security requirements gathering. There are many companies that, under competitive pressure to turn out applications with new features in a short time, relegate security to a lower priority; shortening the development time (Viega, Kohno, & Potter, 2001; Viega & McGraw, 2002; Mead & Stehney, 2005). Facilitating conditions (e.g., organizational support and availability of resources) can have a positive influence on behavioral intention (Venkatesh, 2000).

REFERENCES

Anderson, R. (2001). *Security engineering: A guide to building dependable distributed systems.* Wiley Computer Publishing.

Backhouse, J., & Dhillon, G. (1996). Structures of responsibilities and security of information systems. *European Journal of Information Systems, 5*(1), 2-10.

Baskerville, R. (1988). *Designing information systems security.* John Wiley Information Systems.

Baskerville, R. (1992). The developmental duality of information systems security, *Journal of Management Systems, 4*(1), 1-12.

Charles, B., Moffett, J. D., Laney, R., & Bashar, N. (2006, May). A framework for security requirements engineering. In *Proceedings of the 2006 International Workshop on Software Engineering for Secure Systems SESS '06.*

Connolly, T., & Gilani, N. (1982). Information search in judgment tasks: A regression model and some preliminary findings. *Organizational Behavior and Human Decision Processes, 30*(3), 330-350.

Connolly, T., & Thorn, B. K. (1987). Predecisional information acquisition: Effects of task variables on suboptimal search strategies. *Organizational Behavior and Human Decision Processes, 39*(3), 397-416.

Dacier, M. (1994). *Vers une 'evaluation quantitative de la s'ecurit'e, informatique.* Phd thesis, Institut National Polytechnique de Toulouse.

Davis, A., (1993). *Software requirements: Objects, functions and states.* Upper Saddle River, NJ: Prentice Hall.

Davis, A. (1998). A comparison of techniques for the specification of external system behavior. *Communications of the ACM, 31*(9), 1098-1115.

Devanbu, P. & Stubblebine, S. (2000). Software engineering for security: a roadmap. *In Proceedings of the Conference of the Future of Software Engineering.*

Dhillon, G., & Backhouse, J. (2001). Current directions in IS security research: toward socio-organizational perspectives. *Information Systems Journal, 11*(2).

Ellmer, E., Pernul, G., & Kappel, G. (1995). Object-oriented modeling of security semantics. *In Proceedings of the 11th Annual Computer Society Applications Conference (ACSAC'95).*

Flechais, I., Sasse, M. A., & Hailes, S. M. V. (2003, August). Security engineering: Bringing security home: a process for developing secure and usable systems. In *Proceedings of the 2003 Workshop on New Security Paradigms.*

Gottesdiener, E. (2002). *Requirements by collaboration.* Boston: Addison-Wesley.

Gürses, S., Jahnke, J. H., Obry, C., Onabajo, A., Santen, T., & Price, M. (2005, October). Eliciting confidentiality requirements in practice. In *Proceedings of the 2005 Conference of the Centre for Advanced Studies on Collaborative Research.*

Haley, C. B., Laney, R., & Bashar, N. (2004, March). Deriving security requirements from crosscutting threat descriptions. In *Proceedings*

of the 3rd International Conference on Aspect-Oriented Software Development.*

Herrmann, G., & Pernul, G. (1998). Towards security semantics in workflow management. In *Proceedings of the 31st Hawaii International Conference on Systems Sciences.*

Hickey, A., & Davis, A. (2002). The role of requirements elicitation techniques in achieving software quality. In C. Salinesi, B. Regnell, & K. Pohl (Eds.), *Proceedings of the Requirements Engineering Workshop: Foundations for Software Quality (REFSQ '02)* (pp. 165-171). Essen, Germany: Essener Informatik Beiträge.

Hickey, A. M., & Davis, A. M. (2004). A unified model of requirements elicitation. *Journal of Management Information Systems, 20*(4), 65-84.

Hofmann, H., & Lehner, F. (2001). Requirements engineering as a success factor in software projects. *IEEE Software, 18*(4), 58-66.

Holbrook, H. (1990). A scenario-based methodology for conducting requirements elicitation. *ACM SIGSOFT Software Engineering Notes, 15*(1), 95-104.

Hsia, P., Samuel, J., Gao, J., Kung, D., Toyoshima, Y., & Chen, C. (1994). Formal approach to scenario analysis. *IEEE Software, 11*(2), 33-41.

Lane, V. P. (1985). *Security of computer based information systems.* Macmillan Education Ltd.

Lauesen, S. (2002). *Software requirements: Styles and techniques.* London: Addison-Wesley.

Lee, S.-W., Gandhi, R., Muthurajan, D., Yavagal, D., & Ahn, G.-J. (2006, May). Building problem domain ontology from security requirements in regulatory documents. In *Proceedings of the 2006 International Workshop on Software Engineering for Secure Systems SESS '06.*

McDermott, J. (2001). Abuse-case-based assurance arguments. In *Proceedings of the 17th An-*

nual Computer Security Applications Conference (ACSAC).

McDermott, J., & Fox, C. (1999). Using abuse case models for security requirements. *In Proceedings of the 15th Annual Computer Security Applications Conference (ACSAC).*

Mead, N., & Stehney, T. (2005a). Security quality requirements engineering (SQUARE) methodology. *ACM SIGSOFT Software Engineering Notes, 30*(4), 1-7.

Mead, N. R., & Stehney, T. (2005b). Software engineering for secure systems (SESS)—building trustworthy applications: Security quality requirements engineering (SQUARE) methodology. *ACM SIGSOFT Software Engineering Notes, Proceedings of the 2005 Workshop on Software Engineering for secure systems—building trustworthy applications SESS '05, Volume, 30*(4).

Michailova, A., Doche, M., & Butler, M. (2002). *Constraints for scenario-based testing of object-oriented programs* (Technical Report). Electronics and Computer Science Department, University of Southampton.

Noel, S., Jajodia, S., O'Berry, B., & Jacobs, M. (2003). Efficient, minimum-cost network hardening via exploit dependency graphs. In *Proceedings of 19th Annual Computer Security, Applications Conference* (pp. 86-95). IEEE Computer Society.

Pernul, G. (1992). Security constraint processing during multilevel secure database design. In *Proceedings of the 8th Annual Computer Security Applications Conference.*

Pitts and Browne. (2004). Stopping behavior of systems analysts during information requirements elicitation. *JMIS, 21*(1), 203-226.

Ro"hm, A. W., & Pernul, G. (2000). COPS: a model and infrastructure for secure and fair electronic markets. *Decision Support Systems, 29*(4), 434-455.

Schenk, K., Vitalari, N., & Davis, K. (1998). Differences between novice and expert systems analysts: What do we know and what do we do? *Journal of Management Information Systems, 15*(Summer), 9-50.

Schwartz, M. (2005). *Organizations neglect human factors in security.* Retrieved from http://www.itcinstitute.com/display.aspx?id=363

Sindre, L., & Opdahl, A. (2005). Eliciting security requirements with misuse cases. *Computer Science and Engineering, 10*(1), 34-44.

Siponen, M. (2005a). Analysis of modern IS security development approaches: towards the next generation of social and adaptable ISS methods. *Information and Organization, 15*(4), 339-375.

Siponen, M. (2005b). An analysis of the traditional IS security approaches: implications for research and practice. *European Journal of Information Systems, 14*(3), 303-315.

Siponen, M., & Heikka, J. (2007). Do secure information system design methods provide ..., Inform. Softw. Technol. doi:10.1016/j.infsof.2007.10.011

Standish Group. (1995). *The CHAOS report.* West Yarmouth, MA. available at www.standishgroup.com.

Strens, R., & Dobson, J. (1993). How responsibility modeling leads to security requirements. In *Proceedings of the 1992 & 1993 ACM SIGCAS New Security Paradigm Workshop.*

TCSEC. (1985). *Department of defense trusted computer system evaluation criteria* (TCSEC: DoD 5200.28-STD). Department of Defense.

Thomas, R. K., & Sandhu, R. S. (1994). Conceptual foundations for a model of task-based authorizations. In *Proceedings of the 7th IEEE Computer Security Foundations Workshop.*

van Lamsweerde, A. (2004). Elaborating security requirements by construction of intentional anti-models. In *Proceedings of the International Conference on Software Engineering* (pp. 148-157).

Venkatesh, V. (2000). Determinants of perceived ease of use: integrating control, intrinsic motivation, and emotion into the technology acceptance model. *Information Systems Research, 11*(4), 342-365.

Vetterling, M., Wimmel, G., & Wisspeintner, A. (2002, November). Requirements analysis: Secure systems development based on the common criteria: the PalME project. In *Proceedings of the 10th ACM SIGSOFT Symposium on Foundations of Software Engineering.*

Viega, J., Kohno, T., & Potter, B. (2001). Trust and mistrust in secure applications. *Communications of the ACM, 44*(2), 31-36.

Viega, J., & McGraw, G. (2002). *Building secure software*. Boston: Addison-Wesley.

Viega, J., & McGraw, G. (2004). *Building secure software—how to avoid security problems the right way*. Reading, MA: Addison-Wesley.

Waldron, V. R. (1986). Interviewing for knowledge. *IEEE Transactions on Professional Communications, PC29*(2), 31-34.

Yavagal, D. S., Lee, S.-W., Ahn, G.-J., & Gandhi, R. A. (2005, March). Security: Common criteria requirements modeling and its uses for quality of information assurance (QoIA). In *Proceedings of the 43rd Annual Southeast Regional Conference ACM-SE 43* (Vol. 2).

Yu, E. (1995). *Modelling strategic relationships for process reengineering*. Ph.D. Thesis, Department of Computer Science, University of Toronto, Canada.

Chapter XIX
Do Information Security Policies Reduce the Incidence of Security Breaches:
An Exploratory Analysis

Neil F. Doherty
Loughborough University, UK

Heather Fulford
Loughborough University, UK

ABSTRACT

Information is a critical corporate asset that has become increasingly vulnerable to attacks from viruses, hackers, criminals, and human error. Consequently, organizations are having to prioritize the security of their computer systems in order to ensure that their information assets retain their accuracy, confidentiality, and availability. While the importance of the information security policy (InSPy) in ensuring the security of information is acknowledged widely, to date there has been little empirical analysis of its impact or effectiveness in this role. To help fill this gap, an exploratory study was initiated that sought to investigate the relationship between the uptake and application of information security policies and the accompanying levels of security breaches. To this end, a questionnaire was designed, validated, and then targeted at IT managers within large organizations in the UK. The findings presented in this chapter are somewhat surprising, as they show no statistically significant relationships between the adoption of information security policies and the incidence or severity of security breaches. The chapter concludes by exploring the possible interpretations of this unexpected finding and its implications for the practice of information security management.

INTRODUCTION

It has been claimed that "information is the firm's primary strategic asset" (Glazer, 1993), as it is the critical element in strategic planning and decision making as well as day-to-day operational control. Consequently, organizations must make every effort to ensure that their information resources retain their accuracy, integrity, and availability. However, ensuring the security of corporate information assets has become an extremely complex and challenging activity, due to the growing value of information resources and the increased levels of interconnectivity among information systems both within and among organizations (Garg et al., 2003). Indeed, the high incidence of security breaches suggests that many organizations are failing to manage their information resources effectively (Straub & Welke, 1998). One increasingly important mechanism for protecting corporate information, and in so doing reducing the occurrence of security breaches, is through the formulation and application of a formal information security policy (InSPy) (Hinde, 2002; von Solms & von Solms, 2004). Gaston (1996, p. 175) defines an InSPy as: "broad guiding statements of goals to be achieved; significantly, they define and assign the responsibilities that various departments and individuals have in achieving policy goals."

The role and importance of information security policies and the incidence and severity of security breaches are both topics that have attracted significant attention in the literature, but there is little evidence that these topics have been explicitly linked. Consequently, there has been little empirical exploration of the extent to which information security policies are effective, in terms of reducing security breaches. The aim of this chapter is to help fill this gap by reporting upon the results of a study that sought to empirically explore the relationship between the uptake and application of information security policies and the incidence of security breaches. The remainder of this chapter is organized into the following five sections: a review of the literature and a description of the conceptual framework; a discussion of the research methods employed; a presentation of the findings; a discussion of their importance and finally the conclusions and recommendations for future research.

LITERATURE REVIEW AND CONCEPTUAL FRAMEWORK

This section aims to present a discussion of the literature with regard to the role and importance of the InSPy and the common security threats, which such policies are intended to prevent. The section concludes with a critique of this literature, and the presentation of the conceptual framework for our study.

The Role of the Information Security Policy

The broad aim of the information security policy is to provide the "ideal operating environment" for the management of information security (Barnard & von Solms, 1998), by defining: "the broad boundaries of information security" as well as the "responsibilities of information resource users" (Hone & Eloff, 2002b, p. 145). More specifically, a good security policy should: "outline individual responsibilities, define authorized and unauthorized uses of the systems, provide venues for employee reporting of identified or suspected threats to the system, define penalties for violations, and provide a mechanism for updating the policy" (Whitman, 2004, p. 52).

The InSPy also has an important role to play in emphasizing management's commitment to, and support for, information security (Gaston, 1996; Hone & Eloff, 2002b; Kwok & Longley, 1999). While the InSPy provides the framework for facilitating the prevention, detection, and response to security breaches, the policy document typically is supported by standards that tend to have a more technical or operational focus (Dhillon, 1997).

In recent years, a consensus has emerged both within the academic and practitioner communities that the security of corporate information resources is predicated upon the formulation and application of an appropriate information security policy (e.g., Rees et al., 2003). As Hinde (2002) puts it, the information security policy is now the *sine qua non* (indispensable condition) *of* effective security management. In a similar vein, von Solms and von Solms (2004) note that the information security policy is the *heart and basis* of successful security management. However, while the InSPy may play an important role in effective information security management, there is growing recognition that the policy is unlikely to be a successful security tool, unless organizations adhere to a number of important prescriptions in their policy implementation (Hone & Eloff, 2002b). The following are probably the most commonly cited examples of best practice guidelines:

1. The policy must be widely and strongly disseminated throughout the organization (Hone & Eloff, 2002a; Hone & Eloff, 2002b; ISO, 2000; Sipponen, 2000).
2. The policy must be reviewed and revised frequently (Higgins, 1999; Hone & Eloff, 2002a; Hong et al., 2003).

It also has been suggested that policies must be tailored to the culture of the organization (Hone & Eloff, 2002b; ISO, 2000), well aligned with corporate objectives (ISO, 2000; Rees et al., 2003), and rigorously enforced (David, 2002). While the literature, with respect to the facilitators of effective information security policy utilization, undoubtedly is growing, no previous studies could be found that sought to empirically explore the importance of different success factors. Indeed, there is a very significant gap in the literature with

respect to empirical studies of the role that the InSPy has to play in the prevention of common security threats (Loch et al., 1992; Mitchell et al., 1999; Rees et al., 2003; Whitman, 2004), such as those summarized in the following section.

Threats to the Security of Information Assets

Information resources can retain their integrity, confidentiality, and availability only if they can be protected from the growing range of threats that is arrayed against them (Dhillon & Backhouse, 1996; Garg et al., 2003). Security threats — which have been defined as "circumstances that have the potential to cause loss or harm" (Pfleeger, 1997, p. 3) — come both from within and from outside the organization (Hinde, 2002). For example, common internal threats include "mistakes by employees" (Mitchell et al., 1999) and some categories of computer-based fraud (Dhillon, 1999), while attacks by hackers (Austin & Derby, 2003) and viruses (de Champeaux, 2002) are the most commonly cited types of external threat. The increasing vulnerability of computer-based information systems is underlined by the growing cost of security breaches (Austin & Darby, 2003). For example, Garg et al. (2003) estimate the cost of significant security breaches, such as "denial of service attacks" to be in the range *$17 to 28 million*. Given the growing cost of security breaches, many surveys have been undertaken that have sought to quantify the range and significance of threats that face computer-based information systems. A review of these surveys (Loch et al., 1992; Mitchell et al., 1999; Whitman, 2004) suggests that the breaches presented in Table 1 are probably the most common and most significant threats. While the threats to the security of information systems are both well documented and well understood, there is a continuing worry that such issues are not high on the organizational agenda. As Straub and Welke (1998) note, "Information security continues to be ignored by top manag-

Table 1. Common types of security breaches

Type of Breach	Description
Computer Virus	Computer programs that have the capability to automatically replicate themselves across systems and networks.
Hacking Incidents	The penetration of organizational computer systems by unauthorized outsiders, who are then free to manipulate data.
Unauthorized Access	The deliberate abuse of systems and the data contained therein by users of those systems.
Theft of Resources	Theft of increasingly valuable hardware, software, and information assets.
Computer-Based Fraud	Information systems, especially financial systems, are vulnerable to individuals who seek to defraud an organization.
Human Error	The accidental destruction or incorrect entry of data by computer users.
Natural Disasters	Damage to computing facilities or data resources caused by phenomena such as earthquakes, floods, or fires.
Damage by Employee	Disgruntled employees may seek revenge by damaging their employers' computer systems.

ers, middle managers, and employees alike. The result of this unfortunate neglect is that organizational systems are far less secure than they might otherwise be and that security breaches are far more frequent and damaging than is necessary" (p. 441). Therefore, there is a pressing need for more research that can highlight any strategies or approaches that might reduce the incidence and severity of security breaches.

Conceptual Framework and Research Hypotheses

A summary of the literature suggests that there are growing literatures both with regard to the role of information security policies and the nature and incidence of security breaches. Moreover, there is a general acceptance that the information security policy is an important, if not the most important, means of preventing such breaches (Loch et al., 1992; Mitchell et al., 1999; Whitman, 2004). Perhaps it is surprising that to date there has been little conceptual or empirical scrutiny to determine whether the incidence and severity of security breaches can be reduced through the adoption of an information security policy. The aim of the remainder of this section is to

describe the study designed to fill this gap before articulating the specific research hypotheses and presenting the research framework. It should be noted that a full discussion of the design of the questionnaire and the operationalization of the constructs discussed in this section is deferred to the following section. Given the lack of empirical research in the area, it was felt that an exploratory piece of work that embraced a wide range of issues would be most appropriate. To this end, the aim of the study was to explore how a variety of issues relating to the uptake and application of information security policies impacted upon the incidence of security breaches within large organizations. Based upon our review of the literature, it is possible to hypothesize that a number of distinct aspects of the InSPy might influence the incidence of security breaches. Each of these areas is represented as a significant construct on the conceptual framework (see Figure 1), and each can be linked to a research hypothesis, as described in the following paragraphs:

The Existence of an InSPy. The review of literature highlighted the strength of the consensus with regard to the importance of information security policy in countering security breaches

Figure 1. Conceptual framework

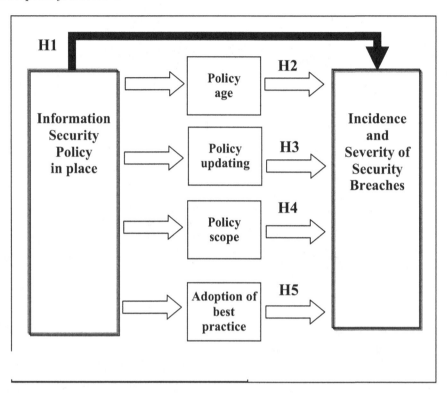

(Loch et al., 1992; Mitchell et al., 1999; Whitman, 2004). Therefore, it is reasonable to propose the following hypothesis:

H1: Those organizations that have a documented InSPy_are likely to have fewer security breaches in terms of both frequency and severity than those organizations that do not.

The Age of the InSPy. The literature has relatively little to say about the longevity of information security policies. However, the following hypothesis articulates the assumption that organizations with a long history of utilizing such policies might be more experienced and, therefore, effective in security management:

H2: Those organizations that have had InSPy in place for many years are likely to have fewer security breaches in terms of

both frequency and severity than those organizations that have not.

The Updating of the InSPy. There is a growing yet empirically untested view within the literature (Higgins, 1999; Hone & Eloff, 2002a; Wood, 1995) that InSPy should be updated regularly. Consequently, the following hypothesis can be proposed:

H3: Those organizations that update their InSPy frequently are likely to have fewer security breaches in terms of both frequency and severity than those organizations that do not.

The Scope of the InSPy: It has been suggested that the scope of the InSPy might vary greatly, depending upon which national or international information security standard has been adopted (Hone & Eloff, 2002b). What is less clear is how the scope of a policy might affect its successful deployment. However, it seems reasonable to propose the following relationship between the scope of the InSPy and the effectiveness of an organization's security management:

H4: Those organizations that have a policy with a broad scope are likely to have fewer security breaches in terms of both frequency and severity than those organizations that do not.

The Adoption of Best Practice: The International Standard (ISO, 2000) has some very clear advice about the factors that are important in ensuring the successful application of the InSPy, most of which have not been covered explicitly by the previous hypotheses. The corollary of this, as presented in the following hypothesis, is that the adoption of these success factors should lead to a reduction in security breaches:

H5: Those organizations that have adopted a wide variety of best practice factors are likely to have fewer security breaches in terms of both frequency and severity than those organizations that have not.

It should be noted that the original intention was to explore whether the active dissemination of an information security policy affected the incidence or severity of security breaches (Hone & Eloff, 2002a; Hone & Eloff, 2002b; ISO, 2000). However, as 99% of our sample reported that they actively disseminated their policies, it was not possible to test this hypothesis. While the hypotheses have been formulated to represent the outcomes that the researchers believed to be the most likely, it was recognized that, in some cases, alternative yet equally plausible results might be produced. For example, it might be that the existence of the InSPy is associated with a high incidence of security breaches in circumstances in which the policy has been implemented in direct response

to a poor security record. The possibility of alternative hypotheses is considered further in a later section.

The urgent need for more research and new insights in the information security domain was recently highlighted by Dhillon (2004), who noted that "information security problems have been growing at an exponential rate" (p. 4). In a similar vein, Kotulic and Clark (2004) argue that "the organizational level information security domain is relatively new and under researched. In spite of this, it may prove to be one of the most critical areas of research, necessary for supporting the viability of the firm" (p. 605). Therefore, it was envisaged that our study might provide some important new insights at the organizational level as to how the incidence and severity of security breaches might be controlled.

RESEARCH DESIGN

In order to explore successfully the five research hypotheses described in the previous section, it was necessary to employ survey methods so that the resultant data could be subjected to a rigorous statistical analysis. The aim of this section is to review how the questionnaire was designed, validated, and ultimately executed, and then to describe the characteristics of the sample.

Questionnaire Development, Validation, and Targeting

A detailed questionnaire was used to collect the data necessary to explore the research hypotheses proposed in the previous section. The questionnaire was organized into the following four sections:

Security Breaches. Respondents were asked to report on the incidence and severity of each of the eight most common types of security breach (see Table 1) that their organizations had experienced over the previous two years. The incidence variable was operationalized as a four-point ordinal scale (0; 1-5; 6-10; > 10), while the severity of breaches was measured using a five-point Likert scale.

The Existence and Updating of the Information Security Policy. This section sought to determine whether a responding organization had a documented InSPy and, if it did, how old it was and how often it was updated.

The Scope of the Information Security Policy. This section of the questionnaire was designed to evaluate the coverage of the information security policy. The respondent was presented with a list of 11 distinct issues, such as disclosure of information, Internet access, viruses, worms, and trojans that an information security policy might reasonably be expected to cover. These items all have been derived explicitly from the relevant International Standard (ISO, 2000) or from a white paper published by the SANS Institute (Canavan, 2003). For each of these issues, the respondent was invited to indicate whether the issue was covered in the policy document only, through the policy document and a supplementary procedure, or not explicitly covered in the InSPy.

Best Practice in Information Security Policy Adoption

The International Standard on information security management (ISO, 2000) suggests that there are 10 distinct factors that might influence the success of an information security policy, such as visible commitment from management and a good understanding of security requirements. For each of these factors, the respondent was asked to indicate the extent to which his or her organization was successful in adopting that factor, using a five-point Likert scale.

As there are few previous survey-based, empirical studies that explicitly address the application of information security policies, it was not possible to adapt specific questions and item measures from the existing literature. Consequently, once a draft questionnaire had been created, it was necessary to subject it to a rigorous validation process. More specifically, the draft questionnaire initially was validated through a series of pre-tests, first with four experienced IS researchers and then, after some modifications, with five senior IT professionals, all of whom had some responsibility for information security. The pre-testers were asked to critically appraise the questionnaire, focusing primarily on issues of instrument content, clarity, question wording, and validity before providing detailed feedback via interviews. The pre-tests were very useful, as they resulted in a number of enhancements being made to the structure of the survey and the wording of specific questions. Having refined the questionnaire, a pilot study exercise also was undertaken, which provided valuable insights into the likely response rate and analytical implications for the full survey.

As an InSPy is essentially a managerial, direction-giving document (Hone & Eloff, 2002b) rather than a technical document, it was recognized that the most appropriate individuals to target were executives with a high degree of managerial responsibility for information systems and technology. Senior IT executives, therefore, were targeted explicitly, as it was envisaged that they could provide the required organizational and managerial perspective. A list of the addresses of IT directors from large UK-based organizations was purchased from a commercial research organization. The decision to target only larger firms (firms employing more than 250 people) was based on the premise that small firms have few, if any, dedicated IT staff (Prembukar & King, 1992). A total of 219 valid responses were received from the 2,838 questionnaires mailed out, representing a response rate of 7.7%. While this response rate was rather disappointing, perhaps it was not surprising, given the increasingly sensitive nature of information security (Menzies, 1993). More recently, in an article entitled, "Why Aren't There More Information Security Studies?" Kotulic and Clark (2004) concluded that "it is nearly impossible to extract information of this nature [relating to information security] by mail from business organizations without having a major supporter" (p. 604). Consequently, while the sample was smaller than had been originally hoped, it was probably as good as could be expected, given the circumstances.

Sample Characteristics and Response Bias

The sample could be characterized in terms of both the size of the responding organizations and the sectors in which they primarily are operating. Of the valid respondents, 44% were employed in organizations having less than 1,000 employees, 33% in organizations with between 1,000 and 5,000 employees, and the remaining 23% in larger organizations with more than 5,000 employees. While the responses also were found to have come from a wide variety of industrial sectors, four were particularly well represented: manufacturing (24%); public services (20%); health (7%); and wholesale/retail (6%). Respondents also were asked to indicate the geographical spread of their organization, as it was envisaged that this might have an impact on the need for a formal information security policy. The majority of responding organizations (50%) operated from multiple locations within the UK, while a further 33% of organizations operated from multiple sites both within the UK and abroad, and the final 17% of the sample were located at a single site within the UK.

When undertaking survey-based research, there is always the danger that the results will be undermined or even invalidated through the introduction of bias. Therefore, it is important that active measures be taken to reduce the likelihood of bias having any such negative effects. In this research, the content validity of the constructs has

been established through the process of initially linking the variables to the research literature and then refining them through an extensive and comprehensive process of pre-testing and pilot testing. Any sample bias introduced through the loss of data from non-respondents is often harder to establish, as the data are not easily obtainable. However, it is possible to approximate this bias by comparing the answer patterns of early and late respondents (Lindner et al., 2001). Consequently, in this study, early and late responses were compared along key dimensions, such as the existence of policy, the age of the policy, the frequency of updating, and severity of breaches, in order to test for non-response bias. An independent samples t-test indicated that there were no significant differences in the profile of responses at the 5% level. These results imply that no detectable response bias exists in the sample and that the results are generalizable within the boundary of the sample frame.

RESEARCH FINDINGS

This section explores the five research hypotheses, as presented in a previous section, through a quantitative analysis of the survey data. Before reviewing the evidence relating to each of these hypotheses, it is important to summarize and discuss the data relating to both the incidence and severity of security breaches, as these two data items are used as the dependent variable throughout the analyses. It is beyond the scope of this chapter to present a detailed, descriptive analysis of the data relating to the uptake and application of information security policies. However, this information is available in a previous paper by the authors (Fulford & Doherty, 2003). Table 2 presents a simple, descriptive analysis of the data relating to the incidence and severity of security breaches.

It is interesting to note that all eight potential types of security breaches have been experienced

Table 2. The incidence and severity of security breaches

Type of Breach	Incidence of Breaches				Severity of Worst Breach					
	Approximate number of breaches in last two years				*Fairly Insignificant*			*Highly Significant*		*Mean value*
	0	**1-5**	**6-10**	**> 10**	**1**	**2**	**3**	**4**	**5**	
Computer virus	6	111	23	77	45	65	47	35	19	2.59
Hacking incident	142	66	1	5	42	21	10	5	4	1.92
Unauthorized access	106	83	13	10	32	42	21	5	7	2.23
Theft of resources	50	123	24	19	43	52	48	20	8	2.38
Computer-based fraud	187	23	0	2	15	10	3	6	2	2.15
Human error	41	85	19	65	32	61	43	23	10	2.48
Natural disaster	160	54	2	1	16	24	9	11	5	2.52
Damage by employees	185	28	0	0	20	8	7	2	2	1.82

within our sample and that there appears to be a relationship between the incidence of breaches and their perceived impact. For example, computer virus and human error are both very common types of breaches, and both have a significant impact, when they do strike. At the other end of the scale, damage by disgruntled employees, hacking incidents, and computer-based fraud all occur infrequently and have a relatively insignificant impact, when they do occur. The only type of breach to break this pattern is obviously natural disasters, which, despite their rare occurrences, do have a significant impact.

The Impact of the Adoption of an InSPy on Security Breaches

The vast majority of respondents (77%) in our sample reported that their organization had a formal, documented InSPy, with the remaining 23% of organizations confirming that they did not. Therefore, it was both possible and desirable to explore the degree of association between the adoption of InSPy and the resultant level of security breaches. The results of a series of chi-squared tests suggest that there is no statistical association between the adoption of InSPy and the incidence of security breaches (see Table 3, columns 2 to 4). An analysis of variance (ANOVA) also was used

to determine whether there was any association between the adoption of InSPys and the severity of each of the distinct types of security breach (see Table 3, columns 5 to 8).

An inspection of the data in Table 3 indicates that there are no statistically significant associations between the existence of an information security policy and either the incidence or the severity of any of the eight types of security breach. This is a particularly surprising result, given the prevailing orthodoxy that the InSPy is the primary mechanism for preventing security breaches (Rees et al., 2003). However, based upon this analysis, hypothesis H1 must be rejected.

The Impact of the Age of the InSPy on Security Breaches

It was envisaged that the greater experience of those organizations that had utilized an information security policy for many years might be manifested in more effective security management practices and, thus, fewer security breaches. As the respondents had been asked to estimate the number of years that their organizations had actively used an InSPy as a simple integer, the degree of association between the age of a policy and the incidence/severity of security breaches was explored using ANOVA (Table 4, columns

Table 3. The relationship between the adoption of InSPy and the incidence and severity of security breaches

Type of Breach	Incidence of Breaches (Chi-Squared Analysis)			Severity of Worst Breach (One-Way ANOVA)			
	Pearson Value	Deg. of Freedom	Two-Sided Prob.	Yes	No	F Ratio	F Prob.
Computer virus	0.730	3	0.878	2.59	2.69	0.215	0.644
Hacking incident	5.733	3	0.111	1.92	1.72	0.422	0.518
Unauthorized access	3.090	3	0.378	2.23	2.00	0.730	0.395
Theft of resources	1.905	3	0.607	2.38	2.51	0.429	0.513
Computer-based fraud	1.892	2	0.300	2.15	2.25	0.036	0.851
Human error	5.388	3	0.144	2.48	2.67	0.743	0.390
Natural disaster	6.469	3	0.089	2.52	2.32	0.361	0.550
Damage by employees	0.003	1	1.000	1.82	2.30	1.210	0.279

Note: A chi-squared test was used to test the association between the four categories of incidence (0, 1-5, 6-10, >10) and the two classes of InSPy existence (yes, no), while ANOVA was used to compare the mean severity of breaches and the two classes of InSPy existence.

Table 4. Relationship between the age of the InSPy and the incidence/severity of security breaches

Type of Breach	Incidence of Breaches (One-Way ANOVA)						Severity of Worst Breach (Correlation)	
	0	1-5	6-10	>10	F Ratio	F Prob.	Pearson Value	Two-Sided Significance
Computer virus	2.0	3.7	3.0	5.1	2.3 .	08	-0.05	0.501
Hacking incident	3.7	4.7	5.0	5.0	.77	.51	-0.05	0.718
Unauthorized access	3.5	3.9	4.5	10.1	6.4	.00**	-0.08	0.443
Theft of resources	4.1	3.7	3.4	7.27	3.7	.01*	-0.20	0.025*
Computer-based fraud	3.9	6.14	-	3.00	2.8 .	07	-0.13	0.513
Human error	3.9	3.5	3.7	4.9	1.2	.31	-0.00	0.963
Natural disaster	4.1	3.82	.8	-	.23	.80	-0.15	0.335
Damage by employees	7.8	8.9	-	-	2.9 .	09	-0.19	0.332

*Note: * Result significant at the 5% level; ** Result significant at the 1% level*

2 to 7) and correlation (Table 4, columns 8 to 9). The findings (see Table 4) indicate that there are two significant associations between the age of the policy and the incidence of security breaches. However, an inspection of this data suggests that in both cases where there is a significant result, the decreased incidence of security breaches is associated with recently deployed policies rather than those that have been in existence for a long time. Consequently, these findings are important,

as they suggest that there may be some complacency creeping into the security practices of those organizations with a longer history of policy utilization. When it comes to associations between the age of the policy and the severity of breaches, there is only one case (theft of resources) where there is a significant association. In this case, there is some support for hypothesis H2, as the Pearson correlation value is negative, indicating that older policies are associated with less severe

Table 5. Relationship between the frequency of updating InSPy and the incidence/severity of security breaches

Type of Breach	Incidence of Breaches (Chi-Squared Analysis)			Severity of Worst Breach (One-Way ANOVA)			
	Pearson Value	Degree of Freedom	Two-Sided Prob.	< Once a Year	?Once a Year	F Ratio	F Prob.
Computer virus	3.157	3	0.368	2.42	2.75	2.71	0.101
Hacking incident	1.679	3	0.642	2.00	1.92	0.065	0.799
Unauthorized access	3.108	3	0.375	2.21	2.25	0.030	0.864
Theft of resources	2.219	3	0.528	2.35	2.42	0.117	0.733
Computer-based fraud	1.098	2	0.577	2.08	2.20	0.052	0.821
Human error	5.253	3	0.154	2.67	2.42	1.467	0.228
Natural disaster	3.237	2	0.198	2.29	2.72	1.450	0.235
Damage by employees	1.198	1	0.274	1.73	1.87	0.087	0.770

Table 6. Relationship between the range of issues covered by the InSPy and the incidence/severity of security breaches

Type of Breach	Incidence of Breaches (One-Way ANOVA)						Severity of Worst Breach (Correlation))	
	0	1-5	6-10	> 10	F Ratio	F Prob.	Pearson Value	Two-Sided Significance
Computer virus	8.0	7.8	7.6	8.4	.79	.49	0.05	0.530
Hacking incident	8.0	7.9	10.0	6.5	.41	.75	-0.04	0.779
Unauthorized access	7.9	8.0	7.9	9.4	.86	.46	0.15	0.169
Theft of resources	7.4	8.0	8.2	9.3	2.4	.10	-0.05	0.536
Computer-based fraud	7.8	9.3	-	5.00	3.4	.04*	0.31	0.122
Human error	8.1	7.9	7.8	8.2	.29	.88	0.02	0.838
Natural disaster	7.9	8.5	3.5	-	3.8	.02*	0.24	0.105
Damage by employees	7.8	8.9	-	-	2.9	.09	0.08	0.678

Note: Result significant at the 5% level

Table 7. One-way ANOVA between the successful adoption of success factors and the incidence/severity of security breaches

Type of Breach	Incidence of Breaches (One-Way ANOVA)						Severity of Worst Breach (Correlation))	
	0	1-5	6-10	> 10	F Ratio	F Prob.	Pearson Value	Two-Sided Significance
Computer virus	3.17	2.95	2.85	2.85	0.42	0.74	0.031	0.699
Hacking incident	2.94	2.93	2.50	1.55	3.05	0.03*	0.120	0.365
Unauthorized access	2.99	2.82	2.76	2.75	1.01	0.39 -	0.070	0.529
Theft of resources	2.87	2.89	3.01	2.91	0.40	0.75 -	0.149	0.097
Computer-based fraud	2.89	2.87	-	2.40	0.27	0.76	0.305	0.138
Human error	2.98	2.87	3.12	2.81	0.99	0.39	-0.189	0.035*
Natural disaster	2.92	2.82	3.20	-	0.50	0.60	0.171	0.255
Damage by employees	2.91	2.86	-	-	0.09	0.76 -	0.088	0.655

*Note: * Result significant at the 5% level*

breaches. However, given that there is no strong or consistent evidence in support of the hypothesis, H2 also must be rejected.

Impact of InSPy Update Frequency on Security

The relationship between the frequency of updating an information security policy and the incidence and severity of security breaches was explored using a chi-squared analysis (Table 5, columns 2 to 4) and ANOVA (Table 5, columns 5 to 8). The frequency with which InSPys were updated was measured using a five-item categorical scale (less than every two years; every two years; every year; every six months; more than every six months). To use this variable in a chi-squared analysis, with the incidence of breaches variable, it was necessary to compress the five original categories into just two (less than once a year and at least once a year), to ensure that the expected frequencies in every cell of the contingency table were greater than five, a prerequisite of the chi-squared approach. Having used a two-category measure of frequency of updating for the chi-squared analysis, it made sense also to use it for the ANOVA in order to make the results more comparable.

The results of the two analyses (see Table 5) indicate that there are no statistically significant associations between the frequency with which the InSPy is updated and the incidence and severity of any of the eight types of security breach; hypothesis H3, therefore, also must be rejected. This result is also surprising in the face of the prevailing orthodoxy that the InSPy will be more effective if updated regularly (Hone & Eloff, 2002b).

The Impact of the Scope of an InSPy on Security Breaches

The scope of information security policies can vary greatly in terms of the numbers of issues

covered, so it was important to explore whether the scope of the policy was associated with the incidence and severity of security breaches. As discussed in a previous section, the scope of the policy was investigated by asking respondents to indicate which issues, from a list of 11 separate issues, were covered in their policies. Consequently, it was possible to create a new variable — total issues covered — that was the sum of the individual issues covered. This new variable, which was in the range 0-11, had a mean of 8.01 and a standard deviation of 2.61. The relationship between the total issues covered and the incidence and severity of security breaches was explored using an ANOVA (Table 6, columns 2 to 7) and a bivariate correlation (Table 6, columns 8 to 9).

The results relating to hypothesis H4 are quite interesting, as there are some statistically significant results. For example, the range of issues covered is associated significantly with the incidence of both computer-based fraud and natural disasters. However, an inspection of the data (Table 6, columns 2 to 5) is inconclusive; while the incidence of breaches is highest in both of these cases in which the issues covered are lowest, the lowest incidence of breaches is not associated with the highest numbers of issues covered. With regard to the severity of threats, there are no statistically significant associations between number of issues covered by the policy and the severity of security breaches. In summary, given that only two out of the 16 individual tests conducted resulted in statistically significant outcomes, there is little in the way of strong evidence in support of hypothesis H4, and, therefore, it must be rejected.

The Impact of the Adoption of Best Practice on Security Breaches

In order to explore effectively the relationship between the adoption of success factors and the incidence and severity of security breaches, it was necessary to derive a summated scale for the 10 success factors. An underlying assumption and fundamental requirement for constructing a summated measure of a metric construct is that the item scales all measure the same underlying construct. This was confirmed by undertaking internal reliability tests using the Cronbach alpha measure, which yielded a statistically significant score of 0.87. Having derived the overall measure for the adoption of best practice, ANOVA and correlation analyses were conducted to explore its association with the incidence and severity of security breaches (see Table 7).

The results of these analyses indicate that there is a statistical association between the summated success factors and security breaches for two out of the 16 tests conducted. Moreover, an inspection of the data provides some evidence in support of hypothesis H5. For example, success in adopting best practice is associated with a low occurrence of hacking incidents, whereas low success in adopting best practice is associated with a high incidence of hacking incidents. In a similar vein, success in adopting best practice is associated with low severity breaches due to human error, whereas low success in adopting best practice is associated with high severity incidents of human error. However, given that only two of the 16 tests were significant, there is insufficient evidence to support hypothesis H5, and, therefore, it must be rejected.

DISCUSSION

It was established in the literature review that the information security policy is now viewed as the basis for the dissemination and enforcement of sound security practices and, as such, should help to reduce the occurrence of security breaches (Loch et al., 1992; Mitchell et al., 1999; Whitman, 2004). Indeed, as Wadlow (2000) notes, "[I]f you ask any security professional what the single most important thing is that you can do to protect your network, they will unhesitatingly

say that it is to write a good security policy." Therefore, it came as something of a surprise in the present study to find almost no statistically significant relationships between the adoption of information security policies and the incidence or severity of security breaches. Consequently, it is important to explore the possible interpretations of this unexpected finding. The implications of this study for the practice of information security management are reviewed in this section, and then its limitations are explored.

Although there is little evidence of any formal, empirical studies that focus on the effectiveness of information security policies, the published literature does provide some clues as to why InSPys might be failing to stem the level of security breaches. Among these, the following are the most plausible reasons for deficient poli and ineffective policy implementationcies.

Difficulties of Raising Awareness. Sipponen (2000) highlights the problems of policy dissemination in the workplace. If employees are not made aware of a policy, then there is a danger that it will become a dead document rather than an active and effective security management tool. Given that nearly all the respondents in our study claimed to be actively disseminating their policies, questions must be raised about the effectiveness of their dissemination strategies, in the light of the consistently high levels of security breach witnessed. As Hone and Eloff (2002b) note, "a common failure of information security policies is that they fail to impact users on the ground" (p. 15).

Difficulties of Enforcement. As David (2002) notes, "having a policy and being able to enforce it are totally different things" (p. 506). Hinde (2002) provides evidence that the problem of policy enforcement might stem primarily from the difficulties of getting employees to read and take heed of policies. As Wood (2000) notes, the expectation that "users are going to look at a centralized information security policy is just unrealistic and bound to lead to disappointing results" (p. 14).

Policy Standards Are Too Complex. Many organizations lack the skills and experience to formulate an information security policy. Therefore, they typically will refer to one of the many international information security standards, such as ISO17799, COBIT, or GMITS (Hone & Eloff, 2002a). While such standards are recognized as a "good starting point for determining what an InSPy should consist of" (Hone & Eloff, 2002a, p. 402), in practice, they can be complex and time consuming to apply (Arnott, 2002).

Inadequate Resourcing. In too many cases, there are "insufficient resources available to devote to the monitoring and enforcement of policies" (Moule & Giavara, 1995, p. 8). Effective security management requires a great deal of time, effort, and money, which many organizations are not prepared to commit.

Failure to Tailor Policies. It has been argued that the security requirements of an organization will be dependent on the types of information being processed (Pernul, 1995) and on the culture of the organization (Hone & Eloff, 2002a). Consequently, an InSPy must be tailored to its organizational context. However, because many organizations rely on international standards as the point of departure for developing a policy, they often apply a generic solution rather than tailor it to their own circumstances.

It is very likely that the factors reviewed previously provide at least a partial explanation of why InSPys are failing to have a significant impact on the incidence and severity of security breaches. However, the drivers for adopting or enhancing an information security policy also might help

to explain why all five of our hypotheses were ultimately rejected. Our basic thesis was that organizations that had formulated a policy that was updated regularly, broad in scope, and adhered to best practice, would have fewer security breaches than those organizations that had not. An alternative thesis might be that, rather than deploying policies to prevent breaches, many organizations might be adopting or enhancing a policy in response to a spate of security breaches. However, if there was any significant evidence in support of this alternative thesis in which the direction of causality is simply reversed, then a large number of statistically significant associations still might have been expected. Consequently, one plausible explanation of our findings is that there is a mixture of drivers; in some instances, policies are doing their job and preventing breaches, and in other cases, policies are being implemented or enhanced in response to a high incidence of breaches.

While the previous discussion might help to explain the apparent ineffectiveness of information security policies, any manager with responsibility for the formulation of his or her organization's information security policy needs to heed the messages that are inherent in these findings. First, the findings suggest that there is no room for complacency; it is not enough simply to produce a policy, even if that policy has a broad scope, adheres to best practice, and is updated regularly. Steps must be taken to ensure that the policy is tailored to its organizational context and then enforced, which, in turn, means that the policy must be disseminated appropriately and well resourced. Moreover, the results suggest that organizations need to be more proactive in evaluating the effectiveness of their policies; when security breaches occur, the policy should be reviewed to determine how such incidents can be avoided in the future. It is particularly important for those organizations who already deploy an appropriate policy and who appear to be following best practice in its application yet still suffer a high incidence of security breaches to evaluate critically their security policy and security practices.

This research also should be of interest to the information management research community. As it is one of the first empirical studies to explicitly tackle the relationship between the information security policy and the level of security breaches, many new variables and item measures have been identified and validated; these might be incorporated usefully in future research. Moreover, the study has highlighted the need for far more research in this area in order to explore further the relationship between the information security policy and security breaches and to determine what steps are needed to improve its effectiveness.

Research into the adoption of sophisticated policies within the organizational context is an ambitious undertaking and, therefore, contains a number of inherent limitations. In particular, the adoption of the survey format restricts the range of issues and constructs that can be explored; the selection of a very narrow sampling frame reduces the generalizability of the results; and, finally, there is potential response bias associated with the single-informant. Moreover, the survey approach cannot help provide meaningful explanations of why no statistically significant findings were derived from our analyses. Consequently, while the study provides many interesting insights, these limitations do highlight the need for follow-up studies to be conducted employing different methods and targeting different populations. When considering future studies, it will be important for researchers to be creative in finding ways to secure organizational buy-in to their studies in order to avoid the difficulties of response witnessed in this and other information security projects (Kotulic & Clarke, 2004).

CONCLUDING REMARKS

The work presented in this chapter makes an important contribution to the information security literature, as it presents the first empirical study of the relationship between the application of information security policies and the incidence and severity of security breaches. The key result of this research is the finding that there is no statistically significant relationship between the existence and application of information security policies and the incidence or severity of security breaches. While a number of plausible explanations have been proffered to help understand this somewhat surprising finding, there is an urgent need for follow-up studies to explore what can be done to improve the effectiveness of information security policies. To this end, a series of follow-up interviews and focus groups to help interpret and explain the results of the quantitative analysis currently are being planned. As the project unfolds, it is anticipated that the findings will help organizations to better understand the value of security policies and to pinpoint the policy areas for prioritization.

ACKNOWLEDGMENT

The provisional version of the research framework upon which this chapter is based was presented at the IRMA Conference (Doherty & Fulford, 2003). The authors would like to thank the chapter reviewers and conference participants for their helpful comments, as these greatly shaped our thinking with regard to this chapter.

REFERENCES

Arnott, S. (2002, February). Strategy paper. *Computing.*

Austin, R.D. & Darby, C.A. (2003, June). The myth of secure computing. *Harvard Business Review.*

Barnard, L. & von Solms, R. (1998). The evaluation and certification of information security against BS 7799. *Information Management and Computer Security, 6*(2), 72-77.

Canavan, S. (2003). An information security policy development guide for large companies. *SANS Institute.* Retrieved from *http://www.SANS.org*

David, J. (2002). Policy enforcement in the workplace. *Computers and Security, 21*(6), 506-513.

De Campeaux, D. (2002). Taking responsibility for worms and viruses. *Communications of the ACM, 45*(4), 15-16.

Dhillon, G. (1997). *Managing information systems security.* London: Macmillan Press.

Dhillon, G. (1999). Managing and controlling computer misuse. *Information Management and Computer Security, 7*(4), 171-175.

Dhillon, G. (2004). The challenge of managing information security. *International Journal of Information Management, 24,* 3-4.

Dhillon, G. & Backhouse, J. (1996). Risks in the use of information technology within organizations. *International Journal of Information Management, 16*(1), 65-74.

Doherty, N.F. & Fulford, H. (2003). Information security policies in large organisations: Developing a conceptual framework to explore their impact. In M. Khosrow-Pour (Ed.), *Information Technology & Organizations: Trends, Issues, Challenges & Solutions, 2003 Information Re-* *sources Management Association International Conference*, Philadelphia, Pennsylvania, May 18-21 (pp. 1052-1053). Hershey, PA: Idea Group Publishing.

Fulford, H. & Doherty, N.F. (2003). The application of information security policies in large UK-based organizations. *Information Management and Computer Security, 11*(3), 106-114.

Garg, A., Curtis, J., & Halper, H. (2003). Quantifying the financial impact of information security breaches. *Information Management and Computer Security, 11*(2), 74-83.

Gaston, S.J. (1996). *Information security: Strategies for successful management.* Toronto: CICA.

Glazer, R. (1993). Measuring the value of information: The information intensive organization. *IBM Systems Journal., 32*(1), 99-110.

Higgins, H.N. (1999). Corporate system security: Towards an integrated management approach. *Information Management and Computer Security, 7*(5), 217-222.

Hinde, S. (2002). Security surveys spring crop. *Computers and Security, 21*(4), 310-321.

Hinde, S. (2003). Cyber-terrorism in context. *Computers and Security, 22*(3), 188-192.

Hone, K. & Eloff, J.H.P. (2002a). Information security policy: What do international security standards say. *Computers & Security, 21*(5), 402-409.

Hone, K. & Eloff, J.H.P. (2002b). What makes an effective information security policy. *Network Security, 20*(6), 14-16.

Hong, K., Chi, Y., Chao, L., & Tang, J. (2003). An integrated system theory of information security management. *Information Management and Computer Security, 11*(5), 243-248.

I.S.O. (2000). *Information technology. Code of practice for information security management, ISO 17799*. International Standards Organization.

Kotulic, A.G. & Clark, J.G. (2004). Why there aren't more information security research studies. *Information & Management, 41*, 5907-607.

Kwoc, L. & Longley, D. (1999). Information security management & modelling. *Information Management and Computer Security, 7* 1), 30-39.

Lindner, J.R., Murphy, T.H., & Briers, G.E. (2001). Handling non-response in social science research. *Journal of Agricultural Education, 42*(4), 43-53.

Loch, K.D., Carr, H.H., & Warkentin, M.E. (1992). Threats to information systems: Today's reality, yesterday's understanding. *MIS Quarterly, 16*(2), 173-186.

Menzies, R. (1993). Information systems security. In J. Peppard (Ed.), *IT strategy for business*. London: Pitman Publishing.

Mitchell, R.C., Marcella, R., & Baxter, G. (1999). Corporate information security. *New Library World, 100* 1150), 213-277.

Pernul, G. (1995). Information systems security: Scope, state of the art and evaluation of techniques. *International Journal of Information Management, 15*(3), 165-180.

Pfleeger, C.P. (1997). *Security in computing*. Englewood Cliffs, NJ: Prentice Hall.

Premkumar, G. & King, W.R. (1992). An empirical assessment of information systems planning and the role of information systems in organizations. *Journal of Management Information Systems, 19*(2), 99-125.

Rees, J., Bandyopadhyay, S., & Spafford, E.H. (2003). PFIRES: A policy framework for information security. *Communications of the ACM, 46*(7), 101-106.

Siponen, M. (2000). Policies for construction of information systems' security guidelines. In *Proceedings of the 15th International Information Security Conference (IFIP TC11/SEC2000)*, Beijing, China, August (pp. 111-120).

Straub, D.W. & Welke, R.J. (1998). Coping with systems risk: Security planning models for management decision making. *MIS Quarterly, 22*(4), 441-470.

von Solms, B. & von Solms, R. (2004). The ten deadly sins of information security management. *Computers & Security, 23*, 371-376.

Wadlow, T.A. (2000). *The process of network security*. Reading, MA: Addison-Wesley.

Whitman. (2004). In defense of the realm: Understanding threats to information security. *International Journal of Information Management, 24*, 3-4.

Wood, C.C. (1996). Writing infosec policies. *Computers & Security, 14*(8), 667-674.

Wood, C.C. (2000). An unappreciated reason why information security policies fail. *Computer Fraud & Security, 10*, 13-14.

This work was previously published in Information Resources Management Journal, Vol. 18, No. 4, edited by M. Khosrow-Pour, pp. 21-39, copyright 2005 by IGI Publishing, formerly known as Idea Group Publishing (an imprint of IGI Global).

Compilation of References

Aaltonen, M., & Wilenius, M. (2002). *Osaamisen ennakointi*. Helsinki, Finland: Edita Prima Oy.

ACM SIGCHI. (1996). *Curricula for human-computer interaction*. Retrieved March 20, 2007, from http://sigchi.org/cdg/cdg2.html#2_3_3

Adams, A., Bochner, S., & Bilik, L. (1998). The effectiveness of warning signs in hazardous work places: Cognitive and social determinants. *Applied Ergonomics, 29*, 247-254.

Adams, J. (1999). *Risk-benefit analysis: Who wants it? Who needs it?* Paper presented at the Cost-Benefit Analysis Conference, Yale University.

Adams, J. (2005). *Risk management, it's not rocket science: it's more complicated* draft paper available from http://www.geog.ucl.ac.uk/~jadams/publish.htm

Adams, J., & Thompson, M. (2002). *Taking account of societal concerns about risk. Framing the problem* (Research Rep. 035). London: Health and Safety Executive,

Advergaming on the blockdot Web site. (n.d.). Retrieved April 27, 2007, from http://games.blockdot.com/basics/index.cfm/.

Advergaming on the innoken Web site. (n.d.). Retrieved April 27, 2007, from http://www.innoken.com/ar_brandgames.html/.

Ahvenainen, S., Helokunnas, T., & Kuusisto, R. (2003). Acquiring information superiority by time-divergent communication. In B. Hutchinson (Ed.), *Proceedings of the 2nd European Conference on Information Warfare and Security* (pp. 1-9). Reading, UK: MCIL, Reading.

Akrich, M. (1992). The de-scription of technical objects. In W. E. Bijker & J. Law (Eds.), *Shaping technology/building society: Studies in sociotechnical change* (pp. 205-224). Cambridge, MA/London: MIT Press.

Alberts, C., & Dorofee, A. (2002, July). *Managing information security risks: The OCTAVE (SM) approach*. Boston: Addison Wesley.

Alexander, I. (2002, September). Modelling the interplay of conflicting goals with use and misuse cases. *Proceedings of the 8th International Workshop on Requirements Engineering: Foundation for Software Quality (REFSQ-02)*, Essen, Germany (pp. 9-10).

Alexander, I. (2003, January). Misuse cases: Use cases with hostile intent. *IEEE Software, 20*(1), 58-66.

America Online and the National Cyber Security Alliance (2004). *AOL/NCSA online safety study*. http://www.staysafeonline.info/news/safety_study_v04.pdf

American Management Association. (2005). *Workplace e-mail and instant messaging survey*. Retrieved March 2006, from http://www.amanet.org/research/

American National Standards Institute (ANSI). (2002). *Criteria for safety symbols* (Z535.3-Revised). Washington, DC: National Electrical Manufacturers Association.

Anderson, A. R. (Ed.). (1964). *Minds and machines*. Prentice Hall.

Anderson, R. (2001). *Security engineering: A guide to building dependable distributed systems*. New York: Wiley.

Antonopoulos, A. M., & Knape, J. D. (2002). Security in converged networks (featured article). *Internet Telephony*, *August*. Retrieved April 15, 2007, from http://www. tmcnet.com/it/0802/0802gr.htm

AOL/NCSA. (2005). *AOL/NCSA online safety study*. America Online and the National Cyber Security Alliance, December 2005. Retrieved March 21, 2007, from http://www.staysafeonline.info/pdf/safety_study_2005. pdf

Applehans, W., Globe, A., & Laugero, G. (1999). *Managing knowledge*. Boston: Addison-Wesley.

Applekid. (author's name). (2007). *The life of a social engineer*. Retrieved April 15, 2007, from http://www. protokulture.net/?p=79

APWG. (2007). *Phishing activity trends report for the month of February, 2007*. Retrieved April 15, 2007, from http://www.antiphishing.org/reports/apwg_report_february_2007.pdf

Argonne (2006). *Simulated 'social engineering' attack shows need for awareness*. Retrieved April 15, 2007, from http://www.anl.gov/Media_Center/Argonne_News/2006/an061113.htm#story4

Arnott, S. (2002, February). Strategy paper. *Computing*.

Ashenden, D., & Ezingeard, J.-N. (2005). *The need for a sociological approach to information security risk management*. Paper presented at the 4th Annual Security Conference. Las Vegas, Nevada, USA.

Association for the Advancement of Artificial Intelligence. (2007). Cognitive science. Retrieved on March 20, 2007, from http://www.aaai.org/AITopics/html/cogsci.html

Athabasca University. (2000). *Ergonomics resources*. Retrieved April 17, 2007, from http://scis.athabascau. ca/undergraduate/ergo.htm

Athanasopoulos, E., & Antonatos, S. (2006). Enhanced captchas: Using animation to tell humans and computers apart. In H. Leitold & E. Leitold (Eds.), *Commu-nications and multimedia security* (Vol. 4237, pp. 97-108). Springer.

Austin, R.D. & Darby, C.A. (2003, June). The myth of secure computing. *Harvard Business Review*.

Awad, E., & Ghaziri, H. (2004). *Knowledge management*. Upper Saddle River, NJ: Prentice Hall.

Axelrod, C. W. (2005). The demise of passwords: Have rumors been exaggerated? *The ISSA Journal, May*, 6-13.

Axelrod, C. W. (2007). The dynamics of privacy risk. *Information Systems Control Journal, 1*, 51-56.

Axelrod, C. W. (2007). Analyzing risks to determine a new return on security investment: Optimizing security in an escalating threat environment. In H.R. Rao, M. Gupta, & S. Upadhyaya (Eds.), *Managing information assurance in financial services* (pp. 1-25). Hershey, PA: IGI Global.

Axelrod, C.W. (1979). *Computer effectiveness: Bridging the management-technology gap*. Washington, D.C.: Information Resources Press.

Backhouse, J., & Dhillon, G. (1996). Structures of responsibilities and security of information systems. *European Journal of Information Systems, 5*(1), 2-10.

Baird, H. S., & Bentley, J. L. (2005). Implicit captchas. In *Proceedings of Spie/IS&T Conference on Document Recognition and Retrieval Xii*.

Baird, H., & Riopka, T. (2004, Dec). ScatterType: a reading CAPTCHA resistant to segmentation attack. In L. L. J. M. D. M. W. A. Y (Ed.), *Vision geometry Xiii. Proceedings of the Spie* (Vol. 5676, pp. 197-207).

Balfanz, D., Durfee, G., Grinter, R., Smetters, D., & Stewart, P. (2004). Network-in-a-box: How to set up a secure wireless network in under a minute. In *Proceedings of the 13ᵗʰ Conference on USENIX Security Symposium* (pp. 207–222). Berkeley: USENIX Association.

Balfanz, D., Smetters, D., Stewart, P., & Wong, H. C. (2002). Talking to strangers: Authentication in ad-hoc wireless networks. In *Proceedings of Symposium on Network and Distributed Systems Security (NDSS)*.

Ball, K. (2006). Expert report: Workplace. In D. M. Wood (Ed.), *Surveillance studies network, a report on the surveillance society for the information commissioner (UK), appendices* (pp. 94-105). London.

Bank, D. (2005). "Spear phishing" tests educate people about online scams. *The Wall Street Journal*. Retrieved March 2, 2006, from http://online.wsj.com/public/article/SB112424042313615131-z_8jLB2WkfcVtgdAWf6LRh733sg_20060817.html?mod=blogs

Barnard, L. & von Solms, R. (1998). The evaluation and certification of information security against BS 7799. *Information Management and Computer Security, 6*(2), 72-77.

Baron, A. (1965). Delayed punishment of a runway response. *Journal of Comparative and Physiological Psychology, 60,* 131-134.

Baskerville, R. (1988). *Designing information systems security*. John Wiley Information Systems.

Baskerville, R. (1991). Risk analysis: An interpretive feasibility tool in justifying information systems security. *European Journal of Information Systems, 1*(2), 121-130

Baskerville, R. (1992). The developmental duality of information systems security, *Journal of Management Systems, 4*(1), 1-12.

Baskerville, R. (1993). Information systems security design methods: Implications for information systems development. *Computing Surveys, 25*(4), 375-414.

Baskerville, R. Investigating information systems with action research. *Communications of the Association for Information Systems, 19*(2). Retrieved October 5, 2006, from http://www.cis.gsu.edu/~rbaskerv/CAIS_2_19/CAIS_2_19.htm

Baskerville, R., & Siponen, M. (2002). An information security meta-policy for emergent organizations. *Journal of Logistics Information Management, 15*(5/6), 337-346.

Baskerville, R., & Wood-Harper, A.T. (1999). A critical perspective on action research as a method for information systems research. *Journal of Information Technology, 11*, 235-246.

Baum, M. (1997). The ABA digital signature guidelines. *Computer Law & Security Report, 13*(6), 457-458.

Beck, U. (1992). *Risk society*. London: Sage Publishers.

Bell, W. (1998). *Foundations of futures studies, vol II, values, objectivity, and the good society*. New Brunswick, London: Transaction Publishers.

Belsis, P., Kokolakis, S., & Kiountouzis, E. (2005). Information systems security from a knowledge management perspective. *Information Management & Computer Security, 13*(3), 189-202.

Bergson, H. (1911). *Creative evolution*. Lanham, MD: Henry Holt and Company, University Press of America, TM Inc.

Berkovsky, S., Eytani, Y., Kuflik, T., & Ricci, F. (2006, April). *Hierarchical neighborhood topology for privacy enhanced collaborative filtering*. Paper presented at CHI 2006 Workshop on Privacy-Enhanced Personalization (PEP2006), Montreal, Canada.

bernz (author's name). (n.d.). *The complete social engineering FAQ*. Retrieved April 15, 2007, from http://www.morehouse.org/hin/blckcrwl/hack/soceng.txt

Betteridge, I. (2005). Police foil $420 million keylogger scam. *eWeek.com*. http://www.eweek.com/article2/0,1895,1777706,00.asp

Birch, D. (1997). The certificate business: Public key infrastructure will be big business. *Computer Law & Security Report, 13*(6), 454-456.

Birchall, D., Ezingeard, J.-N., Mcfadzean, E., Howlin, N., & Yoxall, D. (2004). *Information assurance: Strategic alignment and competitive advantage*. London: GRIST.

Blass, T. (2002). The man who shocked the world. *Psycology Today*. Retrieved March 9, 2006, from http://www.psychologytoday.com/articles/pto-20020301-000037.html

Blizzard entertainment ltd., press release January 2007. (n.d.). Retrieved April 27, 2007, from http://www.blizzard.com/press/070111.shtml

Bloom, E., Schachter, M., & Steelman E. H. (2003). Competing interests in the post 9-11 workplace: the new line between privacy and safety. *William Mitchell Law Review, 29*, 897-920.

Boehm, B. W. (1988). A spiral model of software development and enhancement. *IEEE Computer, 21*(5), 61-72.

Bogner, M. S. (2004). *Misadventures in health care: Inside stories*. Mahwah, NJ: Lawrence Erlbaum Associates.

Booysen, H. A. S., & Eloff, J. H. P. (1995). A methodology for the development of secure application systems. *Proceeding of the 11ᵗʰ IFIP TC11 International Conference on Information Security.*

Borgida, E., and Nisbett, R. E. (1977). The differential impact of abstract vs. concrete information on decisions. *Journal of Applied Social Psychology, 7*, 258-271.

Bowyer, B. (2003). Toward a theory of deception. *International Journal of Intelligence and Counterintelligence, 16*, 244-279.

Boyer, A., Castagnos, S., Anneheim, J., Bertrand-Pierron, Y., & Blanchard, J-P. (2006, December). Le filtrage collaboratif : Pistes d'applications dans le domaine bancaire et présentation de la technologie. *Dossiers de la veille technologique du Crédit Agricole S.A.* : Number 27.

Bresciani, P., Perini, A., Giorgini, P., Giunchiglia, F., & Mylopoulos, J. (2004) Tropos: An agent-oriented software development methodology. *Autonomous Agents and Multi-Agent Systems, 8*(3), 203-236.

Brooks, F. (1995, August). *The mythical man-month: Essays on software engineering, 20th Anniversary Edition* (1ˢᵗ ed.). Boston: Addison-Wesley.

Brostoff, S., Sasse, A., & Weirich, D. (2002). Transforming the "weakest link": A human-computer interaction approach to usable and effective security. *BT Technology Journal, 19*(3), 122-131.

Brunker, M. (2004, September). *Are poker bots raking online pots?* Retrieved April 27, 2007, from http://www.msnbc.msn.com/id/6002298/

BSI. (1993). *DISC PD0003: A code of practice for information security management*. London: British Standards Institute.

BSI. (2002). BS7799-2:2002. *Information security management. Specification with guidance for use*. British Standards Institute.

BSI. (2003). BS15000-2:2003 *IT service management. Code of practice for service management*. British Standards Institute.

Canavan, S. (2003). An information security policy development guide for large companies. *SANS Institute*. Retrieved from *http://www.SANS.org*

Canny, J. (2002, May). Collaborative filtering with privacy. In *Proceedings of the IEEE Symposium on Security and Privacy* (pp. 45-57). Oakland, CA.

Canny, J. (2002, August). Collaborative filtering with privacy via factor analysis. In *Proceedings of the 25th Annual International ACM SIGIR Conference on Research and Development in Information Retrieval (SIGIR 2002)*. Tampere, Finland.

Carnegie Mellon Computer Emergency Response Team (CERT). (2007). *Computer emergency response team statistics*. Retrieved April 25, 2007, from http://www.cert.org/stats/cert_stats.html#incidents

Carstens, D. S., Malone, L., & Bell, P. (2006). Applying chunking theory in organizational human factors password guidelines. *Journal of Information, Information Technology, and Organizations, 1*, 97-113.

Carstens, D. S., McCauley-Bell, P., Malone, L., & DeMara, R. (2004). Evaluation of the human impact of password authentication practices on information security. *Informing Science Journal, 7*, 67-85.

Castagnos, S., & Boyer, A. (2006, April). *From implicit to explicit data: A way to enhance privacy*. Paper presented at CHI 2006 Workshop on Privacy-Enhanced Personalization (PEP 2006), Montreal, Canada.

Castagnos, S., & Boyer, A. (2006, August). A client/server user-based collaborative filtering algorithm: Model and implementation. In *Proceedings of the 17th European Conference on Artificial Intelligence (ECAI2006)*. Riva del Garda, Italy.

Castagnos, S., & Boyer, A. (2007, April). Personalized communities in a distributed recommender system. In *Proceedings of the 29th European Conference on Information Retrieval (ECIR 2007)*. Rome, Italy.

Castells, M. (1996). *The information age: Economy, society and culture: Volume I, The rise of the network society*. Padstow, Cornwall: T.J. International Limited.

Castro, J., Kolp, M., & Mylopoulos, J. (2002). Towards requirements driven information systems engineering: The Tropos project. *Information Systems, 27*(6), 365-389.

CCEVS. (2005). *Common criteria—Part 1: Introduction and general model* (Draft v3.0, Rev 2). Common Criteria Evaluation and Validation Scheme.

CERT. (2002). *Social engineering attacks via IRC and instant messaging* (CERT® Incident Note IN-2002-03). Retrieved April 15, 2007, from http://www.cert.org/incident_notes/IN-2002-03.html

CESG. (1994). *CESG electronic information systems security: System security policies* (Memorandum No.5).

Chan, P. (1999, August). A non-invasive learning approach to building Web user profiles. In *Proceedings of the Workshop on Web Usage Analysis and User Profiling, Fifth International Conference on Knowledge Discovery and Data Mining*, San Diego, California.

Chang, K. (2004, April 6). In math, computers don't lie. Or do they? *New York Times*. Retrieved October 5, 2006, from http://www.math.binghamton.edu/zaslav/Nytimes/+Science/+Math/sphere-packing.20040406.html

Charles, B., Moffett, J. D., Laney, R., & Bashar, N. (2006, May). A framework for security requirements engineering. In *Proceedings of the 2006 International Workshop on Software Engineering for Secure Systems SESS '06*.

Charlesworth, A. (2003). Privacy, personal information and employment. *Surveillance and Society, 1*(2), 217-ff.

Chatziapostolou, D., & Furnell, S. M. (2007, April 11-13). Assessing the usability of system-initiated and user-initiated security events. In *Proceedings of ISOneWorld 2007*, Las Vegas. Washington DC: The Information Institute.

Checkland, P., & Holwell, S. (1998). *Information, systems and information systems—making sense of the field*. Chichester, New York, Weinheim, Brisbane, Singapore, Toronto: John Wiley & Sons Ltd.

Checkland, P., & Scholes, J. (2000). *Soft systems methodology in action*. Chichester, New York, Weinheim, Brisbane, Singapore, Toronto: John Wiley & Sons, Ltd.

Chellapilla, K., Larson, K., Simard, P. Y., & Czerwinski, M. (2005, July 21-22). Computers beat humans at single character recognition in reading based human interaction proofs (hips). In *Proceedings of Ceas 2005—Second Conference on E-mail and Anti-spam*. Stanford University, California, USA.

Chellapilla, K., Larson, K., Simard, P., & Czerwinski, M. (2005). Designing human friendly human interaction proofs (hips). In *Chi '05: Proceedings of the Sigchi Conference on Human Factors in Computing Systems* (pp. 711-720). New York: ACM Press.

Chellapilla, K., & Simard, P. Y. (2005). Using machine learning to break visual human interaction proofs (hips). In L. K. Saul, Y. Weiss, & L. Bottou (Eds.), *Advances in neural information processing systems 17* (pp. 265-272). Cambridge, MA: MIT Press.

Chew, M., & Baird, H. S. (2003). Baffletext: a human interactive proof. In *Proceedings of the 10th IS&T/Spie Document Recognition & Retrieval Conference*.

Chew, M., & Tygar, J. (2005, Jan). Collaborative filtering captchas. In H. S. Baird & D. P. Lopresti (Eds.), *Lecture notes in computer science* (pp. 66-81). Springer Verlag.

Chew, M., & Tygar, J. D. (2004). Image recognition captchas. *Isc* (p. 268-279).

Chia, P.A., Ruighaver, A.B., & Maynard, S.B. (2002). Understanding organizational security culture. In *Proceedings of PACIS2002*, Japan. Retrieved February 20, 2007, from http://www.dis.unimelb.edu.au/staff/sean/research/ChiaCultureChapter.pdf

Chung L., Nixon, B. A., Yu, E., & Mylopoulos, J. (2000). *Non-functional requirements in software engineering.* Kluwer Academic Publishers.

Chung, L. (1993). Dealing with security requirements during the development of information systems. In C. Rolland, F. Bodart, & C. Cauvet (Eds.), *Proceedings of the 5th International Conference Advanced Information Systems Engineering, CAiSE '93* (pp. 234-251). Springer.

Cialdini, R. (2001). *Influence: Science and practice.* Needham Heights, MA: Allyn & Bacon.

Ciborra, C. (2004). *Digital technologies and the duality of risk* (Discussion Paper). Centre for Analysis of Risk and Regulation, London School of Economics.

CMU. (2000). *The captcha project.* Retrieved April 26, 2007, from http://www.captcha.net

Coates, A. L. (2001). Pessimal print—a reverse Turing test. In *Proceedings of the Sixth International Conference on Document Analysis and Recognition (Icdar '01)* (p. 1154). Washington, DC: IEEE Computer Society.

Cobb, M. (2006). *Latest IM attacks still rely on social engineering.* Retrieved April 15, 2007, from http://searchsecurity.techtarget.com/tip/0,289483,sid14_gci1220612,00.html

Cohen, D. (2004). *Consumer front-end to WPA.* Wi-Fi Alliance.

Collins, H.M. (1990). *Artificial experts: Social knowledge and intelligent machines.* Cambridge, MA: MIT Press.

Commission Nationale de l'Informatique et des Libertés (CNIL). (2002). *La cybersurveillance sur les lieux de travail.* Paris.

Cone, E. (2007). Hacking's gift to IT. *CIO Insight, March 7.* Retrieved August 15, 2007, from www.cioinsight.com/article2/0,1397,21087886,00.asp

Connolly, T., & Gilani, N. (1982). Information search in judgment tasks: A regression model and some preliminary findings. *Organizational Behavior and Human Decision Processes, 30*(3), 330-350.

Connolly, T., & Thorn, B. K. (1987). Predecisional information acquisition: Effects of task variables on suboptimal search strategies. *Organizational Behavior and Human Decision Processes, 39*(3), 397-416.

Conry-Murray, A. (2001). The pros and cons of employee surveillance. *Network Magazine, 12*(2), 62-66.

Cooper, A. (1999). *The inmates are running the asylum: Why high-tech products drive us crazy and how to restore the sanity.* Sams Publishing.

Cooper, J. (1989). *Computer and communications security.* New York: McGraw-Hill.

Core Impact. (n.d.). *Core impact overview.* Retrieved April 15, 2007, from http://www.coresecurity.com/?module=ContentMod&action=item&id=32

Cowan, N. (2001). The magical number 4 in short-term memory: A reconsideration of mental storage capacity. *Behavioral and Brain Sciences, 24*(1), 87-185.

CRA. (2003). *Grand research challenges in information systems.* Washington DC: Computing Research Association. Retrieved March 21, 2007, from http://www.cra.org/reports/gc.systems.pdf

CRAMM – CCTA (Central Computer and Telecommunications Agency, UK). *Risk analysis and management method.* Retrieved from http://www.cramm.com/cramm.htm

Cranor, L. F. (2005). *Hey, that's personal!* Invited talk at the International User Modeling Conference (UM05).

Cranor, L. F., & Garfinkel, S. (Eds.). (2005). *Security and usability: Designing secure systems that people can use.* Sebastopol, CA: O'Reilly Media.

Crawford, M. (2006). Social engineering replaces guns in today's biggest bank heists. *ComputerWorld (Australia), May.* Retrieved April 15, 2007, from http://www.computerworld.com.au/index.php/id;736453614

Crockett, L. J. (1994). *The Turing test and the frame problem.* Ablex Publishing Corporation.

Crook, R., Ince, D., & Nuseibeh, B. (2005, August 29-September 2). On Modelling access policies: Relating roles to their organisational context. *Proceedings of the 13th IEEE International Requirements Engineering Conference (RE'05)*, Paris (pp. 157-166).

CSI/FBI. (2006). *Computer crime and security survey.* Retrieved February 2007, from http://www.gocsi.com

CSI/FBI. (2006). *Eleventh annual CSI/FBI computer crime and security survey.* Retrieved August 15, 2007, from http://i.cmpnet.com/gocsi/db_area/pdfs/fbi/FBI2006.pdf

Dacier, M. (1994). *Vers une 'evaluation quantitative de la s'ecurit'e, informatique.* Phd thesis, Institut National Polytechnique de Toulouse.

Dalziel, J. R., & Job, R. F. S. (1997). Motor vehicle accidents, fatigue and optimism bias in taxi drivers. *Accident Analysis & Prevention, 29*, 489-494.

Damle, P. (2002). Social engineering: A tip of the iceberg. *Information Systems Control Journal, 2.* Retrieved April 15, 2007, from http://www.isaca.org/Template.cfm?Section=Home&CONTENTID=17032&TEMPLATE=/ContentManagement/ContentDisplay.cfm

Dardenne, A., van Lamsweerde, A., & Fickas, S. (1993). Goal-directed requirements acquisition. *Science of Computer Programming, 20*(1-2), 3-50.

Darley, J. M. & Latané, B. (1968). Bystander intervention in emergencies: Diffusion of responsibility. *Journal of Personality and Social Psychology, 8*, 377-383.

Data Protection Working Party—DPWP. (2001). *Opinion 8/2001 on the processing of personal data in the employment context* (5062/01/Final).

Data Protection Working Party—DPWP. (2002). *Working document on the surveillance of electronic communications in the workplace* (5401/01/Final).

Data Protection Working Party—DPWP. (2004). *Opinion 4/2004 on the processing of personal data and video surveillance* (11750/02/Final).

Datta, R., Li, J., & Wang, J. Z. (2005). Imagination: a robust image-based captcha generation system. In *Proceedings of the 13th annual ACM International Conference on Multimedia (Multimedia '05)* (pp. 331-334). New York: ACM Press.

David, J. (2002). Policy enforcement in the workplace. *Computers and Security, 21*(6), 506-513.

Davies, B. (2006, October 3). Full proof? Let's trust it to the black box. *Times higher education supplement.*

Davis, A. (1998). A comparison of techniques for the specification of external system behavior. *Communications of the ACM, 31*(9), 1098-1115.

Davis, A., (1993). *Software requirements: Objects, functions and states.* Upper Saddle River, NJ: Prentice Hall.

De Campeaux, D. (2002). Taking responsibility for worms and viruses. *Communications of the ACM, 45*(4), 15-16.

De Millo, R.A., Lipton, R.J., & Perlis, A.J. (1977). Social processes and proofs of theorems and programs. In *Proceedings of the 4th ACM Symposium on Principles of Programming Language* (pp. 206-214).

Dejoy, D.M. (1987). The optimism bias and traffic safety. In *Proceedings of the Human Factors and Ergonomics Society* (Vol. 31, pp. 756-759).

Delbar, C., Mormont, M., & Schots, M. (2003). New technology and respect for privacy at the workplace. *European Industrial Relations Observatory.* Retrieved January 2006, from http://www.eiro.eurofound.eu.int/print/2003/07/study/TN0307101S.html

Denning, D. E. (1998). *The limits of formal security models.* National Computer Systems Security Award Acceptance Speech. Retrieved October 18, 1999, from www. cs.georgetown.edu/~denning/infosec/award.html

Desprocher, S., & Roussos, A. (2001). The jurisprudence of surveillance: a critical look at the laws of intimacy (Working Paper), *Lex Electronica, 6*(2). Retrieved March 2006, from http://www.lex-electronica.org/articles/v6-2/

Detert, J. R., Schroeder, R. G., & Mauriel, J. (2000). Framework for linking culture and improvement initiatives in organisations. *The Academy of Management Review, 25*(4), 850-863.

Devanbu, P. & Stubblebine, S. (2000). Software engineering for security: a roadmap. *In Proceedings of the Conference of the Future of Software Engineering.*

DeWitt, A. J., & Kuljis, J. (2006, July 12-14). Aligning usability and security: a usability study of Polaris. In *Proceedings of the Second Symposium on Usable Privacy and Security (SOUPS '06)* (pp. 1-7). Pittsburgh, Pennsylvania.

Dhamija, R., & Tygar, J. D. (2005). The battle against phishing: Dynamic security skins. In *Proceedings of SOUPS* (pp. 77-88).

Dhillon, G. & Backhouse, J. (1996). Risks in the use of information technology within organizations. *International Journal of Information Management, 16*(1), 65-74.

Dhillon, G. (1997). *Managing information systems security.* London: Macmillan Press.

Dhillon, G. (1999). Managing and controlling computer misuse. *Information Management and Computer Security, 7*(4), 171-175.

Dhillon, G. (2004). The challenge of managing information security. *International Journal of Information Management, 24,* 3-4.

Dhillon, G. (2007). *Principles of information systems security: Text and cases.* Danvers: John Wiley & Sons.

Dhillon, G., & Backhouse, J. (2001) Current directions in IS security research: Toward socio-organizational perspectives. *Information Systems Journal, 11*(2), 127-154.

Dhillon, G., & Torkzadeh, G. (2006). Value-focused assessment of information system security in organizations. *Information Systems Journal, 16*, 293-314.

Dinnie, G. (1999). The second annual global information security survey. *Information Management & Computer Security, 7*(3), 112-120.

DOD. (1985). *DoD trusted computer system evaluation criteria (The Orange Book).* (DOD 5200.28-STD). United States Department of Defense.

Dodge, R., & Ferguson, A. (2006). Using phishing for user e-mail security awareness. In S. Fischer-Hübner, K. Rannenberg, L. Yngström, & S. Lindskog (Eds.), *Proceedings of the IFIP TC-11 21st International Information Security Conference (SEC 2006)* (pp. 454-458). New York: Springer Science + Business Media Inc.

Doherty, N.F. & Fulford, H. (2003). Information security policies in large organisations: Developing a conceptual framework to explore their impact. In M. Khosrow-Pour (Ed.), *Information Technology & Organizations: Trends, Issues, Challenges & Solutions, 2003 Information Resources Management Association International Conference*, Philadelphia, Pennsylvania, May 18-21 (pp. 1052-1053). Hershey, PA: Idea Group Publishing.

Drake, P. (2005). *Communicative action in information security systems: An application of social theory in a technical domain.* Hull: University of Hull.

DSDM Consortium. (2006). White papers. Retrieved October 5, 2006, from *http://www.dsdm.org/products/white_papers.asp*

DTI. (2000). *Information security breaches survey 2000: Technical report.* London: Department of Trade & Industry.

DTI. (2002). *Information security breaches survey 2002: Technical report.* London: Department of Trade & Industry.

DTI. (2004). *Information security breaches survey 2004: Technical report*. London: Department of Trade & Industry.

DTI. (2006). *Information security breaches survey 2006*. Retrieved March 2006, from www.dti.gov.uk

Duffy, R. R., Kalsher, M. J., & Wogalter, M. S. (1995). Increased effectiveness of an interactive warning in a realistic incidental product-use situation. *International Journal of Industrial Ergonomics, 15*, 169-166.

Edworthy, J., & Adams, A. (1996). *Warning design: A research prospective*. London: Taylor and Francis.

Electronic Privacy Information Center (EPIC). (2002). Possible content of a European framework on protection of workers' personal data. *Workplace Privacy*, European Commission. Retrieved October 2005, from //www.epic.org/privacy/workplace

Ellmer, E., Pernul, G., & Kappel, G. (1995). Object-oriented modeling of security semantics. *In Proceedings of the 11th Annual Computer Society Applications Conference (ACSAC'95)*.

EMVCo. (2004). *EMV integrated circuit card specifications for payment systems, Book 2*. Retrieved March 20, 2007, from http://www.emvco.com/

Ericsson, K. A., & Simon, H. A. (1993). *Protocol analysis: Verbal reports as data* (Rev. ed.). Cambridge, MA: The MIT Press.

Espiner, T. (2006). Microsoft denies flaw in Vista. *ZDNet UK, December 5*. Retrieved April 15, 2007, from http://www.builderau.com.au/news/soa/Microsoft_denies_flaw_in_Vista/0,339028227,339272533,00.htm?feed=rss

Eysenck, H. (1947). *Dimensions of personality*. London: Routledge & Kegan Paul.

Ezingeard, J.-N., Mcfadzean, E., & Birchall, D. W. (2003). Board of directors and information security: A perception grid. In S. Parkinson & J. Stutt (Eds.), *Paper 222 presented at British Academy of Management Conference*, Harrogate.

Ezingeard, J.-N., Mcfadzean, E., Howlin, N., Ashenden, D., & Birchall, D. (2004). *Mastering alignment: bringing information assurance and corporate strategy together*. Paper presented at the European and Mediterranean Conference on Information Systems, Carthage.

Faulkner, W. (2000). The power and the pleasure? A research agenda for 'making gender stick.' *Science, Technology & Human Values, 25*(1), 87-119.

Fazekas, C. P. (2004). 1984 is still fiction: Electronic monitoring in the workplace and U.S. privacy. *Duke Law & Technology Review, 15*. Retrieved January 2006, from http://www.law.duke.edu/journals/dltr/articles/PDF/2004DLTR0015.pdf

Feer, F. (2004). *Thinking about deception*. Retrieved March 11, 2006, from http://www.d-n-i.net/fcs/feer_thinking_about_deception.htm

Ferguson, A. J. (2005). Fostering e-mail security awareness: The West Point Carronade. *Educause Quarterly, 28*, 54-57.

Ferraiolo, D., Sandhu, R., Gavrila, S., Kuhn, R., & Chandramouli, R. (2001, August). Proposed NIST standard for role-based access control. *ACM Transactions on Information and Systems Security, 4*(3), 224-74.

Feynman, R. P. (2001). *The pleasure of finding things out*. Penguin Books.

Findlay, P., & McKinlay, A. (2003). Surveillance, electronic communications technologies and regulation. *Industrial Relations Journal, 34*(4), 305-314.

Finnish Government Resolution. (2004). *Strategy for securing the functions vital to society*. Helsinki, Finland: Edita Prima Oy.

Fisher, C., & Lovell, A. (2003). *Business ethics and values*. Harlow, London, New York, Boston, San Francisco, Toronto, Sydney, Singapore, Hong Kong, Tokyo, Seoul, Taipei, New Delhi, Cape Town, Madrid, Mexico City, Amsterdam. Munich, Paris, Milan: Prentice Hall.

Flechais, I., Sasse, M. A., & Hailes, S. M. V. (2003, August). Security engineering: Bringing security home: a process for developing secure and usable systems. In

Proceedings of the 2003 Workshop on New Security Paradigms.

Forrester, T., & Morrison, P. (1994). *Computer ethics.* MIT.

Forrester. (2006). *Forrester research reports.* Retrieved March 2006, from http://www.forrester.com

Forsythe, D.E. (2001). *Studying those who study as: An anthropologist in the world of artificial intelligence.* Stanford University Press.

Franch, X., & Maiden, N. A. M. (2003, February 10-13). Modelling component dependencies to inform their selection. *COTS-Based Software Systems, 2ⁿᵈ International Conference, (ICCBSS 2003)* (pp. 81-91). Lecture Notes in Computer Science 2580. Ottawa, Canada: Springer.

Freeman, S., Walker, M. R., & Latané, B. (1975). Diffusion of responsibility and restaurant tipping: Cheaper by the bunch. *Personality and Social Psychology Bulletin, 1*(4), 584-587.

Friedman, B., & Nissenbaum, H. (1997). Software agents and user autonomy. In *Proceedings of the First International Conference on Autonomous Agents* (pp. 466–469).

Friedman, B., Hurley, D., Howe, D. C., Felten, E., & Nissenbaum, H. (2002). Users' conceptions of Web security: a comparative study. *Extended Abstracts of the CHI 2002 Conference on Human Factors in Computing Systems* (pp. 746-747). New York: Association for Computing Machinery.

Friedman, B., Kahn, P., & Borning, A. (2006). Value sensitive design and information systems. In P. Zhang, & D. Galletta (Eds.), *Human-computer interaction in management information systems: Foundations* (Vol. 4).

Friedman, B., Lin, P., & Miller, J. K. (2005). Informed consent by design. In L. F. Cranor, & S. Garfinkel (Eds.), *Security and usability* (Chap. 24, pp. 495-521). O'Reilly Media, Inc.

Fulford, H. & Doherty, N.F. (2003). The application of information security policies in large UK-based organiza-

tions. *Information Management and Computer Security, 11*(3), 106-114.

Furnell, S. M. (2004). Using security: easier said than done? *Computer Fraud & Security, April,* 6-10.

Furnell, S. M., Bryant, P., & Phippen, A. D. (2007). Assessing the security perceptions of personal Internet users. *Computers & Security, 26*(5), 410-417.

Furnell, S. M., Jusoh, A., & Katsabas, D. (2006). The challenges of understanding and using security: A survey of end-users. *Computers & Security, 25*(1), 27-35.

Furnell, S. M., Katsabas, D., Dowland, P. S., & Reid, F. (2007, May 14-16). A practical usability evaluation of security features in end-user applications. In *Proceedings of 22nd IFIP International Information Security Conference (IFIP SEC 2007)*, Sandton, South Africa. New York: Springer.

Garg, A., Curtis, J., & Halper, H. (2003). Quantifying the financial impact of information security breaches. *Information Management and Computer Security, 11*(2), 74-83.

Garland, D. J., Hopkin, D., & Wise, J. A. (1999). *Handbook of aviation human factors.* Mahwah, NJ: Lawerence Erlbaum Associates.

Gartner (2005). Retrieved April 1, 2007 from http://www.gartner.com/130100/130115/gartners_hyp_f2.gif

Gaston, S.J. (1996). *Information security: Strategies for successful management.* Toronto: CICA.

Gaudin, S. (2007). Hackers use Middle East fears to push Trojan attack. *Information Week, April 9.* Retrieved April 15, 2007, from http://www.informationweek.com/windows/showArticle.jhtml?articleID=198900155

Gaudin, S. (2007). Human error more dangerous than hackers. *TechWeb.* http://www.techweb.com/showArticle.jhtml?articleID=197801676

Gaunard, P., & Dubois, E. (2003, May 26-28). Bridging the gap between risk analysis and security policies: Security and privacy in the age of uncertainty. *IFIP TC11*

18th International Conference on Information Security (SEC2003) (pp. 409-412). Athens, Greece. Kluwer.

Gerber, M., Solms, R. V., & Overbeek, P. (2001). Formalizing information security requirements. *Information Management & Computer Security, 9*(1), 32-37.

getafreelancer.com Web site. (2006). Retrieved April 27, 2007, from http://www.getafreelancer.com/projects/Data-Processing-Data-Entry/Data-Entry-Solve-CAPTCHA.html

Gietzmann, M. B., & Selby, M. J. P. (1994). Assessment of innovative software technology: Developing an end-user-initiated interface sesign strategy. *Technology Analysis & Strategic Management, 6,* 473-483.

Gillies, A.C. (1997). *Software quality: Theory and management* (2nd ed.). London/Boston: International Thomson Computer Press.

Gimp 2.2. (n.d.). Retrieved April 26, 2007, from http://www.gimp.org/

Giorgini, P., Massacci, F., & Mylopoulos, J. (2003, October 13-16). Requirement engineering meets security: A case study on modelling secure electronic transactions by VISA and Mastercard. *The 22nd International Conference on Conceptual Modelling (ER'03)* (LNCS 2813, pp. 263-276). Chicago: Springer.

Giorgini, P., Massacci, F., Mylopoulos, J., & Zannone, N. (2005). Modelling social and individual trust in requirements engineering methodologies. *Proceedings of the 3rd International Conference on Trust Management (iTrust 2005).* LNCS 3477. Heidelberg: Springer-Verlag.

Glazer, R. (1993). Measuring the value of information: The information intensive organization. *IBM Systems Journal., 32*(1), 99-110.

Gligor, V. D. (2005, Sep). Guaranteeing access in spite of distributed service-flooding attacks. In *Proceedings of the 12th ACM Conference on Computer and Communications Security* (pp. 80-96). *Lecture Notes in Computer Science, 3364.*

Global Platform. (2005). *GlobalPlatform smart card security target guidelines.* Retrieved March 20, 2007, from http://www.globalplatform.org/

Golbeck, J. (2002). *Cognitive load and memory theories.* Retrieved April 2, 2007, from http://www.cs.umd.edu/class/fall2002/cmsc838s/tichi/printer/memory.html

Golbeck, J. (2006). Generating predictive movie recommendations from trust in social networks. In *Proceedings of the Fourth International Conference on Trust Management.* USA.

Goldberg, D., Nichols, D., Oki, B., & Terry, D. (1992). Using collaborative filtering to weave an information tapestry [Special Issue]. *Communications of the ACM, 35,* 61-70.

Goldstein, W. M. & Hogarth, R. M. (1997). *Research on judgment and decision-making: Currents, connections, and controversies.* Cambridge, UK: Cambridge University Press.

Golle, P., & Ducheneaut, N. (2005). Preventing bots from playing online games. *Computer Entertainment, 3*(3), 3.

Gollman, D. (1999). *Computer security.* Wiley.

Goodman, S. (1991). *New technology and banking: Problems and possibilities for developing countries, actor perspective.* University of Lund, Sweden: Research Policy Institute.

Google's audio captcha. (2006, November). Retrieved April 29, 2007, from http://googleblog.blogspot.com/2006/11/audio-captchas-when-visual-images-are.html

Gordon Training Institute. *Conscious competence learning model.* www.gordontraining.com

Gordon, L. A., Loeb, M. P., Lucyshyn, W., & Richardson, R. (2006). *2006 CSI/FBI computer crime and security survey.* Baltimore: Computer Security Institute.

Gottesdiener, E. (2002). *Requirements by collaboration.* Boston: Addison-Wesley.

Gragg, D. (2002). A multi-level defense against social engineering. *SANS Institute.* Retrieved September 17, 2003, from http://www.sans.org/rr/papers/index. php?id=920

Gragg, D. (2003). A multi-level defense against social engineering. *SANS Institute Information Security Reading Room.* Retrieved April 15, 2007, from http://www. sans.org/reading_room/papers/51/920.pdf

Graham, D. B., & Allinson, N. M. (1998). *Characterizing virtual eigensignatures for general purpose face recognition.*

Granger, S. (2001). Social engineering fundamentals. *Security Focus.* Retrieved September 18, 2003, from: http://www.securityfocus.com/printable/infocus/1527

Gregoire, J., Jr. (2007). CIO confidential: The Manhattan effect. *CIO Magazine, 20*(9), 30-34.

Grice, G. R. (1948). The relation of secondary reinforcement to delayed reward in visual discrimination learning. *Journal of Experimental Psychology, 38,* 1-16.

Grimm, R., & Bershad, B. (2001). Separating access control policy, enforcement, and functionality in extensible systems. *ACM Transactions on Computer Systems, 19*(1), 36-70.

Gross, D., & Yu, E. (2001, August 27-31). Evolving system architecture to meet changing business goals: An agent and goal-oriented approach. The *5th IEEE International Symposium on Requirements Engineering (RE 2001)* (pp. 316-317). Toronto, Canada.

Guess the google. (n.d.). Retrieved April 27, 2007, from http://grant.robinson.name/projects/guess-the-google/

Gürses, S., Jahnke, J. H., Obry, C., Onabajo, A., Santen, T., & Price, M. (2005, October). Eliciting confidentiality requirements in practice. In *Proceedings of the 2005 Conference of the Centre for Advanced Studies on Collaborative Research.*

Gutmann, P. (2003). Plug-and-play PKI: A PKI your mother can use. In *Proceedings of the 12th USENIX Security Symposium* (pp. 45–58). Berkeley: USENIX Association.

Habermas, J. (1984). *The theory of communicative action, volume 1: Reason and the rationalization of society.* Boston: Beacon Press.

Habermas, J. (1989). *The theory of communicative action, volume 2: Lifeworld and system: A critique of functionalist reason.* Boston: Beacon Press.

Hacker, S. (1989). *Pleasure, power and technology: Some tales of gender, engineering, and the cooperative workplace.* Boston: Unwin Hyman.

Haley, C. B., Laney, R., & Bashar, N. (2004, March). Deriving security requirements from crosscutting threat descriptions. In *Proceedings of the 3rd International Conference on Aspect-Oriented Software Development.*

Hammond, K. R. (2000). *Judgments under stress.* New York: Oxford University Press.

Han, P., Xie, B., Yang, F., Wang, J., & Shen, R. (2004, May). A novel distributed collaborative filtering algorithm and its implementation on P2P overlay network. In *Proceedings of the Eighth Pacific-Asia Conference on Knowledge Discovery and Data Mining (PAKDD04).* Sydney, Australia.

Hardee, J. B., West, R., & Mayhorn, C. B. (2006). To download or not to download: An examination of computer security decision-making. *Association of Computing Machinery: Interactions, 13*(3), 32-37.

Harl (1997). *The psychology of social engineering.* Retrieved March 12, 2006, from http://searchlores. org/aaatalk.htm

Harris, A. J., & Yen, D. C. (2002). Biometric authentication: Assuring access to information. *Information Management &Computer Security, 10*(1), 12-19.

Helander, M. (1997). The human factors profession. In G. Salvendy (Ed.), *Handbook of human factors and ergonomics* (2nd ed., pp. 3-16). New York: Wiley.

Helmer, G., Wong, J., Slagell, M., Honavar, V., Miller, L., & Lutz, R. (2002). A software fault tree approach to requirements analysis of an intrusion detection system. In P. Loucopoulos & J. Mylopoulos (Ed.), *Special Issue on Requirements Engineering for Information Security. Requirements Engineering* (Vol. 7, No. 4, pp. 177-220).

Helokunnas, T., & Kuusisto, R. (2003). Strengthening leading situations via time-divergent communication conducted in Ba. *The E-Business Review, 3*(1), 78-81.

Helokunnas, T., & Kuusisto, R. (2003). Information security culture in a value net. In *Proceedings of the 2003 IEEE International Engineering Management Conference* (pp. 190-194). Albany, NY, USA.

Hensley, G. A. (1999). *Calculated risk: passwords and their limitations*. Retrieved April 2, 2007, from http://www.infowar.com/articles/99article_120699a_j.shtml

Herrmann, D. (2007). *Complete guide to security and privacy metrics*. Boca Raton, FL: Auerbach Publications.

Herrmann, G., & Pernul, G. (1998). Towards security semantics in workflow management. In *Proceedings of the 31st Hawaii International Conference on Systems Sciences.*

Herrmann, G., & Pernul, G. (1999). Viewing business-process security from different perspectives. *International Journal of Electronic Commerce, 3*(3), 89-103.

Hickey, A. M., & Davis, A. M. (2004). A unified model of requirements elicitation. *Journal of Management Information Systems, 20*(4), 65-84.

Hickey, A., & Davis, A. (2002). The role of requirements elicitation techniques in achieving software quality. In C. Salinesi, B. Regnell, & K. Pohl (Eds.), *Proceedings of the Requirements Engineering Workshop: Foundations for Software Quality (REFSQ '02)* (pp. 165-171). Essen, Germany: Essener Informatik Beiträge.

Higgins, H. N. (1999). Corporate system security: towards an integrated management approach. *Information Management & Computer Security, 7*(5), 217-222.

Hinde, S. (2002). Security surveys spring crop. *Computers and Security, 21*(4), 310-321.

Hinde, S. (2003). Cyber-terrorism in context. *Computers and Security, 22*(3), 188-192.

Hinson, G. (2006). Seven myths about information security metrics. *The ISSA Journal, July*, 43-48.

Hirsch, C. (2005). Do not ship trojan horses. In P. Dowland, S. Furnell, & B. Thuraisingham (Eds.), *Security management, integrity, and internal control in information systems.* Fairfax, VA: Springer.

Hodges, A. C. (2006). Bargaining for privacy in the unionized workplace. *The International Journal of Comparative Labour Law and Industrial Relations, 22*(2), 147-182.

Hoeren, T., & Eustergerling, S. (2005). Privacy and data protection at the workplace in Germany. In S. Nouwt, B. R. de Vries, & C. Prins (Eds.), *Reasonable expectations of privacy* (pp. 211-244). The Hague, PA: TMC Asser Press.

Hofmann, H., & Lehner, F. (2001). Requirements engineering as a success factor in software projects. *IEEE Software, 18*(4), 58-66.

Hofstede, G. (1984). *Culture's consequences: International differences in work-related values.* Beverly Hills, London, New Delhi: Sage Publications.

Holbrook, H. (1990). A scenario-based methodology for conducting requirements elicitation. *ACM SIGSOFT Software Engineering Notes, 15*(1), 95-104.

Hollows, P. (2005). Hackers are real-time. Are you? *Sarbanes-Oxley Compliance Journal, February 28*. Retrieved April 15, 2007, from http://www.s-ox.com/Feature/detail.cfm?ArticleID=623

Holz, T., & Raynal, F. (2006). Malicious malware: attacking the attackers (part 1), *Security Focus, January 31*. Retrieved April 15, 2007, from http://www.securityfocus.com/print/infocus/1856

Hone, K. & Eloff, J.H.P. (2002). Information security policy: What do international security standards say. *Computers & Security, 21*(5), 402-409.

Hone, K. & Eloff, J.H.P. (2002). What makes an effective information security policy. *Network Security, 20*(6), 14-16.

Hong, K., Chi, Y., Chao, L., & Tang, J. (2003). An integrated system theory of information security management. *Information Management and Computer Security, 11*(5), 243-248.

Howell, J. (1999). *Introduction to face recognition.* Boca Raton, FL: CRC Press, Inc.

Hsia, P., Samuel, J., Gao, J., Kung, D., Toyoshima, Y., & Chen, C. (1994). Formal approach to scenario analysis. *IEEE Software, 11*(2), 33-41.

Huitt, W. (2003). A systems model of human behavior. *Educational Psychology Interactive.* Valdosta, GA: Valdosta State University. Retrieved March 20, 2007, from http://chiron.valdosta.edu/whuitt/materials/sysmdlo.html

Hussin, H., King, M., & Cragg, P. (2002). IT alignment in small firms. *European Journal of Information Systems, 11*, 108-127.

I.S.O. (2000). *Information technology. Code of practice for information security management, ISO 17799.* International Standards Organization.

Ilet, D. (2005). Inside the biggest bank raid that never was. *Zdnet.* http://news.zdnet.co.uk/security/0,1000000189,39191956,00.htm.

Imagemagick 6.2.8. (n.d.). Retrieved April 26, 2007, from http://www.imagemagick.org/

Ince, D. (1994). *An introduction to software quality assurance and its implementation.* London: McGraw-Hill.

Index of bongard problems. (n.d.). Retrieved April 26, 2007, from http://www.cs.indiana.edu/~hfoundal/res/bps/bpidx.htm

International Labour Office—ILO. (1997). *Protection of workers' personal data.* Geneva.

International Working Group on Data Protection in Telecommunications—IWGDPT. (1996). *Report and recommendations on telecommunications and privacy in labour relationships.* Retrieved January 2006, from http://www.datenschutz-brlin.de/doc/int/iwgdpt/dsarb_en.htm

ISM3. *Information security management maturity model.* www.ism3.com

ISO 17799. (1999). *Information security management — Part 1: Code of practice for information security.* London: British Standards Institution.

ISO. (2000). *BS ISO/IEC 17799:2000, BS7799-1:2000. Information technology. Code of practice for information security management.* International Standards Organisation.

ISO. (2005). *Information technology—security techniques—code of practice for information security management* (ISO/IEC 17799:2005). London: BSI.

ISO. (2005). *Information technology—security techniques—information security management systems—requirements* (ISO/IEC 27001:2005(E)). London: BSI.

ITGI (2003). *IT control objectives for Sarbanes-Oxley.* Rolling Meadows, IL: IT Governance Institute.

ITGI. (2005). *COBIT 4.0: control objectives and management guidelines.* Rolling Meadows, IL: Information Technology Governance Institute.

Ives, B., Walsh, K., & Schneider, H. (2004). The domino effect of password reuse. *Communications of the ACM, 47*(4), 75-78.

Jackson Higgins, K. (2006). *Phishing your own users.* Retrieved April 26, 2007, from http://www.darkreading.com/document.asp?doc_id=113055

Jackson Higgins, K. (2006). *Social engineering gets smarter.* Retrieved April 26, 2007, from http://www.darkreading.com/document.asp?doc_id=97382

Jackson, J. W., Ferguson, A. J., & Cobb, M. J. (2005, October 12-22). Building a university-wide automated information assurance awareness exercise. In *Proceedings of the 35th ASEE/IEEE Frontiers in Education Conference*, Indianapolis, IN, (pp 7-11).

Jahner, S., & Krcmar, H. (2005). *Beyond technical aspects of information security: Risk culture as a success factor for IT risk management.* Paper presented at Americas Conference on Information Systems 2005.

Jaques, R. (2007). *UK smoking ban opens doors for hackers*. Retrieved April 26, 2007, from http://www.vnunet.com/vnunet/news/2183215/uk-smoking-ban-opens-doors

Johnston, J., Eloff, J. H. P., & Labuschagne, L. (2003). Security and human computer interfaces. *Computers & Security, 22*(8), 675-684.

Kan, S. H. (1995). *Metrics and models in software quality engineering*. Boston: Addison-Wesley.

Katsabas, D. (2004). *IT security: A human computer interaction perspective*. Master's thesis, University of Plymouth, UK.

Katsabas, D., Furnell, S. M., & Dowland, P. S. (2006, April). Evaluation of end-user application security from a usability perspective. In K. K. Dhanda & M. G. Hunter (Eds.), *Proceedings of 5th Annual ISOneWorld Conference and Convention*, Las Vegas, USA, (pp. 19-21). Washington DC: The Information Institute.

Kazman, R., Klein, M., & Clements, P. (2000). *ATAM: Method for architectural evaluation (CMU/SEI-2000-TR-004)*. Pittsburgh, PA: Software Engineering Institute, Carnegie Mellon University.

Kelly, M. (2007). Chocolate the key to uncovering PC passwords. *The Register, April 17*. Retrieved April 26, 2007, from http://www.theregister.co.uk/2007/04/17/chocolate_password_survey/

Kesan, J. P. (2002). Cyber-working or cyber-shirking?: a first principles examination of electronic privacy in the workplace. *Florida Law Review*, 289ff.

Killmeyer-Tudor, J. (2000). *Information security architecture: In integrated approach to security in the organisation*. CRC Press.

Kirk, J. (2006). Free CDs highlight security weaknesses. *PC World*. http://www.pcworld.idg.com.au/index.php/id;2055135135;fp;2;fpid;1

Klein, G. (1998). *Sources of power: How people make decisions*, Cambridge, MA: The MIT Press.

Kochanski, G., Lopresti, D., & Shih, C. (2002, September). A reverse Turing test using speech. In *Proceedings of the International Conferences on Spoken Language Processing (ICSLP)*. Denver, Colorado.

Kotulic, A.G. & Clark, J.G. (2004). Why there aren't more information security research studies. *Information & Management, 41*, 5907-607.

Kuhn, T.S. (1962). *The structure of scientific revolutions*. University of Chicago Press.

Kumar, K. G. (2005). *Towards financial inclusion*. Retrieved April 16, 2007, from http://www.thehindubusinessline.com/2005/12/13/stories/2005121301240200.htm

Kuo, C., Perrig, A. & Walker, J. (2006). Designing an evaluation method for security user interfaces: Lessons from studying secure wireless network configuration. *ACM Interactions, 13*(3), 28-31.

Kuong, J. (1996). *Client server controls, security and audit (enterprise protection, control, audit, security, risk management and business continuity)*. Masp Consulting Group.

Kuusisto, R. (2004). *Aspects on availability*. Helsinki, Finland: Edita Prima Oy.

Kuusisto, R. (2006). Flowing of information in decision systems. In *Proceedings of the 39th Hawaii International conference of System Sciences* (abstract on p. 148, paper published in electronic form). Kauai, HI: University of Hawai'i at Manoa.

Kuusisto, R., Nyberg, K., & Virtanen, T. (2004). Unite security culture—may a unified security culture be plausible. In A. Jones (Ed.), *Proceedings of the 3rd European Conference on Information Warfare and Security* (pp. 221-230). London: Academic Conferences Limited.

Kuusisto, T., Kuusisto, R., & Nissen, M.,(2007). Implications of information flow priorities for interorganizational crisis management. In L. Armistead (Ed.), *Proceedings of the 2nd International Conference on I-Warfare and Security* (pp. 133-140). Monterey, CA: Naval Postgraduate School.

Kwoc, L. & Longley, D. (1999). Information security management & modelling. *Information Management and Computer Security, 7* 1), 30-39.

Lahaie, D. (2005). The impact of corporate memory loss. *Leadership in Health Services, 18*, 35-48.

Lane, V. P. (1985). *Security of computer based information systems.* Macmillan Education Ltd.

Langford, D. (1995). *Practical computer ethics.* McGraw-Hill.

Lasprogata, G., King, N., & Pillay, S. (2004). Regulation of electronic employee monitoring: Identifying fundamental principles of employee privacy through a comparative study of data privacy legislation in the European Union, United States and Canada. *Stanford Technology Law Review, 4.* Retrieved March 2006, from http://stlr.stanford.edu/STLR/Article?04_STLR_4

Latour, B., & Woolgar, S. (1979*). Laboratory life: The social construction of scientific facts.* Princeton University Press.

Lau, F. (1999). Toward a framework for action research in information systems studies. *Information Technology & People, 12*(2), 148-175.

Lauesen, S. (2002). *Software requirements: Styles and techniques.* London: Addison-Wesley.

Lee, J., & Lee, Y. (2002). A holistic model of computer abuse within organisations. *Information Management & Computer Security, 10*(2), 57-63.

Lee, S.-W., Gandhi, R., Muthurajan, D., Yavagal, D., & Ahn, G.-J. (2006, May). Building problem domain ontology from security requirements in regulatory documents. In *Proceedings of the 2006 International Workshop on Software Engineering for Secure Systems SESS '06.*

Lehto, M. R., & Miller, J. M. (1986). *Warnings, volume 1: Fundamentals, design, and evaluation methodologies.* Ann Arbor, MI: Fuller Technical.

Leng, T. (1997). Internet regulation in Singapore. *Computer Law & Security Report, 13*(2), 115-119.

Levine, R. (2003). *The power of persuasion.* Hoboken, NJ: John Wiley & Sons Inc.

Lewis, J. (2003). Cyber terror: Missing in action. *Knowledge, Technology & Policy, 16*(2), 34-41.

Leyden, J. (2006). MS anti-spyware labels Symantec as Trojan. *The Register, 14.* Retrieved March 21, 2007, from http://www.theregister.co.uk/2006/02/14/ms_anti-spyware_false_positive

Leyden, J. (2007). Data theft replaces malware as top security concern. *The Register, April 19.* Retrieved April 19, 2007, from http://www.theregister.co.uk/2007/04/19/security_fears_poll/

Linden, J. V. (2004). The trouble with blood is it all looks the same: Transfusion errors. In M.S. Bogner (Ed.), *Misadventures in health care: Inside stories* (pp. 13-25). Mahwah, NJ: Lawrence Erlbaum Associates.

Lindner, J.R., Murphy, T.H., & Briers, G.E. (2001). Handling non-response in social science research. *Journal of Agricultural Education, 42*(4), 43-53.

Linsky, J., Bourk, T., Findikli, A., Hulvey, R., Ding, S., Heydon, R., et al. (2006, August). *Simple pairing* (Whitepaper, revision v10r00).

Liu, L., & Yu, E. (2003). Designing information systems in social context: A goal and scenario modelling approach. *Information Systems, 29*(2), 187-203.

Liu, L., & Yu, E. (2004). Intentional modelling to support identity management. In P. Atzeni et al. (Eds.), *Proceedings of the 23rd International Conference on Conceptual Modelling (ER 2004)* (pp. 555-566). LNCS 3288. Berlin, Heidelberg: Springer-Verlag.

Liu, L., Yu, E., & Mylopoulos, J. (2002, October 16). Analyzing security requirements as relationships among strategic actors. The *2nd Symposium on Requirements Engineering for Information Security (SREIS'02).* Raleigh, NC.

Liu, L., Yu, E., & Mylopoulos, J. (2003, September). Security and privacy requirements analysis within a social setting. *Proceedings of International Conference* on *Requirements Engineering (RE'03)* (pp. 151-161). Monterey, CA.

Loch, K. D., Carr, H. H., & Warkentin, M. E. (1992). Threats to information systems: Today's reality, Yesterday's understanding. *MIS Quarterly, 16*, 173.

Loch, K.D., Carr, H.H., & Warkentin, M.E. (1992). Threats to information systems: Today's reality, yesterday's understanding. *MIS Quarterly, 16*(2), 173-186.

Lodderstedt, T., Basin, D. A., J, & Doser, R. (2002). SecureUML: A UML-based modelling language for model-driven security. *Proceedings of UML '02: Proceedings of the 5th International Conference on The Unified Modelling Language,* Dresden, Germany (pp. 426-441).

Loftus, E. F., Dark, V. J., & Williams, D. (1979). Short-term memory factors in ground control-ler/pilot communication. *Human Factors, 21*, 169-181.

Longbough (1996). *Internet security and insecurity.* Management Advisory Publications.

Lopresti, D. (2005, May). Leveraging the captcha problem. In H. S. Baird & D. P. Lopresti (Eds.), *Human interactive proofs: Second international workshop (HIP 2005)* (Vol. 3517, p. 97). Springer Verlag.

Lortz, V., Roberts, D., Erdmann, B., Dawidowsky, F., Hayes, K., Yee, J. C., et al. (2006). *Wi-Fi simple config specification* (version 1.0a).

Low, J., & Woolgar, S. (1993). Managing the socio-technical divide: Some aspects of the discursive structure of information systems development. In P. Quintas (Ed.), *Social dimensions of systems engineering: People, processes and software development* (pp. 34-59). New York/London: Ellis Horwood.

Luhmann, N. (1999). *Ökologishe Kommunikation, 3. Auflage.* Opladen/Wiesbaden: Westdeutcher Verlag.

Lytz, R. (1995). Software metrics for the Boeing 777: A case study. *Software Quality Journal,* **4**(1), 1-13.

MacKenzie, D.A. (2001). *Mechanizing proof: Computing, risk, and trust.* Cambridge, MA/London: MIT Press.

MacKenzie, D.A. (2004). *Computers and the cultures of proving.* Paper presented at the Royal Society Discussion Meeting, London.

Macromedia Web site. (n.d.). Retrieved April 27, 2007, from http://www.macromedia.com/

Maier, R. (2002). *Knowledge management systems. Information and communication technologies for knowledge management.* Berlin, Heidelberg, New York: Springler-Verlag.

Malaska, P., & Holstius, K. (1999). Visionary management. *Foresight, 1*(4), 353-361.

Marett, K., Biros, D., & Knode, M. (2004). Self-efficacy, training effectiveness, and deception detection: A longitudinal study of lie detection training. *Lecture Notes in Computer Science, 3073*, 187-200.

Mark, R. (2006). Teens charged in VA laptop theft. *Internetnews.* http://www.internetnews.com/bus-news/article.php/3624986

Martin, B. (2004). Telling lies for a better world? *Social Anarchism, 35*, 27-39.

Martins, A., & Eloff, J. (2002). Information security culture. In *Proceedings of IFIP TC11 17th International Conference on Information Security* (pp. 203-214). Cairo, Egypt: IFIP Conference Proceedings 214.

Marx, K., & Engels, F. (1968). *Selected works in one volume.* London: Lawrence & Wishart.

Mayer, N., Rifaut, A., & Dubois, E. (2005). Towards a risk-based security requirements engineering framework. *Workshop on Requirements Engineering For Software Quality (REFSQ'05), at the Conference for Advanced Information Systems Engineering (CAiSE),* Porto, Portugal.

Mayhorn, C. B., Lanzolla, V. R., Wogalter, M. S., & Watson, A. M. (2005). Personal digital assistants (PDAs) as medication reminding tools: Exploring age differences in usability. *Gerontechnology, 4*(3), 128-140.

Mayhorn, C. B., Rogers, W. A., & Fisk, A. D. (2004). Designing technology based on cognitive aging principles.

In S. Kwon & D. C. Burdick (Eds.), *Gerotechnology: research and practice in technology and aging* (pp. 42-53). New York: Springer Publishing.

Mayhorn, C. B., Stronge, A. J., McLaughlin, A. C., & Rogers, W. R. (2004). Older adults, computer training, and the systems approach: A formula for success. *Educational Gerontology, 30*(3), 185-203.

Mayhorn, C. B., Wogalter, M. S., & Bell, J. L. (2004). Are we ready? Misunderstanding homeland security safety symbols. *Ergonomics in Design, 12*(4), 6-14.

McCauley, J. (1997). Legal ethics and the Internet: A US perspective. *Computer Law & Security Report, 13*(2), 110-114.

McCauley-Bell, P. R., & Crumpton, L. L. (1998). The human factors issues in information security: What are they and do they matter? In *Proceedings of the Human Factors and Ergonomics Society 42nd Annual Meeting*, USA (pp. 439-442).

McCune, J. M., Perrig, A., & Reiter, M. K. (2005). Seeing-is-believing: Using camera phones for human-verifiable authentication. In *Proceedings of IEEE Symposium on Security and Privacy*.

McDermott, J. (2001). Abuse-case-based assurance arguments. In *Proceedings of the 17th Annual Computer Security Applications Conference (ACSAC)*.

McDermott, J., & Fox, C. (1999). Using abuse case models for security requirements analysis. *Proceedings 15th IEEE Annual Computer Security Applications Conference*, Scottsdale, USA (pp. 55-67).

Mcfadzean, E., Ezingeard, J.-N., & Birchall, D. (2004). Anchoring information security governance research. In G. Dhillon & S. Furnell (Eds.), *Proceedings of the Third Security Conference*. Las Vegas, Nevada, USA.

McMillan, R. (2006). *Third word exploit released, IDG news service*. Retrieved April 15, 2007, from http://www.techworld.com/applications/news/index.cfm?newsID=7577&pagtype=samechan

Mead, N. R., & Stehney, T. (2005). Software engineering for secure systems (SESS)—building trustworthy applications: Security quality requirements engineering (SQUARE) methodology. *ACM SIGSOFT Software Engineering Notes, Proceedings of the 2005 Workshop on Software Engineering for secure systems—building trustworthy applications SESS '05, Volume, 30*(4).

Mead, N., & Stehney, T. (2005). Security quality requirements engineering (SQUARE) methodology. *ACM SIGSOFT Software Engineering Notes, 30*(4), 1-7.

Mendell, R. L. (2007). The psychology of information security. *The ISSA Journal, March*, 8-11.

Menzies, R. (1993). Information systems security. In J. Peppard (Ed.), *IT strategy for business*. London: Pitman Publishing.

Merleau-Ponty, M. (1968).*The visible and invisible*. Evanston, IL: Northwest University Press.

Messmer, E. (2007). RSA '07: Bruce Schneier casts light on psychology of security. *CSO Online, February 7*. Retrieved August 15, from http://www.networkworld.com/news/2007/020707-rsa-schneier.html

Michailova, A., Doche, M., & Butler, M. (2002). *Constraints for scenario-based testing of object-oriented programs* (Technical Report). Electronics and Computer Science Department, University of Southampton.

Microsoft. (2007). *What's not secure. Help protect yourself: Security in Office tutorial*. Microsoft Office Online, Microsoft Corporation. Retrieved March 21, 2007, from http://office.microsoft.com/training/training.aspx?AssetID=RP010425901033&CTT=6&Origin=RP010425891033

Miller, A. (1991). Personality types, learning styles and educational goals. *Educational Psychology, 11*(3-4), 217-238.

Miller, B. N., Konstan, J. A., & Riedl, J. (2004, July). PocketLens: Toward a personal recommender system. *ACM Transactions on Information Systems, 22*.

Miller, G. A. (1956). The magical number seven plus or minus two: Some limits on our capacity for processing information. *Psychological Review, 63*, 81-97.

Ministry of Defence (MoD). (1997). Requirements for safety related software in defence equipment Retrieved October 5, 2006, from http://www.dstan.mod.uk/data/00/055/01000200.pdf

Ministry of Defence (MoD). (2004). Interim defence standard 00-56. Retrieved October 5, 2006, from http://www.dstan.mod.uk/data/00/056/01000300.pdf

Misra, D., & Gaj, K. (2006, February). Face recognition CAPTCHAs. In *Proceedings of the the Advanced Int'l Conference on Telecommunications and Int'l Conference on Internet and Web Applications and Services (AICT-ICIW '06).* (pp. 122). Washington, DC: IEEE Computer Society.

Misra, D., & Gaj, K. (2006, July). *Human friendly CAPTCHAs—simple games* (Poster). Symposium on Usable Privacy and Security (SOUPS). Pittsburgh, Pennsylvania, USA.

Mitchell, R.C., Marcella, R., & Baxter, G. (1999). Corporate information security. *New Library World, 100* 1150), 213-277.

Mitnick, K. (2002). *The art of deception.* Indianapolis, Indiana: Wiley Publishing, Inc.

Mitnick, K. D., & Simon, W. L. (2002). *The art of deception: Controlling the human element of security.* Indiana: Wiley Publishing, Inc..

Mitrou, E., & Karyda, M. (2006). Employees' privacy vs. employers' security: Can they be balanced. *Telematics and Informatics Journal, 23*(3), 164-178.

Modhvadia, S., Daman, S. et al. (2002). *Engaging the board: Benchmarking information assurance.* Cambridge: Information Assurance Advisory Council.

Mohney, D. (2006). Defeating social engineering with voice analytics. *Black Hat Briefings*, Las Vegas, August 2-3, 2006. Retrieved April 25, 2007, from http://www.blackhat.com/presentations/bh-usa-06-BH-US-06-Mohney.pdf

Montage a google. (n.d.). Retrieved April 27, 2007, from http://grant.robinson.name/projects/montage-a-google/

Morgan, G., Fischhoff, B., Bostrom, A., & Atman, C. (2002). *Risk communication: A mental models approach.* New York: Cambridge University Press.

Mori, G., & Malik, J. (2003). Recognizing objects in adversarial clutter: breaking a visual captcha. In *Proceedings of 2003 IEEE Computer Society Conference on Computer Vision and Pattern Recognition* (pp. I-134–I-141).

Mouratidis, H., Giorgini, P., & Manson, G. (2004, April 13-17). Using security attack scenarios to analyse security during information systems design. *Proceedings of the 6th International Conference on Enterprise Information Systems*, Porto, Portugal.

Mouratidis, H., Giorgini, P., & Manson, G. A. (2003). Integrating security and systems engineering: Towards the modelling of secure information systems. *Proceedings of the 15th Conference on Advanced Information Systems Engineering (CAiSE 03)* (Vol . LNCS 2681, pp. 63-78). Klagenfurt, Austria: Springer.

Mouratidis, H., Giorgini, P., & Schumacher, M. (2003). Security patterns for agent systems. *Proceedings of the 8th European Conference on Pattern Languages of Programs*, Irsee, Germany.

Mouratidis, H., Kolp, M., Faulkner, S., & Giorgini. P. (2005, July). A secure architectural description language for agent systems. *Proceedings of the 4th International Joint Conference on Autonomous Agents and Multiagent Systems (AAMAS05).* Utrecht, The Netherlands: ACM Press.

Myers, G. J. (1979). *The art of software testing.* New York: Wiley.

Myers, M.D., & Avison, D.E. (Eds). (2002). *Qualitative research in information systems: A reader.* London: Sage Publications.

Nair, V., Sofield, A., & Mulbagal, V. (2006). *Building a more inclusive financial system in India.* Retrieved on April 16, 2007, from http://www.diamondconsultants.com/PublicSite/ideas/perspectives/downloads/India%20Rural%20Banking_Diamond.pdf

Naor, M. (1996). *Verification of a human in the loop or identification via the Turing test* [Unknown]. Retrieved April 27, 2007, from http://www.wisdom.weizmann.ac.il/%7Enaor/PAPERS/human_abs.html

Naraine, R. (2006). Voice phishers dialing for PayPal dollars. *eWeek, July 7*. Retrieved April 15, 2007, from http://www.eweek.com/article2/0,1895,1985966,00.asp

Naraine, R. (2006). Hackers use BBC news as IE attack lure. *eWeek, March 30*. Retrieved April 15, 2007, from http://www.eweek.com/article2/0,1895,1944579,00.asp

Naraine, R. (2006). Drive-by IE attacks subside; threat remains. *eWeek, March 27*. Retrieved April 15, 2007, from http://www.eweek.com/article2/0,1895,1943450,00.asp

National Institute of Standards and Technology (NIST). (1992). Computer *system security and privacy advisory board* (Annual Report, 18).

Neumann, P. (1995). *Computer related risks.,* Addison-Wesley.

Newell, A., Shaw, J. C., & Simon, H. (1961) *Information processing language V manual*. Edgewood Cliffs, NJ: Prentice-Hall.

Newman, R., Gavette, S., Yonge, L., & Anderson, R. (2006). Protecting domestic power-line communications. In *Proceedings of Symposium on Usable Privacy and Security (SOUPS)*.

Nielsen, J. (1994). Heuristic evaluation. In J. Nielsen & R.L. Mack (Eds.), *Usability inspection methods* (pp. 25-64). New York: John Wiley & Sons.

Niiniluoto, I. (1997). *Informaatio, tieto ja yhteiskunta, Filosofinen käsiteanalyysi*. Helsinki, Finland: Edita.

Nissenbaum, H. (1999). Can trust be secured online? A theoretical perspective. *Etica e Politica, 2*. Retrieved October 5, 2006, from http://www.units.it/~etica/1999_2/nissenbaum.html

Noel, S., Jajodia, S., O'Berry, B., & Jacobs, M. (2003). Efficient, minimum-cost network hardening via exploit dependency graphs. In *Proceedings of 19th Annual Computer Security, Applications Conference* (pp. 86-95). IEEE Computer Society.

Norman, D. (1980). Twelve issues for cognitive science. *Cognitive Science, 4*, 1-32. [Reprinted in Norman, D. (1981). Twelve issues for cognitive science. In D. Norman (Ed.), *Perspectives on cognitive science* (pp. 265-295). Norwood, NJ: Ablex Publishing Corp.]

Norman, D. A. (1988). *The psychology of everyday things*. New York: Harper & Row.

Northcutt, S. et al. (2002). *Inside network perimeter security: The definitive guide to firewalls, virtual private networks (VPNs), routers, and intrusion detection systems*. Que.

Nosworthy, J. (2000). Implementing information security in the 21st century—do you have the balancing factors? *Computers and Security, 19*(4), 337-347.

Nouwt, S., de Vries, B. R., & Loermans, R. (2005). Analysis of the country reports. In S. Nouwt, B. R. de Vries, & C. Prins (Eds.), *Reasonable expectations of privacy* (pp. 323-357). The Hague, PA: TMC Asser Press.

O'Connor, J., & McDermott, I. (1996). *Principles of NLP. London: Thorsons*.

O'Donovan, J., & Smith, B. (2006, January). Is trust robust? An analysis of trust-bades recommendation. In *IUI 2006*. Sydney, Australia.

OCC. (2006). Customer authentication and internet banking alert (OCC Alert 2006-50). Retrieved April 1, 2007, from http://www.occ.treas.gov/ftp/alert/2006-50.html

OECD. (2002). *OECD guidelines for the security of information systems and networks: Towards a culture of security*. Adopted as a recommendation of the OECD Council at its 1037th session on July 25, 2002. Retrieved April 11, 2007, from http://www.oecd.org/dataoecd/16/22/15582260.pdf

Online Safety Study. (2004, October). *AOL/NCSA online safety study, conducted by America Online and the National Cyber Security Alliance*. Retrieved April 15, 2007, from http://www.staysafeonline.info/pdf/safety_study_v04.pdf

Oppy, G., & Dowe, D. (2005). The Turing test. In E. N. Zalta (Ed.), The *Stanford encyclopedia of philosophy*. Retrieved April 27, 2007, from http://plato.stanford.edu/archives/sum2005/entries/turing-test/.

Organisation for Economic Co-Operation and Development—OECD. (2006). *RFID: Drivers, challenges and public policy considerations* (DSTI/ICCP (2005)19/FINAL).

Orgill, G. L., Romney, G. W., Bailey, M. G., & Orgill, P. M. (2004, October 28-30). The urgency for effective user privacy-education to counter social engineering attacks on secure computer systems. In *Proceedings of the 5th Conference on Information Technology Education CITC5 '04*, Salt Lake City, UT, USA, (pp. 177-181). New York: ACM Press.

Oshri, I., Kotlarsky, J., & Hirsch, C. (2005). *Security in networkable windows-based operating system devices.* Paper presented at Softwares Conference, Las Vegas, Nevada, USA

OST. (2004). *Cyber trust and crime prevention.* London: Office of Science & Technology—UK Department of Trade and Industry. HMSO.

Palmer, C. C. (2001). Ethical hacking. *IBM Systems Journal, 40*(3). Retrieved April 15, 2007, from http://www.research.ibm.com/journal/sj/403/palmer.html

Parizo, E. B. (2005). *New bots, worm threaten AIM network.* Retrieved April 25, 2007, from http://searchsecurity.techtarget.com/originalContent/0,289142,sid14_gci1150477,00.html

Park, D. C., & Skurnik, I. (2004). Aging, cognition, and patient errors in following medical instructions. In M.S. Bogner (Ed.), *Misadventures in health care: Inside stories* (pp. 165-181). Mahwah, NJ: Lawrence Erlbaum Associates.

Parno, B., Kuo, C, & Perrig, A. (2006, February 27-March 2). Phoolproof phishing prevention. In *Proceedings of the 10th International Conference on Financial Cryptography and Data Security.* Anguilla, British West Indies.

Patrice, J. B. J. C. I. C., Simard, Y., & Szeliski, R. (2003). Using character recognition and segmentation to tell computer from humans. In *Proceedings of the Seventh International Conference on Document Analysis and Recognition (ICDAR '03)* (p. 418). Washington, DC: IEEE Computer Society.

Payne, J. W., Bettman, J. R., & Johnson, E. J. (1993). *The adaptive decision maker.* Cambridge University Press.

Peltier, T. (2001). *Information security risk Analysis.* Auerbach.

Peltier, T. R. (2001, January). *Information security risk analysis.* Boca Raton, FL: Auerbach Publications.

Penrose, R. (1989). *The emperor's new mind.* Oxford University Press.

Penrose, R. (1994). *Shadows of the mind.* Oxford University Press.

Perloff, R. (1993). Third person effect research 1983-1992: A review and synthesis. *International Journal of Public Opinion Research, 5,* 167-184.

Pernul, G. (1992). Security constraint processing during multilevel secure database design. In *Proceedings of the 8th Annual Computer Security Applications Conference.*

Pernul, G. (1992, November 23-25). Security constraint processing in multilevel secure AMAC schemata. The *2nd European Symposium on Research in Computer Security (ESORICS 1992)* (pp. 349-370). Toulouse, France. Lecture Notes in Computer Science 648. Springer.

Pernul, G. (1995). Information systems security: Scope, state of the art and evaluation of techniques. *International Journal of Information Management, 15*(3), 165-180.

Perrig, A., & Song, D. (1999). Hash visualization: A new technique to improve real-world security. In *Proceedings of International Workshop on Cryptographic Techniques and E-Commerce (CrypTEC).*

Peters, T. J., & Waterman, R. H. (1982). *In search Of excellence: Lessons from America's best run companies.* New York: Harper and Row.

Pfleeger, C.P. (1997). *Security in computing*. Englewood Cliffs, NJ: Prentice Hall.

Phillips, J. D. (2005). Privacy and data protection in the workplace: the US case. In S. Nouwt, B. R. de Vries, & C. Prins (Eds.), *Reasonable expectations of privacy* (pp. 39-59). The Hague, PA: TMC Asser Press.

Phishers raise their game. (2006). Retrieved April 25, 2007, from http://software.silicon.com/security/0,39024655,39164058,00.htm

Pinkas, B., & Sander, T. (2002). Securing passwords against dictionary attacks. In Ccs '02: Proceedings of the 9th acm conference on computer and communications security (pp. 161–170). New York, NY, USA: ACM Press.

Pitts and Browne. (2004). Stopping behavior of systems analysts during information requirements elicitation. *JMIS, 21*(1), 203-226.

Plewes, A. (2007, March). *VoIP threats to watch out for—a primer for all IP telephony users*. Retrieved April 18, 2007, from http://www.silicon.com/silicon/networks/telecoms/0,39024659,39166244,00.htm

Polat, H., & Du, W. (2004). SVD-based collaborative filtering with privacy. In *Proceedings of ACM Symposium on Applied Computing*. Cyprus.

Popper, K.R. (1963). *Conjectures and refutations*. New York: Harper.

Porter, D. (2003). Insider fraud: Spotting the wolf in sheep's clothing. *Computer Fraud & Security, 4*, 12-15.

Pottas, D., & Solms, S. H. (1995). Aligning information security profiles with organizational policies. *Proceedings of the IFIP TC11 11th International Conference on Information Security*.

Preczewski, S. C., & Fisher, D. L. (1990). The selection of alphanumeric code sequences. In *Proceedings of the Human Factors Society 34th Annual Meeting* (pp. 224-228).

Premkumar, G. & King, W.R. (1992). An empirical assessment of information systems planning and the role of information systems in organizations. *Journal of Management Information Systems, 19*(2), 99-125.

Pressman, R. (2005*). Software engineering: A practitioner's approach* (6th ed.). London/New York: McGraw Hill.

Privacy International. (2006). *PHR2005—threats to privacy* (28/10/2006). Retrieved March 2006, from http://www.privacyinternational.org/

Proctor, R. W., Lien, M. C., Vu, K. P. L., Schultz, E. E., & Salvendy, G. (2002). Improving computer security for authentication of users: Influence of proactive password restrictions. *Behavior Research Methods, Instruments, & Computers, 34*, 163-169.

Provos, N., McClain, J., & Wang, K. (2006). Search worms. In *Proceedings of the 4th ACM Workshop on Recurring Malcode (WORM '06)* (pp. 1-8). Alexandria, VA: ACM Press.

Radu, C. (2003). *Implementing electronic card payment systems*. Norwood: Artech House.

Rankl, W., & Effing, W. (2003). *Smart card handbook*. Chichester, England: John Wiley and Sons.

Rapaport. W. J. (2000). Cognitive science. In A. Ralston, E. D. Reilly, & D. Hemmindinger (Eds.), *Encyclopedia of computer science* (4th ed.) (pp. 227-233). New York: Grove's Dictionaries.

Reason, J. (2002). *Human reason*. Cambridge, UK: Cambridge University Press.

Rees, J., Bandyopadhyay, S., & Spafford, E.H. (2003). PFIRES: A policy framework for information security. *Communications of the ACM, 46*(7), 101-106.

Reeves, B., & Nass, C. (1996). *The media equation: How people treat computers, televisions and new media like real people and places*. Cambridge University Press.

Reich, B. H. & Benbasat, I. (1996). Measuring the linkage between business and information technology objectives. *MIS Quarterly, 20*, 55-81.

Reich, B. H., & Benbasat, I. (2000). Factors that influence the social dimension of alignment between business and information technology objectives. *MIS Quarterly, 24*, 81-113.

Reserve Bank of India. (2005). *RBI announces measures towards promoting financial inclusion*. Retrieved April 16, 2007, from http://www.rbi.org.in/scripts/BS_Press-ReleaseDisplay.aspx?prid=14069

Reserve Bank of India. (2006). *Financial inclusion by extension of banking services—use of business facilitators and correspondents*. Retrieved April 20, 2007, from http://www.rbi.org.in/scripts/NotificationUser.aspx?Mode=0&Id=2718

Roarke, S. P. (2005, July). *Bots now battle humans for poker supremacy*. Retrieved April 27, 2007, from http://www.Foxsports.com

Rodota, S. (2004, September 16). Privacy, freedom and dignity. *Closing remarks at the 26th International Conference on Privacy and Personal Data Protection*, Wroclaw.

Rogers, W. A., Lamson, N., & Rousseau, G. K. (2000). Warning research: An integrative perspective. *Human Factors, 42*(1), 102-139.

Röhm, A. W., & Pernul, G. (1999). COPS: A model and infrastructure for secure and fair electronic markets. *Proceedings of the 32nd Annual Hawaii International Conference on Systems Sciences.*

Rolland, C., Grosz, G., & Kla, R. (1999, June). Experience with goal-scenario coupling in requirements engineering. *Proceedings of the IEEE International Symposium on Requirements Engineering*, Limerick, Ireland.

Ross, B., Jackson, C., Miyake, N., Boneh, D., & Mitchell, J. C. (2005). Stronger password authentication using browser extensions. In *Proceedings of the 14th Usenix Security Symposium, 2005.*

Rui, Y., Liu, Z., Kallin, S., Janke, G., & Paya, C. (2005). Characters or faces: A user study on ease of use for hips. *Hip* (pp. 53–65).

Rui, Y., & Liu, Z. (2003). Artifacial: automated reverse Turing test using facial features. In *Proceedings of the Eleventh ACM International Conference on Multimedia (Multimedia '03)* (pp. 295-298). New York: ACM Press.

Rui, Y., & Liu, Z. (2003). Excuse me, but are you human? In *Proceedings of the Eleventh ACM International Conference on Multimedia (Multimedia '03)* (pp. 462-463). New York: ACM Press.

Russell, D., & Gangemi, G., Sr. (1991). *Computer security basics*. O'Reilley.

Rusu, A., & Govindaraju, V. (2005, Jan). Visual captcha with handwritten image analysis. In H. S. Baird & D. P. Lopresti (Eds.), *Human interactive proofs: Second international workshop* (Vol. 3517). Bethlehem, PA: Springer Verlag.

Ryst, S. (2006, July 11). The phone is the latest phishing rod. *BusinessWeek.*

Sahut, J. M. (2006). Electronic wallets in danger. *Journal of Internet Banking and Commerce, 11*(2). Retrieved April 16, 2007, from http://www.arraydev.com/commerce/JIBC/2006-08/Jean-Michel_SAHUT.asp

Saltzer, J. H., & Schroeder, M. D. (1975). The protection of information in computer systems. In *Proceedings of the IEEE, 63*(9), 1278-1308.

Samarati, P., & Vimercati, S. (2001). Access control: Policies, models, and mechanisms. In R. Focardi & R. Gorrieri (Eds.), *Foundations of security analysis and design: Tutorial lectures* (pp. 137-196). LNCS 2171.

Sanders, M. S., & McCormick, E. J. (1993). *Human factors in engineering and design* (7th ed.). New York: McGraw-Hill Inc.

Sanderson, E., & Forcht, K. A. (1996). Information security in business environments. *Information Management & Computer Security, 4*(1), 32-37.

Sanderson, P. (2006). The multimodal world of medical monitoring displays. *Applied Ergonomics, 37*, 501-512.

Sandhu, R. (2003, January/February). Good enough security: Towards a business driven discipline. *IEEE Internet Computing, 7*(1), 66-68.

Sandhu, R. S., Coyne, E. J., Feinstein, H. L., & Youman, C. E. (1996, February). Role-based access control models. *IEEE Computer, 29*(2), 38-47.

SAR. (2007). A *survey* of sharing information in a search and rescue excercise. A co-operative exercise, where rescue, law and medical organizations and non-governmental organizations rehearsed together in a case of airliner accident at Helsinki airport on January 25, 2007 (Research report not published).

Scalet, S. D. (2007). Alarmed: Bolting on security at Stop & Shop. *CIO Online, March 9*. Retrieved on August 15, 2007, from www.csoonline.com/alarmed/03092007.html

Schein, E. H. (1980). *Organizational psychology* (3rd ed.). Englewood Cliffs, NJ.: Prentice-Hall.

Schein, E. H. (1992). *Organizational culture and leadership* (2nd ed). San Francisco: Jossey-Bass.

Schenk, K., Vitalari, N., & Davis, K. (1998). Differences between novice and expert systems analysts: What do we know and what do we do? *Journal of Management Information Systems, 15*(Summer), 9-50.

Schlienger, T., & Teufel, S. (2002). Information security culture: The socio-cultural dimension in information security management. In *Proceedings of IFIP TC11 17th International Conference on Information Security* (pp 191-202). Cairo, Egypt: IFIP Conference Proceedings 214.

Schneider, S., & Barsoux, J-L. (1997). *Managing across cultures*. London, New York, Toronto, Sydney, Tokyo, Singapore, Madrid, Mexico City, Munich, Paris: Prentice Hall.

Schneier B. (2007) The psychology of security. *DRAFT, February 28*. Retrieved August 15, 2007, from www.schneier.com/essay_155.html

Schneier, B. (1999). *Attack trees modelling security threats*. Dr. Dobb's Journal, December. Retrieved from http://www.counterpane.com/attacktrees-ddj-ft.html

Schneier, B. (2000). *Secrets and lies*. John Wiley and Sons.

Schneier, B. (2003). *Beyond fear: Thinking sensibly about security in an uncertain world*. New York: Copernicus Books, an imprint of Springer-Verlag.

Schneier, B. (2007). All or nothing: Why full disclosure—or the threat of it—forces vendors to patch flaws, *CSO Magazine, 6*(2), 20.

Schneier, B., & Shostack, A. (1998). *Breaking up is hard to do: Modelling security threats for smart-cards*. First USENIX Symposium on Smart-Cards, USENIX Press. Retrieved from http://www.counterpane.com/smart-card-threats.html

Schultz, E. (2002). Network associates drops PGP. *Computers & Security, 21*(3), 206-207.

Schultz, E. E. (2002). A framework for understanding and predicting insider attacks. *Computers and Security, 21*(6), 526-531.

Schwartz, M. (2005). *Organizations neglect human factors in security.* Retrieved from http://www.itcinstitute.com/display.aspx?id=363

Schwartz, P., & Reidenberg, J. (1996). *Data privacy law*. Charlottesville, VA: Mitchie Law Publishers.

Selmi, M. (2006). *Privacy for the working class: public work and private lives* (Public law and legal theory working paper No 222). The George Washington University Law School.

service, N. S. news. (2005, August). *Computer characters mugged in virtual crime spree*. Retrieved April 27, 2007, from http://www.newscientist.com/article.ns?id=dn7865

Shardanand, U., & Maes, P. (1995). Social information filtering: Algorithms for automating "word of mouth." In *Proceedings of ACM CHI'95 Conference on Human Factors in Computing Systems* (Vol. 1, pp. 210-217).

Shaw, E. D., Ruby, K. G., & Post, J. M. (1998). The insider threat to information systems. *Security Awareness Bulletin, 2*- 98. Retrieved September 5, 2007, from http://rf-web.tamu.edu/security/secguide/Treason/Infosys.htm

SHIFT WS#1. (2006). *Group survey.* Conducted in workshop of a project that deals with information sharing in networked crisis management environment (SHIFT = Shared Information Framework and Technology) on November 13-16, 2006 (Research report not published).

Sillers, T.S., & Kleiner, B.H. (1997). Defence conversion: Surviving (and prospering) in the 1990s. *Work Study, 46*(2), 45-48.

Simitis, S. (1987). Reviewing privacy in an information society. *University of Pennsylvania Law Review, 135*, 707-728.

Simitis, S. (1999). Reconsidering the premises of labour law: Prolegomena to an EU refulation on the protection of employees' personal data. *European Law Journal, 5*, 45-62.

Simon, H. (1996). *The sciences of the artificial* (3rd ed.). MIT Press.

Simon, H. A. (1956). Rational choice and the structure of the environment. *Psychological Review, 63*, 129-138.

Simon, H. A. (1982). Economic analysis and public policy. In *book "Models of Bounded Rationality"*: volume 1 and 2: MIT Press.

Simons, D. J., & Chabris, C. F. (1999).Gorillas in our midst: sustained inattentional blindness for dynamic events. *Perception, 28*(9), 1059-1074.

Sindre, G., & Opdahl, A. L. (2000). Eliciting security requirements by misuse cases. *Proceedings of the 37th Conference on Techniques of Object-Oriented Languages and Systems* (pp. 120-131). TOOLS Pacific 2000.

Sindre, G., & Opdahl, A. L. (2001, June 4-5). Templates for misuse case description. *Proceedings of the 7th International Workshop on Requirements Engineering, Foundation for Software Quality (REFSQ2001)*, Switzerland.

Sindre, L., & Opdahl, A. (2005). Eliciting security requirements with misuse cases. *Computer Science and Engineering, 10*(1), 34-44.

Singh, S. (1997). *Fermat's last theorem.* London: Fourth Estate.

Sipior, C. J., & Ward, T. B. (1995). The ethical and legal quandary of email privacy. *Communications of the ACM, 38*(12), 48-54.

Siponen, M. (2000). Policies for construction of information systems' security guidelines. In *Proceedings of the 15th International Information Security Conference (IFIP TC11/SEC2000)*, Beijing, China, August (pp. 111-120).

Siponen, M. (2005). Analysis of modern IS security development approaches: towards the next generation of social and adaptable ISS methods. *Information and Organization, 15*(4), 339-375.

Siponen, M. (2005). An analysis of the traditional IS security approaches: implications for research and practice. *European Journal of Information Systems, 14*(3), 303-315.

Siponen, M. T., & Baskerville, R. (2001). A new paradigm for adding security into IS development methods. In J. Eloff, L. Labuschagne, R. von Solms, & G. Dhillon (Eds.), *Advances in information security management & small systems security* (pp. 99-111). Boston: Kluwer Academic Publishers.

Siponen, M., & Heikka, J. (2007). Do secure information system design methods provide ..., Inform. Softw. Technol. doi:10.1016/j.infsof.2007.10.011

Slovic, P., Fischhoff, B., & Lichtenstein, S. (1986). Facts versus fears: Understanding perceived risks. In D. Kahneman, P. Slovic, and A. Tversky (Eds.), *Judgment under uncertainty: Heuristics and biases* (pp. 463-489). New York: Cambridge University Press.

Sobrado, L., & Birget, J.-C. (2005). *Shoulder surfing resistant graphical passwords.* Retrieved April 15, 2007, from http://clam.rutgers.edu/~birget/grPssw/srgp.pdf

Solove D. J. (2006). A taxonomy of privacy. *University of Pennsylvania Law Review, 154*(3), 477-564.

Solove, D. J. (2004). Reconstructing electronic surveillance law. *The George Washington Law Review, 72*, 1701-1747.

Sorkin, R. D. (1988). Why are people turning off our alarms? *Journal of Acoustical Society of America, 84*, 1107-1108.

Stahl, B.C. (2006). *Trust as fetish: A Critical theory perspective on research on trust in e-commerce.* Paper presented at the Information Communications and Society Symposium, University of York, UK.

Stajano, F., & Anderson, R. (1999). *The resurrecting duckling: Security issues for ad-hoc wireless networks.* Security Protocols, 7th International Workshop.

Standish Group. (1995). *The CHAOS report.* West Yarmouth, MA. available at www.standishgroup.com.

Stanford, J., Tauber, E. R., Fogg, B. J., & Marable, L. (2002). Experts vs. online consumers: A comparative credibility study of health and finance websites. *Consumer WebWatch.* www.consumerwebwatch.org

Stanton, J. M. (2000). Reactions to employee performance monitoring: framework, review, and research directions. *Human Performance, 13*, 85-113.

Starner, T. (2001). The challenges of wearable computing: Part 2. *IEEE Micro*, 54-67.

Stasiukonis, S. (2006). *Social engineering, the USB way.* Retrieved April 15, 2007, from http://www.darkreading.com/document.asp?doc_id=95556&WT.svl=column1_1

Stasiukonis, S. (2006). *How identity theft works.* Retrieved April 15, 2007, from http://www.darkreading.com/document.asp?doc_id=102595

Stasiukonis, S. (2006). *Banking on security.* Retrieved April 15, 2007, from http://www.darkreading.com/document.asp?doc_id=111503

Stasiukonis, S. (2006). *Social engineering, the shoppers' way.* Retrieved April 15, 2007, from http://www.darkreading.com/document.asp?doc_id=99347

Stasiukonis, S. (2007). *By hook or by crook.* Retrieved April 15, 2007, from http://www.darkreading.com/document.asp?doc_id=119938

Stasiukonis, S. (2007). Social engineering, the USB way. *Dark Reading.* http://www.darkreading.com/document.asp?doc_id=95556&WT.svl=column1_1

Stone, B. (2007). Study finds web antifraud measure ineffective. *The New York Times, Feb 5.*

Straub, D., Loch, K., Evaristo, R., Karahanna, E., & Strite, M. (2002). Toward a theory-based measurement of culture. *Journal of Global Information Management, 10*(1), 13-23.

Straub, D.W. & Welke, R.J. (1998). Coping with systems risk: Security planning models for management decision making. *MIS Quarterly, 22*(4), 441-470.

Straub, K. (2004). Cracking password usability exploiting human memory to create secure and memorable passwords. *UI Design Newsletter*, Retrieved April 2, 2007, from http://www.humanfactors.com/downloads/jun04.asp

Strens, M. R., & Dobson, J. E. (1994). Responsibility modelling as a technique for requirements definition. *IEEE, 3*(1), 20-26.

Strens, R., & Dobson, J. (1993). How responsibility modeling leads to security requirements. In *Proceedings of the 1992 & 1993 ACM SIGCAS New Security Paradigm Workshop.*

Stubblebine, S., & van Oorschot, P. (2004, February). Addressing online dictionary attacks with login histories and humans-in-the-loop. In *Proceedings of Financial Cryptography.* Springer-Verlag.

Sturgeon, W. (2005). Foiled £220m heist highlights spyware threat. *Zdnet.* http://news.zdnet.co.uk/security/0,1000000189,39191677,00.htm

Sveiby, K-E. (2001). *A knowledge-based theory of the firm to guide strategy formulation.* Retrieved February 15, 2003, from http://www.sveiby.com/articles/Knowledgetheoryoffirm.htm

Swain, A.D, & Guttmann, H.E. (1983). *Handbook of human reliability analysis with emphasis on nuclear power plant applications. NUREG/CR 1278.* Albuquerque, NM: Sandia National Laboratories.

Symantec. (2007)

Tan, P., Steinbach, M., & Kumar, V. (2005). *Introduction to data mining.* Addison-Wesley.

TCSEC. (1985). *Department of defense trusted computer system evaluation criteria* (TCSEC: DoD 5200.28-STD). Department of Defense.

TechNET. (2006). *How to protect insiders from social engineering threats.* Retrieved April 15, 2007, from http://www.microsoft.com/technet/security/midsize-business/topics/complianceandpolicies/socialengineeringthreats.mspx

The esp game. (n.d.). Retrieved April 26, 2007, from http://www.espgame.org/

Thierauf, R. (2001). *Effective business intelligence systems.* London: Quorum Books.

Thomas, R. K., & Sandhu, R. S. (1994). Conceptual foundations for a model of task-based authorizations. In *Proceedings of the 7th IEEE Computer Security Foundations Workshop.*

Thomson, I. (2006). 'Evil twin' Wi-Fi hacks target the rich. *iTnews.com.au, November.* Retrieved April 15, 2007, from http://www.itnews.com.au/newsstory.aspx?CIaNID=42673&r=rss

Tierney, M. (1993). The evolution of Def Stan 00-55: A socio-history of a design standard for safety-critical software. In P. Quintas (Ed.), *Social dimensions of systems engineering: People, processes and software development* (pp. 111-143). New York/London: Ellis Horwood.

Times, T. (2006, May). *Computer game bot: Archnemesis of online games.* Retrieved August 1, 2006, from http://times.hankooki.com/lpage/culture/200605/kt2006052116201765520.htm

Top myths. (2006). *The 10 biggest myths of IT security: Myth #1: 'Epidemic' data losses.* Retrieved April 15, 2007, from http://www.darkreading.com/document.asp?doc_id=99291&page_number=2

Top myths. (2006). *The 10 biggest myths of IT security: Myth #2: Anything but Microsoft.* Retrieved April 15, 2007, from http://www.darkreading.com/document.asp?doc_id=99291&page_number=3

Treasury Inspector General for Tax Administration. (2007). *Employees continue to be susceptible to social engineering attempts that could be used by hackers* (TR 2007-20-107). Retrieved August 18, 2007, from http://www.ustreas.gov/tigta/auditreports/2007reports/200720107fr.pdf

Trim, P. (2001). Public-private partnerships and the defence industry. *European Business Review, 13*(4), 227-234.

Turing, A. M. (1950). Computing machinery and intelligence. LIX (236).

Turnbull, N. (1999). *Internal control: Guidance for directors on the combined code:* The Turnbull report. London: The Institute of Chartered Accountants in England & Wales.

Tversky, A, & Kahneman, D. (1974). Judgment under uncertainty: Heuristics and biases. *Science, 185*(4157), 1124-1131.

U.S. Department of Homeland Security. (2002). *Federal information security management act.* Retrieved April 2, 2007, from http://www.fedcirc.gov/library/legislation/FISMA.html

UK Information Commissioner. (2003). *The employment practices data protection code.*

United States Secret Service. (2004). *Insider threat study: Illicit cyber activity in the banking and finance sector*. Retrieved September 5, 2007, from http://www.secretservice.gov/ntac_its.shtml

Uzun, E., Karvonen, K., & Asokan, N. (2007). Usability analysis of secure pairing methods. *Usable Security (USEC)*.

van der Raadt, B., Gordijn, J., & Yu, E. (2005). Exploring Web services from a business value perspective. To appear in *Proceedings of the 13ᵗʰ International Requirements Engineering Conference (RE'05)*, Paris (pp. 53-62).

van Lamsweerde, A. (2001, August 27-31). Goal-oriented requirements engineering: A guided tour. The *5ᵗʰ IEEE International Symposium on Requirements Engineering (RE 2001)* (p. 249). Toronto, Canada.

van Lamsweerde, A. (2004). Elaborating security requirements by construction of intentional anti-models. In *Proceedings of the International Conference on Software Engineering* (pp. 148-157).

van Lamsweerde, A. (2004, May). Elaborating security requirements by construction of intentional anti-models. *Proceedings of ICSE'04, 26ᵗʰ International Conference on Software Engineering* (pp. 148-157). Edinburgh: ACM-IEEE.

van Lamsweerde, A., Brohez, S., Landtsheer, R., & Janssens, D. (2003, September). From system goals to intruder anti-goals: Attack generation and resolution for security requirements engineering. *Proceedings of the RE'03 Workshop on Requirements for High Assurance Systems (RHAS'03)* (pp. 49-56). Monterey, CA.

Venkatesh, V. (2000). Determinants of perceived ease of use: integrating control, intrinsic motivation, and emotion into the technology acceptance model. *Information Systems Research, 11*(4), 342-365.

Venkatraman, N., & Camillus, J. C. (1984). Exploring the concept of 'fit' in strategic management. *Academy of Management Review, 9*, 513-525.

Vetterling, M., Wimmel, G., & Wisspeintner, A. (2002, November). Requirements analysis: Secure systems development based on the common criteria: the PalME

project. In *Proceedings of the 10th ACM SIGSOFT Symposium on Foundations of Software Engineering*.

Viappiani, P., Faltings, B., & Pu, P. (2006, June). The lookahead principle for preference elicitation: Experimental results. In *Proceedings of the 7th International Conference on Flexible Query Answering Systems (FQAS 2006) Lecture Notes in Computer Science, 4027*, 378-389. Milan, Italy: Springer.

Viega, J., & McGraw, G. (2002). *Building secure software.* Boston: Addison-Wesley.

Viega, J., & McGraw, G. (2004). *Building secure software—how to avoid security problems the right way.* Reading, MA: Addison-Wesley.

Viega, J., Kohno, T., & Potter, B. (2001). Trust and mistrust in secure applications. *Communications of the ACM, 44*(2), 31-36.

Vijayan, J. (2006). "Human error" exposes patients' social security numbers. *Computerworld.* http://www.health-itworld.com/newsletters/2006/02/14/18209?page:int=-1

Vishing. (2006). *Secure computing warns of vishing.* Retrieved April 15, 2007, from http://www.darkreading.com/document.asp?doc_id=98732

von Ahn, L. (2005). *Utilizing the power of human cycles.* Unpublished doctoral dissertation, Carnegie Mellon University.

von Ahn, L., Blum, M., Hopper, N., & Langford, J. (2003). Captcha: Using hard AI problems for security. In *Proceedings of Eurocrypt* (pp. 294-311).

von Ahn, L., Blum, M., & Langford, J. (2002). *Telling humans and computers apart automatically or how lazy cryptographers do AI* (Tech. Rep. No. CMU-CS-02-117). Carnegie Mellon University.

von Ahn, L., Blum, M., & Langford, J. (2004). Telling humans and computers apart automatically. *Communications of the ACM, 47*(2), 56-60.

von Ahn, L., & Dabbish, L. (2004, April). Labeling images with a computer game. In *Proceedings of the*

SIGCHI Conference on Human Factors in Computing Systems (CHI '04) (pp. 319-326). Vienna, Austria: ACM Press.

von Solms, B. & von Solms, R. (2004). The ten deadly sins of information security management. *Computers & Security, 23*, 371-376.

Von Solms, B. (2000). Information security—the third wave? *Computers and Security, 19*(7), 615-620.

Vu, K. P. L., Bhargav, A., & Proctor, R. W. (2003). Imposing password restrictions for multiple accounts: Impact on generation and recall of passwords. In *Proceedings of the 47th Annual Meeting of the Human Factors and Ergonomics Society,* USA (pp. 1331-1335).

Vu, K. P. L., Tai, B. L., Bhargav, A., Schultz, E. E., & Proctor, R. W. (2004). Promoting memorability and security of passwords through sentence generation. In *Proceedings of the Human Factors and Ergonomics Society 48th Annual Meeting*, USA (pp.1478-1482).

Wadlow, T.A. (2000). *The process of network security.* Reading, MA: Addison-Wesley.

Waldron, V. R. (1986). Interviewing for knowledge. *IEEE Transactions on Professional Communications, PC29*(2), 31-34.

Waltz, E. (1998). *Information warfare: Principles and operations.* Boston & London: Artech House.

Wang, Y., & Kobsa, A. (2006, April). *Impacts of privacy laws and regulations on personalized systems.* Paper presented at the CHI 2006 Workshop on Privacy-Enhanced Personalization (PEP 2006), Montreal, Canada.

Warman, A. (1993). *Computer security within organisations.* MacMillan.

Washkuch, F. (2007). Newspaper: Medical information of 75,000 Empire Blue Cross members lost. *SC Magazine.* http://scmagazine.com/us/news/article/643807/newspaper-medical-information-75000-empire-blue-cross-members-lost/

Web Accessibility Initiative. (n.d.). Retrieved April 29, 2007, from http://www.w3.org/WAI/

Weinberg, G. (1971). *The psychology of computer programming.* New York: Van Nostrand Reinhold.

Weng, J., Miao, C., & Goh, A. (2006, April). Improving collaborative filtering with trust-based metrics. In *Proceedings of SAC'06.* Dijon, France.

Westin, A. (1967). *Privacy and freedom. Talk at the Atheneum.* New York.

White, B. (2006). *The implications of Web 2.0 on Web information systems.* Invited talk, Webist 2006.

White, G. W., & Pearson, S. J. (2001). Controlling corporate e-mail, PC use and computer security. *Information Management and Computer Security, 9*(2), 88-92.

Whitman, M. E., & Mattord, H. J. (2003). *Principles of information security.* Boston, London: Thomson Course Technology.

Whitman. (2004). In defense of the realm: Understanding threats to information security. *International Journal of Information Management, 24*, 3-4.

Whitten, A., & Tygar, J. D. (1999). Why Johnny can't encrypt: A usability evaluation of PGP 5.0. In *Proceedings of the 8th USENIX Security Symposium.* USENIX, Washington, D.C., USA.

Whitten, A., & Tygar, J. D. (1999, August 23-26). Why Johnny can't encrypt: A usability evaluation of PGP 5.0. In *Proceedings of the 8th USENIX Security Symposium,* Washington, DC, USA.

Wickens, C. D. (1992). *Engineering psychology and human performance* (2nd ed.). New York: HarperCollins Publishers.

Wiedenbeck, S., Waters, J., Birget, J. C., Brodskiy, A., & Memon, N. (2005). PassPoints: Design and longitudinal evaluation of a graphical password system. *International Journal of Human Computer Studies, 63*, 102-127.

Wiedenbeck, S., Waters, J., Sobrado, L., & Birget, J. (2006, May 23-26). Design and evaluation of a shoulder-surfing resistant graphical password scheme. In *Proceedings of the Working Conference on Advanced Visual interfaces AVI '06*, Venezia, Italy,(pp. 177-184).

ACM Press, New York: ACM Press. http://doi.acm.org/10.1145/1133265.1133303

Willcocks, L., & Margetts, H. (1994). Risk assessment and information systems. *European Journal of Information Systems, 3*, 127-138.

Wilson, T. (2007). *Five myths about black hats*. Retrieved April 15, 2007, from http://www.darkreading.com/document.asp?doc_id=118169

Wogalter, M. S. & Mayhorn, C. B. (2006). Is that information from a credible source? On discriminating Internet domain names. In *Proceedings of the 16th World Congress of the International Ergonomics Association*. Maastricht, The Netherlands.

Wogalter, M. S. (2006). *Handbook of warnings*. Mahwah, NJ: Lawrence Erlbaum Associates.

Wogalter, M. S., & Mayhorn, C. B. (2005). Providing cognitive support with technology-based warning systems. *Ergonomics, 48*(5), 522-533.

Wogalter, M. S., Dejoy, D. M., & Laughery, K. R. (1999). *Warnings and risk communication*. London: Taylor and Francis.

Wogalter, M. S., Racicot, B. M., Kalsher, M. J., & Simpson, S. N. (1994). The role of perceived relevance in behavioral compliance in personalized warning signs. *International Journal of Industrial Ergonomics, 14*, 233-242.

Wolff, J. S., & Wogalter, M. S. (1998). Comprehension of pictorial symbols: Effects of context and test method. *Human Factors, 40*, 173-186.

Wood, C. W., & Banks, W. W. (1993). Human error: an overlooked but significant information security problem. *Computers & Security, 12*, 51-60.

Wood, C.C. (1996). Writing infosec policies. *Computers & Security, 14*(8), 667-674.

Wood, C.C. (2000). An unappreciated reason why information security policies fail. *Computer Fraud & Security, 10*, 13-14.

Wright, P. (1993). Computer security in large corporations: Attitudes and practices of CEOs. *Management Decision, 31*(7), 56-60.

Wylder, J. (2003). *Strategic information security*. Auerbach.

Xu, J., Lipton, R., Essa, I., & Sung, M. (2001). *Mandatory human participation: A new scheme for building secure systems* (Tech. Rep. No. GIT-CC-01-09). Georgia Institute of Technology.

Xu, J., Lipton, R., & Essa, I. (2000, November). *Are you human?* (Tech. Rep. No. GIT-CC-00028). Georgia Institute of Technology: Georgia Institute of Technology.

Yan, J., Blackwell, A., Anderson, R., & Grant, A. (2004). Password memorability and security: Empirical results. *IEEE Security and Privacy, 2*(5), 25-31.

Yavagal, D. S., Lee, S.-W., Ahn, G.-J., & Gandhi, R. A. (2005, March). Security: Common criteria requirements modeling and its uses for quality of information assurance (QoIA). In *Proceedings of the 43rd Annual Southeast Regional Conference ACM-SE 43* (Vol. 2).

Yu, E. (1993, January). Modelling organizations for information systems requirements engineering. *Proceedings of the 1st IEEE International Symposium on Requirements Engineering* (pp. 34-41). San Diego, CA.

Yu, E. (1995). *Modelling strategic relationships for process reengineering*. Ph.D. Thesis, Department of Computer Science, University of Toronto, Canada.

Yu, E. (1997, January 6-8). Towards modelling and reasoning support for early-phase requirements engineering. *Proceedings of the 3rd IEEE International Symposium on Requirements Engineering (RE'97)* (pp. 226-235). Washington, DC.

Yu, E. (2001, April). Agent orientation as a modelling paradigm. *Wirtschaftsinformatik, 43*(2), 123-132.

Yu, E. (2001). Agent-oriented modelling: Software versus the world. *Agent-Oriented Software Engineering AOSE-2001 Workshop Proceedings* (LNCS 222, pp. 206-225). Springer Verlag.

Yu, E., & Cysneiros, L. (2002, October 16). Designing for privacy and other competing requirements. *The 2ⁿᵈ Symposium on Requirements Engineering for Information Security (SREIS'02)*. Raleigh, NC.

Yu, E., & Liu, L. (2000, June 3-4). Modelling trust in the i* strategic actors framework. *Proceedings of the 3ʳᵈ Workshop on Deception, Fraud and Trust in Agent Societies,* Barcelona, Catalonia, Spain (at Agents2000).

Yu, E., & Liu, L. (2001). Modelling trust for system design using the *i** strategic actors framework. In R. Falcone, M. Singh, & Y. H. Tan (Eds.), *Trust in cyber-societies-integrating the human and artificial perspectives* (pp. 175-194). LNAI-2246. Springer.

Yu, E., Liu, L., & Li, Y. (2001, November 27-30). Modelling strategic actor relationships to support intellectual property management. The *20ᵗʰ International Conference on Conceptual Modelling (ER-2001)* (LNCS 2224, pp. 164-178). Yokohama, Japan: Spring Verlag.

Zakaria, O., & Gani, A. (2003). A conceptual checklist of information security culture. In B. Hutchinson (Ed.), *Proceedings of the 2ⁿᵈ European Conference on Information Warfare and Security* (pp. 365-372). Reading, UK: MCIL, Reading.

Zakaria, O., Jarupunphol, P., & Gani, A. (2003). Paradigm mapping for information security culture approach. In J. Slay (Ed.), *Proceedings of the 4ᵗʰ Australian Conference on Information Warfare and IT Security* (pp. 417-426). Adelaide, Australia: University of South Australia. Avison, D. E. (1989). An overview of information systems development methodologies. In R. L. Flood, M. C. Jackson, & P. Keys (Eds.), *Systems prospects: The next ten years of systems research.*(pp. 189-193). New York: Plenum.

Zaslow, J. (2002). If TiVo thinks you are gay, here's how to set it straight: What you buy affects recommendations on Amazon.com, too; why the cartoons? *The Wallstreet Journal,* Retrieved November 26, 2002, from http://online.wsj.com/article_email/0,,SB1038261936872356908,00.html

Zhang, Z., Rui, Y., Huang, T., & Paya, C. (2004). Breaking the clock face hip. *ICME*(pp. 2167-2170).

Zhao, W., Chellappa, R., Phillips, P.J., & Rosenfeld, A. (2003). Face recognition—a literature survey. *ACM Computer Survey, 35*(4), 399-458.

About the Contributors

Manish Gupta is an information security professional in M&T Bank, Buffalo and also a PhD candidate at the State University of New York, Buffalo. He received his Bachelor's degree in mechanical engineering from the Institute of Engineering and Technology, Lucknow, India in 1998 and an MBA in information systems from the State University of New York, Buffalo, USA in 2003. He has more than ten years of industry experience in information systems, policies, and technologies. He has published three books in the area of information security and assurance (one is forthcoming). He has published more than 30 research articles in leading journals, conference proceedings and books including *DSS*, *ACM Transactions*, *IEEE*, and *JOEUC*. He serves in editorial boards of six international journals and has served in program committees of several international conferences. He has also received advanced certificates in information assurance (SUNY, Buffalo), IT benchmarking (Stanford University), and cyber law (Asian School of Cyber Law). He is listed in *Cambridge Who's Who Among Executives and Professionals, 2007* and *Who's Who among students in American Universities and Colleges, 2003*. He holds several professional designations including CISSP, CISA, CISM, ISSPCS, and PMP. He is a member of ACM, AIS, IEEE, INFORMS, APWG, ISACA, and ISC2.

Raj Sharman is an associate professor in the Management Science and Systems Department at SUNY Buffalo, NY. He received his BTech and MTech degree from IIT Bombay, India and his MS degree in industrial engineering and PhD in computer science from Louisiana State University. His research streams include information assurance, extreme events, and improving performance on the Web. His papers have been published in a number of national and international journals. He is also the recipient of several grants from the university as well as external agencies. He serves as an associate editor for the *Journal of Information Systems Security*.

* * *

C. Warren Axelrod is a senior vice president of U.S. Trust, Bank of America Private Wealth Management, where he is the chief privacy officer and business information security officer. He interfaces with the firm's business units and the parent company to identify and assess privacy and security risks and mitigate them, and to ensure that employees are familiar with and follow privacy and security policies, standards, and procedures. He has worked in many areas of financial services for firms such as SIAC, HSBC, and Pershing. He is involved at both industry and national levels with security, privacy, and critical infrastructure protection issues. He is a member of the FSSCC R&D Committee, the SIFMA Privacy and Data Protection Committee, and the Information Security Subcommittee, and several BITS committees and working groups. He was honored with a *Computerworld* 2003 Premier 100 IT Leaders Award and his department's implementation of an intrusion detection system earned a Best in Class award. Dr. Axelrod represented financial services security interests at the Y2K command center in Washington over the century date rollover. He was a founder of the FS/ISAC (financial services information sharing and analysis center), and served two terms on its Board of Managers. He testified at a congressional hearing on cyber security in November 2001, and contributed to the *Banking and Finance Sector's National Strategy for Critical Infrastructure Assurance*, published in May 2002. Dr. Axelrod is the author of *Outsourcing Information Security* (Artech House, September 2004), and contributed a chapter to *Managing Information Assurance in Financial Services* (IGI Publishing, July 2007). He has published two previous books on computer management and numerous articles on many aspects of information technology, including computer and network security, contingency planning, and computer-related risks. He holds a PhD in managerial economics from the Johnson Graduate School of Management at Cornell University. He has a Bachelor's degree in electrical engineering and Master's degree in economics and statistics from the University of Glasgow. He is certified as a CISSP and CISM, and has NASD Series 7 and 24 licenses.

Anne Boyer is a professor at the Université Nancy 2. She works in the field of artificial intelligence and her research interests include machine learning, real-time decision making, and probabilistic modeling. She is involved in many European projects and international collaborations. She had addressed, in many international conferences, fundamental problems linked to user modeling and information search and retrieval based on an analysis of usages. She combines several approaches such as natural language processing, collaborative filtering, or content-based filtering to deal with scalability, privacy, sparsity, portability, context, trust, quality, and security when designing recommender systems.

Mahil Carr is a doctorate in the area of software engineering from the City University of Hong Kong. He completed his MCA from the St. Joseph's College, Bharatidasan University, Trichy and held the position of director (in-charge), Department of Computer Science, American College, Madurai, for over 3 1/2 years. Currently, Dr. Mahil Carr is assistant professor at the Institute for Research and Development in Banking Technology. Dr. Carr has published in *Information Technology & Management, Journal of Services Research*. His research interests include e-commerce and e-governance.

Deborah Sater Carstens has a PhD in industrial engineering, a BS in business administration from the University of Central Florida, and a MBA from the Florida Institute of Technology. She has been an assistant professor of management information systems since 2003 at the Florida Institute of Technology. Her interests are in information security, human-computer interaction, and system design. She previously was employed for more than 10 years at NASA Kennedy Space Center where she was principal investigator on human factors research projects, industrial engineering for safety program study manager and the process and human factors engineering roadmap manager.

Sylvain Castagnos joined the LORIA laboratory of research in Nancy as a member of University Nancy 2 after obtaining a Master's degree in computer science. He is a third year PhD student in artificial intelligence and his topics of interest include collaborative filtering, user modeling, distributed algorithms, and probabilistic approaches. His work starts from the fact that there are too many information on the Internet. Nowadays, the question is no longer to know where to find information, but how to find the most suitable information in a very short time. A good way to provide useful items consists in generating personalized recommendations within an information system. Through several international publications, he has highlighted the interest of distributing collaborative filtering processes to deal with scalability, privacy, and other industrial constraints.

Steve Clarke received a BSc in economics from The University of Kingston upon Hull, an MBA from the Putteridge Bury Management Centre, The University of Luton, and a PhD in human centred approaches to information systems development from Brunel University—all in the United Kingdom. He is professor of information systems in the University of Hull Business School. He has extensive experience in management systems and information systems consultancy and research, focusing primarily on the identification and satisfaction of user needs and issues connected with knowledge management. His research interests include: social theory and information systems practice, strategic planning, and the impact of user involvement in the development of management systems. Major current research is focused on approaches informed by critical social theory.

Mahi Dontamsetti is president of M3 Security, a security consulting firm. A CISSP, Mr. Dontamsetti currently serves on the board of OWASP-NY/NJ. He is author of a couple of books on wireless technologies and has spoken on security issues at conferences. During his professional career which spans over 15 years, he has held executive leadership positions at Fortune 50 companies such as Lockheed Martin as well as held founding employee status at startups. He has served in the role of CTO, VP, and chief technologist during his career. Mr. Dontamsetti has an MS in computer science from the University of Missouri-Kansas City.

Paul Drake is currently a director within a multinational pharmaceutical organisation. He has over 25 years experience in information technology, 15 of these being aligned with information security, in which has worked in a variety of organisations spanning local authority, utilities, finance and trading, and retail and leisure. He is one of the original authors of the British Standards for information security and sits on the committee that maintains them. He holds a Master's degree in supervisory management and a PhD from Hull University in communicative action in information security systems. In the time left after work, six sigma studies, membership of the British Standards Institute, research, being a husband, and father to two children: He likes to sleep!

Jean-Noël Ezingeard is dean of the Faculty of Business and Law at Kingston University (London). His research is focused on information assurance, information security, and enterprise risk management, topics which he has researched, taught, and consulted about in Europe, North America, and South Africa. His work on information assurance has been used in publications by QinetiQ, Axa, and the Federation against Software Theft. He is a founding member of the British Computer Society's Information Assurance working group. He joined the business school world 9 years ago. Prior to this he worked as a chartered manufacturing engineer (operations management) and a lecturer in computer integrated manufacturing.

Steven Furnell is the head of the Information Security & Network Research Group at the University of Plymouth in the United Kingdom, and an adjunct associate professor with Edith Cowan University in Western Australia. His research interests include the usability of security technology, user authentication, and security management. Professor Furnell is a fellow and branch chair of the British Computer Society (BCS), a senior member of the Institute of Electrical and Electronics Engineers (IEEE), and a UK representative in International Federation for Information Processing (IFIP) working groups relating to information security management (of which he is the current chair), network security, and information security education. He is the author of over 170 papers in refereed international journals and conference proceedings, as well as the books *Cybercrime: Vandalizing the Information Society* (2001) and *Computer Insecurity: Risking the System* (2005). Further details can be found at www. network-research-group.org

Jefferson B. Hardee is a graduate student pursuing his PhD in the ergonomics/experimental psychology program at North Carolina State University in Raleigh, North Carolina. He received his MS in psychology in 2007 and his BS in computer science from North Carolina State University in 2003.

Corey Hirsch is CIO of LeCroy Corporation, headquartered in Chestnut Ridge, New York. He also serves as visiting executive fellow at Henley Management College, UK, in the School of Projects, Processes, and Systems. His research is focused on information security and enterprise risk management. LeCroy is a recognized innovator in these areas, and has been the subject of numerous recent case studies in these and related fields. Dr. Hirsch researches, lectures, e-tutors, and supervises students in competitor intelligence, customer relationship management systems, and managing the ICT function. His practice includes responsibility for development and maintenance of the physical and information infrastructure of LeCroy, a $160M leader in test and measurement instrumentation.

Bogdan Hoanca is an associate professor of management information systems at the University of Alaska Anchorage (UAA). Before joining UAA, he co-founded, started up, and sold a company that builds components for fiber optic communications. He also helped start and consulted with a number of other startup companies in optical fiber communications. He received a PhD in electrical engineering from the University of Southern California in 1999. His current research interests revolve around technology, in particular e-learning and societal implications of technology, as well as privacy and security.

Maria Karyda is lecturer at the University of the Aegean, Greece (Department of Information and Communication Systems Engineering) and member of the Laboratory of Information and Communication Systems Security of the University of the Aegean. She holds a PhD in information systems security management and an MSc in information systems. She has participated in several EU and national funded research projects in the areas of IT security, electronic government, and information systems security management and has also collaborated with many private and public institutions as security consultant. She has published several journal papers and chapters in books and has participated in many international conferences.

Cynthia Kuo is a doctoral candidate in the Engineering and Public Policy Department at Carnegie Mellon University. Her research focuses on how security applications can be designed to minimize end user errors. Previously, she worked as a user experience designer.

Rauno Kuusisto works at the moment as a senior researcher at the Finland Futures Research Centre at Turku School of Economics. He is an adjunct professor of network enabled defense at Finnish National

Defense University, as well. Kuusisto graduated as PhD at Helsinki University of Technology in 2004 on the area of corporate security and futures studies. Kuusisto has general staff officer qualification, as well. He has 30 years experience mainly as a developer and researcher of heavy duty communication systems, intelligence systems, and decision support systems, as well as educating personnel on several degrees up to doctoral programs. He has about 40 scientific publications and research reports on areas of networked management, situation understanding, information in decision-making, and safety and security. Nowadays his interest is directed to networked management, comprehensive information availability for decision-making, and creating futures information. Kuusisto is an active participant of several scientific advisory boards, and he is a conference and journal reviewer.

Tuija Kuusisto works as a chief information officer for the Ministry of Defence in Finland. She is adjunct professor of information management for decision-making at National Defence University and adjunct professor of geoinformatics at Helsinki University of Technology in Finland. Her research interests lay around information, knowledge, and information systems. Her viewpoints to research include management and tactics, software business, and geoinformatics. She has about 60 scientific publications in international and national journals, conference proceedings, and books. She has over 10 years work experience in national and global software business and telecommunications industry and over 10 years work experience in local and national IT administration.

Christopher B. Mayhorn is an associate professor in the ergonomics/experimental psychology program at North Carolina State University in Raleigh, North Carolina. He received his PhD in cognitive/experimental psychology from the University of Georgia in 1999.

Jeremy Mendel is a graduate student pursuing his M.S. in the Psychology Department at Clemson University in Clemson, South Carolina. He received his B.S. in psychology from North Carolina State University in 2007.

Deapesh Misra works as a security analyst with iDefense, a VeriSign company. Previously he worked as a graduate research assistant at the Cryptography and Network Security Implementations Lab in George Mason University. He can be contacted at deapesh@ieee.org.

Lilian Mitrou is assistant professor at the University of the Aegean, Greece (Department of Information and Communication Systems Engineering) and visiting professor at the University of Athens (postgraduate studies program). She holds a PhD in data protection (University of Frankfurt-Germany) and teaches information law and data protection law. She has served as a member of the Hellenic Data Protection Authority (1999-2003) and as advisor to the former Prime Minister K. Simitis in sectors of information society and public administration (1996-2004). From 1998 till 2004 she was the national representative in the EC-Committee on the Protection of Individuals with regard to the processing of personal data. She served as member of many committees working on law proposals in the fields of privacy and data protection, electronic commerce, e-government, and so forth. Her professional experience includes senior consulting and researcher positions in a number of private and public institutions. She has published books and chapters in books (in Greek, German, and English) and many journal and national and international conference papers.

Kenrick Mock received his PhD in computer science from the University of California, Davis, in 1996. He currently holds the position of associate professor of computer science at the University of Alaska Anchorage. His research centers on complex systems, information management, artificial intelligence, computer security, and technological innovations in education. Kenrick has previously held positions as a research scientist at Intel Corporation and as CTO of an Internet startup company, Unconventional Wisdom.

Anup Narayanan is an information security professional and the founding director of First Legion Consulting, an information security management company based in Bangalore, India. His current focus is on developing a framework, that he has christened "HIM-IS" (human impact management—information security), for managing the human impact on information security. He is a CISSP, CISA, and currently pursuing a master's degree in applied psychology. He has more than 8 years of experience in information security and contributes to the development of ISM3 (information security management maturity model).

Marcus Nohlberg used his BSc in information systems to begin working as a consultant in one of Sweden's major Internet firms, but soon found an interest in the business side and received an M.B.A. with a focus on e-business. Still, the lure to specialize further was there, so he got started as an industrial PhD student with a focus on information security at the University of Skövde, Sweden, supported by The Logic Planet AB. His research interest lies specifically in social engineering and the manipulation of humans. His private interests are politics, sport pistol shooting at a national level, his wirehaired dachshund Greta, and general geekiness. He lives in Skövde, Sweden, and his Web page is at: http://www.nohlberg.com

Adrian Perrig is an associate professor at Carnegie Mellon University. He has appointments in the departments of Electrical and Computer Engineering, Engineering and Public Policy, and Computer Science. His research focuses on networking and systems security, security for mobile computing, and sensor networks. Other research interests include human interfaces for security, networking, operating systems, and cryptography.

G. Lawrence Sanders, PhD, is a professor in the Department of Management Science and Systems in the School of Management at the State University of New York at Buffalo. He has also served as a department chair and the chair of the PhD program in the School of Management. He has taught MBA courses in the Peoples Republic of China and Singapore. His research interests are in the ethics and economics of digital piracy, systems success measurement, cross-cultural implementation research, systems development, and decision processes. He has published papers in outlets such as *The Journal of Business*, *MIS Quarterly*, *Information Systems Research*, the *Journal of Management Information Systems*, the *Journal of Strategic Information Systems*, the *Journal of Management Systems, Decision Support Systems, and Decision Sciences*. He has also published a book on database design and co-edited two other books.

Jesse Walker is a principal engineer in Intel Corporation's communications technology lab. His primary interest concerns network security protocols. Dr. Walker served as editor for *IEEE 802.11i*, and has contributed to many other *IEEE 802.11* amendments. He also has contributed to numerous IETF standards. Prior to joining Intel, he worked at Shiva, Raptor Systems, Digital Equipment Corporation, Rockwell International, Datapoint, and Iowa State. He holds a PhD in mathematics from University of Texas.

Ryan T. West is a user experience researcher who has studied enterprise-class systems administration at Microsoft, SAS Institute, and now Dell Inc. He has conducted academic research in risk and decision-making and applied research in areas ranging from medical mistakes to computer security. Ryan West has a PhD in cognitive psychology from the University of Florida.

Index